THE CHALLENGE OF AFRICAN
ECONOMIC RECOVERY AND DEVELOPMENT

Also by Adebayo Adedeji

TOWARDS A DYNAMIC AFRICAN ECONOMY
Selected Speeches and Lectures 1975–1986
Compiled and arranged by Jeggan C. Senghor

The Challenge of
African Economic Recovery
and Development

Edited by
Adebayo Adedeji, Owodunni Teriba
and Patrick Bugembe

With a Foreword by
J. PEREZ DE CUELLAR
Secretary-General of the United Nations

FRANK CASS

First published 1991 in Great Britain by
FRANK CASS & CO. LTD
Gainsborough House, Gainsborough Road
London E11 1RS, England

and in the United States of America by
FRANK CASS
International Specialized Book Services, Inc.
5602 N.E. Hassalo Street, Portland,
Oregon 97213

Transferred to Digital Printing 2004

British Library Cataloguing in Publication Data

The Challenge of African economic recovery and development.
1. Africa. Economic development
I. Adedeji, Adebayo
330.96

ISBN 0 7146 3388 7
ISBN 0 7146 4074 3 (Pbk)

CONTENTS

CONTENTS

CONTENTS

PART SIX

THE LONG-TERM PROSPECTS OF CO-OPERATION
BETWEEN AFRICA AND THE
INTERNATIONAL COMMUNITY

TABLES

CHAPTER 7

Financing of the Implementation of UN-PAAERD

CHAPTER 24

Growth and Structural Change in Africa

CHAPTER 29

*Economic Co-operation in Africa: Role and Relevance of
Regional and Subregional Institutions*

FIGURES

ANNEXES

ABBREVIATIONS*

ACP	African Caribbean and Pacific Countries
ADB	African Development Bank
APPER	Africa's Priority Programme for Economic Recovery, 1986–1990
BDEAC	Development Bank of Central African States
CEAO	Economic Community of West Africa
CEPGL	Economic Community of the Great Lakes Countries
CGs	Consultative Groups organized under the agencies of World Bank
COMECON/ CMEA	Council for Mutual Economic Assistance
DAC	Development Assistance Committee of the OECD
EAC	East African Community
ECA	UN Economic Commission for Africa
ECCAS	Economic Community of Central African States
ECOWAS	Economic Community of West African States
EEC	European Economic Community
ERP	Economic Recovery Programme
FAO	Food and Agriculture Organization
FAL	Final Act of Lagos
GATT	General Agreement on Tariffs and Trade
GDP	Gross Domestic Product
GNP	Gross National Product
IBRD	International Bank for Reconstruction and Development (World Bank)
IDA	International Development Association
IDEP	United Nations Institute for Economic Development and Planning
IGOs	Inter-Governmental Organizations
IMF	International Monetary Fund (Fund)
LDCs	Least Developed Countries
LPA	Lagos Plan of Action
MNCs	Multinational Corporations or Companies
MRU	Mano River Union
NICs	Newly Industrializing Countries
NIEO	New International Economic Order
NGO	Non-Governmental Organization

* Includes only those abbreviations which appear in several Chapters

OAU	Organization of African Unity
ODA	Official Development Assistance
OECD	Organization for Economic Co-operation and Development
OMVG	Organization for the Development of River Gambia
OMVS	Organization for the Development of River Senegal
OPEC	Organization of Petroleum Exporting Countries
PTA	Preferential Trade Area (for Eastern and Southern Africa)
RTs	Round Tables organized under the aegis of UNDP
SADCC	Southern Africa Development Co-ordination Conference
SAF	Structural Adjustment Facility
SAP	Structural Adjustment Programme
SDRs	Special Drawing Rights
TNCs	Trans-National Corporations and Companies
UDEAC	Customs and Economic Union of Central Africa
UDEAO	West African Customs Union
UN	United Nations
UNCTAD	United Nations Conference on Trade and Development
UNDP	United Nations Development Programme
UNESCO	United Nations Educational and Scientific Organization
UNICEF	United Nations Children's Fund
UN-PAAERD	United Nations Programme of Action for Africa's Economic Recovery, 1986–1990
US	United States of America
USAID	United States Agency for International Development
WADB	Central Bank of West African States
WARDA	West African Rice Development Association
WHO	World Health Organization

FOREWORD

Africa has in the last few years been experiencing an economic crisis of unprecedented proportions. In various ways, many governments have formulated programmes and introduced measures to contribute to the process of speedy recovery and long-term development. I have been equally struck by the responses of many thousands of people, acting individually or in groups, to the plight of fellow human beings in Africa who have suffered from famine, hunger and homelessness, resulting from the drought and desertification which have also been one of the root causes of the economic crisis at the continental level.

As is well known, a Special Session of the United Nations General Assembly was, at the request of African Governments, convened from 27 May to 1 June 1986. *The United Nations Programme of Action for African Development, 1986–1990* which was unanimously adopted by the Session analysed the critical economic situation in Africa in all its dimensions. It spelt out policy measures and concrete actions to be taken by African countries at national, subregional and regional levels, particularly in the priority areas identified in *Africa's Priority Programme for Economic Recovery, 1986–1990*. The international community also entered into a wide range of specific commitments, intended to complement the exceptional efforts which African Governments have undertaken to put their economies on course.

The international Conference on *Africa: the Challenge of Economic Recovery and Accelerated Development*, organized by the United Nations Economic Commission for Africa, in June 1987, was a timely opportunity for an assessment of the situation one year after the Special Session.

The present volume, which has put together some of the major papers presented at Abuja, provides a total picture of the African development experience in recent years and pointers for the future. It has also captured the main thrust of the discussion by the over two hundred participants as well as the conclusions reached. I take great pride in recommending it to all those concerned with the destiny of the African continent and especially those in a position to influence that destiny.

Javier Pérez de Cuéllar
New York, 1989   *Secretary-General of the United Nations*

PREFACE

This book presents a number of papers prepared for the International Conference on 'Africa: the Challenge of Economic Recovery and Accelerated Development', held in Abuja, the new capital of the Federal Republic of Nigeria, from 15–19 June 1987. The Abuja Conference was the first of a series of conferences and other activities planned by the United Nations Economic Commission for Africa (ECA) focussing on the implementation of the *United Nations Programme of Action for African Economic Recovery and Development 1986–1990 (UN-PAAERD)*. Since then, ECA has organized the Khartoum Conference on the *Human Dimension of Africa's Economic Recovery and Development* (1988), and in collaboration with non-governmental organizations, African and non-African, an international conference on *Popular Participation in the Development Process* (1989).

Participation in the Abuja Conference was at the highest level, involving African Heads of State and Government, Ministers and high-ranking officials, executive heads and senior officials of United Nations agencies, international, regional and subregional development and financial organizations and institutions, representatives from donor agencies, as well as African and non-African scholars. In all, there were over 200 participants at the Conference, the opening session of which was addressed by H.E. General Ibrahim B. Babangida, President, Commander-in-Chief of the Armed Forces of the Federal Republic of Nigeria; H.E. Denis Sassou Ngouesso, the then current Chairman of the Organization of African Unity and the President of the People's Republic of the Congo; and Madame Monique Landry, Minister of External Relations of Canada. The closing address was given by H.E. Vice Admiral Aikhomu, Chief of General Staff of the Federal Republic of Nigeria. Altogether, seventy-four papers, all extremely stimulating and useful, were prepared for the Conference by officials from African countries, subregional, regional and international institutions, and by individual participants; but only about half of this rich collection are presented in this volume.

In their present form, the papers represent edited versions of what was presented at Abuja; but, as every effort has been made to preserve the essence of the original contributions, the authors alone bear the responsibility for any errors that remain.

ECA wishes to acknowledge with appreciation the generosity of the Federal Republic of Nigeria in co-sponsoring and hosting the Abuja Conference. Most highly appreciated is the personal interest shown by His Excellency President Babangida in the Conference. From the very early stages he provided support and encouragement to the organizers and demonstrated his interest in the success of the Conference. President Sassou Ngouesso was kind enough to take time off from his onerous responsibilities both as current Chairman of OAU and President of Congo to be present at Abuja and to deliver a statement which served as a key point of reference in subsequent deliberations at the Conference. To both Heads of State, the organizers are grateful for their contributions.

The financial contributions of the Government of Canada, the United Nations Development Programme, the Commonwealth Secretariat, the Swedish International Development Authority, the African Development Bank, and the Ford Foundation are also gratefully acknowledged. Finally, ECA is thankful to all authors of papers for the vast wealth of ideas which formed the basis of the Conference deliberations, and to all participants for their overwhelming response to the invitation which was a welcomed manifestation of their genuine concern for and interest in African development and progress.

The world-wide interest shown in the Abuja Conference by the media must also be noted. Nearly fifty journalists from different parts of the world came to Abuja to report on the Conference. Coming as it did exactly a year after the 13th Special Session of the General Assembly of the United Nations which adopted UN-PAAERD, the world was understandably anxious to know what had happened, what was happening and what might follow. Since then, the Secretary-General of the United Nations has submitted to the General Assembly a progress report (1987) and a mid-term review (1988) of the implementation of the Programme. Indeed, the General Assembly at its 43rd Session has undertaken a mid-term review. It was assisted in this exercise by an *Ad Hoc* Committee of the Whole. The conclusions reached were that while most African countries have adopted impressive economic reforms, at both macro and sectoral levels, to foster the recovery and development process, the overall performance of their economies was terribly disappointing in 1986 and 1987 and improved only marginally in 1988. Thus, during these three years of the five-year UN Programme, the standard of living of the average African continued to fall – as it has done consistently since 1980. These poor overall results are due primarily to worsening external factors – the plummetting of commodity prices, the fall in the exchange value of the United States dollar, the high rates of interest, excruciating external debt servicing obligations and the lack of increase in real terms of Official Development Assistance (ODA).

The mid-term review is intended to reinvigorate efforts at implementing the Programme. The extent to which it has succeeded in doing this will be unfolded in the weeks and months ahead. It is hoped that when the time comes to make an overall assessment at the end of the Programme in 1991, positive concrete developments can be reported. If Africa will not have recovered, at least the process will have been set in an irreversible motion.

I would like to thank Agnes Aidoo, Sadig Rasheed, Makhan Sarr and Jean Thisen for their invaluable editorial assistance in the preparation of this volume. I am also extremely grateful to Jeggan Senghor who served as a member of the Steering Committee for the Abuja International Conference, and Carolyn Kiwia, Fantaye Meshehsa, Mehret H. Selassie and Imaculee Nyankiye for their skilful secretarial assistance and the care and patience with which they typed the entire manuscript.

Adebayo Adedeji
UN Under-Secretary-General and
ECA Executive Secretary

Addis Ababa, 1989

NOTES ON THE EDITORS
AND CONTRIBUTORS

Editors

Adedeji, Adebayo is Under-Secretary-General of the United Nations and Executive Secretary of Economic Commission for Africa (ECA)

Bugembe, Patrick K. is Economic Affairs Officer, ECA

Teriba, Owodunni is Senior Regional Adviser on Economic Research and Planning at ECA

*Contributors**

Ake, Claude is Professor of Political Science and Dean of the Faculty of the Social Sciences at the University of Port Harcourt, Nigeria

Amin, Samir is Director of the United Nations University's Programme on Strategies for the Future of Africa, Dakar, Senegal

Ashiabor, Alex is Director, Task-Force on the UN-PAAERD at UNCTAD

Benachenhou, Abdelatif is Director of the International Institute for Educational Planning, Paris, France

Carlsson, Jerker is affiliated to FIDE (Varnamo, Sweden) and Professor of Economic History at the University of Gothenburg, Sweden

Diouf, Makhtar is Professor of Economics at University of Dakar, Senegal

Gambino, Anthony W. is on the staff of the Overseas Development Council, Washington D.C., USA

Hazlewood, Arthur D. is Professor of Economics at Oxford University

Haynes, Richard T. is Donor Co-ordinator for Africa, United States Agency for International Development

Kamba, Walter J. is Vice-Chancellor, University of Zimbabwe

Khalid, Mansour is Vice-Chairman, World Commission on Environment and Development

Ki-Zerbo, Joseph is Professor of History at the University of Cheikh Anta Diop, Senegal

*Other than those who are editors

Luke, David Fashole is Assistant Professor at Dalhousie University, Halifax, Canada

Mazrui, Ali A. is Professor at the University of Michigan, USA

Montasser, Essam is Director of the United Nations African Institute for Economic Development and Planning, Dakar, Senegal

Mutharika, Bingu Wa is Chief, International Trade and Finance Division of ECA

Mwale, Siteke G. is Principal Adviser on Economic and Technical Co-operation to the Government of the Republic of Zambia

Mwanza, Jacob M. is Vice-Chancellor of the University of Zambia

Nana-Sinkam, Samuel C. is Chief, Joint ECA/FAO Agriculture Division of ECA

Odhiambo, T.R. is Director of the International Centre of Insect Physiology and Ecology (ICIPE), Nairobi, Kenya; and currently President of the African Academy of Sciences

Onitiri, H.M.A. is Special Adviser at the United Nations Development Programme

Phillips, Adedotun O. is Professor of Economics at the University of Ibadan and currently Director-General of Nigerian Institute of Social and Economic Research

Rasheed, Sadig is Chief, Public Administration, Management and Manpower Division of ECA

Robson, Peter is Professor of Economics at the University of St. Andrews, Scotland

Sangare, Louis is Chief, Economic Co-operation Office of ECA

Sarr, Makha D.N. is Chief, ECA/UNIDO Joint Industry Division, ECA

Schatz, Sayre P. is Professor of Economics, Temple University, Philadelphia, USA

Sewell, John is President of Overseas Development Council, USA

Shaw, Timothy M. is Professor of Political Science and International Development Studies at Dalhousie University in Nova Scotia, Canada. He has also served as Director of the Centre for African Studies

Sorokine, Ardalion A. is Economist at the USSR Institute of African Studies, Academy of Sciences, Moscow

Tevoedjre, Albert is Secrétaire Général de l'Association Mondiale de Prospective Sociale (AMPS), Geneva, Switzerland

Wheeler, Joseph C. is Chairman, Development Assistance Committee of the Organization for Economic Co-operation and Development

White, Andrew D. is Professor-at-Large, Cornell University, USA

INTRODUCTION

The social and economic situation in Africa has been deteriorating since the late 1960s. The number and intensity of distressing economic features have perpetually increased. Poverty and destitution have become almost endemic. The tempo of increasing mass unemployment and under-employment on the continent has also been accentuated by the rapidly growing population. By the 1980s, Africa had a staggering number of people living in absolute poverty, malnourished and under-fed, and with limited access to basic necessities of life: potable water, shelter, health and education.

Thus, when the Great African Drought Disaster struck during 1983–1985, it merely intensified an on-going economic and social crisis, deepened the economic recession of most of the African countries, and brought many of them to the brink of collapse. It is unfortunate that the drought-induced problems coincided with a very hostile external economic environment, involving a drastic deterioration in the terms of trade, a rise in interest rates and a decline in ODA. Taken together, these shocks interacted to tear apart the basic fabric of whatever balance remained of the African economy; and resulted in chronic balance of payments disequilibria, an unsustainable debt service burden, widespread domestic distortions in production and consumption, as well as highly accentuated disparities in the distribution of an ever-decreasing income and wealth.

It is clear that Africa's growth and development dilemma lay intertwinedly in its fragile social and economic structures, and the unfavourable international environment. On the external side, factors like the collapse in the international prices of primary commodities, the world economic recession, the decrease or, at best, stagnation in real terms in ODA, the volatility and misalignment in the exchange rates of major currencies, mounting debt service obligations and worsening balance of payments deficits contributed in no small measure to the deepening of the African crisis. However, the inability of many African countries to increase the levels of production of goods and services and the standard of living of their people is also largely due to the existing structural rigidities of the African economies. The economic structure in Africa is dualistic, with a very large subsistence sector which,

1

together with the tiny modern agricultural sector, account for 60 to 80 per cent of the GNP. Alongside this broad structure is a relatively small and disjointed mining and industrial sector. The mining sector is often operated by or in uneasy co-operation with TNCs. The industrial sector is usually predominantly consumer-industry dominated, and is invariably dependent on the importation of factor inputs, including even industrial raw materials. Production in this 'modern' enclave is mainly export-oriented and consists of a very narrow range of primary agricultural or mineral products. Economic activities in the production of minerals, fuels and agricultural products for exports are, for the most part, dependent upon imported capital equipment and skills. And, in most cases, only a small proportion of production activities in the modern sector caters for the production of domestic consumption goods. But, even in such cases, the domestic products are limited to satisfying the needs of the small urban-based population.

The structural weaknesses resulting from a very rudimentary and disarticulate relationship between a large neglected subsistence sector and a small, privileged, modern enclave are further compounded and aggravated by the non-availability or misdirection of scarce human and financial resources. Inadequacy of domestic management, failure to mobilise and efficiently utilise national resources, and the enclaved physical and institutional infrastructure exacerbate the fragility of a narrow-based African economy. In most cases, the structure of the African economy is such that productive forces – human, physical and financial – are directed to the maintenance of the historical economic links with the outside world. Basic internal links involving use of products such as food and agricultural as inputs into industry, remain neglected or inadequate. Thus, the broad base of the African economy is, as of now, still undeveloped in terms of supportive institutional and physical infrastructure such as extension services, research, provision of agricultural inputs and implements, storage and transport facilities.

The structurally weak functional and operational linkages among the various economic sectors render the African economies extremely vulnerable, and expose them to changes in the exogenous factors. For example, industries in many African countries depend upon imported machinery and inputs. Many of these industries are not based on local raw materials and have limited capacity to cater for the basic needs of the entire population. Only in a few cases do African industries produce even the needed agricultural implements and other essential inputs. With such lack of organic and functional interdependence, the African economy cannot generate, from within itself, either the momentum for development or the capacity or resilience to withstand external shocks.

The high population growth rates also have structural implications for the African economy. High levels of population growth in the face of declining output of goods and services have resulted in a structural increase in the proportion of the wealth of the region that has to be consumed. This implies that the region as a whole has decreasing resources to finance capital formation for further development. In physical terms, a fast growing population puts increasing pressure on resources like land and forestry, thus leading to a further deterioration in the productivity levels and the balance of the ecosystem. In addition, a high population growth has tended to accentuate the income inequality problem. Presently, it is not uncommon to find cases in Africa where 20 per cent of the population appropriates to itself 60 per cent or more of the total national income. Given the situation where there are more and better facilities, such as houses, schools and hospitals in a few urban centres, increases in income inequalities are bound to bring about greater suffering and misery for an increasing number of people, especially in the neglected rural areas. The situation also serves as a push factor in rural–urban migration whose rates have increased tremendously in the last two decades.

Debt has also become a major constraint to African recovery and development. Relative to the limited resources of the African region as a whole, the rapid escalation of the magnitude of the region's debt is alarming. From a mere level of US$32.3 billion in 1974, Africa's public and publicly-guaranteed outstanding debts, including the undisbursed portion, more than quadrupled to reach about $US230 billion in 1988. While this figure might seem modest relative to that of other debtor regions, it is important to underscore the heavy servicing burden implied. Debt service ratios have soared so fast in so many African countries that the region as a whole has had more than 30 reschedulings in a period of less than three years. Indeed, the ratio of debt obligation to exports is as high as 300 per cent in many African countries. No doubt, such a situation will soon degenerate into total chaos unless urgent action is taken to alleviate the burden of debt repayments.

The realization in the 1970s of Africa's long-term development needs and the necessity to overcome the structural maladjustments and pervasive low levels of productivity in African economies led the Heads of State and Government to adopt, in 1980, LPA and FAL. Underlying the philosophy, principles and objectives of LPA is the achievement of a radical change in the pattern of production and consumption, social and economic transformation, accelerated economic growth and

3

development as well as the integration of the African economies. Rather than improve, however, the economic situation of African countries has deteriorated since the adoption of LPA. Beginning with the deep recession into which they were plunged in 1980, the fragile economies of Africa have experienced poor and dwindling performance typified by chronic food deficits, high costs of energy, deteriorating terms of trade and balance of payments disequilibria, and mounting debt service burdens. It was against the background of the dire situation and complexity of the problems and the extreme scarcity of available resources that the African Heads of State and Government committed themselves to the implementation of a sharply focused, time-bound, practical and operational set of activities, priorities and policies when they adopted APPER, in July 1985. They also called for the convening of a special session of the United Nations General Assembly on Africa's critical economic situation.

The United Nations General Assembly Special Session on the Critical Economic Situation in Africa (27 May to 1 June 1986) provided a unique forum for a concentrated focus by the international community on the region's current difficulties, and prospects for the future. It was a timely, historic session which concluded with unanimous agreement on UN-PAAERD in which African governments reasserted their commitment to spearhead Africa's economic recovery and development, based on APPER, and the international community committed itself to support and complement the African efforts. The question now is whether these programmes of action offer Africa a reasonable chance or promise of economic recovery and accelerated development in the years ahead. UN-PAAERD, of course, means different things to different people. To some people, UN-PAAERD constitutes a new source of ideas for action in overcoming some of Africa's pressing economic problems and difficulties; but, to others, it is nothing more than a mere continuum in the already exhausted stock of existing ideas about Africa's development problematique and its challenges.

In demonstration of its continuing interest and preoccupation with Africa's development, and as part of its contribution to the solution of the continent's socio-economic problems, ECA organized an international conference on *Africa: The Challenge of Economic Recovery and Development* in Abuja, Nigeria, from 15 to 19 June 1987. Coming up a year after the Special Session itself and the adoption of UN-PAAERD, and two years after the adoption of APPER, the Conference provided a much-needed opportunity and platform for the fine-tuning of the continent's recovery and development strategy. In particular, it facilitated a close look at the issues and concerns arising from the Special Session and its outcome, some of which, especially those of implementation and follow-up, required urgent consideration and further elaboration. More specifically, the Conference had the following objectives: (i) to critically assess the real chances for economic recovery and medium-term development in Africa, bearing in mind the fact that little economic progress was made on the continent throughout the 1970s and 1980s despite the adoption of stabilization and SAPs in many countries; (ii) to examine the environment – historical, political, social, scientific and technological – for African economic recovery and development, with a view to highlighting what changes – policy, attitudinal, institutional etc. – are needed and how to bring them about; (iii) to make a comprehensive review of UN-PAAERD with a view to identifying gaps in its diagnosis of the 'critical economic situation' in Africa and the relevance of the remedies proffered; (iv) to assess the extent of implementation of UN-PAAERD so far at national, subregional, regional and international levels; and, (v) to undertake a re-evaluation of the overall prospects of long-term economic development and co-operation in and with Africa.

There is no doubt that the Conference, by placing APPER and UN-PAAERD in their proper historical perspectives and contexts, thereby promoting a deeper understanding of their principles and basis as well as the policy issues and choices involved, has greatly enhanced the real chances of their implementation. Particularly significant was the painstaking examination the Conference undertook of the emerging evidence from specific case studies, and its deliberations on whether or not, and to what extent the programmes were beginning to make the desired impact, and what, if any, were the constraints.

The present volume embodies the highlights of the Conference. It contains some selected papers presented by individual participants at the Conference, and submissions by African countries, regional and subregional institutions, and international organizations. While the structure of the book has been patterned closely after the main themes of the Conference, there are nonetheless significant differences in presentation. For example, there were many interesting papers dealing with the background to the African crisis, its nature and magnitude, which were presented at the Conference but have not featured in the present volume in the belief that it is neither necessary nor appropriate to further elaborate on those aspects of the African situation on which a lot has already been said or published. Instead, the volume takes as its point of departure the presentation at the Conference regarding the responses of the African countries and the international community to

5

the crisis situation, beginning with what Africa did to fashion fresh approaches and to react concretely to the rapid deterioration of its socio-economic well-being. And on this, the broad verdict is that Africa was never under any illusions regarding its sombre situation; nor was there an underestimation of the herculean and gigantic efforts and tasks required to turn around the tides of disequilibria, maladjustments, economic peripheralization, mass suffering and overall social instability on the continent.

Now that the commitments of the African Governments have extended beyond the level of rhetoric, and Africa seems to be right on track with regard to the implementation of the necessary policy reforms and actions, how have Africa's development partners and the international community at large responded? In examining the response of the international community, in Part Two, the fact that Africa's malaise is heavily linked to many exogenous aggravating factors is taken as a basic premise. Most of the Chapter contributions in this part of the book reach beyond the traditional concept of international solidarity and its disproportionate emphasis on humanitarian assistance and aid, in the endeavour to show the extent of the complex ways in which the developments in the international environment as a whole directly impinged and continue to impinge on Africa's progress. And their conclusions, overall, tended to converge on one theme: namely, that the changes in the international environment and the overall response of the international community have so far been generally disappointing and less than adequate or generous.

Logically, the *ex-post* analysis in Parts One and Two is followed in Part Three with reflections on the enabling environment for recovery and transformation of the African socio-economic structures. This, no doubt, is a tall order requiring profound insights into the historical, political, socio-cultural and scientific and technological realities of the 'African entity'. But the Chapter contributions in this Part of the book confront the task with admirable dexterity and persuasion by raising the critical questions: Africa's recovery and development for whom and by whom? What are the objective conditions for African development? To which the following answers are also provided without equivocation: namely, that Africa must look inside itself to rediscover the genuine roots of its being and reality, acknowledge its objective conditions, commit itself to building the right and liberating social, economic and political environment, and, finally, as a continent and people, vow with unstinting determination to selflessly implement the necessary actions and policies to launch and manage the process of change and development.

As a follow-up to the brain-storming in Part Three, Part Four examines the crucial options for Africa in initiating structural change and long-term development. Some of the Chapters concentrate on the SAPs that most African countries have had to adopt in recent years, and, in general, came to the conclusion that the stabilization and structural adjustment programmes proposed to Africa by IMF and World Bank have had and are likely to continue to have very limited success. Which, in effect, is another way of saying that African countries must search for new initiatives which take due account of the emerging internal and external economic and technological dimensions, and that the initiatives must be predicated on immediate and full mobilization accompanied by efficient utilization of the region's abundant resources – natural, human, financial and institutional. As for the long term, there is no mincing of words in the Chapters concerning the need for Africa to adopt a 'new economic theology' founded on the triple pillars of agriculture, industrialization and regional economic co-operation. Such a new economic theology is of course seen, of necessity, as one that has to be firmly rooted in popular, auto-centred, internally articulate and self-propelled economic functionalism.

Fully realizing the strategic importance of subregional and regional co-operation and integration to Africa's development, Part Five is devoted to this issue with some of the Chapter contributions surveying African experiments and experiences in co-operation. At the historical level, the general observation is that most integration efforts have had a superficial focus while most co-operation efforts have been conceived almost exclusively within the framework of market integration, even when the reality of balkanized Africa called for much broader integration at the level of production and infrastructure. At the perspectives level, a number of interesting insights are outlined in the different Chapters regarding the future of African integration, ranging from the classical prescriptions for successful integration to such radical approaches as changing existing subregional co-operation arrangements into political confederations.

Part Six deals with the position of Africa in the international economic system. Its main focus is on what the 'New Deal' implicit in UN-PAAERD means for co-operation between Africa and the international community. Virtually all the Chapter contributions in this Part are pessimistic about the prospects of genuine or robust international support for Africa's reform and recovery programmes and processes. That Africa will perforce remain a part of the international economic system is seen not to be in doubt, but this same reality, we are reminded, forces on Africa an imperative necessity to refocus its energies on producing what it wants to consume and consuming more of what it produces if it is to establish the resilience and the internal strength needed to command respect and strategic importance as a member of an integrated world community.

In the epilogue, in Part VII, the chances and prospects for Africa ever getting out of its current economic doldrums are critically examined against the background of the progress or the lack of it in the implementation of UN-PAAERD, and the mid-term review and appraisal of the Programme carried out in November 1988 by the UN General Assembly at its forty-third session. The crucial conditions to be fulfilled, the factors and forces to be unleashed, and the further actions called for on the part of all the parties concerned with Africa's recovery and development in the remaining two-year period to the end of APPER and UN-PAAERD – 1989 and 1990 – are underscored in this Part.

PART ONE

Africa's Response to the Economic Crisis and Recovery Programmes

INTRODUCTORY NOTE

What has been the nature and scope of the African response to the continent's deteriorating socio-economic situation? Why have the strategies and plans adopted before now failed to redress Africa's underdevelopment or ameliorate its social and eonomic crisis, and what real efforts have been made by the African countries, individually and collectively, to implement APPER and UN-PAAERD in the bid to achieve an economic turnaround and launch Africa on the path of economic recovery and thus lay the foundation for renewed growth? These are the central questions on which the five Chapters in this first part of the volume have attempted to focus in several ways.

In Chapter 1, Rasheed and Sarr provide what amounts to an overview answer, amplified in the contributions in the remaining four chapters. They illustrate the efforts of African countries since the independence years to collectively address the critical economic problems of the continent through a chain of initiatives and comprehensive strategies (the central themes of which are self-reliance, self-sustainment and economic integration and co-operation) but go on to demonstrate how, in addition to lack of the political will to tackle real structural problems and faithfully translate declared intentions into concrete activities, a convergence of domestic policy failings and worsening international economic environment have wreaked havoc upon such efforts. By so doing, they have demonstrated, rather convincingly, that there has been no shortage of African ideas on the critical issues of African development; that African countries have been very good at working together in defining their problems, in proposing appropriate solutions and measures, and, recently, in committing themselves to the implementation of concerted programmes of action.

The inescapable question which arises from the analysis by Rasheed and Sarr, is whether it has not been business as usual on the part of the African countries as far as the implementation of APPER and UN-PAAERD is concerned, or whether the adoption of these programmes constitutes a real watershed against the prevailing background of implementation inertia and gaps between policy commitments and performance in Africa. Chapter 2, by the ECA, provides a comprehensive answer to this question through a wide range of information and data, qualitative and quantitative, on the introduction of policy changes and reforms in African countries in the last one to two years, and the actual measures that have been taken by African countries at the regional level. The unmistakable overall picture emerging from the ECA survey is that of a growing number of individual African countries instituting significant and far-reaching reforms, re-ordering their priorities and adopting new strategies in line with APPER and UN-PAAERD, although the same survey depicts less striking measures and inadequate levels of collective action at the regional level. It is on this emerging trend of reform policies in the individual African countries south of the Sahara that Chapter 3 seeks to give further amplification and specificity by focusing on actions taken at the national level in a select sample of 8 country submissions, covering Gambia, Guinea, Nigeria and Senegal (in West Africa), Botswana and Zambia (in Eastern Africa), and Congo and Rwanda (in Central Africa).

In Chapter 4, Mutharika surveys a number of subregional groupings in Africa which have been used as mechanisms for expanding intra-African trade. His assessment of the achievements of these institutions foreshadows, in a way, Chapter 5 which is devoted to the perspectives of continental political and development finance institutions and subregional economic groupings as far as the African response to the economic crisis and recovery programmes is concerned. Notwithstanding the failings or less-than-impressive record of practically all African co-operation institutions, it is difficult not to conclude from Mutharika's analysis that African countries have made a real start in building multinational institutions for economic integration and trade. The bright future envisioned for subregional institutions by Mutharika is underlined by the indications given in Chapter 5 of concerted subregional approaches to the promotion of recovery, and the co-operation process that has begun to emerge in Africa. Equally encouraging is the refocusing on recovery issues and activities, and the refashioning of programmes of regional institutions revealed by some of the perspectives outlined in this Chapter.

CHAPTER ONE

From the Lagos Plan of Action to the Thirteenth Special Session of the United Nations General Assembly

SADIG RASHEED
MAKHA D.N. SARR

INTRODUCTION

The UN General Assembly has launched three International Development Strategies since 1960, one each for the decades of the 1960s, 1970s and 1980s. Yet Africa, which is expected to benefit from these strategies as one of the most disadvantaged continents, continues to be faced with grave economic and social problems.

The large majority of African countries were still part of the colonial systems of the industrialized countries of Europe when the International Development Strategy for the first United Nations Development Decade was launched in the 1960s. Hence, their specific problems were hardly taken into account; the basic interests of the colonial powers predominated in such areas as trade and finance. Although most African countries achieved independence in the early 1960s, they were faced, during that decade, with the consuming tasks of setting up their basic institutional infrastructure. As a result, they could not provide any substantive inputs into the formulation of the International Development Strategy for the Second United Nations Development Decade.

Africa's development at national, subregional, regional and international levels was hardly on the right path even by the early 1970s. At the national level, the overall performance in many countries showed a downward trend while some of the basic socio-economic infrastructure inherited from the colonial system was deteriorating fast. At subregional and regional levels, the growing national egoism prevented the establishment and strengthening of co-operation in such basic areas as education and training; research; transport, production and marketing of strategic industrial products such as chemicals, metal and engineering goods; and money and finance. At the international level, with the prevailing unjust international economic relations, developing countries, particularly those of Africa, remain negatively affected by deteriorating terms of trade and high interest rates, a situation which made it difficult for many of them to earn the necessary foreign exchange resources for development purposes.

On the basis of the above situation and as far back as 1971, at the beginning of the Second United Nations Development Decade, the ECA Conference of Ministers adopted Africa's Development Strategy for the 1970s.[1] This was followed in 1973 by a Declaration on Co-operation, Development and Economic Independence adopted by the Assembly of Heads of State and Government of OAU at its tenth ordinary session, outlining the basic principles and objectives of Africa's development and Africa's stand with respect to international economic relations.

Another step forward in Africa's continuing search for appropriate solutions to the economic and social problems facing the continent was the adoption, in July 1977, by the Assembly of Heads of State and Government of OAU, of the Revised Framework of Principles for the Implementation of the New International Economic Order in Africa. The Revised Framework, initiated by ECA after the sixth and seventh special sessions of the General Assembly of the UN, was to sharpen Africa's views on the various aspects of a NIEO.

At the end of the 1970s, the preparation for UNCTAD V as well as the preparatory work for the International Development Strategy for the Third United Nations Development Decade gathered momentum, and it was within such a context that some prominent Africans, involved in development issues and policies, science and research, met in Monrovia from 12 to 16 February 1979 in a colloquium to discuss the development prospects of Africa under two main themes, namely: (a) What type of development should Africa aspire to for the year 2000? and, (b) What ways and means should be adopted for this purpose?[2]

Following the Monrovia Symposium, the fifth meeting of the ECA Conference of Ministers responsible for economic development and planning, which took place in Rabat, Morocco, in March 1979, adopted resolution 332 (XIV) on the African development strategy which was subsequently endorsed by the sixteenth session of the Assembly of Heads of State and Government of OAU held at Monrovia in July 1979 and which is now known as the Monrovia Declaration of Commitment.

The African strategy laid emphasis on the three basic principles of self-reliance, self-sustainment and economic co-operation and integration. In other words, African countries committed themselves to base their individual and collective development on endogenous factor inputs, especially natural and human resources, and to ensure that the development process relies mainly on domestic factor endowments.

The LPA, adopted by the second extraordinary summit of OAU held in Lagos in April 1980, was a translation into specific actions of those basic principles of the Monrovia Strategy. The Draft Plan of Action was prepared by the sixth meeting of the ECA Conference of Ministers and covered various sectors such as agriculture, industry, science and technology, natural resources, human resources and transport and communications. It also covered development policies and planning, and economic co-operation and integration.

The above review clearly shows that African countries, individually and collectively through ECA and OAU, have consistently addressed the basic development problems facing the continent. But the economic situation in most African countries has nevertheless continued to worsen in spite of the adoption of LPA and FAL. Domestic economic policy shortcomings, insufficient subregional and regional co-operation, the unfavourable international economic environment and, lately, the severe drought of 1983–1985 have been the major factors behind such deterioration. Indeed, Africa faces the threat of the nightmare of socio-economic disaster by the beginning of the next century unless serious actions are taken to reverse current trends.[3]

The sharp deterioration in the social and economic situation led ECA Conference of Ministers to formulate, in April 1985, proposals on economic recovery and accelerated implementation of LPA.[4] The proposals were adopted in July 1985 by the twenty-first Assembly of Heads of State and Government of OAU as APPER; which programme, in turn, formed the basis of UN-PAAERD adopted by the thirteenth special session of the UN General Assembly in June 1986. Thus, within half a decade or so of LPA, African countries adopted various recovery and adjustment programmes to deal with the escalating crisis.

In what follows, we shall review Africa's continuous response to its economic plight, focusing not only on the relevance of the basic principles of Africa's development objectives but equally also on the adequacy and appropriateness of the actions undertaken by the African countries themselves.

THE BASIC PILLARS OF AFRICA'S DEVELOPMENT STRATEGY

In adopting LPA in April 1980, the African Heads of State and Government clearly outlined the philosophy for Africa's future, and laid down the foundations for the genuine development of the region. Not only did the African Heads of State and Government define, in each sector and in an integrated manner, the actions required to ensure a self-reliant and self-sustained development process, but also, in FAL, they committed themselves to strengthening economic co-operation of their respective countries at multinational and subregional levels so as to establish, by the year 2000, an African Economic Community. Of course, the LPA does not limit itself to domestic issues of African development. External factors have also been taken into account, especially trade and economic co-operation with other regions of the world. In doing so, the African Heads of State and Government were aiming at ensuring that Africa plays the role it deserves in the international scene so that peace prevails and a NIEO emerges.

Self-reliance and self-sustainment are the pre-requisites for any genuine independence. In this regard, the Monrovia Declaration of Commitment had specified the main areas in which ownership and mastery of the major factors of production should be achieved: namely, entrepreneurial and technical manpower; science and technology; food production and supply; internally-located industrial development; transport and communications; and natural resources exploration, extraction and use for development.

The LPA further details actions aimed at ensuring that the socio-economic structures of African countries are such that the efforts required for and the benefits derived from development will be equitably shared among various components of the population, and that African economies no longer rely excessively on export of raw materials but provide the necessary basic intermediate, capital and consumer goods.

In the food and agriculture sector, concrete measures were called for in LPA including the reduction of food losses, the establishment of food security schemes at national, subregional and regional levels and the increase in food production. Other measures of paramount importance were directed at the development of agricultural research and extension services and the provision of adequate incentives to producers with respect to pricing policy of agricultural commodities so as to ensure a better income distribution between rural and urban population, and increased food production.

16

With the above measures, African Heads of State and Government had, as a primary objective, the narrowing of the widening gap between demand and domestic supply of food. For, while Africa had to rely on food aid of 1.5 million tons in 1980 and to import 20.4 million tons of food grain at a cost of over $US5 billion at 1980 prices, it was expected that, in the 1980s and 1990s, the region would have reversed the declining self-sufficiency ratio in cereals registered in the 1960s and 1970s and meet its requirements for other food products such as roots, tubers, pulses, meat, fish, etc.

In 1980, Africa's industrial sector represented only 8.9 per cent of the region's GDP and was characterized mainly by light industries producing a small range of consumer goods. It was small and enclaved with little or no link to the other sectors. Thus, LPA stresses the fact that an internally-located industrialization process is a condition for providing the dynamic forces for the structural transformation of the African economy into a modern and self-sustained one. This implies that strong linkages should be established between industry and other sectors as well as between industrial subsectors through the development of resource-based industries such as chemical, metal, building materials and food industries, as well as engineering core industries. It was expected that by 1985 Africa would have laid the foundation for the development of basic industries, i.e. building, metallurgic, mechanical, electrical and chemical industries. The measures that would enable Africa to achieve self-sufficiency in food-processing, industrial products, clothing and energy by 1990 were also defined. By the year 2000, Africa would need to import only a small percentage of its capital goods requirements while it will be self-sufficient in basic intermediate goods such as fertilizers, cement, iron and steel and aluminium. In short, some concrete measures and actions were recommended in LPA for the achievement of short-, medium- and long-term objectives of industrialization.

Given the inadequacy and poor conditions of Africa's transport and communications infrastructure and the inefficiency of transport services, the African Heads of State and Government have, in LPA, emphasized the importance to be attached to the United Nations Transport and Communications Decade for Africa, 1978–1988 (UNCTACDA) which ECA Conference of Ministers at its meeting in Kinshasa, Zaire in 1977 had requested the UN General Assembly to declare in order to mobilize international support for Africa's transport and telecommunications development. While endorsing the principal goals of the strategy of UNCTACDA, the African Heads of State and Government defined the national, subregional and regional measures that would facilitate the integrated and diversified transport and communications infrastructure required to open up the large number of African land-locked countries and isolated regions, and bring about a more integrated African transport network with faster movement of population and goods by the year 2000. The measures hinged partly on the promotion of local manufacture of transport equipment based on local human and material resources.

While focusing on food and agriculture, industry and transport and communications, which no doubt are the basic sectors for ensuring faster economic growth and development, the LPA also highlights the importance of such factor inputs as human and natural resources as well as science and technology essential for the development of these sectors.

With regard to human resources, LPA has spelt out detailed actions at the national, subregional, regional and international levels designed to ensure that African countries, by the year 2000, would achieve a satisfactory level of self-reliance in trained and technical manpower, such that the necessary skills input, both in productive activities and in the services, would be internally generated. Particular emphasis was put on the training of scientists and technicians, managerial staff as well as small-scale entrepreneurs and in-plant industrial workers. Given the variety and specialization of the skills required, LPA also calls for the development of subregional specialized training institutions and co-operation among African countries in pooling their resources.

Natural resources exploration, exploitation and utilization are the necessary conditions for establishing backward and forward linkages in African economies. The main actions outlined in LPA, in this regard, are aimed at integrating natural resources development within national and multinational development plans, programmes and projects. The LPA not only stresses the necessity for African countries, individually and collectively, to exercise sovereignty over their natural resources, but also to develop the necessary technological capabilities for their exploration and use. Also, to speed up the process of technological mastery, African countries undertook to establish joint facilities for applied research and specialized services, especially engineering consultancy services.

In the field of science and technology, LPA has provided detailed actions to be undertaken in the establishment and strengthening of national and regional institutional infrastructure for science and technology. It has also laid great emphasis on the development of human resources for science and technology so as to build up innovation and productive capacities to absorb and adapt imported tech-

18

nology, including high technology. Specific sectoral actions have also been spelt out with respect to the technologies required for food and agriculture, industry, natural resources, transport and communications, education, health, etc.

This brief review of the main elements of LPA clearly shows that the African Heads of State and Government have clearly defined the changes required in patterns of production, distribution and life-styles so as to fully take advantage of the potentials and possibilities of the region.

The need for strengthening African solidarity was also stressed by African Heads of State and Government in FAL. Indeed, African leaders realized that the balkanization of the continent is one of the main constraints to Africa's socio-economic development and hence attempted in FAL to concretize the relevant provisions of the Charter of the OAU relating to the strengthening of subregional and regional co-operation with the ultimate objective of setting up, by the year 2000, an African Economic Community. The evolutionary stages of the African Economic Community, as indicated in FAL, included *inter alia* the establishment and strengthening of subregional economic groupings as well as sectoral integration through the harmonization of development plans, programmes and projects in such basic sectors as food and agriculture, industry, transport and communications, and energy.

FAL also made provisions for the promotion of bilateral and multilateral joint ventures in production activities, and called for the harmonization of financial and monetary policies with a view to reversing the declining trend in the growth of intra-African trade. Overall, it represented the collective response of African countries to overcome the present balkanization of the region so that a united and strengthened Africa could emerge by the year 2000 and play its deserved role in the international fora.

At the Lagos Summit, African leaders emphasized the need for African countries to participate positively in and influence the decision-making process of international fora. Specifically, the Assembly of Heads of State and Government appealed to all OAU member States 'to participate fully and actively in the international economic negotiations... and in global negotiations based on the LPA ...'.[5] The agenda for such global negotiations should include: (a) international effort to enable Africa to achieve sovereignty over its natural resources; (b) international support for the physical integration of Africa through full co-operation in the implementation of the UNTACDA, 1978–1988; (c) international co-operation to achieve a breakthrough in manpower development in Africa; (d) decolonization of Africa's colonial monetary arrangements and the setting up of an African monetary system; (e) respect for Africa's political independence and the elimination of manipulation of the African economy by outside powers with a view to frustrating the achievement of national and regional economic objectives; and, (f) acceptance by the entire international community that Africa's continued economic backwardness constitutes a danger to world peace and stability and, consequently, an international agreement to provide Africa with the wherewithal to enable her achieve a new national and regional order by the year 2000.[6]

PROBLEMS AND CONSTRAINTS IN THE IMPLEMENTATION OF LPA AND FAL

The worsening international economic environment, endogenous policy shortcomings at national, subregional and regional levels, and deteriorating climatic conditions are some of the major problems and constraints in the implementation of LPA.

The Worsening International Economic Environment

The global economic environment was, in the early 1980s, characterized by a widespread economic recession in developed countries, and this, in turn, contributed to a large extent to a further deepening of the economic crisis which had confronted most African countries at the time LPA and FAL were adopted. Indeed, one year after the adoption of these two documents, the attention of the ECA Conference of Ministers, at its seventh meeting in Freetown, Sierra Leone, in April 1981, was drawn to the rapidly escalating economic crisis in Africa and to the need for devising an African emergency programme of action.[7]

First was the collapse in commodity prices which has resulted in a sharp decline in export earnings which, coupled with an ever-increasing demand for imports, further increased the external trade and current account deficits. Between 1979 and 1981, the prices of some African leading export commodities, such as coffee, copper, cocoa, bananas, vegetable oils and tea, experienced sharp declines, with losses in earnings estimated at $US2.2 billion during the period. Indeed, virtually all other primary commodities exported by Africa experienced similar declines in prices. In real terms, commodity prices in 1982 were at their lowest level since 1940. Between 1981 and 1983 alone, the total value of Africa's exports fell by more than 15 per cent. This trend has continued ever since, with the value of Africa's exports declining substantially by 28.7 per cent in 1986. Inevitably, Africa's current account position has worsened, reaching $US24.7 billion in 1982 and $US21.5 billion in 1986.

A second major characteristic of the worsening international economic environment is Africa's increasing external indebtedness. Both the widening trade gap and the decline in official transfers have forced most African countries to borrow extensively from abroad, with the result that Africa's total indebtedness is estimated to have reached close to $US200 billion at the end of 1986. In addition, such massive external borrowing was made at high interest rates especially since 1981 when they reached about 10.1 per cent and continued to escalate, compared to 4.2 per cent in 1972. Debt-service requirements have become unmanageable and are currently estimated at around $US30 billion for the continent. The number of countries entering into re-scheduling agreements has increased substantially, often to no avail, and arrears continued to accumulate. Indeed, the debt-service ratio is estimated at over 30 per cent, on average, and above 50 per cent for a quarter of all African countries. Thus, debt-servicing has become one of the major impediments to Africa's economic growth and development.

The developments in the international scene since 1980/1981 are such that the main preoccupation of African countries is one of economic and financial crisis management. Because of the external pressures, most of them have failed to embark on the necessary structural changes that would enable them to build the foundations for sclf-reliance and self-sustainment, and disengage from the inequitable post-war world economic order.

Domestic Policy Shortcomings

While Africa's external dependence was increasingly reinforced, as explained above, there were no significant steps by African countries to improve the domestic order. Indeed, non-economic behaviour in patterns of production, consumption and life-styles have continued to prevail in many countries.[8] Consequently, economic performance has been lagging far behind the expectations raised by LPA and FAL.

Although agricultural production accounted for over 70 per cent of the total GDP in the early 1980s, little attention was given to food production; the main concern being the increase in the production of agricultural export commodities. Hence, dependence on food imports and food aid continued to increase, thus wiping out the meagre foreign exchange earnings from exports. More serious was the inadequacy or lack of incentive measures in terms of producer prices, extension services and credit facilities, as a result of which subsistence farming became the dominant feature of African agriculture and the rural–urban migration increased sharply.

In other sectors, the main characteristic of the early 1980s has been the allocation, by many African countries, of scarce resources to projects of national pride that, more often, do not bring any tangible increase in the well-being of the population, or constitute a heavy burden on the public finances because of large subsidies required for sustaining them. The industrial sector, which is essential for the transformation of African economies, has remained small and fragmented with little or no intra- and inter-sectoral linkages. The large number of import-substitution industries created in many African countries during the 1960s and 1970s have turned into important sources of foreign exchange leakages through imports of raw materials, spare parts and skilled manpower.

The expenditure component of African economies has also remained as it was when LPA was adopted. Africa has increasingly continued to consume what it does not produce. The expenditure patterns of the richer class of the population – including leaders and high-level managers – continued to reflect uneconomic and counter-productive ways of life, with extravagant and expensive tastes. As a result, Africa's savings rate in the early 1980s was as low as 18 per cent of GDP, meaning that productive investment, if any, relied mainly on external capital.

The above shortcomings at the national level were compounded by the failure of Africa to concretize the objectives spelled out in FAL. Though a number of subregional economic groupings have been established, subregional and regional integration has remained illusory. As a result, very little progress has been achieved in such areas as the establishment of multinational basic industries, the building of integrated national or multinational multi-modal transport networks, the creation and development of advanced and efficient subregional and regional training and research centres, the increase and diversification of intra-African trade and the formulation of monetary arrangements with a view to preventing large fluctuations in the values of African currencies vis-a-vis the major foreign currencies.

The Impact of the Deteriorating Climatic Conditions

Africa was virtually at the verge of economic collapse in the early 1980s when as many as 34 African countries were, in 1983/1984, hard-hit by a severe and widespread drought. The persistence of drought has led to a serious food scarcity resulting in famine, malnutrition and related diseases, loss of human lives, sharp depletion of livestock and severe water shortages. In 1984 alone, as many as 27 countries were dependent largely on food-aid.[9]

Not only have the consequences of worsening climatic conditions resulted in catastrophe, food-wise; entire economies were gravely affected, with over 150 million people involved. Moreover, the sharp decline in the production of agricultural export commodities has made most African countries entirely dependent on external aid, not only for food and other survival items, but also for resources required to maintain the minimum level of social and administrative services, and for purposes of development.

Such a situation, combined with the worsening international economic environment and the domestic policy shortcomings, constituted a grave concern for the international community since 1984. In this regard, the Secretary-General of the UN launched an initiative in early 1984 to alert the international community to the then escalating social and economic crisis in Africa. At the same time, the African countries have themselves also resolved, as they did in 1980, to formulate, once again, an appropriate and adequate global response to their critical economic situation.

EFFORTS TO COPE WITH THE ESCALATING CRISIS OF THE 1980s

The escalating crisis has forced African countries to take, individually and collectively, far-reaching measures to deal with the rapidly deteriorating economic situation. Actions by most African countries, on an individual basis, have concentrated on measures designed to deal with the immediate plight relating to the drought and the achievement of internal and external equilibrium in the short-run. The collective responses, on the other hand, while recognizing the need for immediate and short-term actions to alleviate the human suffering and misery, and to redress the conditions which gave rise to the short-term crisis, emphasized the root causes of the crisis, both internal and external, and focused on enduring solutions.

The Individual Adjustment Efforts of African Countries

The escalating economic and social crisis has resulted, *inter alia*, in acute balance-of-payments difficulties which, together with the pressing need for external resource flows, have forced African countries to adopt stringent structural adjustment policies and stabilization programmes, often in agreement with the World Bank and IMF.

Indeed, between 1980 and 1984, no fewer than 22 countries negotiated SAPs with the IMF and the World Bank.

The austerity measures that have been adopted within the framework of these programmes have generally included currency devaluation, reduction of public expenditure, reduction of budget deficits, setting of ceilings for government and private sector borrowings from the banking system, curtailment of import demand, removal of subsidies and price controls, liberalization of the economy, limitation of the size of the public sector and improvement in production incentives. Most of the adjustment programmes were of a short-term nature lasting for two years or so, with a built-in component of conditionality. Tied to the SAPs have been attempts to provide debt relief to African countries through debt rescheduling exercises. Experience has however shown that many of the SAPs have been implemented at grave political and social costs, which in some instances have led to the programmes being abandoned or reversed in part.

Overall, the impact of the SAPs has not been particularly favourable. In the majority of cases, they did not succeed in achieving their objectives of restoring internal and external equilibrium, and in bringing about a resumption of steady growth.[10] The fact that the international environment has not been favourable and productive capacity was often curtailed as a result of import reductions and curbs on investment expenditures has contributed to the unsatisfactory outcome of SAPs.

Africa's Collective Response to the Multi-dimensional Crisis

Africa's collective response to the rapidly deteriorating economic and social conditions on the continent has been channelled through the main regional fora; namely, that of ECA and OAU. As stated earlier, one year after the adoption of LPA, the deteriorating economic conditions led the seventh meeting of ECA Conference of Ministers to consider a document entitled: Africa's Rapidly Escalating Crisis – Proposals for a Short-term Immediate Programme for Survival.[11] Also in 1983, the ECA Conference of Ministers, at ECA's Silver Jubilee session, deliberated on the serious economic situation in Africa. Furthermore, as a result of the serious deterioration of economic conditions on the continent, the running themes of the meetings of the ECA Conference of Ministers in 1984, 1985 and 1986 were devoted to the critical economic and social situation in Africa, and to the requirements for African economic recovery and development. This was followed by the twenty-first Assembly of the Heads of State and

Government of OAU which was devoted mainly to the consideration of economic matters, and culminated in the adoption of APPER.

The tenth meeting of ECA Conference of Ministers and nineteenth session of the Commission, which took place from 24 to 28 May 1984, focused on the critical economic and social situation and adopted a Special Memorandum on Africa's economic and social crisis for presentation to the 1984 second regular session of the Economic and Social Council of the UN (ECOSOC) and the twentieth ordinary session of the Assembly of Heads of State and Government of OAU.

The Special Memorandum did not limit itself to the emergency created by the drought situation, although the main preoccupation, in the latter part of 1983 and the beginning of 1984, both of Africa and the international community was with the severe and widespread drought and its outcome. It clearly recognized that the crisis had existed since the mid-1970s as a result of the cumulative impact of a number of adverse factors, both internal and external, and only rapidly escalated and reached a critical level in the early 1980s as a result of the severe drought and the rapidly deteriorating international economic environment manifested in the collapse of commodity prices, the stagnation and decline in official development assistance, the dramatic increase in Africa's external debt, the rising interest rates and debt-servicing costs, and increased protectionism. The Memorandum called for a concerted approach to the problem, involving actions directed at the emergency and short- and medium-term measures focusing on the rehabilitation and reconstruction of the major economic sectors of African economies. In view of the scale and complexity of the problem, it called on the international community to complement and supplement Africa's efforts through the provision of massive assistance and the creation of an environment conducive to development.

Because of the serious concern over Africa's external debt problem, the African Ministers of Finance met in June 1984 to discuss the problem in all its aspects and adopted *The Addis Ababa Declaration on Africa's External Indebtedness*[12] analysing the worsening indebtedness of African countries, its causes and the detailed measures to deal with the problem at national, subregional, regional and international levels. The Addis Ababa Declaration was annexed to the Special Memorandum and presented to the second regular session of ECOSOC during 12 to 17 July 1984. Both at the ECOSOC 1984 summer session and at the General Assembly that followed, an active debate on the African crisis took place and a strong expression of support for Africa was voiced. Indeed, a Declaration on the critical economic situation in Africa was adopted by the thirty-ninth session of the General Assembly which called on the international community and the UN System to take specific measures to assist African countries in dealing with the crisis. The Special Memorandum was also approved by the Assembly of the Heads of State and Government of OAU and formed the basis for a Declaration by the Heads of State and Government on the critical economic situation in Africa.

The worsening of the economic situation in Africa further prompted ECA Conference of Ministers to devote its 1985 meeting to the discussion of the crisis. Subsequently, the Conference adopted a *Second Special Memorandum by the ECA Conference of Ministers: International Action for Long-term Development and Economic Growth in Africa*[13] for presentation to the 1985 regular session of ECOSOC, and a document entitled: *Recommendations of the ECA Conference of Ministers Concerning the Economic Issues on the Agenda of the Twenty-First Ordinary Session of the Assembly of Heads of State and Government of OAU.*[14]

In the Second Special Memorandum, the African ministers responsible for economic development and planning stated as follows:

> We are deeply convinced that unless the factors underlying Africa's economic and social crisis are attacked at the root through durable and long-term structural transformation measures, as enunciated in the LPA and the FAL, the current emergency will become a permanent, structural phenomenon and the hope for transforming Africa from its current pitiful state into a viable economic community capable of achieving a growing measure of self-reliant and self-sustained growth and development, will be a fantasy. The time is most opportune for an attack on the root causes of Africa's underdevelopment and a start on the required long-term structural adjustment measures. Unless we act with the seriousness that the problem deserves and act now, Africa will have no future to speak of or to look forward to.[15]

The recommendations of the ECA Conference of Ministers concerning the draft agenda of the twenty-first ordinary session of the Assembly of Heads of State and Government of OAU gave an overall assessment of the implementation of LPA and the economic performance of the African region for the period 1980–1985, and proposed measures for the accelerated attainment of the objectives of LPA and FAL; a special programme of action for the improvement of the food situation and rehabilitation of agriculture; and measures for dealing with Africa's external debt. Proposals for establishing a common platform of action by African countries were also made. These recommendations were subsequently adopted, with certain modifications, by the Steering Committee, Council of Ministers and the twenty-first Assembly of the Heads of State and Government of OAU as APPER.

APPER was formulated as a concrete programme for reconstruction and rehabilitation, and as a basis for medium- and long-term structural transformation of the African economies towards self-reliant and self-sustaining growth and development. The Programme was based on the LPA and designed to lay the foundation for the achievement of the objectives of the latter by concentrating on a set of priority activities and policies to be implemented during 1986–1990, at the centre of which is the food and agriculture sector. Agricultural transformation was seen as the means for spearheading the breakthrough in structural transformation. Strong linkages between agriculture, on the one hand, and industry and the economic infrastructure, on the other, were seen as crucial for agricultural transformation while combating drought and desertification and the development of human resources were singled out as other priorities.

While committing themselves to the implementation of the measures contained in APPER, the African leaders were very much aware of the limitations imposed by an unfavourable international economic environment and of the need for the international community to be fully involved in solving Africa's economic crisis. Thus, in their resolution on the African economic situation accompanying APPER, the Assembly of Heads of State and Government of OAU requested that a special session of the UN General Assembly be convened on the critical economic situation in Africa. In their Declaration on the critical economic situation in Africa, the Heads of State and Government also called for an international Conference on Africa's external indebtedness to be convened as a matter of urgency to provide a forum for Africa's international creditors and the African countries to discuss Africa's external debt problem with a view to arriving at appropriate solutions.

It is evident from the foregoing that Africa's collective responses to the economic crisis have been both timely and appropriate. Furthermore, the collective responses have managed to attract the attention of the international community, particularly at the UN fora. ECA's first and second Memoranda formed the basis for a discussion on the African crisis at the ECOSOC's 1984 and 1985 regular sessions. The Declaration on the critical economic situation in Africa, adopted by the UN General Assembly in 1984, took note of the Declaration on the critical economic situation in Africa and the resolutions adopted by the Heads of State and Government of OAU at its twentieth ordinary session, held in November 1984. Acting on the request of the African Heads of State and Government, the UN General Assembly decided to convene from 27 to 31 May 1986 a special session at ministerial level to consider in depth the critical economic situation in Africa.[16]

AFRICA AND THE THIRTEENTH SPECIAL SESSION OF THE UN GENERAL ASSEMBLY

The decision of the UN General Assembly to convene a special session for an in-depth consideration of the critical economic situation in Africa afforded the continent a unique opportunity to put its case before the international community with a view to mobilizing international support for the efforts to surmount the crisis. Never before had a special session of the UN General Assembly been organized to discuss the problem of any one particular region of the world.

Africa's Submission to the Thirteenth Special Session of UN

A comprehensive analytical document entitled *Africa's Submission to the Special Session of the United Nations General Assembly on Africa's Economic and Social Crisis*[17] was prepared by ECA and OAU, and adopted by the first extraordinary session of ECA's Conference of Ministers, which was specifically convened in Addis Ababa, Ethiopia from 28 to 30 March 1986. The *Submission* was also adopted on 31 March 1986 by the Council of Ministers of OAU at its fifteenth extraordinary session. It was subsequently presented to the *Ad Hoc* Committee of the Whole as Africa's collective response. As it turned out, *Africa's Submission* was indeed the main and major substantive preparatory document for the Session. Africa's *Submission* involved close co-operation between ECA and OAU, which included the mounting of joint ECA/OAU missions to all African countries. Extensive consultations were also undertaken with the international community, including the UN system at all levels.

The *Submission* analysed the nature of the African crisis, the potentials for future development and the actions required both from the African Governments and people and from the international community to achieve recovery and development. It was, in essence, a translation of APPER into an action-oriented programme that is required to bring about a process of rehabilitation, recovery and development during the period 1986–1990.

The financial requirements of APPER were clearly specified in the document on the basis of data collected from member States by the joint ECA/OAU missions. One hundred and twenty eight billion US dollars are required to finance the Programme during 1986–1990, of which $US82.5 billion or 64.4 per cent would be covered from domestic sources, while $US45.6 billion or 35.6 per cent was expected from external sources. The resource requirements were highest for agriculture ($US57.4 billion) followed by other sectors in support of agriculture ($US60.1 billion), human resources development ($US7.2 billion) and drought and desertification ($US3.4 billion). The *Submission* made it clear that the support required from the international community for the successful implementation of APPER should be seen as a special assistance to a special priority programme, and does not in any way represent the total external requirements of the continent's recovery and development efforts. In addition to the gap of $US9.1 billion annually, the document estimated that the debt-servicing requirements will amount to between $US14.6 billion and $US24.5 billion annually, and called on the international community to bridge this gap through additional resource flows and debt-relief measures.

While recognizing the need for effective commitment at the national level, *Africa's Submission* called for the establishment of joint co-operative actions between Africa and the international community to enable Africa to achieve its objectives. This concept of forging a shared partnership or compact between Africa and the international community, in which each side is called upon to commit itself to certain actions, was a novel approach which helped a great deal in arriving at a consensus at the special session. On the one hand, Africa re-affirmed its determination to implement APPER and undertook to make genuine efforts to improve the management of its economies, pursue policy reforms and mobilize domestic resources. On the other, the *Submission* called on the international community to accept APPER as the basis for development priorities during 1986–1990; improve the arrangement for international economic co-operation; make the external environment more favourable to Africa's rehabilitation, recovery and growth efforts; alleviate the debt-burden through lasting debt-relief measures; and provide extensive international support to implement APPER in general. An element of reciprocal responsibility in following up and evaluating the implementation of the agreement was included. In calling for the establishment of a compact between Africa and the international community, the *Submission* thus emphasized the principles of mutual commitments and co-responsibility.

The United Nations Programme of Action for African Economic Recovery and Development, 1986–1990

The UN-PAAERD, which was adopted by consensus by the thirteenth special session, is largely based on *Africa's Submission.* The negotiations preceding UN-PAAERD were fraught with difficulties and the very process of arriving at a compromise was such that Africa was not in a position to insist on the inclusion of three elements, namely: (i) outright endorsement of APPER by the international community; (ii) commitment from the international community to provide financial assistance in specific dollar terms to African countries for the implementation of APPER and for ameliorating the debt-servicing requirements as requested; and, (iii) commitment from the international community to provide lasting solutions to the debt problem along the lines specified in the *Submission.*

In spite of these limitations, however, the unanimous adoption of UN-PAAERD represents, from an African perspective, a great success for Africa. UN-PAAERD does provide a unique framework for co-operation between Africa and the international community. The real issue is whether Africa and its major partners are ready to undertake the various actions and honour the various commitments embodied therein.

CONCLUSION

The foregoing review of the socio-economic situation in Africa begs a fundamental question to which an explanation ought to be provided: Why is it that in spite of the comprehensive and sound strategies that have been adopted at various fora, Africa has consistently been confronted with a deepening social and economic crisis? We can think of four broad explanations.

Failure to Address the Structural Nature of the Crisis

No doubt, the drought calamity and a host of adverse exogenous factors have contributed, in no small measure, to the further deepening of Africa's socio-economic crisis since 1980. This notwithstanding, it is essential to recognize that Africa's basic problems are structural in nature and are to be sought in the internal structural imbalances of the African economies and their excessive outward orientation and overt external dependence. The production structure of African countries is lopsided in the sense that it is heavily dominated by export-oriented agriculture, a small industrial base – only marginally linked to the region's natural resource base – and a mining sector almost totally dependent on external finance, technology and management, and whose output is destined for export in a raw or, at best, semi-processed form. It is obvious that such a production structure lacks the healthy internal dynamism and sectoral interdependence that are necessary for generating steady growth. The overdependence on external markets for the export of a narrow range of agricultural and mineral products whose prices have been falling continuously, and the increased dependence on imports whose prices have been steadily increasing, have resulted in serious structural trade and financial imbalances. Unless these fundamental weaknesses are addressed, there is little hope that the African economies could become buoyant, self-reliant and less vulnerable to internal and external shocks.

Regrettably, post-independence development policies and strategies have done very little to tackle these structural problems. More recently, as the crisis escalated, the capacity of the African countries to pursue meaningful policies became weakened. The combined effects of the disastrous drought and the adverse external conditions and shocks have led African countries to follow, on an individual basis, survival policies merely designed to enable them to cope with the emergency situation and with short-term considerations. So much so that the post-1980 years in Africa are perhaps best described as years of crisis management.

Failure to Reflect Declared Strategies and Policies in the Countries' Political and Socio-economic Structures

The political and socio-economic structures of African countries that emerged, following independence in the early 1960s, are well known and need therefore no extensive review. However, some salient features should be borne in mind. First, the macro-structure of the African colonial economy was characterized by a profound dichotomy between rural and urban areas. While the life-styles and aspiration of the latter were focused on European patterns of consumption, the rural population was deprived of the most essential basic social and economic infrastructure, such as schools, health centres, clean water, etc. Moreover, the bureaucratic fortress of the cities, built up as an 'edifice' of the newly gained sovereignty, was such that most policy measures and decisions only helped to widen the economic and social disparities between the urban and rural areas.

Second, following independence, there has been a proliferation of bilateral aid agencies. Most African countries were offered assistance programmes aimed at building up their administrative and economic infrastructure for development, but these assistance programmes often worked at cross purposes and have not always been directed towards productive activities. The misuse of bilateral aid has created a situation of aid-dependency in many countries, whereby both recurrent and development budgets depended heavily on external resources. Hence, since independence, a mentality of dependency has developed in many African countries, and the more technical assistance and financial aid provided, the greater has been the need for more aid.

Third, the emerging post-independence political and administrative structures in many African countries have not enabled governments to effectively manage development. The inadequacies of human resource base and policies, the lack of endogenous administrative and managerial capacities and inappropriate financial, administrative and managerial policies and practices have greatly undermined the ability of African Governments to manage their economies. The fact that the last two-and-a-half decades have witnessed a considerable expansion in the size of the public sector as well as the role of that sector in the development process has made these constraints particularly costly.

Public enterprises have, in general, been performing poorly in most countries and have been a drain on scarce national resources. In many countries, the public services are overstaffed, inefficient and totally devoid of a development orientation. Political patronage and ethnic loyalties have subverted merit and bred nepotism and inefficient recruitment policies. The lack of administrative ethics and higher costs of living have often led to an attitude of nonchalance, and promoted corruption. All these factors have contributed to the malaise of the public services. Added to that is the fact that in many instances these services lack the sense of direction and purpose as their goals and functions are often not structured in a manner that would render their functioning effective.

The political and administrative structures have made it difficult to develop and implement rational management systems, with lengthy and cumbersome decision-making processes. Thus, substantial resources, both human and financial, have been wasted. The lack of sound organizational and management methods in the various socio-economic sectors, coupled with the mounting economic and financial difficulties, have brought most of Africa's public services to a state of near chaos. Consequently, an increasing number of expatriates from bilateral and multilateral donors have taken over high-level administrative and managerial posts in African countries.

Politicians have tended in general to undermine the authority of public institutions by disregarding the rules and regulations which govern their operations, and it is no wonder therefore that the capacity of governments to deal with complex issues of development policy and manage the development effort has been ineffectual in many instances. The rapid turn-over of political regimes, governments, ministers and senior public officials as well as the frequent reordering of the portfolios of ministries have added to the administrative chaos and hampered the efficacy of development policies and strategies.

The aforementioned domestic structures and practices are clear impediments to the implementation of the commitments made by African Governments in various fora since the late 1970s. With over 80 per cent of the population marginalized; with an aid-dependent mentality; inadequate and sometimes counter-productive public services, management and organizational systems; and an externally-dependent economic structure, the objectives of self-reliance and self-sustainment naturally remained mere slogans. This is why a new style of leadership and more effective administrative structures and systems that are development-oriented and free from the crippling deficiencies of the past must emerge if any developmental goals are to be meaningfully implemented.

Failure to Translate African Solidarity into Concrete Collective Actions

African countries have repeatedly expressed their full commitment to economic co-operation. As a result, many economic groupings have been set up in various African sub-regions. The river basin authorities, for example, have specific objectives of common exploitation of water resources. In addition, many countries have entered into bilateral or multilateral agreements for the joint management of services and infrastructure inherited from the colonial administrations, particularly railways, airlines and postal services. But, generally, the main objective of the sub-regional organizations is to achieve economic integration through co-operation in various sectors.

While the above arrangements constituted a step forward towards the objectives laid down in FAL, their functioning has been greatly hampered by interstate conflicts that have no relevance to economic co-operation. Hence, the hopes that were created by the emergence of viable communities have quickly vanished, a case in point being the EAC. Presently, the CEAO is threatened by national egoisms, while other similar viable multinational enterprises, especially in the transport sector, have been dismantled or are on the verge of bankruptcy because of selfishness and lack of interest by member States.

The main advantages of subregional economic groupings in developing countries in general and African countries in particular are the gains expected by member States from intra-union specialization, particularly in the establishment of large-scale industries. Yet, in practice, existing subregional groupings have tended to concentrate on trade and customs issues, while the production base remained narrow and externally oriented. African countries have, therefore, to realize that political commitment to intra-African co-operation can be effective only through integrated industrial and infrastructural projects and through common development of their technological capabilities. Only such integration schemes can survive the political divergencies or differences among countries, which often lead to the weakening of subregional organizations.

Debilitating Effects of the Unfavourable External Economic Environment

The collapse in commodity prices, the sustained deterioration in Africa's terms of trade and the serious external debt situation have all contributed to a deepening of the African crisis and have weakened the capacity of African countries to successfully deal with it.

As long as the African economies continue to be excessively outwardly oriented, the external economic environment will continue to play a major role in influencing Africa's chances for economic recovery or otherwise. No matter how successful Africa becomes in raising production and productivity, low export prices and the adverse terms of trade will wipe out any likely gain from attempts at increasing export revenues and narrowing the trade deficits. Also, unless a lasting solution is found to the serious debt and debt-servicing problems, the already unmanageable size of the debt-servicing requirements will make a sheer mockery of any attempts at maintaining investment and import levels. Furthermore, even if African countries were to succeed in adopting appropriate policies aimed at achieving an increased measure of national and collective self-reliance, the efforts will become futile without the needed improvements in the international economic environment. The efforts of the African countries to reform and introduce policies required to generate steady recovery and development are a necessary rather than sufficient condition. This is why Africa must unite firmly in pressing for the creation of favourable conditions in support of Africa's initiatives and in ensuring that such initiatives do not remain futile.

Both APPER and UN-PAAERD have raised new hopes for the African people, and it is encouraging to note that since the adoption of these programmes, many African countries have embarked on courageous reforms, including the reordering of investment priorities; the strengthening of overall co-ordinating structures for development and domestic financial resources mobilization mechanisms; improvements in the management of the economy, especially public financial management; better control of resource allocation; encouragement of production and productivity; and promotion of greater participation of indigenous private sector in the development process. Such measures, coupled with improved weather conditions, have undoubtedly been the main reasons for the signs of recovery that are evident in many African countries, particularly non-oil exporting countries, in 1986. However, the measures must be sustained and expanded with a view to bringing about structural transformation of the African economies and the reform of institutions and attitudes if the fundamental aspects of the economic crisis are to be addressed. In spite of the unfavourable international economic environment, and while adopting co-ordinated and concerted approaches to face the challenge of the adverse economic environment and pressing for changes in that environment, African countries must make a determined effort to push ahead with the task of recovery and sustained development.

NOTES

1. ECA Resolution 218 (X).
2. See, 'What Kind of Africa by the Year 2000?' *Final Report on the Monrovia Symposium of the Future Development Prospects of Africa Towards the Year 2000*; OAU/ILO Publication 1979.
3. See, *ECA and Africa's Development 1983–2008: A Preliminary Perspective Study, Economic Commission for Africa*, April 1983.
4. Recommendations of the ECA Conference of Ministers Concerning the Economic Issues on the Draft Agenda of The Twenty-First Ordinary Session of the Assembly of Heads of State and Government of OAU, E/ECA/CM.11/Rev.1, April 1985.
5. Resolution on the participation of Africa in international negotiations. Annex III of the LPA. Organization of African Unity, 1980.
6. Adebayo Adedeji, *Africa and the International Order: A Reassessment*, December 1979.
7. See, *Africa's Rapidly Escalating Economic Crisis: Proposals for a Short-term Immediate Programme for Survival*, E/CN.14/CONF/81/01, ECA, January 1981.
8. See, *ECA and Africa's Development 1983–2008 – A Preliminary Perspective Study*, ECA, *op. cit.*
9. See, *Critical Economic Situation in Africa*. Report of the Secretary-General of the United Nations, E/1984/68, 26 April 1984, and A/39/594, 23 October 1984.
10. See, for example, *Survey of Economic and Social Conditions in Africa, 1982–1983*, pp.135–156 (E/ECA/CM.10/4), April 1984; *The Implications of Structural Adjustment and Stabilization Programmes on Long-term Growth and Develop-*

ment in African Least Developed Countries, Issues for Consideration (E/ECA/LDCs.7/EXP.6/4), 31 March 1987.
11. *Ibid.*
12. Report of the Regional Ministerial Meeting on Africa's External indebtedness, E/ECA/CM.11/5, 11 March 1985.
13. E/ECA/CM.11/77/Rev.1, May 1985.
14. E/ECA/CM.11/80/Rev.1, *op.cit.*
15. E/ECA/CM.11/77/Rev.1, *op.cit.* p.8.
16. United Nations General Assembly resolution 40/40, 2 December 1985.
17. OAU/ECM/2XV/Rev.2, E/ECA/ECM.1/Rev.2, ECA, United Nations 1986.

CHAPTER TWO

Survey on the Implementation of APPER and UN-PAAERD

ECA SECRETARIAT

INTRODUCTION

As already stated in the preceding chapter, the thirteenth special session of the UN General Assembly on the African economic crisis had before it an African submission which set out a new and unique approach to launching social and economic growth in African countries. The *Ad Hoc* Committee of the Whole examined the African submission alongside other documents which had been submitted to the Special Session. On 1 June 1986, the Special Session adopted by consensus a resolution on the UN-PAAERD. The resolution, *inter alia*, urged all governments to take effective action for the rapid and full implementation of UN-PAAERD and requested the organizations and bodies of the UN system to participate fully to support the implementation of the Programme of Action. The Secretary-General was also requested to monitor the implementation of the Programme and to submit progress reports to the General Assembly at its forty-second and forty-third sessions.

The effective and timely implementation of APPER and UN-PAAERD is crucial to Africa's economic recovery. Hence there is an urgent need to establish or strengthen national implementation and follow-up mechanisms. Indeed, given the importance of national mechanisms for the successful implementation of UN-PAAERD, it was necessary to conduct a survey to ascertain concrete and effective mechanisms that African countries have established or strengthened to ensure a rapid and vigorous implementation of APPER and UN-PAAERD.

In order to monitor the implementation of the Programme at the national and subregional levels year-to-year, it was necessary to obtain information on the situation existing in 1986 and any proposed national initiatives to restructure development planning programmes, the mechanisms for monitoring them and the mobilization of resources. With this in mind, the ECA administered a questionnaire to all member States.

It should be noted that monitoring on a regular and continuing basis of any development programme is necessary for its success. In APPER, the African countries themselves recognized the importance of monitoring. They stated that 'it is absolutely essential that a machinery be put in place to monitor on a continuing basis the implementation of the Priority Programme so as to ensure that problems and bottle-necks are identified at an early stage and corrective measures instituted without delay'. They emphasized that *post-facto* evaluation of programmes had often proved too late for remedial action to be taken. Member States themselves agreed that follow-up and evaluation mechanisms should be set up at the national level and the terms of reference of each mechanism should include the review and evaluation of progress in the implementation of agreed commitments both on the part of the donor community and national governments.

Immediately after the Special Session, the Secretary-General of the UN set up two special bodies: the Steering Committee, with the Director-General of Development as Chairman, the Executive Secretary of ECA as Vice-Chairman and the Regional Director of UNDP as Secretary, to oversee the implementation of UN-PAAERD, and a UN Inter-agency Task Force, with the Executive Secretary of ECA as Chairman and the Deputy Executive Director of UNICEF as Vice-Chairman, was also set up as an operational arm of the Steering Committee. Both bodies were to assist the Secretary-General in monitoring the implementation of UN-PAAERD and thus enable him to report to the forty-second and forty-third sessions of the UN General Assembly in accordance with resolution S-13/2.

In order to keep up the momentum generated by the Special Session, the second extraordinary session of the ECA Conference of Ministers which took place in October 1986 devoted part of its discussions to the question of monitoring the UN-PAAERD. Resolution ES-2/4 of 16 October 1986 passed by the Conference *inter alia* strongly urged member States to implement speedily and fully the measures and policy reforms which they had committed themselves to in UN-PAAERD and APPER and also called on the Executive Secretary of ECA to further intensify his efforts in assisting member States in the successful implementation, monitoring and evaluation of UN-PAAERD and APPER. The resolution also urged member States to complete urgently the ECA questionnaire on the implementation of APPER and UN-PAAERD. The Executive Secretary of ECA was requested on the basis of this questionnaire to prepare an in-depth and comprehensive report for consideration of the ECA Conference of Ministers at its ordinary session of April 1987, for consideration by the OAU Steering Committee and the 1987 Assembly of Heads of State and Government of OAU as well as the General Assembly of the UN at its forty-second session as part of the Secretary-General's progress report.

The issuing of the questionnaire just five months after the adoption of UN-PAAERD was to enable ECA to ascertain whether member States had established a continuous process for the follow-up, evaluation and co-ordination of its implementation at the national level. Such information would assist ECA to prepare a composite picture of the implementation status of UN-PAAERD in the base year 1986 and would thus provide baseline information against which progress can be measured in later years. It will also assist member States to identify key areas where their implementation lags behind that of other countries in the region.

RESPONSES

The questionnaire was designed in five parts:

> Part I – General Issues Related to the Implementation of APPER and UN-PAAERD
> Part II – Immediate measures
> Part III – Short/medium-term measures
> Part IV – Financial resources mobilization
> Part V – Modalities and mechanisms for implementation and monitoring of APPER and UN-PAAERD.

It was structured in such a way as to obtain information on the main priority areas of the two Programmes. These are: (a) Food and agriculture; (b) Other sectors in support of agriculture, rehabilitation and development of agro-related industries, development of transport and communications, trade and finance; (c) Drought and desertification; (d) Human resources development, planning and utilization; (e) Policy reforms improving the management of the economy, other policy measures, population policy, participation of the people in development, women and development; and, (f) Refugees and displaced persons.

The questionnaire closely followed the structure of both APPER and UN-PAAERD in order to ensure that the mechanisms and policy reform issues dealt with under the different areas of concentration of the two programmes are adequately covered. A simplified approach in questionnaire design was followed usually requiring respondents to mark one of the two boxes. In a few cases, such as efforts to create or to strengthen financial institutions under part IV of the questionnaire, responding governments were asked to give examples.

The questionnaire was handed over to the Ministers who attended the second extraordinary session of the ECA Conference of Ministers convened in Addis Ababa from 13 to 16 October 1986. In addition copies were sent to member States through the normal official channels. The UNDP Resident Representative in each African country was also given a copy to enable him to follow up with the appropriate government ministry to ensure an early return of the completed questionnaire. In addition, ECA staff members on missions to countries were asked to follow up. By the middle of May 1987, 36 member States, i.e., 72 per cent of ECA's total State membership had responded to the questionnaire. These were: Algeria, Benin, Botswana, Burkina Faso, Burundi, Cameroon, Cape Verde, Central African Republic, the Comoros, the Congo, Egypt, Equatorial Guinea, Ethiopia, the Gambia, Ghana, Guinea-Bissau, Lesotho, the Libyan Arab Jamahiriya, Liberia, Madagascar, Malawi, Mali, Mauritius, Morocco, the Niger, Nigeria, Rwanda, Sao Tome and Principe, Senegal, Sierra Leone, Somalia, the Sudan, Togo, Uganda, the United Republic of Tanzania and Zambia. One or two countries which returned their questionnaires without completing them but attached government statements which unfortunately could not be used to supply the relevant information have not been included. Twenty-two of the responding countries were LDCs; thus 81 per cent of all LDCs in Africa completed the questionnaire. The distribution of the countries by subregion is as follows:

Subregions	Number of countries	Those who returned the form	
		Number	%
Indian Ocean Island countries	4	3	75
East Africa	9	7	78
Southern African States	8	4	50
Central Africa	7	5	71
Sahel	9	7	78
Non-Sahel West Africa	8	6	75
North Africa	5	4	80
Total	50	36	72

It is also interesting to look at how many of these countries are sub-Saharan. As defined by the World Bank, 39 African countries are sub-Saharan. If that definition is adopted, 82 per cent of sub-Saharan countries responded to the questionnaire. However, the World Bank classification excludes countries like Cape Verde, the Comoros, Djibouti, Equatorial Guinea, Sao Tome and Principe and Seychelles. If these are taken into account, then 71 per cent of the sub-Saharan countries responded to the questionnaire.

In December 1986 the UN Inter-agency Task Force on the follow-up of UN-PAAERD appointed a group of three experts to prepare a report on improving information flows on the follow-up process of African economic recovery and development. This mission visited nine African countries and held discussions with high government officials in eight of them on the need for information for monitoring the UN Programme at national, subregional and regional levels. The mission took the opportunity to remind governments which had not responded to the questionnaire about the importance of completing the questionnaire as soon as possible.

The information contained in the questionnaire has been computerized and will be up-dated every year to ensure that up-to-date information is available at ECA on actions being taken at the national, subregional and regional levels to implement UN-PAAERD. The analysis should be read in conjunction with the Survey of Economic and Social Conditions in Africa, 1985–1986 (E/ECA/CM.13/3) and the ECA/ADB Economic Report on Africa, 1987.

ANALYSIS

The results of the survey are shown in Tables 2.1–2.6. In the following sections, the highlights of the country responses are given.

General Issues Related to the Implementation of APPER and UN-PAAERD

The UN resolution, in asking the African countries to implement the UN Programme of Action, implied that national perspectives and initiatives formed the principal basis for the implementation of the UN-PAAERD. It is therefore necessary to look at some of the general issues which have arisen or are likely to arise in the implementation of the Programme at the national level.

It should be noted that many African countries have a variety of on-going national programmes embodied in either long-term development plans or short-term policy perceptions. These programmes are normally drawn up by the Ministry of Planning with the assistance of the sectoral ministries. In order to ensure that UN-PAAERD is being successfully implemented, it was necessary to investigate whether any actions had been taken with respect to (i) the integration of the strategies, policies and priorities of APPER into the individual national development plans and policies and the immediate realignment of existing national programmes (e.g. development plans, and structural adjustment and stabilization programmes) to the strategies and priorities of APPER and UN-PAAERD; (ii) the incorporation of the UN-PAAERD priorities in the annual budgets; and, (iii) the reorientation of external assistance towards UN-PAAERD-derived national priorities.

Among the principal criticisms levelled at the functioning of national planning mechanisms is that programme formulation tends to be limited to the technical level and most development plans and policies do not reflect priority needs of basic economic urgency. The private sector is also generally ignored. In the survey which was carried out by ECA, it was shown that out of the 36 African countries which responded to the questionnaire, 72 per cent had discussed APPER and UN-PAAERD at the cabinet and other policy formulation levels. Most of the countries (just over 78 per cent) had discussed the two documents at the technical planning level. When the private sector level is considered, it is clear that very little had been done to discuss these two programmes at that level. Only 14 per cent of the countries had done so. This seems to reinforce the view that private sector participation in the development process is often ignored and that development policies and preparation of plans and programmes are generally limited to the public sector. It could also be inferred that popular participation in plan formulation is rare. There is a general problem of the public awareness of important regional documents like the LPA, APPER and UN-PAAERD. It is obvious from reports by ECA staff travelling to African countries that both APPER and UN-PAAERD are not known by high officials of important national sectoral ministries and departments who are supposed to take them into account in preparing their sectoral plans. There is need, therefore, to have an effective mechanism at the national level for disseminating such documents. APPER and UN-PAAERD should be popularized in order to increase the awareness of these programmes in Africa. In this exercise, maximum use of the media such as radio, television and newspaper should be made. In this connection, it should be noted that the UN is already informing the international community about UN-PAAERD by publishing the African Economic Recovery Newsletter.

At the time of the adoption of APPER and UN-PAAERD, several African countries were implementing their own ongoing national development plans with their own national priorities. One of the objectives of the ECA questionnaire was to check whether the national priorities conform in general to those set at the regional level in APPER and UN-PAAERD and, where they do not, whether the plans have been refocused to reflect these priorities. For development plans formulated after APPER and UN-PAAERD, information was sought on whether those plans had together with their corresponding budgets taken into account APPER and UN-PAAERD priorities.

The survey shows that in at least one area, a number of countries have taken specific action. Ninety-two per cent of the countries had indicated that their priorities under UN-PAAERD, namely, food and agriculture, development of other sectors supporting agriculture (particularly agro-industries, transport and communications, trade and finance), drought and desertification and human resources development have been incorporated into the current national development plans where applicable. Eighty-six per cent of the countries have already reflected these priorities in their budgets. It should be noted in this context that in the original submission of APPER a number of countries indicated that while the other priority areas were relevant to their countries' programmes, drought and desertification was not. Most of the countries indicated that food and agriculture was the number one priority followed by other sectors in support of food and agriculture, human resources development and drought and desertification in that order.

With respect to investments in agriculture, 61 per cent of the countries indicated that they had achieved the target of investment in agriculture; namely, that it should constitute 20–25 per cent of total public investment. Of those who indicated that they had not achieved this, 79 per cent plan to do so by 1990, 14 per cent had no intention of doing this and 7 per cent did not state any intentions. These responses generally agree with the figures given on total investment and investment in agriculture in the 1986 budget as well as from the corresponding data on the current plan, where these were supplied.

Many countries had adopted stabilization, structural adjustment and overall economic rehabilitation programmes. Macro-economic management programmes being currently pursued by countries are: stabilization programme (39 per cent), structural adjustment programme (69 per cent) and overall economic rehabilitation programme (50 per cent). The information supplied in the questionnaire, however, did not make it easy to describe the main content of the programme followed, particularly the main policies, the resources required and the impact on the country's recovery. General statements were made such as: both stabilization programme and the SAP laid emphasis on demand management policies; export-led industrialization; agricultural diversification; tourism; objectives and policies to increase the output of food and export crops through appropriate incentives for production, marketing and resource availability; rehabilitate the physical infrastructure in support of directly productive activities; increase capacity utilization in industry; restore internal and external balance by pursuing prudent fiscal, monetary and trade policies; restructuring of public boards and corporations; fiscal and monetary adjustments; devaluation of currency; and structural adjustment in all sectors of the economy. In one case an attempt was made to indicate the resource requirements namely: 'an average of about $US 1.2 billion annually will be required to cover the import bill for three consecutive years', but in general the request contained in the questionnaire to 'briefly describe the main contents of the programme followed, indicating the main policies, resource requirements and impact on your country's recovery' was ignored.

However, a lot is known of SAP from other sources and thus a more complete picture of some of the measures described above and their impact can be described. In its Joint Programme of Action submitted to its Development Committee in 1984, the World Bank outlined plans to deal with adjustment policies and comprehensive development programmes. The objectives of SAPs were: to stimulate output and exports especially in the field of food and agriculture, to correct distortions in exchange rates and producer prices, to improve marketing policies and institutions, to reduce the size of the public sector and generally to shift the terms of trade in favour of agricultural production and rural incomes.

SAPs have been in existence in some countries for a number of years now and their impact is being felt. In the short term, there has been a sharp rise in the prices of basic foods at the same time as there has been a decline in the purchasing power of public sector employees and other urban dwellers. In fact, in at least two countries the salary and wage levels for public servants are not enough to live on. On the other hand, it is claimed by some economists that the situation in these countries would have been worse without SAPs.

The medium and long-term impact of these adjustment policies needs to be studied by African Governments and the World Bank. The World Bank is planning to conduct surveys in a selected number of African countries to assess the social dimensions of its structural adjustment policies in sub-Saharan Africa. ECA is playing the lead role in the Inter-agency Task Force effort to organize in October 1987 in Libreville, Gabon, an international conference on the Human Dimension of Recovery and Development. It is important that these two exercises should be linked. Fortunately, the World Bank and UNDP are both members of the United Nations Inter-agency Task Force.

In general, it appeared from the responses to part I of the questionnaire that many countries had taken action in line with the principle of UN-PAAERD except in the area of the involvement of the private sector in the recovery effort and the mobilization of the people in support of it.

Immediate Measures

For the effective implementation of UN-PAAERD, it was proposed that certain immediate actions or measures regarding certain priority areas should be taken. The purpose of these measures was to enable African countries to cope with future emergencies and catastrophes. It appears from the responses to the questionnaire that with respect to food and agriculture, about half of the African countries had already taken action and a further 30 per cent propose to take action before the end of the programme. The percentage of countries which had taken action on three main categories are:

- Creation and/or maintenance of national emergency preparedness mechanism (50 per cent);
- Instituting effective early-warning system (47 per cent);
- Establishment of national food security system (53 per cent).

With respect to other sectors in support of agriculture, the majority of countries covered (78 per cent) had already taken action or measures on the maintenance and development of feeder, access and service roads and small bridges. Nineteen per cent propose to take action by 1990. Eighty-six per cent had adopted price incentives for agricultural products. With respect to rehabilitation and upgrading of existing industrial plants 64 per cent of the countries had already taken action.

A crucial area of concern under UN-PAAERD is the proposal to reverse the brain drain. In this area only, 28 per cent of the countries had taken action. A further 33 per cent intend to take action by the year 1990. These figures are rather disappointing in view of the need to retain trained manpower to help in the process of economic recovery and development. The precise measure(s) countries have taken include: economic incentives only (3 per cent); political and economic incentives (3 per cent); ensuring good working conditions (8 per cent); ensuring good working conditions and political incentives (3 per cent);

ensuring good working conditions and economic incentives (17 per cent); and ensuring good working conditions, political incentives and economic incentives (17 per cent).

The following percentages reflect the number of countries which had taken action in the other areas under other sectors in support of agriculture:

	Per cent
Improvement of internal distribution channels	67
Undertaking reafforestation programmes	86
Controlling deforestation	75
Controlling soil erosion and/or salination	64
Controlling overgrazing and/or over-exploitation	56

With respect to soil erosion and/or salination, the detailed responses can be classified as follows:

	Per cent
Controlling soil erosion only	31
Controlling salination only	6
Controlling soil erosion and salination	19

Again with respect to overgrazing and/or over-exploitation, the responses were:

	Per cent
Controlling overgrazing only	8
Controlling over-exploitation only	11
Controlling both overgrazing and over-exploitation	31

Since just under half of the countries responding have not taken action, there is need for further investigation to ensure that for those countries overgrazing and over-exploitation do not constitute major problems. Otherwise, some form of action has to be taken.

Prior to UN-PAAERD, a number of African countries had already taken action in the area of macro-economic policy reforms to redress economic imbalances especially related to exchange rates, subsidies, size of the public sector, wages and salaries. At the time of the survey, about 72 per cent of the countries had taken action in the areas of reduction of subsidies, 67 per cent on public employment freeze, 56 per cent on exchange rate adjustment and 50 per cent on wage and salary freeze or reduction.

At the subregional level, only 33 per cent of the countries indicated that they are taking part in regional crops protection agencies while 28 per cent indicated their intention to participate in such subregional networks by 1990. A slightly higher number of countries (39 per cent) were co-operating in national early warning systems.

From the returns to the questionnaire, it appears in general that immediate measures had been taken to deal with the African economic crisis.

Short/Medium-Term Measures

After analysing Africa's critical economic situation, APPER and UN-PAAERD laid considerable emphasis on short- and medium-term measures to assist in Africa's economic recovery and development. In this section, the short- and medium-term measures are considered. As stated in UN-PAAERD, the main objective of the medium-term measures will be 'to give a new impetus to agricultural development in order to achieve increasing levels of productivity and production'. It should however be noted that these efforts in the agricultural field will succeed only if there are parallel developments in the areas of rehabilitation and development of agro-related industries, transport and communications and trade and finance, control of drought and desertification and human resources development, planning and utilization.

At the national level, 75 per cent of the countries indicated that they had raised substantially the level of investment in food and agriculture. Nineteen per cent had plans to do this by 1990. Seventy-two per cent had already established or strengthened agricultural credit institutions and 25 per cent more propose to do so by 1990. Fifty per cent of the countries had already taken action in providing incentives to encourage rural savings and 36 per cent more propose to do so by the end of the plan period. In the area of land reform and land reclamation, 50 per cent and 42 per cent of the responding countries respectively have already taken action.

In the field of mechanization and modernization, a number of actions had already been taken. This includes the introduction of mechanization of agriculture (67 per cent), development, dissemination and encouragement of use of modern inputs and methods (89 per cent), improving and expanding storage capacity (72 per cent) and the strengthening or creation of a network of agronomical research stations (75 per cent). With respect to development, dissemination and encouragement of the use of modern inputs and methods, the detailed responses can be summarized as follows:

47

	Per cent
High-yielding varieties	8
High-yielding varieties and pesticides	8
Modern low-cost irrigation methods and pesticides	3
Modern low-cost irrigation methods, high-yielding varieties and pesticides	11
Sound crop rotation systems and pesticides	3
Sound crop rotation systems, high-yielding varieties and pesticides	14
Sound crop rotation systems, modern low-cost irrigation methods, high-yielding varieties and pesticides	42

It is obvious that countries are using a variety of methods to increase productivity in agriculture. With respect to high-yielding varieties, the following crops were identified: Maize (47 per cent of the countries), sorghum (25 per cent), rice (22 per cent), vegetables (14 per cent), 11 per cent each for cotton, potatoes, beans, coffee and groundnuts, 6 per cent for cocoa and 3 per cent each for sugarcane, cereals without specification, tobacco, cassava, yam, rubber and wheat. It is however not possible to distinguish between use of modern inputs and use of improved seeds or crop varieties in the responses given. It is clear that most efforts in these directions in African countries have been directed towards maize and sorghum.

It appears from these results, therefore, that African countries have taken seriously the provisions in UN-PAAERD which are aimed at giving new incentives to agricultural development in order to achieve increasing levels of productivity and production. Another area of interest is extension services. Only 53 per cent had provision of incentives to extension workers. Also, 64 per cent had taken action to strengthen laboratory facilities. With respect to small farmers support, especially women food producers and rural youth, 72 per cent had already established assistance programmes while 22 per cent intend to do so in the very near future.

Other actions to be taken in the second main area of concern, namely, other sectors in support of agriculture, include processing of raw materials and intermediate inputs (47 per cent of countries had initiated action), development of local capacity for project design and preparation (67 per cent) and national training programmes (92 per cent). The detailed breakdown of the information on training is as follows:

Per cent

National workshops for training and training abroad   3
National workshops for on-the-job training   3
National workshops for training, training abroad and
   on-the-job training   92

Thus, it is obvious that most African countries completing the questionnaire combine all three types of training.

Other measures taken include the rehabilitation and maintenance of existing modes of transport and communications (83 per cent), with 17 per cent planning to take action by 1990. However, with respect to production of spare parts for the overhaul, repair and maintenance of public vehicles, machinery and equipment, only 28 per cent of the countries had taken action and 36 per cent intend to do so by the end of the plan period. Thirty-six per cent did not state their intention and they can be subsumed among the countries where no action is planned in the foreseeable future. This is an area which therefore deserves urgent attention by African countries.

Surprisingly, the responses to the question on better management of water resources showed that only 61 per cent have already taken action. This relatively low percentage is surprising because of the recent drought which affected a large number of African countries. The situation is even worse with respect to the improvement of drainage in irrigated areas for which the percentage is 53. The situation improves in other areas related to the protection of the environment (67 per cent), reorientation of the educational system to meet development needs (64 per cent) and intensification of efforts to promote mass literacy and adult learning (83 per cent). It is unsatisfactory for arrangements for reduction of dependence on non-African experts (50 per cent) but satisfactory for development and encouragement of indigenous enter-preneurial capabilities (64 per cent). The details of the arrangements for reduction of dependence on non-African experts are as follows: arrangements with African countries with trained manpower surplus (8 per cent), programmes for universities and polytechnics (33 per cent) and the combination of the above two approaches (25 per cent). Thus, most of the arrangements for reducing reliance on non-African experts involve training nationals in universities and polytechnics both within and outside the country.

One of the areas of concern to African countries is the management of the economy. It is recognized that project and plan monitoring capabilities are generally weak in most countries. There is also the question of public accountability and proper use of resources. The questionnaire attempted to find out what action had been taken in these areas. Eighty-nine per cent of the countries responded that action had already been taken to improve the management of the economies of the countries. Eight per cent plan to do this before 1990. The measures taken include all of the following: ensuring accountability, improving public financial management, control of wastage and resource misallocation and rationalizing the functioning of the public sector enterprises (72 per cent of the countries), and improving financial management, control of wastage and resource misallocation and rationalizing the functioning of public sector enterprises (19 per cent). Three per cent of the countries had taken action on improving financial management, ensuring accountability and rationalizing the functioning of public sector enterprises. With respect to measures to encourage the private sector, 78 per cent had already taken action with the rest expecting to do so by 1990. Responses on types of measures taken to encourage the private sector can be classified as follows:

	Per cent
Denationalization and privatization	3
Denationalization, privatization and investment incentives	8
Investment incentives and provision of infrastructure	8
Privatization, investment incentives and infrastructure	6
Denationalization, privatization, investment incentives and infrastructure	8
Privatization and establishment of industrial estates	3
Privatization, industrial estates and investment incentives	3
Industrial estates, privatization, denationalization and investment incentives	8
Industrial estates, investment incentives and infrastructure	25
Industrial estates, privatization, investment incentives and infrastructure	11
Industrial estates, denationalization, privatization, investment incentives and infrastructure	19

Thus, 44 per cent of the countries had encouraged the private sector through some denationalization, 67 per cent through privatization, 89 per cent through investment incentives, 72 per cent through provision of infrastructure and 67 per cent through the establishment of industrial estates.

Seventy two per cent had established a national population policy and 86 per cent had already undertaken measures to integrate women into the development process. The elements of population policy include: establishment of a national population commission (14 per cent of the countries); formulation of a comprehensive rural development policy to stem rural–urban migration (14 per cent); the combination of the above two elements (31 per cent); context-specific population redistribution resettlement policies (3 per cent); a combination of formulation of a comprehensive rural development policy and context-specific population redistribution/resettlement policies (11 per cent); and a combination of a national population commission, a comprehensive rural development policy and population redistribution/resettlement (19 per cent). A careful examination of the responses shows that they reflect explicit population policies only. It also shows that there has been a major shift in the perceptions of African Governments with respect to population questions in the recent past. Now, more member States have formulated fairly comprehensive population policies.

With respect to the integration of women into the development process, the following are the details of the responses given: instituting specific programmes for enhancing the role of women in development (14 per cent); granting of incentives to encourage involvement of women (8 per cent), and a combination of the above two approaches (72 per cent).

In the context of both APPER and UN-PAAERD, many initiatives have already been taken in the area of medium-term measures to deal with Africa's economic crisis and the policy reforms which African leaders regard as necessary to change Africa's image as a continent with chronic economic problems to one of sustained growth and hope. The monitoring of the situation in subsequent years will determine whether the interpretation of the information collected in this section of the questionnaire turns out to be accurate.

Financial Resource Mobilization

In their submission to the thirteenth special session of the UN General Assembly, the African countries stressed that they fully accepted their responsibility of being the principal actors in the promotion of African economic recovery and development and thus the major part (more than 64 per cent) of the resources needed to implement UN-PAAERD would come from them. In the survey by ECA to find out the efforts which were being made to mobilize domestic resources, the results revealed that in 83 per cent of the countries action had been taken to increase savings. With respect to increasing savings, three main approaches have been followed: efforts to create or strengthen financial institutions only (11 per cent), policies adopted to encourage savings only (6 per cent) and greater budget surplus only (3 per cent). In addition, 61 per cent of the countries have adopted a combination of the first and second approaches, 3 per cent the second and third, and 14 per cent all three approaches. Thus, for each of the approaches, the following are percentages of countries that have actually taken action:

Per cent

Efforts to create or strengthen financial institutions	86
Policies adopted to encourage interest rates	83
Greater budget surplus	19

Examples of financial institutions which were given as having been created or strengthened are: investment banks, agricultural credit banks, rural banks, building finance corporations and special banks (e.g. for housing). Policies adopted to encourage interest rates include high deposit rates and partial or total tax rebates on interest earned on savings.

With respect to the efficient utilization of domestic resources, 92 per cent of the countries had already taken action and the remaining 8 per cent intend to do so by 1990. The measures which have been taken under this general heading are: controlling financial wastage and enhancing financial management (17 per cent), controlling wastage, enhancing financial management and controlling of imports (8 per cent), controlling financial wastage, enhancing financial management, controlling imports and ensuring that essential commodities are given priority (50 per cent), enhancing financial management, controlling imports and ensuring that essential commodities are given priority (8 per cent) with the other combinations of factors already listed above not exceeding 6 per cent of the countries. Thus, the following are the percentages of countries that have taken action under each of the measures listed under efficient utilization of domestic resources:

Per cent

Controlling financial wastage	83
Enhancing financial management	92
Controlling import of non-essential commodities	75
Ensuring that essential commodities are given priority	72

With respect to external resource mobilization, actions had been taken in the following areas: measures for export promotion (72 per cent); diversification of trade direction including research in products and markets and inclusion of commercial attaches in diplomatic missions (61 per cent); measures to increase foreign aid and ensure effective utilization of technical assistance (81 per cent) and measures to improve investment climate (81 per cent).

A more detailed breakdown of the responses is available in respect of measures to increase foreign aid and ensure effective utilization of technical assistance, and measures to improve investment climate. Under the former, 61 per cent of the countries had taken action in all the following four areas: better project identification and preparation; provision of competent local counterparts; meeting recurring cost component; and instituting technical assistance and aid co-ordinating apparatus. Fourteen per cent had taken action in project identification, provision of competent local counterparts and instituting technical assistance and aid co-ordinating apparatus. Less than six per cent had taken action in any of the remaining combinations. To sum up, the following are the percentages of countries that have taken action in respect of the various measures listed:

	Per cent
Better project identification and preparation	92
Provision of competent local counterparts	81
Meeting recurrent cost component	72
Instituting technical assistance and aid co-ordination apparatus	75

This seems to suggest that most countries are exploring all avenues for mobilizing external assistance.

In the second area of measures to improve the investment climate, 11 per cent of the countries had taken action to liberalize the investment codes. The same percentage had taken action to provide special incentives for priority areas, 19 per cent have combined the two approaches already listed. In addition, 17 per cent had taken action to liberalize the investment codes, provide special incentives for priority areas and tax havens while 28 per cent have combined the preceding three approaches with measures to benefit from the expertise, resources and technical know-how of multinationals. Six per cent of countries had taken action to liberalize the investment code, provide special incentives for priority areas and implement measures to benefit from the expertise, resources and technical know-how of multinationals and 3 per cent had taken action or had plans to liberalize investment codes and tax havens. Thus, the percentage of countries that have taken action on each of the various measures proposed is as follows:

	Per cent
Liberalization of investment codes	83
Tax havens	47
Special incentives for priority areas	81
Measures to benefit from the expertise, resources and technical know-how of multinationals	33

Since the questionnaire dealt with non-statistical information, nothing is available from the responses to show whether the requirements stated in APPER for either domestic or foreign assistance mobilization are in course of being met. Evidence from other sources however suggests that unless urgent action is taken neither the domestic nor the external resources expected under UN-PAAERD will be forthcoming in full and this will lead to a serious short-fall in plan implementation. Statistical information will be available from the initiatives now being taken by the UN Inter-Agency Task Force to improve information flows on the follow-up process to UN-PAAERD, and this will be used in future studies.

Modalities and Mechanisms for Implementation and Monitoring of APPER and UN-PAAERD

With respect to modalities and mechanisms which assist the implementation and monitoring of UN-PAAERD, the survey showed that a high proportion of the countries had set up technical apparatus for national and project planning. A little more than half of the countries had established national economic councils (58 per cent). A clear picture of the level and composition of these bodies could not be gauged from the responses received. However, the National Economic Council is usually an interministerial committee or a sub-committee of the cabinet presided over by the Vice-President or the Minister of finance and/or planning. Only 44 per cent of the countries had Economic Review Commissions, though in a few cases they differ from National Economic Councils only in name but not in composition. The Economic Review Commission is however usually not a sub-committee of cabinet. It is broadly based and in some countries includes, in addition to government officials, representatives of the private sector and labour.

However, almost all countries (94 per cent) possessed a technical apparatus for national and project planning. Seventy-eight per cent of the countries surveyed had a central planning agency, departmental/

regional planning unit and project identification and preparation mechanism all functioning simultaneously. Six per cent each have either only a central planning agency or central planning agency together with a project identification and preparation mechanism functioning and 3 per cent had a central planning agency with departmental planning units only. Thus, for each of the possible mechanisms under technical apparatus for national and project planning, the following are the percentages of countries already possessing the relevant organizational unit.

	Per cent
Central Planning Agency	92
Departmental Regional Planning Units	81
Project identification and preparation mechanisms	83

With respect to emergency relief and rehabilitation, 56 per cent of the countries had established or intend to establish mechanisms to define policy, specify areas of priority concern, follow-up and monitor implementation. Fourteen per cent have plans to do so by 1990. The types of mechanisms set up are as follows:

	Per cent
Early warning systems only	11
Emergency relief only	8
Early warning and emergency relief	22
Emergency relief and rehabilitation	3
Early warning, emergency relief and rehabilitation	19

Thus, for each type of emergency, relief and rehabilitation mechanism, the following is the corresponding percentage of countries:

	Per cent
Early warning	53
Emergency relief	53
Rehabilitation	22

This shows that the majority of countries have an emergency relief or early warning mechanism. However the position with respect to rehabilitation is still unsatisfactory.

The mechanisms for monitoring the overall plan and also the flow and repayment of foreign loans had been established in 81 per cent of the countries. Eighty-three per cent of the countries had established mechanisms for national aid co-ordination and public debt management. Six per cent have in place only a mechanism for national aid co-ordination while 14 per cent have only a body for public debt management. With respect to monitoring popular participation mechanisms, 83 per cent of the countries had already taken action. Fifty-eight per cent of the countries have mechanisms for both sensitizing the public on development issues and direct public works. Twenty-five per cent have mechanisms for sensitizing the public on development issues and 3 per cent have a direct public works mechanism only. With respect to joint monitoring and follow-up mechanisms UNDP RTs exist in 39 per cent of the countries, the World Bank in 39 per cent, Paris Club in 36 per cent and the London Club 19 per cent. Eleven per cent of the countries had an ad hoc consultative machinery for APPER while 17 per cent have a variety of other arrangements.

CONCLUSIONS AND RECOMMENDATIONS

The survey was able to achieve a 72 per cent response rate. This is normally regarded as satisfactory in mail surveys. However, in view of the priority African countries themselves attach to APPER and UN-PAAERD and the need to monitor the implementation of these programmes and to ensure their effectiveness, more countries should have responded to the questionnaire. Nevertheless, it is worth noting that the responding countries constitute 78.3 per cent of the total population of the 50 ECA member States and account for 86.7 per cent of total GDP. The following are some of the main conclusions and recommendations arising from the responses to the questionnaire.

Under general issues related to the implementation, a number of macro-economic management programmes of unspecified duration had been undertaken in many African countries. By 1986, about half of the responding countries had each in place a stabilization or structural adjustment or an overall economic rehabilitation programme or a combination of two or more of these programmes. The target in APPER for African countries to increase their overall investment in agriculture to 20–25 per cent of total public investment had been achieved by most countries.

APPER and UN-PAAERD made specific recommendations for immediate measures to be taken in respect of the priority areas. With respect to the recommendations relating to food and agriculture, over 72 per cent of the countries had taken at least one measure, that is, either the creation or maintenance of national emergency preparedness mechanism or instituting effective early-warning system or establishment of national food security system. Under other sectors in support of agriculture, 97 per cent of the countries had taken at least one measure. The measures recommended were rehabilitation and upgrading of existing industrial plants, maintenance and development of feeder, access and service roads and small bridges, adoption of price incentives for agricultural products, improvement of internal distribution channels, measures to reverse the brain drain, undertaking reafforestation, controlling deforestation or soil erosion or salination or overgrazing or over-exploitation.

With respect to macro-economic policy reforms to redress economic imbalances, 89 per cent had taken at least one action. The four areas identified were exchange rate adjustment, reduction of subsidies, public employment freeze, wage and salary freeze or reduction.

At the subregional level, 53 per cent of the countries had taken action in establishing regional networks of crop protection agencies or mechanisms for co-operation among national early warning systems or both.

In order to realize the objectives of APPER and UN-PAAERD, a number of short- and medium-term measures were proposed under *Food and Agriculture*. All countries had taken action, at least in one of the five areas listed. Under *Investment*, 94 per cent had taken action in at least one of the following areas: raising substantially the level of investment, establishment or strengthening of agricultural credit institutions, provision of incentives to encourage rural savings, land reform and land reclamation. Under *Mechanization and modernization*, 83 per cent of all countries had taken at least one measure. The two measures identified were introduction, where appropriate, of mechanization of agriculture and development, dissemination and encouragement of the use of modern inputs and methods. Under *Storage*, 72 per cent of the countries had taken action in improving and expanding storage capacity. With respect to *Research and extension services*, 86 per cent of the countries had taken at least one measure out of the three listed. These are: strengthening or creation of a network of agronomical research stations, provision of incentives to extension workers and strengthening of laboratory facilities. Finally, with respect to *Small farmer support*, 72 per cent of the countries had taken action in establishing assistance programmes for small farmers, especially women food producers and rural youth.

A number of recommendations were also made in respect of short- and medium-term measures for *Other sectors in support of agriculture*. All countries had taken at least one action out of the 12 proposed. The proposed measures were: processing of raw materials and intermediate inputs; development of local capacity for project design and preparation; national training programmes, rehabilitation and maintenance of existing modes of transport and communications; production of spare parts for the overhaul, repair and maintenance of public vehicles, machinery and equipment; better management of water resources; improvement of drainage in irrigated areas; protection of environment; reorientation of the educational system to meet development needs; intensification of efforts to promote mass literacy and adult learning; arrangements for reduction of dependence on non-African experts; and development and encouragement of indigenous entrepreneurial capabilities.

Under *Policy reforms*, all countries had taken action in at least one of the following areas: improving the management of the economy, encouraging the private sector, formulation of a national population policy and measures to integrate women in the development process.

Another major area of concern to African Governments is financial resource mobilization. African countries had undertaken to mobilize the greater part of the financial resources required for implementation of APPER and UN-PAAERD. All countries had taken at least one action to mobilize domestic or external resources. With respect to domestic resource mobilization, 97 per cent of the countries had taken one financial measure or adopted policies in respect of the following areas: increasing savings and efficient utilization of domestic resources. With respect to external resource mobilization, 94 per cent of the countries had similarly taken action in at least one of the following areas: measures for export promotion, diversification of trade direction including research in products and markets and inclusion of commercial attaches in diplomatic missions or measures to increase foreign aid and ensure effective utilization of technical assistance and measures to improve investment climate.

The fifth major area which received attention in the survey was the *Modalities and mechanisms for implementation and monitoring of APPER and UN-PAAERD*. All countries had established at least one of the following mechanisms: a national economic council, economic review commission, technical apparatus for national and project planning, emergency relief and rehabilitation and overall plan monitoring. These are national level organs. For joint monitoring and follow-up plans 69 per cent of the countries had taken at least one measure in: *Ad hoc* consultation on APPER, UNDP RT, World Bank CG, Paris Club and London Club.

The above picture shows that the majority of African countries are serious with their economic recovery programmes. There are, however, some areas of concern. These areas can be defined as those where only half or less of the countries that had responded to the questionnaire had taken action. The first category is that relating to creation and/or maintenance of national emergency preparedness mechanism, instituting effective early warning systems, establishment of mechanism for co-operation among national early warning systems in relation to food and agriculture and establishment of regional networks of crop protection agencies. In view of the African food crisis of 1983–1985 one would have expected that at least those African countries that were affected by drought and famine would by now have put in place the necessary mechanisms which would warn them of impending disaster and which would trigger off the necessary institutional mechanisms for ameliorating the situation. Regrettably, as the responses from the countries themselves show, this is not the case. Concerted efforts are therefore required at national, subregional and regional levels to assist those countries that have not yet done so to set up the appropriate emergency preparedness mechanisms.

Another area which deserves special attention relates to measures to reverse the brain drain. Only 28 per cent of the countries had taken any of the listed measures to try to reverse the brain drain. It had been recognized that some of Africa's problems are due to lack of an adequate number of trained manpower in critical fields. Yet in these same fields there are large numbers of Africans working outside the region, mainly in the developing countries and the oil-rich states of West Asia. The trend seems to be continuing. In spite of attempts to stem the flow of immigrants into Western Europe and North America, there is no evidence yet that these have substantially reduced the outflow of trained high-level manpower to the two regions and the oil-rich states of Western Asia.

There is, thus, the need for governments to take the necessary measures to ensure that effective actions are taken to reverse the brain drain. It may be mentioned that, with the exception of a few African countries where emigrants' remittances play a large role in their economies, for most countries the brain drain seriously affects the performance of the economy. Unfortunately, the survey had shown that 39 per cent of the countries have no intention of taking any action in this area even by the year 1990. It is important for these countries to reconsider their position and to see what practical steps can be taken to reverse the brain drain.

The other critical area is land reform (50 per cent) and land reclamation (42 per cent). In some countries these are critical issues inhibiting the development of agriculture. Unless they are dealt with, the objective of increased agricultural production which is one of the underlying themes of both APPER and UN-PAAERD cannot be achieved.

Another area of concern is the processing of raw materials and intermediate inputs and the production of spare parts for the overhaul, repair and maintenance of public vehicles, machinery and equipment. The survey had shown that only 47 per cent of the countries had taken action to process raw materials and intermediate inputs while 28 per cent only had in place plants for the production of spare parts etc. These measures were identified by African Governments as very essential for the development of the agricultural sector but appear to have been neglected. If no urgent action is taken to remedy the situation, the main objectives of APPER and UN-PAAERD would not be realized.

The results of the survey also show that 83 per cent of the countries have set up a mechanism for popular participation in development. It is not clear from the survey what these mechanisms are actually doing because, as may be recalled from Table 2.1, the private sector does not appear in most African countries to have been consulted in respect of APPER and UN-PAAERD and, by implication, in respect of national development programmes. If there was real popular participation in development efforts one would normally have expected the private sector to have been involved.

The information provided in the questionnaire gives the impression that in many areas of APPER and UN-PAAERD, African Governments have taken action. The questionnaire however did not seek information on how effective these actions have been. For example, in the African region, there are 18 RTs and 14 CGs but the mere existence of these bodies neither implies that they are active nor, even if they are active, that they are effective instruments for monitoring national economic recovery programmes.

African Governments are therefore urged to re-examine their existing or envisaged mechanisms for project planning, overall plan monitoring and economic review to ensure that they are effective in playing their role in delineating areas of priority, taking follow-up action and monitoring plan and programme implementation.

In the current survey, which is a baseline one, emphasis has been on qualitative information but there are now other initiatives being taken within the UN family to obtain both non-statistical and statistical information to monitor the implementation of UN-PAAERD at the national, sub-regional and regional levels. The responsibility for monitoring national programmes is however that of the African Governments. And for this they need not only effective monitoring mechanisms but also the necessary information (both quantitative and qualitative) which will enable them to assess the progress being made in programme implementation.

The twenty-second session of the Commission and thirteenth meeting of ECA Conference of Ministers adopted resolution 603 (XXII) of 27 April 1987 in which it requested the Executive Secretary of ECA 'to prepare a more comprehensive report on the implementation of UN-PAAERD and APPER in 1987 including an assessment of the contribution of the international community and submit it to the twenty-third session of the Commission and fourteenth meeting of the Conference of Ministers'. In order to do this, ECA requires relevant information on the implementation of UN-PAAERD and APPER from national, subregional, regional, intergovernmental and non-governmental organizations which are participating in the implementation of the two programmes.

It may be recalled that the UN Inter-Agency Task Force had in December 1986 appointed a group of three experts, one each from ECA, UNICEF and FAO, to prepare a report on 'Improving information flows in the follow-up process to African Economic Recovery and Development'. It should be noted that the main objectives of information gathering in this context are *inter alia* as follows:

(a) To monitor the process of the implementation of UN-PAAERD and to prepare reports on this to the UN, OAU and other relevant bodies;

(b) To use the information so gathered to mobilize timely and effective external and domestic resources for the implementation of the UN-PAAERD;

(c) To provide relevant information to the African Governments and the international community on progress in the implementation of UN-PAAERD at the national, subregional and regional levels.

The experts group's report which covered both statistical and non-statistical information is under consideration by the UN Inter-Agency Task Force. It is expected that the Task Force will come out soon with its recommendations on the information system which should be set up. The recommendations are expected to cover objectives and purposes of information gathering, identification of relevant information, administrative mechanics of information flows and information dissemination. When the system is set in place, more comprehensive reports on the implementation of UN-PAAERD and APPER can be prepared for the consideration of all relevant bodies.

TABLE 2.1

GENERAL ISSUES RELATED TO THE IMPLEMENTATION OF
APPER AND UN-PAAERD

Subheading and text of the question	Number of countries			
	Yes	No	Not stated	Not applicable
Internalization of APPER and the UN-PAAERD in development efforts				
Have these programmes been discussed in your country at:				
− the cabinet or any other top policy formulation body level?	26	1	9	0
− the technical planning organs level?	28	2	6	0
− the private sector level?	7	8	21	0
Reorientation of national programmes				
There are four areas of priority action at the national level in APPER and UN-PAAERD				
Has your country incorporated these priorities in:				
− the current plan?	33	0	3	0
− the State budget?	31	0	5	0
Investment targets				
Increasing overall level of investment by government in agriculture to 20–25 per cent of public investment				
Has your country achieved this target?	22	14	0	0
If no, does it intend to achieve this target by 1990?	11	2	1	22

TABLE 2.2
IMMEDIATE MEASURES

Heading/subheading and text of the question	Number of countries		
	Already taken	Proposed to be taken by 1990	Not stated
At the national level			
(a) *Food and agriculture*			
Creation and/or maintenance of national emergency preparedness mechanism	18	10	8
Instituting effective early-warning system	17	12	7
Establishment of national food security system	19	12	5
(b) *Other sectors in support of agriculture*			
Rehabilitation and upgrading of existing industrial plants	23	6	7
Maintenance and development of feeder, access & service roads and small bridges	28	7	1
Adoption of price incentives for agricultural products	31	4	1
Improvement of internal distribution channels	24	12	0
Measures to reverse brain drain	10	12	0
Undertaking reafforestation programmes	31	4	1
Controlling deforestation	27	7	2
Controlling soil erosion and/or salination	23	7	6
Controlling overgrazing and/or over-exploitation	20	12	4
(c) *Macro-economic policy reforms to redress economic imbalance*			
Exchange rate adjustment	20	3	13
Reduction of subsidies	26	5	5
Public employment freeze	24	3	9
Wage and salary freeze or reduction	18	4	14
At the subregional level			
Establishment of regional networks of crop protection agencies	12	10	14
Establishment of mechanisms for co-operation among national early warning systems	14	12	10

TABLE 2.3
SHORT- AND MEDIUM-TERM MEASURES

Heading/subheading and text of the question	Number of countries		
	Already taken	Proposed to be taken by 1990	Not stated
(a) *Food and agriculture*			
(i) *Investment*			
Raising substantially the level of investment	27	7	2
Establishment or strengthening of agricultural credit institutions	26	9	1
Provision of incentives to encourage rural savings	18	13	5
Land reform	18	10	8
Land reclamation	15	9	12
(ii) *Mechanization and modernization*			
Introduction, where appropriate, of mechanization of agriculture	24	5	7
Development, dissemination and encouragement of the use of modern inputs and methods	32	4	0
(iii) *Storage*			
Improving and expanding storage capacity	26	8	2
(iv) *Research and extension services*			
Strengthening or creation of a network of agronomical research stations	27	8	1
Provision of incentives to extension workers	19	9	8
Strengthening of laboratory facilities	23	9	4
(v) *Small farmers support*			
Establishment of assistance programmes for small farmers, especially women food producers and rural youth			
(b) *Other sectors in support of agriculture*			
Processing of raw materials and intermediate inputs	17	11	8
Development of local capacity for project design and preparation	24	9	3
National training programme	33	3	0

TABLE 2.3 continued

Heading/subheading and text of the question	Number of countries		
	Already taken	Proposed to be taken by 1990	Not stated
Rehabilitation and maintenance of existing modes of transport and communications	30	6	0
Production of spare parts for the overhaul, repair and maintenance of public vehicles, machinery and equipment	10	13	13
Better management of water resources	22	11	3
Improvement of drainage in irrigated areas	19	8	9
Protection of environment	24	10	2
Reorientation of the educational system to meet development needs	23	10	3
Intensification of efforts to promote mass literacy and adult learning	30	5	1
Arrangements for reduction of dependence on non-African experts	18	8	10
Development and encouragement of indigenous entrepreneurial capabilities	3	7	6
(c) *Policy reforms*			
Improving the management of the economy	32	3	1
Measures to encourage the private sector	28	8	0
Formulation of a national population policy	26	8	2
Measures to integrate women in the development process	31	4	1

TABLE 2.4

FINANCIAL RESOURCE MOBILIZATION

Heading/subheading and text of the question	Number of countries		
	Already taken	Proposed to be taken by 1990	Not stated
(a) *Domestic resource mobilization*			
Increasing savings	30	6	0
Efficient utilization of domestic resources	33	3	0
(b) *External resource mobilization*			
Measures for export promotion	26	7	3
Diversification of trade direction including research in production and markets and inclusion of commercial attaches in diplomatic mission	22	8	6
Measures to increase foreign aid and ensure effective utilization of technical assistance	29	5	2
Measures to improve investment climate	29	5	2

TABLE 2.5

MODALITIES AND MECHANISMS FOR IMPLEMENTATION
AND MONITORING OF APPER AND UN-PAAERD

Heading/subheading and text of the question	Number of countries		
	Already taken	Proposed to be taken by 1990	Not stated
(a) *National level organs*			
National Economic Council (level and composition of membership)	21	6	9
Economic Review Commission (level and composition of membership)	16	1	19
Technical apparatus for national and project planning	34	1	1
Emergency, relief and rehabilitation mechanism	20	5	11
Overall plan monitoring mechanisms	29	5	2
Mechanisms for monitoring the flow, utilization and repayment of foreign assistance	30	1	1
Popular participation mechanisms	30	1	5
(b) *Joint monitoring and follow-up mechanisms*			
Ad-hoc consultation for APPER	4	6	26
UNDP Round Table	14	8	14
World Bank consultative group	14	4	18
Paris Club	13	4	19
London Club	7	3	26
Other	6	1	29

TABLE 2.6

NUMBER OF COUNTRIES WHICH TOOK AT LEAST ONE MEASURE
UNDER EACH SUBHEADING OF THE QUESTIONNAIRE ON THE
IMPLEMENTATION OF APPER AND UN-PAAERD

Subheading	Number of countries which took at least one measure mentioned under this subheading
PART II. *Immediate measures*	
2.1 At the national level	36
(a) Food and agriculture	26
(b) Other sectors in support of agriculture	35
(c) Macro-economic policy reforms	32
2.2 At the subregional level	19
PART III. *Short- and medium-term measures*	36
(a) Food and agriculture	36
(i) Investment	34
(ii) Mechanization and modernization	36
(iii) Storage	26
(iv) Research and extension services	31
(v) Small farmers support	26
(b) Other sectors in support of agriculture	36
(c) Policy reforms	36
PART IV. *Financial resources mobilization*	36
(a) Domestic resource mobilization	35
(b) External resource mobilization	34
PART V. *Modalities and mechanisms for implementation and monitoring of APPER and the UN-PAAERD*	36
(a) National level organs	36
(b) Joint monitoring	25

CHAPTER THREE

Country Case Studies

OWODUNNI TERIBA (ed.)

INTRODUCTION

The overall picture from the evidence in Chapter 2 is that many African countries have seriously embarked on the implementation of the policies, programmes and priorities enshrined in APPER and UN-PAAERD. However, greater specificity to this emerging trend is needed. This is provided in this Chapter in the form of eight country case studies which provide details of the strenuous efforts which have taken place at the national level and the qualitative changes in force or under way in policies, programmes and the management of the economy.

It is important however to remember that the policy changes and reforms that have taken place in Africa in the last one to two years have been embarked upon often with the support of and in agreement with the World Bank and the IMF, within the framework and context of the Structural Adjustment Programmes of these two institutions. Indeed, SAPs predate APPER and UN-PAAERD, and have been in existence for several years in a number of African countries. The programme elements invariably included severe austerity designed to curtail demand and restore balance-of-payments equilibrium, while the measures have generally included currency devaluation, reduction of public expenditure and removal of subsidies. Hence, SAPs have not always been coterminous with APPER and UN-PAAERD in scope nor convergent with the latter in objectives. The selected case studies in this Chapter relate to the general experience of individual African countries with the implementation of policy changes and reforms both within the general framework of APPER and UN-PAAERD, and in connection with SAPs.

BOTSWANA

Agricultural Development

Agricultural development policy has continued to shift emphasis from livestock development to arable production in the current Development Plan. During the earlier years, following independence, a concerted effort was made to develop the livestock industry because Botswana's climate and soils give livestock production a distinct advantage over crop production. The Government has now decided that more attention should be given to the arable subsector which, due to the severe climatic conditions in Botswana and an almost complete absence of surface water, requires a more intensive and innovative process for successful development. Additionally, the drought has emphasized the vulnerability of Botswana in terms of dependence on outside sources of food supplies and served to strengthen the determination to pursue domestic food production.

The approach the Government has taken in recent years to improve arable production has been to enlarge the rain-fed arable projects that were started during the Fifth Development Plan and to introduce an innovative element into this concept. Rain-fed farming in Botswana has been largely limited to small-scale operations in Eastern Botswana and yields are quite low due to poor soils and unreliable rainfall. Assistance to farmers has generally taken the form of subsidizing inputs such as seeds, fertilizers, fencing, stock, water, farm implements and draught power. In keeping with Government's commitment to improve arable production, a programme involving the opening up of a new area in northern Botswana where the nature of the soil and remoteness of the area have prevented earlier development by small farmers has been initiated. The area was opened up and financial assistance provided to experienced farmers willing and able to operate on a large scale. The results, after two years of development, are encouraging. Although early development involves only large-scale enterprises, longer-term plans include the development of small-scale enterprises as well.

Another innovative approach to improved arable production is the examination of the rivers in the northern part of the country for possible irrigation development. Studies are under way at present to determine the feasibility of irrigation development on the fringes of the Okavango Delta as well as flood plains on the Chobe River.

The proceeds from livestock sales go directly to the farmers, and these incomes, with their attendant multiplier effects, help to increase rural purchasing power and stimulate rural development and employment opportunities. Livestock represents a major national resource and remains the cornerstone of the agricultural sector. Government support for livestock continues in the form of disease control, ranch development, breed improvement and research. Ranch development programmes are designed to commercialize the livestock industry in terms of improved husbandry methods and better management of cattle and land. It is hoped that success in these areas over the longer term will improve the quality of Botswana's rangelands which will, in turn, increase their productivity in terms of animal product sales.

In addition to arable lands and cattle development, the Government continues to encourage and support diversification in agricultural production. Such efforts involve small-stock programmes to encourage improved management and husbandry techniques, as well as marketing assistance. Assistance and encouragement by Government to poultry producers in Botswana has worked well, with the result that the country has become self-sufficient in poultry meat and egg production, and imports of these products are no longer required. Dairying and pig husbandry are supported and encouraged but feed requirements are such that their rapid development becomes difficult. Also, in the case of dairy animals, the technical expertise needed to operate a successful dairy are often lacking. Nevertheless, there are successful dairy operators in Botswana and support for their continued efforts in this area continues. Fisheries has also been a strongly supported small industry and, considering the limited water resources in Botswana, has shown encouraging progress. Government has supported this industry by providing financial assistance to fishermen, and through marketing technical back-up.

Food Security Measures

Botswana has just gone through a sixth season of severe drought conditions, and the longest period of drought in recorded history. Up to the end of April 1986, the average national rainfall deficiency was 23 per cent below the long-term average. During the last two seasons, the deficiencies were 37 per cent and 34 per cent respectively. Harvesting is now in progress and is forecast to produce about 20,000 metric tons of cereals, the same as in the last two years, and about 10 per cent of the national needs for staple grains. Much of the rest, about 70 per cent of total grain requirements, will come from commercial imports. However, the Government will again run an extensive feeding programme and has requested donor assistance for the final 20 per cent of

71

total grain needs. This amount will be distributed through clinics and schools.

There is a four-pronged approach to drought relief, and each of the programmes is considered to be complementary to the others in maintaining the health of the population, ensuring a quick recovery from the drought when the rains arrive, reducing asset losses in rural areas, and ensuring that farmers can continue to cultivate. It is hoped that rural incomes can be quickly restored by this comprehensive approach. There will also be a two-year recovery programme after the drought is declared over, during which the drought programmes will be gradually phased out.

Long-term Measures to Combat Drought

Botswana has developed a national food strategy involving, in particular: improvement in the data base and monitoring strategies for arable agriculture; household food consumption and nutrition; drought relief and contingency planning; post drought recovery; and, national food security through grain and financial reserves.

At present, Botswana is working to combat the effects of drought in several other directions such as:

(a) Through SADCC Regional Early Warning System and Regional Reserve Fund;

(b) Long-term improvements to the Labour Based Relief Programme. The cash that this Programme injects into the rural areas has been vital to the maintenance of the rural economy, for instance, through keeping solvent the small traders who stock, among other things, food products. Since levels of unemployment are not going to be reduced quickly in the rural areas, the use of labour-intensive techniques is being encouraged; and

(c) Raising agricultural productivity throughout the country, so as to increase the output and returns of the largely rural population.

Transport and Communications

Since the adoption of APPER in July 1985, which coincides with Year One of Botswana's Sixth National Development Plan (NDP-6), we have been through two full Plan-years and have just commenced Year Three of NDP-6. In 1985/86, P82.9 million was expended on the Transport and Communications Sector, in 1986/87 P129 million was spent on the sector. On the average, the Transport and Communications sector is the largest development budget sector.

Major development highlights of the sector include roads, civil aviation, telecommunications and railways. The roads subsector has consistently been given priority in view of the geographical vastness of Botswana and the predominantly sparse population settlement pattern. Within the roads subsector, rural roads, secondary roads improvement and feeder roads construction have been earmarked as core factors in their contribution to general economic development. Prior to 1985, Botswana had largely completed its major trunk road network from the north to the south thus connecting Botswana to Zimbabwe and Zambia. Plans have been formulated for connecting western Botswana both from Gaborone in the south towards Namibia via Ghanzi and from Francistown in the north towards the Okavango, with eventual connection towards Mamuno (Namibia border) again via Ghanzi. The objective of these developments is to integrate western Botswana, which is a major cattle farming area, into the country's mainstream economic development, which now appears concentrated on the eastern rail/road axis from south-to-north.

Recognizing the vital role of air transport in economic activity in vast landlocked countries, such as Botswana, a new international airport has been built and commissioned in the capital to ensure a safe outlet should transit land corridors pose problems. The level of various long-haul and regional air services that currently link Botswana with the outside world since the completion of the new international airport vindicates the decision. It is planned to link this with satellite airports in remote areas of the country to allow Botswana greater flexibility in speedily responding to the needs of the population, again within the context of Botswana's geographical vastness and sparse human settlements. A new airport at Kasane is being planned and construction will commence in 1988 to improve access to the far north of Botswana and facilitate economic development, specifically in the fields of tourism and agriculture. The improvement of rural aerodromes and airstrips will continue to form part of the civil aviation development programme throughout the Sixth National Development Plan.

Botswana has established an independent railway organization which is in the process of taking over railway operations in Botswana from National Railways of Zimbabwe. Major infrastructural investments were completed, such as rehabilitation of 120 kilometres of track, procurement of 20 new locomotives and construction of a maintenance depot. Other measures still being implemented include rehabilitation and improvement of signalling and telecommunication systems, procurement of 450 units of rolling stock, continuation of track rehabilitation as well as staff training. The railway network is vital for local and transit traffic and it remains the Government's objective to ensure its efficient performance.

Telecommunications subsector has been expanded by implementing a major development programme which included a microwave trunk network in the eastern part of the country connecting major centres, establishment of a local and international switching centre in Gaborone, and improvement of international connections both regionally and worldwide. A feasibility study to determine the needs, appropriate technology, and costs involved to provide more access to telecommunication in rural areas is to be embarked upon.

Employment and Human Resources Development

Two very important areas of initiative that strongly impact on employment generation are: (a) direct support for industrial development; and, (b) major increases in the educational level and the technical skills of the work force.

First, the cornerstone of the Government's direct assistance for employment generation is the Financial Assistance Program (FAP) which has been operational for the past five years. It represents a significant allocation of government resources for the direct encouragement of productive activities and the assistance is directed towards new job-creating investment. During its first five years of operation, it is estimated that FAP created nearly 7,000 new employment opportunities. During the next five years, it is expected that the number will increase by an additional 12,000 jobs.

A series of major initiatives have been taken in the areas of education and skill training which will significantly raise the educational and skill level of the work force and aid employment creation. First is the expansion of junior secondary education so that each student will have nine full years of free education. This will ensure that all Botswana citizens are better prepared to enter the work-force or to continue education and skill training. Increased skill training activities are also being initiated through four new modern vocational technical centres which will shortly open and each of which will have a capacity for 270 students. In a parallel effort, and with the co-operation of private industry, a new major apprenticeship and industry training effort has begun. In addition, the enrolment at the Polytechnic is to be expanded from 600 to 1,500 students in the early 1990s. Plans also call for the number of intakes into the youth brigades for vocational training to double to 1,200 during this period and for university enrolment to increase from 1,600 to 3,400.

Industry and Trade

Botswana's open, trade-oriented economy is based on a small but dynamic private sector actively encouraged by government policies and programmes and supplemented, where necessary, by direct government involvement through parastatal organizations.

The success of Botswana's trade and industry, and the attraction of foreign investors and technology largely depends on maintaining a suitable investment climate. Recognizing this, the Government has committed itself to free enterprise, a strong national currency, a liberal foreign exchange policy and favourable fiscal and monetary policies and other incentives.

The Ministry of Commerce and Industry has the portfolio responsibility to promote the development of the commercial and industrial sectors of the economy through its departments of commerce and consumer affairs (DCCA), industrial affairs (DIA), and trade and investment promotion agency (TIPA) with their variety of public policy instruments, and the aim of enhancing socio-economic progress. In order to achieve this, the Government puts a lot of emphasis on measures to increase the diversification of the economy with corresponding growth in income-earning opportunities, develop local entrepreneurship, and increase participation in all sectors and levels of business.

Some of the government institutions formed to promote industry and commerce are:

(a) the Botswana Enterprises Development Unit (BEDU) whose objective is to increase direct participation of Botswana in all sectors and at all levels of industry and trade;

(b) the Rural Industrial Officers Cadre (RIO's) which is the main agency responsible for co-ordinating the activities of small business extension agencies directed towards promoting industry in the rural areas. It also offers training and other types of assistance to rural producers at district level, and is instrumental in implementing the non-agricultural small-scale FAP projects in rural areas;

(c) the Rural Industries Promotion (RIP) which is a non-profit organization founded through the Ministry of Commerce and Industry. The RIP operates the Rural Industries Innovation Centre (RIIC) at Kanye and the one-stop service Centre for agriculture in Palapye. RIP develops, adapts and disseminates technologies appropriate for improving living conditions for rural dwellers;

(d) Business Advisory Services (BAS) which is a programme of direct consultancy and advisory services to local traders; in addition, it provides courses and seminars to the business community. BAS co-operates with BEDU and RIO's to provide Integrated Field Services for small-scale commercial and industrial firms on a national basis;

(e) Trade and Investment Promotion Agency (TIPA) which is the focal point for trade and investment promotion activities, and acts as a one-stop source of information and advice to potential investors. It also organizes participation in trade fairs and exhibitions, and it prepares and circulates information to the business community. TIPA supports established industry and commerce through its support for local Chambers of Commerce and Industry;

(f) National Development Bank (NDB), which is responsible to the Ministry of Finance and Development Planning, lends money to industry and commerce as well as agriculture;

(g) Botswana Development Corporation (BDC), which is a para-statal organization responsible to the Ministry of Finance and Development Planning, identifies commercially and industrially viable opportunities for exploitation preferably with private sector partners;

(h) Botswana Technology Centre (BTC), responsible to the Ministry of Finance and Development Planning, is a focal point in the field of appropriate technology. Its purpose is to assist in the choice and adoption of technology, working from its international information resource capacity. It is particularly attuned to the needs of small-scale industry and promotes the search for technologies suitable for Botswana. It works closely with BEDU and RIIC;

(i) The Industrial Extension Co-ordinating Committee (IECC) is formed by all the institutions listed above in order to facilitate rationalized individual efforts and complement them more effectively with Government policies as implemented by BEDU;

(j) The Industrial Development Advisory Committee (IDAC) defines and formulates industrial policy objectives and strategies, and also co-ordinates and monitors implementation of industrial policy objectives and projects.

Government is taking steps to clarify the licensing system, to define more precisely the products concerned, to co-ordinate the data gathering aspects more closely with the Central Statistics Office, with a view to using licensing as a means of promoting orderly industrial growth.

CONGO

The sharp drop in the price of oil and the rate of exchange of the US dollar to the CFA Franc, as well as the difficulty of slowing down public recurrent and capital expenditures in line with the decline in available domestic resources have caused significant internal and external imbalances in the Congolese economy. This prompted the Government to adopt, in June 1985, a coherent and global programme for the recovery of economic equilibrium. Congo's SAP also took into account all the objectives of APPER and UN-PAAERD.

For the purpose of harmonizing the programmes, APPER and UN-PAAERD were discussed in the Congo at the level of the Party, which initiates national policy, and at the level of the Government, which ensures its execution. The programmes were also communicated to the technical planning bodies. In the same way, the conformity of the national programmes to APPER and UN-PAAERD was ensured by the incorporation into the national programmes of the priorities of the two programmes, namely: food and agriculture, development of other agricultural support sectors, notably the agro-industries, transport and communications, and the development of human resources.

With regard to investment goals, the share of investments devoted to agriculture rose from 16.3 per cent in the 1986 budget to 24 per cent in the 1987 investment budget. This means that Congo has achieved the APPER objective of an increase in the general level of investments in agriculture to 20–25 per cent of all public sector investment.

At the end of 1985, when SAP had just been set up, Congo was confronted with a sudden worsening of the oil situation, which was totally unexpected. In fact, the average price of a barrel of crude oil fell from $US25.5 in 1985 to $US12.7 in 1986, and the average exchange rate of the dollar dropped from 449 CFA francs to 346 CFA francs during the same period. The State oil revenues, which amounted to 220 billion CFA francs in 1985 were reduced by half in 1986 and will be only 30 to 40 billion CFA francs in 1987. This sudden reversal of the state of the economy prompted the strengthening of SAP in May 1986, by emphasizing the following principal objectives:

(a) The restoration of the balance of public finance and the balance of payments, through a reduction in and better utilization of Government expenditure, and through an improvement in the collection of fiscal revenue;

77

(b) The revamping of the State sector and its restructuring by concentrating efforts on certain enterprises;

(c) The adoption of a reflationary policy.

Thus, among the various measures included in SAP were: the giving of priority to the rehabilitation of existing investments; the winding up of certain enterprises with negative value-added; staff retrenchments; the review of certain monopolies; price readjustments; the reorganization of State intervention in agriculture; the strengthening of the institutional framework which ultimately involved calling in private partners.

Based on the guidelines defined in SAP, the following actions have been initiated:

(a) A significant increase in producer prices of agricultural commodities in order to stimulate production;

(b) A drastic reduction in capital and recurrent expenditure in order to limit the State budget deficit, while preserving most of our development objectives;

(c) International negotiations to obtain a rescheduling of the public debt and thereby avoiding a breakdown in our financial and economic relations with the outside world;

(d) A case-by-case examination of the situation of State enterprises and the introduction of appropriate measures.

The 1987–1988 interim programme is not a plan in the same manner as the 1982–1986 plan which is a detailed, calculated package of coherent projects based on a global strategy. It is essentially a package of guidelines, options and measures, for the most part, deliberately general and designed to give rise to well-defined actions and measures during the years 1987 and 1988, taking into consideration existing constraints. It gives priority to a policy of support to the rural sector, with emphasis on agriculture, livestock breeding, fisheries and, to a certain extent, forestry.

State intervention is conceived to focus on support measures for rural production and the development of various private initiatives. In addition to a number of economic policy measures which have already been taken in 1986; namely, the increase of the prices of agricultural commodities, the winding up of the OCV and GCC monopolies, etc., such intervention will include, notably, the following: the production of improved seeds; technical support centres; agricultural extension; research and experimentation; a programme for the development and distribution of farm implements; a feeder roads programme; a price policy guaranteeing remunerative prices for the producer, as well as measures aimed at developing and facilitating the marketing of domestic products; a customs tariff policy designed to protect domestic production; and an agricultural credit policy to be carried out concurrently with the setting up of a production development programme.

Moreover, a number of rural production support actions have been initiated (food crop projects at Kindamba, Inoni Falaise, the AGRI Congo project, etc.). In short, the main options for the interim investment programme include the pursuit of recovery measures which will affect the sectors that make for growth (agriculture, livestock breeding, fisheries, forestry, small and medium-sized enterprises (SMEs), cottage industries).

Economic recovery in the State sector remains a basic objective in which all forms of social organization of production are expected to participate, thus establishing the basis for the construction of the national economy, e.g. farmers, individual producers or producers grouped into co-operatives, and nationals engaged in private enterprise. The strategy adopted to this end consists of several essential axes: the rebalancing of the State and private sector roles in economic activity and the reforming of the incentives framework of the economy to stimulate private initiative in agriculture, wood and the small and medium-scale private enterprises; the adjustment of public expenditure to the available financial resources while ensuring more effective State intervention; and the definition of a sectoral strategy relating primarily to the production sector and education and training.

Monitoring Mechanism

At the institutional level, the following have been created in order to ensure the monitoring of the implementation of APPER and UN-PAAERD: a National Monitoring Committee; and a technical Follow-up Committee. The National Monitoring Committee is presided over by the Minister of Foreign Affairs and Co-operation and the Vice-President is the Minister of the Plan. In order to ensure at the technical and political levels the execution and monitoring of SAP, a SAP Steering Committee has been created, with the Prime Minister as chairman.

THE GAMBIA

Prior to launching of the ERP in August 1985, the Gambia like many developing countries pursued its national development priorities and goals within the context of comprehensive development plans. However, with the increased deterioration in economic circumstances and the setting in of very serious macro-economic imbalances, which by their very nature resulted in plan implementation going off-track, it became imperative to institute comprehensive programmes to rehabilitate the economy for sustained economic recovery and growth.

Also, prior to the ERP, efforts were made to redress economic imbalances within the context of IMF Standby Adjustment and Stabilization programmes. Two such programmes were implemented in the period 1982/83 and 1984/86. However, despite these efforts at adjusting and stabilizing the economy, the Gambia continued to experience extreme budgetary and balance-of-payments difficulties which by mid-1985 reached crisis levels. By then, foreign exchange earnings were so low that the country could not meet the cost of domestic imports of essential commodities like rice and petroleum, and also the rising debt obligations. The difficulties were further compounded by low production levels for cash and food crops, with the former reaching an all-time low of 45,000 tons of marketed output in 1984/85. The very serious food deficits were supplemented by food aid assistance from external donors.

A comprehensive diagnosis of the situation showed that the economy was facing structural bottlenecks which needed far-reaching policy measures in order to deal with the crisis facing the economy and also achieve medium-term economic recovery. It was in this regard that the Gambia detailed an action programme to serve as a framework for discussion with the international donor community on a joint strategy for sustainable economic recovery and growth. Following intensive consultations and in collaboration with the World Bank, the IMF and the United Kingdom Overseas Development Administration, the Gambia's ERP was launched in 1985. The ERP is a comprehensive action strategy for overcoming the major imbalances in the economy over the short- and medium-term and for laying the basis for sustained growth over the longer-term. Over the initial two years (1986–87), the programme is designed to achieve: (a) financial and balance-of-payments stability; (b) maximum short-term expansion of output; (c) elimination of major exchange rate and price distortions; (d) curtailment and rationalization of the over-extended public sector; and, (e) creation of a climate conducive to the longer-term growth of the private sector.

In its *statement of development policy*, the Government outlined the long-term objective of the ERP, which is to promote over a period of years sustained economic growth through progressive alteration in the structure of the economy. The statement further outlined the direction to achieve this structural adjustment through:

(a) Diversification of production and exports;

(b) Increasing the degree of food self-sufficiency, including increased consumption of traditional coarse grains;

(c) Balancing the size of the public sector in line with the productive base of the economy;

(d) Improving public investment planning in order to increase its productivity and ensure a proper balance with recurrent public outlays; and,

(e) Reforming the system of credit and financial intermediation to support the growth and diversification of the private sector.

To facilitate dialogue with the international community, the Gambia presented its ERP to a donor's conference convened in London in September 1985. The donors accepted the programme as an important and politically courageous set of policy adjustments. They also recognized that, for this programme to succeed, substantial short-term balance-of-payments support and a Paris Club rescheduling of the Gambia's external debt are critically important. Since the London donor's conference, the Government has steadfastly adhered to its commitment in implementing the various measures of the ERP which have been further elaborated and refined into a time-bound and monitorable action programme.

In order to introduce a realistic exchange rate for the efficient allocation of resources, a fundamental reform of the exchange system was implemented. A flexible interbank market system was introduced in January 1986 under which the exchange rate of the local currency, the Dalasi, was permitted to float freely. In support of this system, exchange control procedures were liberalized. And the system, since its introduction, has been operating satisfactorily. It has increased the confidence of the private sector in the banking system with increased inflow of foreign exchange into the system. The thriving street operations in foreign exchange prior to the introduction of the system have abated drastically.

It is however recognized that an essential element for a flexible exchange rate system is a flexible pricing policy for key commodities in the economy whose prices are Government-administered. Consequently, there has been a pass-through of exchange rate movements in the upward adjustment of prices. The importation, marketing and pricing of such commodities as rice were also liberalized from a monopoly situation by the Gambia Produce Marketing Board to the private sector. Although, initially, prices rose dramatically as the private sector was adjusting to the new situation, the market has now stabilized with more certainty in the availability of and price levels for rice.

In order to ensure adequate returns to assets held in local currency form, the Government pursued a prudent credit policy stance and adopted a flexible interest rate policy. The latter was also meant to increase mobilization of domestic financial resources within the banking system. Interest rates were increased and a weekly tender system for Treasury Bills was introduced.

The thrust of the policies and actions for the agricultural sector, which accounts for a third of GDP and 85 per cent of domestic exports, and which will remain the principal engine of growth for the foreseeable future, is to reverse its weak performance. Given its critical position in the success of the ERP, the Government so far has implemented substantial increases in producer prices; improved the performance of the main credit institution – the Gambia Co-operative Union; reviewed subsidies on consumer foodstuffs (particularly on imported rice); and introduced an increasing measure of protection for domestic cereal producers with a view towards enhancing food self-sufficiency. Given the importance of an efficient Ministry of Agriculture towards improving the performance of agricultural production, the Ministry is being restructured in order to define an appropriate and manageable focus for it. Other policy measures implemented for increased agricultural production involved improvements in the availability and delivery of certified seed, increased application of fertilizer, focusing research programmes on farming systems, cultural and cropping patterns and the development of integrated crop/livestock extension services.

To increase the economic base of the Gambia through the exploitation of the productive potentials available in fisheries, livestock, horticulture, tourism and manufacturing activities, a number of incentives packages have been implemented for these areas including revision of the Development Act with a view to improving its effectiveness as an investment incentive.

The Government recognized the urgent need to restructure the public sector in order to improve its productivity and its capacity to implement the economic recovery programme. It also recognized the need to bring the size of the public sector in line with the productive potential of the economy. It was in this regard that, following a comprehensive review of the public sector, a large reduction in the number of public employees was instituted. The size of the civil service was reduced by 14 per cent and a comprehensive administrative reform and staff development programme launched. The thrust of these reforms is to reverse unproductive public service expansion and institute a smaller, adequately remunerated, better managed and better organized civil service. Service delivery and maintenance of productive assets will also be improved by instituting direct cost recovery policies.

To facilitate improvements in the performance of public enterprises, the Government has already launched programmes to: (a) Systematically divest Government holdings in commercial sectors; and, (b) Increase the autonomy and accountability of public enterprises through the use of performance contracts. Three such contracts have already been entered into between Government and three public enterprises.

In order to meet the overriding objective of the ERP for the achievement of a substantial improvement in the productivity of public investments and ensure that recurrent cost implications of new investments are sustainable in the light of projected medium-term fiscal constraints, the Government has revised its public investment programme for the period 1986/87 to 1988/89 which has given emphasis to projects with net foreign exchange generation or saving potential; rehabilitation and maintenance projects; and long-term investments in education and basic health services to develop the Gambia's human capital. The Government has also instituted the system of three-year rolling investment programmes.

Donor response in support of the Gambia's comprehensive and far-reaching programme of economic reforms so far has come from the World Bank, the British Overseas Development Administration, the ADB and the Saudi Fund, who have rendered financial support for the country's SAP. The IMF has also rendered Standby Programme, Structural Adjustment Facility and Compensatory Financing Facility assistance. Other balance of payments support has been received from the Government of the Netherlands and the United States of America. The country has also been to the Paris Club for debt rescheduling. Most of these were commitments made during the London Donor's Conference held in September 1986.

GUINEA

In September 1985, the authorities of the Second Republic launched the Economic and Financial Recovery Programme (PREF), covering about 30 months, with the following two objectives: (a) reorganization of public finance; and, (b) laying of the foundation for profound changes in the rules governing the economy of the country.

Alongside the PREF, and with the same objectives in view, the Government drew up a medium-term development strategy whose twin guiding principles can be summarized as follows:

(a) To encourage private individual and collective initiatives so long as they fit in with the general policy laid down by the state; and,

(b) To pursue state divestiture from the productive system, while strengthening its essential responsibilities as pilot, arbiter, and promoter of investments necessary for the emergence and development of productive activities.

Economic and Financial Measures

The non-convertibility of the national currency, the distortions caused by the artificial pricing structure, and the unbearable burden of the external debts were the main obstacles to be overcome as soon as possible in order to restore minimum activity and the confidence of the international economic community and financiers.

Following the devaluation and change of currency on 6 January 1986, with the Guinean franc replacing the syli, a system of weekly foreign exchange auction was introduced.

In order to guard against the risks of exchange rate fluctuations, the Government has adopted measures aimed at increasing foreign exchange supply and enlarging the range of operations eligible to bid at the auctions organized by the Central Bank. The current exchange rate of the Guinean franc is FG430 to $US1.00.

Measures have been taken in connection with price adjustments aimed at arriving gradually at cost pricing through: (a) economic liberalization; (b) return to normal tax system; and (c) realistic public tariffs (cost recovery).

The new Customs Tariff which came into effect on 15 January 1986 and was amended on 1 July 1986, is simpler than the previous one, and rates have been reduced, particularly import rates. The ordinary rate of import duties and taxes is now 18 per cent.

The monetary authorities decided to apply a credit policy which takes into account inflation and exchange rate fluctuations in order to stimulate savings. Three lines of credit (IDA, EEC and CCCE) were opened for SMEs and agricultural enterprises.

The rescheduling of public debt (about 40 per cent of the total) owed to the members of Paris Club was negotiated in April 1986. Guinea secured the consolidation and rescheduling of its arrears on

31 December 1985 and of the debts due or which will become due between 1 January 1986 and 28 February 1987. The total amount thus negotiated was $US 168 million. For the rest of the debt, owed mainly to the Eastern countries, the Arab countries and uninsured creditors, negotiations are progressing actively, even though they appear to be delicate and may take quite some time to conclude. Priority is presently given to soft (or concessionary) loans.

Structural Reforms

In order to stimulate private initiatives, the State had to divest itself, as rapidly as possible, from most of the productive activities and restructure the key sectors.

The restructuring involved the liquidation of State corporations which were a bottleneck or entirely irremediable. The liquidation of the following state banks (excluding the Central Bank) and their replacement with private or joint-venture banks was decided upon on 23 December 1985: Banque Internationale pour le Commerce et l'Industrie de la Guinée (BICIGUI); Société Générale des Banques; Banque Internationale de l'Afrique de l'Ouest (BIAO); and Banque Islamique de Guinée. It also involved the revival of viable enterprises either by privatizing them or by making them semi-public enterprises. This phase of the programme, particularly ambitious, is proceeding at a pace slower than expected because of institutional problems including lack of personnel and appropriate supervision of those available.

Under its divestiture policy, the state decided to liquidate the obviously irremediable industrial units and privatize most of the other enterprises. Only a small number of public utilities will remain under state control, i.e. water (DEG), railway (ONCFG), electricity (SNE), and the State Press. The privatization programme for industrial sector is behind schedule due to a wait-and-see attitude on the part of foreign investors (lack of funds or confidence?).

The administrative reform concerns the gradual setting up of an efficient administration, by scrapping 30,000 posts in the public service; establishment of the Office for the Reconversion of Civil Servants; selection and training of employees who will be pursuing their careers in the new Public Service; and, lastly, the introduction of new procedures and economic and financial measures (examples: Investment programming, National Accounting, etc...).

The legislative and statutory reform consists of unprecedented efforts aimed at making the state a 'Law State' with the enactment of codes and laws regulating economic activities. So far, the following have been enacted into law or are in the process of being promulgated:

Investment Code; Petroleum Code; Fishing Code; Trade Code; Electricity Code; Public Market Code; and New Accounting Plan.

NIGERIA

The internalization of some of the features of UN-PAAERD in Nigeria preceded the adoption of that programme by the Special Session of the United Nations General Assembly as well as that of its forerunner – APPER. For example, as far back as April 1982, the country had embarked on a stabilization programme to arrest emerging disequilibria in its domestic and external economic relations. The visible structural problems were caused on the internal front by low levels of productivity, cultivation of inappropriate consumption patterns, corrupt and bad economic management, on the one hand, and by destabilizing external factors such as collapse of commodity prices, adverse terms of trade, increasing protectionism on the part of advanced industrialized countries and the crippling effect of rising level of external debt servicing obligations, on the other hand. The economic stabilization measures, which were reinforced in 1984 and 1986, were aimed, among other things, at:

(a) Stimulation of the domestic economy with special emphasis on self-reliance in food production and reactivation of local industries;

(b) Reasonable improvement in the balance of payments by clearing the backlog of short-term arrears;

(c) Mobilization of both external and domestic financial resources;

(d) Development of rural areas with a view to stemming the rural/urban migration;

(e) Maintenance of price stability; and,

(f) Management of external debt.

The adoption of such stabilization measures had led to a substantial increase in the level of Government capital budget allocation to agriculture and agriculture-related projects from 11.9 per cent in 1985 to 17.9 per cent in 1986.

However, such austerity measures were not comprehensive enough and did not go far enough to revamp the economy and set the foundations for future growth as they were not potent enough to overcome the economic crisis and the structural imbalances. It was for this reason that the Government recognized the need to fully embrace the tenets of APPER and UN-PAAERD by supplementing its austerity measures with policies aimed at overcoming the pronounced structural weaknesses in the economy. The crucial policy reforms embarked upon within the framework of APPER and UN-PAAERD culminated in the adoption of SAP from July 1986 to June 1988. The macro-economic management policies contained in SAP were designed to correct distortions in prices (particularly the price of foreign exchange), streamline and de-emphasize cumbersome administrative controls, and rely increasingly on market forces to regulate economic activities so as to generally encourage efficient and rising level of private investment and production.

SAP formed the cornerstone of policy reforms embarked upon by Nigeria within the framework of APPER and UN-PAAERD. It was conceived right from the beginning as a two-year policy measure, from July 1986 to June 1988, and was designed to turn the national economy around with a view to resetting it on a healthy course of reconstruction, growth and development. The main features of SAP, whose effective implementation started only in October 1986 with the launching of the Second-Tier Foreign Exchange Market (SFEM), are as follows:

(a) Strengthening of the hitherto strong demand management policies;

(b) The adoption of measures to stimulate domestic production and broaden the supply base of the economy;

(c) Adoption of a realistic exchange rate policy;

(d) Further rationalization and restructuring of tariffs in order to aid industrial diversification;

(e) Move towards improved trade and payments liberalization;

(f) Reduction of complex administrative controls simultaneously with a greater reliance on market forces;

(g) Adoption of appropriate pricing policies, especially for petroleum products and public enterprises; and,

(h) Encouragement of rationalization and privatization of public sector enterprises.

These features show that SAP is a balanced programme. On the one hand are policy reforms designed to correct macro-economic price distortions in the economy with a view to restructuring the pattern of demand and supply of goods and services. On the other hand are several measures to be put in place to stimulate domestic production and broaden the supply base of the economy, particularly in the area of export.

Demand Management Measures

The demand management measures contained in SAP include, among other things, the following: (a) Monetary and credit targets; (b) Fiscal deficit limit; and, (c) Incomes guidelines.

The tight monetary policy included in SAP, with ceilings and guidelines on monetary and credit targets, was aimed at achieving an improvement in the balance of payments and at controlling excessive demand for foreign exchange on the second-tier foreign exchange market. In this connection, the expansion of the banking system's credit to the domestic economy was restricted in the second half of 1986 to 7.6 per cent and in 1987 to 4.4 per cent, consistent with an increase in the level of money supply of 0.3 per cent in 1986 and 11.8 per cent in 1987. With the overall ceiling, the expansion of credit to the Government was limited to 7.4 per cent in 1986 and 1.5 per cent in 1987.

The implementation of such measures has so far resulted in a 'liquidity squeeze' and the 'inadequacy' of new investments which could reduce unemployment, strengthen effective demand, expand production capacity and accelerate the economic recovery which the adoption of SAP is intended to accomplish in spite of the fact that the credit ceilings for 1986 were far exceeded, with the private sector overshooting its limit by over 20 per cent as shown below:

	March 1986	September 1986	December 1986	March 1987
	billions of naira			
1. Credit to the private sector (net)	14.300	15.847	17.365	17.549
2. Credit to the Government (net)	18.830	19.130	19.455	20.600
3. Total credit to domestic economy (net)	33.130	34.976	36.820	38.149

No one uniform conclusion can be drawn from the out-turn of credit ceilings in the implementation of SAP so far. In fact, empirical data from which any conclusive remark can be deduced is 'inadequate'. While one school of thought has contended that the action of some banks in exceeding their entire credit ceilings for 1987 by March is an indication of the over-restrictiveness of the credit limit and guidelines, another has attributed the same to imprudent banking policy and lack of desire to comply with necessary directives because penalties for infringement are not positive enough. Another argument to justify default in this regard is that importers require more credit because they require more naira per dollar unit of import as a result of the continued depreciation of the naira which, in turn, is due to inadequate funding of the SFEM and the poor prospects for the balance of payments in 1987.

However, the real problem, long outstanding before SAP, is the inaccessibility of particular sectors and groups to available credit even when foreign exchange earnings pose no constraint. These are in areas relating to small and medium-scale indigenous enterprises, particularly in the agricultural and industrial/manufacturing sectors. The inability of these categories of borrowers to avail themselves of bank credit poses a bottleneck which is negating the growth objectives of SAP, and thus calls for appropriate institutional reforms in the existing machinery for channelling credit to these categories of borrowers.

The fiscal policy reform included in SAP stipulates that the Government budget deficit is to be held at 4 per cent of the GDP in 1986 and below 3.5 per cent in 1987. The cut-back in Government expenditure to be brought about in the fiscal deficit limit is to be achieved through other limits imposed on public sector wage increase which is not to exceed 10 per cent during SAP period, and other areas as follows:

(a) Nominal rise in the Federal Government expenditure;

(b) Real increase in expenditure on materials and supplies (3 per cent in 1987);

(c) The pegging at 50 per cent of their 1985 level of transfers and loans to parastatals;

(d) The limiting of budgeted investment expenditure, including loans to parastatals to be kept at naira 3.3 billion in 1986 and 1987;

(e) The ending of the practice by the Federal Government, from 1987, of issuing debt on behalf of State Governments and allowing them to float public bonds on their own behalf; and,

(f) The limiting of the growth in net credit to the Government including net credit to the States to a maximum of 7.4 per cent in 1986 and 1.5 per cent in 1987.

Such a cut-back in Government expenditure, which ignores the effect of relative price changes occasioned by SFEM on public sector purchases, cannot but adversely affect the productivity of that segment. In addition, it has also produced a serious liquidity squeeze within the public sector. The illiquidity caused by the situation described above is aggravated further by another liquidity problem imposed on the economy by the large domestic debt owed by Government to the private sector and whose amortization is greatly constrained by the fiscal deficit limit. All these factors, taken together, unwittingly may have constituted impediments to new investment and business expansion in the private sector.

It is the expectation of SAP that all prices, including factor prices, would be deregulated to allow the determination of their equilibria levels largely by free market forces. The only restriction is the one imposed on public sector wage increase which is expected not to exceed 10 per cent during SAP period. The combination of restraint on wages and salaries with a high level of unemployment under inflationary conditions has produced major declines in real incomes. This has also resulted in a reduction in the effective demand for goods and services that should have been translated into new investments through the acceleration principle. The recently approved upward revision of fringe benefits and tax-cuts in the 1987 Budget are yet to be implemented. Similarly, the assumed adjustment of wages and salaries by 10 per cent under SAP has not been implemented.

Policy Measures to Stimulate Domestic Production

The other elements of SAP can be compressed into two as follows: (a) Adoption of a realistic exchange rate policy through the operation of SFEM; and (b) Adoption of appropriate pricing policies especially for petroleum products and public enterprises. These policy measures, like the demand management policies, perform overlapping functions. On the one hand, they have the potential for dampening effective demand and producing a deflationary effect. On the other hand, they are designed to stimulate domestic production and broaden the supply base of the economy, particularly in the area of exports.

As a main feature of SAP, Nigeria opted for the introduction of SFEM on 29th September 1986 rather than outright devaluation in its endeavour to attain a realistic and sustainable exchange rate for the naira. The two-tier exchange rate system allowed for public debts to be serviced under the official exchange rate, which is the rate in the first-tier market, while all other exchange transactions are to be carried out at SFEM rate. It is stipulated that the exchange rates in the two markets should be unified within a period of nine months.

The naira–dollar exchange rates fluctuated widely in the first five bids on the market from a low of naira 5.0584 = \$US1.00 in the second week to a high of naira 3.4999 = \$US1.00 in the third week and averaged naira 4.1517 = \$US1.00 during the period. Thereafter, the rate appreciated persistently from naira 4.1775 = \$US1.00 at the 5th bidding session to naira 3.0005 = \$US1.00 at the 11th session. Further appreciation to naira 2.900 at the 12th bidding was pushed down to naira 3.2000 by the Central Bank of Nigeria. As at the end of December 1986, the exchange rate was naira 3.300 = \$US1.00. However, from January, the naira depreciated persistently against the dollar to above naira 4.00 = $US1.00 by May 1987 despite the switch from marginal rate determination to the Dutch Auction method in April.

Based on the purchasing power parity thesis, the view in some quarters is that the naira is appreciably under-valued and that the prevailing SFEM rate may not be a realistic value. This argument is reinforced by the appreciation of most currencies of the world against the dollar. It would appear that the funding of SFEM and the psychology of the market have been the key factors influencing the second-tier rate attained. This is because funding has been low relative to original projections. There has been a drastic reduction in the average weekly supply of foreign exchange to the SFEM from $US 65 million in the last quarter of 1986 to about $US 35 million since March 1987 compared to the weekly average of 100 million naira envisaged by SAP. The continuation of the country's high level of debt-service ratio despite its success at debt rescheduling partially accounts for the low funding of SFEM. Another reason for underfunding of SFEM is the poor prospects of balance of payments for 1987.

A communication gap between the market (Government) and the people about the long-term course of events and the sustainability of funding may lead psychologically to hoarding and spurious demand for foreign exchange, which may produce artificially high rates of exchange. This is likely to pose severe short-term production/ supply base problems for the domestic economy. It is also likely to lead to a deviation on the pattern of use of purchased foreign exchange from the objective of promoting local substitutes to replace imported goods. For SAP to produce the intended result, it would be necessary that the exchange rate of the naira be unified at a realistic value based on its purchasing power parity with all factors taken into consideration.

The deadline indicated in SAP document for the Government views to be issued on the modalities of implementing the rationalization of public sector enterprises, which is June 1987, is yet to pass. Meanwhile, Government transfers and loans to parastatals have been pegged each year of the Programme at 50 per cent of their 1985 level while the committees set up by Government on the rationalization of public sector enterprises are working to complete their various assignments with a view to facilitating the issuance of necessary modalities for implementation within the target date. The issues to be addressed in the report are to include, among other things, the following: (a) Reduction of the burden imposed by parastatals on the dwindling resources of Government; (b) Enhancement of the efficiency of parastatals; (c) Improving the generally poor returns on overall Government investment; and, (d) Withdrawal of Government from activities that are best suited for the private sector.

There is also a need for Government to take a definite decision as well as implement a phased withdrawal of subsidies, especially of petroleum products, and utility services such as electricity, telephones, water, etc., so as to rationalize their uses and avoid unnecessary wastage by consumers.

Food and Agriculture

The Government has continued to give pre-eminence to food, agriculture and rural development in the 1987 budget which spans the middle of SAP period. The centrepiece of national policy on food and rural development programme is the small-scale farmer, the fundamental objective being to move rapidly towards self-reliance and self-sufficiency in the production of basic staples of grains, tuber, vegetable oil and fibre in the framework of a rising nutritional standard.

The Government will in the course of 1987 launch a National Food Security and Storage Scheme aimed at creating 500,000 tons farm and off-farm storage in order to reinforce the major policy measures and programmes announced in the 1986 Budget in respect of food and agriculture. Innovative decentralized network of small-scale and medium-scale storage facilities owned and operated by farmers' groups and private individuals will be employed in place of hitherto established large-scale integrated silo complexes for intra- and inter-seasonal stabilization of food stocks and prices. Other areas of policy thrust in the fiscal year 1987 shall include: (a) The launching of a new national small farmers credit programme to bring seasonal credit to farmers at the grassroots, as well as post harvest loans to ease cash flow squeeze; (b) The continuation of existing sectoral and commodity credit guidelines; (c) The development of a food market information dissemination service to provide the Nigerian food system with routine information so as to facilitate the free flow of farm produce from surplus producing areas to deficit states within the context of one Nigeria National Food Market; (d) The formulation of a National Nutrition Policy to attain nutrition norms and targets; and, (e) The general implementation of the articulated programmes of the established directorate of foods, roads and rural infrastructure in the fields of crops, livestock, fruits, vegetables, rural housing, rural health, rural education and social organization, the provision of rural infrastructural facilities such as the construction and effective maintenance of a national network of rural feeder roads as well as the implementation of a national rural water supply scheme, and a national rural markets programme within the framework of the rural feeder road programme and a rural electrification programme with emphasis on rural agro-industrialization.

The need to enable small and medium-scale farmers and business to men gain access to credit cannot be over-emphasized. Given the extent of leakages of local investment funds abroad through imports of capital goods – machinery, equipment and raw materials – by the large-scale enterprises, these small and medium-scale enterprises whose products have high local content should be the main focus of attention if economic growth is to be resumed as well as indigenized. With the abolition of the commodity boards, there is also a need to put in place special commodity financing arrangements in order to sustain domestic production.

Development of Other Sectors Supporting Agriculture, Exports and Agro-based Industries

The activities of the non-oil export subsector are strategic to the success of SAP since not only will they generate scarce foreign exchange, they will also expand domestic supply of goods and services as well as generate employment, especially through active encouragement of small-scale industries. The incentives to be given to export-oriented activities under SAP include, among other things: (a) subsidies to exporters of manufactured goods; (b) creation of an export development fund; (c) export expansion grant; (d) export adjustment fund; and, (e) duty draw back/suspension scheme.

It was expected that, with SFEM, a revised tariff structure would be introduced for a period of 12 months. In addition, a comprehensive review of tariffs is being undertaken and the revised structure is expected to be put in place in the course of 1987. The purpose of this rationalization and restructuring of tariffs is to liberalize trade and payments as well as aid the promotion and diversification of industrial activities. The initial restructured tariffs at the inception of SFEM ranged between 10 and 20 per cent, in the case of industrial raw materials, as against the former range of 15–20 per cent. For capital goods, the range was raised from 5–10 per cent to 10–20 per cent in order to encourage the development of local capital goods industry. Furthermore, the number of prohibited items has been reduced from 73 to 16.

Improvement in transport and telecommunications modes is one of the areas of emphasis in APPER and UN-PAAERD for bringing about economic recovery and accelerated development in Africa. It is for this purpose that the 1987 Federal Budget places emphasis on efficiency and effectiveness in the transport sector as an essential aid to facilitate the activities of the productive sectors of the economy. To achieve this, the Budget places priority on repair, maintenance and rehabilitation of existing road networks and vehicles as well as support to water and rail transportation. In addition, the Government will further encourage competition between Nigeria Airways and domestic private airlines.

In view of the role of the agricultural sector in the on-going efforts to restructure and diversify the productive base of the economy, the Government places top priority on finding solutions to the problems of drought and desertification. It is for this reason that increased provision of infrastructural facilities to bring more drought-affected areas under cultivation and protect land resources from desert encroachment, soil erosion and flood is made one of the main objectives of agricultural development policies and programmes under the Fifth Development Plan to be launched later in 1987. The medium to long-term objectives in this sector also include, among others, the combating of ecological problems such as drought, desertification and flood.

Government has continued to emphasize the role of education and human resources development in the socio-political and economic transformation of the country. Towards this end, the Government provided special funds for the rehabilitation of Universities, grants for educationally-disadvantaged states, funds for the provision of science equipment, women's education, education of the gifted, and reactivation of the Federal Scholarship and Students Loan Schemes, in the 1986 budget. Owing to dwindling resources, the Government has readjusted its educational priorities in 1987 to cover only key areas of education. These include the rehabilitation of the Federal Polytechnics and Colleges of Education, the provision of a few more technical colleges and the continuation of the development of the four special programmes (women, nomads, science and the gifted) started in the 1986 fiscal year.

In addition, established human resources training institutions or manpower development agencies such as the Nigerian Institute for Policy and Strategic Studies, the Administrative Staff College of Nigeria, the Centre for Management Development and the recently set up National Centre for Economic Management and Administration have continued to run courses, seminars and workshops aimed at the development of human resources of various cadres already in employment.

Mobilization of Domestic and External Financial Resources

The Government has been making every effort to mobilize domestic and external financial resources since 1986 for expanded production. While the Government recognizes that better interest rates are likely to attract depositors both at home and abroad, it is very conscious that they must not be allowed to be fixed so high as to be inimical to the interest of small and medium-scale entrepreneurs. With this in mind, the Government has raised the maximum lending rate from 13 per cent to 15 per cent while floor rates of 10 per cent and 12 per cent were set respectively for savings and time deposits during the course of the 1986 Budget. This policy is continued in 1987 leaving the banks free to negotiate higher interest rates, within the new monetary and credit policy/guidelines.

One of the aims of SAP was to make the investment and general economic climate attractive enough for foreign capital to flow freely into Nigeria. Towards this end, adequate provision was made to facilitate repatriation of capital, dividends and interest that accrue from investment brought into the country through SFEM.

The monitoring of the operation of SAP is not closely effected at present. What is currently being done by the Inter-ministerial Committee set up to monitor SAP is based on the data requirements of the World Bank and IMF. Such monitoring relates only to financial aggregates. Yet if SAP is to bring about desired growth along the lines envisaged in the document, it is imperative that the trends in the structural changes taking place in the economy in real terms be closely and regularly monitored. This will lead to timely and necessary modifications of policies, targets, programmes, etc. that are not accomplishing the desired goals.

The country has also set up another permanent interministerial committee to monitor and assess external assistance received by Nigeria within the framework of APPER and UN-PAAERD.

RWANDA

The period of preparation of the Fourth Economic, Social and Cultural Development Plan, 1987–1991, coincided roughly with the period of reflection on the practical direction to be given to UN-PAAERD. The broad lines of UN-PAAERD were indeed adjusted to reflect the national socio-economic reality and act as a backdrop for the Fourth Development Plan, adopted by the 'Comité Central du Mouvement Révolutionnaire National pour le développement' (MRND). To initiate the structural transformation of its economy, Rwanda thus adopted the main orientations indicating the priority areas where it intends to deploy and mobilize resources, both domestic and external, for the realization of the various objectives of its economic development policy during the five-year period, 1987–1991. Certain actions recommended by UN-PAAERD have already been implemented; others are being implemented or will be implemented gradually over the five-year period (1987–1991) and in accordance with a rolling and revisable investment programme.

Rwanda's development strategy for the 1987–1991 period aims, then, at:

(a) Restructuring and stimulating national economic growth around one basic objective, that of food self-sufficiency, understood in the sense of a strategic objective that should lead the national economy to a point where it can generate within itself a process, a self-stabilizing dynamism, capable of producing simultaneously the volume of goods and services needed both for the welfare of people and for the maintenance and expansion of the potentials for production, especially of food; and,

(b) Formulating sectoral strategies to support the basic strategic objective of food self-sufficiency, and strategies to achieve the ultimate objective of increased security in the satisfaction of vital needs: agriculture, industry and crafts, economic infrastructure (energy, water, transport), education and training, population, health, area planning, trade and finance, etc.

In Rwanda, the challenge of food self-sufficiency has been made the basic strategic goal of the Fourth Development Plan, towards which will converge what we have defined as sectoral strategies and what UN-PAAERD calls 'agriculture support measures'. To carry this strategy through, Rwanda has opted for a model known as 'rural self-development', which emphasizes the stimulation, expansion or consolidation of production and, hence, manpower development activities on family holding which form the fabric of the Rwandese socio-economic landscape. By self-development, then, we mean the strengthening of existing activities and the encouragement of new activities that will enable each individual to expand his production capacity and, consequently, increase his income.

But what is Rwanda actually doing or intending to do in the short and medium term to cope with the pressing food problem and to develop agriculture? Regarding immediate measures, Rwanda has since 1983, with the aid of the EEC, embarked upon the experiment of implementing a food strategy, and is on the point of finalizing arrangements for the building up of an emergency food stock. The warehouses are already completed and institutions capable of managing this stock also exist; for example, OPROVIA (an institution responsible for the processing and marketing of food products) and TRAFIPRO co-operative, both of which have an extensive collection and distribution network. All that needs to be done is to supplement the market regulating activity of these institutions, including the working capital replenishment mechanisms. The working capital funding require-ments are estimated at FRW 100 million, that is about $US1.25 million, to feed 300,000 persons for some forty days, the time needed to organize large-scale relief. Furthermore, consultations are under-way to set up a national storage and distribution system, with the technical assistance of the International Trade Centre (ITC) financed by the Swiss Government.

It is to be noted that steps have already been taken to launch studies on the various parameters which herald climatic changes. The results should make it possible to take prompt action to aid regions and populations affected by the effects of an abnormally prolonged drought.

Regarding medium-term measures, nearly $US50 million are spent each year in Rwanda as investments in agriculture, i.e. the equivalent of 13.5 per cent of total investment expenditures for the 1982–85 period. This amount will be doubled before the end of this decade so as to step up food production mostly through rapid intensification and regional specialization in crops. Appropriate provisions have also been made to promote non-agricultural activities in rural areas. This will offer job opportunities for the surplus labour force which creates under-employment on the family holdings, and, by so doing, increase the effective demand for foodstuffs.

Market forces regulate prices of agricultural commodities in Rwanda, in general, and of foodstuffs, in particular. However, severe fluctuations in food prices have been observed in recent years. These have been due to surplus production (the case of potato in 1985/86) or shortfalls in production due to drought (the case of beans in 1984). In order to guarantee the farmer a stable price, the Government has, in the first instance, fixed floor prices for a number of agricultural commodities. These prices are, however, not being applied on the market. To reduce the impact of price fluctuations on the smooth running of the economy, in general, and on the income level of peasant producers, in particular, the Government is finally experimenting with a series of measures which in themselves are flexible enough but will gradually lead to greater regularity in the growth of the economy. These measures range from a storage policy, on the one hand, to the determination of the production cost of agricultural commodities, on the other. As a result, 'remunerative' prices, reflecting costs actually incurred, and market conditions are calculated to serve as reference points for agricultural production programmes, which will form part of the 'annual programmes'. Government intervention also takes the form of incentives, through credit and tax policy.

Within the Fourth Development Plan, the incentives system is based on a series of indirect measures of an economic nature. Resort to government regulation is either non-existent or temporary. Among these measures, the following may be mentioned:

(a) The food aid marketing policy, which must henceforth avoid allowing prices of local commodities to depreciate;

(b) The establishment, currently under-way, of an agricultural credit system, whose management structure is still to be defined, but which, it is hoped, will meet the many small financing requirements of agricultural and para-agricultural activities in which the commercial banks are not interested; and,

(c) Livestock development, the strategy for which revolves around two major actions. First, the establishment of modern ranches in suitable natural areas. These ranches will also serve as a means of raising yields of milk products and meat, and as centres for the dissemination of pasture improvement techniques as well as techniques for the manufacture and sale of enriched feed. Two such agro-pastoral projects have already been executed, with the help of the World Bank, for the development of the regions of Mutara (OVAPAM) and Gishwati (GBK). Second, the introduction, on a wider scale, of the 'cow loan' facility for the small farmer. This will help raise the nutritive value of children's food while constituting an additional source of income for peasant families, not to mention the natural manure it will provide for farms.

Mechanization, in the real sense (mechanical ploughs, combine harvesters, tractors, etc.) is, with few exceptions, unsuited to Rwanda. The country is exceptionally hilly and the terrain is very rugged. Farms are very narrow and broken up into small plots; the average area is 1.2 ha consisting of five fields. The use of modern equipment is uneconomic, at the best of times. The same applies to produce-processing equipment, with the exception of the agro-food industry but, there again, on a 'small scale'. The most profitable processing activity at the moment but one where attempts at modernization have not yet yielded the expected results is the making of beer from banana, fortunately a very widespread activity which helps to offset shortages of imported brewers' cereals.

The introduction of fertilizers and pesticides is unfortunately still limited, owing to the high prices of these imported inputs, the weaknesses of the agricultural extension system and also, sometimes, the unsuitability of these inputs to the nature of the soil and the crops. The results of traditional methods are, most of the time, not far from those obtained at high cost through these modern methods; hence the marked scepticism of peasant farmers.

During the Fourth Plan, a nitrate fertilizer factory will be built which will use as raw material methane gas from Lake Kivu. A pesticides factory will also be built. Also, research and agricultural extension will soon be closely associated so that they can complement each other. A loan has been obtained from the World Bank (IDA) to help reorganize and develop the resources and activities of the Institut des Sciences Agronomiques du Rwanda (ISAR). This will help extend the system for monitoring the application of agricultural research findings while giving greater substance to technical packages disseminated by extension agents. Still in connection with agricultural intensification, the new investments code contains explicit provisions aimed at exempting from customs duties all equipment and sundry raw materials required for the manufacture and distribution of fertilizers.

Irrigation systems are at the moment not an absolute necessity for agriculture in Rwanda where, on the average, every peasant farmer is able to make two harvests annually. On the other hand, deforestation is becoming a real menace for the ecology and for the protection of soil fertility; and landslides are constant threats to families who possess only 60 to 80 acres for subsistence. An extensive programme has been launched as part of our 'umuganda' operations to start replacing all felled trees, to improve the calorific quality of species and to introduce constructional timber species in anticipation of the development requirements of wood-workers who are expected to play an important role in eliminating imports of furniture and metal equipment.

In the particular case of Rwanda, to improve the distribution of agricultural commodities, it is necessary first to increase sales outlets, improve the means of transport and make credit more widely available to tide farmers over the lean period between harvests without mortgaging future crops. It often happens that the farmer, when he needs immediate cash to meet expenses that cannot be deferred, is obliged to sell off his produce cheaply and buy it back later at a higher price. This creates serious price fluctuations on the market, which affect the poorest, disorganize production programmes and upset the food balance. The institution of reinforced buffer stocks will help improve matters; hence the importance the authorities attach to keeping supplies stable and maintaining prices within reasonable limits. Efforts are being made by the rural population, as part of communal labour, to build, develop, and maintain feeder roads throughout our communes. This facilitates the collection and evacuation of farm produce to the various markets of our nascent towns. The Public Works Department, on its part, endeavours to build trunk roads linking the chief towns.

SENEGAL

Senegal has embarked upon the implementation of a programme of social and economic development measures for the period 1986–1989 in line with UN-PAAERD.

At least one third of the twenty programmes of priority measures which constitute the basic core of the Eighth Development Plan are in the area of food and agriculture. These include: promotion of self-sufficiency among rural producers; improvement of the environment and agricultural production; attainment of food security throughout the country; the fight against desertification; and mastery of water resources.

Planned investments in the primary sector (agriculture, fisheries, water and forests, rural and agricultural irrigation) represent around 32 per cent of the Plan's total investments, while the investments in agriculture in particular represent some 14.7 per cent. Also among the financial measures taken by Senegal is a series of reforms concerning food and agriculture, on the one hand, and the agricultural support sectors, the struggle against drought and desertification and the mobilization of human resources, on the other hand. These reforms mean the implementation of new sectoral policies, such as the new agricultural policy adopted in 1985, and the new industrial policy which is currently in the first phase of implementation.

The fundamental objective of the new agricultural policy is the promotion of food self-sufficiency at the same time as the strengthening of technical crops through the implementation of the following measures: (a) A readjustment of the method of rural supervision linked to the implementation of a contractual policy between the State and rural development enterprises; (b) An improvement in the supply of inputs and the reorganization of trading channels through the decontrol of the marketing of inputs and outputs; and, (c) A policy of processing, and the encouragement of the consumption of local cereals by means of an appropriate pricing system.

The measures currently being undertaken in the framework of the implementation of medium and long-term adjustment programmes relate notably to: (a) the rationalization of Public Investment Policy; (b) an improvement in the performance of state enterprises; and, (c) better financial management.

Senegal has taken a number of institutional measures aimed at easing the constraints on the implementation of its national programme. The reforms have been at the level of Government as well as in respect of new policies directed at the primary and secondary sectors of the economy.

As part of the national monitoring mechanism for the implementation of the Medium and Long-term Adjustment Programme (MLAP) in Senegal, which was set up in 1985 and whose structures have been complemented in the context of the implementation of the UN-PAAERD, there are three councils or committees.

First, there is the Inter-ministerial Supervisory Council whose task it is to help the Government to implement and control the execution of the MLAP as contained in the Senegalese Government's general policy declaration presented at the first meeting of the Consultative Group on Senegal held in Paris on the 13th and 14th December 1984. The Inter-ministerial Council has, in particular, the task of: following the implementation of the Government's general policy objectives as well as sectoral strategies; initiating studies and action programmes necessary for this purpose; co-ordinating the actions of the different ministerial departments; and following the implementation of the Action Plan put into operation by the Government. The Council meets once every three months under the chairmanship of the Head of State. In the absence of the Head of State, the Council is chaired by the Minister of the Plan and Co-operation.

Second, there is the Technical Follow-up Committee responsible for monitoring the MLAP. The committee, directed by a co-ordinator assisted by a team of Senegalese and foreign experts, has specifically the tasks of: taking charge of the Consultative Group secretariat; ensuring liaison with the co-ordinating committee of investors set up following the Consultative Group's recommendations; ensuring control of the effective implementation of the Action Plan and the guidelines fixed by the Government in its declaration of general policy; collaborating with the relevant administrative services in the preparation of sectoral meetings and programmes on economic and financial negotiations with the investors; setting up a schedule of follow-up indicators; and helping to publicize the Government's economic programmes.

Third, there is the Inter-ministerial committee for the implementation of MLAP and UN-PAAERD whose responsibility it is to ensure proper liaison between the Inter-ministerial Supervisory Council and the MLAP technical follow-up committee. The committee meets at least once a month under the chairmanship of the Minister of the Plan and Co-operation.

In order to carry out economic recovery programmes efficiently, structural reforms have been made at the level of certain Ministerial Departments and, principally, at the level of the Ministry of the Plan and Co-operation and the Ministry of Economy and Finance. The aim of these reforms is to harmonize the procedures for dealing with development projects and strengthen the technical capacity of these two ministerial departments in the functions of co-ordinating the economic and financial measures in the framework of the new strategies.

ZAMBIA

The Government of Zambia has since 1983 been implementing macro-economic policy reforms supportive of the agricultural sector, culminating in the introduction of an auction system of foreign exchange allocation. Since then, there has been a massive devaluation of the local currency against the US dollar. Simultaneously, there has been a reduction in subsidies and public employees and restricted wage and salary increases. At the regional level, an early warning system for SADCC region was established in Harare, Zimbabwe, in 1986. However, only two countries – Zambia and the United Republic of Tanzania – have national early warning systems; the other members do not. Until all member states establish national early warning systems, the subregional programme will not be very functional. Zambia collaborates closely with regional crop protection agencies, e.g., the Red Locust Eradication Centre based in Nairobi, Kenya. In the field of livestock protection, she works closely with the Bovine Regional Research Centre in Gaborone, Botswana, and the small livestock centre in Nairobi, Kenya.

In the short and medium term Zambia hopes to continue the programmes by undertaking the following measures:

Food and Agriculture
The aim in this sector is to increase the levels of savings (especially rural savings) and investment through wider coverage of Credit Union and Savings Association (CUSA) mobile banks and the establishment of

new credit institutions. Land reclamation activities in an attempt to reverse land degradation have also been intensified.

The Zambian Government has since independence encouraged mechanization of agriculture by establishing land clearing and tractor hire units. However, high maintenance costs rendered a lot of machinery obsolete. Since APPER, a major rehabilitation programme for tractors and land-clearing equipment has been embarked on. Notwithstanding, it has become clear that small-scale farmers will not be able to afford the increased charges for these services. The only way this group of farmers can therefore afford to increase hectares under cultivation and crop output is by use of draught power. The Government is helping in ox-training for this purpose. For many years now the Government has improved and expanded storage capacities. Since APPER, a storage master plan has been drawn up.

Recent droughts have, however, proved that as long as agricultural development continues to depend on rainfall, all the above measures are easily rendered useless. To ameliorate the effects of drought, steps have been taken to establish a low-cost irrigation fund to help farmers construct dams, canals, etc.

Zambia has had a strong network of regional research stations and laboratory facilities. This has enabled us to develop our own drought-resistant seed varieties for maize, sorghum, sunflower and groundnuts. There also exists an on-going traditional crop research programme. The new maize seed varieties are now being exported to neighbouring countries.

To date, no gender-specific programme has been set up by the Government for women food producers. However, one province (Western) is experimenting with a project aimed at increasing incomes of female-headed households, 'Peoples Participation Project' (PPP). In other areas, studies are underway to assess the number of people in a similar situation and the nature of their constraints. There is an ongoing rural youths programme and steps are being taken to strengthen it.

Two provinces (Southern and North-Western) are practising 'train-and-visit' extension services under donor support, but the Government has not adopted it at national level because it is extremely expensive to run.

Other Sectors in Support of Agriculture

The Government intends to intensify measures already being undertaken in this area, i.e., the rehabilitation of transport infrastructure and manufacturing. Additional measures in the short and medium term include reduction of dependence on non-African experts and encouragement of indigenous entrepreneurial capabilities. We hope to achieve the former through intensified subregional co-operation. Concentration on the teaching of science-based subjects at higher levels and the promotion of small-scale industries will all go a long way towards achieving the latter objective. The Project Planning and Evaluation Unit (PPEU) of the Ministry of Finance will be strengthened in order to develop local capacity for project design and preparation.

Also, plans are underway to set up a central engineering workshop to produce spare parts for the overhaul, repair and maintenance of public vehicles machinery. If it goes according to plan, it should become operational by 1990.

Human Resources Development

In this area, a number of programmes and projects which commenced before the adoption of APPER and UN-PAAERD were continued during 1986. Among them is the maternal and child health and family planning which began in 1983. This project aims at improving the health of mothers and children by strengthening the National Maternal Child and Family Planning Programmes within primary health care. It also aims to assist the Ministry of Health to increase delivery points.

The Government accepted a recommendation of the 1985 salaries and incomes commission (Love II) to set up a National Manpower Council. The composition of the Council is currently being considered. Another action in this area is the setting up of the School of Demography at Unza. Both moves will go a long way towards strengthening human resources development.

Policy Reform

Immediate macro-economic policy reform measures taken were exchange rate adjustment and reduction of subsidies. Between October 1985 and the same period in 1986, the kwacha rate against the US dollar depreciated by 523 per cent. This came about as a result of letting market forces determine the weekly rate in an environment of a predetermined foreign exchange supply. And, because Zambia is greatly dependent on imports, such massive devaluation led to escalation in inflation rates. The withdrawal of subsidies added new pressure to domestic prices.

During 1987 the Government has instituted measures to appreciate the local currency by adopting a 2-tier auction system. Under the new system, Government transactions, i.e., debt servicing, essential imports of medicines and education requirement, Zambia Airways IATA bills and Zam Oil requirements will purchase their foreign exchange at a rate of between ZK9–12.50 to 1 $US. Commercial transactions of other institutions and individuals will continue on old lines without an upper limit.

In addition, the Government has taken measures aimed at reducing the civil service through early retirement. Incentives are being worked out to help those affected by this policy to go into self-employment such as agro-business where they can help create gainful employment for others. The Government intends to continue with the programmes of improving the management of the economy, i.e., liberalizing the exchange rate market, removal of price ceiling and subsidies on all crops except maize, and will strengthen the activities of Foreign and Joint Monitoring Centre.

Financial Resources Mobilization

Zambia has already created or strengthened financial institutions by liberalizing commercial banks interest rates. During the last parliamentary session (January–March 1987), legislation was passed increasing interest rates on deposits. Under the Income Tax Amendment Act of 1987, marginal tax rates were reduced. Both measures are aimed at increasing domestic savings.

Simultaneously, the Government has taken measures to increase the surplus on the Government budget by increasing revenue and cutting expenditure. Also, measures aimed at increasing efficient utilization of domestic resources, ensuring that essential commodities are given priority, strict fiscal discipline, and liberalization of prices and imports have been instituted.

Measures have been instituted to increase foreign exchange earnings as well. Thus, the Government of Zambia has endeavoured to promote exports through the formation of an Export Promotion Board, depreciation of the local domestic currency and lower tax rates for exporters. Also, a new Investment Act was enacted in 1986 which sets out attractive incentives for foreign investors. Under the Act, exporters of non-mineral commodities are allowed to retain 50 per cent of export earnings derived therefrom. Incentives are given to those who invest in priority sectors of the economy and the rural areas. The Act also lays down the rules for the transfer of technology into the country and remittances of income abroad.

Diversification of trade from developed countries into regional markets has commenced. Both SADCC and PTA countries have proved willing trading partners. Other measures in this area have aimed at increasing effective utilization of technical assistance through better project identification and preparation; provision of local counter-parts; meeting recurrent cost component; and instituting technical assistance and setting up an aid co-ordination apparatus, the Joint Monitoring Committee.

Modalities and Mechanism for Implementation and Monitoring of APPER and UN-PAAERD

The Zambian Government has established a policy organ, the National Economic Development Council composed of the Joint Central Committee and Cabinet, and chaired by the President. Regular economic reviews are undertaken by the planning wing of the Ministry of Finance.

There also exists a technical apparatus for national and project planning comprising the regional planning, project identification and preparation units as well as sectoral units. Overall plan monitoring is done by these same units and the Joint Monitoring Committee, if the project has foreign funding. The Government has not yet established emergency food relief and rehabilitation mechanism; however, discussions on the subject have commenced.

Co-ordination and monitoring the implementation of the ERP is done by the following joint monitoring organs: *Ad hoc* consultation for APPER; UNDP Round Table; World Bank CG; Paris and London Clubs. At the meeting of the Multinational Programming and Operational Centre (MULPOC) held in Lusaka, Zambia, in February 1987, member countries appointed Lusaka MULPOC to monitor both APPER and UN-PAAERD in the sub-region.

CHAPTER FOUR

The Contribution of Subregional Institutions Towards Intra-African Trade, Economic Recovery and Development

BINGU WA MUTHARIKA

INTRODUCTION

Since 1960, there has been considerable progress towards the establishment of African subregional institutions for intra-African trade. While most of the subregional institutions embrace all possible sectors and subsectors of the economies of member States, trade has been the centrepiece in the orientation of the major groupings. Among such institutions may be found the economic communities, customs unions, monetary unions, preferential trade areas and river basin unions.[1] The motivation behind all these joint efforts is to maximize development potentials and to increase intra-African trade.[2] Even during the colonial days, some forms of integration were achieved, largely based on the need to ease administrative problems. These groupings included the East African Common Services Organization; the South African Customs Union; the Federation of Rhodesia and Nyasaland; French Equatorial Africa; French West Africa.[3] Similarly, the African countries were grouped in currency zones which were 'pegged' to the metropolitan currencies.[4]

Subregional integration is not therefore new to Africa. During the early days of pan-African militarism, several groupings were established as rallying points against colonialism. These included the *Brazzaville Group*, the *Monrovia Group* and the *Cassablanca Powers*. The Pan Africanists envisioned a united Africa in which there would be integrated planning for social and economic development, common education institutions and, indeed, a common army.[5]

The role of subregional institutions in the promotion of intra-African trade as the 'mainstay' for an African strategy was given prominence when the African Heads of State and Government adopted the LPA and the FAL in 1980. There was a call for all African countries to create subregional preferential trade areas or similar institutions not later than December 1984.[6]

Before 1980, ECOWAS, CEAO, and UDEAC were established with objectives which included intra-African trade promotion. Since the adoption of LPA several new institutions have been established to promote intra-African trade. These include PTA, ECCAS, CEPGL, SADCC, and the Indian Ocean Island Commission. The Federation of African Chambers of Commerce and several subregional chambers of commerce have also been established to enhance the involvement of the private sector in the development and expansion of intra-African trade.

A critical question is what role the subregional institutions play in Africa's development. The purpose of this chapter is to review, briefly, the mechanisms and role of these subregional institutions in the development and expansion of intra-African trade as a means of enhancing Africa's economic recovery, growth and development within the overall framework for UN-PAAERD.

TYPES OF SUBREGIONAL TRADE INSTITUTIONS

Subregional trade institutions in Africa have essentially assumed the following forms: customs unions; preferential trade areas; economic communities; and other trade promotion mechanisms.

Customs Unions

Customs Unions have been among the oldest institutions to be established in Africa to promote intra-African trade. A customs union is an agreement between two or more member states to facilitate trade among them through the removal of tariffs levied on imports from other members of the Union.[7] There are two such unions. The first is UDEAC, comprising Cameroon, Central African Republic, Congo, Equatorial Guinea and Gabon. The second is the South African Customs Union established in 1910 and made up of South Africa, Botswana, Lesotho and Swaziland. The UDEAC treaty aims at developing economic integration of the member states through the gradual establishment of a common market and common external tariff. It also provides for the removal or reduction of tariffs and non-tariff barriers to inter-state trade and the harmonization of customs legislation, fiscal policies, industrial development and planning policies.[8] Another objective is to seek co-operation in transport and communications, tourism, rural development, investment laws and regulations, and science and technology. The South African Customs Union, on the other hand, has somewhat limited objectives in the area of abolition of tariffs and non-tariff obstacles and ensuring free movement of goods, services and persons among the member states of the Union. The Rand Currency Area ensures the smooth functioning of the customs union.

Preferential Trade Areas

A preferential trade area is an agreement by which a group of countries agree to provide preferential treatment to selected goods originating from member states by according a gradual reduction of tariffs over a given period until a zero tariff level is reached for those goods.[9] Essentially, a preferential trade area should involve the exchange of existing goods and services among the member states. However, in the case of Africa, the institution tends to embrace all major economic sectors approximating an economic community. A specific case in point is the PTA.[10] Recently, the North African countries have also taken a firm decision to establish a preferential trade area among them. The PTA for Eastern and Southern Africa covers a wide range of activities envisaged by its eleven protocols.[11] In addition, there are two special protocols in respect of Botswana, Lesotho and Swaziland and on special provisions in respect of the Comoros and Djibouti. The PTA Treaty provides for a wide spectrum that takes into account the peculiar geographical locations, economic situations and political problems in which some of its members find themselves.

The principal objective of these arrangements is to ensure a faster rate of industrialization of the area. Member states are generally free to impose any level of import duties on third parties as their individual policies dictate.[12] Thus, in line with the overall aspirations of its members, the PTA's objective is 'to promote co-operation and development in all fields of economic activity particularly in the fields of trade, customs, industry, transport, communications, agriculture, natural resources and monetary affairs with the aim of raising the standard of living of its peoples, of fostering closer relations among its member states, and to contribute to the progress and development of the African continent'.[13] As can be appreciated, this objective is much wider than that envisaged in traditional free trade areas.[14] To attain this objective, the member states agreed, *inter alia*, to 'gradually reduce and eventually eliminate as between themselves customs duties in respect of imports of selected commodities produced within the

Preferential Trade Area'.[15] For this purpose, countries established common rules of origin with respect to products which shall be eligible for preferential treatment.[16]

Economic Communities

The establishment of economic communities is another form of subregional institution in which intra-African trade plays a prominent role. Four African subregional economic communities need specific mention. These are ECOWAS; CEAO; ECCAS; and CEPGL.[17] The EAC which was established in 1967 between Kenya, Uganda and Tanzania has now been dissolved. The main issue to stress is that all these economic communities assert the perceptions expressed in the Pan-African movement of ensuring rapid economic development through collective self-reliance.[18] The aims and objectives of these economic communities are all-embracing and broadly aspire to promote and enhance social and economic development through close co-operation among the member states in all fields of social and economic activity such as transport and communications, energy, agriculture, natural resources, trade, customs, industry, monetary and financial matters, human resources development, tourism, education, culture, science and technology, and to ensure free movement of persons within the community.[19]

Other objectives of the economic communities include the following: to assist in the eventual establishment of an African Common Market; to initiate and organize African trade fairs and co-ordinate the participation of its members and African businessmen in trade fairs and trade events; to collect, analyse and disseminate trade, production and technological information in Africa and promote the exchange of trade missions within Africa; to assist in the training of African economists and technicians, especially business managers and trade personnel; to act to settle such trade disputes that may be brought before it by its members, to co-ordinate and harmonize the activities and views of its members with a view to safeguarding their interests within international circles and with respect to third parties; and to undertake consultancy services and research with respect to its objectives.

THE SUBREGIONAL INSTITUTIONS AND AFRICAN
ECONOMIC RECOVERY: EXPECTATIONS AND ASPIRATIONS

The Rationale

Before analysing the major trade objectives of the subregional institutions identified in Section I of this Chapter, a brief word about the motivation behind their creation would serve as a useful reference background. Several factors have interacted to form the rationale for subregional trade institutions.

The first major factor was the collapse of the colonial regimes following the political independence of a large number of African countries in the 1960s. This created an inevitable yawning gap in the expectations of the African peoples.[20] In this regard, it should be pointed out that subregional institutions, especially those in the expansion of intra-African trade, have been greatly influenced by the collapse or modifications in the trade and economic groupings created during the colonial period. During the colonial era, trade within such groupings did not necessarily follow factor endowments or comparative cost advantages.[21] Nevertheless, there was still a basic assumption that the creation of a larger trade or economic block would result in increased economic activity and growth through greater market and industrial opportunities.[22]

The second motivating factor has been the new policy of socio-economic and political consciousness brought about by independence and the expression of 'negritude', resulting in the call of 'Africa for the Africans'.[23] In order to understand this, one must recall that in typical African traditional society, people lived and worked together, be it in the construction of dwelling places, or in cultivating their fields, or harvesting their crops. The fruits of their common endeavours were shared in such a way that none of the people could get advantage over the rest of the group. The people lived on the principle that 'what happens to one, happens to all'.[24] With the advent of Western idealism, the principle of co-operation and integration in Africa has only changed in form and character but the rudiments remain the same, namely, to assert the sense of belonging and purpose. In recent years, the destabilization of the 'front line' African States by South Africa has brought the countries in the area closer than before in their endeavours for economic self-reliance and independence.[25]

The third major motivation arises from the bitter recognition that the international community is not prepared to come to full grips with the problems of world poverty and hunger facing many of the developing countries, especially those in Africa. As one distinguished African leader put it, 'thus far, most of the attempts at finding extra-African remedies to our problems have met with some rude rebuff. The developed countries made it clear through the various UNCTAD conferences, the North-South Dialogue, even through the ACP-EEC Lome Conventions that the new international economic order that the Third World seeks is both unacceptable and a threat to their survival'.[26]

The lesson to draw from these three interrelated factors is that the African subregional institutions are seen both as a challenge and a response to the impotence of the international economic system to address itself adequately to the trade problems facing the African countries. They have to be seen as an effort not only to promote collective self-reliance through intra-African trade, but also as a means of promoting real development through concrete programmes of industrial development and forging socio-economic linkages within Africa.[27]

The Objectives

Subregional institutions are envisioned as mechanisms for developing and expanding intra-African trade so as to enhance collective self-reliance and self-sustaining growth. These institutions are expected to play a vital role in the socio-economic transformation of the African economies and help alleviate mass poverty through sustained recovery and growth. At the same time, these groupings are expected to provide the necessary responses to the adverse effects of the international trading system on the African economies by providing the required diversification of the production and marketing base. Thus, it is firmly believed that co-operation would strengthen the collective bargaining position of the African countries vis-a-vis other Third World countries.

Essentially, the major objectives of the subregional trade institutions may be classified into the following three broad categories.

(a) *To enhance social and economic development through the reduction or elimination of all forms of trade barriers.* This objective includes measures towards subregional free trade, and elimination of all obstacles to intra-African trade, especially in coffee, pulses, sugar, meat, maize, fish, oilseeds, rice, wheat, tea, sorghum and vegetable oils. To this end, all goods and services, including food products originating from other countries in the grouping, are exempted from regulatory non-tariff barriers except for health requirements.

(b) *Establishment of institutions, mechanisms and measures for facilitating and developing intra-African trade.* These include agricultural and non-agricultural commodity exchanges; specialized marketing organizations for major export commodities; African associations of state trading organizations; national chambers of commerce and the Federation of African Chambers of Commerce; expanding the activities of the Association of African Trade Promotion Organizations; subregional trade and development banks; African multinational marketing enterprises; multinational shipping lines to promote intra-African trade; and free movement of persons.

(c) *Market integration to achieve economies of scale.* This objective includes the adoption of various protocols on agriculture, industry, transport and communications, customs legislations, transit trade, etc. These are intended to improve the production and distribution structures, and take advantage of forward or backward linkages. Subregional trade institutions have also another objective of assisting in the adoption of a common position in multilateral trade negotiations of interest to the member states of these subregional groupings.

Within the three objective scenarios established in the preceding paragraph, the subregional trade institutions must also be seen as an effort towards a shift from the present export of primary commodities to more self-reliant production, marketing and distribution structures to include: reducing Africa's dependence on external factor inputs whenever feasible, especially in the production for intra-African markets; establishing information systems which will enable African buyers to increase their knowledge of supply sources in the subregions and on current trading conditions. Other objectives include adjustments in prices, payment arrangements, quality and delivery periods with a view to enabling African suppliers to be competitive and to get better conditions for their imports; and the training of African importers with the aim of upgrading their skills in subregional purchasing and import management techniques as well as training exporters in export marketing techniques including costing and pricing.

Another objective is to reduce or eliminate excess capacities in industrial production and manufacturing directly linked to the size of subregional markets through trade liberalization at the bilateral and multilateral levels. The improvement in the trade facilitating measures, such as simplification of documentation and procedures, and transit agreements for intra-subregional trade, is another way in which the subregional groupings contribute towards development. The establishment of national, subregional and all-Africa trade fairs, as a means of forging contacts between producers and African buyers, has been a critical outcome of the above objectives.

REVIEW OF ACHIEVEMENTS OF SUBREGIONAL TRADE INSTITUTIONS

In reviewing the achievements of the subregional trade institutions discussed above, it is important to bear in mind the objectives of each institution. There is, therefore, no common yardstick for measuring the success or failure of each grouping, although the following broad criteria would serve a useful purpose.

Industrialization through Market Integration

It is almost a tautology to state that the basic objective of industrialization of any country or group of countries is to optimize the utilization of domestic natural resources, including minerals, through an orderly and planned growth of industrial production capacities. Yet this is important in all cases of joint industrial development.[28] A basic problem arises in the definition of industries for joint exploitation. It is generally held that industries which use minerals or natural resources or produce basic chemicals, petrochemicals, fertilizers and engineering goods are called 'heavy industries' whereas the rest would be 'medium' or 'light' industries.[29] This distinction is very important because it affects the trend of thought on the entire question of industrial location as a means of balancing the costs and benefits from integration.

A point to stress is that the industrialization of the subregional groupings has engendered the process of domestic market restructuring which increases opportunities for trade in manufactured goods, agricultural processed goods and raw materials.[30] This fact was recognized even during the colonial era when groups of African countries were intricately linked with the metropolitan economies and hence required no integration with other colonial territories to expand their industrialization schemes.[31] There has been an awareness of the need to analyse in detail the following issues to ensure an adequate agro-industrial policy: pricing policy for industrial products; taxation of raw material products especially export crops and food crops; distribution, storage and transportation; the production and supply of agricultural inputs including extension services and agricultural credit for small holder farmers; and the development of local technologies in agro-industries especially in the rural areas.[32]

The awareness of the 'opportunity cost' of industrialization for the integrated markets has also acquired a new significance. For instance, in the PTA, Zimbabwe is the most industrialized country followed by Kenya. The issue is whether these countries would industrialize anyhow outside the PTA market. The problem which arises involves the selection of the best industrial package through the establishment of PTA enterprises that would enable the area as a whole to progress economically.[33] Therefore, a careful analysis is being made of the industrial licensing policy so as to ensure that factory locations and optimal sizes ensure a regional balance.[34] Such an analysis also includes the pricing of subregional goods; the structure and levels of protection for infant industries; import substitution policy; and tax incentives.[35]

Increasing Productivity through Import Substitution

Intra-subregional trade involves both trade creation and trade diversion more especially with a protected market environment.[36] This is achieved through import substitution in which some countries (Nigeria, Cote d'Ivoire, Kenya, Zimbabwe) have been able to take advantage of the subregional markets; especially in manufactured goods such as textiles, food including breakfast cereals, dairy products and plastics. Future opportunities also exist in trade in energy and oil.

The main manufactured goods which are sensitive to subregional market structures include cement, footwear, fertilizers, plastic goods, soap, canned meat, diary products, electrical equipment, paints and cellulose, textile goods, sugar, soda ash, beverages, cigarettes and cigars, salt. This broad production base and the diversity in the manufacturing industries provide a comparative advantage and a much greater opportunity for intra-African trade than generally appreciated.[37] In the agricultural sector, the major export commodities include cereals, tobacco, coffee, cotton, sugar cane, beef, hides and skins, tea, sisal, beans, cashew-nuts, spices, vegetable fibres, wood pulp, bananas, livestock, edible oils and fats. A full-scale and in-depth analysis of the supply and demand patterns of the area including food habits and consumer preferences is being undertaken as a matter of priority to assess the trade opportunities within the subregional groupings.

Technological Diffusion

A potential area of contribution of subregional institutions to growth is through technological diffusion. This would involve Joint Research and Development and the adaptation of foreign technologies to local needs. In recent years, some countries have been sharing the research results in animal breeding, improved seeds and in the control of pests and animal diseases. There is a full awareness that factor mobility is determined by the level of technological diffusion.[38] Consequently, attempts are being made at several levels to enhance technological development by sharing technology and technical co-operation in all fields. This includes training for the development of local technical and managerial skills to perform functions currently undertaken by the foreign expertise.[39]

The technology programmes are designed to take into account the following aspects: (a) the need to develop auxiliary technologies and related functions such as machine tool industries, spare parts and components and agricultural inputs, (b) the creation of joint technology testing and standardization centres so as to link agricultural needs with rural development as well as small scale or cottage industries,[40] (c) the development of integrated technological receptive centres to assess the appropriateness of technology acquired from TNCs into the subregions including alternative sources of such technology. This undoubtedly will promote a long-term strategy for self-reliance in this field.[41]

Subregional Economies of Scale

Directly linked to technological diffusion are opportunities for attaining economies of scale in industry and agriculture, including processing opened up by subregional trade institutions.[42] An essential factor in agricultural development is that it provides increased processing in order to diversify the export base and to increase the export earnings.[43] The countries have agreed to harmonize their activities in agricultural research and production and in the export of crops, livestock, fish and forest products. Food processing will become an important aspect in subregional trade and this fact is now fully recognized at all policy levels.

The same is true with regard to manufacturing industries. While the assessment of the expansion of intra-African trade directly attributable to subregional institutions is not an easy matter, it is true that the given pace of industrial growth of the member states of these groupings determines the extent of the economies of scale.[44] Bearing in mind that a number of these trade institutions have been in existence or operational for less than five years or so, it is hardly surprising that economies of scale have not been fully explored and that the level of intra-African trade continues to be very small indeed.

CRITICAL PROBLEMS OF SUBREGIONAL TRADE AND GROWTH

Despite the creation of subregional trade institutions, Africa is still a long way from developing the level of intra-African trade that can support economic recovery and self-sustaining growth. Paradoxically before the creation of these institutions intra-African trade was about 8 per cent of total trade in 1975. From the latest statistics now available, trade among African countries has averaged about 4 per cent of Africa's total trade annually between 1981 and 1985, a much lower share than in the seventies. During this period, the value of intra-African trade in absolute terms had fluctuated between US2–3 billion dollars annually out of total annual exports ranging between $US 56 and 75 billion.

Several problems can be identified as being critical to the development and expansion of intra-African trade through the sub-regional institutions, but for purposes of this brief expose, only a few are highlighted drawn from individual and overall experiences of these groupings:

Extroverted Character of African Economies

The member States of these groupings individually or collectively face tremendous constraints in reordering the dynamics of economic growth within a subregional market structure so as to increase the opportunities for viable and profitable domestic investment and industrialization.[45] It is generally the case that the trade policy of the individual African countries is biased in favour of the expansion of the export base for the overseas market in the pursuit of foreign exchange. Hence, the full and rational utilization of natural resources for domestic and intra-African trade expansion is hampered by such pursuits.

Perceptions and Expectations

The first critical problem arises from the perception and outlook of the member States themselves in terms of their expectations of what advantages these subregional trade institutions are supposed to bring to their economies. For instance, an examination of the National Development Plans of the countries within PTA, ECCAS, ECOWAS, CEAO and CEPGL shows no reference to subregional development objectives and priorities. In other words, what is implemented at the national level may often be at variance with the subregional objectives. There seems to be an obvious dichotomy in the government policies in that while expecting benefits from these institutions they are reluctant to take measures that would maximize the benefits therefrom.[46] Part of this problem has to do with the harsh economic conditions because of inherent problems which reduce the advantages that any country can derive from such integration efforts.[47] The fact that many of the economic groupings never actually took off the ground despite the declaration of intent from their sponsors is a reflection of this problem.[48]

Trade Adjustment Policies and Competitiveness

The second problem is the issue of adjustment in the trade policy and structures to take full advantage of the subregional markets. One of the most pressing tasks in enhancing the competitiveness of African products for intra-African trade is the establishment of trade liberalization mechanisms such as preferential trade areas, economic communities, customs unions and subregional Federations of Chambers of Commerce. It is a fact that very little attention has been paid to the restructuring of the agro-industrial business policy so as to ensure adequate food supply and raw materials for industries.[49] Agricultural development, in which competitiveness is greatest, continues to be pursued almost in total isolation from the other sectors of the economy.

Moreover, competitiveness of the indigenous enterprises with foreign firms has been negligible because of the low key support provided to them by the governments.[50] At the same time, commercial banks are still biased against such traders in their financing and credit allocations. Hence, private economic operators constitute the missing link in trade liberalization, in the process for the establishment of all those economic groupings. It is also important to stress that the restructuring of subregional markets through the integration of industrial ventures would have a dramatic effect on the competitiveness of African made products.[51] It would also provide opportunities of rehabilitating the presently underutilized industrial capacities, and thereby reducing fixed unit costs through economies of scale.

Demand and Supply Functions

The third critical factor relates to the lack of linkages between supply and demand functions for the subregional markets; the absence of backward and forward linkages and consumer preferences and habits. The interaction between supply and demand (the supply and demand function) determines the degree of success of integrated industries in a subregional framework. In the case of Africa no full assessment has been made of the real purchasing power for certain locally produced goods and services within the subregional markets against potential supply. Moreover, there has been no real effort to standardize trade information and its useability to ensure that all potential traders, regardless of the trade systems followed in their countries, understand in the same way about a given product in terms of specifications and quality controls.

A related problem in this regard is the lack of trade and investment information coupled with insufficient and ineffective contacts between African businessmen. African producers/exporters, or importers/consumers, do not have enough information on markets for their products and the availability of products from other countries. African traders need to capture the markets by strongly influencing African consumers with well conceived advertising messages based on goods of an internationally accepted standard and quality.

The Role of Externalities

The fourth critical impediment to intra-African trade is the role of externalities, especially the activities of transnational corporations (TNCs) and foreign firms.[52] It is a fact of life that TNCs encourage the exports of primary commodities and minerals and the imports of manufactured and capital goods including food. TNCs continue to play a dominant role in the major economic sectors of the member States.[53] At the same time TNCs reinforce the production of cash crops and minerals by the African countries to the detriment of food and other staple agricultural commodities especially those badly needed for internal consumption. Moreover, TNCs foster the international division of labour which created serious distortions within the economies of the African countries by encouraging urban development against rural development.

Externalities in African subregional groupings also work in a different sense. The donor community has no interest in intra-African trade expansion. Consequently they are not only unwilling to finance such activities but also often give advice to member States contrary to the objectives under the treaties for subregional trade institutions. In the context of the subregional trade, it has been difficult to control the trade flows within the area so long as the trade structures and the supporting services such as transport and communications, banking, insurance and export credit and financing institutions are still largely controlled by TNCs.[54] Moreover the attitudes of aid donors, bilateral agencies and international organizations also affect the pace and thrust of the integration schemes.[55]

NEW DIRECTIONS IN SUBREGIONAL DEVELOPMENT
STRATEGIES

From the foregoing analysis, a simple but critical scenario emerges with regard to prospects for intra-African trade as 'Engine for Growth'. This is that although prospects for intra-African trade are indeed enormous, African countries have to take appropriate measures to fully make use of the subregional trade institutions which they have created. There is evidence to suggest that intra-African trade prospects could be bright and rewarding provided certain structural adjustment and policy reforms are adopted and implemented specifically aimed at capturing the subregional market.

It is a sad fact that presently the African subregional markets are mainly exploited by foreign firms and transnational corporations who flood them with foreign goods which outcompete the local products. In order to become competitive and to reverse the trends, African governments would need to adopt a number of willed and interrelated policies described in the next few paragraphs.

The first is the structural reorientation in goods and services through the mounting of an intensive 'Buy African Goods' campaign so that this trend towards external sources can be reversed. In short, African governments have to persuade themselves to think of subregional markets before looking to other markets. To achieve this measures should include: (i) the re-orientation of subregional production policies and plans so as to give priority to the processing of raw materials available within Africa, to create backward and forward inter-sector linkages and to link demand and supply; (ii) the promotion of productive investments through appropriate incentives to both local and foreign investors, the establishment of capital mobilization mechanisms, including the re-orientation of the existing banking systems towards the financing of indigenous inward looking productive activities and to promote intra and interregional co-operation in investment financing; (iii) the harmonization of quality and technical standards within the region; (iv) the training of skilled manpower including technicians and managers.[56]

The second is linkage of activities of subregional institutions with the overall policies aimed at the improvement of distribution mechanisms which might be achieved through the participation of the subregional trade promotion institutions in the implementation of trade policies. This should involve dealing with the problems of unreliability of African supply sources especially when this involves other African countries. Also this should involve the following activities: the accelerated construction of transport and communications networks linking African countries; the establishment and/or strengthening of transit arrangements backed by multinational guarantees; the promotion of long-term purchasing and counter-purchasing arrangements including multinational marketing enterprises and state trading organizations which would generate new distribution networks; the creation of trade financing mechanisms including export credit facilities and integrated intra-African networks of commercial banks.

The third is the encouragement of increased private participation in subregional trade promotion activities, marketing, storage and distribution. This proposition is based on empirical evidence that one of the main reasons for the low levels of intra-African trade is the lack of goods to trade with. The range of products available for trading continues to be very restricted while the quality is often dubious and not matching with established consumer tastes and preferences. Small production units and business traders, who are best suited to reach the poor, are generally not provided with the incentives to take advantage of the economies of large-scale production. Moreover, in many cases they are also incapable of acquiring or absorbing the required technology for the subregional markets. It is therefore necessary for African governments in restructuring their production for intra-African trade, to develop new forms of dialogue with the private entrepreneurs, both foreign and indigenous, to see how the latter can play a more positive role in intra-African trade expansion.

The fourth aspect, which is perhaps most critical, relates to the theory of production and pricing policies in intra-African trade.[57] Presently such policies not only distort trade flows but make African goods far less competitive than they really ought to be. This is aggravated by exchange rate adjustment policies in the industrialized countries which may lower prices of imports vis-a-vis domestically produced goods.[58] Pricing policy is essentially the art of fixing or manipulating prices of certain goods and services to attain predetermined objectives.[59] This naturally takes into account the outlays on factor inputs, market environmental constraints and local absorption capacity. The problem of pricing policies of intra-African trade transactions in many African countries is that they are often out of alignment with the real market constraints.[60] Empirical research shows that subregional trade is also hampered by, among other things, the uncompetitiveness of products due to high cost of production, inappropriate pricing, lack of quality control, standardization, inadequate advertising and packaging. It is also observed that prices of African products, especially manufactured products, tend to be much higher than those of equivalent items imported from other parts of the world.

The production for intra-African trade not only suffers from distortions in the distribution structures within the trade groupings, but also from 'trade diversion' rather than 'trade creation' to the extent that local goods become either unavailable or expensive compared with foreign goods.[61] The problem of pricing policy is exacerbated by factors such as the low level of productivity due to cumbersome work procedures, inadequate technology, below standard skills and social problems. There is also the question of oversized industries with large idle (excess) capacities which dramatically increase their unit cost-price, coupled with inappropriate packaging and handling methods resulting in unattractive merchandise. Similarly prohibitive costs of transportation and transit due to poor transport facilities also play havoc on the subregional market. Therefore, a new pricing policy in intra-African trade should be the sine qua non of a new intra-African trade policy.

There is no evidence to suggest that the above policies will necessarily remove all impediments to intra-African trade but it is true to argue that if implemented, they would greatly improve the direction of such trade in the coming years. In summary therefore, the following policy measures would also significantly enhance prospects for intra-subregional trade: progressive reduction and eventual removal of trade and customs barriers to intra-African trade especially those affecting cash crops specifically those mentioned in the LPA;[62] direct government support and strengthening subregional institutions for trade promotion; and improvements in intra-African trade information and marketing systems and systematically monitoring and evaluating trade performance. Furthermore, new commitments ought to be made to encourage the free movement of people, especially African traders and economic operators for the purpose of promoting intra-African trade. It is also suggested that where circumstances permit, governments should give priority to African bidders in the tenders for the provision of goods and services offered by or originating from other African countries.[63]

SUMMARY OF CONCLUSIONS

From the foregoing brief expose some conclusions can be drawn on the contribution of subregional institutions to intra-African trade. The first conclusion is that over the past 25 years or so, Africa has made considerable progress in the establishment of subregional institutions for intra-African trade. These include Customs Unions; Preferential Trade Areas; Economic Communities and other forms of co-operation in trade. Institutionally, these have succeeded in raising the political and social awareness of African governments in matters relating to subregional co-operation and collective self-reliance. However, the biggest problem is that subregional objectives are generally not incorporated in the national development plans of the member States, and subregional institutions have made little or no impact on socio-economic growth and development. Moreover, in terms of their contribution to intra-African trade, the success has been encouraging only in limited cases such as the PTA in Eastern and southern Africa, and less than satisfactory in the cases of both ECCAS and ECOWAS. In fact, statistics show in general that the share of intra-African trade in Africa's total trade has generally been declining from 8–10 per cent in the 1960s to less than 5 per cent in the 1980s.

The second conclusion has to do with factors inhibiting intra-African trade. These range from the perceptions both economic and political, by African countries of subregional trade co-operation to rigidities in the policies, structures and distribution mechanisms for intra-African trade. It is important to stress that part of this problem arises from the conceptualization of costs and benefits of these institutions as seen from the national perspective. Another reason for the lukewarm approach is that despite the adoption of the LPA, a good number of African countries still face serious constraints in restructuring their production and distribution policies away from commodity exports for foreign exchange earnings to manufactured goods for intra-African trade. This is because in the latter case prospects for foreign exchange earnings are not readily determined. The role of externalities (donor community and transnational corporations) especially in investments and resource flows also adversely influences decisions towards intra-African trade. Hence, propositions for intra-African trade are less attractive to many African countries.

The final conclusion to draw from this chapter is that paradoxical as this may sound to external observers, the future of subregional institutions is rather bright. This is so because despite the constraints to subregional trade institutions enumerated earlier, intra-African trade is still very high on the African agenda for development. There is a new awareness among African policy makers that the development and expansion of intra-African trade offers an alternative option toward real economic recovery and growth. Therefore, subregional trade institutions still have a critical role to play in moulding the future trade structures in Africa. They provide a sound framework in each grouping for balancing growth and development; scientific and technological diffusion; diversification of the manufacturing base through appropriate adjustments in macro-economic policies. In a practical sense, these institutions offer the best opportunities for implementing and monitoring a true 'Buy African Goods' campaign. These institutions also form the framework on which the proposed African Common Market and the African Economic Community would be structured.

NOTES

1. In all, there are presently about 120 regional and subregional co-operation and integration schemes ranging from all-embracing schemes to those with limited objectives (see ECA, Directory of Intergovernmental Organizations in Africa).
2. See also Peter Robson, *Economic Integration in Africa*, London, George Allen and Unwin Ltd., 1968, pp.25–26.
3. The major colonial powers in Africa were Britain, France, Belgium, Portugal, Italy, Spain and West Germany.
4. For instance, the Sterling Zone, the Franc Zone, the Escudo Zone.
5. For instance, statesmen such as Kwame Nkrumah envisaged the establishment of a United States of Africa as the ultimate goal for Africa.
6. See chapter 7, on Trade and Finance, in the Lagos Plan of Action.
7. For a full theory of customs union see Jacob Viner, *The Customs Union Issue*, New York Carnegie Endowment for International Peace, 1950, pp.41 et. seq. and J.E. Meade, *The Theory of Customs Union*, Amsterdam, North-Holland Publishing Company, 1956.
8. Cf. R.G. Lipsey and Kelvin Lancaster, 'The General Theory of the Second Best' in *Review of Economic Studies*, vol. XXIV(i), No. 63, 1956–57, pp.11–33.
9. Compare with the Latin American Free Trade Association (LAFTA) in Sidney Dell, *Trade Blocs and Common Markets*, London, Constable & Co. Ltd, 1963, pp.198–227.
10. PTA membership presently covers Comoros, Djibouti, Ethiopia, Kenya, Lesotho, Madagascar, Malawi, Mauritius, Seychelles, Somalia, Swaziland, Tanzania, Uganda, Zambia and Zimbabwe.
11. These protocols are on (1) Reduction and elimination of trade barriers on selected commodities to be traded within PTA; (2) Customs co-operation within PTA; (3) Rules of origin for products to be traded between the members of PTA; (4) Re-export of goods within PTA; (5) Transit trade and transit facilities; (6) Clearing and payments arrangements; (7) Transport and Communications; (8) Co-operation in the field of Industrial Development; (9) Co-operation in the field of agricultural development; (10) Simplification and harmonization of trade documents; (11) Protocol on standardization and quality control.
12. For a full theory of optimum tariffs and retaliation see N. Kaldor, 'A Note on Tariffs and the Terms of Trade' in *Economica*, N.S. vol. VII, No. 28, November 1940, pp.377–380 and also T. de Scitovsky, 'A Reconsideration of Theory of Tariffs' in *Review of Economic Studies*, vol. IX, No. 20, 1942, pp.89–110.
13. See *Treaty for the Establishment of the Preferential Trade Area of Eastern and Southern African States*, Article 3.
14. Cf. Treaty establishing the EFTA and CARIFTA which covers essentially the same matters and the Treaty of Montevideo establishing the Latin American Free Trade Association (LAFTA).

15. See Article 4 of the Treaty. A common list was also agreed in the protocol on trade barriers dividing the goods into six groups with varying degrees of tariff reductions.
16. The protocol on the rules of origin stipulates that goods shall be deemed to have originated within PTA if at least 51 per cent of the equity holding in the venture belongs to the nationals of the member States; that the goods have been produced in the member States, and the c.i.f. value of raw materials used and imported does not exceed 60 per cent of the total cost of materials used; and where goods are produced essentially from imported raw materials the value added does not exceed 45 per cent of ex-factory cost.
17. *ECOWAS* is composed of the following sixteen countries: Cape Verde, Niger, Senegal, Gambia, Mauritania, Mali, Guinea, Guinea Bissau, Sierra Leone, Liberia, Burkina Faso, Cote d'Ivoire, Benin, Ghana, Nigeria and Togo. *CEAO* is made up of seven countries: Senegal, Mauritania, Mali, Cote d'Ivoire, Burkina Faso, Benin, Niger; *ECCAS* comprises the following countries: Burundi, Cameroon, Central African Republic, Congo, Gabon, Equatorial Guinea, Rwanda, Sao Tome and Principe, Chad and Zaire. *CEPGL* comprises Burundi, Rwanda and Zaire.
18. See especially Article 2, paragraph 1 (b) and paragraph 2 of the *Charter of the Organization of African Unity*.
19. See also R.F. Mikesell, 'The Theory of Common Markets and Developing Countries' in P. Robson (ed), *International Economic Integration*, Harmondsworth, Penguin Books Ltd., 1971, pp.168–170.
20. For a full analysis of these issues see B.W.T. Mutharika, *Toward Multinational Economic Co-operation in Africa*, New York, Praeger Publishers, 1972, Chapter I.
21. However, it is known that the former colonial groupings had more intra-trade among their members than is currently the case.
22. See, for instance, the LPA, pp.83–87 which calls for the establishment of an African Common Market and Preferential Trade Areas as a means of promoting regional development.
23. See for instance, Colin Legum, *Pan-Africanism*, New York, Praeger Publishers, 1963, pp.13–23.
24. This aspect is fully developed in Bingu Wa Mutharika, *Fundamentals of African Economic Thought (challenges, choices and responses)* (forthcoming).
25. SADCC was established as a direct response to South Africa.
26. See statement by Dr. Kenneth D. Kaunda, President of Zambia, at the signing ceremony for the PTA Treaty, Lusaka, Zambia, 21 December 1981.
27. See also OAU, *LPA for the Economic Development of Africa – 1980–2000*, pp.5–9.
28. For an analysis of this issue, see B.W. Mutharika, 'A case study of Regionalism in Africa' in *Regionalism and the New International Economic Order*, UNITAR, Davidson Nicol, Luis Echeveriria and Aurelio Pecchi (eds), New York, Pergamon Press, 1981, pp.91–113.
29. See, Rana K.D. Singh, 'Note by the Secretariat of UNIDO' in UNIDO's monograph No. 13 on *Appropriate Industrial Technology for Basic Industries*, pp.3–11.
30. Cf. the EFTA Convention and Article I (Revised) of the GATT Treaty; Treaty of Montevideo establishing LAFTA and the Treaty establishing the Central Africa Customs and Economic Union (UDEAC).
31. In fact, as is well known, most colonial possessions were oriented towards the production of primary commodities geared to requirements for raw materials in European industries.
32. See also World Bank, *Accelerated Development in sub-Saharan Africa* (an agenda for action), Washington D.C., U.S.A., 1981, pp.45–80.
33. See, for instance, I.D.M. Little, 'Regional Integration Companies as an approach to Economic Integration' in P. Robson (ed), *International Economic Integration*, *op. cit.*
34. See UNIDO, *Inceptive Policies for Industrial Development*, Vienna, March 1, 1970.
35. For a full exposition of these issues, see G.T. Stigler, and E. Baldwin (eds), *Readings*

in Price Theory, New York, D. Irwin, 1952; E.A.G. Robinson, *The Structure of Competitive Industry*, Cambridge, Cambridge University Press, 1958, pp. 140–155; M.C. Kemp, 'The Mill-Bastable Infant Industry Dogma' in *Journal of Political Economy* LXVIII. No. 1, February 1960, pp.65–67; B. Van Arkadie, 'Import substitution and export promotion as aids to industrialization in East Africa', in *East African Economic Review*, vol. I (New Series), 1964, pp.40–56; and Murray D. Bryee, *Policies and Methods for Industrial Development*, New York, McGraw-Hill, 1965.

36. See H.G. Johnston, 'An Economic Theory of Protectionism, Tariff Bargaining and the Formation of Customs Unions' in P. Robson (ed.), *International Economic Integration, op. cit.*, pp.99–141.

37. On comparative costs see Harry G. Johnson, *Money Trade and Economic Growth*, London, George Allen and Unwin Ltd, 1964, pp.28–45.

38. See, for instance, Jack Barson, *Industrial Technologies for Developing Countries*, New York, Praeger Publishers, 1969; and UNIDO, *Transnational Corporations and the Processing of Raw Materials: Impact on Developing Countries* (ID/B/209), 21 April 1978.

39. See also ECA, *Developing Local Technical and Managerial Capabilities for Dealing with Transnational Corporations in Africa*. (A note by ECA secretariat) (ST/ECA/TNC/3), July 1981.

40. The African Regional Centre for Technology (ARCT) and African Regional Organization for Standardization (AROS) were established to deal with those aspects.

41. See also Sidney Dell, *A Latin American Common Market?* London, Oxford University Press, 1966, pp.15–35.

42. See also Jack Goody, *Technology Tradition and the State in Africa*, London, Oxford University Press, 1971, pp.21–56.

43. SADCC's aim in this field is to ensure regional food security and agricultural development as a means of economic liberation in Southern Africa. See SADCC, *Regional Co-ordination in Food and Agriculture*, Blantyre, Malawi, November 1981.

44. See also E.A.G. Robinson, *The Structure of Competititve Industry*, Cambridge University Press, 1958, pp.59–70.

45. See also M.E. Jhighan, *The Economies of Development Planning*, Viskes Publishing Company, Uttar Pradesh, India (13th Revised Edition).

46. See also UNCTAD, *The Distribution of Cost and Benefits of Integration Among Developing Countries* (TD/B/4/3), 27 September 1972.

47. See for instance, A.H. Birch, 'Opportunities and Problems of Federation' in C. Leys and P. Robinson (Eds.) *Federation in East Africa*, Nairobi, Oxford University Press, 1956, pp.21–23.

48. For a full discussion of the assessment of costs and benefits of co-operation, see Bingu Wa Mutharika, *Toward Multinational Economic Co-operation in Africa, op.cit.*, chapter 9; and Peter Robson, *Economic Integration for Africa, op. cit.*, pp.84–93.

49. For instance, strategic agricultural commodities such as tobacco, cotton, sugar cane, maize, livestock, tea, coffee, groundnuts, beans and lentils, spices, sisal, tropical hardwood, wood pulp, bananas, hides and skins have been essentially governed by external market factors. Agricultural processing is largely in the hands of transnational corporations whose policies in this field do not tally with the national policies.

50. For a full analysis of this issue see E.A.G. Robinson, *The Structure of Competitive Industry, op.cit.*, pp.152–154.

51. For a full analysis of relationships between supply and demand functions see Joan Robinson, *The Economics of Imperfect Competition*, London, MacMillan and Co. Ltd, 1969, pp.47–91.

52. See also UNCTAD, *The International Market Power of Transnational Corpora-*

tions (UNCTAD/ST/MD/13), 14 April 1978.

53. For a full analysis of TNCs issues, see UNCTC, *Transnational Corporations in World Development: A Re-examination* (E.C.10/38); and Richard J. Barnet and Ronald E. Muller, *Global Research: The Power of the Multinational Corporations*, New York, Simon and Schuster, 1974, chapter 7.
54. See ECA, *Transnational Corporations in Africa: Some Major Issues* (E/ECA/UNCTC/21). The absence of the real desire by TNCs to abstain from frustrating the PTA efforts would be a real test in the success of this Organization.
55. For instance, until quite recently, the UNDP, the World Bank and bilateral donors were reluctant to consider subregional projects for financing. Even now, their approach is very cautious.
56. See ECA, *Africa's Trade Relations: Some Major Issues* (E/ECA/TRADE/53), March 1987, p.17.
57. For an earlier theory of pricing, see C.J. Stigler and K.E. Boulding (eds.), *Readings in Price Theory*, Homewood, Illinois, Richard D. Irwin, Inc, 1952. This treatise, together with subsequent amplifications, gives adequate background on pricing.
58. See also Ronald I. Mackinson: 'The Exchange Rate and Macro-economic Policy Changing Postwar Perceptions', in *Journal of Economic Literature*, vol. 19, June 1981, pp.531–557.
59. See also Paul A. Samuelson and Anthony Scott in *Economics* (Fourth Canadian Edition), McGraw-Hill Ryerson Limited, 1975, pp.43–63.
60. *Ibid*, pp.64–81.
61. J.S. Mill, *Principles of Political Economy*, London, Ashley Publishers, 1929, p.127 *et. seq.*
62. These include cereals, coffee, pulses, sugar, meat, fish, oilseeds, tea, vegetable oils, etc.
63. See also *Report of the Ninth Session of the Conference of African Ministers of Trade* (E/ECA/OAU/TRADE/33), March 1987.

CHAPTER FIVE

Regional and Subregional Perspectives

OWODUNNI TERIBA (ed.)

In focusing on the regional and subregional perspectives to the African economic crisis and recovery programmes, this Chapter features some of the papers submitted to the Abuja Conference by African regional and subregional institutions. Collectively, the papers provide illuminating searchlights on underlying principles and issues of strategy as well as practical approaches and policy measures with regard to economic recovery and development.

OAU AND AFRICA'S RECOVERY AND DEVELOPMENT*

When the OAU was established in May 1963, there were 32 independent states, and 30 signed the OAU Charter in Addis Ababa, Ethiopia. The founder Members were: Algeria, Benin, Burkina Faso, Burundi, Cameroon, Central African Republic, Chad, Congo, Cote d'Ivoire, Egypt, Ethiopia, Gabon, Ghana, Guinea, Libya, Liberia, Madagascar, Mali, Morocco, Mauritania, Niger, Nigeria, Rwanda, Senegal, Sierra Leone, Somalia, Sudan, Tanzania, Togo, Tunisia, Uganda and Zaire. It is noteworthy that when Ghana became independent in 1957, there were only 8 independent African States; namely, Ethiopia, Guinea, Liberia, Libya, Morocco, Sudan, Tunisia, and the United Arab Republic (Egypt). Today, there are 51 independent African States, 50 of which are Members of the OAU.

From its inception in May 1963, the OAU has been concerned not only with political matters, but also with economic affairs. The OAU Charter indicates that one of the objectives of the Organization is to work for the improvement of the welfare of the African peoples. Similarly, the Charter provides for the establishment of a Department concerned with economic affairs. Over the years, the Department of

---

* Part of the submissions by the General Secretariat of the OAU

Economic Affairs has been strengthened progressively as more and more economic decisions have been adopted by the Assembly of Heads of State and Government, particularly since 1973, ten years after the establishment of the Organization.

The First Conference of the Independent African Heads of State and Government, meeting in Addis Ababa, Ethiopia (22 to 25 May, 1963), adopted important resolutions on 'Areas of Co-operation in Economic Problems'. The most important aspects of these resolutions concerned the appointment of a preparatory economic committee to study and submit its findings to Member States, questions concerning the establishment of a common external tariff to protect the emergent industries and the setting up of a raw materials price stabilization fund; the restructuring of international trade; a progressive freeing of national currencies from all non-technical external attachments and the establishment of a pan-African monetary zone; and the ways and means of effecting the harmonization of existing and future national development plans. Furthermore, the Conference welcomed the then forthcoming World Conference on Trade and Development which was expected to examine international trade problems in relation to the economic development of emerging nations. Finally, the Conference urged all States concerned to conduct concerted negotiations, with a view to obtaining from the consumer countries real price stabilization and guaranteed outlets on the world market, so that the developing countries may derive considerably greater revenue from international trade. These issues are still as important today as they were some twenty-five years ago. They constitute the core of both the internal and external economic policy of African countries.

Since that First OAU Summit, the OAU and ECA have made continuous efforts to seek solutions to the old as well as the new problems facing African countries as they strive for social and economic development. Several major conferences have been held since then to discuss these issues. The most important Conferences include the following. In February 1971, the ECA Conference of Ministers, at its first meeting, convened in Tunisia and adopted Resolution 218(X) entitled 'Africa's Strategy for Development in the 1970s'. This document provided the basis for additional serious thinking within the ECA Secretariat about the process of economic growth and development in Africa. In May 1973, the OAU, ECA and ADB jointly convened the African Ministerial Conference of Trade, Development and Monetary Problems. The report of this Conference formed the basis of the OAU's 'African Declaration on Co-operation, Development and Economic Independence' (otherwise known as the Addis Ababa

Declaration of 1973) which was adopted by the OAU Assembly of Heads of State and Government at its 10th Ordinary Session on the 10th Anniversary of the founding of the OAU. In May 1976, the Executive Committee of the ECA Conference of Ministers adopted the 'Revised Framework of Principles for the Implementation of the New International Economic Order in Africa'. This same document was adopted in December 1976 at the Extraordinary Session of the OAU Council of Ministers meeting in Kinshasa. The Assembly of OAU Heads of State and Government, meeting in Libreville in July 1977, endorsed that document.

The main argument of this document[1] is that any international order, whether economic, social, political or cultural, is a reflection of the interactions of national orders. The world system is a combination of national systems, and its ultimate strength is determined by the strengths of the dominant national systems. The old order was born and sustained by the dominating national systems of the Western industrial societies which were and are based on strong domestic policies. Such policies operate principally on the domestic market for factor inputs for production and distribution as well as on the determinants of the levels and components of consumption.

Following from the argument in the document, several recommendations were made. First, that there was need for the acquisition of knowledge of the natural resources of each member State not only as a basis for determining the profile of development and economic growth, but also for designing the programmes of manpower development to underpin such development and economic growth. Second, that there was need to design an appropriate industrialization strategy for the use of the abundant mineral and agricultural resources available in the continent. Third, that there was need for deliberate encouragement of domestic production of producer goods as inputs into food and agriculture, industry, building and construction, transport and communications, and other services. Finally, that there was need to bear in mind constantly the linkages between agriculture, industry and the services, including the infrastructure of transport and communications, and the use of such linkages as a basis of planning and plan implementation. The other central point made in the Revised Framework is that there is an inevitable link between national and collective self-reliance as a basis of self-sustaining and internally-generated development and economic growth.

It is important to emphasize that the ideas contained in the Revised Framework have formed the very core upon which those in the LPA and FAL were subsequently erected.[2]

In continuation of its involvement with economic development of Africa, the OAU, in co-operation with the ECA, and with the financial support of the UNDP, convened a colloquium in February 1979 in Monrovia, Liberia, on Perspectives of Development and Economic Growth in Africa up to the Year 2000. Some of the major conclusions of that colloquium formed the basic text of the book entitled 'What Kind of Africa by the Year 2000?'[3] – a book which was to prove influential subsequently. Most of the recommendations therein were incorporated in the Declaration of Commitment by the OAU Heads of State and Government, adopted at the Sixteenth Ordinary Session held in Monrovia from 17 to 20 July 1979. The Declaration was entitled: 'Monrovia Declaration of Commitment of the Heads of State and Government of the Organization of African Unity on Guidelines and Measures for National and Collective Self-reliance in Social and Economic Development for the Establishment of a New International Economic Order'.[4]

It is necessary to quote the Declaration of Commitment substantially. The Heads of State and Government said as follows: 'In adopting this Declaration, we recognize the need to take urgent action to provide the political support necessary for the success of the measures to achieve the goals of rapid self-reliance and self-sustaining development and economic growth, and declare as follows:[5]

(i) We commit ourselves, individually and collectively, on behalf of our governments and peoples, to promote the economic and social development and integration of our economies with a view to achieving an increasing measure of self-sufficiency and self-sustainment;

(ii) We commit ourselves, individually and collectively, on behalf of our governments and peoples, to promote the economic integration of the African region in order to facilitate and reinforce social and economic intercourse;

(iii) We commit ourselves, individually and collectively, on behalf of our governments and peoples, to establish national, subregional and regional institutions which will facilitate the attainment of objectives of self-reliance and self-sustainment;

(iv) More specifically, we commit ourselves, individually and collectively, on behalf of our governments and peoples, to:

    (a) give an important place to the field of human resources development by starting to eliminate illiteracy;

    (b) put science and technology in the service of development by reinforcing the autonomous capacity of our countries in this field;

(c) achieve self-sufficiency in food production and supply;

(d) implement completely the programmes for the United Nations Transport and Communications Decade for Africa;

(e) realize the subregional and regional internally-located industrial development;

(f) co-operate in the field of natural resources control, exploration, extraction and use for the development of our economies for the benefit of our peoples and to set up the appropriate institutions to achieve these purposes;

(g) develop indigenous entrepreneurship, technical manpower and technological abilities to enable our peoples to assume greater responsibility for the achievement of our individual and collective development goals;

(h) co-operate in the preservation, protection and improvement of the natural environment;

(i) ensure that our development policies reflect adequately our socio-cultural values in order to reinforce our cultural identity; and,

(j) take into account the dimension of the future in the elaboration of our development plans including studies and measures aimed at achieving a rapid socio-economic transformation of our states.

(v) We hold firmly to the view that these commitments will lead to the creation, at the national, subregional and regional levels, of a dynamic and interdependent African economy and will thereby pave the way for the eventual establishment of an African Common Market leading to an African Economic Community.

(vi) Resolving to give special attention to the discussion of economic issues at each annual Session of our Assembly, we hereby call on the Secretary-General, in collaboration with the Executive Secretary of the ECA, to draw up annually specific programmes and measures for economic co-operation on subregional, regional and continental bases in Africa.'

These Declarations form part of the Preambular Section of the LPA.

The Sixteenth Ordinary Session of the Assembly of Heads of State and Government of the OAU decided to hold a Special Economic Summit in Lagos, Nigeria, and this was done in April 1980. The Lagos Economic Summit adopted the 'LPA for the Implementation of the Monrovia Strategy for the Economic Development of Africa'.

The LPA has proved to be of considerable interest in Africa and the rest of the world. It was adopted by the Eleventh Special Session of the United Nations General Assembly meeting, in August and September 1980, and subsequently by the General Assembly at its Ordinary Session in the same year. The document is now part of the New International Development Strategy.

In July 1985, five years after the adoption of the LPA, the Assembly of Heads of State and Government of the OAU, meeting in Addis Ababa, took stock of what the member states had done by way of implementing the LPA. The Assembly concluded that 'Although the philosophy, principles and objectives of the LPA have been accepted by the member states as a whole, their underlying concerns have not always been translated into concrete action or reflected in national development plans of member states. Indeed, efforts were made here and there to tackle the substantial imbalances which characterized several sectors of the economy, particularly agriculture and food, drought and desertification control, literacy, industry and so on. Nevertheless, if most of the measures recommended in the LPA had been implemented, the ravaging effects of the current world recession and drought on African economies would certainly have been minimized.'[6]

The Assembly then identified a number of principal obstacles and constraints which hindered the effective implementation of the LPA as follows:[7]

First, the colonial economic structures inherited by most African countries have proved difficult to be changed radically for African development as called for in the LPA. These colonial economic legacies have been compounded by a host of other related international factors including the collapse in commodity prices, a stagnation and decline in ODA in real terms, the unprecedented high interest rates, the shift to a regime of sharp fluctuations of exchange rates, and increased protectionism.

Second, national development plans and annual budgets of most African countries have tended to perpetuate and even accentuate the dependency of our economies on foreign resources (financial and human), and have led to the misallocation of domestic resources through reduced shares for such high priority areas as agriculture, manpower, industry and massive expenditure on foreign consumer goods and non-productive investment projects.

Third, there has been lack or inadequacy of skilled manpower, leading to the importation of a large number of foreign technicians and managers.

Fourth, a large number of extraneous factors, not foreseen when drafting LPA, have affected the implementation. Such factors include the widespread, severe and persistent drought, acceleration of desertification process, persistent and destructive cyclones, intensification of destabilization attempts from South Africa on neighbouring African States.

Finally, a number of structural and political obstacles have impeded the implementation. These include outward-oriented economies, lack of complementarity, narrow economic base, etc. Others are conflict situations, inadequate political will, failure to honour commitments made jointly, and extraneous circumstances.

Having identified the problems concerning the implementation of the LPA, the Assembly of Heads of State and Government of the OAU then adopted the APPER, the main focus of which was to choose particular sectors in the LPA and to concentrate on those sectors. The Food and Agriculture sector was identified as the priority of priorities sector for action. All the other sectors were concerned only in so far as they supported the food and agriculture sector.

The other priority area was Africa's external indebtedness. The Assembly argued that the recovery programme could not go far as long as the problem of Africa's external indebtedness was not tackled.

In APPER, the measures for common action among member States of the OAU were outlined. Also specified in APPER are: (i) conditions for integration; (ii) areas of priority action in different fields and at all levels; (iii) follow-up measures and mechanisms at the national, subregional and continental levels; and, (iv) the effects of the destabilization policy of the racist regime of South Africa on the economies of the Southern African States, and the measures to deal with them at the national, subregional, regional and continental levels.

One other major action taken by the Assembly was the establishment of a high level OAU Permanent Steering Committee whose terms of reference were provided as follows:[8]

(i) To follow up decisions of the Twenty-first Assembly of Heads of State and Government on Economic Matters and the monitoring of the implementation of the Declaration on APPER and Resolutions of the Twenty-First Assembly of Heads of State and Government on the Critical Economic Situation in Africa;

(ii) To pay permanent attention to issues concerning the economic development of Africa;

(iii) To assist in defining and co-ordinating the positions of the member

States in the preparation for major international negotiations and within the major international institutions; and,

(iv) To deal with any other issue submitted to it by the current Chairman of the OAU or the Council of Ministers.

In adopting APPER, the Assembly also adopted a Resolution on the African Economic Situation and called for, among other things, the convening of a special session of the United Nations General Assembly on the critical economic situation in Africa. The Secretary-General of the United Nations acceded to the call and the Special Session was convened in New York from May 27 to June 1, 1986.

In preparation for the Special Session, the OAU Permanent Steering Committee, the Council of Ministers and the ECA Conference of Ministers convened many meetings and prepared a document entitled: *Africa's Submission to the Special Session of the United Nations General Assembly on Africa's Economic and Social Crisis.*[9]

This document outlines the nature and scope of Africa's social and economic crisis, and indicates the quantitative amount of resources required to implement APPER over a five-year period. It also indicates the amount of resources the African governments themselves had indicated would be forthcoming to implement APPER. Finally, the gap between the required and available resources was estimated, and this balance is what the international community was called upon to supplement. In addition, the document also discussed areas of policy reforms, as indicated in APPER.

ADB AND DEVELOPMENT FINANCING IN AFRICA*

The history of development shows that in economically backward countries development institutions were created by Governments to fill specific *gaps* in the development process. It was believed that such deliberate action would accelerate development so as to catch up with other fast developing countries.[10] In other words, the missing ingredients in the development process were to be substituted by other factors which could be provided by the state.[11] However, the mere filling of observed gaps by creating development institutions was not adequate to accelerate development. This was particularly so in times of economic crises, and in countries characterized by high levels of non-monetized output, wide preference for holding wealth in the form of real assets, dormant entrepreneurial activity, undeveloped human resources, etc. What was required, it was argued by Patrick,[12] was for

---

* Part of a paper submitted by B.C. Muzorewa of ADB

financial institutions not only to satisfy emerging demand but to *actively* seek demand for their services in a 'supply-leading' manner. Given such a behaviour and a conducive macro-economic policy environment, financial intermediation was expected to explain a large part of the growth in savings, entrepreneurship and in the GDP. At least, a high and positive correlation is expected to exist between these variables.

In the African case, a whole range of financial institutions were created at independence to fill specific gaps. At the continental, subregional and national levels, development banks or corporations were established to mobilize and seek productive investments of the resources. In the light of these actions, what has been the record of performance? The limited literature available on the study of the role of financial institutions in African development indicates little discernible relationship between financial intermediation and economic development or growth.[13] More recent evidence seems to show the limited capacity of financial institutions in Africa to mobilize domestic resources, particularly in the rural areas.[14] Obviously, more rigorous research using more recent data is required. However, it appears that the institutions created in Africa have largely behaved in an uninnovative manner, uninfluenced by the supply-leading or active-behaviour theory, in contrast to the situation in Asia, particularly South Asia.

At a time when economic deterioration is taking place in Africa, financial institutions cannot afford to passively wait for demand for their services. The institutions have to re-orientate their operations, by actively mobilizing resources, identifying projects or programmes, preparing them and, at times, participating in their execution. Entrepreneurship, skilled manpower and management have to be activated from their dormant state. Research into new methods and technologies needs to be intensified. As close as they are to governments, national development finance institutions need to be involved in economic policy analysis, formulation and implementation. In short, innovative behaviour in all these areas has become imperative, if development finance institutions are to justify their existence in countries facing economic collapse.

At the continental level, how has the ADB, the only such institution at this level, responded to the challenge facing Africa? The answer lies in an important policy statement by the President of the ADB, immediately after attending the OAU Summit at which APPER was adopted. ADB, he declared, was to be seen not just as a development financing institution but, more than that:

Our Bank should rise to this challenge, re-examine conventional approaches and techniques, generate new ideas and methods and, in the process, transform itself into a new Bank, more responsive to the times, forward-looking, imaginative and effective.[15]

The first concrete measure in the new re-orientation of ADB relates to the size of resource mobilization. Given the magnitude of the resources required to implement APPER, the management of ADB has requested a 200 per cent increase in the capital resources of the Bank, and approval has been given in principle. When this is combined with a matching increase in the resources of its soft-loan affiliate – the African Development Fund (ADF) – and co-financing, the ADB Group is expected to lend at a rate of about $US2.3 billion per year during the next five years. The significance of the role of the ADB Group in the economic recovery and development of Africa cannot, therefore, be over-stated. However, to achieve this objective, new methods of lending are imperative. In this connection, the ADB Group has already introduced non-project lending which is most appropriate for the needed structural transformation of African economies.[16] To cope with this type of lending, economic policy analysis and continuous dialogue with member countries will be required. Towards this end, ADB has recently restructured its services and is increasing its relevant staff.

It must be pointed out, however, that the traditional project-lending approach will continue to dominate the operations of ADB even though it is placing new emphasis on projects and programmes which either generate or save foreign exchange, with concentration on agriculture and supportive sector activities. In addition to making foreign exchange available for essential imports and external debt servicing, an expansion in exports, both traditional and non-traditional, would considerably enhance the potential of regional member countries to mobilize domestic resources. Expansion in export production, however, would need to be supported by export financing – a facility the ADB is seriously considering. Lack of export credits at lower cost, among other factors, has placed African exporters at a disadvantage, at a time of critical shortage of foreign exchange. Therefore, this new activity by the Bank could greatly assist member Countries in expanding their exports.

Other than the Bank's contribution through the above operations, indirect contribution can also be made in the area of domestic resource mobilization through a variety of channels. In this connection, it needs to be stressed that mobilization of domestic savings takes different approaches, depending on the net benefits attached to the techniques by the country concerned.[17] In some economies, the fiscal technique is the main vehicle for mobilizing surpluses. As the ADB study on domestic resource mobilization in Africa suggests, taxation in these countries needs to be examined and rationalized, and the Bank may wish to provide advice in this area within the context of policy-based lending.

However, in other economies, cost-benefit analysis may indicate that domestic resources would most efficiently be mobilized through capital markets (both securities and non-securities markets). In this area, the Bank's role is not entirely new. Traditionally, ADB has been involved in promoting development and other finance institutions in Africa through equity participation, lines of credit and support of the Association of African Development Finance Institutions. But more could be done in this area by way of innovation.

For instance, the Bank could study the possibility of promoting what are called *Development Savings Banks*, which combine the features of Provident Funds (i.e., compulsory accumulation of savings by the money income earning population, including farmers) and those of Unit Trusts (i.e., means of providing investment opportunities for the average person).[18] The ultimate goal of such institutions is equitable distribution of wealth and incomes, greater domestic resource mobilization and an increase in personal savings going into equity investments.[19]

More life insurance and pension funds institutions could also be promoted as was the case with Africa Re-insurance. Life and pension premium incomes have proved to be very important sources of long-term domestic savings the world over; yet, in most African countries, such premiums constitute only a small proportion of insurance company income.

In connection with promotion of financial institutions, ADB has some innovative role to play in the development of capital markets, particularly securities markets.[20] The latter institutions play a critical role in mobilizing foreign and domestic savings and channelling them into productive investment. The fact that only a handful of securities markets exist in Africa poses a great challenge to ADB Group. It would, therefore, have to be more active in promoting the development of capital market institutions through, among others, direct equity participation in and lending to medium- and large-scale private enterprises through the International Finance Corporation's (IFC) type of mechanism. For, without a viable private industrial sector, the supply of securities is bound to be limited, and evidence shows that this is one of the main reasons for failure of capital markets. Technical assistance and advice to member countries on approaches to the development of capital markets and the private sector would be necessary. ADB would have, first, to commission a study and hold seminars for regional member countries on the development of capital markets.[21] ADB's study on domestic resource mobilization is clearly a step in the right direction. For the new forms of lending being introduced to be able to assist in these areas, appropriate staff structures would have to be in place.

There are other new areas of support ADB is actively studying. Among these is direct support (through an IFC-type of institution) for the growth of the private sector, which is essential for the growth of capital markets and enhancement of the potential for effective domestic resource mobilization. It is commendable that a Division within ADB has already been created for the purpose of promoting the private sector in countries requesting such assistance. Towards the same goal, the participation by the ADB, the IFC and the UNDP in the African Project Development Facility, the aim of which is to assist African entrepreneurs to identify and prepare viable projects and to assist them in seeking financing, is a clear testimony to the active and innovative behaviour of these three development institutions. Such behaviour is indispensable under the current economic crisis in Africa.

In summary, it is necessary to reiterate that the existence of development and other finance institutions alone is not adequate to promote economic recovery and development. Indeed, the contribution of financial intermediaries to growth in Africa appears so far to have been insignificant, and the institutions involved would have to adopt innovative and active behaviour if their role in promoting recovery and development were to be meaningful.

The ADB Group is beginning to show signs of active behaviour through a substantial increase in its lending programme and promotional services. However, more still has to be done in the area of promotion of domestic resource mobilization through support, for instance, of savings banks and the development of capital markets in regional member countries.

The strategy of focusing attention on the removal of internal or domestic constraints or rigidities, as contained in APPER, can only be regarded as the most important sign of hope that, in future, continental financing will play its full role in promoting economic recovery and development in Africa. However, development and other financial institutions would need to re-orientate their operations in order to cope with the demands on them to finance projects and programmes for speedy economic recovery and development. Further, the external environment (i.e., increased concessional capital flows and greater access of African exports) would need to be much more favourable in support of actions at the domestic level.

APPROPRIATE STRUCTURES OF REGIONAL ECONOMIC ORGANIZATIONS: THE CASE OF SADCC*

It has been argued that if regional organizations are to attract the material support of their member states, they must implement programmes which directly address national priorities and concerns. This approach, which largely entails the co-operation of national plans, requires the maximum possible participation of member states in project identification and implementation. One of the factors which militate against meaningful regional co-operation is excessive centralization, with large bureaucracies far removed from the day-to-day problems of the member states. This fosters a relationship of 'we' and 'they' between national policy-makers and the regional bureaucrats, with the attendant effect of weakening the commitment of governments and their institutions.

SADCC seeks to achieve this, in part, through the decentralization of its structures, so that each member state has responsibility for the co-ordination of at least one sectoral programme. As far as possible, member states are assigned sectors which are important to their own economies and in which they, potentially, have competence. It is necessary to emphasize that this co-ordination goes beyond simply providing a domicile for the administrative activities of the sector: it makes the respective co-ordinating governments politically accountable for the performance of the sector for which they are responsible. Each member state has to use its own resources, including staff, augmented where necessary by external technical assistance, to discharge its regional responsibilities. Usually, a member government will create a 'sector co-ordinating unit' in an appropriate Ministry to carry out this function. When the co-ordinating unit has developed a sufficiently large portfolio of implementable projects (as opposed to studies) it may be turned into a 'regional institution or commission'. In this case, all member states contribute to the budget of the regional institution and its staff are recruited regionally, although the co-ordinating State remains politically accountable for the sector. This arrangement allows SADCC to maintain a relatively small central

* part of the submissions by the General Secretariat of SADCC

Secretariat to carry out programme co-ordination and ensure the implementation of the decisions of its policy organs.

Furthermore, although the co-ordination and planning of projects and the mobilization of resources are carried out regionally, individual member states are responsible for the implementation and operation of the projects located on their territories. This means, for instance, that if a road linking two countries is considered to be of regional importance, each member state will be responsible for the construction of the section falling within its own territory. All financial and other obligations thus devolve on the participating member states, separately. In this context, the decision-making process emphasizes consensus in order to guarantee the maximum possible commitment of all member states.

Another feature of SADCC which ensures the involvement of member states is the priority given to the maximum use of national structures and institutions to perform regional functions. The organization mobilizes resources to enable the member states concerned to strengthen these institutions so that they can undertake additional regional functions. Other member states use the facility on terms agreed during the design of the project. New regional institutions are only established where no appropriate facility exists in the member states which can be strengthened to perform a regional function. This approach is very much in line with the directive of the LPA that no new multinational institutions should be created unless their creation has been thoroughly examined and only after the possibilities offered by national institutions or existing multinational ones, have first been fully considered.

It is important to note that in this arrangement the ownership of most of the assets created will remain with individual member states. The organization itself owns very few physical assets and is not directly involved in the financing of projects. This minimizes one of the main factors which have undermined regional co-operation efforts elsewhere: the distribution of regionally-owned physical assets among the member states.

A potential danger of this approach is slow implementation, since all the participating states must agree that the project in question is of priority. The consensus-building process may, therefore, involve lengthy consultations and trade-offs but, once secured, agreement will ensure the full practical support of all concerned.

Another important factor which impinges on the effectiveness of regional organizations is their size. There must be an optimal size of regional organizations beyond which the diseconomies of scale set in. If regional programmes should be based on national plans and policies, the complex process of reconciling the various national priorities must impose a limit on the size of subregional organizations. Decision-making in a regional organization constantly involves striking compromises among member states. Therefore, in determining the optimal size of a regional organization, the following factors should be taken into account: (a) Shared political objectives; (b) Geographical proximity and a history of relations across national boundaries; (c) Potential for, or the existence of a minimum level of economic and physical infrastructure across national boundaries; (d) Common major natural features such as river basins, lakes and coastlines; and, (e) Complementarity of resource endowment.

Although these criteria may increase the number of subregional organizations foreseen in the LPA, their application would lead to more cohesion, which is a necessary condition for successful economic co-operation.

SUBREGIONAL RECOVERY PROGRAMMES: THE CASE OF ECOWAS*

The ECOWAS initiative to have West Africa adopt a subregional ERP was motivated by the following factors: (i) every ECOWAS member state stood in need of an economic recovery and structural adjustment programme; (ii) countries would gain by coming together to discuss and appreciate the magnitude and seriousness of the economic crisis; (iii) a minimum set of remedial measures needed to be adopted by each member state; (iv) synchronised and simultaneous action in some areas would be more effective than unco-ordinated and isolated individual national initiatives; (v) joint action at the subregional level in some sectors would supplement national recovery efforts; and, (vi) a common subregional recovery programme would be an additional measure that could attract additional external assistance to fill the considerable resource gap. It was on the basis of considerations such as these that the issue of subregional economic recovery was raised at the Seventh Summit of the ECOWAS Authority of Heads of State and Government in November 1984, at Lome. In what came to be known as the 'Lome Declaration on Economic Recovery in West Africa', the ECOWAS Authority recognised the need to adopt a subregional recovery programme that addresses both short-term and long-term socio-economic problems, and identified a series of actions to be undertaken at national and Community levels.

* Part of the submissions by the ECOWAS Secretariat

In the Lome Declaration, the West African Heads of State and Government pledged their individual and collective political and financial support to:

(i) adopt a common strategy for economic development, based on a joint plan of action for the subregion, so as to make the best possible use of the resources;

(ii) promote the rehabilitation of the productive sectors of their national economies;

(iii) adopt and implement appropriate adjustment policies to combat the worsening balance of payments situation;

(iv) adopt, as soon as possible, measures to encourage the creation of an ECOWAS Monetary Zone, to promote stable monetary and financial conditions for a sustained growth of the regional economy;

(v) take necessary measures to ensure the achievement of food self-sufficiency, the rationalisation of manufacturing industries and the improvement of their productive capacity. In the field of agriculture, every effort was to be made to implement the decision relating to the establishment, on a zonal basis, of committees for agricultural development;

(vi) continue to pursue the current Community policies on infrastructural development in transport and communications, aimed at the promotion of social and economic intercourse among the peoples of the subregion;

(vii) initiate immediate joint action to combat desertification through the implementation of Community reafforestation programmes;

(viii) adopt collective measures to minimize the effects of unemployment within the Community;

(ix) take concerted action in the application of the findings of research institutions in the field of developmental problems in the subregion and provide these institutions with all the facilities necessary for the successful performance of their functions.

On the basis of the desires expressed in the Lome Declaration, the ECOWAS Institutions embarked upon an exhaustive study of both the immediate causes of the economic crisis and the basic structural problems facing the economies of the West African subregion. This analysis led to the formulation of a two-part economic recovery programme. The first part of the programme consists of short-term measures to alleviate the effects of the global recession and achieve a revival of the national economies in the short run. The second part contains medium-term measures designed to lay the foundation for sustained growth and initiate the process of structural transformation required for the effective development of the West African economies.

Economic integration groupings of the Third World are mainly concerned with the long-term development problems of their member countries; their co-operation programmes, therefore, tend to reflect less the short-term needs of national economies. ECOWAS felt the time had come to depart from this practice and to be much more responsive to the immediate and pressing problems of the West African states. Apart from the reasons enunciated above, it was recognized that the economic crisis was threatening the very survival of many countries, and everything needed to be done to help the countries hold the crisis in check.

Coverage of Programme

In line with these major concerns, the Short-term ERP adopted by the ECOWAS Council of Ministers in November 1986 focused attention on priority sectors and measures which are crucial in the context of the current West African economic situation. The ERP concentrates on tackling the acute food situation and declining agricultural production, in general, control of drought and desertification, water resources development and management, and the rehabilitation of infrastructural facilities and productive capacity. In addition, attention is paid to policy reforms to improve economic management as a whole, and public sector performance in particular. Other areas of concern that the ERP addresses are sound fiscal and monetary policies to curb inflation and eliminate domestic price distortion, correction of the over-valuation of weak national currencies, significant improvements in the balance of payments position and putting a check on the rising external indebtedness of the member states.

The above measures are the now-familiar policies contained in national economic recovery programmes, and one might rightly wonder whether the ECOWAS programme was to be a substitute for national action. As indicated earlier, not all the sixteen member states had committed themselves to a serious economic rehabilitation exercise by 1984. The aim of the Community was to create awareness for the need to take the challenge of the economic crisis seriously and to ensure that the minimum package of policy actions was adopted by each member state. The short-term Programme is consequently divided into two parts: action to be taken at the national level by each member State, and measures to be undertaken by the Community, at the subregional level.

Action at National Level

The part of the ECOWAS ERP to be executed at the national level was meant in effect to provide a check-list which would serve as a guideline for the formulation of individual national recovery programmes. These measures, recommended by the Community, were to be modified to fit the specific requirements of each country. For it is recognised that, although all the countries are going through an economic crisis, the severity of the different economic difficulties varies from country to country, and, therefore, different priorities would need to be established within the national recovery programmes. The important point was that the Community was able to get all the sixteen West African states to commit themselves to implement national economic recovery programmes.

Subsequent developments have proved that, with or without the involvement of the IMF and the World Bank, all the countries of the subregion have made concerted efforts to rehabilitate their economies. The encouragement and guidance these countries received at the subregional (ECOWAS), continental (APPER) and international (UN-PAAERD) levels contributed in no small way to the adoption of a series of bold economic reform policies within the past three years. The recent assessment of the economic situation carried out by the ECA had concluded that the positive economic growth registered since 1985 cannot be attributed solely to the good rains. Credit is also given to the national governments for adopting recovery measures which have entailed, in many cases, massive exchange rate adjustments, drastic cuts in public expenditure, privatisation of state enterprises and the dismantling of various economic controls.

Action at Community Level

The purpose of the Community-level measures is to supplement efforts being made at the national level and to assume responsibility for those measures which achieve greater effectiveness if co-ordinated and executed jointly. To a very large extent, the programme elements reflect those subregional measures agreed upon in APPER. The sectors covered by the Community are: food and agriculture, ecological preservation, transport, industry, energy, trade, tourism, culture, economic management, money and finance, and external indebtedness.

In the field of food and agriculture, the following Community actions are envisaged: creation or strengthening of Community centres for production of selected cattle-breeding stock and improved seeds;

harmonisation of livestock development programmes of West African IGOs; production of a subregional map on water and agro-pastoral resources; participation in subregional programmes on animal diseases control; promotion of co-operation in assessment of subregional fishery resources; promotion of increased intra-Community trade in fish products; co-ordination and assistance with establishment of national early warning systems; establishment of subregional agricultural information systems; assistance with establishment of a system for organising emergency food-aid and relief schemes on a bilateral and multilateral basis; organisation of systems for receiving, transporting and delivering emergency food-aid and other relief assistance; co-ordination of food security systems; harmonisation of pricing policies on major staple foods; and organization of subregional seminars and workshops to debate major agricultural issues and encourage exchange of information between member states.

In the area of natural environment and ecological preservation, the Community is to formulate a comprehensive subregional Plan to be used as guidelines by West African IGOs. The plan would also enable ECOWAS to co-ordinate their activities and identify issues and areas not adequately covered by these IGOs. ECOWAS is requested to develop close working relations with these IGOs to improve current programmes on drought and desertification control, water resources and meteorological studies, and soil erosion control. The Community is to encourage the involvement and participation of non-member Countries in the programmes of the IGOs to enhance their effectiveness. ECOWAS is also to lend its support to the IGOs in their search for international assistance, including multilateral resources such as is available under the Regional Fund of the EEC.

The short-term Community level measures adopted in the transport sector revolve round an accelerated implementation of some of the ECOWAS co-operation activities in this sector. The programme calls for the monitoring of the application of harmonised road legislation, and the functioning of the Motor Vehicle Third Party Liability Insurance Scheme (Brown Card). The Community is to devise means for improving transit facilities for moving goods within the subregion. The assistance being given in the construction of the Trans-West African Highway Network is to be stepped up, as is continued encouragement to West African airlines to co-ordinate and harmonise their operations.

The regular ECOWAS industrial co-operation programme focuses attention on some selected priority subsectors and the short-term recovery measures adopted in this sector relate to the food and agro-allied industries. The Community is to conduct an exhaustive evaluation of the agro-chemical, agricultural tool and food processing subsectors and to increase its assistance towards the establishment or expansion of enterprises in these subsectors.

The Community short-term measures in the energy sector emphasise conservation and efficiency in the utilisation of energy. Some of the specific measures are: (i) continuation of the Community energy conservation programme, including the electric-generating plant audit scheme; (ii) assistance with the rationalization and increased yield of existing oil refineries; (iii) increased search for better utilisation of new and renewable sources of energy; and (iv) co-operation between oil producing and non-producing countries.

The objective of the short-term trade policies is to increase intra-Community trade. ECOWAS is requested to accelerate the utilisation of harmonised customs documents, finalise the harmonisation of the ECOWAS-Mano River Union liberalisation schemes, and ensure the effective application of a single Community Trade Liberalisation Scheme. Every encouragement is to be given to the Federation of West African Chambers of Commerce in its efforts to strengthen co-operation among the business communities of the subregion. ECOWAS is further requested to expedite action on the harmonisation and programming of national trade fairs organised in West Africa.

As a complement to national reforms to improve economic management and to cut down on government expenditure, ECOWAS is requested to assist in a study of West African IGOs with a view to making proposals for their rationalization. Such rationalization is also to ensure the maximisation of the contribution of subregional co-operation to the development of the West African economy.

In the field of monetary and financial co-operation, the Community is to step up the preliminary studies for the establishment of a single monetary zone for West Africa. Meanwhile, closer co-operation between the central banks of the subregion and their greater use of the West African Clearing House is to be encouraged. The Community is to be used in the identification of additional sources of financial assistance for meeting the financial requirements of the national and Community recovery programmes.

Managing External Indebtedness

Finally, the Community is to bring its member states together, through the organisation of an international conference, to debate the issue of West Africa's external indebtedness. The conference is to determine the effects of the debt burden on the economies of the member states. Another aim of the Conference should be to provide general guidelines on debt management and to determine tolerable limits for external debt service and debt ratios compatible with development requirements.

Short-term Investment Programme

Some of the short-term recovery measures agreed upon for implementation at national and Community levels have to be translated into concrete projects. The ECOWAS Recovery Programme, therefore, includes one hundred and thirty-six projects. The total cost of the Investment Programme is estimated at $US926 million. Forty projects, estimated at $US548.5 million, are of a regional nature while the remainder are national projects. All the projects are drawn from national programmes; that is, each project is sponsored by a member state or a number of member states.

The projects are drawn from the following priority sectors: rural development (consisting of drought, desertification and erosion control, plant protection, livestock and crop production), transport, communications, energy and industry. All the selected projects are either on-going or have reached the implementation stage and are capable of contributing to the recovery of the economies within the next three years. Other criteria used for the selection of the projects include the use of local raw materials, promotion of regional integration, satisfaction of basic needs and supporting rural development.

At the Community level, regular co-operation programmes have been adjusted to reflect the priority and urgency accorded to particular projects. For example, there has been a heightened awareness for achieving greater monetary co-operation to complement national monetary reform measures, and, during the past twelve months, every effort was made to complete the studies on the creation of a single monetary zone and the improvement of the West African Clearing House. Similarly, a joint ECA/ECOWAS Report on the rationalisation of West African IGOs has been completed which, it is hoped, will contribute to making subregional integration a more effective tool for West African development. Mention may also be made of collaborative efforts in respect of agricultural pricing policies, food processing industries, subregional programmes on energy conservation (plant audits) and the implementation of the Community transport programme.

ECOWAS Medium-term Measures

The ERP outlined above is cast within the framework of a longer-term programme which goes beyond the exigencies of the prevailing economic crisis. The Programme limits itself to the short-term component of the Community's entire programme, in the sense that it addresses itself to the immediate problems of the national economies, but the ECOWAS programme is also concerned with basic structural issues.

The Medium-term Programme, which is to be fully developed after due consideration has been taken of the evolution of the subregional economic situation and the implementation of the short-term programme, has these objectives: consolidate the achievements of the short-term programme, especially concerning major policy reforms; continue with re-organisation of economic management; and initiate structural transformation and economic re-orientation needed for accelerated and sustainable development.

Since the Medium-term Programme is a prelude to a long-term development programme, it is based on the development philosophy adopted by the countries of West Africa: subregional integration and collective self-reliant development. The emphasis of the short-term programme on agriculture, rural development and related support measures is not just to redress the acute food and ecological problems of the subregion. It is a recognition that sustainable development must be based on the primary sector where the bulk of West African wealth is.

A mechanism involving Community and national planning experts has already been adopted by ECOWAS for monitoring and assessing the implementation of the Recovery Programme. One of the tenets of the Medium-term Programme is the cultivation of the habit in national policy-makers to see economic development in a subregional context. The Medium-term Programme envisages the formulation of a masterplan for West African development with the active participation of officials of all the sixteen countries. Particular emphasis is given to staple food crop production, industrial crop production, livestock and artisanal fishing, rural infrastructure, water resource management, agro-industry, transport and communications, energy development, domestic and intra-Community trade, money and payments arrangements, external indebtedness and balance of payments.

The Medium-term Programme is largely an indicative one which will evolve and continue to guide future action. Indeed, the Community's effort in the entire economic recovery undertaking provides a general framework to guide individual member states. Some of these countries are quite far advanced with their recovery programmes and are already considering programmes of longer duration and more development-oriented. The pragmatic approach adopted by the Community enables it to guide and be guided by developments within the member states.

NOTES

1. The summary of the argument in the document and the recommendations are adapted from Julius O. Aiyegbusi, 'The Role of the UN Economic Commission for Africa (ECA) in the Evolutionary Process of Development and Economic Growth in Africa – An Assessment' in Duri Mohammed, ed., *African Perspective in the New International Economic Order* (Nairobi: Bookwise Limited 1984). A more extensive discussion on the importance of this document is found in Adebayo Adedeji, 'The Monrovia Strategy and the LPA: Five Years After' in Adebayo Adedeji and Timothy Shaw, ed., *Economic Crisis in Africa: African Perspectives on Development Problems and Potentials* (Boulder: Lynne Rienner Publishers, Inc., 1985).
2. This point is emphasized by both Adedeji, *op.cit.* and Aiyegbusi.
3. See OAU, 'What Kind of Africa by the Year 2000?' (Addis Ababa: OAU 1980).
4. For more background information on the OAU involvement in this matter, see OAU Resolution CM/Res.722 (XXXIII).
5. The citation is from the LPA, paragraph 3.
6. *Africa's Priority Programme for Economic Recovery, 1986–1990 (APPER)*, Paragraph 8.
7. The following reasons for the failure to implement the LPA are summarized from *APPER, op.cit.*, paragraphs 14–18.
8. See *APPER*, para.111.
9. OAU, *Africa's Submission to the Special Session of the United Nations General Assembly on Africa's Economic and Social Crisis* (Addis Ababa: OAU, 1986).
10. Gerschenkron, A., *Economic Backwardness in Historical Perspective* (Cambridge, Mass., 1966).
11. Gerschenkron, *op. cit.*
12. Patrick, H.T. 'Financial Development and Economic Growth in Underdeveloped countries', *Economic Development and Cultural Change*, vol.14, No.2, 1966, pp.174–198.
13. Bhatia, R.J. and Khatkhate, D.R., 'Financial Intermediation, Savings Mobilization, and Entrepreneurship Development: The African Experience', *IMF Staff Papers*, vol.22, No.1 (March 1975), pp.132–158.
14. ADB, Domestic Resource Mobilization, *op. cit.*
15. N'Diaye B., Speech on the occasion of his investiture as President of African Development Bank Group, Abidjan, 31 August 1985.
16. ADB, A Proposal for the Fourth General Increase in the Bank's Capital, Document ADB/IC – IV/86/02 (Abidjan, April 1986).
17. Gurley, J.G., 'Financial Structures in Developing Economies', in Krivine, D. (ed.), *Fiscal and Monetary Problems in Developing States: Proceedings of the Third Rehovoth Conference* (N.Y., Praeger Publishers, 1967), Chapter 6.
18. Loganathan, C., *Development Savings Banks and the Third World – A Tool for the Diffusion of Economic Power* (London, Praeger Publishers, 1973), provides detailed features of this model for domestic resource mobilization.
19. Loganathan, *ibid.*, p.39.
20. As stated in A Proposal for the Fourth General Capital Increase in the Bank's Capital, *op. cit.*, p.3.
21. The Asian Development Bank has already commenced along these lines. See ADB, *Capital Market Development* (Manila, 1985).

CONCLUDING REMARKS

In Africa, there has been no underestimation of the enormous tasks and sacrifices required to arrest the continent's persistent economic and social deterioration and lay the foundation for a self-reliant and self-sustaining process of development. It was indeed the realization of Africa's development needs and the necessity to overcome structural maladjustments and pervasively low levels of productivity on the continent that led to the adoption of various regional plans and programmes of action since 1980. What has been lacking, all along, is the political will and earnest resolve to institute the necessary reforms and implement the appropriate measures. Now, all that would seem to have changed, with the reforms and restructuring activities and policies that have actually accompanied the adoption of APPER and UN-PAAERD at the national level, and the concerted subregional approaches to recovery and development that are beginning to emerge.

In line with their total commitment to APPER and UN-PAAERD, African countries have instituted a number of wide-ranging policy reforms, involving not only the re-ordering of priorities but also the adoption of new strategies to address issues of economic stabilization and recovery. Several of them have also embarked on serious structural adjustment with a focus on increasing economic efficiency, improving macro-economic management, reforming the public sector and the exchange rate. Africa, it would appear, is, at least for once, matching its rhetoric with its deeds, and its promises with its performance by fulfilling its own part of the compact entered into on June 1, 1986 with the rest of the world at the end of the Special Session of General Assembly devoted to African economic crisis. Sufficient time must of course elapse to permit the emergence of established trends, but the record to date of African Governments' implementation of UN-PAAERD is commendable. It is no longer Africa's inaction that is halting the progress towards recovery on the continent.

It also has to be realized and appreciated that policy reforms and adjustment exercises of the type now underway in Africa require a great deal of financing, especially in terms of foreign exchange which most African countries do not currently have. Sweeping reforms have never been easy or costless, anywhere, or without political risks and

151

social strains and stress. And, in Africa, there are indications already that the attendant social costs may be very, very formidable if not unbearable for many countries, and that the process and burden of adjustment has been made more difficult rather than helped by the problems of excruciating debt burdens, declining export incomes and external financial inflows. Thus, the fact that the African governments and institutions can no longer be said to lack a willed future for the recovery and accelerated development of their economies, or that there exists a strong determination on their part to continue with the implementation of APPER and UN-PAAERD, does not mean that their immediate troubles are over or that their long-standing structural problems will automatically disappear or be assuaged.

PART TWO

Response of the International Community to the African Economic Crisis and Recovery Programmes

INTRODUCTORY NOTE

The overall response of the international community to the African economic crisis must be judged against the background of the aggravating factors, the most serious of which are the persistent international economic recession, the decline in commodity prices, adverse terms of trade, the heavy burden of debt and debt servicing obligations, the decline in financial flows, increased protectionism, high interest rates, and, in the light of the commitments entered into in UN-PAAERD, the alleviation and the redressing of these problems. In the five chapters in this part of the book, the external constraints and requirements of Africa's development are examined in varying details while the extent to which the international community has honoured the commitments entered into in UN-PAAERD is evaluated.

In Chapter 6, Ashiabor reviews developments in the external environment since the adoption of UN-PAAERD and assesses the extent to which they have been supportive or inhibitive of African efforts. His prognosis for the future of Africa's external economic relations is not in the least bright, as he foresees expansion in world output and trade to continue to be slow for the rest of the 1980s and for protectionist measures to increase while prices of primary commodities of interest to Africa improve only marginally, if at all, thus further exacerbating the continent's trade and current account balances and the debt problem.

By far the greatest portion of the resources needed for the financing of APPER will be provided domestically in Africa. Yet, as Schatz points out in Chapter 7, even the modest external resource requirements of APPER far exceed the external resource flows currently available or likely to become available to Africa, and call into question the issues of autonomy, ideology and choice of development orientation as far as Africa is concerned. Other aspects of the required international support for Africa, relating in particular to improvements in aid co-ordination and donor assistance programmes and improvements in world trade, especially in agricultural products, are discussed in Chapter 8 by the World Bank.

In Chapter 9, Wheeler gives an overview of the resource flows to Africa in the recent past and reviews the initiatives by the international

155

community relating to the African debt problem. But more significant, perhaps, are his recommendations on measures needed to support structural adjustment programmes, and improve aid administration and the delivery of technical assistance. This is the more so, viewed against the background of SAPs-oriented initiatives and assistance of the US towards African recovery and development, detailed in Chapter 10 by Haynes and Haykin, and the views of the socialist countries on co-operation with Africa expatiated on by Sorokine in Chapter 11.

CHAPTER SIX

The External Environment and the Prospects for African Economic Recovery and Accelerated Development

A. ASHIABOR

INTRODUCTION

The measures by which the international community could support African development efforts are spelt out in paragraph 17 of UN-PAAERD. They include, *inter alia*, improving the quality and modality of external assistance and co-operation, improving the external environment, supporting Africa's policy reform and ensuring that African countries are assisted to deal with their financial constraints in such a manner that debt service burden does not undermine their efforts to establish the basis for sustainable growth.

The term 'external environment' has been used in recent analyses to represent all those exogenous economic variables which influence developments within the national economy. Paragraph 17 of UN-PAAERD gives a fairly representative coverage of the main constituent elements of the external environment some of which are already referred to in the preceding paragraph.

This chapter, however, limits itself essentially to paragraph 17(b)(i) and (ii) of UN-PAAERD. Also, some elements of paragraph 17(c) on supporting Africa's policy reform, such as increased support for LDCs, are briefly discussed. The discussion of the external environment and its effects on African economies and prospects for UN-PAAERD will concentrate on three broad aspects; namely, growth trends in the world economy, international trade, especially trade in primary commodities, protectionism and access to markets, and debt and international resource flows.

The reasons for this restricted coverage are, firstly, that the elements covered in paragraph 17(b)(i) and (ii) of UN-PAAERD relate essentially to UNCTAD's work and areas of competence. Secondly, other issues such as improving the quality and modality of aid and supporting African policy reforms will be dealt with in other chapters. Thirdly, there is a need for brevity, even though because of the interdependence of issues, references to factors outside the limited coverage may be expected.

CURRENT TRENDS IN THE GLOBAL ECONOMY

Because of the high dependence of many African economies on external trade, changes in global economic activity have a substantial influence on their economic performance. In particular, expansion or contraction of economic activity in the OECD countries which account for more than 60 percent of African exports exert strong influence, not only on the balance of payments and reserve positions, import and debt service capacity, but also on fiscal receipts, personal incomes and even monetary aggregates in many African countries. It is against this background that changes in output in the industrialized countries, especially developed market economy countries, must be viewed.

At the time of adoption of APPER in 1985, there was high expectation that the sharp drop in oil prices would stimulate a more dynamic growth in world output. It was thought that lower oil prices would encourage the developed market economy countries to take bolder measures to stimulate their economies without fear of reviving the inflationary pressures of the 1970s. However, these hopes have not materialized. On the contrary, economic expansion in the developed market economy countries slowed down in 1986 and the first few months of 1987, and prospects for a vigorous recovery remain dim for the rest of the year. Instead, a number of asymmetries have become apparent. The weak performance of OECD economies has persisted against a background of low inflation. In spite of a decline in interest rates and some recovery in business profits, rates of investment have remained low. Policy stance in many developed market economy countries continues to be relatively restrictive despite high levels of unemployment (8 per cent) and capacity under-utilization. Several factors account for some of the disappointed hopes for a post-1985 recovery in the global economy.

In the first place, the effect of the oil price drop on real expenditures was marginal, mainly because the possible gains to consumers were siphoned off by governments and businesses. The former did so through increased taxes on imported oil products. For instance, on the average, petrol prices in the six major OECD countries[1] declined by 15.4 per cent in 1986 over 1985 whereas, if taxes were excluded, businesses took advantage of the fall in crude oil prices to raise profit margins. These policies only reinforced the substantial shifts in demand already generated by earlier oil price booms.

But the continued weakness in oil and non-oil primary commodity prices in 1986 and early 1987, coupled with the sharp rise in debt service payments, also constrained developing countries' demand for the exports of the industrialized countries. Moreover, recent exchange rate realignments leading to a large depreciation of the American dollar and upward adjustments in the Japanese yen and the Deutschmark have dampened output growth prospects in the latter countries without, as yet, stimulating growth to any noticeable degree in the US.

Meanwhile, the slow growth of output in the leading market economy countries in 1986 and the prospects of a world economy in the doldrums or on the brink of a recession have also depressed demand for raw materials and output growth in the developing countries, especially in Africa. UNCTAD Secretariat calculations, within the framework of the System for Interlinked Global Modeling and Analysis (SIGMA) developed in UNCTAD, give an indication of output growth in 1985 and 1986 and prospects for 1987. The estimates and forecasts are based on a number of assumptions; mainly, that interest and exchange rates will remain at end-first quarter levels for the rest of the year, and that OPEC petroleum production will be within the limits set at the October 1987 meeting of OPEC.

Under those assumptions, growth in the volume of world trade is expected to slow down to 3.3 per cent in 1987 from 4.9 per cent in 1986. Lower growth rates of import volumes in the developed market economy countries and an absolute decline in the case of developing countries will be important factors in this development. The terms of trade of the industrialized countries will improve while those of the developing countries, including Africa, will continue to deteriorate due principally to the further deterioration in the 'real'[2] prices of non-oil commodities where a decline of almost 10 per cent was forecast for 1987.

The overall policy changes and the response of the developed market economies are not likely to make any significant impact on the balance of payments and structural disequilibria in those countries before 1988. Their current account surplus could turn into a small deficit, with both Japan and the Federal Republic of Germany reducing their surplus and the United States reducing its deficit by some $US2 billion in 1987. For the developing countries, the overall deficit in 1987 remained much the same as for 1986. African countries' current deficits, which rose to $US24.7 billion in 1986, improved somewhat but remained at a substantially high level of some $US21 billion. Current account deficits of sub-Saharan African countries are estimated to have deteriorated sharply in 1986 ($US16 billion from $US4.8 billion in 1985) and improved marginally in 1987 to $US11.8 billion (see Table 6.1).

TABLE 6.1
WORLD OUTPUT BY MAJOR COUNTRIES AND COUNTRY GROUPINGS,
1980–1987
(percentage change)

Country or Country Group	1980–1985 (Annual Average)	1985	1986	1987 (a)
World	2.3	3.2	2.9	2.8
Dev.market economy countries (b)	2.2	3.0	2.4	2.4
Developing countries	1.4	2.4	3.3	3.0
North Africa	2.7	2.8	1.0	2.6
Other Africa	−0.5	2.3	0.6	0.7
Other African countries, excl. Nigeria	2.1	2.5	2.9	2.9
China (c)	9.8	12.3	7.4	7.5
Socialist Countries of E. Europe (d)	3.5	3.2	4.3	4.1

Source: UNCTAD Secretariat calculations. Forthcoming in Trade and Development Report 1987

Notes:
(a) Estimates
(b) Gross domestic product/gross national product
(c) National income
(d) Net material product

As a consequence of these developments, growth in world output is expected to stagnate at the 1986 level of 2.9 per cent or slightly below. Output growth in developing countries is estimated at 3.3 per cent for 1986 and 3.0 per cent for 1987 compared with 2.4 per cent for the developed market economy countries. Sub-Saharan African countries, excluding Nigeria, will record only marginal advances over 1985 (2.9 per cent for 1986 and 2.7 per cent for 1987). But this picture changes drastically when Nigeria is taken into account. Growth rates for sub-Saharan Africa, including Nigeria, dropped sharply from 2.3 per cent in 1985 to 0.6 and 0.7 per cent respectively in 1986 and 1987 indicating the vastly contractionary effects of the fall in oil prices and export volumes on the Nigerian economy.

Agriculture continues to be the main determinant of output growth in sub-Saharan Africa.[3] Some encouraging improvements were recorded in food production in the recent past in response to the vigorous policies of some African countries and improved weather conditions. However, the situation remains disquieting over the long term in regard to African countries' ability to maintain food production growth at levels above population growth. Despite the fact that African agriculture has performed reasonably well, repercussions of external developments on other sectors of the economy have constrained overall economic performance.

OUTPUT PERFORMANCE IN SELECTED AFRICAN COUNTRIES

In Zambia, for example, the persistence of weak copper prices led to drastic falls in export earnings, intensifying the contractionary impact of the courageous structural adjustment policies initiated in 1985. Despite encouraging developments in food production, expansion in economic activities slowed down as urban incomes declined and production costs rose sharply in the wake of trade and price liberalization measures. Increasing difficulties and the social unrest that accompanied the austerity programme forced the Government to reverse most of the key elements of the IMF-supported adjustment programme in 1987.[4] Zaire, on the other hand, has adhered strictly to the IMF/World Bank-supported programme although growth continued to be slow as projected foreign investment inflows were not realized. With the country becoming a net exporter of financial resources, the Government decided to limit repayments of interest to 10 per cent of export receipts in order to arrest the situation.

Even the structurally more diversified economies such as Zimbabwe and Cote d'Ivoire have not been immune to the vicissitudes common to sub-Saharan African countries. In Zimbabwe, the bumper harvests of 1985 were not repeated in 1986 and, with foreign exchange restraints, manufacturing output growth had to be compressed. Similarly, Cote d'Ivoire registered a slow-down in agricultural output after relatively better performance in 1985, and the weak performance of the agricultural sector was not compensated for by other sectors. By the end of the year, the boom in coffee prices in 1986 had petered out. By early 1987, in the face of a deterioration in the situation caused by continued weakness of commodity prices and rising debt service, the Government was obliged to announce its inability to meet debt service payments.

161

In Ghana, the bold policies of the authorities to restructure the economy to correct past policy failures through, *inter alia*, the liberalization of trade and prices, introduction of incentives and mobilization of savings, yielded results. Vigorous output growth was recorded in 1984 and 1985. Cocoa production in particular responded well to these policy changes and Ghana began to recapture part of its lost market share. Food production also benefitted from these policies, helped also by improved weather conditions. However, the economy continues to operate under heavy constraints – depressed commodity prices; heavy debt service payments due between now and 1990; and low capacity utilization due to lack of adequate inputs and technical obsolescence of equipment. Output grew even though at a lower pace in 1987. However, the drastic cuts in social expenditures and necessarily stringent limitations on money wages are causing concern among both the Government and low income and disadvantaged groups. Besides, a return of poor rainfall conditions could aggravate the country's problems.

Kenya and other countries of East and Southern Africa benefitted from improved terms of trade which helped to raise output. But, in these countries too, growth will slow down as commodity prices resume their decline or stagnate at historically low levels.

For the North African countries, GDP growth dropped to 1.0 per cent in 1986 from 2.8 per cent in 1985. These countries, which (excepting Morocco) are mainly net oil-exporters, were particularly subject to influences in the oil market. Only Algeria showed a positive growth rate in 1986, and this relatively better performance was probably due to the more diversified structure of its economy as crude oil exports account for no more than one-third of hydrocarbon exports. The increasing share of refined products and natural gas in exports and improvements in domestic production have cushioned the economy against the depressive effects of the drop in crude oil prices.

Egypt on the other hand is in a different situation. It is a highly indebted oil-exporting country and, therefore, very much exposed to developments in oil markets. Moreover, remittances from Egyptian workers in other oil-exporting countries have also declined significantly as those countries themselves face a slow-down in demand and prices. These developments have put serious strains on Egypt's balance of payments and output growth.

Morocco on the other hand (a net oil-importer) benefitted from the decline in oil prices and improved agricultural production which helped it to limit its import bill. In spite of the weakness in export markets, these developments, coupled with the relative decline in international interest rates and an increase in private transfers, enabled Morocco to improve its current account deficit and at the same time maintain some growth in 1986. Output growth strengthened in 1987.

Thus, for both Africa itself and the rest of the world, output growth performance has been below expectation although individual country performances varied. The developed market economies especially failed to provide the engine of growth through expansion of output even though conditions appear to warrant it especially in the leading surplus countries.

INTERNATIONAL TRADE IN PRIMARY COMMODITIES

A second major element in the external environment relates to international trade. For Africa, and especially for a large number of sub-Saharan African countries, this means international trade in primary commodities. These countries depend on primary commodity exports for more than 60 per cent of export revenues. Many of them have narrow economic structures with not more than three (sometimes one or two) commodity items accounting for the bulk of foreign exchange earnings. Thus, changes in international markets for primary commodities have far-reaching effects on their economies. Even the oil-exporting countries of Africa have not escaped the destabilizing effects of massive swings in commodity prices.

Since the beginning of the 1980s, primary commodity prices have continued a decline (only broken briefly in 1984) and have now reached their lowest levels since the Great Depression. Already in 1983, at UNCTAD VI, the UNCTAD Secretariat tried to draw the attention of the international community to these trends. Their potentially adverse effects on the economies of commodity-exporting countries and the consequences for international trading relations and debt service were also highlighted.[5] However, the weak signs of apparent recovery on the horizon in the last quarter of 1983 deflected attention from the problem. It was also held that 'trickle down effect' of recovery in the industrialized countries would lead to a recovery in the developing countries.

Today, the recession in primary commodity prices remains as ever, even worse. The UNCTAD combined index of principal commodity exports of African developing countries (1979–81 = 100) has dropped 24 percentage points in terms of current dollars and SDRs from its 1979–1981 base (Table 6.2).

All the main commodity groups have shown continued signs of weakness during the period 1983 to date. In particular, between 1985

TABLE 6.2

COMBINED INDEX OF FREE MARKET PRICES OF PRINCIPAL
COMMODITY EXPORTS OF DEVELOPING AFRICA (a)
1983–1987
(1979–1981 = 100)

Period (b)	In terms of current US dollars (c)	In terms of SDRs
1983	84	98
1984	89	109
1985	82	101
1986	85	92
1987 Jan–April	76	76

Source: UNCTAD Secretariat calculations
Notes:
(a) Free market prices, excluding long-term contract or preferential prices
(b) Monthly average
(c) Weighted according to the relative importance of each group in the value of exports
of African countries in 1979–81

(when APPER was adopted) and April 1987, prices in all the broad groups have fallen sharply except in the cases of food and beverages, and agricultural raw materials where the strengthening of coffee prices (in 1986), in the former case, and the firmness of cotton prices, in the latter, resulted in marginally better prices above 1985 (see Table 6.3).

In the food and tropical beverages group, prices dropped by 12 per cent between 1983 and 1987 (Table 6.3). The performance of the sub-groups was varied, with 10 per cent decline for food and 14 per cent for beverages. Within the food group, banana was the only product of export interest to African countries which enjoyed price rises between 1983 and 1987. Export prices for this commodity fell by 10 per cent between 1983 and 1985, but recovered strongly by 37 per cent to levels above those at 1983. Sugar prices, on the other hand, after dropping to levels below cost of production of even the most efficient producers in 1985 following the earlier failure of the International Conference on Sugar, picked up strongly in 1986 and 1987. This was due partly to supply rationalization policies in some producer countries and recent increased purchases by the USSR (from Cuba) and China.

In the beverages sub-group, price performance was varied. Coffee (robustas) prices, after rising sharply in 1986 as a result of tightness of supplies induced by weather conditions in Brazil, dropped to a level in 1987 which is 21 per cent below 1983. Despite the underlying supply

TABLE 6.3

INDICES OF FREE MARKET PRICES OF PRINCIPAL COMMODITY
EXPORTS OF DEVELOPING AFRICA (a) BY COMMODITY GROUPS,
1983–1987, IN TERMS OF CURRENT DOLLARS
(1979–1981 = 100)

Period (b)	Food and Tropical beverages	Food	Beverages	Vegetable oil/oilseeds	Agricultural Raw materials	Mineral ores metals
1983	84	68	84	81	88	81
1984	93	56	97	111	90	76
1985	83	51	87	79	83	76
1986	94	56	99	50	80	74
1987	74	61	75	51	89	76
Average	86	58	89	74	86	77

Source: UNCTAD Secretariat calculations
Notes:
(a) Same as for table 6.2
(b) Same as for table 6.2

overhang, cocoa prices rose somewhat in 1984 in reaction to the drought and bush fires in West Africa. However, they have since resumed their downward course reflecting market fundamentals and weak demand generally. Tea prices have not escaped the depressive effects of global market trends either. After a sharp rise of 48 per cent in 1984, prices dropped equally steeply in 1985 by 43 per cent, and the decline has persisted through 1987. Vegetable oils and oilseeds, after a brief rally in 1984, suffered the worst decline of any commodity group.

Both agricultural raw materials and mineral ores and metals prices have also remained at low levels or maintained a declining trend. While phosphate rock prices have remained largely unchanged, iron and manganese ores and copper dropped by an average of a further 10 per cent from 1983 levels. For the African countries which depend largely on oil exports,[6] the dramatic changes in oil prices in recent years have had traumatic destabilizing effects. Between 1982–1985, oil prices dropped in real terms by 11 per cent. But, in 1986 alone, real prices dropped by a further 55 per cent reflecting the collapse of the OPEC price arrangements. After further attempts by OPEC member States to establish market equilibrium, prices have now settled at levels well below those of 1983. Even these prices are only expected to hold somewhat so long as OPEC member states observe production quotas and non-OPEC members voluntarily refrain from upsetting the market with further supplies. The sharp fluctuations in prices have created vast problems for the economies of Nigeria, the Libyan Arab Jamahiriya, Gabon, Congo and Egypt and caused serious adjustment difficulties.

The reasons for the collapse of commodity markets in the 1980s are well-known.[7] They include structural and technological changes in the industrialized countries, weak growth in the developed market economies, abundance of supplies due to lagged response to earlier price rises. In the case of oil prices, the fundamental changes in energy-use triggered off by the oil price rises, the capacity expansion of producers and the oil dependence generated by the boom of earlier years appear to have created conditions of fundamental disequilibrium between supply and demand. This could take some time to eliminate. In the meantime, oil-exporting African countries will be faced with serious problems of adjustment, much in the same way if not more seriously than their non-oil exporting counterparts.

Protectionism

The tensions generated in international trade as a result of the asymmetries mentioned earlier have created a protectionist mood among the leading trading partners. Even the developing countries have not escaped the protectionist onslaught from the developed countries. Most of Africa's primary commodity exports, in their raw and un-processed forms, enjoy relatively free entry to markets of the OECD countries. However, tariff and especially non-tariff barriers escalate sharply with the degree of processing. Thus, a number of African countries with fairly diversified economic structures such as Zimbabwe face problems of market access for their manufactures.

But the major problem of protectionism for African countries arises from the increasing use of non-tariff barriers which are more discreet and therefore difficult to monitor or even predict. Also the protectionist policies of the EEC with regard to certain agricultural commodities have been known to be partly responsible for the overall excess of supply over demand in the food items, as well as in vegetable oils and oil seeds. These protectionist policies distort comparative advantage and create undue difficulties of market access for developing countries, in particular, including African countries.

Terms of Trade

As a result of these developments, the terms of trade of most developing countries have deteriorated sharply especially since 1985 (see Table 6.4). Although no separate figures are available for the African subregion, developments relating to the developing countries can be expected to apply with greater adverse effects to Africa.

Developing countries' terms of trade worsened by almost one quarter in 1986, mainly reflecting oil market developments. For non-oil developing countries, the deterioration in terms of trade was much smaller in 1986. However, the situation was expected to worsen in 1987 and, possibly, in 1988.

TABLE 6.4

ANNUAL PERCENTAGE CHANGE IN VOLUME AND PRICES OF WORLD (a) TRADE CLASSIFIED BY MAIN COUNTRY GROUPS, 1985-1987

Country or country groups	1985 Actual	1986 Estimated	1987 Forecast
World export volume	2.4	4.0	3.0
Developed market-economy countries			
Export volume	3.5	1.7	3.4
Terms of trade	1.0	9.9	0.2
Purchasing power of exports	4.5	11.8	3.6
Import volume	5.4	7.7	4.0
All developing countries			
Export volume	−0.4	10.0	1.7
Terms of trade	−0.9	23.2	−2.6
Purchasing power of exports	−1.3	15.5	−0.9
Import volume	−3.3	7.9	−1.6
Oil-exporting developing countries (b)			
Export volume	−3.3	13.2	−3.2
Terms of trade	0.3	31.2	−1.2
Purchasing power of exports	−3.0	22.1	−4.4
Import volume	−5.7	19.7	−9.9
Net oil-importing developing countries (c)			
Export volume	2.7	7.4	3.0
Terms of trade	−1.9	−0.3	−3.7
Purchasing power of exports	0.7	1.1	1.1
Import volume	−1.9	3.2	2.8

Source: UNCTAD Secretariat calculations based on official national and international sources, in forthcoming *Trade and Development Report* 1987.
Notes:
The terms of trade calculations for groups of countries have been made by the UNCTAD Secretariat using a methodology briefly described in the UNCTAD Handbook of International Trade and Development Statistics, Supplement 1985 (United Nations publication, Sales No.E.F.85.11.D.12), p.536.
(a) Excluding China and the socialist countries of Eastern Europe.
(b) Major petroleum exporters plus Bolivia, Egypt and Malaysia.
(c) All developing countries except oil-exporting developing countries as defined above.

Current Account Balances

Current account balances of African countries have reflected these influences. Corresponding with the overall position of developing countries,[8] North African countries' current account deficit rose from $US0.6 billion in 1985 to $US8.0 billion in 1986 and are expected to improve only marginally to $US7.1 billion in 1987 (Table 6.5). The other African countries' external accounts show similar levels of deficit except that the fluctuations between 1985 and 1987 are not so dramatic. It is worth noting, however, that the deficit of these countries increased in 1987 as compared to a slight improvement for the countries of North Africa.

Debt and External Resource Flows

The developments described above have seriously exacerbated the debt problems of many African countries. Not only has the quantum and incidence of debt increased rapidly in recent years but, given the elements of the external environment, the debt burden has become a major hindrance to Africa's development process.

TABLE 6.5
CURRENT ACCOUNT BALANCES (a): MAJOR COUNTRIES AND COUNTRY
GROUPS, 1985–1987
(Billions of US dollars)

Country or country groups	1985 Actual	1986 Estimated	1987 Forecast
Developed market-economy countries	−27.7	11.4	−2.3
Developing countries	−22.4	−43.7	−39.1
North Africa	−0.6	−8.0	−7.1
Other Africa	−4.9	−8.7	−9.1
China	−11.4	−7.8	−7.5
Socialist countries of Eastern Europe (b)	2.4	−2.2	−0.9
Statistical discrepancy (c)	−59.1	−42.3	−49.8

Source: UNCTAD Secretariat calculations, based on official national and international sources.
(a) Goods, services and private transfers.
(b) All countries, territories and areas not included in other groups.
(c) The statistical discrepancy is composed of a (usually negative) discrepancy on merchandise trade, mainly due to timing asymmetries, and a positive discrepancy on services reflecting, in the main, under-reporting of interest income, receipts from sales of transportation services and remittances.

Debt Service Problems

The debt service figures doubled between 1978 and 1985. Interest payments in particular rose threefold, reflecting both the sharp rise in interest rates (though now declining) and the fall in exports. But even these figures mask the real extent of the debt burden of many countries which have debt service ratios of over 50 per cent, and are, like the Sudan and Uganda, among the poorest in the world in terms of *per capita* incomes. As noted earlier, not even countries such as the Cote d'Ivoire are able now to cope with the crushing effects of debt on incomes and development.

On the basis of present policies, future prospects look equally gloomy and no real relief is in sight even up to 1985 according to a simulation exercise undertaken by the UNCTAD Secretariat.

TABLE 6.6

SELECTED DEBT INDICATORS FOR SUB-SAHARAN AFRICAN
COUNTRIES (a), 1978–1985 (PERCENTAGES)

	Debt/ Exports	Debt and service exports	Interest payments/ exports
1978	133.3	11.6	4.2
1979	149.0	14.0	6.3
1980	134.4	14.0	7.6
1981	158.1	15.2	9.1
1982	185.0	16.2	11.1
1983	207.6	17.7	12.3
1984	198.6	18.3	13.6
1985 (b)	225.2	22.0	13.8

Source: UNCTAD Secretariat calculations
(a) Excluding Nigeria
(b) Estimates

The projections in Table 6.7 show that, even on the restricted assumption of a minimum annual average GDP growth rate of 2.5 to 2.6 per cent, the debt/GDP ratio will rise by a third by the end of the period covered by UN-PAAERD and continue to 106.8 per cent in 1995. Similarly, the debt/exports ratio will also rise from 212 per cent in the opening period to 376 per cent in 1990, and by a further 52 per cent to 428 per cent in 1995. Reflecting the conditions of the external environment described, the ratio of payments deficit to total exports of goods and services will worsen from 38 per cent now to between 53 and 56 per cent in 1990–1995. The projections for the LDCs (27 of which are in Africa) follow the same pattern although the rates of increase are smaller. The relatively lower ratios of interest to GDP reflect the high proportion of concessionary lending to the LDCs most of which are African. Nevertheless, the Table shows that debt and balance-of-payments problems will continue to constrain the development efforts of the LDCs as well as other African countries.

TABLE 6.7
SELECTED DEBT INDICATORS FOR NON-OIL DOMINANT
COUNTRIES (a) MEDIUM-TERM PROJECTIONS UP TO 1995
(Percentage ratios)

	1984–1986	1990	1995
Africa (b)			
Base line scenario			
Average annual GDP Growth	–	2.5–2.6	–
Ratio of interest payments to GDP	3.1	4.9	5.8
Debt to GDP	66.9	91.0	106.8
Interest payments/exports	12.6	20.3	23.3
Debt/exports	272.5	376.4	428.3
Current account balance/exports	–38.1	–53.4	–55.7
All least developed countries			
Base line scenario			
Average annual GDP Growth	–	2.8–2.7	–
Ratio of interest payments to GDP	1.4	1.5	1.8
Debt to GDP	57.6	63.2	72.7
Interest payments/exports	8.4	8.9	10.3
Debt/exports	342.3	368.6	411.5
Current account balance/exports	–63.3	–65.4	–76.8

Source: UNCTAD Secretariat calculation based on SIGMA Projections
(a) Non-oil dominant developing countries comprise all developing countries other than the seven countries for which exports of fuel and lubricants (SITC 3) accounted for at least 85 per cent of total exports of goods and services and the share of mining and quarrying was over 35 per cent of GDP during 1980–1983. The seven countries are Iraq, Kuwait, the Libyan Arab Jamahiriya, Oman, Qatar, Saudi Arabia and the United Arab Emirates.
(b) Excluding Algeria, the Libyan Arab Jamahiriya and Nigeria.

Outflow of Resources to IMF

A disquieting new feature of short-term multilateral debt is the fact that there is now a net outflow of resources from Africa to the IMF. This development calls into question the relevance of IMF's rules and practices to the present-day situation of many low-income countries, including those in Africa.[9]

Table 6.8, for example, shows that net purchases by African countries from the IMF declined sharply from SDRs 2.3 billion in 1982 to just SDRs 258 million in 1985.

Between 1986 and 1987, African countries transfered on a net basis three and a half times as much money to IMF as they received in 1985. Already in 1985, eleven low and middle income African countries[10] were in a net repurchase situation vis-a-vis the IMF. Such a situation has arisen because the rules and practices of IMF, which were designed only for short-term temporary balance of payments adjustments, have become incapable of solving the more complex issues of growth and adjustment now facing many of the developing countries. Should such a situation persist without appropriate review and adjustment, it will call into question the relevance of the Fund and its modus operandi to the real needs of developing countries.

TABLE 6.8

IMF PURCHASES AND REPURCHASES OF DEVELOPING AFRICAN COUNTRIES (SDR MILLIONS)

Year/Period	Purchases (1)	Repurchases (2)	Net (1)–(2)
1947–81	6,530.9	2,629.2	3,901.7
1982	2,620.7	273.0	2,347.7
1983	1,939.9	425.6	1,514.3
1984	1,225.9	552.7	673.2
1985	1,025.0	766.5	258.5
1986	776.8	1,472.4	−695.6
1986 I	203.6	389.4	−185.8
II	143.2	358.4	−215.2
III	136.1	361.4	−225.3
IV	293.9	363.2	−69.3
1986 December	105.8	81.0	24.8
1987 January	–	78.1	−78.1
1987 February	9.0	156.5	−147.5

Source: IMF: *International Financial Statistics*, Vol. XL, No.4, April 1987, pp.28–31.

Resource Flows

Complete figures on net medium- and long-term financial flows to Africa are available up to 1984, and some estimates are available also for 1985 (see Table 6.9). These data show that total net financial flows (concessional and non-concessional) declined in 1983 and 1984. Non-concessional flows declined rather sharply. But concessional flows, after a temporary slow down in 1983, increased especially strongly in

1985. This was in response to the African situation. In particular, concessional flows to the African LDCs increased substantially. This increase is expected to continue in the coming years but the pace will depend on the evolution of the world economy, especially output in the developed market economies.

Total American aid to Africa[11] for instance is expected to decline in 1987 but rise modestly in 1988 still to a level below 1986.[12] However, there appears to be a clear trend towards increased development assistance to the LDCs, especially African LDCs. In 1985, DAC technical assistance to African LDCs was $US1.3 billion. Concessional assistance, consisting of DAC and OPEC sources, was $US5.7 billion. Concessional assistance from all sources, including private flows from DAC countries in 1985, was equivalent to 70 per cent of these countries' aid inflows compared with 45 per cent in 1980.

The Nordic countries[13] and Netherlands continue to put up the leading performance in terms of net development assistance from DAC member countries to developing countries and multilateral agencies (Table 6.10). These countries reached or exceeded the ODA target of 0.7 per cent of GNP in 1985. In a number of other countries, ODA performance was above average[14] ratios for 1985. The average[15] performance for all DAC member countries has declined from 0.35 (half of the target) in 1982 to 0.31 in 1985.

The foregoing analysis shows that the current evolution and prospects attending the main elements of the external environment do not augur well for the attainment of the objectives of UN-PAAERD.

CONCLUSIONS

The following observations emerge from the analysis, assuming no major changes in the policies of the industrialized countries:

(a) World output growth has been slow and is expected to be slow for the rest of the decade given the policy stance of the authorities in the leading industrial countries and the unresolved asymmetries which have emerged;

(b) World trade expansion will consequently be slow and commodity prices especially will continue to be low or improve only marginally towards the end of the decade;

(c) Given the serious adjustment problems facing the US and the understandable desire of the authorities to redress the situation, protectionist pressures will increase unless especially strong measures are taken, especially by surplus countries, to liberalize

TABLE 6.9

NET MEDIUM- AND LONG-TERM FINANCIAL FLOWS (a) TO DEVELOPING COUNTRIES IN AFRICA, 1978–1985
(billions of current US dollars)

	1978	1981	1982	1983	1984	1985b/	annual growth rate c/ (per cent)	
							1981–1985	1981–1985
Concessional	11.47	12.80	12.98	12.75	13.86	16.75	7.9	1.4
1. Official flows	10.75	12.09	12.08	11.83	12.64	15.15	6.7	1.2
Bilateral	8.13	9.11	9.20	8.82	9.50	11.45	6.8	1.5
OECD	5.24	7.57	7.78	7.57	8.69	10.71	10.0	7.5
OPEC	2.65	1.37	1.24	1.11	0.68	0.59	18.4	23.6
Multilateral	2.62	2.98	2.88	3.01	3.14	3.70	6.6	8.8
2. Private grants	0.72	0.71	0.90	0.92	1.22	1.60	23.5	5.3
Non concessional	12.87	11.53	12.79	9.10	5.96	–	–	8.3
1. Official flows	7.23	6.56	6.29	5.18	5.59	4.12	10.2	8.0
Bilateral	6.58	5.77	5.33	4.01	4.33	2.81	15.7	9.0
Official export credits	0.70	0.85	1.01	0.59	0.39	0.19	30.4	1.3
Officially supported export credits	5.10	3.52	2.89	2.91	1.11	1.10	24.6	15.9
Other official	0.78	1.40	1.43	0.51	2.83	1.52	2.9	15.5
Multilateral	0.65	0.79	0.96	0.17	1.26	1.31	14.7	1.4
2. Private flows	5.64	4.97	6.50	3.92	0.37	–	–	8.9
Direct investment	1.31	2.22	2.74	1.06	0.02	–	–	13.5
Capital markets	4.33	2.75	3.76	2.86	0.35	–	–	18.3
Net flows	24.34	24.33	25.77	21.85	19.82	–	–	4.9

Source: UNCTAD secretariat estimates based on OECD, *Geographical Distribution of Financial Flow to Developing Countries* and other data from the OECD and UNCTAD sources.

Notes:
(a) Excluding aid from CMEA countries since data from official sources are not available on a systematic basis but including aid from countries other than members of DAC and OPEC.
(b) Estimates
(c) Deflated by the DAC GNP deflator.

173

TABLE 6.10

NET OFFICIAL DEVELOPMENT ASSISTANCE FROM DAC-MEMBER COUNTRIES TO DEVELOPING COUNTRIES AND MULTILATERAL AGENCIES AS A PERCENTAGE OF GNP, 1978–1985

Country	1978	1980	1982	1983	1984	1985a/
Countries which reached or exceeded the 0.7 per cent target in 1985:						
Norway	0.88	0.84	0.98	1.09	1.02	1.03
Netherlands	0.88	1.02	1.08	0.91	1.02	0.91
Sweden	0.89	0.79	1.02	0.84	0.80	0.86
Denmark	0.75	0.74	0.76	0.73	0.85	0.80
Countries with ODA ratio above in the DAC average in 1985:						
Belgium	0.55	0.51	0.59	0.59	0.57	0.55
France b/	0.32	0.38	0.48	0.48	0.52	0.54
Canada	0.52	0.43	0.41	0.45	0.50	0.49
Australia	0.55	0.48	0.56	0.49	0.46	0.49
Germany, Federal Republic of	0.35	0.42	0.46	0.47	0.44	0.46
Finland	0.16	0.22	0.30	0.32	0.36	0.39
Austria	0.26	0.23	0.34	0.23	0.28	0.37
United Kingdom	0.46	0.35	0.37	0.35	0.33	0.34
Countries with ODA ratios below the DAC average in 1985:						
Italy	0.14	0.17	0.24	0.24	0.33	0.31
Switzerland	0.20	0.24	0.25	0.31	0.30	0.31
Japan	0.23	0.32	0.28	0.32	0.35	0.29
New Zealand	0.34	0.32	.	0.28	0.25	0.25
Ireland c/	–	–	–	–	0.22	0.24
United States	0.22	0.24	0.24	0.20	0.20	0.19
Total DAC member countries b/						

Source: UNCTAD secretariat calculations based on OECD, Development Co-operation, various issues.

Notes: (a) Provisional
    (b) Excluding French aid to overseas departments and territories and including Ireland's aid for 1984 and 1985.
    (c) Ireland joined the DAC in November 1985.

174

and expand output in the advanced industrialized market economies;

(d) These difficulties will indicate that total aid funds will not rise substantially between now and the end of the decade. On the other hand, the major donors will be more selective regarding recipient and policy linkage of their aid;

(e) This could intensify rather than diminish the trend towards bilateralism; and,

(f) The debt problem will grow and become intractable unless substantially new solutions are found to meet the pressing problems of all developing countries, including African debtors.

For the African countries, the decline or stagnation in output growth and the present overhang of excess supply of both oil and non-oil commodities could mean a further decline in foreign exchange availability. As many of the African countries currently undertaking strong and socially difficult adjustment programmes have now pushed their imports to levels which cannot permit further reductions without serious social and political consequences, debt default could increase and more countries could be forced to abandon such needed adjustment programmes.

As regards the objectives of UN-PAAERD itself, clearly the developments in the external environment described above cannot be said to be supportive of UN-PAAERD. If anything, they have constrained the efforts of many African countries. Without a radical change in the attitudes and policy stances of the leading industrial countries towards issues of international economic co-operation, the courageous efforts of African countries to deliver on their own part of the compact implied by UN-PAAERD will be frustrated by developments in the international environment. UN-PAAERD could end in disappointed hopes for Africa.

NOTES

1. France, Federal Republic of Germany, Italy, Japan, United Kingdom and United States.
2. Sometimes referred to as the import purchasing power of non-oil primary commodities, i.e. commodity prices in relation to prices of manufactured goods in international trade.
3. Because of the size of the Nigerian economy and the dominance of oil exports, discussions of sub-Saharan Africa in this section excluded Nigeria which is discussed in brief below.
4. See also 'West Africa: Kaunda's May Day Call': *West Africa Magazine*, London, 25 May 1987, p.1006.

5. UNCTAD: TD/273 June 1983.
6. Algeria, Angola, Congo, Gabon, Nigeria, the Libyan Arab Jamahiriya, Tunisia, Egypt.
7. UNCTAD: Commodity Survey 1986 (TD/B/C.1/284) of 14 November 1986.
8. Except East Asia which recorded surpluses.
9. See Maurice J. Williams: 'Should IMF Withdraw From Africa?' in *Policy Focus*, 1987, No.1, Overseas Development Council, Washington D.C., March 1987.
10. These countries are: Zambia, Madagascar, Liberia, the Sudan, Sierra Leone, Mauritania, Uganda, Ethiopia, Tanzania, Zimbabwe, Cote d'Ivoire: Maurice J. Williams, *op. cit.*
11. Excluding Egypt.
12. See Carol Lancaster, 'Foreign Aid: Annual Budget Battle Resumes' in *Policy Focus*, 1987, No.3, Overseas Development Council, Washington D.C., April 1987.
13. Denmark, Norway, Sweden.
14. Belgium, France, Canada, Australia, Federal Republic of Germany, Finland, Austria, United Kingdom.
15. Italy, Switzerland, Japan, New Zealand, Ireland, United States.

CHAPTER SEVEN

Financing of the Implementation of UN-PAAERD

SAYRE P. SCHATZ

In addressing the need for improvement in African economic performance, it is well to recognize that the record has not been one of continuous crisis. For sub-Saharan Africa, the period from 1950 to 1977 was a long phase of modest economic growth and development. Though less than satisfactory, economic performance could not be called poor. The simple average growth rate was 4.1 per cent per annum over the span of years, and real income per capita steadily increased.

The crisis in African development started about 1977, when economic growth fell off sharply from the previous 4.1 per cent for sub-Saharan Africa to 1.8 per cent for the 1977–1984 period. This has been a period of falling real income per capita.[1]

The crisis phase arose from external factors – more precisely, from the impact of external forces upon economies that had for some time been functioning in a less than satisfactory manner.[2] There were no continent-wide changes in domestic factors that could account for the sudden drop in African growth rates. Moreover, the drop-off in developing country economic performance was worldwide. The average real GDP growth rate for all developing countries fell from 6.2 per cent (1968–1977) to 3.2 per cent (1978–1984).[3] Unfavourable external development – curtailment of export volumes when more developed country income slowed its growth and then declined, terms of trade deterioration as world markets softened, huge increases in real interest rates, reductions in the availability of foreign credit, sudden cuts, especially for Africa, in ODA, etc. – harmed all less developed countries, particularly the least developed, and, for Africa, converted lacklustre economic performance into crisis.

Thus, the immediate task for Africa to return to a more satisfactory development performance requires improvements in the external spheres. This chapter deals with the fundamental issues relating to financing.

NO CORRECT FIGURES

The attached Tables provide considerable financial data on the financing of African development efforts, but the first point to make is that there is no such thing as a correct set of figures regarding external resource requirements. Even profound analysis and unlimited data cannot yield amounts that are 'correct' or 'necessary' or 'sufficient'. By the nature of the issue, this is impossible. The very concept of a correct set of figures is fallacious.

The concept implies discontinuity. Rather than a continuum of uses for funds, it implies that deviations from the correct amounts would generate discontinuous effects. Reductions would cause the sacrifice of substantial benefits, while increases would bring little additional benefits. The implausibility of the concept can best be demonstrated graphically.

In figure 7.1(a), the 'correct' set of external resource inflows is represented by point B. Reducing inflows below the correct amount B causes the loss of high marginal benefits, shown by the curve segment AB. But increasing resources would provide little additional benefit, shown by the curve segment CD (segment BE would represent additional benefits in a less severe statement of the correct-amount concept). This is unrealistic. A more reasonable representation of reality is shown by the continuous curve in figure 7.1(b). The downward slope signifies a gradually diminishing marginal productivity of resource inflows. There is no kink or sharp discontinuity; within the range of realistically possible external resource inflows, increases in resources will normally facilitate increases in production and vice versa.

Thus, the 'correctness' of any set of figures is a minor issue. Questions about the accuracy of the numbers do not constitute a valid reason for withholding aid or a commitment to aid.[4] Even the highest external resource inflows that can realistically be hoped for will leave appalling poverty. It is erroneous and harmful to think that there is a correct amount that will be adequate.

All of this is related to the notion, developed some three decades ago, that poor countries have only a limited absorptive capacity for capital. Like the earlier concept of the backward-sloping supply curve of labour, it has some plausibility. Some theoretical level of wages would be high enough to cause the labour supply curve to bend backwards; similarly some theoretical level of external resource inflows would be high enough to cause a negative (or a sharp drop in) marginal productivity of capital. However, in the general neighbour-

FIGURE 7.1
EXTERNAL RESOURCE INFLOWS: RELATION BETWEEN AMOUNT
AND MARGINAL EFFICIENCY

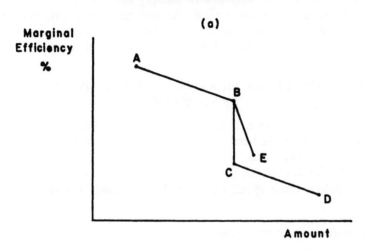

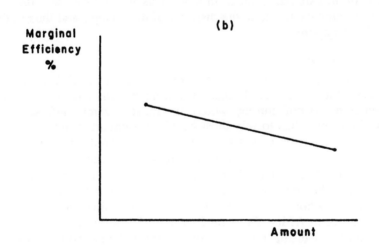

hood of wages actually available, the labour supply curve did not generally bend backwards. And in the general neighbourhood of external resources available, there is no evidence to support the hypothesis of an extremely low or sharply discontinuous drop in the marginal productivity of capital. As the backward-bending-supply notion provided a rationale for low wages, the limited-absorptive-capacity notion provides a rationale for low external resource inflows.

NEED FOR FOREIGN FINANCING: THE MULTIPLIED COSTS OF STRINGENCY

That Africa needs external resource inflows is generally recognized. The point to be made here is that shortfalls in such inflows generate costs much greater than the shortfalls themselves. For purposes of exposition, let us consider the effects of reductions in external resource inflows below some specified level. There would be three layers of costs.

Direct reduction in real income

The real income available to the country would be directly cut by the reduction in external resource inflows. This would take the form of a cut in foreign exchange at the disposal of the country and thus in the supply of imports.

Secondary reductions

The fall in imports of raw materials, intermediate goods and spare parts for domestic firms would cause a secondary reduction in domestic production. Manufacturing would be most severely affected, for manufacturing tends to rely most heavily on imported inputs, but all kinds of enterprises would be affected. There would also be a substantial impact on agriculture if imports of fertilizers, pesticides and other agricultural inputs were curtailed. Government effectiveness would also be impaired. Consider some of the ways that difficult external conditions, since the later 1970s, have affected government performance in Africa. Governmental energies were diverted to crisis containment, causing more routine though not unimportant government activities to suffer. Inability to achieve desired results harmed government morale, with the result that 'individual and institutional managerial capacities [were] eroded'. Simple lack of revenues sometimes crippled government operations when there was the capacity to do better. In agriculture, for example, 'extension services in several countries cannot sensibly advise use of fertilizer, insecticides, implements or improved seed because none of these is available'. Competent personnel, particularly in health and education, were immobilized because 'lack of adequate government revenue or import capacity means that drugs, textbooks, kerosene for fridges, desks and chairs, paper and pencils, beds and medical equipment, vehicles and fuel cannot be provided in adequate quantities for the personnel to function properly...'.[5]

Tertiary reductions

The import curtailment necessitated by foreign exchange stringency does not occur automatically. The requisite policies cause a tertiary reduction in real income. Import reductions could be achieved by tightening fiscal and monetary policies, with or without devaluation, or by adopting or tightening trade and exchange controls. The former alternative works by curtailing national income enough to cut imports to the level of funds available. This might well involve a severe domestic recession.[6] The control alternative would also entail tertiary costs. Even if administered perfectly, there are both allocational and administrative costs. A country's capital stock is doubly impaired; first, by the low rate of investment associated with low income (and investment rates in Africa are now lower than in any other region of the third world);[7] and, second, by reductions in resources devoted to maintenance, repair and rehabilitation of existing capital stock. The political effects can also be severe.[8]

EXTERNAL RESOURCE REQUIREMENTS

This chapter deals with only two issues drawn directly from the financial data presented in the Tables: the magnitude of the external resource requirements and the degree of dependence upon such resources. In this section, we estimate the total external resource inflows called for by the ECA and OAU. We begin our calculation with the resource requirements of APPER, which are shown (on a country-by-country basis) in Table 7.1 and (in more aggregated form) in Tables 7.2 and 7.3. Amounts are for the entire five-year period 1986–1990.

Total external resource inflows required for APPER amount to $US45.8 billion. The largest share, about 65 per cent, is needed by the 29 lower-income sub-Saharan African countries designated as eligible for IDA assistance. The mid-income sub-Saharan African countries call for approximately 22 per cent, while North Africa requires about 11 per cent of the total.

APPER requirements, however, constitute only a portion of Africa's

TABLE 7.1
RESOURCES FOR APPER, 1986–1990 BY INDIVIDUAL COUNTRIES
($US millions, for the five-year period)

	Resources already mobilised			Resources planned to be mobilised			Total of likely available resources	Total Cost of program	Resource gap
	Domestic (1)	External (2)	Subtotal (3)	Domestic (4)	External (5)	Subtotal (6)	(7)	(8)	(9)
BENIN	0.0	0.0	0.0	265.4	0.0	265.4	265.4	924.3	658.9
BURKINA FASO	0.0	242.8	242.8	0.0	197.9	197.9	440.7	839.1	398.4
BURUNDI	0.0	440.5	440.5	0.0	143.7	143.7	584.2	912.4	328.2
CENTRAFRICAN REPUB.	71.2	328.5	399.7	0.0	0.0	0.0	399.7	675.2	275.5
CHAD	0.0	0.0	0.0	0.0	0.0	0.0	0.0	392.9	392.9
ETHIOPIA	0.0	0.0	0.0	2,897.9	0.0	2,897.9	2,897.9	4,880.6	1,982.7
GAMBIA	7.8	15.2	23.0	0.0	0.0	0.0	23.0	157.4	134.4
GHANA	0.0	517.0	517.0	946.0	2,712.0	3,658.0	4,175.0	4,724.0	549.0
GUINEA	102.0	0.0	102.0	0.0	0.0	0.0	102.0	840	738.0
GUINEA BISSAU	21.6	44.2	65.8	0.0	0.0	0.0	65.8	160.4	94.6
KENYA	91.0	73.0	164.0	375.0	417.0	792.0	956.0	1,197.0	241.0
LESOTHO	0.0	0.0	0.0	26.7	31.7	58.4	58.4	119.6	61.2
LIBERIA	0.0	0.0	0.0	14.0	0.0	14.0	14.0	374.0	360.0
MADAGASCAR	46.3	67.3	113.6	76.0	97.1	173.1	287.7	872.0	584.3
MALAWI	0.0	0.0	0.0	83.4	255.7	339.1	339.1	849.9	510.8
MALI	59.4	17.7	77.1	0.0	290.7	290.7	367.8	539.1	171.3
MAURITANIA	49.0	0.0	49.0	0.0	809.0	809.0	858.0	1,221.0	363.0
MOZAMBIQUE	95.0	500.0	595.0	600.0	0.0	600.0	1,195.0	2,595.0	1,400.0
NIGER	31.1	482.2	513.3	0.0	0.0	0.0	513.3	1,204.6	691.3
RWANDA	0.0	0.0	0.0	239.9	723.6	963.5	963.5	1,251.2	287.7
SENEGAL	68.3	449.0	517.3	0.0	0.0	0.0	517.3	777.3	260.0
SIERRA LEONE	42.0	0.0	42.0	0.0	0.0	0.0	42.0	219.1	177.1
SOMALIA	0.0	0.0	0.0	147.0	675.3	822.3	822.3	1,458.6	636.3
SUDAN	0.0	0.0	0.0	1,252.0	911.0	2,163.0	2,163.0	2,913.0	750.0
TOGO	123.5	186.6	310.1	0.0	0.0	0.0	310.1	1,001.9	691.8
UGANDA	0.0	0.0	0.0	77.4	1,087.0	1,164.4	1,164.4	2,500.1	1,335.7
TANZANIA	823.0	148.0	971.0	3,484.0	664.0	4,148.0	5,119.0	5,832.0	713.0
ZAIRE	1,095.0	0.0	1,095.0	1,951.9	1,415.0	3,366.9	4,461.9	5,220.0	759.0
ZAMBIA	0.0	0.0	0.0	105.9	0.0	105.9	105.9	557.3	451.4
Totals, IDA-Eligible	2,726.2	3,512.0	6,238.2	12,436.6	10,430.7	22,867.3	29,106.5	44,652.6	15,546.1

182

TABLE 7.1 (continued)

	NA	NA	NA	NA	NA	NA	NA	NAL	NAL
ANGOLA	4.2	0.0	4.2	0.0	45.9	45.9	50.1	142.2	92.1
BOTSWANA	0.0	0.0	0.0	0.0	289.0	0.0	0.0	3,619.0	310.0
CAMEROON	0.0	64.7	0.0	3,020.0	0.0	3,309.0	3,309.0	1,317.1	0.0
CONGO	0.0	64.7	64.7	0.0	0.0	0.0	64.7	1,381.5	1,252.4
COTE D'IVOIRE	0.0	0.0	0.0	331.6	0.0	331.6	331.6	1,784.2	1,049.9
GABON	1,324.3	0.0	1,324.3	0.0	0.0	0.0	1,324.3	99.0	459.9
MAURITIUS	2.6	12.8	15.4	52.1	10.3	62.4	77.8	0.0	21.2
NIGERIA	8,724.0	596.0	9,320.0	0.0	1,117.0	1,117.0	10,437.0	12,437.0	2,000.0
SWAZILAND	0.7	0.2	0.9	0.2	0.2	0.4	1.3	3.2	1.9
ZIMBABWE	1,246.9	0.0	1,246.9	1,424.4	1,782.5	3,206.9	4,453.8	5,601.9	1,148.1
Totals, Mid-Income	11,302.7	673.7	11,976.4	4,828.3	3,244.9	8,073.2	20,049.6	26,385.1	6,335.5
Totals, S.S.A.	14,028.9	4,185.7	18,214.6	17,264.9	13,675.6	30,940.5	49,156.1	71,037.7	21,881.6
ALGERIA	5,520.0	0.0	5,520.0	22,080.0	0.0	22,080.0	27,600.0	27,600.0	0.0
EGYPT	2,871.0	700.0	3,571.0	14,335.0	0.0	14,335.0	17,906.0	21,467.0	3,561.0
LIBYA	1,097.8	0.0	1,097.8	4,406.5	0.0	4,406.5	5,504.3	5,504.3	0.0
TUNISIA	122.8	30.4	153.2	491.4	121.8	613.2	766.4	1,375.1	608.7
Totals, North Africa	9,611.6	730.4	10,342.0	41,312.9	121.8	41,434.7	51,776.7	55,946.4	4,169.7

TABLE 7.2

APPER RESOURCE REQUIREMENTS AND SOURCES, 1986–1990

($US billions, for the five-year period)

	Resources Required	Resources Already mobilised			Resources planned			Total resources planned and mobilized (13+16)	Resource gap (10-17)	Resource gap as % of resources required (18/10)x100
		Domestic	External	Total	Domestic	External	Total			
	(10)	(11)	(12)	(13)	(14)	(15)	(16)	(17)	(18)	(19)
IDA ELIGIBLE (29 countries)	44.7	2.7	3.5	6.3	12.4	10.4	22.8	29.1	15.5	35.0%
MID-INCOME SSA except Nigeria (9 countries)	13.9	2.7	0.1	2.6	4.8	2.1	7.1	9.6	4.3	31.0
NIGERIA	12.4	8.7	0.6	9.3	0.0	1.1	1.1	10.4	2.0	16.0
MID-INCOME SSA	26.3	11.3	0.7	11.9	4.8	3.2	8.1	20.0	6.3	24.0
SSA (39 countries)	71.0	14.0	4.2	18.2	17.3	13.7	30.9	49.1	21.9	31.0
OTHER SMALL COUNTRIES	1.1	0.1	0.1	0.2				0.2	0.9	78.0
NORTH AFRICA	55.9	9.6	0.7	10.3	41.3	0.1	41.4	51.8	4.2	8.0
TOTAL, AFRICA	128.1	23.7	5.1	28.8	58.6	13.8	72.4	101.2	26.9	21.0%

TABLE 7.3
APPER DOMESTIC AND EXTERNAL RESOURCES, 1986–1990
($US billions for the five-year period)

	Domestic resources planned or mobilised (11+14) (20)	External Resources			External Resources as % of resources required (23/10x100) (24)
		planned or mobilised (12+15) (21)	Resource gap (18) (22)	Total (21+22) (23)	
IDA ELIGIBLE (29 countries)	15.2	13.9	15.5	29.5 (64.4%)	66.0%
MID-INCOME SSA (except Nigeria)	7.4	2.2	4.3	6.5 (14.3%)	46.9
NIGERIA	8.7	1.7	2.0	3.7 (8.1%)	29.9
MID-INCOME SSA	16.1	3.9	6.3	10.2 (22.4%)	39.0
SSA (39 countries)	31.3	17.9	21.9	39.7 (86.8%)	55.9
OTHER SMALL COUNTRIES	0.1	0.2	0.9	1.0 (2.3%)	94.2
NORTH AFRICA	50.1	0.9	4.2	5.0 (11.0%)	9.0
TOTAL, AFRICA	82.3	18.9	26.9	45.8	35.8%

external resource requirements. Another major financial need arises from the continent's large debt-servicing obligations (Tables 7.4 and 7.5). Scheduled payments (interest and amortization of principal) amount to $US71.9 billion, $US35.6 billion to official creditors and $US36.3 billion to private creditors. Obligations of the lower income sub-Saharan African countries constitute $US20.1 billion of this total, of the mid-income Sub-Saharan African countries $US25.6 billion, and of North Africa $US26.0 billion. Scheduled debt service thus exceeds considerably (by 57 per cent) the total of all external resources requested for APPER.

The magnitude of the debt-service obligations necessitates some form of debt relief, such as rescheduling to stretch out payments, interest-rate reductions, debt write-offs, conversion of debt into equity holdings, etc. Table 7.6 presents rough working-hypothesis estimates. Relief needs on official debt are estimated at $US45 billion. On obligations to private creditors, the rough estimate of debt-relief that might be made available is $US10 billion. The same Table presents a rough regional breakdown of the totals. Debt-relief estimates at $US55 billion are naturally smaller than debt-servicing obligations, but, even so, they are larger than the $US45.8 billion APPER request.

There is a third major need for external resource inflows for non-APPER imports. The APPER request is for external resources to 'cover the import content of the priority programmes'. These are for 'specific assistance to the implementation of APPER', and do not include imports needed for other purposes.[9] Here, we refer to that portion of other imports which lie beyond the countries' ability to pay; these are non-APPER imports requiring external financing.

Calculation of non-APPER imports requires some specification of the total volume of imports needed. This has been provided by the already cited World Bank study, which specified that 'at a minimum, imports per capita should return to their level of 1980–1982' for all countries except Nigeria, for which a level substantially below that of 1980–1982 is assumed.[10] Such a level of imports is considered necessary to enable Africa 'to continue its progress towards economic development'; these imports are needed 'to halt the trend of decline in per capita consumption by 1990 and achieve some growth thereafter. This minimum objective would require a GDP growth rate of at least 3–4 per cent a year by 1990'.[11]

The external resource requirements for non-APPER imports have been calculated in Table 7.8. World Bank calculations were used to estimate the total foreign exchange gap, i.e., the total external resource requirement. From this we subtracted the external resources needed

TABLE 7.4

DEBT SERVICING REQUIREMENTS, 1986–1990, INDIVIDUAL COUNTRIES
($US millions for the five-year period)

	Official creditors			Private creditors			Total		
	Interest (25)	Principal (26)	Subtotal (27)	Interest (28)	Principal (29)	Subtotal (30)	Interest (31)	Principal (32)	Total (33)
BENIN	39.9	94.8	134.7	43.8	198.9	242.7	83.7	293.7	377.4
BURKINA FASO	47.3	115.7	163.0	3.5	17.6	21.1	50.8	133.3	184.1
BURUNDI	66.8	97.5	164.3	3.6	23.8	27.4	70.4	121.3	191.7
CENTRAFRICAN REPUBLIC	29.8	70.2	100.0	4.1	13.0	17.1	33.8	83.3	117.1
CHAD	6.3	16.5	22.8	0.0	0.4	0.4	6.3	16.9	23.2
ETHIOPIA	124.5	356.3	480.8	48.3	115.8	164.1	172.7	472.2	644.9
GAMBIA	15.4	42.4	57.8	7.2	20.7	27.9	22.6	63.1	85.7
GHANA	122.7	307.8	430.5	12.4	43.5	55.9	135.1	351.3	486.4
GUINEA	94.3	494.6	588.9	10.9	64.6	75.5	105.2	559.2	664.4
GUINEA BISSAU	12.4	46.0	58.4	0.9	8.7	9.6	13.3	54.7	68.0
KENYA	552.7	709.2	1,261.9	119.7	374.2	493.9	672.4	1,083.4	1,755.8
LESOTHO	16.1	30.0	46.1	0.6	3.3	3.9	16.7	33.3	50.0
LIBERIA	133.3	229.9	363.2	30.7	143.2	173.9	164.0	373.1	537.1
MADAGASCAR	221.7	544.8	766.5	83.3	273.9	357.2	305.0	818.7	1,123.7
MALAWI	90.4	122.4	212.8	19.6	87.6	107.2	110.0	210.0	320.0
MALI	74.5	340.3	414.8	7.2	18.5	25.7	81.7	358.8	440.5
MAURITANIA	132.8	527.0	659.8	21.0	69.7	90.7	153.8	596.7	750.5
MOZAMBIQUE	273.0	1,326.0	1,599.0	0.0	0.0	0.0	273.0	1,326.0	1,599.0
NIGER	100.9	171.8	272.7	40.2	140.0	180.2	141.1	311.8	452.9
RWANDA	20.3	54.1	74.4	0.0	0.0	0.0	20.3	54.1	74.4
SENEGAL	271.0	487.8	758.8	82.3	233.5	315.8	353.3	721.3	1,074.6
SIERRA LEONE	25.0	83.8	108.8	10.1	36.8	46.9	35.1	120.6	155.7
SOMALIA	96.2	452.0	548.2	9.5	26.0	35.5	105.7	478.0	583.7
SUDAN	847.6	1,459.5	2,307.1	192.5	756.8	958.3	1,040.1	2,265.3	3,305.4
TOGO	108.4	243.0	351.4	18.4	76.2	94.6	126.8	319.2	446.0
UGANDA	81.1	248.0	365.1	9.0	46.9	55.9	91.1	330.9	422.0
TANZANIA	229.5	714.4	943.9	53.3	208.2	261.5	282.8	922.6	1,205.4
ZAIRE	914.9	1,378.3	2,293.2	128.5	546.7	675.2	1,043.4	1,925.0	2,968.4
ZAMBIA	444.6	808.2	1,252.8	104.6	406.1	510.7	549.2	1,214.3	1,763.5
Totals, IDA Eligible	4,748.8	10,840.1	15,588.9	960.6	3,557.5	4,518.1	5,710.2	14,397.8	20,108.0

(continued overleaf)

187

TABLE 7.4 (continued)

ANGOLA	520.0	1,275.0	1,795.0	0.0	0.0	0.0	520.0	1,275.0	1,795.0
BOTSWANA	112.5	140.8	253.3	14.0	10.9	24.9	126.5	151.7	278.2
CAMEROON	346.2	574.4	938.6	60.6	262.1	322.7	424.7	836.6	1,261.3
CONGO	144.8	348.9	493.7	139.2	603.0	742.2	284.0	951.9	1,235.9
COTE D'IVOIRE	808.4	997.9	1,806.3	783.5	2,114.3	2,897.8	1,591.9	3,112.1	4,704.1
GABON	71.1	139.1	210.2	147.9	411.4	559.3	219.0	550.5	769.5
MAURITIUS	90.7	150.6	241.3	13.3	46.4	59.7	101.0	197.0	298.0
NIGERIA	904.4	1,276.4	2,180.8	2,207.3	9,316.7	11,524.0	3,111.7	10,593.1	13,704.8
SWAZILAND	47.9	62.7	110.6	1.7	7.9	9.6	49.6	70.6	120.2
ZIMBABWE	263.1	201.0	464.1	222.6	720.3	942.9	485.7	921.3	1,407.0
Totals, Mid-Income	3,327.1	5,166.8	8,493.9	3,590.1	13,493.0	17,083.1	6,914.1	18,659.9	25,574.0
Totals, S.S.A.	8,075.9	16,006.9	24,082.8	4,550.7	17,050.5	21,601.2	12,624.3	33,057.7	45,682.0
ALGERIA	762.8	2,363.1	3,125.9	2,083.9	8,435.6	10,519.5	2,846.7	10,798.7	13,645.4
EGYPT	2,266.4	3,537.7	5,804.1	627.2	2,494.0	3,121.2	2,893.6	6,031.7	8,925.3
LIBYA	0.0	0.0	0.0	0.0	0.0	0.0	0.0	0.0	0.0
TUNISIA	792.8	1,581.6	2,374.4	248.2	766.8	1,051.0	1,077.0	2,348.4	3,425.4
Totals, North Africa	3,822.0	7,482.4	11,304.4	2,995.3	11,696.4	14,691.7	6,817.3	19,178.8	25,996.1
TOTALS, AFRICA	12,673.6	24,692.6	37,366.2	7,721.0	28,080.0	35,801.0	20,394.6	52,772.6	73,167.2

188

TABLE 7.5

DEBT SERVICING REQUIREMENTS, 1986–1990

($US billions for the five-year period)

	Official creditors			Private creditors			Total		
	Interest (34)	Principal (35)	Subtotal (36)	Interest (37)	Principal (38)	Subtotal (39)	Interest (40)	Principal (41)	Total (42)
IDA ELIGIBLE (29 countries)	4.7	10.8	15.6	1.0	3.6	4.5	5.7	14.4	20.1
MID-INCOME SSA except Nigeria (9 countries)	2.4	3.9	6.3	1.4	4.2	5.6	3.8	8.1	11.9
NIGERIA	0.9	1.3	2.2	2.2	9.3	11.5	3.1	10.6	13.7
MID-INCOME SSA	3.3	5.2	8.5	3.6	13.5	17.1	6.9	18.7	25.6
SSA (39 countries)	8.1	16.0	24.0	4.5	17.0	21.6	12.6	33.1	45.7
OTHER SMALL COUNTRIES	0.1	0.2	0.2				0.6	0.2	0.2
NORTH AFRICA	3.8	7.5	11.3	3.0	11.7	14.7	6.8	19.2	26.0
TOTAL, AFRICA	12.0	23.6	35.6	7.6	28.8	36.3	19.5	52.4	72.0

TABLE 7.6
ESTIMATED DEBT RELIEF REQUIREMENTS, 1986–1990
($US billions, for the five-year period)

	Official debt relief (43)	Private debt relief (44)	Total debt relief (45)
IDA ELIGIBLE (29 countries)	15.7	3.5	19.2
MID-INCOME SSA except Nigeria (9 countries)	4.9	1.1	6.0
NIGERIA	4.4	1.0	5.3
MID-INCOME SSA	9.3	2.1	11.3
SSA (39 countries)	25.0	5.5	30.5
OTHER SMALL COUNTRIES	0.4	0.1	0.5
NORTH AFRICA	19.6	4.4	24.0
TOTAL, AFRICA	45.0	10.0	55.0

for APPER and for debt-relief. What remains is the external resource requirement for non-APPER imports.[12]

None of the non-APPER-import figures can be considered as more than working-hypothesis estimates, but the most reliable of these, given the nature of the World Bank study, are for sub-Saharan Africa. For the 29 poorer countries, external resource requirements for non-APPER imports are $US27.9 billion (almost the same amount as for APPER); for the 10 mid-income countries, $US23.4 billion (considerably greater than APPER needs); for sub-Saharan Africa as a whole, non-APPER-import needs at $US51.3 billion considerably exceed the APPER requests of $US39.7 billion as well as debt-relief requests of $US30.5 billion. The estimates of non-APPER imports for Africa as a whole, which are even rougher than those for sub-Saharan Africa, amount to $US92.4 billion. This is almost equal to the combined continent-wide external resource requirements for APPER ($US45.8 billion) plus debt relief ($US55 billion).

TABLE 7.7

FOREIGN EXCHANGE NEEDED AND EARNED, 1986–1990
WORLD BANK ESTIMATES AND AUTHOR'S PROJECTIONS
($US billions, per annum)

	Foreign Exchange Needed					Foreign Exchange Earned (Exports)	ERR Needed (50–51)
		Scheduled debt servicing			Total		
	Imports	Interest	Amortization	Total	Total		
	(46)	(47)	(48)	(49)	(50)	(51)	(52)
IDA ELIGIBLE (29 countries)	142.5	15.0	19.0	34.0	177.5	100.0	77.5
MID INCOME SSA except Nigeria (9 countries)	95.0						
NIGERIA	62.5						
MID INCOME SSA	157.5			32.5	190.0	145.0	45.0
SSA (39 countries)	300.0			66.5	367.5	245.0	121.5
OTHER SMALL COUNTRIES							
NORTH AFRICA							
TOTAL, AFRICA							

TABLE 7.8

ESTIMATE OF NON-APPER IMPORTS, 1988–1990

($US billions per annum)

	ERR – OAU Basis			ERR Needed WB Basis (52) (56)	Non-APPER Imports (56–55) (57)
	For APPER (23) (53)	For debt relief (45) (54)	Total (53–54) (55)		
IDA ELIGIBLE (29 countries)	29.5	19.0	48.7	76.5	27.9
NON INCOME SSA except Nigeria (9 countries)	6.5	6.0	12.5		
NIGERIA	3.7	5.3	9.0		
MID INCOME SSA	10.2	11.3	21.5	45.0	23.4
SSA (39 countries)	39.7	30.5	70.2	121.5	51.3
OTHER SMALL COUNTRIES	1.0	0.5	1.5		0.8
NORTH AFRICA	5.0	24.0	29.0		40.4
TOTAL, AFRICA	45.8	55.0	100.8		92.4

Thus, total external resource requirements far exceed those for APPER. They are, respectively, for the 29 IDA-eligible countries of sub-Saharan Africa, $US76.6 billion and $US29.5 billion; for the mid-income countries, $US45.0 billion and $US10.3 billion; and, for all of sub-Saharan Africa, $US121.5 billion and $US39.7 billion. The figures for all Africa, which are the least reliable, show total external resource requirements ($US193.2 billion) which are more than four times the magnitude of APPER requirements of $US45.8 billion.[13]

RELATIVE ROLE OF EXTERNAL AND DOMESTIC RESOURCES

Here we seek a measure of the degree to which Africa's desire for economic recovery and accelerated development is dependent upon external resource inflows. Since APPER resource requirements (external plus internal) constitute only a portion of overall resource requirements, we have to go beyond APPER. We consider instead two broader ways of measuring the degree of African dependence upon external sources during the 1986–1990 period.

Comparing external resource requirements to total foreign exchange requirements, including those that will be earned from African exports of goods and services, provides one index of external dependence.

Relevant though limited information is provided by Table 7.8 which is based upon World Bank data and estimates for sub-Saharan Africa. Total foreign exchange needs, including debt-servicing obligations, are estimated by the World Bank study as follows: $US177.5 billion for the IDA-eligible countries, $US190 billion for the mid-income countries and thus $US367.5 billion for sub-Saharan Africa. Of these totals, it is estimated that foreign exchange earned will be $US100 billion for the poorer countries, $US145 billion for the mid-income countries and thus $US245 billion for sub-Saharan Africa. This leaves necessary external resource inflows of $US77.5 billion, $US45 billion and $US121.5 billion respectively. The data necessary for making similar estimates for North Africa are unfortunately not presently available.

Thus, the foreign-provided share of Africa's total foreign exchange needs for 1986–1990 is substantial: 43.7 per cent for the low-income countries of sub-Saharan Africa, 23.7 per cent for the mid-income countries and 33.1 per cent for sub-Saharan Africa altogether. But it can be argued that this tends to overstate the degree of African dependence upon external assistance and that a broader measure provides a better gauge.

Overall Dependence

We turn to a comparison of external resource requirements to the total resources required for the functioning and development of the African economies, i.e. to the total resources to be used for the interrelated purposes of private consumption, private investment and government activities. Stated simply, we compare external resource requirements to GDP.

Table 7.9 relates external resource requirements, 1986–1990, to GDP in 1984. Unadjusted (and therefore overstated) figures for sub-Saharan Africa show that 14.3 per cent of GDP would be provided externally, while 85.7 per cent would be provided domestically. The corresponding proportions for the low-income countries would be 24.7 and 75.3 per cent, while for mid-income countries they would be 8.3 and 91.7 per cent.

Two adjustments are required however; one for price-level changes in the donor countries, as the raw figures compare external resource inflows at later (1986–1990) prices to African GDPs at earlier (1984) prices, and the other for growth adjustment, as external resource inflows are properly compared to concurrent rather than the smaller 1984 GDPs. These double adjustments are made in column 64 of Table 7.9, albeit conservatively, on the assumption that donor country price levels rise at an annual 4 per cent rate and that African aggregate GDPs continue to grow at the low 1.8 per cent rate averaged over the 1977–1984 period.

The importance of domestic resources is clear; for sub-Saharan Africa as a whole, 88.4 per cent of the total resource requirement is to be provided domestically (77.9 per cent for the low-income countries and 93.3 per cent for the mid-income countries), for North Africa, the domestic portion is 91.1 per cent, and for all of Africa, it is 89.5 per cent. It should also be well noted that the external resource figures are requests; actual external resource inflows will almost surely be smaller, and, therefore, domestic resource provision will be greater than what these figures indicate.

While external resource requirements are substantial, the great bulk of the resources needed for the functioning and development of the African economies, even for the most indigent and dependent countries, is to be provided domestically. 'The bulk of Africa's development inevitably will be paid for by Africans through improved productivity and through the development of their own resources'.[14]

TABLE 7.9

TOTAL EXTERNAL RESOURCE INFLOWS REQUESTED BY OAU, 1986–1990
($US billions, for the five-year period)

	APPER (23) (58)	Debt Relief (45) (59)	Non-APPER Imports (57) (60)	Total (23+45+47) (61)	GDP-1984 (62)	Annual ERR as % of GDP Unliquidated (63)	Adjusted (64)
IDA ELIGIBLE (29 countries)	29.5	19.2	27.9	76.6	62.1	24.7%	20.1%
MID INCOME SSA except Nigeria (9 countries)	6.5	6.0		12.5	34.2	7.3	
NIGERIA				9.0	74.2	2.4	
MID INCOME SSA	10.2	11.3	23.4	44.9	108.4	8.3	6.7
SSA (39 countries)	39.7	30.5	51.3	121.5	170.5	14.3	11.6
OTHER SMALL	1.0	0.5	0.8	2.3	0.5	90.7	
NORTH AFRICA	5.0	24.0	40.4	69.4	127.6	10.9	8.9
TOTAL, AFRICA	45.7	55.0	92.4	193.2	298.6	12.9%	10.5%

THE QUALITY OF THE DATA

There are substantial limitations on the quality of the financial data. For one thing, the individual-country programmes that comprise APPER (which provides the core set of financial figures) are fractional. They constitute merely parts of broader implicit programmes of each country. All sorts of government activities that strongly influence economic performance are omitted from APPER; 'in many countries' the focus is primarily on government's directly productive activities. Also omitted is private investment; in APPER, 'emphasis is placed on public investment programmes'.[15]

Thus the amounts that will actually be devoted to APPER are not independent of sums for other purposes. Actual expenditures will be functionally related to funds available for debt relief, for non-APPER imports, and for other government activities besides those APPER comprises. Thus, APPER figures can only be interpreted as domestic and external revenues that would be allotted to the Priority Programmes if additional unspecified amounts were available for a number of other purposes.

Another limitation arises from the fact that APPER is a compilation of policies and programmes of 50 individual countries. These underlying individual-country plans are of varying quality, drawn up with varying degrees of care, and based on information of varying degrees of comprehensiveness and accuracy; they also represent varying degrees of governmental commitment. In some cases, their grounding in reality is open to question. They may merely represent wish lists, and estimates of expenditures and revenues may have been hastily constructed for the purpose of the APPER exercise. In sum, the overall APPER figures can be no more reliable than the estimates provided by the individual countries, each making its calculations in its own way, with widely differing degrees of care, competence, and available information.

A further limitation is that the APPER figures are not firm; not all the governments, it appears, are serious about the estimates that APPER comprises. Of course, no government will be bound by preliminary planning sums, but the APPER figures seem especially soft.

When we go beyond APPER, the roughness of the estimates becomes greater and more apparent. Debt-relief requirements on official debt were estimated by the ECA/OAU as somewhere between $US7 billion and $US11 billion, a very wide range, and no explanation was offered of the basis for the estimates, leaving the inference that it was a seat-of-the-pants hunch. With respect to non-APPER imports, the basis for the calculations (the return of imports per capita to differing specified levels) is arbitrary.

To recapitulate: (a) APPER programmes are fractional; (b) being a compilation of 50 individual country estimates, APPER can be no more solid than its components; (c) the degree of governmental commitment to the country programmes is uncertain; (d) the underlying country estimates are of varying degrees of reliability; and, (e) on external resource requirements beyond those for APPER, the estimates are even more unreliable.

AUTONOMY, IDEOLOGY AND DEVELOPMENT ORIENTATIONS

There is conflict between a desire for national autonomy and a need for foreign advice or assistance. Effective advice, even if completely pressure-free, influences decisions and, thus, in some sense impinges upon autonomy.

But impingements upon African autonomy in the present circumstances go beyond the persuasive effects of good advice. The potential providers of funds have made it abundantly clear that the flow of concessional finance depends upon the adoption by recipient countries of acceptable policy reform. Potential donor countries and international institutions have been quite explicit about this. Even if its effects are positive, such conditionality weakens autonomy.

Conditionality also involves the possibility that the resource providers will impose their own ideology. This is, in fact, occurring at present. It seems so evident to many resource providers in the North that what is needed in Africa is movement towards a laissez-faire economy that they see 'policy reform' as synonymous with such movement.

This, however, is an ideological rather than a social-scientific perception. While there may be information about the immediate causes of specific problems, proposals regarding the best way to deal with African problems are seldom supported by solid evidence. For example, assuming that some economies would benefit from a more active private sector, one might seek to promote this in either of two quite different ways: through a subsidence in government activism and a movement towards laissez-faire; or, through increased and reformed government activism directed towards nurturing private business. Conditionality might allow external ideology to affect such decisions regarding a country's economic development orientation, and this should be explicitly recognized.

Three principal development orientations vie for attention in Africa today: laissez-faireism, nurture capitalism and socialism.

Laissez-faireism states the belief that a retreat from government activism is the major means of improving the quality of a country's economic performance. It stresses the benefits of reliance on free markets, on the profit incentive and on the growth of the private sector. Free market pricing is crucial not only for products but also for inputs, including labour and foreign exchange. Exchange rates particularly should be allowed to approach their natural levels, for artificially overvalued exchange rates are especially damaging. Tariffs and other forms of protection should be cut back. The country should move towards a regime of free trade.[16]

Nurture capitalism constitutes an alternative development orientation within a capitalist framework. Like laissez-faireism, it relies on private enterprise to play an important role, and on price and profitability incentives. However, it states the belief that unmodified free-market price and profitability incentives are often insufficient or misleading, and that an African economy that relies on these alone will not generate sufficient development thrust. Instead, the state must often take an active role in advising, assisting, fostering and nurturing private enterprise that would not otherwise materialize or survive. While recognizing that ill-advised or corrupt government activities have often been harmful, the nurture capitalist believes that reformed government activism is both possible and necessary.[17]

Then there is the socialist alternative. There are difficulties in specifying just what socialism is. There is much disagreement and indecisiveness among the radicals about what countries, if any, are socialist and about many propositions concerning the characteristics of a socialist country.[18] There are also difficulties in evaluating the performance of developing countries that call themselves socialist. Nevertheless, socialism cannot simply be dismissed; it is one of the major competing orientations in the real world.

Differing development orientations are in contention. Whatever the circumstances regarding autonomy and external ideology, African judgments on the relative efficacy of these orientations must be made.

CONCLUSION

Conceptually, there can be no such thing as a correct set of figures on Africa's external resource requirements. Nevertheless, the costs of resource paucity are great; they amount to a multiple of any shortfall. External resource requirements extend beyond those called for by

APPER; they include also resources for debt relief and for non-APPER imports. Despite grave limitations in the quality of the data, it is clear that these combined needs far exceed the external resource inflows currently being made available. Thus, Africa is dependent on external resources, and this involves issues of autonomy, ideology and choice of development orientations. The dependence should not be exaggerated, however. By far the largest portion of the resources needed for the functioning and development of the African economies will be provided domestically.

NOTES ON TABLES

A. *Sources*

1. Source for Tables 7.1–7.5: OAU, Africa's Submission to the Special Session of the United Nations General Assembly on Africa's Economic and Social Crisis, Document OAU/ECM/2XV/Rev.2, 30–31 March 1986.
2. Source for Table 7.6: *ibid.*, and estimates by the author.
3. Source for Table 7.8: World Bank, financing adjustment with growth in sub-Saharan Africa, 1986–1990 (World Bank, Washington, D.C., 1986), and estimates by the author.
4. Source for Table 7.7: preceding tables.
5. Source for Table 7.9: OAU, *op.cit.*, and preceding tables.

B. *Other general notes*

1. IDA-eligible countries are the 29 poorest countries of sub-Saharan Africa; they are eligible for assistance from the International Development Association.
2. Tables 7.1 and 7.4 do not include the six small, mainly island economies: Cape Verde, Comoros, Djibouti, Equatorial Guinea, Sao Tome and Principe and Seychelles. These countries are included in some of the other tables under the heading 'other small countries'.
3. The OAU did not include data for Morocco. This affects the figures for North Africa in all of the tables.
4. Other abbreviations: ERI for external resources inflows; ERR for external resources required.

C. *Notes on specific Tables*

Table 7.6

1. Author's estimate of official debt relief (column 43) was made as follows: total official debt relief requested over the five-year period is $US35 billion to $US55 billion (Organization of African Unity, p.25). Author uses the midpoint, $US45 billion, as an approximation. He then made the rough assumption as a working hypothesis that the debt relief needed for each group of countries is proportional to the total estimated costs of each group's programmes.
2. Author's estimate of private debt relief (column 44) was made as follows: the ECA and OAU indicate that scheduled annual servicing of private debt will be between $US7 billion and $US11 billion and request debt relief. He makes a conservative and rough estimate that debt relief will be $US2 billion per annum. The breakdown among groups of countries is made on the same assumption as that used for column 43.

Table 7.7

1. Data in column 46 are for imports of goods and services excluding interest.
2. Import needs in column 46 are calculated by the World Bank on the assumption that it is necessary to restore per capita imports for all countries except Nigeria to the 1980–1982 level. For Nigeria, a level substantially below that of 1980–1982, closer to the levels of the late 1970s, is assumed. World Bank, *Ibid.*, p.42.
3. Scheduled debt-servicing figures (columns 47, 48 and 49) are amounts expected after rescheduling.

Table 7.8

1. Non-APPER imports consist of imports other than those needed for APPER which are needed to restore overall imports to the levels specified in Note 2, Table 7.7.
2. Non-APPER imports have been estimated as follows:
   (a) ECA and OAU estimates of external resource requirements, which do not include non-APPER imports, are presented in columns 53–55;
   (b) World Bank estimates of external resource requirement, which do include non-APPER imports, are presented for sub-Saharan Africa in column 56;
   (c) It is assumed that the difference between these two sets of data constitutes a rough estimate of non-APPER imports for sub-Saharan Africa and its two constituent groups, column 57;
   (d) For the other two rows in column 57, North Africa and 'other small countries', it is assumed that the ratio of their non-APPER imports to those of sub-Saharan Africa is the same as the ratio of the size of their APPER programmes to those of Sub-Saharan Africa.

Table 7.9

1. *Adjustments for column 64*
   It is assumed that donor-C price levels rise at an annual 4 per cent rate and that African aggregate GDPs continue to grow at the 1.8 per cent rate of the 1977–1984 period. Thus, column 63 figures are divided by 1.23.

NOTES

1. Source of data: World Bank, *World tables*, The Third Edition, Volume I – *Economic data* (Baltimore, Johns Hopkins University Press, 1983) and other World Bank sources. Faber and Green also see a more unfavourable phase starting in the late 1970s. Using UNCTAD data, they date the crisis stage from 1979. Mike Faber and Reginald H. Green, 'Sub-Saharan Africa's Economic Malaise: Some questions and answers', in Tore Rose (ed.), *Crisis and recovery in sub-Saharan Africa* (Paris, OECD, 1985). The first phase may have begun earlier than 1950; this was the first year for which World Bank data were available. The growth rate referred to here is the unweighted average annual increase in gross national product.
2. Sayre P. Schatz, 'External versus Internal Causation of the Crisis in African Development,' *Journal of Modern African Studies*, Vol.25, No.2, June 1987.
3. International Monetary Fund, *World Economic Outlook*, April 1986 (International Monetary Fund, Washington D.C., 1986).
4. Some donor countries have expressed misgiving because it is unclear how the African figures have been calculated. *New York Times*, 27 May 1986, p.A12.
5. Faber and Green, pp.18 and 19.
6. Thus, the World Bank has been pleading for 'substantially higher donor assistance'

to Africa in order to achieve 'adjustment with growth'. The World Bank, *Financing Adjustment with Growth in sub-Saharan Africa 1986–1990* (Washington, The World Bank, 1986), p.7.

7. *Ibid.*, p.35.
8. Sayre P. Schatz, 'Laissez-Faireism for Africa?' *Journal of Modern African Studies*, Volume 25, No.1, March 1987.
9. ECA/OAU, Africa's Submission to the Special Session of the United Nations General Assembly on Africa's Economic and Social Crisis (OAU/ECM/2XV/ Rev.2) (Addis Ababa, 1986), pp.68 and 69.
10. World Bank, *ibid.*, p.42.
11. *Ibid.*, p.2. The OAU also speaks of increasing imports to at least the 1980 level, *op.cit.*, pp.25–68.
12. For a fuller explanation see the 'Notes on the tables'.
13. The Overseas Development Council and the Council on Foreign Relations, both of the United States, have stated that Africa needs twice as much aid as it received in 1986, and that it will continue to need $US16 billion to $US20 billion in annual aid through the rest of this century. *New York Times, ibid.* See also 'Compact for African Development: Report of the Committee on African Development Strategies', in Robert J. Berg and Jennifer Seymour Whitaker (eds.), *Strategies for African Development* (Berkeley, University of California Press, 1986).
14. *Ibid.*, p.581.
15. ECA/OAU, pp.73 and 75.
16. For more on laissez-faireism and a critique, see Schatz, 'Laissez-Faireism for Africa?'.
17. For more on nurture capitalism, see Schatz, *Nigerian Capitalism* (Berkeley, University of California Press, 1977), pp.3–8 and ff., and Crawford Young, *Ideology and Development in Africa* (New Haven, Yale University Press, 1982), pp.189–190.
18. Keith Griffin and John Gurley, 'Radical Analyses of Imperialism, the Third World, and the Transition to Socialism: A Survey Article,' *Journal of Economic Literature*, XXIII, 3 Sept. 1985, p.1136.

CHAPTER EIGHT

Africa's Economic Recovery and Support from the International Community

THE WORLD BANK

INTRODUCTION

UN-PAAERD consists of two central elements:

(a) The commitment of the African countries to launch national and regional programmes of economic development as reflected in APPER, 1986–90;

(b) The response of the international community to support the African development efforts.

Under APPER, African Governments, individually and collectively, reaffirmed their primary responsibility for the economic and social development of their countries, identified areas for priority action and undertook to mobilize domestic resources for the achievement of these priorities. The priorities identified in APPER include: stimulating agricultural recovery and production, improving public sector management, addressing the human resources development and other long-term constraints to sustainable growth.

The international community fully supports these priorities and the broad policy orientation of APPER and the operational recommendations of UN-PAAERD adopted by the Special Session. Indeed, over the last few years, reports on sub-Saharan Africa prepared by the World Bank and endorsed by the World Bank/IMF Development Committee as well as other reports by the OAU, ECA and ADB have reached the same conclusions about the long-term nature of the African crisis and have made similar policy recommendations to African Governments and donors. Like APPER, an earlier ECA report of 1983[1] and the World Bank's Joint Programme of Action[2] of September 1984 emphasized the dual priority of vigorous medium-term adjustment policies and of comprehensive development strategies addressing the longer-term constraints to development, i.e. programmes to develop human resources and institutional capacity, introduce appropriate environmental policies, improve agricultural research and support technological progress. The Joint Programme of Action also focused attention on the on-going decline in overall resource flows and recommended concerted action by the donor community to increase financial support and to improve aid co-ordination for African programmes of adjustment and development. The same message was included in the 1986 World Bank report entitled *Financing Adjustment with Growth in sub-Saharan Africa, 1986–1990*. This report commended efforts made by African Governments to correct economic distortions, improve the incentive environment and implement comprehensive adjustment policies. The report urged the donor community to provide the additional concessional assistance needed to help restore the per capita import capacity of African countries to the 1980–1982 level and presented detailed estimates of external financing requirements for sub-Saharan countries for the period 1986–1990. These estimates were broadly comparable with those prepared by the OAU and ECA for the UN Special Session.[3]

UN-PAAERD called on the international community to undertake complementary action to support Africa's recovery and development efforts in two areas:

Improvements in the External Economic Environment – It recommended that many of the external factors which affect African economies need to be addressed and examined in the competent international forums. It spoke of the need for the international community to evolve and implement policies conducive to sustained, equitable and non-inflationary growth, including the expansion of trade through, *inter alia*, the elimination of protectionism, particularly non-tariff barriers, in accordance with existing commitments, the adoption of measures which encourage African exports and diversification programmes and improved market access, especially for tropical products, within the framework of the GATT.

Improvements in the Level, Quality, and Co-ordination of Aid – UN-PAAERD stressed the need for extensive international support for the priorities and policies that Africa has identified as necessary and on which many African countries have already embarked. African countries need assistance to enable them to achieve a speedier recovery and long-term development. It called for the international donor community to increase assistance to Africa and improve its quality and effectiveness.

This Chapter will discuss: (a) Improvements in aid co-ordination as a means for mobilizing more donor support and improving the efficiency of donor assistance programmes; and, (b) Improvements in world trade, particularly in agriculture, given its predominant role in African economies.

IMPROVING THE EFFECTIVENESS OF AID CO-ORDINATION AND DONOR ASSISTANCE PROGRAMMES

Recent Developments in sub-Saharan Africa

Since 1983–1984, a growing number of African countries have taken action to improve incentives for increasing agricultural production, devalue real effective exchange rates, rationalize the public sector, and implement other policies aimed at restoring growth. There are now 28 countries in Africa, accounting for about three-quarters of the Region's population and GDP, which have adjustment programmes underway or are about to launch such programmes. Yet, much remains to be done. In some countries, e.g. Cote d'Ivoire, Ghana, Senegal, Togo and Zaire, adjustment efforts have been underway for several years. The challenge for these countries and for the donor community is to support the deepening of adjustment programmes on a sustained basis. In other countries, for example, Chad, Central African Republic, the Gambia, Equatorial Guinea, Sierra Leone, and the United Republic of Tanzania, the adjustment process has barely begun and the initial momentum needs to be strengthened and supported. A major encouraging development has been the emergence of a far-reaching reform effort in Nigeria.

Donor Support

Multilateral and bilateral donors are supporting these programmes with increased commitments and accelerated disbursements. Firm data for concessional aid flows in 1985 shows a large increase over 1984; gross disbursements of grants and concessional loans to all sub-Saharan Africa appear to have risen by almost 17 per cent, although about half of the increase can be attributed to emergency food aid. Preliminary figures for 1986 suggest further increases in concessional flows. Countries implementing adjustment programmes are the main beneficiaries. For 22 IDA-eligible countries with adjustment programmes, total net concessional aid flows (excluding food aid, which probably declined) are tentatively estimated to have increased by $US800 million, or some 24 per cent over 1985 levels. The World Bank, through IDA and the Special Facility for Africa (SFA), increased disbursements by 80 per cent in 1986 over 1985 and is responsible for almost $US500 million of this increase. For all of sub-Saharan Africa, disbursements of IDA and SFA rose to $US1.4 billion in 1986, compared to $US0.9 billion in 1985 and to an annual average of only $US0.7 billion during 1982–1984. Policy-based, quick-disbursing operations now account for more than 50 per cent of World Bank-managed concessional assistance. The EEC, in the context of the Lome III Agreement, ADB and several major bilateral donors are also increasing the share of their aid programmes in support of policy reforms. Close to half of IDA-8 resources and a high proportion of the IMF's Structural Adjustment Facility will be allocated to sub-Saharan Africa.

Despite on-going and anticipated increases in multilateral and bilateral aid flows, current projections indicate that a large number of low-income sub-Saharan African countries will be unable to mobilize the overall resource flows necessary to maintain adequate import levels and achieve even a modest growth in per capita income and consumption levels. Recent World Bank estimates indicate that an additional annual average of $US700 million over and above foreseen aid flows would be required to prevent per capita consumption from declining in 1987–1989 in just six countries: Madagascar, Niger, Senegal, the United Republic of Tanzania, Zaire, and Zambia.

Mounting Debt Problem

Two major factors explain the shortage of external capital – the decline in non-concessional and private loans, and the rapid increase in debt-service obligations and payments. Addressing the mounting external debt problem is essential for recovery and growth. For low-income sub-Saharan African countries, the debt-service ratio rose by almost half, between 1980 and 1985, and would have been much higher had it not been for a large number of reschedulings (17 countries in 1984–1986) and, in some cases, a build-up of arrears that often disrupted needed adjustment efforts. Nor is the situation expected to improve. For some fifteen countries with prolonged debt problems, even continued rescheduling with the liberal terms currently practised will leave their debt burden unmanageably high at the end of the century. For thirteen of these countries, the large and growing multilateral share (including IMF) of debt service payments – 51 per cent in 1985 – means that past solutions to debt problems will not work for them. The situation is worse in 1986–1988, when these payments will exceed $US1 billion per year, accounting for as much as three-quarters of actual debt-service payments. Dealing with this debt-service problem will require new flows of aid and/or innovative debt relief.

Improving the Effectiveness and Co-ordination of Assistance

The current situation in Africa underscores the importance of increasing external assistance on an urgent and co-ordinated basis. If African countries are to be successful in reorienting their economies and restoring growth, not only are additional external resources required, but the effectiveness of donor assistance programmes and aid co-ordination need to be improved.

There is strong support and a basic consensus on the actions that are needed to improve the effectiveness of aid co-ordination on the part of African Governments, bilateral donors, and multilateral institutions.

This consensus is reflected in the recommendations in:

(a) UN-PAAERD, which incorporates the recommendations for improving the level, quality, and the co-ordination of aid contained in APPER;

(b) DAC's Guiding Principles for Aid Co-ordination, which were approved at the DAC high-level meeting in December 1986, and,

(c) World Bank's April 1986 report on improving the effectiveness of aid co-ordination in sub-Saharan Africa, prepared at the request of the Development Committee, which expressed support for the actions already taken by the international community to strengthen aid co-ordination and '... urged the Bank to continue to exert leadership when taking or participating in further initiatives along the lines set forth in the report ...'.[4]

Before discussing the major recommendations of these Reports, there follows below a brief review of the substantial improvements in aid co-ordination in Africa over the last few years.

Increase in Aid Co-ordination Activities

In the early 1980s, African countries began to recognize the need for policy reforms in order to arrest their continuing economic decline as well as 'donor fatigue' reflected in declining net external flows. As the recovery programmes were launched, however, the need for more donor support and the importance of better co-ordination became crucial. There was a substantial increase in aid co-ordination activities, which is clearly reflected in the increase in the number of active World Bank-chaired CGs and UNDP-sponsored RTs. During the period

1980–1982, only five CGs were active in Africa, i.e. meeting on a regular basis every twelve to eighteen months. In 1983–1984, three inactive CGs started up again (Ghana, Kenya, and Zambia) and two new CGs were established (Senegal and Somalia). Since 1985, three new CGs have been established (Guinea, Malawi, and Mauritania) and two more have been reactivated (Morocco and Tanzania). There are now 16 CGs in Africa, of which 11 are scheduled to meet in 1987. Similarly, the number of RTs increased rapidly. New RTs were initiated in five countries in 1984 and another three in 1985. At the present time, there are eighteen RTs in Africa and nine RT meetings are scheduled for 1987. There was also a major increase in sector meetings and various local aid co-ordination meetings. Annex 8.1 provides information on the current status of CGs, RTs, and other aid co-ordination arrangements.

Primary Role of the Recipient Country in the Aid Co-ordination Process

As the recovery programmes gained momentum, it became increasingly apparent that the recipient country has to be at the centre of the aid co-ordination process. Effective aid co-ordination requires the recipient country to articulate and implement a realistic adjustment and investment programme, and to monitor aid and other financial flows. Many African governments, recognizing this need, requested technical assistance to strengthen their economic management capacity. UNDP, IMF, World Bank[5] as well as a number of bilateral donors are support ing various activities to help African Governments improve the planning and management skills in order to restructure their economies.

While many African Governments still find it necessary to rely on external expertise to help with economic policy management, they are giving high priority to making more effective use of national personnel and strengthening their local institutions. They are also assessing critically their technical assistance needs for institutional development and are calling for better co-ordination of such assistance provided by various donors.

Improving the Effectiveness of Aid Co-ordination in Support of Medium-Term Programmes of Adjustment for Growth

Although there have been significant improvements in aid co-ordination in recent years, the effective implementation of medium-term adjustment programmes requires a far more comprehensive and sustained effort by both donors and recipient countries. UN-PAAERD, DAC's

Guiding Principles for Aid Co-ordination and World Bank's reports recommend improvements in four areas which are discussed below: (a) A multi-year comprehensive approach by recipient and donors; (b) Greater discipline in adhering to public investment priorities; (c) Provision of adequate levels of quick-disbursing assistance and co-ordination of policies in support of adjustment lending; and, (d) Strengthening aid co-ordination mechanisms, with particular emphasis on monitoring.

(i) *Multi-year comprehensive approach to development strategies and resource requirements.* Many African countries have launched adjustment programmes, but the process of adjustment is a long-term process. African Governments have the major burden of implementing key policy and structural changes on a sustained basis. They need to develop coherent multi-year public investment and expenditures programmes with an appropriate balance between maintenance and new investments and with adequate attention to long-term aspects of development. Family planning, education, health and resource conservation are vital in this respect. This task is extremely difficult because it involves: addressing problems relating to adjustment and growth that have accumulated over two decades, strengthening or restructuring institutions, and coping with fragile political systems. Each Government must not only take responsibility for implementing its own appropriate adjustment programme but it must be ready to review the progress of its programmes with the donors. In addition, the country must give high priority and take an active role in improving aid co-ordination.

Donors, for their part, cannot encourage recipient countries to undertake multi-year adjustment and investment programmes without providing adequate financial packages. Donors must be willing to adopt a comprehensive approach and support a medium-term framework for their assistance programmes. A more comprehensive approach to financial flows is needed, especially in those sub-Saharan countries which have protracted debt-servicing problems. Donors need to better harmonize their decisions with regard to debt relief and new aid, and provide meaningful envelopes of resource availabilities which will permit recipient countries to implement their medium-term adjustment and investment programmes. While it is recognized that some donors lack legislative authority to make multi-year commitments, even indicative levels of future aid can help in medium-term planning.

World Bank and IMF are now developing, with individual countries, joint Policy Framework Papers (PFPs). These papers reflect the Government's intentions over the next several years regarding the main features of its adjustment and investment programmes and the associated financing requirements. These PFPs can serve as a basis for discussion in CG and RT meetings. The PFPs, supplemented by other documentation prepared by the World Bank, for example Public Investment and Expenditure Reviews, can form the basis for medium-term donor country assessments of both the development programme and its financial requirements. The donor country is stressed in this context because the development framework and the financing plan for each recipient country require adherence by aid agencies as well as by export credit agencies.

(ii) *Support of multi-year public investment and expenditure programmes and priorities.* Rationalizing public investment programmes is a central element of the restructuring process. Public investment and expenditure programmes must reflect national priorities and be brought in line with resource availabilities. The sectoral composition needs to be properly balanced and clear-cut criteria established to assure that only high-priority viable projects and programmes are financed. The World Bank is providing technical assistance to many African countries, for example, Ghana, Guinea, Kenya, Madagascar, Mauritania, Senegal, Somalia, Togo, Zambia and Zaire, to help them develop three-year rolling Public Investment Programmes. The World Bank is also undertaking its own review of these multi-year programmes, identifying the core investment and expenditure programmes which can serve as a framework for mobilizing donor support. Since 1983, World Bank has undertaken 36 public investment and expenditure programmes reviews in 27 sub-Saharan African countries, and some 20 reviews were planned for 1987 and 1988.

Donors and recipients must exercise more discipline and work within agreed public investment and expenditure programmes which have been reviewed and agreed to at CG and/or RT meetings. Project selection should be based on rigorous economic evaluation and donors must avoid financing overdesigned, non-viable projects. Viable projects which are not priorities and even fully-financed marginal projects should be deferred. This is a continuing problem and requires constant monitoring, because some donors do not always adhere to these criteria and to a core public investment programme. Similarly, in utilizing export credits, discipline must be exercised to ensure that such credits are in line with the recipients' investment priorities and the adjustment programme.

(iii) *Need for increasing levels and better co-ordination of adjustment-related assistance.* There is a continuing need for better co-ordination among donors with regard to policy dialogue and for the timely provision of adequate levels of adjustment lending within a multi-year framework. As indicated above, World Bank/IMF PFPs can provide the outline of the resource requirements and the CGs and RTs will continue to serve as the mechanisms for mobilizing additional donors' resources. IDA-8 resources, however, will barely maintain the level of lending to Africa in real terms achieved by the combination of IDA and Special Facility lending in the last two years, despite the agreed increase in Africa's share of IDA-8. Fast-disbursing aid is required to finance essential imports, e.g. fertilizer, seeds, fuels, spare parts and wage goods to keep the adjustment process going and to maintain basic consumption levels. Such assistance is also needed to offset the decline in non-concessional flows and the growing increases in the debt-service burdens in many African countries. Special relief is needed for some 15 countries in Africa with protracted debt-problems.

Donors' aid budgets need to be increased and refocused to support adjustment programmes. Co-financing should be expanded and the CG process needs to be strengthened through the establishment of mechanisms to monitor donors' performance regarding their aid commitments.

A number of alternatives are currently under study with regard to addressing the need for expanding adjustment assistance and concessional debt relief for African countries implementing comprehensive adjustment programmes. In any future arrangements in support of adjustment lending, one important feature of the Special Facility merits being retained, whereby bilateral donors earmarked a significant amount of their assistance programmes for co-financing in support of multi-year adjustment programmes for an agreed list of eligible countries and operations.

(iv) *Strengthening aid co-ordination mechanisms – particularly monitoring.* CG and RT Meetings: Considerable improvements have already been introduced into CG and RT[6] operations. However, several additional changes which have been recommended are listed below:

(a) While recognizing the role of lead multilateral agencies, more extensive participation by the key bilateral and other donors is encouraged in the review of a country's adjustment and public investment and expenditure programmes. Such participation is essential to ensure the emergence of a genuine consensus on a recipient country's development policies and programmes;

(b) Donors need to provide more precise commitment/disbursement information concerning their current aid operations and future levels of assistance. World Bank has prepared standard aid indication forms which are distributed to donors in advance of CG meetings. The Tables, when compiled, should help to improve the monitoring of donors' performance and allow better planning by the recipient countries; and,

(c) CG and RT meetings should facilitate a more frank and substantive exchange of views on key policy issues and problems; more critical reviews of recipient countries' investment and expenditure programmes, greater discussion of the aid implications of recipient countries' stabilization and structural adjustment programmes and more harmonization of aid flows and debt relief options. The chairman of such meetings should aim for operationally relevant conclusions which will allow for more effective monitoring.

These improvements have already been introduced in a number of CG meetings and World Bank plans to extend their application to other CGs.

Sector meetings: The number of sector meetings has increased dramatically in recent years. For example, in 1986, sector meetings were held in 12 sub-Saharan countries. With few exceptions, World Bank has taken the lead in helping the recipient country to organize these meetings and to prepare the necessary documentation. Donor participation is self-regulating inasmuch as only interested donors participate in specific sector meetings. The links between CG and RT meetings and the sector meetings need to be strengthened to ensure proper integration of the sector strategy with the country's overall development strategy. Sector meetings should seek a consensus among the donors concerning the sector strategy, investment priorities, institutional and policy changes required, and mobilize additional resources for the sector. Here again, co-financing can provide a good vehicle for co-ordinating donors' operations.

Local aid co-ordination: In most sub-Saharan countries donors meet informally but regularly under the chairmanship of the UN Resident Representative or the World Bank Representative. The degree of participation by the host Government varies among countries. With resident missions in 25 sub-Saharan countries, World Bank's ability to support such meetings is expanding and is being further strengthened by the addition of resident economists in many of the Bank's missions.

Joint monitoring committees: Various forms of Joint Monitoring Committees (JMCs) have been established in a number of sub-Saharan countries including Ghana, Kenya, Senegal, the Sudan, Zambia and Zaire. The mandates and the experience of these JMCs vary a great deal. For example, some JMCs just provide for an exchange of information between donors and the host country. Others are handling the sector meetings. With very few exceptions, however, these committees are not systematically monitoring the implementation of the Government reform programmes and donors' performance regarding their aid commitments.

UN-PAAERD and World Bank's recent reports on sub-Saharan Africa stressed the critical role of effective monitoring for implementing a multi-year framework of adjustment and assistance. Effective monitoring requires that it be joint and include representatives of the Government and the donors. It must also be comprehensive and provide timely and adequate reporting on its overall financial requirements as well as the performance of donors in meeting their aid commitments.

The strengthening of the monitoring mechanism remains one of the major requirements for improving aid co-ordination. World Bank is prepared to work with individual host countries and other donors to help establish more effective JMCs. These Committees, to be effective, need to work in the countries, meet on a regular basis and follow-up and supplement the work of CG and RT meetings. One alternative would be to convert local aid groups into such monitoring committees. This would require high-level commitment from the recipient Government, technical support from the donors as well as accepting the discipline that effective monitoring implies.

IMPROVEMENTS IN THE WORLD ECONOMY – LIBERALIZING TRADE IN AGRICULTURE

In 1986, the world economy enjoyed the fourth consecutive year of recovery from the deep recession of 1980–1982. Given the interdependence of economies, if the recovery is to continue and expand, better policies are needed by both industrial and developing countries to reduce market distortions and trade barriers and thereby foster higher levels of international trade and capital flows which, in turn, will stimulate economic growth.

The interdependence of economies is clearly evident in the agricultural sector. Public policies in both developing and industrial countries greatly influence the growth of agriculture and rural incomes and extend far beyond national frontiers. Furthermore, agriculture accounts for a very significant share of the labour force, GDP, and exports in developing countries. This is particularly true in Africa where agriculture accounts for over 70 per cent of the labour force; about 40 per cent of GDP and over 65 per cent of the exports (see Table 8.1). Agriculture, therefore, will play a major role in determining the course of growth of the developing countries' economies for decades to come. Within a country and throughout the world, improved agricultural policies which permit more liberal trade are needed to improve the resource allocations and raise real incomes.

TABLE 8.1

AGRICULTURE'S SHARE OF GDP, EMPLOYMENT, AND EXPORTS,
SELECTED YEARS, 1964–1984
(percent)

	Share of agriculture					
	GDP		Employment		Exports (a)	
Country group	1964–66	1982–84	1965	1980	1964–66	1982–84
Low-income countries	42.8	36.3	76.0	72.0	58.6	32.8
Africa	46.9	41.3	84.0	78.0	70.7	68.4
Asia	42.5	35.7	74.0	71.0	54.0	25.9
Middle-income oil exporters	21.8	14.8	62.0	50.0	40.8	13.6
Middle-income importers, excluding major exporters of manufactures	25.2	18.0	63.0	53.0	54.2	44.8
Major exporters of manufactures	19.3	12.1	50.0	36.0	56.9	20.2
Developing countries	30.2	19.9	66.9	63.2	52.3	22.0
Industrial countries	5.1	3.1	13.7	7.1	21.4	14.1

Source: World Development Report 1986, p.3.
Notes:
Data for developing countries are based on a sample of ninety countries.
(a) Includes re-exports.

Agricultural Production

Agricultural output has grown rapidly in many developing countries during the past fifteen years. The growth in food production was faster in developing countries than in the industrial countries and East European non-market economies largely because of the 'Green Revolution' (see Table 8.2). This revolution began in the mid-1960s with the development of high-yielding varieties of wheat and rice which were so productive that it was profitable for farmers to utilize better farming methods, more fertilizers, and for both governments and farmers to invest in irrigation. China and India expanded cereal production at the rate of 3.2 and 4.1 per cent a year, respectively, with both rates exceeding their population growth. However, the Green Revolution left some areas, especially in Africa, largely untouched. Nevertheless, it demonstrated the enormous impact of technological change. The fact that Africa still lags far behind in yields, suggests that with the right technological packages plus price and marketing incentives, Africa can experience significant increases in agricultural production in the future.

One cannot, however, be too sanguine about the state of world agriculture because of existing trade and pricing policies. Given the fact that most agricultural goods are traded in world markets, all countries have opportunities to increase their incomes by specializing in products in which they have a comparative advantage. The strides made by developing countries in agriculture during the past few decades indicate that developing countries as well as industrial countries can benefit from an efficient system of world trade. Yet, trade barriers in industrial countries have become more restrictive and many developing countries pursue policies that inhibit the growth of agricultural output and rural incomes.

The 1986 World Development Report of World Bank focused on trade and pricing policies in world agriculture. It examined agricultural policies of developing and industrial countries, stressing their interdependence and the potential for large gains from more liberal trade in agriculture.

Priorities in Developing Countries

In many developing countries, both macro- and micro-economic policies have hindered agricultural development. Low producer prices and overvalued exchange rates have discouraged domestic agricultural production and exports. It is ironic that, in many developing countries, although the farmers account for a large share of GDP and exports, Government intervention results in policies which discriminate against agriculture. Low food prices are used to subsidize consumers, particularly in urban areas. However, these subsidies distribute benefits widely across income classes and are inefficient and costly instruments for helping the poorest people. Well-targeted food distribution programmes are more effective in reaching especially disadvantaged groups.

Many developing countries have begun to reform their agricultural

214

TABLE 8.2

GROWTH OF AGRICULTURAL PRODUCTION BY MAJOR COMMODITY GROUP, 1961–1984

(average annual percentage)

	Beverages		Food		Raw materials		Total agriculture	
	1961–70	1971–84	1961–70	1971–84	1961–70	1971–84	1961–70	1971–84
Developing countries	-0.4	1.9	2.2	3.2	4.5	2.3	2.4	3.0
Low-income countries	1.9	1.2	1.3	3.2	5.7	3.8	1.9	3.3
Africa	2.3	-0.5	2.6	2.0	6.0	-1.8	3.0	1.2
Asia	1.2	3.6	1.2	3.4	5.7	4.3	1.8	3.6
Middle-income oil exporters	3.5	0.5	3.0	3.1	1.5	-0.9	2.7	2.2
Middle-income oil importers	-2.9	2.8	3.5	3.2	4.8	1.0	2.9	2.9
High-income oil exporters	-6.8	0.6	4.9	14.6	8.0	-0.5	5.0	14.1
Industrial market economies	0.9	0.4	2.9	2.1	-4.9	0.4	2.2	2.0
East European non-market economies	5.3	7.0	3.6	0.5	4.3	1.9	3.7	0.7
World	-0.3	1.9	2.7	2.4	2.2	2.0	2.5	2.3

Source: World Development Report 1986, p. 3.

Note: Data are weighted by the 1978–1982 world export unit prices to permit cross-country comparisons. Growth rates are least squares estimates. Beverages comprise coffee, cocoa and tea. Food comprises cereals, sugar, meat, poultry, roots and tubers, pulses, fruits and vegetables. Raw materials comprise cotton, jute, rubber and tobacco.

policies and are experiencing good results. In sub-Saharan Africa, in 1986, with favourable weather conditions and improved policies, agricultural production increased by almost 3 per cent. Food production kept pace with population growth, and only a few countries are expected to require exceptional food aid in 1987. There is ample evidence that agriculture can be a dynamic sector in Africa and can contribute very significantly to growth in real incomes, employment, foreign exchange earnings and the alleviation of poverty.

Agricultural Policies in Industrial Countries

The 1986 World Development Report analyzed the agricultural trade and pricing policies of the industrial countries and their costs and benefits, both domestically and internationally. It points out that the agricultural support policies of the industrial countries have surprisingly little effect on farmers' income in the long run while imposing a heavy cost on their taxpayers and consumers.

In the EEC, for example, $US23.5 billion was spent in 1984 on agricultural price supports. In the US, this spending is also very significant with agricultural subsidies expected to average $US20 billion a year in the period 1968–1988. The main aim of all this spending is to raise farmers' incomes and keep them from fluctuating. Some stability has probably been achieved, but it is doubtful that high product prices have raised farm incomes in the long term and maintained the farmers on the land. In the US, net farm income as a proportion of farmers' total income, fell from 58 per cent in 1960 to 36 per cent in 1982. In Japan, whose small-scale farming is more important, farm households derived 75 per cent of their income from non-farm sources in 1980.

International Consequences

The effects of industrial countries' agricultural policies spill over onto the rest of the world. By expanding output and depressing domestic demand, their policies reduce world prices and distort the relative prices of agricultural and manufactured goods. By granting special trading privileges and subsidizing exports, industrial countries help destabilize international markets and amplify commodity price fluctuations. The 1986 World Development Report noted that, with global liberalization of agricultural policies, the industrial and developing countries would together gain about $US64 billion annually – more than double the annual level of ODA from OECD countries, which averaged about $US27 billion annually during 1980–1984. The adage that 'Trade is better than Aid' is clearly demonstrated with regard to agriculture.

Many of the international initiatives to increase the benefits of agricultural trade, including international commodity agreements and special trade preferences, often address the symptoms rather than the problem itself – inappropriate policies in both the industrial and developing countries. For example, international commodity agreements are costly and often degenerate into efforts by producer groups to raise rather than stabilize prices and incomes. Compensatory arrangements, such as IMF's Compensatory Financing Facility, are superior instruments for promoting stability in earnings. Regional schemes which provide trade preferences to a limited number of countries can erode the interest of the beneficiaries in promoting general trade liberalization.

Increased trade liberalization will help developing countries attain faster rates of economic growth and will also bring benefits to industrial countries as well. Less government intervention will help stabilize international prices and assist all countries in attaining their common objective of more stability in farm incomes and prices.

Preparations are underway for negotiations regarding agricultural protection in a new round of GATT negotiations. There seems to be increasing recognition that existing agricultural policies will lead to higher and higher costs of protection and greater instability in agricultural markets and trade. The 1986 World Development Report concluded that:

> What Governments must be willing to negotiate about are the degrees of protection provided by their domestic price and income support programmes and the effects that these programmes have upon production, consumption, exports and imports and international market prices.

CONCLUSION

Over the last several years, there have been substantial improvements in aid co-ordination. However, to be effective, co-ordination must evolve with changing requirements. An increasing number of African countries have launched medium-level adjustment programmes which require a more comprehensive and sustained aid co-ordination effort than has been evidenced to date. This Chapter outlined a series of recommendations for strengthening aid co-ordination aimed at mobilizing more donor support and improving the efficiency of assistance programmes. World Bank stands ready to join with recipient countries and donors to implement these recommendations. Most of them are not new, but their implementation has lagged far behind the implementation of adjustment programmes by many African countries. Unless there is sustained action to increase overall external flows, including the provision of innovative debt relief, and to improve the co-ordination of aid, Africa's reform and growth programmes will fall far short of their goals. Such a prospect is not acceptable in a continent where, in most countries, per capita income levels today are no higher than they were twenty years ago.

World Bank strongly supports an expansion and liberalization of the world trading system to help stimulate economic growth. In this connection, the Report of the President of the World Bank to the Development Committee in April 1987 pointed out that the GATT Uruguay Round provides an excellent opportunity to liberalize trade in agriculture and change agricultural policies through improving market access and the reduction of production and export subsidies. Given the significance of industrial country agricultural policies to both developed and developing countries' economic prospects, the President's Report called on the Ministers 'to consider how they can strengthen the resolve of their Governments to modify agricultural policies and promote freer trade in agriculture'.

NOTES

1. ECA and Africa's Development, 1983–2008. A Preliminary Perspective Study, April 1983.
2. Toward Sustained Development in sub-Saharan Africa: A Joint Programme of Action, August 1984.
3. APPER estimated that net transfers to Africa should reach about $US9 billion annually, in addition to appropriate measures to help African countries meet their debt-service obligations of about $US15–25 billion a year. Full implementation of the Bank's recommendations – an increase of $US2.5 billion of official development assistance over and above the increase already in sight – would result in net transfers to sub-Saharan Africa equivalent to $US9–12 billion annually during the period 1986–1990.
4. Development Committee Press Communique, September 29, 1986.
5. World Bank is providing substantial amounts of technical assistance to help African Governments improve their economic policy management through a variety of mechanisms including: the Bank's country economic and sector work (CESW); IDA-financed technical assistance projects, which are currently supporting institutional development and training in 28 sub-Saharan countries in such critical areas as policy analysis, public investment programming, debt management; the special programme involving the assignment of Bank staff members as advisers concerned with policy analysis and planning; and, lastly, the Bank is the executing agent for UNDP-financed technical assistance projects supporting economic planning in 12 countries in sub-Saharan Africa.

6. UNDP has recently made a series of recommendations to strengthen RTs and to enhance its capacity to perform its co-ordination more effectively including, *inter alia*: emphasis on policy reforms; the strengthening of UNDP staff; a more selective approach to the choice of countries and participants; improved analysis and in-country follow-up; better preparation and organization of the RT meetings with UNDP chairmanship of the meetings and closer collaboration with the World Bank.

ANNEX 8.1
AID CO-ORDINATION MECHANISMS IN AFRICA

	CGs		RTs		Joint coordinating mechanisms	Sector meetings	Local aid coordination efforts
	First/since 83 Meetings	Forthcoming Meetings	Past Meetings	Forthcoming Meetings			
Angola							Meetings focusing on emergency supply management, and rehabilitation issues are held weekly.
Benin	1980		Feb/Mar 1983		Formal fortnightly meetings of the "Comite Mixte" have taken place since Jan 1984. France, Germany,EEC, UNDP FAO, WFP, and the World Bank participate.	Forestry (Mar 1983); Nangbeto Dam (Feb 1984) Principal roads (Apr/Jun1984); Tourism and cultural sub-sectors (Jun 1984); Health (Oct 1984); Rural development (Mar/Aug 1985), Dassa-Parakou highway (Mar 1986); Transport (Mar 1987); Telecommunications (planned spring 1987); Quarterly meetings take place on water supply and sanitation sector.	
Botswana					Under consideration		Government handles own aid coordination. Periodic informal meetings of donors. Semi-formal local coordination meetings with govt. participation, in drought relief, environment, and food aid.

220

ANNEX 8.1 (cont.)

Burkina Faso	Jul 1987 1/	Govt. has organized informal coordination meetings with donors active in the health sector. The World Bank chaired a health sector meeting in Jan. 1987.	Donor coordination takes place in emergency food aid, regular food aid, NGOs, and infrastructure projects.
BBurundi	Feb.1984	Education mini RT to be scheduled; Energy under consideration	Informal monthly donor meetings to share information. Ad hoc sectoral meetings with full Government participation.
Cameroon			Occasional informal meetings hosted by France, U.K. and the World Bank
Cape Verde	June 1982 / Dec 1986	Water planned lets June 1987	Regular formal meetings among agencies of the UN system, including UNDP, WFP, UNICEF, FAO and WHO
C.A.R.	Jun 1980 / Jun 1987	Transport and petroleum sector meetings to be coordinated by the World Bank	
Chad	Dec 1985	Weekly meetings in the health sector. Cotton (May 1986); Petroleum refineries (Jul 1986); Food (Dec 1986); Transport (planned May 1987).	
Comoros	Jul 1984		

ANNEX 8.1 (cont.)

	CGs		RTs				
	First/since 83 Meetings	Forthcoming Meetings	Past Meetings	Forthcoming Meetings	Joint coordinating mechanisms	Sector meetings	Local aid coordination efforts
Congo							No regular aid coordination mechanism
Cote d'Ivoire						Annual meeting between World Bank/UNDP on agricultural research and forestry	No formal aid coordination at the local level
Djibouti			Nov 1983				
Eq.Guinea			Apr 1982	Jul 1987			
Ethiopia	1971 1973					Transport sector meeting planned. WFP-initiated Govt/donor metings in the reforestation and soil conservation sectors	Local consultation on emergency relief assistance have been frequent
Gabon							No formal local consultation mechanism
Gambia			Nov 1984 Sep 1985 2/		Regular bi-monthly meetings of donors and government	Health (Dec 1984); Fisheries (Jun 1985) Agriculture and water (scheduled for Mar/ Apr 1987)	

ANNEX 8.1 (cont.)

Ghana	1987 Mar 1987 Nov.1983 Dec.1984 Nov.1985	Regular meetings of the Joint Monitoring Committee Chaired the government. Central project monitoring unit also established	Industry (May 1986); Eduction and health Sep1986); Water (planned Apr 1987); Transport (planned May 1987).	Monthly local donor meetings
Guinea	Apr 1986 3/ May 1987		On-going consultations in agriculture, transport, power and water, prior to CG. Agriculture (planned Apr 1987; other sector meetings to be planned	Monthly local donor meetings
Guinea Bissau	May 1984 Feb 1985 2/ Apr 1985 2/		Health (Feb 1986): Agriculture and fisheries (planned May 1987); Water supply and sanitation (to be scheduled)	Semi-annual meetings for local aid coordination activities
Kenya	1970 Jan/Feb 1984 Apr 1986	Joint Monitoring Committe organized after 1984 CG. Subcommittee on Agriculture meets frequently.	Agricultural (Apr 1986)	World Bank representative chairs frequent but irregular meetings of donors on health, population, agriculture. Other ad hoc meetings also held
Lesotho	May 1984		Water and sanitation (Jun 1985); Integrated rural development and employment generation (Jul 1986).	Monthly donor meetings led by UNDP. "Government/Donor Coordination Committee to Monitor Utilization of Food Aid and Other External Assistance Related to the Drought" established in June 1985
Liberia	Oct 1983 5/			Informal contacts among local donors, particularly in the agricultural and health sectors

ANNEX 8.1 (cont.)

	CGs		RTs		Joint coordinating mechanisms	Sector meetings	Local aid coordination efforts
	First/since 83 Meetings	Forthcoming Meetings	Past Meetings	Forthcoming Meetings			
Madagascar	1982 Apr 1983 Nov 1984 Apr 1986	Dec 1987				Road rehabilitation (Sep 1986); Fisheries (1985); Frequent meetings on irrigation. Periodic meetings on agricultural policy	Informal local meetings organised by the World Bank's resident representative
Malawi	Jan 1986	Oct/Nov 1987 1/	Feb 1984		Development Coordination Committee established as result of 1986 CG. Sectoral committees being established; transport sector committee active	Health (Jun.Sept 1986)	Monthly informal donor coordination meetings organized by UNDP
Mali			Dec 1982 Nov 1985	late 1987 3/		Power (Jun 1986, Mar 1987); Industrial dev't. (Oct 1986); Agricultural price policies (planned Apr 1987); Rural development (tent.late 1987).	In-country RT review chaired by UNDP/Govt in December 1985. Joint govt/donor group on food aid and cereals policy reform meets regularly
Mauritania	Nov 1985	1986				Fisheries, water supply and irrigation are planned for 1987	World Bank/UNDP sponor regular meetings of donors
Mauritius	1980 May 1985					Sugar sector (Feb 1987)	Occasional informal meetings organized by UNDP
Morocco	1970s Jan 1985 Mar 1987						

224

ANNEX 8.1 (cont.)

Mozambique	July 1987			
Niger		Jun 1987		Agricultural policies (Feb 1987): Transport (plan.Apr 1987): Health (plan.Apr./May 1987)
Nigeria	May 1971			Quarterly health care meetings
Rwanda		Dec 1982		NGOs (Jun 1985): High-ways (Sep 1985): Indu-stry (Jan 1986): Water- and sanitation (Jan 1986,Mar 1987): Agri-culture (May/Dec 1986) Population and nutri-tion (Aug 1986):Agr. Extension (Feb 1987): Mining (tent.May 1987): Census/PHN (tent.late 1987)	Monthly meetings with full govt. participation chaired in rotation by donor repre-sentatives
Sao Tome & Principe		Dec 1985	Jul 1987 2/	Interministerial Committee, under chairmanship of the Head of State, periodically reviews progress in the implementation of the "Action Plan."A technical monitoring unit provides support	May 1986: rural develop-ment, fisheries, energy water, transport, and problems of geographical isolation, NGO's (Nov 1986)
Senegal	1984 Mar 1987			Telecommunications(Dec 1984): Energy (Jan 1985): Agriculture and DWS power (Jun 1985): Human resources (Sep.Nov.1986): Household energy conser-vation, Transport (Dec 1986): Education. Tourism (scheduled spring 1987): Industry (planned Dec 1987): Water supply (planned 1988).	Bi-monthly meetings of all donor representatives.Joint donor/govt commission on aid counterpart.

ANNEX 8.1 (cont.)

	CGs		RTs		Joint coordinating mechanisms	Sector meetings	Local aid coordination efforts
	First/since 83 Meetings	Forthcoming Meetings	Past Meetings	Forthcoming Meetings			
Seychelles							No formal local aid coordination
Sierra Leone	May 1987 1/						UNDP organizes occasional meeting of donors
Somalia	1983 Jan 1985 2/ Nov 1985 Apr 1987					Regular sector meetings in forestry and livestock since 1982;Bardere Dam aid coordination (planned Nov 1987)	Regular meetings of local donors co-chaired by World bank and UNDP
Sudan	1983 Dec 1983				Joint Monitoring Committee which was set up after last CG is no longer active		World Bank resident representative organizes regular meetings of government and donors
Swaziland							Monthly informal local donor meetings
Tanzania			1978 Jun 1986	July 1987		Transport/railways (Feb 1987)	Informal monthly meetings of principal donors chaired alternately by UNDP and World Bank representative. Govt. has established aid coordination office
Togo			Jun 1985	Mar 1987 3/		Agriculture and rural development (Mar 1986). Infrastructure, Transport, Social, Health and Human resources (Oct 1986)	

ANNEX 8.1 (cont.)

Country	Date			
Uganda	1969 Jan 1984	"Joint Donor Coordination Committee on External Resources" established to improve management of financial resources provided by external donors		Government aid coordinator. Quarterly donor meetings
Zaire	Dec 1983 Apr 1986 May 1987	"Commission de Suivi" established to follow-up the recommendations of CG. meets twice a year	Highways (Mar 1985); GECAMINES (Sep 1985) Transport, Energy and Agriculture (to be determined)	Local representatives meet informally about once a month
Zambia	1978 May 1984 Jun 1985 Dec 1985 2/ Dec 1986	Established a Joint Monitoring Committee in 1984. A project tracking system is being put into place to assist donor coordination	One JMC Meeting dealt with agricultural research and extension	Informal meetings organized by EC representatives and EC member countries with occasional govt. observers
Zimbabwe	see 7/			Regular informal meetings of local donor representatives, often with government participation. Several joint working groups

1. Tentative date
2. Balance of payments meeting chaired by World Bank
3. Meeting on economic reform chaired by World Bank
4. Interim meeting: Round Table follow-up
5. Inter-Governmental Group for Liberia (IGGL) will replace RT: the US will chair, and World Bank and UNDP will provide technical support and help the Government prepare documentation.
6. Interim meeting: Non-project finance
7. ZIMCORD first met in 1981, with a review in 1983.

227

CHAPTER NINE

Sub-Saharan Africa and OECD Member States

JOSEPH C. WHEELER

This Chapter looks at sub-Saharan Africa from the point of view of the aid donor community of the OECD member states, particularly members of the DAC.[1] Each African country has its unique natural endowments, economic circumstances and history. Consequently, there are severe limitations on any process of generalization. Likewise, donors vary widely in economic capability, geo-political concerns and approaches to development. Nevertheless, it is difficult to avoid generalizing about both Africa and the donor community. I hope the reader will forgive me if some generalizations do not fit particular country or donor circumstances.

THE CHALLENGE

The world has come to recognize the enormous challenge facing sub-Saharan Africa. Over the next three decades Africa must triple food output to meet the needs of an unusually fast-growing population. This comes after a generation when per capita food production went down on average by more than 1 per cent a year.

Within thirty years Africa must increase the number of places for first-year primary school students to 30 million. DAC countries today contain about 700 million people compared with less than 500 million in sub-Saharan Africa, but have only 10 million children entering school each year. The proportion of children to total population in Africa is four times that of the DAC countries.

On the average, sub-Saharan Africa still loses one out of every ten new-born babies in the first year. While this is substantially lower than the figure for twenty years ago, it is generally accepted that no country needs to have an infant mortality rate this high. African countries will be making a concerted effort to improve the health of their citizens in the decades ahead. Africa faces critical problems of environmental

228

deterioration, including deforestation, desertification and soil loss, which will gain increasing attention from decision-makers over the coming decades.

Over the next 30 years Africa will need employment opportunities for another 300–400 million working-age people. Since most of these jobs will be in the private sector, African Governments will give increasing attention to the policy environment and infrastructure resources needed to encourage rapid creation of employment opportunities.

With all these long-term development challenges, Africa enters the period with its hands at least partly tied by a combination of conditions arising from an awful drought, earnings diminished by sluggish world growth in trade and structural changes in commodity markets, and the need to service an accumulation of debt.

There is little that can be added to what has been written about the financial conditions of African countries in the preceding chapters. Surely, it would help if world growth accelerated, if protectionism were diminished, if interest rates went down, and if terms of trade improved. Indeed, anyone concerned about African development knows that these are often most important factors. But most of these factors will be affected by decisions unrelated to policies designed specifically for Africa. It is resource flows which can be affected by donor decisions and, to a considerable extent, by the African countries themselves. This chapter will therefore concentrate on volume of flows, the efficiency of their use and their role in supporting African country structural adjustment.

RESOURCE FLOWS TO AFRICA

Most of the resources to cope with Africa's monumental challenges will come from Africa itself. But substantial outside financing will also be needed. Let us look at the current situation on resource flows to Africa as reflected in OECD statistics (see Table 9.1 for a summary of available data on total net resource flows to sub-Saharan Africa).

DAC divides 'total net resource flow' into three major categories: official development finance; total export credits; and private flows. Total net resource flows to sub-Saharan Africa in 1985 are estimated to have been about $US16 billion.[2] This amount is from all sources, public and private, and includes aid not only from DAC countries but also from OPEC and CMEA countries. The components of this total will be discussed from the figures in Table 9.1.

Private Flows

Total private flows in 1985 were about $US2.5 billion. Commercial private flows were only $US1.1 billion. Commercial flows were down from levels which in 1979 and 1981 exceeded $US3.5 billion. The reduced levels reflect the private sector's more pessimistic perception of creditworthiness in light of very high levels of indebtedness, reductions in commodity prices and other economic circumstances. One could guess that private flows would be unlikely to reach earlier levels for several years. Yet, in the long run, private commercial flows will be critical to the financing of rapid African growth.

The first commercial private flows to recover are likely to be those owned by Africans themselves. Exchange rates, interest rates, prices, marketing systems and other factors will affect profitability, and when these become positive, Africans are likely to repatriate funds now lodged in developed countries' banks or stock markets. When Africans find it profitable to invest in Africa, the rest of the world will follow.

Note that under 'other private' flows, OECD includes primarily grants by NGOs. These are privately contributed grant funds which have tended to increase over the years. Now estimated by the OECD Secretariat at nearly $US1.0 billion for sub-Saharan Africa, they represent a welcome and significant supplement to ODA.

Total Export Credits

Export credits in 1985 are estimated to have been about $US0.6 billion. This is down from a level reached in the 1979–82 period of about $US2.0 billion. Again, these reductions reflect a perception of lowered credit worthiness, in this case by government agencies rather than by the private sector. The reductions probably also reflect less demand by sub-Saharan countries for non-concessionally funded imports. It is unlikely that either borrowers or lenders will press for higher levels until debt servicing–export ratios are greatly improved.

Official Development Finance

Total Official Development Finance (ODF) is made up of two categories: ODA and other Official Development Finance (other ODF). Total ODF in 1985 was about $US12.9 billion. This was the highest level ever reached. (Early estimates for 1986 suggest a further increase in total ODF to about $US16.0 billion or about $US13.1 billion at 1985 prices and exchange rates.) The portion of the 1985 level which is listed in OECD statistics as 'other ODF' is $US1.8 billion. This represents financing which does not meet the concessionality criteria of

TABLE 9.1
TOTAL NET RESOURCE FLOWS TO SUB-SAHARAN AFRICA
(Current US$ billion)

	1978	1979	1980	1981	1982	1983	1984	1985	1986	1986(b)
I. OFFICIAL DEVELOPMENT FINANCE (ODF)	7.2	8.9	11.1	10.9	11.6	11.4	12.7	12.9	16.0	13.1
1. Official Development Assistance (ODA)	6.3	7.9	9.2	9.4	9.5	9.6	9.9	11.1		
A.Bilateral	4.4	5.7	6.7	6.8	7.0	7.0	7.0	7.8		
(a) OECD Countries	3.7	4.8	5.8	5.8	5.8	5.6	6.1	6.8		
(b) OPEC Countries	0.5	0.7	0.6	0.6	0.8	0.9	0.4	0.5		
(c) CMEA Countries	x	x	0.1	0.2	0.2	0.3	0.3	0.3		
(d) Other Countries	0.2	0.2	0.2	0.2	0.2	0.2	0.2	0.2		
B. Multilateral	1.9	2.2	2.5	2.6	2.5	2.6	2.9	3.3		
2. Other ODF	0.9	1.0	1.9	1.5	2.1	1.8	2.8	1.8		
of which: Multilateral	0.4	0.4	0.5	0.5	0.6	0.7	0.8	0.8		
Bilateral	0.5	0.6	1.4	1.0	1.5	1.1	2.0	1.0		
II. TOTAL EXPORT CREDITS	1.4	2.0	1.9	1.9	1.9	1.1	0.2	0.6	0.6	0.5
1.OECD Countries Including short-term	1.4	2.0	1.8	1.8	1.8	0.1	0.2	0.5		
2. Other countries	x	x	0.1	0.1	0.1	0.1	x	0.1		
III. PRIVATE FLOWS	3.8	4.9	3.4	4.6	3.9	2.3	0.3	2.5	2.3	1.9
1. Direct Investment (OECD)	1.0	1.5	0.1	1.5	1.0	0.9	0.4	0.3	0.4	
2. International bank sector	1.5	2.0	2.0	2.0	2.0	0.5	-1.0	0.8	1.0	
3. Total bond lending	x	x	x	x	x	x	x	x	x	
4. Other Private (a)	1.3	1.4	1.3	1.1	0.9	0.9	0.8	1.4	1.5	
TOTAL NET RESOURCE FLOWS (I+II+III)	12.4	15.8	16.4	17.4	17.4	14.8	13.2	16.0	18.9	15.5

Source: OECD
Notes: (a) Including grants by Non-Governmental Organizations (NGOs)
(b) At 1986 prices and exchange rates.

TABLE 9.2

TOTAL NET RECEIPTS OF ODA FROM ALL SOURCES BY REGION AND SELECTED DEVELOPING COUNTRIES

Region, major recipients (a)	Percentage of total ODA			Percentage of DAC bilateral ODA 1985	Share in total population 1984(f)	ODA receipts		ODA as percentage of recipient's GNP		Per capita income 1984(f)	GNP annual average growth rate per capita 1974-84(f)
	1975-76	1980-81	1985	1985	1984(f)	1985 $ billion	Annual change 1980 to 1985	1980-81	1983-84(f)	1984(f)	1974-84(f)
	%	%	%	%	%	(d)	%	5	%	$	%
SUB-SAHARAN AFRICA	**21.1**	**27.5**	**31.9**	**30.4**	**11.4**	**9.5**	**3.4**	**4.3**	**5.0**	**430**	**-2.1**
of which: Sahel group(c)	4.0	4.6	5.6	5.5	0.9	1.7	(5.0)	-	19.5	210	0.4
Sudan	1.5	2.1	3.8	3.3	0.6	1.1	14.1	7.8	9.8	340	-2.2
Tanzania	1.6	2.4	1.6	1.9	0.6	0.5	-6.4	13.4	14.3	210	-1.7
Zaire	1.2	1.4	1.1	1.1	1.8	0.3	-5.3	7.6	8.4	140	-3.4
Kenya	0.8	1.4	1.5	1.7	0.5	0.4	2.0	6.3	7.5	300	-0.1
Ethiopia	0.7	8.0	2.4	2.1	1.2	0.7	27.6	5.5	7.5	110	-0.5
Somalia	0.7	1.4	1.2	0.8	0.1	0.3	-4.0	28.4	24.1	260	1.6
Ghana	0.6	0.6	0.7	0.5	0.3	0.2	1.2	3.9	3.8	380	-3.9
Rwanda	0.5	0.5	0.6	0.5	0.2	0.2	3.1	12.8	10.0	280	2.4
Madagascar	0.4	0.8	0.6	0.5	0.3	0.2	-4.0	7.7	6.7	260	-3.9
Zambia	0.4	0.9	1.1	1.1	0.2	0.3	0.7	7.3	8.2	470	-2.8
Mozambique	0.3	0.5	1.0	1.1	0.4	0.3	12.2	3.7	4.6	360	-4.3
Cameroon	0.7	0.8	0.5	0.6	0.3	0.2	-9.7	3.3	2.3	810	3.0
Cote d'Ivoire	0.6	0.6	0.4	0.6	0.3	0.1	-9.9	1.9	2.2	610	-2.3
Nigeria	0.4	0.1	0.1	0.1	2.7	0.0	-2.0	0.1	0.1	770	-2.9
Congo	0.4	0.3	0.2	0.2	0.0	0.1	-5.0	5.0	5.5	1,130	4.1
Reunion	1.7	1.9	1.3	1.8	0.0	0.4	-5.0	29.2	21.5	3,700	0.8
SOUTH ASIA	**23.3**	**17.2**	**15.5**	**11.8**		**4.6**	**-3.3**	**2.3**			
of which: India	10.3	6.9	5.1	2.6	20.8	1.5	-6.6	1.2	0.9	260	2.4
Pakistan	6.3	3.2	2.5	2.1	2.6	0.7	-8.2	3.4	2.1	410	2.9
Bangladesh	4.5	4.1	3.9	3.2	2.7	1.2	-2.1	8.8	9.8	130	1.9
Sri Lanka	0.9	1.3	1.6	1.7	0.4	0.5	4.5	9.2	8.6	360	3.3

TABLE 9.2 (continued)

	13.3	13.2	13.2	12.9	( )	3.9	1.3	0.6	( )	( )	( )
OTHER ASIA AND OCEANIA	13.3	13.2	13.2	12.9	( )	3.9	1.3	0.6	( )	( )	( )
of which: Indonesia	4.0	3.3	2.0	2.6	4.4	0.6	-8.7	1.3	0.9	540	3.9
Indochina (e)	2.0	1.6	0.5	0.4	2.0	-	-	-	1.2	230	4.4
China	-	0.9	3.1	2.9	28.6	0.9	70.0	0.1	0.3	310	5.8
Philippines	1.1	1.2	1.6	2.2	1.4	0.5	10.2	0.9	1.2	660	1.1
Thailand	0.7	1.4	1.6	2.0	1.4	0.5	2.8	1.2	1.1	850	4.1
NORTH AFRICA AND MIDDLE EAST	29.3	26.4	23.3	-	-	-	-	-	-	-	-
of which: Egypt	12.8	4.6	5.9	8.6	1.3	1.8	5.0	5.4	4.7	730	6.3
Morocco	1.4	3.3	2.8	1.6	0.6	0.8	-1.3	5.8	2.6	670	1.9
Tunisia	1.2	0.8	0.5	0.6	0.2	0.2	-6.9	2.8	2.4	1,270	3.0
Israel	3.2	2.8	6.6	10.1	0.1	2.0	17.3	4.4	5.8	5,060	0.2
Jordan	2.7	0.4	1.8	0.4	0.1	0.5	-15.8	34.3	17.8	1,280	6.3
Syria	3.5	5.4	2.1	0.1	0.3	0.6	-18.2	11.4	5.0	1,840	2.4
LATIN AMERICA AND CARIBBEAN	9.9	10.0	12.8	15.5	10.8	3.8	9.4	0.4	0.5	1,730	0.0
of which: Bolivia	0.4	0.6	0.7	0.7	0.2	0.2	3.6	4.0	5.1	410	-3.5
El Salvador	0.2	0.5	1.2	1.2	-	0.4	29.0	3.8	7.4	-	-
SOUTHERN EUROPE	1.5	3.6	1.4	1.6	( )	-	-	-	-	-	-
of which: Turkey	0.6	2.9	0.6	0.7	-	-	-	-	-	-	-
TOTAL	100.0	100.0	100.0	100.0	100.0	29.9	0.1	1.1	1.1	730	1.9

Source: OECD

Notes: (a) ODA from DAC Members, multilateral donors, and to the extent known, OPEC donors. No data are available on CMEA net disbursements.

(b) Least developed countries and all other countries with an average per capita GNP in 1983 of less than $700

(c) Comprises Cape Verde Islands, The Gambia, Burkina Faso, Mali, Mauritania, Niger, Senegal and Chad.

(d) Excludes unallocated funds, i.e. those not allocated by individual recipient country, which are estimated at some $1 billion. Includes aid from DAC and OPEC countries but excludes CMEA and other countries.

(e) Comprises Kampuchea, Laos and Vietnam

(f) Not yet available for 1985

EODA. The most important example would be financing from the regular funds of the World Bank (as opposed to the very concessional IDA funds). Although lower than in 1984, the $US1.8 billion level was at roughly the same level as had been made available under this category over the four earlier years.

ODA, on the other hand, represented $US11.1 billion of the $US12.9 billion total. This was higher than earlier levels. Representing as it did in 1985, 70 per cent of total resource flows in the short run, it is the most important factor. The point to underline is that this concessional assistance has been a steady and increasing source of funding for Africa while private commercial flows and export credits have fluctuated sharply in the light of changing economic circumstances. Furthermore, these funds are provided on grant or very concessional terms.

The prospects for future ODA to sub-Saharan Africa are for continuing modest increases. The portion of world-wide aid going to Africa has increased from about 20 per cent to about 30 per cent over the past decade. We tentatively guess that the proportion of total bilateral aid going to sub-Saharan Africa will not continue to increase substantially. However, since we estimate ODA will increase moderately at perhaps 2 per cent per year, ODA flows to sub-Saharan Africa should also increase moderately.

It is worth looking at aid flows from the point of view of the recipients. Taking DAC bilateral, OPEC and multilateral ODA together, OECD statistics suggest that sub-Saharan Africa is now receiving 5 per cent of its GNP from aid (see Table 9.3). For low-income sub-Saharan Africa, over 10 per cent of GNP comes from aid. For some countries, the proportion is much higher. For example, the Sahel group is receiving about 20 per cent of GNP in aid, and Somalia is receiving 24 per cent of GNP in aid. Thus, reasonable questions can be raised about the implications of such high levels of aid dependency if extended for a long time.

By way of perspective, total GNP in sub-Saharan Africa is less than the GNP of Spain. Also by way of perspective India, with substantially more people than sub-Saharan Africa and a per capita income only slightly higher than the sub-Saharan low-income country average, received net ODA in 1985 of about $US1.5 billion – compared with a net ODA of $US11.1 billion for sub-Saharan Africa.

TABLE 9.3

TOTAL DISBURSED LONG- AND SHORT-TERM DEBT OF SUB-SAHARAN COUNTRIES AT YEAR END, 1975–1986 BY SOURCES AND TERMS OF LENDING ($US BILLION)

	1975	1979	1980	1981	1983	1982	1983	1984	1985	1986
Long-term debt										
I. OECD countries and capital markets	10	24	28	30	32	36	39	38	43	51
A. ODA	4	5	6	6	6	6	6	7	9	11
B. Total exports credits	4	12	15	15	16	16	18	18	23	28
Guaranteed bank credits	–	–	–	–	–	6	7	7	9	9
Other export credits	–	–	–	–	–	10	11	10	14	14
C. Financial markets	2	6	7	8	9	14	15	14	13	12
Banks	2	6	7	8	9	13	14	13	13	–
Bonds	–	1	1	1	1	–	–	–	–	–
D. Other private	–	–	1	1	1	–	–	–	1	–
II. Multilateral	3	7	8	10	11	12	14	15	18	20
of which: concessional	2	4	5	6	7	7	8	9	11	11
non-concessional	1	2	3	4	4	5	6	6	6	6
III. Non-OECD creditor countries	3	7	8	9	10	10	11	11	11	11
Sub-total: Long-term debt	16	38	44	49	54	58	64	64	74	82
of which: concessional	7	14	16	18	20	20	22	23	–	–
non-concessional	8	23	28	30	34	37	42	40	–	–
Short-term debt										
Banks	–	–	–	–	–	8	7	6	7	10
Export credits	–	–	–	–	–	3	3	2	2	3
Sub-total: short-term debt	–	–	–	–	–	10	10	8	10	13
Total External debt	–	–	–	–	–	68	73	74	82	95
Memorandum item										
Use of IMF credit	–	–	–	–	–	4	5	5	6	–
Other identified liabilities	–	–	–	–	–	1	–	–	–	–

Source: OECD

AFRICAN DEBT

Debt is an important issue in Africa although African debt represents less than 10 per cent of the world-wide debt portfolio. In a number of individual countries the requirements for debt-service financing are so high that special forms of relief will clearly be needed. Total sub-Saharan debt, both short- and long-term, at the end of 1986 was about $US95 billion (Table 9.3). However, aggregating debt figures for the continent is of questionable usefulness. For many countries, debt servicing is being successfully managed. For others, the best we can say is that the problem is being put off. Many of the important decisions related to debt renegotiations are arrived at in the Paris Club for official debt and the London Club for private debt.

DAC has taken the position that those making decisions about debt should be well informed about the status of SAPs and the availabilities of other resources. The point here is that, in connection with any one country situation, and in addition to the country government, there are a number of circles of decision-making, including the increasingly well co-ordinated structural adjustment discussions with World Bank and IMF, the debt discussions in the Paris and London Clubs, the processes of RTs and CGs, the individual decision-making of each bilateral donor. Since debt decision-making is made in such a wide variety of places, the minimum we can ask of ourselves is that all decision-makers have the best possible understanding of the requirements, and of what other decision-makers are doing.

There seems to be a widening acceptance that, in some cases, actions will be required which go beyond recent practice. For example, the Communique of the April 10, 1987 Washington meeting of the Development Committee, chaired by the Honourable B.T.G. Chidzero, Minister of Finance, Economic Planning and Development of Zimbabwe, recognized that many countries, 'especially in sub-Saharan Africa, face severe problems of indebtedness. Ministers stressed the need for larger concessional flows and agreed that for many of these countries additional measures were needed to improve their capacity to service their debts and at the same time undertake growth-oriented programmes'.

Similarly, the Interim Committee of the Board of Governors of IMF on April 8, 1987 said the following:

> Committee members expressed special concern about the plight of low-income countries. The Committee emphasized that it is

crucial for these countries to implement major reforms which, to be fully effective, will need to be accompanied by additional financing on concessional terms. In this connection, the progress with operations under IMF's Structural Adjustment Facility was welcomed. Committee members noted the forthcoming review by the Executive Board of the SAF and they expressed their hope that arrangements under the Facility would serve to elicit from bilateral and multilateral donors the necessary additional financial support. In this general context, the Committee also urged creditor Governments, as a matter of priority, to consider means for granting exceptional financial relief with respect to official credits in cases, including particularly sub-Saharan Africa, where such relief is necessary to support and encourage far-reaching economic reforms in highly indebted low-income countries ...

Close co-operation between IMF and World Bank was welcomed. Committee members noted that increased lending from multilateral development banks had contributed importantly to debtor country financing. They noted with appreciation the continuing efforts and new initiatives of the Paris Club to tailor rescheduling agreements to the circumstances of individual countries and stressed the importance of necessary flexibility on the part of export credit agencies in resuming or increasing cover for countries that are implementing comprehensive adjustment programmes.

While the ministers in the Development and Interim Committees have so far not been very precise on what additional measures might be taken, the recognition of the problem is a welcome step. Since the Development and Interim Committees met in April, the Paris Club has been continuing the dialogue. Already, the Paris Club has agreed that, in some cases, grace periods can be extended.

Most recently, the Council of the OECD, meeting at ministerial level in Paris on May 13, 1987, after declaring on issues of improving growth prospects, macro-economic policies and structural adjustment policies in their own countries, spoke of relations with developing countries. They said, *inter alia*:

Even more constraining are debt problems among low-income countries. Proposals have recently been made by OECD countries for additional action to reduce the debt servicing burden of the poorest countries, especially in sub-Saharan Africa, undertaking strong growth-oriented adjustment programmes. Early results

237

from the current discussions among creditor governments will be urgently sought ...

For poorer developing countries, provision of adequate concessional finance is essential. OECD countries' record in this respect is already substantial but should be further enhanced. The volume and forms of aid must be commensurate with the growing requirements of policy reform programmes and broader development efforts. The new DAC guiding principles for using aid to support improved development policies and programmes and strengthening aid co-ordination with developing countries are welcomed.

It is quite clear that the international community will be giving these issues more urgent attention in the coming months. In its further consideration of the sub-Saharan debt issue, it seems likely that special attention will be given to the problems of about a dozen countries which are carrying out SAPs and which have debt-servicing/export ratios in excess of 25 per cent. No combination of measures so far put forward will adequately deal with the problems of accumulated debt of at least some of these countries.

SUPPORTING STRUCTURAL ADJUSTMENT

Over the past several years, a majority of African countries have embarked on SAPs. Of course, no country – developed or developing – can escape the need for structural adjustment. Slow agricultural growth and unmanageable debt were the symptoms which signalled the need for special action in many African countries. The resolve of the African community toward reform was well reflected in UN-PAAERD and has been demonstrated in the practical steps taken since that time, usually in close consultation with IMF and World Bank as well as with many other donors. These reform programmes often require forms of aid which many donors have found difficult to provide, such as quick-disbursing funds for spare parts and raw materials needed to achieve fuller utilization of existing capacity – both public and private and including industry, agriculture and public infrastructure. Exchange rate reforms, including foreign exchange auctions, designated to provide fully adequate funds to the private sector at realistic exchange rates, have also needed financing. Some donors have made very special efforts to accommodate their policies and procedures to be responsive to the special needs of SAPs. Others have so far abstained from this kind of support on the grounds that their resources are minimal or because of strong preferences for utilizing their scarce funds in support of a project portfolio. A recent important event has been Japan's May, 1987 announcement of intention to provide significant additional support to African low-income countries. It is not clear what the requirements will be for additional quick-disbursing funds. Many African countries have found adequate levels of sufficiently flexible money to provide the support they needed for structural adjustment. Others have not. It will be important to bring an increasing sense of urgency to the process of identifying unmet needs for structural adjustment, as a basis for further consideration by donors and recipients of how aid can be used most effectively to support structural adjustment.

In discussions in the DAC, attention has been drawn to the fact that the donor countries from time to time lack discipline in keeping within agreed investment schedules. It is argued that, after long and careful analysis, African countries have adopted lists of highest priority projects which should receive first call on available financing. In one case, it was alleged that a donor country agreed with an African country to proceed with a project not on the priority list only weeks following agreement on the list within a structural adjustment process. Of course, the obvious point is that it takes two to make such an agreement and that the African country, being the requesting country, must take its full share of responsibility. Since one cannot doubt the seriousness of the African country's minister of finance in putting the list forward on behalf of his government, this example points to the need for systems within African governments of horizontal co-ordination of aid negotiations – avoiding a situation where aid is negotiated by a number of competing ministries dealing outside a policy framework with donors who, themselves, may not have been very close to the structural adjustment negotiation. Also, it is clear that to the extent donors are brought into structural adjustment discussions, they will be more committed to the results. Anyway, donors recognize the need to respect the discipline of the structural adjustment process. This was agreed at last December's DAC High-Level Meeting which emphasized 'the need for continuing discipline by both recipients and donors in adhering to carefully appraised and productive investment programmes ...'. (See Annex 9.1 for DAC's agreement on 'Aid for Improved Development Policies and Related Aspects of Aid Co-ordination'.)

Over the past two years of debate about structural adjustment, a consensus has been reached that our goal is adjustment with growth. Beyond that is the idea of 'adjustment with a human face'. DAC members expressed their view in their guiding principles for aid co-ordination (cited above) as follows: DAC Members 'agree that structural adjustment programmes should take fully into account equity and income distribution issues and would like to see more explicit addressing of budget and strategy issues in human resources questions such as education, health and population, as well as environment'. In practice, this has proved difficult to achieve. In structural adjustment negotiations, inevitably, the critical issues such as exchange rate policy, budget levels, and price policy have taken the time and attention of the participants. While statistics on the impact of structural adjustment on education, health and nutrition are difficult to gather, it seems to be generally agreed that adjustment has often slowed growth in these areas or even caused backward movement. The damage is magnified by the fact that progress in these areas is generally correlated with progress in achieving a demographic transition which, in turn, is relevant to achieving an environmental balance. African governments and donors share an interest in giving this problem more attention.

ISSUES FOR DONORS AND RECIPIENTS IN AID ADMINISTRATION

With ODA representing over 10 per cent of low-income Africa's GNP, we must ask ourselves how we can make the best use of these precious funds. The first question any observer must ask is whether or not the African countries are organized to receive this amount of assistance.

In African governments a high priority is placed on the staffing of central banks and ministries of finance. It is not so immediately apparent that governments place equally high priority on the staffing of aid negotiations. Some of us who have worked in other parts of the world have seen governments appoint as aid co-ordinators senior civil servants of calibre and rank comparable to the person assigned to manage finance and the central bank. This person usually has direct access to a senior minister and meets frequently with the prime minister. Yet, in Africa, where aid dependence is much higher, there is a perception in the donor community that aid co-ordination and negotiations are dealt with as lower priorities.

It is frequently the case that the aid co-ordination function is spread among a number of ministries. For example, some donors might deal with the ministry of foreign affairs, the World Bank usually deals with the ministry of finance, other donors might deal with the ministry of planning, and still others with the functional ministries. Various specialized agencies of the UN often deal directly with functional ministries. In many cases, no one person in the government has overall co-ordination responsibility. In too many cases projects are agreed to by Heads of State or ministers of foreign affairs dealing with their donor country counterparts without adequate reference to project economies or agreements on priorities.

In one country which will remain nameless, the result of this dispersion of decision-making authority was the accumulation of a portfolio of projects which, under constrained budgetary circumstances, the government was manifestly unable to utilize. The government could not afford the local costs during the construction phase. Nor could it afford needed funds for operation and maintenance of public sector facilities once the projects were completed.

Another result of weak aid co-ordination is implementation delays. Recently, millions of dollars in structural adjustment funds were being held up because the recipient country did not provide a bank account number for the deposit. Some donors are deciding not to provide more funds because unexpended obligations are too high.

It would be wrong to suggest that all of the forces favouring lack of co-ordination and sluggish decision-making are in the recipient government. Donors gravitate to that portion of the government which will come up with the kinds of answers which will be best received back home. They often lack crispness in getting decisions, particularly when local staff is limited, or lack needed delegation of authority.

One of the problems with unco-ordinated decision-making is the fact that a variety of criteria are applied in the decision-making process. A line ministry, following the old adage about 'a bird in the hand is worth two in the bush', would be more interested in getting the project agreed and completed on the assumption that a completed project will get needed funds for operations one way or another. Funds are then provided to a lower-priority project because an unused project would become a political embarrassment both at home and abroad.

If consulted, a ministry of finance would be particularly concerned about the budgetary implications of a project. It would also be concerned about financial policy issues and would look to see whether procurement procedures were followed which would achieve good value for money. Further, a ministry of finance would know that a short route to insolvency is borrowing foreign exchange to finance a series of unproductive projects. But, if not, these considerations might not be given appropriate attention.

A ministry of planning, looking to the longer run besides issues of interest to the ministry of finance, would be particularly interested in the relation of projects to longer-term planning criteria and to the sustainability aspects of projects. They would ask whether a project simply 'provides a fish' or rather 'teaches how to fish'. A ministry of planning might well be interested in whether a health project would actually change the health condition of the population as opposed to providing a high-cost service to a few people in the capital city. They would probably be more interested in a public health-oriented project than a curative-oriented project. But, if not consulted, their concerns might not be considered.

Low quality decision-making by the donor and recipient communities can never be justified. But, in a time when an especially high degree of austerity is forced upon us, the need to assure the best possible quality of decision-making within a co-ordinated process where good development criteria are adequately considered is manifest.

One of the special attributes of African assistance is the large number of sources. It is not untypical these days for a relatively small African country to be receiving ODA from some thirty official aid agencies in addition to an untold number of non-governmental agencies. In the DAC we have been giving increasing attention to the question of co-ordination. Whenever co-ordination is spoken of, we find ourselves coming back to the fundamental point that we are providing assistance to sovereign countries who should be making their own decisions and, therefore, should be at the centre of the co-ordination process. This is why it is so critically important that sub-Saharan countries should organize themselves more and more effectively to deal with the donor community.

Certainly, there is no one 'right' way to organize to receive aid more efficiently. It is not argued that all decisions must be made in one office. Rather, it is argued that aid decisions should be made within a policy framework determined by the receiving government and that decisions should be made which are consistent. It is no longer satisfactory for governments to receive aid with conflicting policy prescriptions. We recall the case in one country where, following the criteria of three different donors, three different credit policies were being implemented simultaneously. It would be to African countries' advantage to develop aid co-ordination capacity able to represent views vigorously to the donors. At the same time, donors' willingness to adjust policies or use their money some other way needs to be increased.

DAC countries have discussed the possibility of simplifying procedures in order to make it easier for recipients to deal with the large number of donor spigots. For example, one could imagine the donor community agreeing to utilize a developing country's own planning documents as a basis for project planning. To do this, however, it would be necessary for the recipient country to have such documents and to be willing to modify them in order to meet the minimum requirements of prudent donor decision-making.

Another example would be in the field of audit. There are now in many African countries reputable and well-experienced audit firms which could be called upon to audit aid projects. It would be important that the recipient government has an audit process which satisfied the minimum needs of most of the donor community. In such a case, it would be reasonable for the developing country to raise the issue with the donor community. Similar progress might be made in the field of procurement.

TECHNICAL ASSISTANCE

One other aspect of assistance deserves special mention. This is the whole area of what is commonly called technical assistance. Including free-standing technical assistance, amounts associated with capital projects and amounts provided by NGOs, the total technical assistance effort in sub-Saharan Africa would be measured in billions of dollars. Technical assistance plays a critical role in the training of people and in the provision of expertise. But, because it is provided from a multitude of sources in small amounts and because it gains even less attention from the fragile co-ordination mechanisms of the recipient govern-ments, there is the danger that technical assistance may not be achiev-ing all that we would hope for. Many African countries have become increasingly concerned by the apparent difficulty in achieving more self-sufficiency in the operations of government. Expatriates often continue in decision-making positions long after independence. One finance secretary, in talking about technical assistance, said that there are two kinds of long-term consultants he worries about. First, he worries about long-term incompetent consultants – those individuals who turn out not to be right for the job they were brought in to do. Everyone agrees that they are not needed. But the other kind of consultants he worries about are the excellent ones who come into a ministry, do a fine job and then leave without having changed the capacity of his own country's people to do the job themselves. He argued for long-term relationships with institutions in the donor country where he could go from time to time for short-term advisory services of the highest calibre. This would cost less and be more effective in building the capacity to make decisions among his own officers. However, this finance secretary went on to say that in his government only a few ministries had strong enough leadership to make good use of such institutional relationships.

It would, of course, be wrong to conclude that all long-term consultants should be eliminated. Rather, one would like to ask whether the time has not come for technical assistance to be taken more seriously. Does it not serve the benefits of a carefully thought-through government policy? Does it not deserve much more programming attention in which the objectives of the assistance are carefully thought about? Might we not want to organize technical assistance behind more significant institution-building kinds of objectives in which the donor and the recipient institutions enter into longer-term undertakings which would lead to attainment of self-sufficiency?

It has often been stated that one way of achieving technical assistance programming which is more oriented to institution-building would be to base such programming on carefully thought-through sector or subsector plans. These are often not available, but the question must be raised as to whether it would not be worth the investment of time and planning staff to consider subsectors in these more strategic terms.

Let us take the example of agricultural research. In many countries there is a recognized need for more agricultural research, yet there is lacking an inventory of all that is currently being undertaken. Research institutions doing the same thing are separately seeking funds from outside sources. Operating as separate cells, they are not getting the benefits of networking among themselves. There is a lack of national research strategy. Vertical agencies are unco-ordinated in particular geographic regions. A strategic planning process within a ministry of agriculture, involving the research facilities of the country along with the agricultural education facilities and the agricultural extension facilities resulting in a talked-through subsector strategy for agricultural research, would provide the basis for more efficient use of national resources as well as better co-ordinated technical assistance. If, in a particular country, the donors most interested in helping in this area were involved in the subsector planning process, they would be more likely to support the result and, furthermore, might well make substantive contributions based on their experience in other countries. With a series of subsector strategies for critical areas, there would be a basis for organizing technical assistance to achieve more important results, greater efficiency and the tailoring of technical assistance to an institution-building mode rather than simply to provide on-the-spot advice on a current basis.

One advantage of subsector strategies is their potential for raising subsector goals to the political level. It is hard to get the attention of the public and/or the government administration to such general goals as 'improving research' or 'improving health'. But sub-sector campaigns to 'double wheat production' or 'increase immunization levels to 75 per cent' have provided an organizing vehicle to top management in many countries. While care must be taken to avoid one goal driving out others, which may be less quantifiable but even more important, often the careful articulation of very precise objectives has made possible significant achievements at surprisingly low cost. While most subsector strategies could not be suitably organized behind such specific goals, it is worth looking for opportunities.

We should recognize, of course, that individuals on both the recipient side and the donor side often see benefits in the present anarchy. Recipient institutions accept technical assistance for the vehicles or equipment which come with it – or salary topping and travel and study opportunities. Donor personnel are often creating their own jobs. Consulting firms seek business. The point is that these private objectives need to be controlled in the public interests of recipient governments and donors alike. It will be for the recipients to take the lead in improving technical assistance programming. And it is most likely that donors will be willing to co-operate.

CONCLUSIONS

With these general comments, let us conclude by suggesting the following measures which African governments and donors might work together to implement:

(a) Both donor and recipient communities should act within the framework of SAPs where they exist. Rolling three-year investment schedules which may have been adopted should be respected. Where developing country ministries or donors wish to sponsor projects to be included in the next revision of the investment schedule, the process of project priority setting should be transparent so that the cabinet and Head of State will be able to make decisions with maximum information on the table;

(b) Donors should continually review the opportunities to respond to SAPs with quick-disbursing funds. Recipients should actively seek higher priority in donor portfolios for funding needed to support structural adjustment. Where projects are agreed to be appropriate, opportunities to finance them in ways which take account of on-going structural adjustment measures should be sought. For example, in times of budget and foreign exchange stringency, it may be appropriate for donors to finance a higher than usual proportion of local costs. For poorer countries, grants or very concessional terms are more appropriate. Where existing capacity is not being well used or maintained, priority should be given to maintenance, spare parts and raw materials;

(c) African governments should call to the attention of the donor community information on the impact of structural adjustment on education, health, population, nutrition and environment programmes. While solutions may not be easy, information and dialogue could lead to improved strategies and more support in these areas;

(d) Recipients and donors should work together to make CG and RT processes more effective. But these are only an aspect of the total process of dialogue and co-ordination. Recipients should welcome co-ordination efforts among donors and afford opportunities for donors to discuss issues frankly. While exchange of information should be encouraged, this is only one aspect of co-ordination. In the end, decisions must be made among alternative policies or programmes, and the recipient governments must make these decisions;

(e) African governments, as a measure to achieve greater control over the use of scarce resources, should each decide to give a higher priority to the aid process. They should appoint one highly-placed person of exceptional ability to be in charge of aid. This person should have staff resources, should operate in very close co-ordination with other ministries, especially with finance and planning, and should have direct access to the cabinet. All aid should be co-ordinated by this officer. While negotiations on small aid programmes could be delegated to other ministries, all aid should be required to operate within government policy. No project should be approved unless its financial implications, both during implementation and subsequent operational phases, have been considered by budget and planning authorities. All donors should either deal with the aid co-ordinator or be specifically authorized to deal with another ministry, which in turn, would be expected to operate within established policies and to keep the co-ordinating unit fully informed. African governments should develop cadres of trained aid negotiators – people who understand the legal and policy issues and know donors' procedures and negotiating goals. Donors are willing to finance the training of aid-negotiating staff;

(f) African governments should insist that each technical assistance

246

intervention be planned with a clear objective in mind. This should usually be an institution-building objective which will increase self-sufficiency; and,

(g) As rapidly as possible, where they do not already exist, subsector strategies should be articulated as a framework within which both country and donor programmes can operate. These should be undertaken with the co-operation of donors to the subsector. Long-term goals should be clearly stated and measures designed to reach them. Subsector strategies should be designed within the framework of budget realities, with needed attention to cost recovery and decentralized responsibility.

In summary, there is consensus that African countries face difficult structural adjustment issues and that support is needed for the bold efforts now being implemented. In addition to improvements in the world economic environment, donors can help by debt relief measures, provision of aid which supports structural adjustment efforts and an increased volume of aid. Recipients can help by improving aid decision-making. Proper measures of discipline and flexibility are needed by all sides. With dialogue on these matters increasing, there is reason to hope that significant progress will take place in the coming years.

NOTES

1. DAC members are Australia, Austria, Belgium, Canada, Commission of the European Communities, Denmark, Finland, France, Germany, Ireland, Italy, Japan, the Netherlands, New Zealand, Norway, Sweden, Switzerland, the United Kingdom and the United States.
2. For 1986, the figure is estimated to be $US18 billion. Because of the significant change in exchange rates in real terms, however, this represents a modest decrease from the 1985 level.

Aid for Improved Development Policies and Related Aspects of Aid Co-ordination

INTRODUCTION

The need to use aid more systematically to support improved development policies and programmes of developing countries and the related problems of aid co-ordination has for some time been a central theme in the work of the DAC. This work is an essential element of the efforts of DAC members to improve the effectiveness of aid in achieving development goals and objectives. At DAC's high-level meeting held in December, members reviewed recent work on this subject and approved a series of guiding principles designed to give general guidance and direction to a collective effort at improved aid co-ordination with developing countries. The text of these guiding principles and the considerations which led to their adoption is set out in the section that follows. The remainder of the annex provides a factual account of recent developments, which form the background from which these conclusions have emerged.

CONCLUSIONS OF DAC HIGH-LEVEL MEETING OF 1986

Nature of the Problem

Much of recent DAC work has been concerned with the problems of adapting aid to support improved development policies by developing countries and the related problems of aid co-ordination. These problems were summarized in Twenty-Five Years of Development Co-operation: A review, along the following lines.

The number of development assistance institutions operating in developing countries has expanded substantially in recent years. Two dozen donor governments, some ten multilateral development banks and funds, 19 UN agencies and several hundred NGOs currently provide development assistance. Some donors use more than one administrative unit to channel aid funds to recipient countries. Additionally, export credit agencies and commercial banks provide finance to countries they judge to be creditworthy.

The funds made available from external sources vary greatly as to their financial terms and other conditions (procurement regulations, end-use controls, counterpart requirements, etc.). Donor preferences for particular sectors, projects and approaches are also often different. In addition, there are differences among donors in their willingness to provide certain kinds of aid, and in the degree of their involvement in managing the aid delivery process. Several donors maintain full-time field staff in recipient countries to administer aid programmes. Others work mainly through resident diplomatic missions, augmented in some cases by regional aid offices and in all cases by visiting development specialists.

Adding further to the complexity of the aid process is the wide variety of needs for aid to help finance capital projects in many different sectors involving different planning and executing agencies: to provide technical assistance for strengthening local management, research, training and other institutions; and to provide funds for essential imports, such as fuel, other production inputs, spare parts and, in some cases, food.

To ensure that this complex process, involving divergent sources and diverse activities, interrelates effectively with the recipient country's own resources and programming processes requires an extraordinary organizational effort. Frequent donor—recipient consultations on policy and procedural issues are required to establish agreed purposes, approaches, administrative systems and supporting measures for each aid project or programme.

Aid effectiveness has been impaired in a number of instances where a recipient's limited planning or administrative capacity was unequal to the demands of aid management. In some cases, the aid received may have been substantial in the aggregate but nonetheless short of the critical mass because of insufficiently concerted planning and concentration of resources.

Moreover, experience has shown that for aid to make a lasting contribution to the economic and social well-being of developing countries, it must be concerned not only with the proper selection, design and implementation of individual projects and their economic and institutional sustainability, but also with the support of broader sectoral and national efforts and policies.

Policy decisions cannot and should not be imposed from outside. Donors must strive to understand the political, institutional, economic and social considerations that affect the recipient's capacity to undertake policy adjustments. Closer working relations and co-operation are most likely to evolve from intimate donor knowledge of the political and socio-economic context of the recipient country and from the provision of aid on an increasingly assured, continuous and predictable basis.

For donor advice in the policy and programming dialogue to be credible, it must be consistent as well as competent and reflect full understanding of the variety of economic and other constraints facing the developing country. A profusion of conflicting advice from a multiplicity of donors can be counter-productive. Policy reform efforts are most likely to be fruitful when they are concentrated on key problem areas and when the responsible authorities – central and sectoral – assume responsibility for policy analysis and decisions. It is a basically unhealthy situation if developing countries have to rely heavily and repeatedly on donors to carry out their policy analysis and programme planning.

Guiding Principles for Aid Co-ordination with Developing Countries

It is against the background of the above considerations that DAC members have, at their 1986 high-level meeting, adopted the following principles. These principles must be used flexibly to meet the diversity of specific situations; they apply mainly to developing countries which depend heavily on external assistance and need the support of international aid co-ordination arrangements to ensure effective use of resources. DAC members recognize that developing countries themselves are responsible for setting their policies and priorities, and that central responsibility for aid co-ordination lies with each recipient government.

(i) *Donor co-operation to help developing countries establish and implement improved policies and carefully appraised investments and expenditure programmes.* Developing countries need well-designed policies and carefully appraised investment and expenditure programmes for effective and co-ordinated use of both their national and external resources.

DAC members recognize the importance of the World Bank/IMF-led process of working with developing countries in the articulation of SAPs. They welcome the recent shift in the orientation of SAP towards growth. They agree that SAPs should take fully into account equity and income distribution issues and would like to see more explicit addressing of budget and strategy issues in human resources questions such as education, health and population, as well as environment. They note that SAPs can make a contribution to creating the conditions which, in the medium term, may encourage a resumption of private flows to developing countries.

DAC members underline the need for aid agencies to help developing countries strengthen their analytical and management capacity to design and implement effective policies and programmes. DAC members also recognize the need for greater participation by bilateral aid agencies in assisting developing countries in their efforts to improve their policies and programmes, and in providing the often costly preparatory analytical work. While multilateral agencies are well placed to assist in this field, bilateral donors also have a role to play, especially at the level of sectors where they have special expertise to offer. DAC members will review the need to stengthen their capacity to make contributions to this area.

DAC members emphasize the need for continuing discipline by both recipients and donors in adhering to carefully appraised and productive investment programmes. Such programmes will provide a particularly useful basis for aid allocations if they have been the subject of careful review and discussion with donors with the help and advice of the international financial institutions. The regular review of these programmes offers an opportunity to examine progress and to consult on priorities. They are a good basis for aid co-ordination.

DAC members acknowledge the desirability of providing adequate financing to developing countries undertaking effective policy reform efforts. This will often require making available quick-disbursing funds for the financing of urgent import requirements. Indications by donors of medium-term funding prospects will facilitate structural reform efforts and will, in turn, be facilitated by such efforts.

There is a need to put more emphasis, in the period immediately ahead, on rehabilitation and improved use of existing capacity. Programmes for these purposes will often have a higher priority than launching large new projects. DAC members recognize the need to make realistic provision for recurrent cost and maintenance requirements but with agreement for step-by-step advance towards self-reliance.

DAC members recognize the special merits of having several donors work together with a recipient government in the co-financing of important projects and sector programmes. They will attempt to reduce administrative burdens by relying as much as possible for appraisal on a bilateral or multilateral lead agency.

Export credits may, in selective cases, be helpful also in the low-income countries but great care must be exercised to ensure that development goals and the discipline of carefully appraised investment programmes are taken fully into account.

External debt servicing obligations have major financing implications for many countries. Debt relief exercise by the Paris Club should be based on full information of the nature and requirements of growth-oriented medium-term structural policy reform efforts.

(ii) *Further steps to improve arrangements for aid co-ordination.* DAC members reaffirm their determination to co-operate closely with recipient countries, international institutions and other donors in international aid co-ordination arrangements working towards operationally relevant conclusions, based on genuine consensus.

DAC members accept the need for close co-operation between recipient governments and the multilateral lead agencies but feel that the processes of consultation and co-ordination should provide an opportunity for bilateral donors to express their views during the formative stages of policy and programme consultations between aid-recipients and the international agencies.

Full and frank exchanges of pertinent information on on-going and planned activities among donors, and between donors and recipients, are essential to the successful co-ordination and effective use of aid.

DAC members appreciate the recent improvements in the organization of CGs and RTs and invite the lead agencies to pursue their efforts in the following directions:

(a) Encouraging greater participation by bilateral donors in the consultations preceding CGs and RTs making use of local groups where possible; such participation is essential to ensure the emergence of a genuine consensus on recipient country development policies and programmes;

(b) Revising the format of CG meetings to facilitate more frank and substantive exchanges of views on key policy issues and problems; more careful review of recipient investment plans with a sharper focus on sectoral policies and investment programmes; fuller discussion of the aid implications of recipient SAPs; and taking into account all elements determining recipients' overall financial situation, including trade prospects and debt service requirements;

(c) To be more concerned with the identification and programming of technical assistance needs and priorities which are often as important as financial needs; UNDP has a special role to play in this regard and should participate fully in the CG processes;

(d) Recording of conclusions reached at CG and RT meetings, as summarized by the Chairman, in a detailed and action-oriented manner, and making them available promptly to interested parties, including local co-ordination groups;

(e) Ensuring effective follow-up with respect to actions stemming from CG and RT meetings, specifically regarding donor statements of aid intentions and recipient statements of policy reform intentions through, *inter alia*, sectoral and other in-country meetings.

DAC members are encouraged by UNDP's recent progress in strengthening the RT process and enhancing its capacity to perform its co-ordination role more effectively through, *inter alia*: encouraging developing countries to participate actively; emphasis on policy reforms; the strengthening of UNDP staff; a more selective approach to the choice of countries and participants; improved analysis and in-country follow-up; better preparation and organization of RT meetings through closer collaboration with World Bank; encouraging adequate representation by recipients and donors, and with UNDP chairmanship of the meetings. RTs can be further strengthened if, in the first phase of the process, UN specialized agencies can be represented by UNDP and if DAC members' representatives reflect this position in the appropriate bodies of the specialized agencies.

It was recognized that the second phase of the RT process, i.e. the larger and more open meeting at the country level, can be particularly useful in confirming the resolve of the government to push ahead with its adjustment policies by providing it with an opportunity to indicate its policy commitments in a broad setting. Donors in turn have an opportunity to announce their support for the programme.

DAC members underline the need to strengthen aid co-ordination at the local (i.e. recipient country capital) level, and to establish stronger links between central and local co-ordination arrangements. Central co-ordination arrangements should give the lead to local and sectoral co-ordination, *inter alia*, by identifying issues to be addressed at the local/sectoral level. Policy dialogue should be an intrinsic element of aid co-ordination at the local/sectoral level. Recipient governments should be at the centre of the process. The participation of appropriate officials from the recipient government's line agencies is essential but, for decisions reached on sector aid policies or programmes, it is important for the government's central finance and planning authorities to be involved.

There has been considerable expansion of local co-ordination activities recently. Progress has been made at the level of exchange of information, avoiding project duplication and promoting joint activities; but more needs to be done, especially in relating aid to carefully appraised and reviewed investment programmes, and in developing and implementing sector policies and programmes. DAC members welcome the establishment of recipient-led local mechanisms for the purpose of ensuring more effective monitoring and co-ordination. Such local mechanisms need clear mandates.

DAC members stress the importance of improved sectoral approaches, involving the preparation of and support for carefully appraised investment and expenditure programmes taking capital and recurrent cost-financing prospects realistically into account. There is also the need to explore prospects for more sector grouping of assistance (both technical and capital) to improve its efficiency, thereby also reducing administrative burdens, all around, through improved work-sharing and harmonization of procedures. An important tool to achieve this objective is the use of aid co-financing arrangements.

DAC members acknowledge the need for greater involvement of the regional development banks in policy dialogue and reform, particularly at the sector level, when they are important donors. It is important that they work within the macro-economic policy framework and co-operate closely with World Bank or UNDP, as appropriate.

Regional approaches to co-ordination, as they have been evolved particularly in Africa within the framework of CILSS/Club du Sahel and SADCC in looking at aid needs in a regional context and encouraging regional co-operation, can be an essential complement to country-level co-ordination.

DAC members are fully aware of the need to avoid overburdening the administrative capacity of recipients. While effective action to streamline the administration of aid will not be easy, they should seek opportunities to harmonize and simplify the requirements they exact from recipient governments, especially by making greater use of studies and reports already prepared by others or worked out by an agreed lead agency. This may entail modifications to legislative and administrative requirements.

DAC members recognize the staff implications of improved co-ordination, particularly the need to have staff with appropriate economic and policy expertise in support of this function. Effective participation both in the policy dialogue and in aid programming at the local level will be facilitated by the presence of policy-oriented staff stationed in recipient countries in which individual members have major aid interest. This may require strengthening the staff in the field, including the redeploying of some staff, adjustments in personnel training and recruitment policies and effective use of private expertise.

DAC members underline the essentiality of strengthening developing countries' institutional capacity to design and implement effective policies and programmes, and to manage their development processes. Competent central government institutions are essential to establish an effective policy framework, but broader institutional development efforts are required at all levels of government, including sectoral and local levels. These efforts should also take into account the capabilities and potential of the private sector and the requirements it has for institutional development to better enable it to make its full contribution.

DAC members will take appropriate action within their own organizations to implement the principles set out above. They will, from time to time, take stock in the DAC of the progress being made.

CHAPTER TEN

The United States Assistance Strategy for Africa

RICHARD J. HAYNES
STEPHEN M. HAYKIN

INTRODUCTION

At the closing ceremony of the UN Special Session on the critical economic situation in Africa on June 1, 1986, the Administrator USAID briefly outlined how the US planned to work with African countries and the donor community in a partnership to stimulate economic recovery and renewed growth in Africa. He pledged to focus and concentrate US assistance on the highest priorities identified at the meeting and to find the most effective and efficient ways to implement these priorities with the resources at hand. He expressed the belief that US programmes are moving in the right direction and that the Government is marshalling US resources to maximize the quality of its assistance to Africa.

THE THREE PRIORITY GOALS OF US ASSISTANCE TO AFRICA

The three priority goals to which US assistance is directed are: (a) economic restructuring; (b) agricultural growth; and, (c) human resources development.

To put the US foreign assistance programme in perspective, we should first briefly elaborate our views of the priority goals. A comparison of these priorities with those articulated in UN-PAAERD under the item 'Commitment to a Common Point of Reference' reveals the most fundamental similarity. The agreement on these priorities by the UN members is, in our view, the signal achievement of the Special Session.

The US Government sees economic restructuring as the number one priority for Africa. Nothing short of this will spark renewed growth. The US strongly supports the bold steps for policy reform called for in

UN-PAAERD. Economic stabilization is absolutely necessary, but we all know it must be accompanied by reforms which produce jobs and growth. Each country will employ different means to achieve stabilization, but the increased role for price signals, competitive markets and the private sector to spur income and development is fundamental.

The second priority for Africa is the development of agriculture – the principal engine of growth. UN-PAAERD and previous documents of OAU and ECA should be commended for their renewed commitment to agriculture. To attain lasting growth of the agriculture sector, progress in the following four areas is vital:

(a) The establishment of a favourable policy framework to support small farmer production and marketing;
(b) The availability of appropriate technologies to farmers that require them. Such technologies call for a substantial and long-term commitment to research;
(c) agricultural marketing, with particular emphasis to the expansion of the grain trade among African states; and,
(d) Finally, to assure sustained agricultural growth, proper attention must be paid to better management of Africa's natural resources, including programmes to slow and halt the environmental degradation which undermines efforts to increase agricultural production.

Development of Africa's human resources is US Government's third priority. To make economic policy reforms and agricultural development work, we must never lose sight of the most important resource of any country – its people. Child survival is a key programme. Another is provision of family planning services. And development of women's capacities is essential as is their full integration into all economic assistance activities.

To carry out these three priorities, Africa will need to mobilize all its available resources; in particular those which were perhaps not so apparent to us in the past. For example, the potential energy and resources of the African private sector is enormous. Clearly, its strengths have not been fully marshalled. The community of NGOs is a resource capable of generating significant levels of public and private resources for development.

THE US RESPONSE TO UN-PAAERD

The recent 1983–1985 drought, crop failures, food shortages, famine and subsequent relief efforts focused the attention of the world on

Africa's economic and social crisis. Under President Reagan's leadership, the US was one of the major participants in the emergency relief effort, providing over $US2 billion in food, relief and recovery assistance from 1984 through 1986. Very gratifying to this administration was the extent of the outpouring of support from private citizens and the private sector in response to the needs of the African people, support which complemented nicely what we were doing through official channels.

We have all learned many lessons from that tragedy and we have reached the common conclusion that African states and the international community had to come together to redefine the economic priorities of Africa and to devise a programme for dealing with the underlying causes of the crisis. The UN Special Session on Africa and the Action Programme adopted were the historic outcome of that collaboration.

Following on the Special Session, President Reagan established a White House Task Force to conduct an inter-departmental review of US economic policies and programmes for sub-Saharan Africa. The task force considered a number of issues, among which were: the role of US assistance; the co-ordination of aid programmes with other international donors; trade policies and how they can be adjusted to support economic growth; international lending institutions and debt policies; enhancing the role of US private citizens; and, most significantly, making Africa's indigenous private sector the spark to ignite real economic growth.

Last March, the President approved the recommendations of the Task Force and launched an initiative aimed at ending hunger in sub-Saharan Africa through economic growth and private enterprise development – we call this the 'Ending Hunger Initiative'. Much of US assistance to Africa already is directed toward increasing food production. The major change for us is to make ending hunger, through economic growth, the central focus of all our assistance efforts. We want to support African efforts to develop open, stable, efficient and growing economies capable of ending the threat of periodic famine once and for all. From now on, each US assistance programme effort will be justified by how it contributes to this greater goal. Through the establishment of this unifying policy framework, we believe the effectiveness of all our programmes will be enhanced, regardless of the level of funding available.

There are many elements to the programme developed by the Task Force which encompass an array of policy and programme proposals. In summary the major elements are:

(a) More flexible bilateral foreign assistance legislation for Africa. The US Congress is presently considering this legislative proposal, the 'Development Fund for Africa';
(b) More flexible food aid programmes to be offered on grant terms to countries undertaking viable programmes of economic reform;
(c) US support for efforts to increase multilateral funding for economic reform through an enlarged IMF Structural Adjustment Facility (SAF). At the Venice Summit in 1987, the Western leaders recognized the importance of the problem of African debt and welcomed a proposal for a three-fold expansion of the SAF;
(d) US support for more favourable Paris Club debt rescheduling conditions for low-income countries undertaking programmes of economic reform;
(e) A more tightly integrated and co-ordinated US agency management structure designed to ensure that all US assistance programmes and policies affecting Africa are consistently applied in support of growth and private sector development;
(f) Negotiation, through IMF/World Bank policy framework process, of long-term compacts with each sub-Saharan African country that establishes long-term structural adjustment and reform programmes;
(g) Promotion of continued and improved access to world markets for the exports of low-income sub-Saharan nations in recognition of good performance; and
(h) Mobilization of the US private sector to complement African and donor efforts.

THE DEVELOPMENT FUND FOR AFRICA

In the last few years, USAID has been reconsidering and reviewing its development strategy for Africa in an effort to develop a clearer appreciation of both the economic constraints facing the continent and the way we should be organized as an institution to address them. USAID has been working closely with the US Congress to develop the legislation that will enable it to concentrate its resources to support UN-PAAERD.

To this end, as part of the Ending Hunger Initiative, a bill has been introduced into the US Congress titled 'the African Famine Recovery and Development Act', as part of the 1988 budget request. This legislation would establish the Development Fund for Africa (DFA) as a unique section of the United States Foreign Assistance Act. The

257

following are some of the significant features proposed as part of the DFA:

(a) Funds for Africa would be reserved exclusively for Africa and could not be reallocated to other geographical regions;
(b) Funds for Africa would be authorized for five years, a change from the usual one or two years authorization;
(c) Funds for Africa would be so-called 'no-year funds', meaning they would remain available from one year to the next. This would allow us to make commitments based completely on programme merit rather than being subject to year-end pressures;
(d) With only minor exceptions, funds for Africa would no longer be allocated by specific functions, but may be directed to programme or project assistance as required; and,
(e) Food aid programmes would be offered on all-grant terms, including ocean freight, to countries undertaking significant programmes of economic reform.

The legislation would also require that USAID supports the expansion and strengthening of the development efforts of African and US private and voluntary and non-governmental organizations. At least 15 per cent of USAID's funds are required to be reserved for the programmes of approved US and indigenous voluntary and non-governmental organizations.

Another significant feature of the legislation, which we believe is illustrative of its underlying goal of providing assistance as effectively and expeditiously as possible, is that procurement of goods and services would be untied. This provision would only apply to sub-Saharan Africa under US foreign assistance legislation.

The importance of donor co-ordination is also recognized by the legislation. In addition to calling for strengthened donor co-ordination and, in particular, leadership by the African states, the DFA provides for funding to assist the African states to increase their capacity to participate more effectively in donor co-ordination efforts at the country, regional and sector levels.

SUPPORTING POLICY REFORM

Policy reform is a major component used by all African Governments to reactivate and stimulate economic growth. Thus, it follows that a cornerstone of UN-PAAERD and the US Ending Hunger Initiative is the support of African Governments' policy reform programmes. The US sees policy reforms not as ends in themselves, but rather as means to promote economic growth and development. As such, support for policy reforms must be balanced with technical, financial and commodity assistance to overcome the economic and institutional obstacles faced by farmers, workers, consumers, and those who would invest in Africa's future.

The United States' policy reform strategy centres on the restructuring of economic decision-making. It seeks the shift of economic power from its concentration in central Governments to private entities and local communities. This strategy has the following three major thrusts: (a) encouraging private enterprise while reducing the role and improving the efficiency of the public sector; (b) expanding the use of competitive markets; and, (c) improving the capacity of individuals and local organizations to participate in their own development.

While the US is a strong supporter of policy reforms, it recognizes that the most important roles are played by Africans themselves and by their Governments. Furthermore, the US recognizes the substantial contributions of IMF, World Bank, ADB, UNECA and other donors, and looks forward to continuing co-operation with them.

The US is providing support to active policy reform programmes in more than 20 African countries. Of these countries, most have IMF programmes and many have World Bank Structural or Sectoral Adjustment Programmes. Mali and Somalia are two examples of such countries in which the US has co-operated extensively with other bilateral and multilateral donors to support reform programmes. About half of all US bilateral resources for Africa in 1987 will support economic reform programmes. These supports are carried out through a wide range of programmes.

Since 1985, $US150 million have been committed to provide support to 12 countries through the US African Economic Policy Reform Programme (AEPRP). For instance, in Mauritius, Senegal and Zaire, AEPRPs are designed to increase private sector activity by reducing tariffs and marginal tax rates while in Mali, AEPRP aims at improving fiscal policy as well as the climate for private investment. Increasingly, policy conditionality is being attached to Commodity Import Programmes (CIPs) and cash grants. For example, CIPs between 1982 and 1985 and a 1986 cash sales programme supported public sector and foreign exchange market reforms in Somalia. Through 'policy support' measures associated with our food aid programmes, African countries have agreed to additional policy reforms. Furthermore, technical assistance is provided for policy analysis, the design of reform programmes and related training.

To date, the major reforms carried out in SAPs have concentrated on liberalizing markets. The commonalities among US-supported reforms include the following:

(a) Reducing overvaluation of currencies through devaluation and promoting the development of open foreign exchange markets;
(b) Liberalizing agricultural markets, raising price incentives for food producers and reducing costly government subsidies to food consumers;
(c) Reducing redundant and non-productive public sector employment, while promoting private enterprise and employment; and,
(d) Rationalizing government's taxation and investment spending and improving cost recovery in the provision of public services.

Great strides have been made in several African countries as a result of policy-based assistance supported by the US. At the same time, United States' experience with reform programmes in recent years has been sobering. We acknowledge the difficulties encountered by African states in the face of structural adjustment and reform programmes, particularly at this time when trade prospects look bleak and the debt burden is crushing.

USAID actively engages in collaborative monitoring and evaluation of programmes; it helps to support to increase the likelihood of their success. Although it is always difficult to compare actual experience with scenarios that might have occurred, recent studies provide evidence of progress in promoting economic growth and development through reform programmes. Favourable impacts have included: higher levels of agricultural and aggregate output (GNP); larger incomes for small farmers; export growth and reduction of balance-of-payments deficits; improvements in resource allocation; and greater opportunities for investment and employment in the private sector.

The experience of African countries with reform programmes supported by the US and other donors is summarized below with reference to several critical concerns:

Agricultural Production

Through reforms in agricultural pricing and the reduction of state control of commodity markets, food production has been increased in countries such as Somalia and Zambia. Price and market reforms, combined with better input supplies and access to credit, contributed to output growth in Zimbabwe.

Farmers' Behaviour

Farmers responded to changes in incentives. There is clear evidence that farmers responded to freer markets and price signals and made choices that maximized their welfare. They adjusted to improved market signals by rechannelling their energies back into agriculture, by expanding land and labour use, and by using resources more efficiently – altering the mix of inputs they use and diversifying crop production.

Incomes of Small Farmers

The major beneficiaries of policy reforms in the agricultural sector have been small-holders. Policy reforms fostered increases in the volumes of cereals marketed by small farmers. Overall, small farmers dramatically increased their share of all grain marketed in Somalia, Zambia and Zimbabwe; as a result, small farmers' incomes were higher than they would have been without reforms.

Private Sector Activity

Policy reforms have contributed to the expansion of private sector activity, employment and efficiency in Somalia and Zambia, and in Mali's cereals subsector.

Economic Growth

Macro-economic and sectoral policy reforms have enhanced GDP performance in countries such as Kenya, Mali, Somalia and Zambia. Yet, macro-economic progress has been slow. Most countries, a notable exception being Somalia, have seen the negative effects of bad weather, falling export prices and debt overwhelm the positive effects of increased efficiency and investment.

Government Budgets

Market restructuring and spending reforms helped African Governments in their efforts to cut budget deficits. By reducing the role of public enterprise, improving performance and reducing employment, the public sector is cutting costs, as in Mali and Somalia. But producer price supports and consumer subsidies continue to burden the public sector in many countries.

Balance-of-Payments

Reform programmes have had favourable effects on balance-of-payments. Reforms in the agricultural sector helped countries such as Somalia and Zambia to develop new export markets. Devaluations had the intended effects of increasing domestic production and exports thereby reducing imports. There is evidence of increasing reliance on domestically produced agricultural inputs. Scarce foreign exchange

261

appears to be allocated more rationally, contributing to more efficient input use in agriculture and increases in industrial output.

Equity

There is promising evidence that policy reform programmes have had a positive effect on distributional equity. Reforms have helped some countries to reduce the urban bias of their economic systems with small farmers and workers in the non-formal sectors achieving gains.

The US clearly recognizes the difficulties associated with the adoption of policy reform programmes. Experience suggests the following conclusions:

(a) Even without formal reform programmes, structural adjustment has taken place. Ghana and Guinea are examples of countries which undertook reforms when various factors led to *de facto* adjustment;

(b) Zambia's SAP gave the impetus to real growth in the agricultural sector; but continuing financial pressures and problems in reform implementation were overwhelming;

(c) Price interventions are extremely difficult to manage. Most agricultural reform programmes link market liberalization with support of producer prices and reductions in consumer subsidies. In general, supporting high producer prices in the face of supply gluts is too much of a drain on Government resources. Both Somalia and Mali were forced to suspend price support activities. Zimbabwe, too, has been forced to reduce its support prices in the face of enormous grain production. Yet, as the Zambian experience so dramatically illustrates, reductions in food subsidies are certain to encounter the opposition of consumers when their buying power is eroded; and,

(d) While being essential to the structural adjustment process, reforms that raise the costs of imports, such as devaluations, and those that reduce Government expenditures, such as subsidies on food, health and education require careful scrutiny and targeted interventions to safeguard the most economically vulnerable populations. In this regard, USAID's role has been supportive: food aid to Mali, Somalia, Guinea and Zambia has helped to avert shortages during the reform process. Local currencies generated through the sales of food aid have helped to relieve financial pressures on Governments during transition periods. Commodity Import Programmes have provided balance-of-payments support, supplied critical inputs and also generated local currencies for further development uses. Cash grants have also helped African countries by reducing balance-of-payments pressures while reforms were taking place.

Outlook for US Assistance

The initiative to end hunger underscores the US commitment to continuing support of policy reforms in Africa on both a bilateral and multilateral basis. The US will place emphasis on assistance to countries seeking to build or maintain economic conditions conducive to economic growth. The proposed DFA will provide greater flexibility in directing US assistance to the removal of policy constraints to growth and development. It would also provide greater continuity through longer funding commitments.

Although the objectives of future US assistance for policy reforms will be consistent with those of the past, as progress is made, new concerns are likely to rise to the fore. To date, the major reforms carried out in SAPs have concentrated on liberalizing markets. The next generation of policy reforms will undoubtedly be much more complicated and could well centre on such activities as regulatory reform and increasing the efficiency of the public sector.

THE DEBT ISSUE

The US is aware of the cloud that hangs over African economic recovery. Debt-servicing requirements for African countries are heavy and resources needed for investment and growth are being used to service old obligations. However, there are a number of points we should remember. African economies have not grown fast enough to generate the money to pay for development. To a certain extent, this is because much of the borrowed money was used for consumption or for questionable investments. It is also true that some Governments followed policies which discouraged exports. In the last analysis, the central problem is to move the world economy to higher growth which means expanding international markets. The slow-down in growth in the OECD countries has been accompanied by a technological transformation. Copper is being replaced by fiber optics; sugar by corn products. The future holds promise for new materials such as superconductors; new agricultural technologies in genetic engineering; new advances in robotics.

Specifically with respect to debt, we have supported the stretching out of terms in the Paris Club to ten years grace and ten years repayment. We led the way in the concentration of IMF Trust Funds in the SAF for African LDCs. All of our development assistance pro-grammes have been converted to grants. Over 30 per cent of our assistance takes the form of fast-disbursing balance-of-payments support, and we are looking for ways to provide additional help.

We know that these actions have not solved the problem. We are presently looking for imaginative ways of alleviating the African debt problem without bringing down the international financial institutions which have served the LDCs so well. The US is exploring all options. Up to now we have not found any magic elixir that will make debt go away. We are committed to helping Africa grow again. We are com-mitted to acting forcefully and imaginatively. When the drought hit Africa, we were in the vanguard of those providing the needed assistance. Even though the debt crisis is not only much more invisible, but also much less amenable to easy solutions, we shall not ignore its cost in human suffering.

FOOD AID IN SUPPORT OF STRUCTURAL ADJUSTMENT

As previously mentioned, in keeping with the spirit of the Presidential initiative to end hunger in Africa, we are rethinking the role of food aid in the US assistance programme and, in particular, how food aid can be a positive support to structural adjustment and policy reform pro-grammes. In Guinea, Senegal, Madagascar, Mali and Somalia – among others – US food aid programmes are closely linked to policy reform efforts. At the same time, we recognize the need to target food aid to the vulnerable, poorer populations who in certain instances are being asked to bear a significant burden with regard to structural adjustment reforms, such as those arising from the removal of food subsidies or the freeing of food prices. Structural adjustment must have a 'human face' to temporarily ease pressures on the poor while adjustments are being worked out. Among the basic requirements to make such food programmes successful however are strong local institutions to manage the activity. We see a major role here for both local and foreign private voluntary and non-governmental organizations on whom we rely as key collaborators with the African states and the foreign donors in administering food aid programmes.

There is also a very valuable role for food aid to play in facilitating trilateral trade arrangements between African states. The US has already had some success in making possible the shipment of surplus maize from one African nation to another, paid for in effect by shipments of US food to the exporting nation. We are looking into possibilities to institutionalize such arrangements within the framework of structural adjustment/policy reform programmes. With thoughtfulness and imagination, food aid can play a positive and most supportive role in adjustment efforts.

While we look to an expanded role for food aid in Africa, we are very mindful of avoiding the negative impact of excessive food import on local markets. We recognize the need for all donors not to be overly zealous with their food shipments. A number of US programmes incorporated technical assistance for improved data collection and analysis of food production and for more accurate determination of import needs.

USAID provided Africa with an estimated $US300 million in food assistance in 1987. This represents about 38 per cent of the approximately $US790 million in total US assistance for Africa in 1987.

SUPPORT TO THE AGRICULTURAL SECTOR

Certainly a key to the ultimate success of the United States initiative to end hunger, almost by definition, is assistance to Africa's agricultural sector. As our second priority, the development and support of agriculture goes hand-in-hand with our first support of economic restructuring. Activities promoting agriculture sector reform, agricultural research and the strengthening of private market links receive the greatest emphasis in our programmes.

We have been looking at USAID agricultural efforts in the past year, evaluating them in collaboration with our African partners and World Bank with the goal of arriving at a better understanding of what USAID does best as an institution, what are the key problems our host-countries believe we should focus on, and what kinds of changes we have to make internally to make our efforts more effective and assure that limited resources go as far as possible.

In addition to supporting basic pricing and marketing reforms, and encouraging privatization of parastatals and development of other incentives, we are encouraging our African partners to undertake programmes to improve their agricultural technology. This will give farmers, especially small farmers, a better chance to take full advantage of the economic opportunities that are becoming available to them.

To this end, about 30–35 per cent (about $US48 million in 1987) of the USAID funds devoted to agriculture in Africa are going to agricultural research and schools of agriculture. Our focus is both on technology-producing and adapting countries as well as on collaboration with the international agricultural research centres – of which the

International Institute of Tropical Agriculture in Nigeria is an example – and universities such as Dachang University in Cameroon. In particular, we are working with African agricultural education institutions and universities to improve their capacities to undertake essential research and develop better technologies.

Some recent results should be noted. Sorghum yields in Sudan and Cameroon from improved varieties are significant; yields in low rainfall areas of Northern Cameroon are up 44 per cent. In Zaire, improved cassava has resulted in substantial increases in yields, and in Northern Shaba maize production and marketing has greatly increased due to a successfully integrated package of improved seeds, extension services, roads, and market liberalization.

Our analysis of the agricultural situation has indicated to us that investments, to merely increase the supply of food and other agricultural commodities, will not be as effective as they can be without accompanying improvements in access to local and regional markets where farmers can both sell their produce and buy consumer goods. Thus, in close collaboration with various African partners and other donors, we have been increasingly supporting market links development.

We recognize that rehabilitation and maintenance of transportation systems are vital elements of this effort, but we also believe that other donors play the predominant role here. We are also exploring ways to help promote small- and medium-scale enterprises in support of agriculture, economic diversification and employment.

Natural resources management support will be an increasing part of US agricultural assistance activities in future years. Better management of Africa's renewable natural resources, especially land, water and fuel wood will be at the heart of this effort. African nations are increasingly recognizing that the degradation of their natural resource base is undermining both food and energy production, particularly among the rural poor. We are working at an increasing pace on these problems with our partners, and are currently providing about $US40 million per year for natural resource-related activities.

Drought and famine preparedness is also a continuing priority that grows directly out of our recently shared experience with the African famine. It is inevitable that emergencies brought on by the failure of rains will continue to arise. We intend, therefore, to continue active participation with African states, international organizations and other bilateral donors to support a famine early warning system. We will also co-operate in the strengthening and maintenance of the organizations in the member countries to be ready when the next emergency arises. Similarly, we remain committed to active measures to control locust and grasshoppers. Altogether, $US10 million has been budgeted this year for such activities.

HUMAN RESOURCE DEVELOPMENT

Africa's growth potential remains significantly inhibited because of high population growth rates and high rates of infant mortality. The problems of malnutrition and disease continue to restrain progress. To increase human productivity and to help better balance the requirements of population, food and natural resources, USAID will continue an active programme of focused assistance for our third priority development challenge, human resources development. Currently, our annual assistance to all these areas totals about $US185 million, of which $US80 million will support educational activities with the major emphasis on expanding the pool of middle- and senior-level professional, technical and managerial cadres. Critical manpower gaps in areas such as agricultural research, extension, engineering and economics are the primary targets of USAID education assistance.

Population programmes are increasing, with requests for USAID assistance for voluntary family planning activities now coming from 40 countries and $US55 million programmed for population activities in 1987. These programmes continue to stress the integration of family planning into public health systems and the development of private sector services.

Health activities will receive $US50 million with efforts centred upon the treatment of childhood communicable diseases, diarrhoea and malaria through immunization, oral rehydration therapy and nutrition programmes.

PROGRAMME IMPLEMENTATION

In implementing its priority programme, USAID must contend with very strict budget guidelines and adhere to effective programme management principles. Unfortunately, US resources for Africa are unlikely to increase significantly over the coming years. The total resources for USAID in 1988 will be approximately the same as that of 1987, that is a little under $US800 million. This will force even more selectivity and concentration in the use of our resources, and require strong adherence to important programme principles, in particular the following:

(a) Programmes will be concentrated in fewer areas of highest priority;
(b) Country resource allocations will increasingly take into account country performance in restructuring and managing their economies;
(c) Non-project, policy-conditioned assistance – and fewer projects – will be increasingly favoured;
(d) We will seek to reinforce the growth-creating capacity of the private sector, broadly defined. This will permit African Governments to focus the role of the public sector on those limited areas which it is best suited to manage;
(e) A closer partnership with private voluntary organizations and the US Peace Corps will serve as the primary means for continued support for critical local-level project activities; and,
(f) Improved donor co-ordination will be actively pursued and supported, especially at the sectoral level and with in-country representatives, under the leadership of the African host-country Governments.

DONOR CO-ORDINATION

Representatives of African Governments and the aid donors are now working more closely together than ever before to better harmonize and co-ordinate assistance programmes at all levels. The consensus has been growing that not only is co-ordination desirable, which of course it is, but that co-ordination is essential if the ambitious development and reform programmes we have undertaken are to succeed.

Within the past year, donors formally achieved consensus on and pledged support to the active co-ordination of their assistance programmes under the leadership of African Governments. For the US, active co-ordination, especially within African borders, is given the highest priority. We pledge to support the efforts of African nations to strengthen co-ordination of assistance programmes, and, where appropriate, will make technical assistance resources available to support co-ordination and planning efforts. We trust that other bilateral and multilateral donors and international financial institutions will similarly collaborate with Africa.

We all know that co-ordination is difficult and challenging, both to the African states, who must lead the effort, and to the donors, who must respond to that leadership, as they jointly work out mutually acceptable programmes designed to achieve well thought-out goals. With available funds falling short of Africa's requirements for development resources, none of us can afford to misdirect one dollar to non-essential or poorly planned projects and programmes.

To work at all, donors and recipient countries must adopt, within their own administrations, co-ordination policies which move beyond simple supportive rhetoric. Stronger collective efforts by recipient countries, donors and international institutions are required to establish and implement well designed and carefully appraised investment and expenditure programmes. With such programmes in hand, it is essential that donors then give them the support and financing they deserve.

Co-ordination sometimes means giving things up. For both donors and recipients, it might mean giving up a pet project and directing more resources to programme funding in support of policy reform, the area wherein clearly lies the most pressing need of many African states. If, under African leadership, the participants in co-ordination exercises have identified programme funding as the priority goal to be met, donors in all fairness have to make every effort to shape their assistance to be supportive, and respond appropriately. Africa cannot afford the luxury of 'business as usual' when it comes to the allocation of scarce resources today. Co-ordination is clearly a challenge to all of us, but it is one we all recognize we must accept.

CHAPTER ELEVEN

The Challenge of Africa's Economic Recovery and the Concept of International Economic Security

A.A. SOROKINE

INTRODUCTION

Up till now the global environment has not been conducive, to say the least, to the solution of Africa's economic and social problems. The mounting arms race build-up, an acute lack of confidence and security in international economic relations, the present-day unequal and unjust world economic order – all these factors practically negate the efforts of African and other developing countries in the struggle for a better future. At the Special Session of the United Nations General Assembly, the international community committed itself to adequately supplement Africa's efforts to sustain her economic recovery and development. As is known, much has been done in this field. But, it is obvious still that much more has yet to be done to justify the hopes of African countries.

What urgent tasks come to the fore of the international community in this regard? What are optimum ways of tackling them? What is the contribution of the Soviet Union to solving the problems of Africa and what new opportunities exist in this field?

In this chapter, an attempt will be made to comment on these questions, if not answer them. Such an attempt will be guided by the evidence obtained in the course of implementation of UN-PAAERD, and with due regard to the realities of the modern world.

The available data show that the implementation of UN-PAAERD has encountered serious difficulties. They are due to a wide range of factors, including drought which still lingers in some parts of the region. But one can hardly deny the fact that the root causes are lack of adequate resources and, on the whole, relatively low efficiency in the use of the resources mobilized.

INADEQUATE RESOURCE FLOWS

With regard to the lack of adequate resources, historical experience shows that even carefully elaborated development programmes prove to be hard to fulfil because of the limited resources actually set aside for their implementation. UN-PAAERD may suffer the same fate unless the present-day trends are reversed. As a matter of fact, the net resources inflow to the region at best stagnated in the first half of the eighties.[1] Subsequently, as can be judged for instance from the evidence provided by the findings of the Second Extraordinary Session of ECA held in October 1986, things were getting worse rather than better. As a result, Africa remains a low recipient of aid compared with Asia in the 1960s and 1970s.[2] The fact that the international community has not yet matched its commitments to provide substantial resources in support of UN-PAAERD is also corroborated in the recently adopted Addis Ababa Declaration of African Ministers responsible for trade and development.[3]

Of special concern is the increasing outflow of Africa's resources to developed capitalist countries. Enormous damage to her resources is inflicted by the self-interested and egoistic activities of TNCs, by non-equivalent exchanges and inequitable trade, and by numerous discriminatory and restrictive measures, sanctions and embargoes.

The industrial profits of TNCs have long since surpassed their capital investment. In the period 1970–1982 alone, the repatriation of these profits from Africa equalled $US24 billion whereas the overall sum of direct investment as of the end of 1981 was no more than $US15.5 billion.[4] This means that TNCs operate in Africa with a minimum expenditure of their own resources and that they actually invest, not new capital, but only a part of the profits received there.

African countries are also being plundered at the external trade turnover stage. The prices of practically all main export commodities continue to fall. According to the estimates of the Club of Rome, raw material producers in the developing countries receive now only 15 per cent of the sum paid by the final customer for the products manufactured from those materials.[5] In 1986 when export prices literally collapsed, Africa's export earnings declined from $US60.6 billion in 1985 to $US44.3 billion. At the same time, African countries have had to pay more and more for their imports because of the rise in the prices of many industrial goods. The mechanism of the so-called scissors manifested itself in a new sharp deterioration of the terms of trade (in 1985 – 5.6 per cent, and in 1986 – 27.9 per cent for the continent as a whole).[6] These adverse developments actually deprive African countries of the resources needed to sustain development and seriously complicate the payments situation in many of them. To make things even worse, recent years have seen the strengthening of protectionist measures in the developed capitalist countries – Africa's major trading partners.

This noose of indebtedness is being further tightened around the economies, vulnerable as they are, of African countries to the point of strangling them. Their foreign debt burden to the capitalist states and banks amounts to nearly $US200 billion, which is twice as much as their average annual export revenues. African countries have to use, on the average, about 30 per cent of their GDP and, for some, over 50 per cent to meet their debt and interest payments. For the region as a whole, the absolute amount needed is up to $US24 billion annually.[7] Many countries have accumulated substantial arrears. Rescheduling arrangements and other debt-related measures implemented from time to time can only grant a little breathing-space to the debtors.

The resultant annual net outflows of financial resources from Africa now exceeds $US9,000 million. Incidentally, African countries need exactly the same amount in annual external aid in order to solve their urgent problems, as was pointed out at the thirteenth special session of the UN General Assembly. For 1986, even more graphic evidence is furnished by Adebayo Adedeji in chapter 34 in this book.[8] As a matter of fact, Africa has actually turned or, rather, has been forced to turn into a net supplier of resources to the developed capitalist countries.

In this regard, it is pertinent to repeat the question Mrs. G.H. Brundtland, Norwegian Prime Minister, asked last autumn: 'Where is the common sense in the fact that industrialized countries, even at the height of the flow of aid to Africa, were taking more money out of the stricken continent than they were putting in?'[9] Obviously this can be the common sense only for those who pursue their own selfish ends at the expense of others.

For African countries such a policy is fraught with huge external budget deficits, growing debt burden, curtailment of investment programmes and overall deterioration of the living standards of their population. Suffice it to say that an acute shortage of resources in many countries has led to substantial slow-down in capital formation, with a drop of 5 per cent in 1985 added to that of 3.6 per cent recorded during the period 1980–1984.[10] Keeping this in mind, can one seriously talk about adding further impetus and dynamics to the process of economic recovery and development in Africa? Of course not.

Unfortunately, there is not much hope that things will change for the better in the near future. As Mr. McNamara put it in his ECA Jubilee lecture delivered at the twenty-first session of the Commission in April 1986, 'the external financial flows that will be needed in the second half of this decade to support whatever further structural adjustments the African Governments are prepared to undertake, are simply not now in prospect'.[11] This is mainly because the process of structural and technological reorganization which is now underway in the economies of major capitalist countries will continue to have a very adverse impact on developing countries.

Specifically, it entails a steady decline in the demand for raw materials and some industrial exports of the developing countries. Of special concern in this regard is the fact that most of the causes accounting for this trend are of a long-term nature. Among these are: diminishing consumption of raw materials and energy per unit of GDP due to technological innovations and other resource-saving measures; increasing utilization of the so-called secondary resources; and accentuation of protectionist actions in the major capitalist countries.

As a result of these adverse developments, not only are the developing countries confronted with a highly unfavourable and deteriorating situation in the world market, but they are virtually being ousted from it. Suffice it to say that, between 1981 and 1985, the share of Africa in the import trade of the developed capitalist countries fell by 18.6 per cent and, in the export trade, by 27 per cent.[12] Despite measures taken by African countries in the 1980s to curtail the production of some raw materials, the prices of most of them, as has been mentioned, continue to fall. Under such conditions, more losses in the export earnings of the developing countries are just unavoidable.

Coupled with it is the slow-down of private capital transfer to African countries. Two main reasons account for that. First is the growing demand for capital and high rates of profit in the major capitalist countries themselves which is directly connected with the process of structural and technological reorganization of their economies and protectionist policies. Second, Africa's debt service is expected at $US25 billion a year between 1986–1990.[13] In short, unless these trends are reversed, African countries will most likely continue to be net suppliers of capital to the developed capitalist countries.

STRUCTURAL ADJUSTMENT PROGRAMMES

Lack of adequate external resources is not the sole cause of the difficulties encountered in the course of implementation of APPER and UN-PAAERD. Another major cause is the low efficiency in the use of the resources actually mobilized. As is known, APPER and UN-PAAERD set African countries the task of restructuring their economies in order to achieve a sound solution of economic and social problems confronting them.[14] However, some donor countries and organizations try to push African countries to a type of restructuring which hardly conforms to the goals of the two Programmes.

In this connection, one can recall the criticisms levelled by some delegates to the second extraordinary session of the ECA against IMF and World Bank whose SAPs give rise to constraints which tend to diminish or negate measures undertaken by African countries, especially in the sector of agriculture.[15] And it is no wonder, since these programmes 'have been designed exclusively to protect the short-term interests of creditors'.[16]

They call for further sacrifices from the African countries but do not address the need for symmetrical adjustment or, rather, restructuring of the international economic environment on a just and democratic basis. They call for curtailing of the public sector on the erroneous assumption that low efficiency is inherent in the public ownership of capital and in planned management of the economy, and fail to recognize that privatization is not a panacea for Africa's economic ills. Not to be lengthy, I will just quote the Addis Ababa Declaration of African Ministers responsible for trade and development, which says: 'The very complexity of the situation points to the inappropriateness, if not irrelevance, of economic models based on harmonious, steady growth paths as possible outcomes of market processes. If we seek a balanced, conflict-free and relatively even development process, then, in all probability, we need to consciously plan for it.'[17] Not curtailment of the public sector but its consolidation, wider application of the planning methods in the economy, enhancing the efficiency of management, and active mobilization of the population – as the experience of the USSR and other socialist countries show – are prerequisites of economic recovery in Africa.

This having been said, one cannot but arrive at the conclusion that the underlying causes of the crisis situation in Africa on the whole remain intact up till now. Africa continues to occupy an unequal, subordinate position in the system of international capitalist division of labour. And what is more, the relations of dependence and oppression are being reproduced on an extended scale. In fact one can say that, under the impact of structural and technological changes in the centres of the world capitalist economy, the present-day neo-colonialist system is evolving to a new, more sophisticated system of exploitation. The core of this process is the growing transnationalization of the world capitalist economy and hence the building-up of contradictions between TNCs, on the one hand, and national and state forms of the political organization of society in developing countries, on the other. The phenomenon is of particular significance because the question now is whether African countries succeed in resisting the onslaught of neo-colonialist forces and uphold their sovereign right to independent development or whether they succumb to it with all the ensuing consequences.

In such conditions, the situation in Africa today remains as serious as ever, and cannot but cause concern for the international community. As Adebayo Adedeji has put it, 'it will be premature to conclude that Africa is now out of the economic doldrums'.[18] The economies of the majority of African countries are still beset by considerable difficulties. Last year's modest gains in the recovery process were seriously undermined by a new sharp deterioration of the situation in the world market. In 1985 the total regional output, for the first time in the 1980s, surpassed the 3 per cent level (in 1980–1984 on the average 0.8 per cent). But, in 1986, the rate of growth again fell to a mere 1.3 per cent. And, for that matter, the increase, insignificant as it is, was mainly attributable to the cessation of the drought and improvement of the weather conditions. As a result, Africa's capability to resist possible natural calamities and ups and downs of the international economic environment remains very low.

Then, a question arises: is there a real way out of Africa's economic crisis? The answer is of course yes, subject to the following four conditions:

(a) Constructive approaches to the problems of Africa and concrete actions on the part of major capitalist countries and aid agencies. What is needed now is a new political mentality. It is an objective necessity determined by the realities of our increasingly interdependent world, in part by the fact that the urgent solution of Africa's problems would not only promote Africa's interests but global interests as well;

(b) Mobilization of adequate external resources and their efficient utilization in the interests of African peoples. The task, here, is two-fold: how to ensure an adequate resource inflow to Africa and, at the same time, how to maximally reduce capital outflow from the region. Undoubtedly, this problem cannot be solved without radical restructuring of the present-day system of international economic relations on a just and democratic basis;

(c) Availability of an efficient and comprehensive international strategy of assistance to Africa which will provide, not only for objectives and priorities, but for a concerted approach to Africa's most burning problems; and,

(d) Establishment, on a global and democratic basis, of an efficient mechanism for mobilization and co-ordination of the efforts of the world community to sustain Africa's economic recovery and development.

SOVIET UNION STRATEGY FOR AFRICAN ECONOMIC RECOVERY

Then, what are the optimum ways of tackling these tasks? In our opinion, a series of large-scale foreign policy proposals, put forth by the Soviet Union in the last few years, provide a sound conceptual basis for it. The Soviet Union believes that an end to the arms race, a substantial reduction of military budgets and a reallocation of part of the funds thus saved to meet the socio-economic needs of the newly-independent states are a key condition for ensuring a successful solution to the problems facing these countries. As Mikhail Gorbachev noted in his message to the Conference on Disarmament, 'It is disarmament that, by releasing huge physical and intellectual resources, will permit their switching to aims of construction, economic development and prosperity'.[19]

Disarmament and development are vital to the newly-independent countries. Yet, their accelerated development in the foreseeable future is simply impossible without large financial injections on a democratic basis. It has been estimated that African countries would require at least $US150 billion for the period up to the year 2000 in order to stimulate economic growth. And these funds could be secured if the senseless waste of resources for military purposes is stopped.

Given the present conditions, when humanity has not yet succeeded in combating hunger, illiteracy and diseases, the huge resources allocated by the militarists to the development, production and deployment of the most sophisticated weapons of mass destruction, and to the extension of the arms race into outer space, seem to be even more sinister and outrageous. Creations of man and his intellect should be used for the benefit of mankind and not for its annihilation. The old principle 'arms instead of development' must be replaced with a new one – i.e. 'disarmament for the sake of development'.

The second key component of the Soviet concept of international assistance to developing countries is international economic security, the resolution on which the Soviet Union proposed as far back as the fortieth session of the UN General Assembly. Subsequently it was further substantiated and developed in Mikhail Gorbachev's Statement of January 15, 1986, in the Soviet memorandum 'States' International Economic Security as Major Condition for Invigorating World Economic Relations' and in the documents adopted by the XXVII Congress of the Communist Party of the Soviet Union (CPSU).[20]

This concept aims at creating a system of international economic security, which would equally protect each state from all forms of discrimination. Its range of principles also comprises renunciation of the policy of economic blockades and sanctions if this is not directly envisaged in the recommendations of the world community; joint quest for ways for a just settlement of the problem of debts; establishment of a new international economic order guaranteeing equal economic security to all countries; elaboration of principles for utilizing part of the funds released as a result of a reduction of military budgets for the good of the international community, in general, and of developing nations, in particular; and the pooling of efforts in exploring and making peaceful use of outer space and in resolving global problems on which the destiny of civilization depends.

The concept of international economic security does not replace the basic documents of UN General Assembly on the establishment of a new international economic order. It aims at giving an impetus to the quest of common elements in different approaches to the solution of the world economic problems. As was emphasized at the XXVII Congress of the CPSU the realization of this concept 'alongside disarmament can become a dependable pillar of international security in general'.[21] In turn, an end to arms race is a necessary prerequisite to the creation of a system of international economic security which would be a reliable guarantee that the neo-colonialist exploitation of developing countries will be stopped. A major step towards the establishment of an international economic security system could be made through the realization of the proposal made at the XXVII Congress of the CPSU to the effect that a global forum should be convened to discuss, on a comprehensive basis, all the problems that impede the development of world economic ties.

Developing countries, whose economic security is most vulnerable, acknowledge the importance of and the urgent need in ensuring international economic security. The Conference of the OAU, held in Harare in 1986, demonstrated that African countries stand for the elimination of threats of nuclear war, and for disarmament; that they are out against colonialism, neo-colonialism and racism; and that they support the rights of people to independent development and the idea of restructuring international economic relations on the principles of equality and justice. The fact that African countries attach growing importance to the problems of confidence-building and economic security in international economic relations is also reflected in a number of other documents adopted at various high-level meetings and conferences.[22]

Re-channelling of resources from the arms race to economic growth and international economic security are two crucial, but not the sole, components of the Soviet concept of international assistance to developing countries. The Soviet Union also calls for global co-operation, constructive international teamwork as the only solution to the many contradictions of the modern world. As was recently re-emphasized by the Soviet leaders: 'Africa for the Soviet people is not an arena of confrontation between East and West. It is a field for international co-operation which is so needed for solving such urgent problems facing African peoples as eradication of hunger and diseases, overcoming economic backwardness and uplifting of living standards, and protection of environment. The Soviet Union takes an optimistic view of the possibility of such co-operation.'[23]

It is obvious that major differences set the two words – socialism and capitalism – apart. Of course, this fact to a large degree complicates the solution of such an urgent problem as the establishment, on a global and democratic basis, of an efficient mechanism to mobilize and co-ordinate the support of the international community to African countries. But there is no alternative to co-operation on the international scene. As Mikhail Gorbachev told the Party Congress: 'The course of history and of social progress require even more insistently that there should be constructive and creative interaction between states and peoples on the scale of the entire world. Not only does it so require, but it also creates requisite political, social and material premises for it.'[24]

Socialist countries' concept of solving the problems of newly-independent states was further developed at the session of their Political Consultative Committee held in Berlin in May 1986. The document 'On Overcoming the Backwardness and Establishing a New International Economic Order' adopted at the session re-emphasizes the fact that it is just impossible to ensure economic and political stability in the world without carrying out decisive measures aimed at preventing further deterioration of economic and social conditions in developing countries and overcoming their backwardness. In this regard, they call for fundamental changes in political mentality and international practices, for just international practices and division of labour.

Socialist countries consider practical steps towards armaments reduction and disarmament to be *sine qua non* of the successful solution of the economic problems confronting the developing countries. There exists a close interrelation between disarmament and development, and it is only disarmament and reduction of military budgets that can provide huge additional resources needed to sustain economic recovery and sound development. That's why Socialist countries attach particular importance to the International Conference on the Interrelation between Disarmament and Development which is to be convened under the aegis of the UN.

Socialist countries consider that the fundamental solution of the problem of external indebtedness, which of late has acquired a distinctly political meaning, is possible only by way of restructuring the international economic relations on the principles of justice and democracy.

UN-PAAERD contains a number of concrete proposals aimed at solving the problem of indebtedness. Specifically, it proposes to reduce debt-servicing payments to a share of export earnings that would not impair the process of social and economic development; to abstain from protectionist policies; to lower interest rates; to stabilize currency exchange rates; to reorganize the international monetary system; and to democratize international financial institutions.

Socialist countries deem it necessary that the responsibility of ensuring the global solution of the external indebtedness problem rest with UN as was envisaged by the Forty-first session of the UN General Assembly. Socialist countries also consider it an urgent necessity to ensure a steady supply of commodities to the world markets, as well as a just correlation between the prices of raw materials, agricultural products and industrial commodities. Socialist countries are ready to broaden, in different forms, their economic co-operation with developing countries on the basis of long-term agreements which would take into account the capabilities as well as the needs of national economies, and thus add stability and new vistas to the economic relations between the two groups of countries. They again reiterate their readiness to share their experience in solving the burning economic and social problems, paying due regard to the peculiarities of the developing countries' economies and their specific international environment.

SOVIET ECONOMIC AND TECHNICAL ASSISTANCE
TO AFRICA

Socialist countries have not just proposed a sound conceptual basis for a new approach on the part of the international community to the problems of developing countries. Their stance has been embodied in their comprehensive and mutually beneficial trade and economic co-operation with African countries. Socialist countries co-operate with them in many spheres. Particularly important is their diversified economic and technical assistance in the development of independent national economies. Take, for instance, the Soviet Union. Its economic and technical assistance to African countries is not aimed at establishing economic control over their natural resources and economy. Nor does the Soviet Union abuse its economic power. The co-operation is based on the long-standing, time-tested principles of international relations created by socialism – i.e., the complete and actual equality of the parties concerned, respect of sovereignty, non-interference in internal affairs and mutual beneficence.

The main objective of the Soviet Union's economic and technical co-operation with independent African states and other developing nations is to contribute towards their economic independence through the development of national economies, industrialization, promotion of new industries and expansion of the existing capacities.

The Soviet Union promotes economic relations with those African countries which are interested in this co-operation; it gives them economic and technical assistance, regardless of their political systems and orientation. Today, the Soviet Union has signed intergovernmental agreements on economic and technical co-operation with 37 developing countries of Africa. Besides, economic and technical assistance is given to some African nations outside the framework of intergovernmental agreements. Likewise, the scope and dimensions of the Soviet Union's economic assistance to Africa are rapidly expanding. Since 1970, they have increased more than six-fold. In 1985, the total volume of Soviet economic aid to African countries came up to $US1.7 billion.[25] More than 330 projects have been completed in Africa with Soviet assistance, while another 300 are currently underway or designated for construction.

The Soviet Union has intergovernmental trade agreements with 40 countries of the region. To make the trade relations more stable the

Soviet Union engages in the signing of long-term programmes. Such programmes, for the period up to 1990, have been signed with Algeria, the Libyan Arab Jamahiriya, Morocco, Mozambique, Tunisia and Ethiopia.

The successful development of economic relations between the Soviet Union and African countries is largely due to the existence of long-term programmes of economic co-operation and of joint inter-governmental commissions whose activities put Soviet Union's economic and technical assistance on a planned basis. Soviet–African co-operation, therefore, acquires the character of stable division of labour that makes it possible for the African countries to plan the utilization of their resources for the attainment of the socio-economic objectives and goals.

An important feature of the Soviet–African economic co-operation lies in the fact that the constructed projects belong primarily to the public sector and, as a rule, constitute its backbone. Another feature is the comprehensive approach of Soviet organizations to project implementation, from the designing and construction stage to the personnel training stage, and their assistance in the operation process. Soviet organizations usually participate in foreign projects by providing credits which are an efficient instrument for the promotion of equitable and mutually beneficial co-operation between the Soviet Union and African countries.

Taking into account the objective difficulties facing developing countries, the Soviet Union has of late expanded the scale of its credits to them. From 1983 to 1985, when the difficulties in their financial position reached an unprecedented level, the annual volume of credits granted by the Soviet Union increased 2.7 times. Moreover, in some cases, the Soviet Union meets the requests of developing countries and reschedules credit arrangements. In 1981–1985, such deferments were granted to almost 20 countries. The credit aid provided by the Soviet Union and other socialist countries does not result in the accumulation of external indebtedness to the level that constitutes a serious burden for the recipient countries. Moreover, it cannot accumulate developing countries' external debts beyond the repayable limit. It is not by chance that the socialist states account only for 3 per cent of all developing countries' external indebtedness.

Taking into account the financial difficulties of African countries, the Soviet Union in many cases accepts as payment traditional export commodities as well as products of the industries set up with Soviet assistance. Soviet credits are sometimes paid in national currencies which are also used to buy local products. Mutual benefits are ensured best when projects are built on the compensatory or buy-back basis, and compensatory agreements have been concluded with Guinea, the Congo, Mali, Morocco, Mozambique, and Ethiopia while there are plans for similar agreements with a number of other African countries.

Job-orientation of the Soviet economic and technical assistance fully takes into account the requests of the Governments concerned, and their concepts of socio-political and economic development. Another specific feature of the Soviet Union's aid lies in its production-oriented and integrated nature. Such an approach makes it possible to gradually shape territorial and industrial complexes in African countries – e.g., the Aswan high dam and power generating complex in Egypt, the metal works in Nigeria, the bauxite plant in Guinea, etc.

Industries and power production account for some 75 per cent of the overall assistance. Over the period of 1987–1990, business ties with the countries of Africa in industry are to be expanded considerably. This measure will correspond to the African states' strategic policy charter in the Industrial Development Decade for Africa in the 1980s and in LPA. Some major projects are to be built or retooled in Algeria, Egypt, Ethiopia, Ghana, Morocco, Mozambique, Nigeria, Zimbabwe and other countries.

Given the aggravation of the food problem on the continent, the Soviet Union has stepped up its economic and technical assistance to these countries in developing their agriculture and other sectors in the agro-industrial complex. This assistance involves 155 projects in 16 African countries, and with over 60 projects already commissioned. The share of the technical assistance in this field will increase to 20 per cent of the total volume of Soviet assistance to African countries.

As regards training of personnel, the continent has about 100 different educational institutions built and equipped with Soviet aid, including 10 higher educational establishments and more than 80 vocational and technical colleges and centres. Over 450,000 specialists and skilled workers have been trained, while 30,000 of them have been educated at Soviet higher and secondary specialized institutions. At present, 22,000 African students study in the Soviet Union. One should also stress the economic aspect of training national personnel. Today, African countries have to hire thousands of specialists and skilled workers at a cost of $US20,000–$US50,000 a year per person. It is easy to calculate that by having trained 450,000 national specialists and skilled workers the Soviet Union helped African countries to save some $10 billion a year.

The Soviet Union also renders emergency aid to African countries to combat drought, flood and other natural calamities. The Soviet Union relief aid to Ethiopia alone amounted to more than $US150 million to combat the consequences of the drought of 1984–1985.

In general, the outlook for Soviet–African economic and technical co-operation in the second half of the 1980s and in the 1990s is favourable.

At present, a process of restructuring has begun in the Soviet Union. The economic management system that has taken shape over the last decades is being changed. Social changes are also taking place throughout the country. These efforts are aimed at accelerating the country's socio-economic development; upgrading socialism in line with the latest forms of social structure by developing democracy; and ensuring a continued improvement in the Soviet people's standards of living and its intellectual advancement. The international significance of this process is tremendous. The implementation of the programme for accelerating the socio-economic development of Soviet society and of the foreign policy approved by the twenty-seventh CPSU Congress will, undoubtedly, contribute to the cause of peace and progress in the international arena. The process of restructuring opens up new vistas for a broader Soviet participation in the international division of labour and for closer co-operation with other countries. In part, measures aimed at improving the management of the external economic relations and developing such a promising form of co-operation as joint enterprises will undoubtedly help to contribute to the efforts of African countries to solve their urgent problems. The solution of these problems is a hard task, but they can and must be attained by concerted efforts on the part of African countries and the international community.

NOTES

1. E/ECA/CM.13/3. *Survey of Economic and Social Conditions in Africa, 1985–1986*, p.52.
2. E/ECA/CM.2/L. *Draft Report of the Second Extraordinary Session of the Commission/Second Extraordinary Meeting of the Conference of Ministers*. Addis Ababa, Ethiopia, 13 to 15 October, 1986, p.30.
3. E/ECA/CM.13/47. *Addis Ababa Declaration of African Ministers Responsible for Trade and Development Preparatory to UNCTAD VII*, p.2.
4. UNCTAD. *Handbook of International Trade and Development*, 1985. Table 5; Investir dans le tiers monde. OECD. P., 1983, p.31.
5. *Za Rubezhom*, 1986, nr.8, p.8.
6. World Bank. *World Development Report* 1986. Washington, D.C. p.25; E/ECA/CM.13/3. *Survey of Economic and Social Conditions, 1985–1986*, p.39.
7. *Ibid.*, pp.18–19.
8. Adebayo Adedeji, 'The Challenge to the International Community of Sustaining

Africa's Economic Recovery'.

9. 14/H/0788 B/GHB/16.09.86 – 03. World Commission on Environment and Development. Opening Address by Mrs. G.H. Brundtland at the sixth meeting of the Commission, Harare, Zimbabwe, p.4.
10. E/ECA/ECM. 2/L. *op.cit.*, p.8.
11. Robert S. McNamara. *The Challenge facing the Continent of Africa*, 1986, p.2.
12. E/ECA/CM.13/3. *Op.cit.*, pp.A-56, A-61.
13. E/ECA/CM.13/47. *Op.cit.*, p.1.
14. OAU, *Africa's Priority Programme for Economic Recovery 1986–1990*. Published by FAO, 1985, p.15.
15. E/ECA/ECM.2.L. *Op.cit*, pp. 29, 30, 32.
16. E/ECA/CM.13/47. *Op.cit.*, p.3.
17. *Ibid.*, p.46.
18. Adebayo Adedeji, *Op.cit.*
19. *Pravda*, February 21, 1986.
20. *Pravda*, January 16 and 28, 1986; Materialy XXVI syezda Kommunisticheskoi partii Sovetskogo Soyuza (Party Congress Documents). Moscow, Politizdat Publishers, 1986.
21. Materialy XXVII syezda ..., p.65.
22. See, for example, E/ECA/CM.13/47. *Op.cit.*, pp.51–52.
23. *Pravda*, May 25, 1987.
24. Materialy XXVII syezda ..., p.20.
25. Calculated on the basis of UN methodology. A/F-13/10, May 28, 1986, p.6.

CONCLUDING REMARKS

Despite the critical nature of the impact of exogenous factors on Africa's recovery and development efforts, the overall response of the international community has so far been less than adequate and generally disappointing.

As a result of declining commodity prices, Africa lost in 1986 alone about $US19 billion in export earnings. Yet no concrete actions have been undertaken by the international community to stabilize the export earnings from African commodities, and no serious measures have been undertaken to provide meaningful and lasting solutions to the crippling debt and debt-servicing burden or to provide external resources on the scale required to support the recovery and growth efforts in Africa. Indeed, the overall net resource flows to Africa actually stagnated in 1986 and fell in 1987 in comparison with 1985 while trade barriers in industrialized countries have become even more restrictive. These developments are clearly not in line with either the spirit or the letter of the commitments which the international community entered into under UN-PAAERD and are bound to frustrate attempts at bringing about recovery and development on the continent. This is not to deny of course the laudable efforts and steps by a number of individual donor countries and agencies.

Unless the international community is willing to collectively take positive steps to improve the international economic environment and provide the required support to Africa through sustained actions, Africa's chances for recovery and development will indeed be dim, the tasks involved made more painful and arduous, and the costs, in terms of human suffering, greater.

PART THREE

The Enabling Environment for African Economic Recovery and Transformation

INTRODUCTORY NOTE

Important as the external economic environment and the assistance of the international community to Africa's recovery may be, African domestic efforts are no doubt the most crucial. Thus, the renewed efforts of Africa and Africans must stem from a realistic and thorough assessment and appreciation of the historical, political, socio-cultural, scientific and technological conditions of the continent which greatly influence the success or failure of economic development. Any diagnosis of the African crises, to be meaningful, must indeed include these multiple dimensions, and must uncover the strengths and weaknesses, constraints and positive social forces entailed in them since the positive elements constitute in effect the enabling environment for African economic recovery and transformation. The seven chapters in Part Three undertake the necessary diagnosis from the various critical viewpoints.

Central to all the arguments of the contributors is the question: recovery and development for whom? To which the unequivocal answer is: for the African people, the vast majority of whom are disadvantaged politically, socially and economically either as rural dwellers or as women. This admittedly makes the required transformation in Africa a monumental task but, as it clearly emerges, this is a task that nonetheless must be undertaken if a truly endogenous foundation is to be laid for sustainable growth and development.

Ki-Zerbo, in Chapter 12, traces the major changes and movements that have occurred in Africa's political, economic, social and cultural history and which have left a certain legacy to present-day Africans. His analysis shows how positive developments in political formation, people's participation, economic organization and integration, science and technology, social and cultural expression from the earliest times became overshadowed by the persistently negative effects of the slave trade and European colonization which wrought profound structural changes in the African society. The political dimension of this situation is elaborated and reflected upon in Chapter 13 in which Ake analyses the implications of political power accumulation in the post-colonial

African state. He argues that a further development of inherited colonial authoritarianism by African leaders has led to a paradoxical depoliticization of economic and social processes, repression, militarism, inefficiency and mass alienation which serve as constraints on genuine development, and, by so doing, attempts to lend credence to the underlying view that the continent's current crisis is essentially political in origin and character.

A peculiar negative effect of Africa's contact with Europe has been the emergence of the apartheid state of South Africa whose destabilization policy is analysed by Mwale in Chapter 14. The Black African majorities in South Africa and Namibia and the people of the independent frontline and neighbouring states suffer tremendous human, economic and military losses and disruptions on account of race, history and geographical position. This, as Mwale concludes, makes their development extremely problematic, despite the collective efforts that are increasingly undertaken to solve the problems. In the long run, he sees apartheid as doomed not only because of South Africa's serious moral weakness, but also due to the unsustainable internal economic, political and social costs of apartheid.

In Chapter 15, Mazrui and White analyse a number of germane socio-political conditions and propose ways of achieving transformation in three particular areas: relations between the sexes (domestic or gender revolution), technology and know-how (skill revolution) and different forms of power (power revolution). The importance of solidarity and co-operation among African states and between them and other countries of the South is stressed especially in the areas of skill and power. Still on the required internal transformation, Luke, in Chapter 16, echoes some of the issues raised by Ki-Zerbo and Ake concerning the disjointed relationship between the modern African state, its personalized rulership and pluralistic society, as well as the dependent and marginalized position of Africa in the world economy. The considerable challenge to development management and its reform in such a context is the main focus of the chapter by Luke.

For Africa's development to be meaningful it has to be sustainable. Hence, the last two Chapters of Part Three analyse the essential requirements especially in the areas of science and technology and environment. In Chapter 17, Odhiambo argues for the mobilization and sustenance of African scientific and technological know-how to meet the social needs of the society. The same point is greatly amplified by Khalid in Chapter 18 wherein he stresses, among the causes of Africa's development crisis, the lack of harmony between economic (predominantly growth) policies, social needs, particularly of the poor and marginalized segments of the population, and the limitations of the ecosystem. Thus, proposals are made in these two Chapters for developing and strengthening the role of science and technology and environmental protection in a manner that is responsive to urgent social needs, and also utilizes indigenous capabilities and potentialities for long-term sustainable development.

CHAPTER TWELVE

Historical Perspectives

JOSEPH KI-ZERBO

The stakes are clear: the question is who is going to manage the current changes in Africa's economy and in whose interest? Can history help to find the diagnosis for Africa's helplessness? At least it helps to detect the roots at one time, i.e. in the third dimension without which the analysis of the crisis is likely to be uninteresting, static and even transitory. History provides the film and the direction which implies the contemporary image.

Indeed, a crisis is in itself not an evil; if it is a growth imbalance, for example, it is a difficult but necessary change like puberty. However, if the crisis seriously undermines the deep-seated metabolism of the society, then it assumes a different dimension. History enables us precisely to qualify better the rhythm and nature of the changes, and to identify which group causes them and/or manages them in its own interest.

Certainly, Africa's economic crisis is largely induced and caused from outside; but we should not drown it in alibi. After all, we were perhaps not able to stop the contamination. But today, we have a diagnosis for our disease; we know the remedies to be applied, some of which are within our reach. If, therefore, the evil is spreading, let us have the courage to examine ourselves. We cannot expect that those who take advantage of the status quo would transform the evil merely through philanthropy.

The current crisis does not arise out of economic conditions; it is structural. It is a crisis of civilization for all continents; for Africa, however, it is also a question of survival. For Africa, it is the height of a negative process inherent in the quasi-servile function that she has been called upon to fulfil since the 17th century. This negative function is maintained through domestic and external changes and continuities. It is in relation to this role, endured and accepted by Africans, that any economic data should be viewed. If, for example, an African country records a leap in the growth rate of its cash crop exports, this performance becomes positive only if the latter enables it in future to change the function it fulfils. Otherwise, that country would be applauded for playing excellently the negative role assigned to it. Growth in dependency is often growth *of* dependency; but the negative role in question cannot be analysed in terms of mere dependency.

The drama of Africa is that it is the only continent to have accumulated negative internal and external changes and continuities for so long, to such an extent that one could almost claim that there is no crisis in Africa, because all that is happening now had happened already on our continent and falls within a plurisecular line. The only crisis is the acceleration in the rhythm of the difficulties in Africa. The problem is, by dint of enduring the same difficulties, the critical threshold towards economic coma is almost crossed.

Recovery is, therefore, possible only through the elimination of the discovered negative tendencies, in the interest of continuity and positive changes, in order to find once again, from the history of the continent, the tracks of an ascending road. Such is the aim of this expose.

POSITIVE CHANGES[1]

Certain positive changes have marked the history of Africa. These changes took place before the colonial era and can serve today as landmarks for analysis and action.

Inside Africa

Within the African system itself, and independently, changes resulting from confrontations among the opposing social forces took place. By those successive economic and cultural transformations, Africans moved away from the village clans to chiefdoms, kingdoms and empires. Even at the latter stage, decisive changes occurred, for example, in West Africa between the ancient Ghana model (10th century) and the Gao model (16th century) through the Mali model (14th century). Between the barter system by means of the 'silent trade', described by Masudi in the 10th century, and the complex structures of the productive and market system of Western and Central Sudan in the 15th century, there were considerable endogenous and progressive changes involving innovations and splits. As a matter of fact, in the 15th century, that system included varied and additional productions, according to the ecological and geographical areas, including manufactured products such as the textiles and molten glass from special sands finely worked in Nupe (Nigeria). The marketing systems were especially sophisticated.

At the level of political economy and public institutions, the action of Biton Coulibaly of Segou (1712–1755), who created a state from age groups and provided it with operational structures (such as taxes, army and tribute), shows in a real-life situation the African ability to create and change in the face of imperative historical needs. Everywhere, African societies were animated by an internal dynamism sometimes marked by noteworthy splits. A number of structural adjustments were made through endogenous initiative.

Through Reaction to Changes from Outside

From the time of the Atlantic Slave Trade onwards, memorable or obscure splits caused by Africans were observed, either through open secession or armed struggle, or through partial disengagement involving collaboration and resistance. Two models illustrate the two options. One was the fugitive model which had been initiated in Africa and which assumed its dimensions across the Atlantic in the Quilombos, Palenques, Mocambos, and others, some of whom constituted autonomous states which survived for generations or even centuries. On the other hand, in Africa itself, at the same time as those multiple armed struggles were taking place, other kingdoms like those of Abomey or Kumasi (Ashanti) through qualitative internal changes were adapting their economies (including the use of monopoly) to the implacable course of events and depending on slave trade to replenish their armaments in the form of guns. But a number of them, through a more or less imposed structural adjustment, were able to replace the slave trade with the 'illicit' trade in palm oil. The bureaucratized economy of pre-colonial Dahomey reduced the impact of the slave trade on the socio-political structures and ensured the stability of prices and the cowrie currency for one and a half centuries, especially through the establishment of a kind of free port at Ouidah.

From then onwards, other wide-ranging original structures, sometimes at great human cost were created by the Africans. Such were the changes which took place in the Nguni society under the auspices of Shaka, and the multi-form upheavals the African leaders faced in the 19th century at the time of the colonizers, viz Mirambo, El Hadji Omar, Samory, Menelik II of Ethiopia, the conqueror of the Italians at Adowa in 1896 and the maker of 'modern Ethiopia'.

We shall count among the positive splits a number of experiences recorded *after the achievement of political independence*, because we do not possess the necessary retreat into time to judge them, and because on the whole, despite the enormous effect of independence in the world, there has been no fundamental economic change for the African continent, either because of the type of independence granted, or because it had been obtained or wrested only in a scattered manner or, better still, because the objective social conditions were against it: for example the contrast between the militant nationalist groups and the legatee classes of the colonial regime.

The first decade of independence, which corresponded with a period of favourable economic circumstances and a cold war between the super powers, was the fantastic period of a fatal dizziness during which the African fish took the bait of donations, loans, bank credits and subventions to balance the budget, from all parts of the world. All the means were available to link African executives and leaders definitively to the outside world through ready means, indeed through emoluments. Countries or leaders resistant to association or integration with the dominant western system generally had limited room to manoeuvre: there was the quarantine by the public and private sponsors, dispensers of growth mistaken for 'development'. They almost never found a valid alternative except very often bitter disappointments in the Eastern bloc.

Almost all experiences of economic splits marked by nationalizations, creation of national currencies, public offices for external and/or internal trade, exchange control, etc. resulted in a return to the fold and toeing the line for the countries concerned, i.e. a return to the established order. Only the oil-producing countries or custodians of 'noble' minerals like uranium, gold, copper, bauxite, chrome, germanium and beryllium could hold out longer, although not without coming up against obstacles which have become chronic: social upheavals, political instability, militarization, dictatorships, and so on.

Behind the official declaration of non-alignment, almost all African countries have aligned themselves with the 'laws of the market'. In concrete terms, it meant that African economies were maintained within the framework of the 'colonial pact'. They were by 'vocation', according to the ideological term used but in fact by historical dictate, condemned to the production of plant and/or mineral raw materials and the revenue invested was intended to bring about the economic 'take-off'. People were swimming right in Rostow's theory of the 'stages of growth'; the profits obtained were used notably to purchase from the North equipment and inputs, and to secure the services of experts or office studies and patents needed for all sectors of economic life. Industries were almost always limited to the branches of import substitution, the bureaucratic, military and social sectors. There was an immense historical misunderstanding, not to say a formidable fool's bargain (which functions still), where more than 70 per cent of the aid returns to the donor; where both ends of the economic chain are held by the countries of the North which unilaterally regulate the purchase prices of both the products sold and the manufactured goods bought by Africans.

Planning, under conditions of frequent ignorance of the basic data and lack of control of most of the parameters of growth, beginning from domestic and external prices, amounts to a mere catalogue of projects frequently 'recommended' by the experts or sponsors. Sometimes, it is a string of charities from varied sources without any co-ordinated orientation or internal coherence. Thus, it is not surprising that, twenty-seven years after independence, no fundamental economic change has taken place in almost all African countries, irrespective of their ideological options. Almost everywhere there is still the identifying profile of the formerly colonized economy, which could be noticed for example in the external trade structure of those countries: copper accounts for 91 per cent of Zambia's exports and 66 per cent of Zaire's exports; iron ore accounts for 86.5 per cent of Mauritania's exports and bauxite 87 per cent of Guinea's exports.

With regard to the rulers, they are made up sometimes of wealthy social classes animated by the basic appetite of beginners; sometimes of clear-minded and trustworthy leaders, but powerless before the bronze laws of the system (investment code, monetary conventions, obsolete international legislations, oligopoly of the multinational corporations, and the rest). The positive results obtained by certain leaders or social groups from hard struggle since independence are to their honour; but that does not change the structure of the system. Many take refuge in the bedridden economies maintained out of bankruptcy under the conditional serum of the World Bank or the IMF, supported by the innumerable prostheses of bilateral or multilateral exceptional and emergency aid, although the tendency for public aid in particular is on the decline.[2]

NEGATIVE CHANGES

Among the negative or potentially negative changes in relation to the African historical process, we can mention four: demography, deterioration of the ecosystem, food upheavals and socio-cultural disturbances.

African Demography

This is one of the key parameters in the ecological, economic and social change. Now, Africa's population, with its present 3 per cent annual growth rate, should double in about 25 years to about 900 million. It would have experienced two major changes in four centuries.

The first major change was caused by the impact of the Slave Trade (mainly western) in which African groups actively took part, but which was powerfully activated notably by the economy of plantations across the Atlantic as from the 17th century. The strong periods of that haemorrhage were the 18th century (about 50 per cent of the collection) and the 19th century (about 30 per cent). Its volume is still a topic for debate among experts. Depending on whether or not the effects induced by the vacuum created are taken into account, people speak of 30 to 80 million people carried away from the continent during that period. All should admit, however, that, despite the introduction of American maize and cassava by the Portuguese, the haemorrhage of the Slave Trade replaced by the massacres, massive transfers of labour or the genocides of the colonial period, caused substantial loss which has removed the African from his hold on nature and lowered his enthusiasm below the level of procreation and creation, vital for his role as a historical actor.[3]

The second major change, though ambiguous, is taking place. Whereas certain European countries are dangerously growing old and can no longer maintain the rate of biological regeneration, Africa, which accounts for two-thirds of the LDCs, is also the continent which, thanks to the high birth rate but notably low death rate mainly among children, is experiencing a 'galloping' population growth. This change, which has many positive aspects, also poses considerable short- and medium-term problems such as the upkeep, health, education, housing and employment for all those young people who give to the African pyramid-shaped age structure both a reassuring and disquieting foundation. 'It is through children that we are immortal', say the Africans. More prosaically, the child is often the only capital to transmit a living social security account.

However, a population not based on an active economy is likely to give the African continent away to international charity, more especially as two aspects stand out sharply at present. These are the massive transfer of African populations to the forest areas which contained perhaps 20 per cent of the population in the 15th century, and urbanization, termed 'savage' (4–10 per cent, according to the regions; 7 per cent in the Sahel); now, this urbanization was qualitatively different from that in Europe in the 19th century because it was not functional. It neither met the real needs of attraction towards a labour market in the urban industrial sector, which was embryonic, nor aided an increase in rural productivity. The African town, with its unproductive village quarters, constitutes one of the elements of the dismantling of the productive system. For about two decades now, certain African countries have embarked on family planning. Is it the beginning of the third period for African demography?

Deterioration of the Eco-system

The humid tropical forest area in Cote d'Ivoire has reduced from 15 million hectares, at the beginning of the century, to 3 million in 1985. During that period, the Sahara desert advanced by 1 to 1.5 million hectares each year. These two processes are signs of desertification which is spreading also to north, east and southern Africa, unless there is a gigantic campaign for reafforestation and regeneration of the soil and underground water sheds for which there are no means at the moment, financially or socially. Lifestyles and even civilizations (great and semi-nomadic) are disappearing. Colonization, with the violent expansion of cash crop farming, has also worsened the process. In the life span of a human being, one notices the extinction of certain plant and animal species. Now, nature is not only a factor, but also a powerful economic actor. Despite the fact that African Nature had been the oldest to be exploited in the world (man first appeared in Africa!), it appeared to the first voyagers and explorers as teeming with multiform life. In the *Senegalese Sketches* Abbot Boillat mentions the existence of hordes of big game in the Cape Verde which irresistibly remind us of rupestrine paintings of the desolate stretches of the Sahara of today.

Population growth, not to mention the nuisance of 'modern' economy, such as the reckless experimentation with pesticides on the continent, can also threaten African nature and cause self-destruction. Nature is linked to farming, food customs, traditional pharmacopoeia and medicine, religion, and so on. A day will come when perhaps the break will be irreversible. Tourism, which has taken a short-term useful up-turn for the balance of payments of certain countries, may offer an opportunity to safeguard the natural milieu; but it could also worsen the negative breaks with nature and farming in Africa.

Food Upheavals

If distortions in Africa's population growth date back several centuries and if threats to the continent's ecological equilibrium go back a thousand years and have been renewed, notably through colonization, the chronic and ever-rising food shortages constitute a recent phenomenon which is nevertheless linked to the first two. Between

1970 and 1980, food production in Africa decreased by 7 per cent. For 35 years now, importation of grains which was very negligible just after the Second World War, i.e. before independence, has been on the ascendancy. Certain countries import 50 per cent of their food requirements.

This is the result of a long process and an interaction of structural and economic factors: inadequate rainfall, overgrazing, curtailing of fallow periods, education that uproots one from his environment, urban migration, but especially suicidal agricultural policies which exploited the defenceless African rural milieu in the face of its non-African competitors who were themselves largely protected. The negative effects of the macabre oscillation of world prices have been passed on to the farmer without making him benefit from the increases; the idea is to reduce to the lowest level for the urban consumer the prices of food products. Farmers obtain a meagre portion of the money earned by the state marketing and stabilization enterprises in the form of input subventions, instead of paying them a fair price for their harvest. Sometimes, up to 84 per cent of fertilizers go into coffee, tea and sugarcane cultivation. Too soon, the authorities banked on heavy industry to the detriment of the food sector.

African farmers experienced in times past memorable famines which sometimes served as chronological landmarks in the rural societies till the 20th century. The texts of the Tarikhs of Niger and Sudan inform us also about the numerous famines linked to the natural or political calamities of the 16th and 17th centuries. But, on the whole, from the prehistoric times and antiquity when North Africa was the granary of Rome till the arrival of the Arabs and Portuguese who bear witness to the great abundance of food products, Africa presented a picture of a continent of plenty where food was varied and nature was made use of to embellish and enrich it. At the beginning of the 20th century in certain Sahelian countries, it was a shame to consume the year's harvest in its entirety as the granaries generally contained reserves dating back one to four years or even seven years.

The chronic food deficits signify a 'red light' that in turn signals a serious malfunctioning of the African economic system and the most glaring failure of most independent African states. Certainly, some of the causes of this deficiency date back to the colonial times when cash crop farming was excessively favoured in terms of financing, research and various inputs, to the disadvantage of food production. But precisely this negative change could and should be rectified through a positive break on the part of African leaders. The contrary was the case. That disastrous negligence was also encouraged in certain leaders by the importation of food; hence the well-known retort of a very irresponsible 'Leader': 'why should we produce what we can buy?'

External food aid itself, which is still very much supported because it answers the pressure of excess production in the North, may, through the reflexes and habits it creates, develop a mentality of dependence in the assisted, unfavourable for African production. The big rallies of the youth, singing and dancing to gather money in order to save a half-starved Africa, have become a common sight in contemporary circles. The states concerned have become more and more interested in the problems of weather forecasting and the logistics of emergency aid.

But one aspect which is often ignored is advanced research into the sector of high-yielding seeds. It is forgotten that from the outset, it was the countries of the South which first selected the plants that serviced the 16th century and have since been recognized, acclimatized and improved upon in the countries of the North. The Prussian naturalist, Humbolt, on his return from his voyages in the equinoctial America in 1799, wrote 30 volumes. Thirty plants, which make up 95 per cent of the food of the people living on earth, originate in the Third World today. About a dozen of them make up 75 per cent of the food caloric content of man. The countries of the North, which have experts and especially sufficient laboratories, collect the wild and indigenous varieties in Africa into their seed and gene banks and develop, through genetic engineering, high-yielding hybrid varieties which are then sold to African countries. Now, the secret about those hybrids is that they reproduce only once, and we cannot therefore dip into the seeds of the harvest. In other words, the African dependence on a dish of rice or maize is likely to be transferred to the more strategic dependence on the seeds themselves.

Negative Socio-cultural Changes

These also have an impact on the recovery and development envisaged. Let us select two: the personalized centralization of power and the realms of culture, law, training and communication.

Local decentralization and autonomy, which were common in Africa up to the 20th century, are giving place to *systems which are more and more centralized and bureaucratic* where corruption steps in.

In fact, with the exception of a few cases in North Africa (Moroccan Maghzen, Pharaonic, Ptolemanic, Arab and Ottoman Egypt), and even in those cases, the system of power in Africa was generally founded on the delegation of authority (in exchange for a 'tribute') and self-management of the communities. That policy was born out of an option and/or a technical necessity (for example, the lack of a corps of educated civil servants and the lack of wheeled vehicles or fire arms). Thus, the Mansa (sovereign) of 14th-century Mali was induced to grant religious freedom and autonomy demanded by the gold diggers of Boure, for fear of seeing a fall in production. In North Africa, the vitality of the tribal groups (Kabila) offset the centralized power, and when the latter encroached excessively on their rights, the masses withdrew to the religious communities (Zaouias) and the marabout associations.

The unanimity, which is almost always demanded by African political powers and which tends to obstruct the economic initiatives of people, is in fact a break in tradition. Without being democratic in the contemporary Western sense of the word, without escaping from the episodes of personal tyranny, oligarchy of clans, age groups or secret societies, tradition functioned on the basis of participation of groups in decision-making and its implementation. Moreover, the usual rule, sometimes stronger than the law in a modern state, was imperative on all without exception.

Now, the African cultural landscapes, like the continent's forests, are being dismantled and torn apart. In the areas of development and land law, family law or obligations, the activities of daily life are irresistibly invaded by the spirit and the letter of the legal systems of the North, despite the subdued and sporadic resistance where the religious element plays a certain role.

The socio-cultural sphere in the colonial system was the object of a different legislation according to which the colonizer opted for assimilation (France, Portugal, and to a certain extent Belgium) or for separation (Great Britain). Nevertheless, the practical application of the system and the way the masses perceived it would be the same. A certain degree of break with the indigenous society would also be demanded from the executives directly associated with management. That negative break of the African executives with their socio-cultural basis was a historical phenomenon of the first order though difficult to determine chronologically. It was a groundswell where the educational system reproduced the models of the North, where the lifestyles of the rich countries were illustrated and permanently proposed by the aggressive and omnipresent media, and where the almost clandestine rejection of African languages played an important role.

The colonial malthusian and mimetic school was only a by-product of the overall system. Despite its reforms and the spectacular improvement in the quantitative results, the school of independent Africa is far from helping to resolve the economic problems through adequate internal and external profitability. As an overall producer of the unemployed, the school is culturally a malignant tumour in the social set-up and poses more problems than it can solve. Thus, the African historical process allows us to note many more negative splits than positive changes, likewise with continuties.

POSITIVE CONTINUITIES

Among the positive constants that run through African history, there are two which have from time immemorial struck observers. They are the non-capitalist structures and the traditions of resistance.

Non-capitalist Structures

Here also, the positive meaning is contradictory because what is involved is not metaphysical Africanity but the product of a peculiar history. As a matter of fact, what makes Africa different from other continents is its late entry into the capitalist system which functioned on its soil until the 20th century in a mediate and marginal way. For this reason, pre-capitalist structures remain 'fresher' and more dynamic in Africa than elsewhere, but at the same time more vulnerable on account of the sharp contrast in the balance of power. This explains why the structures no longer function as they did before the introduction of the capitalist system based on the individualization of the 'homo economicus' (money, credit, wage earning, private ownership, price generalization). In many African countries, before the colonial invasion, the sale of the most precious things (land, water, medicine, title of nobility) was forbidden.

This deviating logic, which characterizes another society with different values, is still used as a reference if not as a rule by many African groups not involved in the new production ratio based on rationality of price and profit. The area of operation of the famous informal sector is wider than was originally believed, even though it is often confused with capitalist structures. Long neglected by economists, this sector forms part of the African traditional way of thinking. Indeed, in areas not governed by foreign laws, traditional solidarity, even though suppressed and rejected by 'market laws', shows remarkable vitality. It serves not only as a basis for exchanging gifts and services in the rural areas but also as social guarantee against the hazards of life in the slums of African cities. It also serves as an ideological basis for development policies, as varied as community development, African socialism and *Ujaama Vijnini*. In short, non-capitalist African mutual trade set-up constitutes a factor which must be taken into consideration, even if its scope is limited by national frontiers and if its ambiguous nature makes it at times a capitalism *lumpen* of the shanty towns. Some of its aspects are today used for effective development, particularly by NGOs.

Traditions of Resistance

This is another form of exceptional positive continuity: rejection of injustice and oppression. As far back as the Egypt of the Pharaohs, mention was made of strikes by workers at the pyramid sites. In 15th- and 16th-century, Morocco, the Zaouias (Muslim brotherhood) attracted the rebellion of people and, at times, crystallized insurrections. It is this many-sided capacity for resistance that prompted the colonizers of Africa to prefer taxation to annexation and genocide, and indirect to direct rule.

The most concrete example of such continuous rejection is given to us by the people of South Africa. Right from the time the Dutch first landed on the Cape in 1652, they were resisted by the Hottentots who were determined to defend their land and interests. Over the years, these economic and socio-cultural interests have been seriously undermined through the plundering of the land, the mines, the labour, and the denial of elementary freedoms. Each revolt against these injustices has, until today, been severely repressed, thanks to the complicity of firms and Western countries with vested interests in that country. The powerful drive of capitalism led, way back in 1913, to successful strike action by white trade unionists, followed by that of the black mine workers. Periodically, and with a growing number of people, this resistance gained momentum as evidenced by the civil war the country was nearly plunged into in 1920 and 1923, the strike by the dockers in 1946 and in 1972–1973, and the alliance of young intellectuals and workers formed in Soweto in 1976, which was a prelude to the present alliance of national and workers movements. Indeed, South Africa is the only African country where the working class is in the majority compared to the peasantry and the middle class. It is also the only country whose liberation would have, on the continent's overall economic development, a much more decisive positive impact than the negative effects it now has on the economies of the frontline states. Despite their relegation to bantustan concentration camps and townships, the people of South Africa are waging a relentless economic liberation struggle which cannot be dissociated from the struggle for 'Black Consciousness'. Another concrete example of economic struggle which dates back thousands of years is that of Egypt faced with, as it is, the dangers posed by its geographical position between three continents, particularly for the control of the trans-continental spice trade during the time of Sultan Mamluk and his successors.

As a matter of fact, the two forms of positive continuities which we have just cited are, as it were, contradictory. The persistence of pre-capitalist solidarity tends to attenuate and partially absorb the antagonism generated by the expansion of capitalism in Africa, whereas Africa's tradition of resistance resulted in confrontation. The latter is sustained and activated by a series of negative continuities which can be traced in the history of the continent.

NEGATIVE CONTINUITIES

Weakening of African Labour Force

This has been one of Africa's characteristics for many centuries. From time immemorial, slavery was rampant in North Africa. However, this slavery gained momentum with the extraction of the 'black mineral', resulting in a serious drain on manpower and energy on the continent. The two world wars further weakened the African labour force with the recruitment of soldiers and the 'war effort' imposed on the continent. France alone recruited 200,000 men from Africa during the 1914–1918 war. This led to famine and rebellion. Added to this, following the independence of African countries, there were compulsory intra-African migrations resulting in the displacement of millions of persons (50 per cent of the world figure) due to ecological, economic or political reasons.

Mention should also be made of the migration of African workers which constitutes a considerable loss and a drain on manpower. This forms part of the growth strategy of the developed countries but not part of the development strategy of African countries. Within the same context is explained the increasingly massive exodus of African intellectuals, experts and scientists, trained with African money, who desert the continent, thereby further increasing the management, research and invention capacity of the developed countries.

Everything is happening as though Africa has for several centuries been witnessing, powerlessly, the plundering of its resources. From the historical point of view, the art of bleeding Africa white has been perfected, as evidenced, first, by the changes in the economic structural development of the developed countries and, second, by the reactions from the Africans themselves.

Europeans since the fifteenth century have been interested in the development of the trans-Saharan trade, general mercantilism and

305

collection of scarce and precious products based on weight/value ratio. The most valuable of these products was 'ebony'. Another form of Africa's exploitation began with industrial capitalism. The abolition of slavery was followed by the development of the mining industry (50 per cent of Africa's overall exports in 1913 were mining products) and of cash crops to feed European factories. Territories were conquered and occupied, and the most fertile lands expropriated to ensure regular supply for these factories. It was not by coincidence that Great Britain, the first industrial power, was at the vanguard of actions initiated and the ideological speeches made in this regard: abolition of slavery, 'illicit trade' and writing of theses on the duty of the West based on the dual mandate which the 'powers' gave themselves at the Berlin Conference (1884–1886) namely, to bring to Africans the benefits of material and moral civilization and exploit Africa's wealth. It was on that score that Lugard proposed the system of Indirect Rule, so that the mandate to exploit did not over-shadow the mandate to civilize.

Correlatively, it was also not by coincidence that South Africa which had the greatest exploitation capacity, as was then envisaged, was the first to experience the development of the mining industry, and the first to prove the incompatibility between the mandate to exploit and the mandate to civilize.

As far as colonization is concerned, it was no longer the African who was cheaply sold or bought but rather his labour, through some kind of 'black mineral' refining. Thus, for about one century, colonization which was widespread in Africa, extorted perhaps as many hours of labour from Africans as the Slave Trade did in four centuries. In the Congo of King Leopold, for instance, the entire population was subjected to the collection of rubber under well-known bloody conditions. The manual collection persisted, for as long as it was considered more economically profitable than any other form of collection, into the 20th century, from the time of the spice trade to that of shea butter in the atomic era. For centuries, investment in Africa was too low to enable the African worker to keep body and soul together. To compel the latter to work, a whole legal, administrative, financial and police arsenal was deployed: forced labour, compulsory work, poll-tax, development of new requirements, monetarization and unequal trade.

Capitalism became finance-oriented and monopolistic, in which banks, currencies and prices, particularly the price of money, played a leading role. As far back as the 16th century, the Portuguese indulged in monetary and inflationist practices by transporting whole loads of cowrie from the Indian Ocean into West Africa, and King Chezo of

Dahomey had to fight against this economic subversion in the 19th century. However, these practices were nothing compared to the arsenal used in the contemporary world where uneven domestic trade, characteristic of African countries, is linked with uneven external trade: high interest rate, devaluation, exchange rate war, price manipulation by clearing houses, marketing boards and international money market, and protectionist practices.[4]

The price of the African worker is no longer determined, as was the case in the Goree slave market in the 18th century, by inspecting his teeth. Rather, by an anonymous and remote decision, the price of his labour is determined by the fall in the price of the produce of the farmer, so long as the ruling class, African or non-African, is not affected. The Sahel farmer to whom a trader comes to buy an unharvested crop of millet, and from whom the trader takes back part of the money by selling him a crate of beer is, objectively speaking, transformed into an agricultural wage earner on his own farm. Only a well-to-do farmer who employs agricultural wage earners can be truly considered as making profit. What this boils down to is that, from the structural point of view, the present system undermines the pre-capitalist African systems of ownership and labour, and the 'structural re-adjustment' policies only perpetuate this tendency.

Science and Technology

A second historical constant or continuity that can be traced is the slow pace of the scientific and technological development in Africa. Talking about 'backwardness' is out of the question for, as far as science and technology are concerned, the African continent was until the 15th century, as the works of Cheikh Anta Diop have shown, a net exporter of science and technology ranging from the pre-historic time to the tremendous breakthrough by Egypt during the time of the Pharaohs and the valuable contributions made by the Arab/Berber and Muslim world.

The use or absence of scripts contributed particularly to scientific elaboration and accumulation of knowledge. Today, if it is observed for example that 70 per cent of the water pumps installed in the villages no longer function, it is because, since independence, we have not made full use of science and technology. Instead of going in for 'turn key' factories, Africa should have gone in for factories that use local raw materials. By refusing to embark on scientific discoveries and preferring simply to consume the fruits thereof, we have turned our back on our own scientific and technological heritage. As proven by the award of some recent patents, certain serious diseases are cured more rapidly and effectively by African medicines which, though used more often by over half of the population, *are not considered as* a public utility. It is only a few decades ago that efforts were deployed or redeployed to take stock of Africa's achievements in the fields of medicine and pharmacopoeia, soils,[5] plant and animal sciences, and climatology, not to mention social sciences in which recent works by historians have shown in which way the African approach could make a contribution.

As a matter of fact, science is not like the promethean fire snatched from heaven by only one continent. It is a common heritage of mankind; it is also a social product that appears in given historical circumstances and has increasingly become an economic and strategic property which, like money, is being jealously guarded by the developed countries. Science and technology which are linked with the problem of global industrialization will not be handed out to Africa by the industrial countries which favour the present international division of labour. Some of the advice to Africans to develop the 'food self-sufficiency sector' is malicious. Agro-industry should constitute one of the means to face up to the challenge. As far back as the Middle Ages, Sudan was exporting cotton goods while East Africa was exporting to India Sofala iron which, according to Al Idrisi, in the 12th century defied any comparison in terms of abundance and malleability. As far as industrialization is concerned, the North of the continent is well provided for.

Ideological Cover

The historian cannot help but observe the recurrence or negative continuity of some paradigmatic themes by which the vigilance of Africans was almost always put to sleep with semantics being introduced from time to time to subject the enlightened to anaesthesia which is vital for the surgical operation going on. To that extent, three major concepts have been formulated since the 16th century, namely, salvation, progress and development.

(a) *Salvation* – A major part of the Slave Trade was carried out under the guise of spiritual salvation. By evoking this spiritual salvation, many slave traders arrogated to themselves the right to chain human beings wallowing in servitude with a view to liberating their souls.

(b) *Progress* – From the 18th century, known as the century of Enlightenment, the concept of progress or of a secular or even anti-religious humanism, which can be traced back to Greek heritage through the Renaissance, advocated a progress which served as a framework and was the force behind the formulation of the scientific, rational, evolutionistic and productivistic hypothesis of the industrial capitalist era. In the name of progress and freedom, the slave trade of the previous century was condemned, and well-meaning people called for the colonization of Africa and the propagation therein of the benefits of civilization considered as the mechanical product of science.

(c) *Development* – Following the colonial experiences and the shocks of the two world wars, the ideas of progress and civilization were seriously undermined. During the two world wars, Africa had contributed in no small way to the victories of the democratic forces. This is why the 'development' of the colonies for exploitation purposes gave way, after a short period characterized by the concept of growth, to the idea of progress strongly advocated through the UN System. The concept of development has today become one of under-development in so far as the under-development of some is used as fertilizer for the development of others. The concept is therefore wrong because it does not project the reality.

PERIODIZATION

Any periodization is relative. However, the chronology of evolution through changes and continuities which we have just outlined can help bring into focus the economic itinerary of the African continent. Five periods can be identified.

The first covers the initial period from the origins to the 15th century. It is the era when Africa was open to the outside world but, at the same time, very much in control of internal and external changes such as saharization, Hyksos, peoples of the sea, Hellenization, Romanization, Arabization, Bantu expansion, development of metal industry and plant selection, organization of major trade circuits and 'medieval' university education.

The second period was from the 15th century to the end of the 19th century (colonization). This period was the continuation of the previous one as far as the independence of most of the African social set-ups were concerned. However, this second period has something that makes it different from the previous one in that it revealed the negative role of the continent *vis-à-vis* the outside world from the demographic, ecological, economic and cultural viewpoints. In this connection, the beginning of the 18th century can be considered as a turning point just as was the abolition of the slave trade, 1834–1848, and the beginning of the 'illicit trade'.

The third period was from 1885 (Berlin Conference) to 1945 (end of the second world war). It was the era of direct and immediate dependency in all fields: dispossession of individual and collective self. It was also the period of the great European depression which began in 1873 and which gave impetus to colonial expansion characterized by the Berlin Conference (1885), the war effort during the first world war, the major crises of the 1930s which led to the development of the colonies and their greater integration within the metropoles and, lastly, the war effort of the second world war which led to some sporadic industrialization aimed at national self-sufficiency.

The fourth period was from 1945 to 1973. It was the period of political and ideological conquests but of no change in the established economic order characterized by North–South financial flows. The post-war years were the period of cold war which increased the negotiating power of the African countries such as Nasser's Egypt and, to some extent, Nkrumah's Ghana. There were also the Korean war, Dien Bien Phu, Bandung (1955) and independence of African countries sometimes attained through armed struggles as in Algeria. Mention should also be made of the economic influence of the Eastern bloc on some countries following their independence (such as the supply of goods based on the barter system and arms).

The fifth period started in 1973. It was the period of crises, characterized by radical changes in the ecology, energy supply and economies of African countries and, in particular, by the visible changes or reversal in the financial flows from South to North. At the beginning of this period and following the effects of drought and the 'oil shock' experienced by the non-oil-producing countries, some partial or symbolic gains were made. These include the Declaration of the New International Economic Order (1973), the Declaration on the Economic Rights and Duties of States (1974) and the first Lome Convention (1978). Mention should also be made of the adoption of LPA and the establishment of SADCC. From 1983, however, climatic conditions and the debt situation, not to mention internal wars, over-armament and South Africa's subversion, plunged several African countries once again into structural crisis.

Other divisions into periods are possible; as far as the expectations of the people are concerned, the years of independence were considered as a turning point. When then did disillusionment set in?

Though Africa has experienced a general deteriorating situation, progress has been made in certain economic sectors of some countries.

However, it should be pointed out that while some African countries stagnate or regress, other continents or countries progress, thus making the African continent more dependent on the outside world. Similarly, while Africa largely contributed to the positive structural changes of other continents (for example, the role of the Slave Trade in the development of the capitalist system which in turn colonized the continent), in Africa itself, except in South Africa, there are no powerful financiers to invest in productive ventures.

With the absence of industry generating industry, the continent suffers economic backwardness and shows signs of early decay characterized, for example, by unemployment among cadres and over-consumption of luxury and basic commodities.

PROSPECTS

Africa is not lost. The centuries of exploitation, though painful, are centuries of experience. By the very nature of certain raw materials it produces, Africa is an indispensable partner whose weight should be reckoned with. Besides, important infrastructures were set up by the colonial powers and during the early years of neo-colonialism. The integration of Africans into the world movement is in itself a good thing provided that this is done within the context of real power sharing. In no way should the crisis serve as a basis for perpetuating the negative role played by Africa in the world economy. Now, the continent is threading a difficult path, not only because its share in world production is declining even in respect of products in which it has specialized (for example, cocoa fell from 34 per cent in 1975 to 24 per cent in 1985 and cotton from 17 per cent to 10 per cent between 1970 and 1980), and not only because at the beginning of 1980 each African country exported only 60 per cent of what it exported in 1970, taking into account the population growth, but also because the structural ills of the African economy remain and because its primary role persists, and this increases its dependence on the ouside world.

What is to be done? Three conditions can help Africa take a qualitative and positive turn: Africa's deep-rootedness in its cultures, African integration and justice.

Socio-cultural Basis

Africa's recovery is not a mere question of applying economic technique, much less financial techniques. To be able to recover, Africa must gather its forces and brace itself. Breaking away from the system of exploitation is possible only under certain conditions. In order to

311

recover you must have the will to do so. This presupposes an authentic socio-cultural rootedness. In fact, to break away from the outside world while you are without roots can only lead to one fate: that of a ship which has sunk. You cannot ask the ship to refloat itself, neither can you ask it to sail against the tide. Only a deep-rooted tree can stand and grow all by itself.

Besides, a break with the outside world can only be partial and functional: we have a lot to receive and especially to learn from the developed countries, whose experience contains some major lessons for mankind. Indeed, what is involved is not clinging to past cultural values, but concrete self-affirmation which must be expressed through agricultural journals, various media, art, religion, education, research, sport, private law, contact with nature and rapport between the sexes, use of African languages, etc. All these are not at variance with development. Indeed, culture is the best agricultural fertilizer. It is in this way that culture is vital for development.

African Integration

To break away and starve in solitude only to come back one day to experience more inhuman enslavement is to act like an irresponsible person. There is an African proverb which says that 'when you cross the river as a group you do not have to be afraid of crocodiles'. As a matter of fact, the power of negotiation depends on the strong cohesion of the African countries, not through verbal statements but through the formulation of strategies which should be implemented. At Yamoussokro in February 1987, for instance, the Ministers of the West African Monetary Union (UMOA) advocated collective negotiations and not individual negotiations with IMF. A Minister from an agricultural raw material-producing country demanded 'fair price' for his country's product which would eliminate the problem of the debt crisis. In other words, the North has to embark on some structural adjustment. This it will not do when Africa does not speak with one voice.

Nevertheless, Africans have memorable experiences of integration. For example, cowrie was an African currency used by about 20 countries. Its devaluation was only precipitated in the 19th century with the discovery of deposits in Zanzibar and of steamers. Trans-Saharan trade from the Mediterranean to the Sahel, extending to the forest and the gulf of Guinea, was entirely controlled for a thousand years by African political leaders and merchants. Ashanti and Hausa business men from Kano and Nupe controlled an area of operation extending from the Kola forest to the Fezzan oasis in Libyan Arab Jamahiriya. The Euro-African Almoravids included Berbers, Blacks and Arabs over an area extending from Senegal to the banks of Ebre in Spain, and the Almohad model of unity of the Maghreb still remains one of the culminating points of North African history. From the 16th to the 18th century, there was a continental commercial network stretching from the Atlantic Ocean to the Indian Ocean. The articles traded included mainly ivory and copper in the form of small crosses. This trade was carried on by coloured and black 'pombeiros' and African 'babaris' shuttling between Congo or Angola and Mozambique. In the Kingdom of Kazembe, they met Arabo-Swahili merchants from Zanzibar.

The present partitioning of Africa, particularly the dismantling of some colonial establishments by the Africans themselves in the wake of independence, is a fundamental obstacle to the continent's economic recovery. This does not mean that the current borders recognized by OAU should be removed. What it means is that we should have the courage to transcend them and work towards true sovereignty, sovereignty of non-dependence.

Europe, whose states in a not too distant past were ravaged by wars in which at least 75 million people died, is now in the process of rebuilding itself in all areas: parliamentary, governmental, monetary, agricultural, scientific, educational, etc. A European university is in the process of being established in Paris. Now, the value of goods manufactured by Africa for export (with the exception of South Africa) is equivalent to only 5 per cent of the industrial exports of Belgium alone! Compared with the purchasing power of European citizens, the market for 200 million citizens of ECOWAS would be reduced to 25 or 30 million. No solution whatsoever will be found to some serious problems like genuine industrialization and youth employment without regional or subregional African integration.

Justice

Obviously, this does not involve the transformation of the various forms of democracy on the continent, but the safeguarding, through the application of some inviolable principles, of some basic human rights (freedom and justice) and the establishment of a common law which is no respecter of individuals or groups of people. Even the Pharaoh was subjected to the judgement of Osiris. Any artificial unanimity is a mask that deceives only those who wear it.

CONCLUSION

The above are the necessary and adequate basic conditions for Africa's real recovery. The fulfilment of these conditions depends on the

Africans and should not be confused with unpredictable external resources which have strings attached. Any assistance increases dependency. Only in this way will Africa's deplorable image, for which we are all responsible, change for the better. Way back in the 18th century, Montesquieu, while talking about Africans, said: 'These people are not imaginative, so to speak; their laws have no other principles than those based on primitive morals, and no consistency other than that based on indolence and blindness.'[6] Today, millions of people throughout the world have the same opinion about Africans.

There is need, therefore, to ponder over the following statement by Gandhi: 'Our non-co-operation is not directed against the English or the West, but rather against the materialistic civilization which breeds greed and the exploitation of the weak by the strong. Our non-co-operation leads us to become introvert, expressed through the refusal to co-operate with the English administrators under conditions imposed on us. We say to them: come and co-operate with us on conditions laid down by us and we all, as well as the whole world, shall benefit from this co-operation.'[7] China's 'self-reliance policy' seeks to achieve the same objective. This obviously requires the pooling of forces: not only the credit balance of the balance of payments.

When in 1958 we were campaigning for independence for the French African countries, I received the following reply from one of the African leaders of the time: 'How do you expect us to gain independence? Economically we have nothing!' I retorted by saying that he was himself condemning colonization since he observed that after 65 years of colonization, we have nothing economically speaking. One year later, this politician became the leader of one of the independent countries. Given that thirty years after 'acceding to international sovereignty' we still have nothing, economically speaking, can we say that he was right? Of course not! First, because there are sectors where African countries made considerable progress. In Nigeria in the 1930s, there were 12 hospitals for 4000 Europeans as against only 52 for over 40 million Africans. In Nigeria, at independence, there was not a single kilometre of tarred road. He was also wrong because, in so far as Africans have still not changed the economic role of the continent, they should recognize that there are several forms of dependency and should pursue the struggle (which is a historic struggle) for the attainment of complete independence bearing in mind that political independence is only a tool in this direction, a means but not an end.

It is necessary, above all, to return to the major propositions, most of which are contained in LPA but which still remain only on paper. It is time that Africans again seize their opportunities for, as the proverb says, 'when you jump into the fire, there is still another jump ahead'.

NOTES

1. The positive nature of the splits or continuities was obviously not absolute; it is a question of a historical and dialectical assessment.
2. Special mention should be made here of the EEC policy of co-operation which has attempted to renew co-operation (STABEX, MINEX) without changing its nature.
3. P. Curtin, *The Atlantic Slave Trade – A Census*, Madison, 1969, L. M. Diop, 'Le Sous-peuplement de l'Afrique Noire', *Bulletin de l'IFAN*, 40B, No. 4, October 1978. J.E. Inikori, *Forced migrations: the Impact of the Export–Slave Trade on African Societies*, London, 1982, pp.13–60. P.E. Lovejoy, 'The Volume of the Atlantic Slave Trade – A Synthesis', *Journal of African History*, XXIII, 1982, pp.473–501.
4. Uneven trade is the first factor that contributed to the misery in many countries of the Third World. The present international division of labour compels developing countries to produce to satisfy the needs of the industrialized countries and not their own, thus perpetuating the order established at the time of colonialism. See, E. Pisani, *La main et e'outil*, R. Lafront, 1984, page 40.
5. The traditional agricultural system which to some people appears logical but irrational can even be described as scientific in some cases, where despite an unfavourable ecology, the land supported large human densities. At worst, the farming methods yielded food crops commensurate with the efforts made, if not with the area cultivated.
6. *Encyclopedia*, Supplement, T.I. Amsterdam, 1780, page 194.
7. M. Gandhi, *Tous les hommes sont frères*, Editions Fallimard, p.208.

CHAPTER THIRTEEN

How Politics Underdevelops Africa

CLAUDE AKE

INTRODUCTION

We are never going to understand the current crisis in Africa, much less contain it, as long as we continue to think of it as an economic crisis. What is before us now is primarily a political crisis; its economic consequences are serious, but they are nonetheless incidental. Not only is the crisis essentially political in character, it is also political in its origin. It has arisen largely from a political disposition; namely, a tendency to depoliticize economic interactions and processes. The attempt to depoliticize economic matters has unleashed powerful social forces, including a form of political competition which has rendered the task of overcoming underdevelopment virtually impossible. The dynamics and effects of the process of depoliticization are roughly as follows:

(a) As politics is repressed, it becomes more and more primary and marginalizes everything else, including economic development;

(b) As politics becomes primary, the premium on political power rises and political competition becomes increasingly intense, leading to the militarization of not only politics but also society, to the detriment of economic development; and,

(c) The depoliticization of economic processes expresses and reinforces the contradictions between the rulers and the ruled, and their mutual alienation; it leads to the dissociation of public policy from public interest and, finally, stalls the struggle against imperialism.

Since these factors are essentially the explanation of the current crisis in Africa, it is necessary to treat them in some detail. In particular, we need to examine the objective conditions which formed and gave impetus to the process of depoliticization in Africa. We should note however that the inclination to depoliticize is not something which is new to Africa. Some of its objective conditions were already there, fully formed at the time when the African countries became independent.

Three elements were particularly important in shaping these conditions. The first was political authoritarianism. Since colonialism was an arbitrary seizure of the territory and resources of the colonized, and a concerted assault on their history and culture, it was obliged to rely predominantly on force. One implication of the doctrine of the civilizing mission was that colonized people needed to be ruled by others and could not responsibly be granted the usual civil liberties. By its very nature, colonialism did not and could not have liberal politics.

The second was the exclusiveness of claims to rulership. Political competition in the nationalist period was the clash of two exclusive claims to rulership which made politics a zero-sum game. These two factors made the very practice of politics, paradoxically enough, the very negation of politics; at any rate, politics was practised with the intent of ending politics; that is, to gain power and use it to bar all other claims to power and even to rights.

The third element was that, with few exceptions, the nationalist leadership which inherited power, for good reasons, believed that their interests were served by de-radicalizing the nationalist movement while maintaining its unity. So they convinced themselves and tried to convince others that there were no serious political differences and no basis for political opposition. Apoliticism was elevated to the level of an ideology while the political structures became ever more monolithic.

THE HEGEMONY OF POLITICS

The political structures and political ideologies which were used to effect depoliticization are all too familiar. It is important to take note of the paradoxical relation between the process of depoliticization and the objective conditions prevailing in Africa. On the one hand, the disposition to depoliticize expressed in the most natural way, indeed inevitably, salient realities of the African situation. Some of these have already been mentioned. On the other hand, the process of depoliticization was at odds with other realities which were equally salient. Specifically, the societies which were being depoliticized were heterogeneous and fragmented, sometimes to the point of being incoherent. For instance, economically, the various regions and sectors of the typical African post-colonial economy looked outwards and lacked complementarity. Politically, differences rather than similarities increasingly dominated political life once the colonial regime was removed, showing that common resentment of its character was an important basis of political cohesion during the nationalist era. Most African countries are really a hotch-potch of nationalities or peoples who had little in common with each other before colonialism brought them under a common domination. Lastly, the mounting evidence that political independence had not done much for popular aspirations and popular interests undermined the legitimacy of the political leadership and sharpened class conflict.

The implication of depoliticization is to deny the existence of these serious differences, to disallow their legitimate expression and collective negotiation. However, the process does not remove the differences, it merely represses them while the frustrations of those affected grow, calling for ever more repression. That is how it has come about that, in most of our continent, political repression has become the most characteristic feature of political life, and domination and subordination the salient political relationship. All this means that political power becomes particularly important and the struggle for it gets singularly intense.

How this situation contributes to our underdevelopment is easy to see. The struggle for power has become so intense and so absorbing that it has overshadowed everything else, including the pursuit of development. The appearances suggest that development is our major preoccupation. It is not, and cannot be – at least for most of our leaders. They are, as it were, in a state of siege and their first concern – sometimes it seems to be the only one – is to survive and to reproduce their domination.

There are two major ways in which this situation underdevelops Africa. The first lies in the incompatibilities between the pursuit of development, on the one hand, and the quest for survival and the reproduction of existing forms of domination over development, on the other. The damaging effects of this conflict are everywhere. It leads to the misuse of manpower resources and to inefficiency and corruption. Invariably, appointments into positions of power, even when they are positions which demand specialized knowledge, tend to be made by political criteria, particularly by regarding these appointments as part of survival strategy. Each time such an appointment is made, the conflict between survival, on the one hand, and efficiency and development, on the other, is reproduced. The damage to efficiency and development arises not only from the special performance criteria and likely incompetence of the persons so appointed but also from the general demoralization of the technically competent people serving under them who are often frustrated by their subordination to the supervision of people who are powerful but inept, and whose concerns are often quite different from their own. Here lies the bane of African ministries and parastatals: ignorant and incompetent people used obstructively and wastefully at the very top of our institutions, while competent people are wasted. So we lose at both ends.

A related economic problem of our leaders' concern with survival is the channelling of resources into unproductive uses. Important development projects may be initiated for the wrong reasons; they may, on account of political considerations, be located in places where they are least beneficial economically. There are familiar cases where important contracts and licences have been given to politically-significant people who are unable to execute them successfully or who sell them to other contractors in circumstances which defeat the national interest. Sometimes, well-paid positions are created just to give jobs to people whose political support is considered important. The country pays for no service rendered; worse, it pays for nuisance value. In some cases, people are overpaid for what they do in order to keep them happy, creating demoralizing disparities between reward and effort.

The crisis of survival appears to be jeopardizing the whole notion of a development strategy. Can people trying to function in a state of seige as is the case with most of our leaders have a development strategy in the first place? That is doubtful. A development strategy is a comprehensive programme of social transformation. It calls for a great deal of confidence in the leadership and a great deal of commitment; it calls for a great deal of clarity and concentration of purpose for the society at large, and it calls for social consensus especially on the legitimacy of the leadership. These are not features that are commonly seen in Africa. A development strategy changes too many things and not necessarily in a way that supports the survival of the leadership nor even in ways that are predictable. In this sense it runs against the instincts of a leadership whose preoccupation is to survive and to maintain the political *status quo*.

One of the most amazing things about the literature on development in Africa is how readily it assumes that everyone is interested in development and that when our leaders proclaim their commitment to development and fashion their impressive development plans and negotiate with international organizations for development assistance, they are really for development and for getting on with it. Those making this assumption forget the primacy of power and its conflict with other goals. Why should an African leader, or any other leader for that matter, embark on a course of social transformation just because it is good for his country if it is bad for his own survival? When we think of development, we are thinking of the objective interests of society and the paradox is that it is often the leaders who are in no position to think of the objective interest of the society. For thinking in this way is profoundly a democratic commitment which cannot usually be expected of leaders, a special interest invariably distinguished by the privilege of power and status. By virtue of their position, leaders suffer the disadvantage of confusing what maintains the existing social order, which they dominate, and what is in the national interest. And they are tendentially suspicious of change, all the more so when it is the fundamental type of change that development strategies in Africa envisage.

Finally, we need to remember some of the implications of development for the interest of our leaders. As has already been mentioned, some of our leaders have been more interested in taking advantage of the social order inherited from the colonial era rather than in transforming it. To all appearances, some of our leaders are consciously a comprador bourgeoisie. Others are more nationalistic but find that their economy is locked into a dependency relation with metropolitan economies and that trying to unlock it could undermine not only their chance to accumulate but, more importantly, their prospects of survival.

In these circumstances, it is not surprising that where development is pursued at all, its pursuit is full of ambiguities and contradictions. It is never really clear whether the pursuit of development is merely a posture. In the past, we have taken these postures on their face value and made too much of them. In so far as we have been critical of development strategies in Africa, our criticisms have run in the direction of their sloppy conception, their value orientations, inadequate translation of ideas into projects, poor implementation, their failure to come to grips with the obstacles created by imperialism, and so on. We have not raised the question of the contradiction between survival and social transformation. Once we raise this question we begin to see that it is doubtful whether development is, or has ever been, on the agenda in some of our countries.

The second aspect of the economic consequences of the struggle for survival can be summed up as the militarization of social life. The militarization of society is the outcome of the overvaluing of political power in Africa and the intense struggle to obtain and keep it. This has transformed politics in Africa into warfare. In this competition every form of force is mobilized and deployed: the winners have the prospect of near-absolute power and the losers not only forgo power but face a real prospect of losing liberty and even life. As politics changed from reliance on argument to force, its vocabulary and its organization also changed. The political formations in most of Africa are, for all practical purposes, armies in action. And this is in itself an economic problem. In a society in which the political formations are organized as warring armies, differences are too hard, the scope for co-operation too limited; there is too much distrust and life is too raw to nurture commerce and industry.

The militarization of social life in general and politics in particular has reached its logical culmination in military rule in most of Africa. This too has not helped the course of development. Here again we confront another reality shrouded in confusion and misrepresentation. When Africa started drifting towards military rule, the inclination of most African leaders as well as scholars was to rationalize it, and this has led us to a point where it has become increasingly difficult to separate rationalization from explanation. Economists argued that the economic development of backward societies called for political authoritarianism and that military rule provided an excellent model of this requirement. Some have argued that many African countries were too divided and that they needed a coherent and forceful organization such as the military to hold together and to develop their potential. Some invoke the inefficiency and corruption of the civilian govern-ments in Africa to which the military supposedly offered a better alternative by virtue of its discipline.

However, after a long experience with military rule in Africa, we have very few illusions left. Maybe we can now begin to see the disadvantages of military rule especially on economic development. The military is a very specialized body whose purpose is very specific and whose entire character is defined solely by this purpose. When the military gains political power it does the only thing it knows how to do; namely, to deploy force and maintain discipline. That is, until politics captures it. For once the military assumes power – that is, enters politics – politics captures it and it immediately begins to reflect, on an increasing scale, the social contradictions of the society. Then the same features which discredited the civilian political formations and political regimes begin to assert themselves in the military. Needless to say, they generally prevail because the military does not exist in abstraction, but is itself an integral part of the society and its contradictions.

While the general problems of military rule are interesting and relevant, we should focus here on the economic effects of the militariza-tion of society at large, a phenomenon which also occurs under civilian rule. Two of the important implications of this phenomenon should be noted. First, militarization means the application of a great deal of coercion to social life. Order and conformity are maintained not so much through consensus as through violence and fear. The conformity thus achieved is invariably confused with consensus; a leadership out of touch with its people has no chance of remedying this handicap. It goes on perpetrating all manner of arbitrariness on the people in the name of the people as the society divides into two hostile camps which are increasingly unable to communicate. From the point of view of the society at large, the salient political features of militarization are as follows: there is no expression of popular interest and no mobilization of their consensus, and there is no accountability of leadership.

That this is the political condition prevailing in most African countries is well known. What is not so well known, and needs to be, is the enormous significance of this condition for development. Now, the people are the stuff of development in every sense. If development is to mean anything at all, it must mean the development of their potentialities. But development is not really possible if it is not participatory. External agents may facilitate this process but they cannot, even with the best of intentions, consummate it; in the final analysis, a people develops itself through its own exertions or not at all. Where development is not participatory it can only be the development of alienation and domination.

And that is largely what is happening in Africa. The people who talk most about development and who make and implement development policies are the leadership, the international development agencies and the multinational corporations. But these are not the people who need development. More importantly, they are not the people who understand the need for development. These are people who are educated, live commodiously and have a great deal of choice. They do not know hunger and poverty and the daily rigours of the struggle for existence among the poor. But, more importantly still, the interests of these people are at odds with those of the subordinate peoples of Africa. In most cases, our leaders monopolize power and the good things of life, they seem more interested in survival and accumulation than the development of society which some of them often relate to exploitatively, sometimes in alliance with imperialism.

The international agencies in Africa are here to sell a world view and to reproduce the domination of the nations who effectively own them. The multinationals are in Africa for profit and no more.

So, the very people who speak for development and make development policies are the people least suited for this role. The workers and peasants of Africa who are the whole point of development have no say in development strategies. This takes us back again to the disturbing question: is development really on the agenda in the first place? At this point I am inclined to answer: not really. The interests which inform prevailing development strategies are invariably in conflict with popular interests; the developmental relevance of these strategies is obscure. There is no relationship between public policies and social needs. The populace are merely the means to the ends of narrow interests; they are not, as they should be, the end and the inspiration of the development process. Coercion ensures their conformity but also the withdrawal of their commitment and the mobilization of their energy without which there can be no development. As long as these political conditions remain, we shall continue to flounder even if the international situation becomes more favourable. We shall continue to confuse ideology with reality and form with content, and we shall continue to march backwards.

There are some aspects of this analysis which need to be made more explicit because they reveal more clearly how politics underdevelops Africa. Only two of them will be dealt with here. First is the fact that the high value placed on power and its concentration constrains the economy in highly undesirable ways. Leaders who want to monopolize political power as exclusively as some of our leaders wish to do have to monopolize economic power too or at least prevent opponents and potential rivals from commanding substantial economic resources for such resources easily become a source of political power. Accordingly, fairly successful entrepreneurs are watched and harassed for fear that they may become centres of opposition; and this happens even when they do not show signs of political ambition. These circumstances, in turn, divert them to politics as they seek accommodation with those in power. There is a double disadvantage here for the economy. First, the counter-productive suspicion and harassment of some of the more enterprising and productive members of the society. This is generally compounded by their distraction from productive activity. When they begin to get into politics they soon find that if they are successful, politically, wealth will come easily often without even the trouble of entrepreneurial activity. The general effect is to pressure people away from productive activity.

Another side of this is that, in an attempt to control the economy, some of our leaders tend to overregulate economic activity. Over-regulation complicates the activities of entrepreneurs and sometimes discourages productive investment. It creates large and expensive bureaucracies. Overregulation is all the more damaging in the context of those countries which are supposedly running a capitalist system. It has played a major role in making these budding capitalist economies inefficient and unproductive.

Finally, nationalization has been extensively used as a means of bringing the economy under the control of the political leadership. There is no African country, socialist or capitalist, that does not have a large public sector and this is due partly to the political ambitions of the political leadership. There are good reasons for nationalizing sectors of the economy, although some of the nationalization was also done for very bad reasons including the need for total power. In any event, the burden of our bloated public sector, ruthlessly exploited and badly run, has contributed a great deal to our current economic crisis.

The second problem is this: because the political struggle is so intense and so absorbing, politics becomes, for the political leadership and the entire political class, the means of livelihood. The livelihood is provided by the use of state power for appropriation and accumulation. As accumulation with state power has come to be the norm for the political class, the premium on political power has become higher still. It is no longer just power that is at stake but also wealth. This development is one of the major causes of economic stagnation in Africa. The use of state power for accumulation means, of course, the abuse of state power; above all, it means corrupt practices – the award of contracts to those who will pay the highest kickbacks; the inevitable non-performance in the execution of the contract; the sale of jobs to people who are too incompetent to carry them out successfully; the sale of import and export licences to the highest bidders to the detriment of national interest; and the evasion of exchange controls, quality standards, administrative procedures, import and export duties and the payment of the appropriate fees to officials, etc. These practices have contributed in no small measure to the impoverishment of the state and the failure of development programmes.

Perhaps the most unfortunate economic effect of accumulation by state power is its effect on the working of capitalism in Africa. Clearly, it has played a major role in institutionalizing a singularly unproductive brand of capitalism in Africa. The historical role of capitalism in developing the productive forces is not very much in evidence in Africa. This is partly because it is not necessary to generate wealth by acting capitalistically, that is, by raising capital, investing in some productive activity and then profiting from the sale of the goods or services arising from this investment. Some of our leaders have discovered a shorter and safer way; namely, the use of state power. One does not have to raise and risk capital, and one does not have to contend with the rigours and uncertainties of running an enterprise; one simply uses one's power within the state apparatus to sell one's official power for private gain. Once established within the political class, the circumventing of orthodox capitalistic behaviour makes the routine acceptance of corruption a way of life. Apart from that, it leads to the cynical rejection of any possible relation between reward and effort.

INTERNATIONAL DIMENSIONS

African politics and their relation to the prospects of development cannot be fully understood outside the international context. International social forces are part of the syndrome under review here. To begin with, international agents were highly instrumental in fostering the apolitical attitudes that have paradoxically made politics and political power all important. Multinational corporations, UN agencies, World Bank and IMF approach economic development without much regard for its political context. They have cultivated the myth that development projects and development strategies are politically unproblematic and that bringing political considerations to bear on them is an undesirable complication. They encourage the view that the problems of underdevelopment are quite clear and that the measures required to deal with them are obvious, even if there may be some constraints on resource availability for effecting these measures.

This was precisely the line that most of our leaders adopted shortly after independence; many of them continue to follow this line even now. It became the major rationale for political authoritarianism as it was argued that since the problems and the measures required were not in dispute, the way was open for the co-operation of everyone. The argument was soon extended to justify the stifling of all forms of political dissent and the herding of everyone into one political monolith.

Even this extension too was encouraged by the international agencies. They had refused to see or to acknowledge the political and ideological biases of their perspectives on development. But the biases were there and highly consequential for the prospect of the development and the welfare of the country. Among the assumptions common to them are the following: a strong preference for capitalist solutions and a capitalist economy; implicit acceptance of the existing socio-economic order; indifference to distributive or participative development; and preference for incremental change and a strong antipathy to revolutionary change. Most significantly, there is also the common assumption that anything which contradicts these biases is bad and should be resisted or removed as an obstacle to development. In recent years, IMF and World Bank have made this very clear. Some leaders, professed socialists and capitalists alike, have been using the same rationale for their political repression.

It is not merely the attitudes and biases of the international agencies that are at issue here. Their policies and operations have been a major reinforcement of the political tyranny that is plaguing Africa today. Consider the multinational corporations for instance. The vanguard of capitalism, they cannot by their very nature be interested in distributive or participatory development. When they insist on a favourable investment climate they have in mind certain political conditions. These include the willingness of the political class to co-operate with their profit-making projects, a proposition which sometimes brings this class into conflict with popular interests. They include a commitment on the part of the political class to rule with a strong hand and to keep labour and its demands under control and to shun welfarist measures. Their hearty participation in an economy usually reflects and reinforces a climate of reaction, class conflict and repression.

Both World Bank and IMF contribute to the same effect. Their SAP which has become the standard fare for ailing economies readily illustrates this. The programme has certain standard features:

(a) It liberalizes the economy, which means that it increases the competitive edge of the better off;
(b) It seeks the removal of subsidies and social welfare measures that help the poor;
(c) It insists on a drastic reduction of government expenditure and public consumption; and,
(d) It redistributes incomes and opportunities against labour and in favour of capital, and, within the capitalist class, from the lesser capitalists to the bigger ones.

There is no way of implementing the SAPs without political repression. Even so, the programme is so hostile to popular interests, so prone to cause suffering that the use of repression has not always been able to prevent popular insurrections against these programmes. World Bank and IMF have contributed as much as anything else to the political conditions which underdevelop Africa. Being in a position to exercise power without accountability or responsibility, and having apparently convinced themselves that they are practising an objective science, they remain happily indifferent to the harm they cause.

Recent developments are worrying, for they suggest that the international system will be even more prone to reinforce reaction, repression and underdevelopment in Africa. The world has become closer and more interdependent but this has not necessarily produced greater understanding or co-operation. On the contrary, at certain levels, it is producing a great deal of stress and conflict. The sense of shrinking physical space has led to a more rigorous defence of the turf, particularly among the bigger powers, and there is a great deal of nationalism. In a world of increasing proximity and technologically-induced competitive efficiency, there is a growing sense of insecurity about keeping what one has which has led to more aggressive acquisitiveness.

The Third World countries are making a more determined bid for a greater share of the world's resources at a time when stagflation and the arms race are diminishing the prospects for concessions on the part of the powerful nations. These circumstances have sparked off a new wave of imperialism inclined to more stringent domination and the use of cruder means.

It is not possible or necessary to examine the many important implications of this development for Africa. I will discuss one only and very briefly. It would appear that the West has decided to co-opt some Third World countries. These are the countries such as Brazil and Mexico which have either attained a high level of economic development or/and have historical or cultural affinity to the West. The West will not bother with the poorer Third World countries, including those of Africa, except in cases where they are of significant strategic importance.

However, not bothering with them does not mean leaving them alone. It means that the West will not invest heavily in them and co-opt them into the club of prosperous nations. What the West intends to do – and this intent is already clear enough – is to subordinate them completely, to de-radicalize them and to ensure that they do not become a threat to the existing international order. Accordingly, progressive forces will come under heavy pressure and radical regimes will be subverted. These commitments will put the West unequivocally on the side of reaction and repression thereby making our escape from underdevelopment all the more difficult.

CONCLUSION: WHAT IS TO BE DONE?

What to do about the political underpinnings of economic backwardness in Africa is a difficult question and also an easy one. It is easy because the analysis of the issues readily and unambiguously suggests answers. It is difficult because the people best placed to effect the answers are an integral part of the problem and many of them benefit from it.

As far as the political constraints themselves are concerned the way to remove them can, I believe, be summed up in one word, democratization, not procedurally but in substance. Such democratization will entail the following:

(a) A redistribution of political power away from the regime and in favour of civil society;
(b) A re-orientation of public policy away from special interests and towards common interests. This will mean in effect taking the interests of the subordinate classes as the measure of all things;
(c) Accountability of power to those over whom it is exercised;
(d) Effective popular participation in decision-making at all levels;
(e) Reduction of the economic rewards of political power. In the capitalist countries, this will entail a considerable degree of destatization. In the socialist countries it will entail a shift from state ownership to social ownership of the means of production; and,
(f) Collective self-reliance among African countries and the advancement of collective struggle against imperialism.

These things are easier said than done. There are strong objective forces against their implementation. For one thing, they are largely contrary to the interest of those in power who are currently in a position to implement them. For instance, those in power will be weakened by a redistribution of power from the regime to civil society. Nor can they be expected to support accountability and popular participation especially when they have tended to use power corruptly. The same dilemma applies at the international level. Imperialism will not rethink its interests and modalities of operation for the good of Africa.

Despite these problems, the situation is by no means hopeless. There are powerful factors on the side of Africa too and these are getting more compelling. Because it is cruder and because it comes at a time when the differences between Africa and the West are already so sharply defined, the new imperialism is raising consciousness, forging common identities and promoting common anti-imperialist struggles. I am convinced that the atmosphere is better now for co-operation among African countries. In particular, the strategy of collective self-reliance outlined in LPA is becoming more attractive with each passing day. It is a potentially effective strategy for dealing with the current crisis and the new realities of the international environment.

On the domestic scene, our hope must lie in the lessons of experience and our ability to exploit them. Through the disasters of the last 30 years, we have gleaned some insight into who we are and what this has meant to us; we are clearer about what can be done and about the problems and prospects of the major ideas and policies which have governed our lives. There cannot be many people on whom the consequences of the militarization of social life is completely lost. Nor can there be many who miss the harsh judgement of history on our development strategies, strategies which have left us, in some important respects, worse off than we were 20 years ago and which have increased our marginality in the global order. We can all see the consequences of disenfranchizing workers, peasants and women, of harassing them with self-serving policies from the top to the point when their traditional abilities to cope are undermined. We know now, or should know, that when we banish politics in a society ridden with contradictions, it comes back with a vengeance and undermines everything including peace and progress and the security of those who seek to banish it.

However self-evident these realities might seem, some of our leaders may not recognize them and, if they do, it is unlikely that it will change their behaviour to any significant degree. But that is not as important or as tragic as it may seem. What is important is that even such leaders have to act within the constraints of the new objective conditions which they have helped to create. The objective conditions constrain us by their own logic, by the fact that they are redefining what can be.

I think it is fair to say that they have now demonstrated that certain ways of proceeding are not viable and they are becoming more and more hostile to such ways. They have shown and continue to show that there is no development in mass demobilization and alienation, that wanton coercion and power without accountability promise only more barbarism, that there can be no salvation in an alliance with imperialist forces. By demonstrating these realities, objective conditions are also reshaping our consciousness, shedding light on new and more promising paths of movement, although the general picture is admittedly still quite blurred. One illumination which has emerged is that development has to be concretely democratic in the way we conceive it and the way we pursue it, or it will never come to be. Despite the hostility of the international environment and the enormous force which reaction is able to deploy, the prospects are somewhat better for the democratic forces who understand what should have been clear all along, that development is profoundly a collective enterprise. If we combine this democratic approach on the national level, we might at last have a winning strategy. We need to find one before it is too late and it is very late already.

CHAPTER FOURTEEN

The Consequences of Political Destabilization in Southern Africa for Economic Recovery in the Subregion

SITEKE G. MWALE

INTRODUCTION

The issue of 'the consequences of political destabilization in Southern Africa on economic recovery in the subregion' needs addressing for two important reasons.

First, the OAU Economic Summit in Lagos in 1980 paid particular attention to the armed struggle for the liberation of Namibia and the elimination of *apartheid* in South Africa in the wake of an escalation of destabilization tactics by South Africa on the front-line States of Angola, Botswana, Mozambique and Zambia. To this end, the Summit observed that the independence of Zimbabwe has ushered in renewed and desperate attempts by the Pretoria racist regime to arrest the tide of history and to perpetuate the *status quo* in Namibia and South Africa itself. The Summit pledged to pursue, with vigour, the liberation of the last remaining outposts of exploitation, racism, colonialism and *apartheid*. Second, destabilization in all its forms has to be recognized as an inhibiting exogenous factor in implementing any country's programme of economic and social development. In the annex to the resolution No. A/RES/S-13/2 adopted by the UN General Assembly, based on the Report of the *Ad Hoc* Committee of the Whole of the thirteenth special session, the policy of economic destabilization perpetrated by the racist minority regime in South Africa and its illegal occupation of Namibia is singled out as one of the aggravating factors to the persistent economic crisis in Africa.

During its twenty-first session the Assembly of Heads of State and Government of OAU, meeting in Addis Ababa from 18 to 20 July 1985, adopted APPER to pave the way for national and collective self-reliant and self-sustained growth and development on the African continent. The programme consists of: (a) measures for an accelerated implementation of LPA and FAL; (b) special action for improvement of the food situation and the rehabilitation of agricultural development in Africa; (c) measures for alleviating Africa's external debt burden; (d) measures for a common platform for action at subregional, regional, continental and international levels; and, (e) measures for action against the effects of the destabilization policy of South Africa on the economies of the Southern African States.

In its report entitled *Financing Adjustment with Growth in Sub-Saharan Africa, 1986–1990,* World Bank gives credit to the renewed determination by Africa's own regional institutions leading to a positive change in attitudes towards development policy. Both ECA and OAU have been commended for adopting a theme for Africa's economic recovery which stresses the importance of agriculture, the need for new industrial policies, a bigger participating role for the private sector, a closer look at the demographic factors affecting developing economies in their policy reforms to reduce macroeconomic disequilibria and to increase economic efficiency, and the role of incentives in economic management. But the report also outlines major problems in the following terms:

> at the same time, the year (1986) saw a number of important changes in the international economy that affected the performance and prospects of the developing countries ... the developing countries experienced a marked slow-down in export growth and declines in their terms of trade. Per capita incomes in sub-Saharan Africa deteriorated further, and the highly indebted countries faced increasing difficulties in adjusting their economies to the available finance.

At this juncture, it is important to point out that independent states in the Southern African subregion have experienced serious problems in their programmes of economic development and political stability due to their historical linkage and geographical proximity to *apartheid* South Africa.

The transfer of technology from Western Europe to South Africa has, over the years, enabled South Africa to develop its industrial and economic infrastructure at the expense of its neighbours. The colonial legacies of Portugal and Britain have left Angola, Botswana, Lesotho, Malawi, Mozambique, Swaziland, Zambia and Zimbabwe dependent upon South Africa thereby making it difficult for these countries to pursue a truly independent economic development policy. The fact that six out of eight states neighbouring South Africa (i.e. Botswana, Lesotho, Malawi, Swaziland, Zambia and Zimbabwe) are land-locked and invariably dependent upon South Africa for their transport and communications has made it very difficult for the implementation of their development priorities. Recently, some of them, particularly Botswana, Mozambique and Lesotho, have had the devastating impact of drought, desertification and floods to add to their outstanding economic problems.

Apart from the above problems, the deliberate economic and political destabilization policy of South Africa on those states has been a definite inhibiting, destructive and demoralizing factor in the sub-region. There is hardly a single country in Southern Africa that has lived in an uninterrupted atmosphere of peace during the past 20 years. Angolans, Mozambicans, Namibians and Zimbabweans have endured long and violent liberation struggles. Due to her geo-political position, Zambia has paid a high price for supporting the liberation struggle. The liberation war still continues in Namibia and dissident groups in Angola, Mozambique and Zimbabwe operate with varying degrees of support from South Africa.

In its paper entitled *An Illustrative Assessment of the Cost of Destabilization* submitted to OAU Summit in 1985, SADCC estimated, *inter alia*, that as a result of destabilization, there were already about 300,000 refugees and displaced persons in the subregion. Moreover, the continued state of destabilization of the neighbouring states by South Africa would inevitably lead to continued flows of refugees and the resultant need to channel more emergency aid to Southern Africa. In terms of costs and losses to these countries, South Africa's aggression and destabilization has been in excess of $US 10 billion for the period 1980–1986. The costs and the areas of loss caused by this form of destabilization include:

(a) Loss of human and livestock life and property;
(b) Damage to infrastructure including roads, railways, bridges, powerlines, factories, agricultural fields;
(c) Loss incurred in diverting resources to defence spending; war damage repairs, and disrupted supplies of essential goods and raw materials; and,
(d) The cost of keeping refugees and displaced persons resulting from South Africa's disruptive activities.

In recent years, the countries that have been directly affected by the Southern African conflict include those designated by the fate of the colonial history as front-line States; namely, Angola, Botswana, Mozambique, the United Republic of Tanzania, Zambia and Zimbabwe together with other African states neighbouring South Africa such as Malawi, Lesotho, and Swaziland. For ease of reference, I have chosen the acronym ASNSA (African States neighbouring South Africa) to include all affected countries in the subregion.

The front-line states have, over the years, earned the distinction of representing and often speaking on behalf of OAU as a *de facto* sub-committee of its Summit. On matters concerning *apartheid* and decolonization, they have become both a contact group and a reliable rear base for liberation movements in their struggle for independence, freedom and social justice. But, in the process, ASNSA have become targets of unprovoked armed attacks and destabilization by the *apartheid* regime of South Africa which has taken revenge on them for its failures to wipe out opposition from its own oppressed black nationals who are determined to achieve equality and social justice.

THE PROBLEM AND ITS ROOT CAUSES: A HISTORICAL PERSPECTIVE

South Africa's policies have been under scrutiny in the UN since that Organization's inception and, prior to that, the League of Nations. The United Nations' onslaught has been two-pronged, focusing on Namibia, on the one hand, and on South Africa's domestic policy of *apartheid*, on the other.

From the outset, it must be established that *apartheid* is the root cause of the conflict in Southern Africa and the reason for South Africa's war with its own people within its borders, and its undeclared war against neighbours opposed to its policies. Allied to this is the fact that both violence and destabilization, in all their various forms, are inherent in *apartheid*. Therefore, it is imperative to delve into the background of *apartheid* and then look at the tactics and machinations applied in South Africa's total strategy and its overall effects on the development of the entire subregion. Only through this method of empirical verification can we find suitable solutions to the Southern African crisis.

In this respect, our attention is immediately drawn to the colonial setting of South Africa and the subsequent rise of the Afrikaner Broederbond secret society – resisting British rule, on the one hand, and opposing any rights for the black Africans, on the other. For the Afrikaner Broederbond founded in 1918 and dedicated to the ideology of white supremacy has become the driving force behind the Nationalist

Party since 1948 and, with it, the growth of segregation into *apartheid* with all its diabolical legislation that has shaped South Africa into the constitutional oddity that it is today.

It is important to note that all the past Prime Ministers of South Africa since 1948 such as Malan, Strijdom, Verwoerd and Vorster – including State President Pieter Botha – belonged (and still do, in the case of President Botha) to this Afrikaner elite. But more important is the fact that in 1938, the Broederbond created a Nazi-type organization, the Ossewa Brandwag (Ox-Wagon Brigade), set up on military lines which supported Hitler's Germany during the Second World War and conducted armed sabotage in South Africa to disrupt its own country's participation in the anti-fascist war.

That the Afrikaner Broederbond has an all-pervading influence on the economic, political and social policies of South Africa is a factual reality. But what needs to be explained is the deep-rooted and over-riding fear of the black man – swart gevaar – which has led the white man (both Afrikaner and British) to rule South Africa with the arrogance, emotion, suspicion and brutality that are institutionalized in *apartheid*. The white man's fear has always been one of social change and how it should come about – the fear of a revolution – the revolution of the black masses overthrowing their white masters. Hence, all South Africa's policies over the years, bizarre or far-fetched as they are, have been primarily designed to prevent that revolution. South Africa continues to believe that, by the introduction of reforms ('petty' *apartheid*) particularly in controlled portions and early enough, a bloody revolution can be prevented. As a result of this pre-occupation, it is now common knowledge that any state or group opposed to South Africa's own solution instantly becomes an adversary and, in the case of African states neighbouring it, the reward is aggression, sabotage and other forms of destabilization.

Up to and including the mid-1970s, South Africa's policy was centred around attempts to frustrate and even wipe out activities by liberation movements in Portuguese Angola and Mozambique, UDI-Rhodesia and Namibia, and as well as inside South Africa itself. The Portuguese territories of Angola and Mozambique together with UDI-Rhodesia and Namibia acted as buffer states to South Africa. This resulted in what was known as the *Pretoria–Lisbon–Salisbury Axis* or the *Unholy Alliance*.

During that period, the apparent shield provided by a ring of buffer states gave South Africa enough courage and security to embark upon its so-called 'outward looking' policy of 'dialogue' – aimed at winning over allies from within OAU. The failure of 'dialogue' ushered in a new

South African strategy in which proxies such as UNITA in Angola, MNR in Mozambique, MUSHALA in Zambia, etc., were used not only in the destabilization of the subregion but also in the reinforcement of the sanctions that South Africa had imposed on its neighbours.

At this point, it is important to emphasize that in the intervening period between the collapse of Portuguese colonialism in Angola and Mozambique and the independence of Zimbabwe, South Africa attempted yet another regional strategy in which it expanded its military capacity and, at the same time, launched its diplomatic détente initiative, known as the Southern African Constellation of States (CONSAS).

The Southern African Constellation of States, mooted by South Africa in 1978, was to consist of South Africa itself, the homeland states of Transkei, Bophuthatswana and Venda; neighbouring states of Botswana, Lesotho, Swaziland, Malawi, Zimbabwe and, possibly, Mozambique. It was intended to form an anti-Marxist bastion/buffer south of the Cunene–Zambezi divide, as a regional security and economic bloc of between 7 to 10 States.

The shaping of the current environment of conflict and political destabilization in Southern Africa was heightened by an imminent conflict between South Africa's concept of CONSAS and the grouping of nine independent African States known as SADCC in 1980 – thus, shattering the CONSAS dream in the process. The latter was quickly followed in 1982 by a larger grouping of 15 countries called PTA. In addition, other associations of a bilateral nature in the form of Joint Permanent Missions of Co-operation have also strengthened the bonds of solidarity against South Africa's destabilization tactics. Suffice it to mention at this stage that the failure of CONSAS weakened South Africa as a regional power determined to dominate the subregion by fuelling dissidence, sabotage and economic chaos in the front-line states.

South Africa's strategy is simple: that is, to use both direct and indirect methods to smash the stability of the front-line states and slow down the development of SADCC while striking at the African National Congress (ANC), the South-West Peoples Organization (SWAPO) and other liberation movements together with their host nations. This is South Africa's policy of *swaardmag* (Power of the Sword) as a counter-revolutionary warfare strategy of destabilization.

In this strategy, South Africa wants to internationalize the conflict by capitalizing on the East–West ideological conflict. At the same time, South Africa wants a show-down with the front-line States – knowing very well that the economies and politics of these countries would suffer severely. In essence, South Africa's 'total strategy' policy which involves the mobilization of all forces – political, economic, diplomatic and military – has a regional objective aimed at creating and maintaining a dependence that will be economically lucrative and politically submissive enough to act as a bulwark against the imposition of international sanctions against *apartheid*.

This combination of tactics against neighbouring states has varied from state to state depending on its political, economic and military vulnerability. For instance, in the case of Botswana, Lesotho and Swaziland (also known as the BLS states), South Africa's economic and political grip is overwhelming in that these states belong to the Southern African Customs Union (SACU) and, with the exception of Botswana, to the Rand monetary zone of which South Africa is the dominant member. All the three BLS states have over the years been subjected to direct attacks and other forms of destabilization for little or no apparent reason.

The apparent failure in its previous strategies has since hastened South Africa to re-evaluate its 'foreign policy' without changing its fundamental belief that reform of *apartheid* will avert a bloody revolution inside South Africa. Today, South Africa has embarked upon a new diplomatic-cum-military offensive which aims at diverting world attention from *apartheid* as the root cause by pointing to the presence of the Soviet Union in the subregion as a great threat to Western interests and South Africa's role of protecting them. In short, South Africa has rekindled the traditional East–West ideological conflict in the hope of prolonging and justifying its obnoxious system of *apartheid* with all its concomitant evils.

DESTABILIZATION: ITS BEGINNINGS AND DIMENSION

As it has already been stated earlier on, destabilization is inherent in the policy of *apartheid* itself. It is a strategy which has increased with intensity as *apartheid* has also extended its ugly tentacles to strangle its own black population and to flout, with impunity, all peaceful efforts by the international community to get South Africa to vacate Namibia unconditionally in order for the people of that country to accede to full political independence, in accordance with UN Security Council resolution 435 of 1978.

South Africa's destabilization strategy, just as *apartheid* itself, has its roots in colonialism. In evolving the economic rationale of imperialism, the British colonialists devoted much time to segregation.

Cecil John Rhodes, the Premier of British Cape Colony, when introducing a 'Native Bill for Africa' in 1894, declared:

> My idea is that natives should be kept in these native reserves and not mixed with the white men at all ... in the past, we have made mistakes about native representation. We intend to change all that ... we are going to be lords of this people and keep them in a subject position. They should not have the franchise because we do not want them on an equality with us. These are my politics on native affairs and these are the politics of South Africa ... We must adopt a system of despotism, such as works so well in [British] India, in our relations with the 'Barbarians of South Africa'.

And, as if to echo his country's founding racist pioneers, President Pieter Botha in an interview on black rule, on 12 April 1987, categorically stated:

> I am not prepared to sacrifice my rights so that the other man can dominate me with his greater numbers.

Destabilization can be considered as a multi-dimensional factor if looked at from different angles. Here, credit must go to Adebayo Adedeji who, in his *The African Development Problematique*, states:

> There is, however, the other side to the political destabilization problematique. We have talked about political destabilization arising from continued poor economic performance. However, we must not forget that poor economic performance can also be the product of political instability – whether endogenous, like the frequent military coup d'etats that have afflicted sub-Saharan Africa since independence, or exogenous, like the policy of political destabilization being flagrantly pursued by South African authorities against the front-line States of Southern Africa.

From the outset, there is an imperative need to understand the endogenous seedlings that form the basis of destabilization. First, South Africa is virtually a slave plantation. Confined to mine compounds or ghettos in prison-like conditions, the workers are not allowed to bring their families with them while working under contracts. In order to overcome the chronic shortage of labour in the gold mines, South Africa recruits labour from some independent African neighbouring states who are sent back to their homes after their contracts. Second, the notorious Group Areas Act, which removes all

337

non-whites from the centres of all towns and cities for resettlement in rigorously segregated ghettos on the outskirts of large cities or into Bantustans, creates so much insecurity for a black population which is already subjected to other inhuman severities. This method has been rigorously applied to force poverty-stricken Bantustans into total subjugation. Likewise, the *apartheid* regime uses contract African labour as a device to force its neighbouring states to accept *apartheid* or else have their nationals repatriated.

The havoc that the notorious Group Areas Act causes internally also overflows into some of South Africa's neighbouring states dependent upon it. Health, education and employment are typical examples. For instance, the 1983 WHO publication, *Apartheid and Health*, shows *apartheid* to be the cruellest calculated assault on the health of a people over an extended period of time, ever known to have been devised by man. What the WHO publication reveals is a situation in which the African people, indigenous black South Africans and those from ASNSA recruited as cheap labour, hitherto healthy and energetic prior to the advent of the white man, have been systematically impoverished to the extent of living under the most miserable circumstances in the world. On the other hand, South African education for blacks has been dysfunctional for national development. This is particularly so because, as noted by IMF recently, it has helped to pauperize millions and has created major discrepancies in skills essential to national development.

Here now lies the racial confrontation in South Africa. Many Afrikaners have full faith in *apartheid*. According to a report from the South African Human Sciences Research Council in August 1984, 90 per cent of the Afrikaners approved of separate schooling for black and white children; 85 per cent agreed that different races should use different public facilities; 92 per cent still favoured an electoral system which excludes blacks; nearly 77 per cent supported the Group Areas Act that legalizes residential segregation, and 80 per cent supported the Bantustan or homeland policy.

During the same period, liberation movements such as ANC of South Africa, the Pan-African Congress (Azania), SWAPO (Namibia) and many others have found it inevitable to support armed struggle after the failure of a negotiated settlement through international organizations. There is a period of unrest among youths and labour unions in South Africa. The black masses in South Africa and Namibia have said 'enough is enough' and have regarded all reforms by the *apartheid* regime as delaying tactics. The introduction of the Three-tier Parliament has been regarded by the blacks and the majority of South

African Asians and 'Coloureds' as an assault on their unity by the *apartheid* regime in the same manner as the creation of Bantustans.

One cannot discuss the spate of politcal destabilization acts without looking at the role of super-power global interests, i.e. East–West ideological confrontation. For it is within this context that South Africa has ventured to win the sympathies of the US and Western Europe. Conversely, it is also within the context of the support that the Soviet Union and other Eastern countries have invariably rendered to liberation movements in the Southern African subregion. Indeed, it is this ideological cold war which has to a great extent influenced the attitude of the developed North towards the developing South in its obligation to assist the latter in eradicating poverty and all its offshoots. We have often heard of countries of the developed North that have refused to give aid to particular countries of the developing South because they are 'Communists'.

In the Southern African situation, we are very much conscious of the impasse over Namibia because of the 'linkage' of its independence to the withdrawal of Cuban troops in Angola and the support given to UNITA's insurgence against the People's Republic of Angola. Many students of politics view the policy of constructive engagement in Southern Africa as a serious attempt on the part of the US to be identified as a big brother against any socio-political in-roads by the Eastern bloc into a hitherto exclusive Western bloc 'territory'. Thus, in the process, Namibia becomes a 'sacrificial lamb' in the struggle for regional and global influence by the two super-powers. By the same token, the economic infrastructure of South Africa has become paramount in the choice of what form and to what extent sanctions should be applied. In the US, the Reagan Administration has been quite categorical over sanctions. In his address before a convocation at Carleton College in Northfield, Minnesota, in the US, Ambassador Michael H. Armacost, Under-Secretary of State for Political Affairs, put this issue succinctly, thus:

> Africa was for years a continent happily insulated from the East–West military competition. The presence of Cuban troops has destablized Angola and compounded the difficulty of resolving Angola's Civil War. It extended Soviet power into the Region. It thereby challenges our own strategic interests; it establishes an unfortunate precedent ... we have succeeded in securing South African agreement that if the Cuban problem in Angola can be resolved, South Africa will agree to carry out international agreements for Namibia's independence. We have similarly

> brought the Angolan Government to agree to the principle of Cuban withdrawal ... this agreement will mean an end to Cuba's destabilizing presence in Angola and South Africa's threats to Angola's security and will help promote independence for Namibia ...

It is quite clear from the above syllogism that the hierarchy of national interests and the quest for global influence have determined super-power rivalry in the South African crisis.

On its part, South Africa has taken advantage of this East–West ideological confrontation not only to justify its *apartheid* policies inside Namibia and within its national borders but also to carry out its strategy of political, economic and security hegemony throughout the sub-region.

South Africa's preoccupation with the destabilization strategy has not only caused havoc to the economies of its neighbouring African states but has also created a war psychosis which has become a threat to international peace and security. Recently, it has been ascertained that despite denials from South Africa and cover-ups by its allies, the *apartheid* regime possesses the capability to manufacture nuclear weapons. Dr. A. Visser, Member of the South African Atomic Energy Board once lamented: 'We should have such a [nuclear] bomb to prevent aggression from loud-mouthed Afro-Asiatic States ...'.

In another revelation, Dr. A.I. Roux, President of South Africa's Atomic Board, confirmed as far back as 1976 thus: 'We can ascribe our degree of advancement today in large measure to the training and assistance so willingly provided by the United States.'

In August 1982, US Secretary for Commerce, Malcolm Baldridge, admitted in a letter to former Senator Charles Percy, then Chairman of the Senate Foreign Relations Committee, that his agency had approved five export licences from May 1980 to May 1982 for nuclear-related materials to South Africa.

The implications of these facts for the African states neighbouring South Africa, for the continent of Africa and for the whole world are enormous and frightening. Moreover, the nuclear alliance between South Africa and its allies has repercurssions for the whole nuclear balance between the two super-powers. Above all, these facts show how very determined *apartheid* South Africa is to stay in power to the extent that it is prepared to use these awesome weapons rather than accept the inevitable and cede power to the black majority.

DEPENDENCE – THE SCOURGE OF AFRICAN ECONOMIC DEVELOPMENT

As it is now quite clear, the economic development or lack of it for the Southern African subregion has, in large measure, been greatly affected by the 'dependence' of the independent African states on South Africa. In fact, the entire spectrum of destabilization has been focused on this weakness. Thus, South Africa's subregional and regional objective is solely to impose and maintain a dependence upon it by the entire area which will be *economically* lucrative and *politically* submissive.

The economic importance of the subregion to South Africa is massive, particularly in the areas of trade, transport and communications. South Africa runs a visible trade surplus with eight of the nine countries in the subregion totalling close to $US 2.0 billion per year. However, dependence on South Africa has varied from country to country, both in substance and origin. Suffice it to reiterate that six out of the nine neighbouring states are land-locked and depend on South Africa's ports for their exports and imports. As part of its colonial legacy, the subregion has been subjected, hugger-mugger, to a whole series of links centred around South Africa. Some of these defy economic logic but yet still continue to exist.

But it is in the area of transport and communications where dependence is predominant. This is reflected in the use of South African roads, railways and ports for overseas trade. The destabilizing policy of South Africa and especially the support of the armed bandits in Mozambique and Angola in the sabotage and destruction of the Mozambican railways and the Benguela railways in Angola has counterbalanced the efforts of the African states to reduce their dependence on the South African transport system. Tables 14.1 – 14.3 emphasize the glaring problem of dependence on South Africa's trade routes that should be changed in order for the African states neighbouring South Africa to achieve collective self-reliance.

It must be pointed out that because of the colonial legacy, trade links and other commercial relationships between most of the states in the subregion and South Africa and also with the former colonial powers have been stronger and more developed than the intra-regional links among these states.

In short, the mechanisms of dependence, as outlined above, have progressively become both South Africa's preoccupation and effective means of dominance. Through various links, agreements and other outstanding arrangements with its neighbours, South Africa has over the years acquired a central position which it uses or abuses to the detriment of its peace-loving neighbours. For instance, South Africa provides staff in management positions for transport enterprises and authorities throughout the subregion. Furthermore, the dominant position of South Africa means that it is the nearest main centre in respect of technological services, acquisition of spare parts and other types of technical and consultancy services. Thus, dependence in these areas exists equally or even more in relation to Western Europe and the US.

TOWARDS ECONOMIC RECOVERY: A PROGRAMME OF SURVIVAL FOR SOUTHERN AFRICA

As early as 1974, when the Portuguese authorities had announced their surprise decision to hand over political power to Angola and Mozambique and other African colonial possessions, His Excellency Dr. Kenneth David Kaunda, President of the Republic of Zambia, spoke of the day when independent states of Southern Africa would address the issue of 'liberation – not liberation from political oppression but liberation from poverty'. Indeed, by 1977 the ECA Lusaka-based Multinational Programming and Operational Centre for Eastern and Southern African States (MULPOC) was established with a membership of 18 countries, namely Angola, Botswana, Djibouti, Ethiopia, Kenya, Lesotho, Malawi, Mozambique, Somalia, Swaziland, Uganda, the United Republic of Tanzania, Zambia, Zimbabwe and the offshore Islands of the Comoros, Madagascar, Mauritius and Seychelles. On the basis of other MULPOCs, the Lusaka-based MULPOC was intended to function as a means of *implementing Africa's new development strategy which, at the subregional level, required the MULPOCs to assist in generating and concretizing the process of economic integration in the subregions they served as a first and pragmatic step towards the creation of a regional common market and, ultimately, an economic community.*

A few years later, in 1982, PTA was established with headquarters in Lusaka, Zambia. The launching of PTA was both Lusaka-MULPOC's brain-child and its priority project. With a membership of 15 States, namely Burundi, the Comoros, Djibouti, Ethiopia, Kenya, Lesotho, Mauritius, Malawi, Rwanda, Somalia, Swaziland, Uganda, the United Republic of Tanzania, Zambia and Zimbabwe, PTA has since embarked upon *the promotion of co-operation and development in all fields of economic activity particularly in the fields of trade, customs, industry, transport, communications, agriculture, natural resources and monetary affairs* ... . In essence, by its numerical strength and commitment to its Treaty, PTA became the first step and main vehicle for the realization of a work programme leading to the fulfilment of the objectives of LPA and FAL.

The role of subregional organizations in combating destabilization from South Africa has become increasingly crucial. Small wonder that the establishment of SADCC in 1980, with a membership of nine countries, namely Angola, Botswana, Lesotho, Malawi, Mozambique, Swaziland, the United Republic of Tanzania, Zambia and Zimbabwe was hailed as a courageous challenge to counteract the domination and destabilization strategy of *apartheid* in South Africa.

However, the performance of SADCC member states since 1980 has been adversely affected by the military aggression and economic destabilization of racist South Africa. The implications of destabilization for the subregion have been in the form of reduction in productive capacity, economic growth and development. Other economic consequences of destabilization are: (a) Reduction in employment; (b) Increase in consumer prices as a result of shortfalls in supply, revenue and the resultant rise in budget deficits; (c) Extra defence expenditure of approximately $US 3.6 billion for the period 1980–1985; and, (d) Expenditure of approximately $US 660 million on refugees for the period 1980–1985.

In spite of this, the outcome of the 1980 SADCC Lusaka Conference was the Lusaka Declaration – SOUTHERN AFRICA: TOWARDS ECONOMIC LIBERATION – committing the member states to work collectively towards the integration of their economies in order to achieve economic liberation and regional self-reliance. The Lusaka Declaration emphasizes the following broad objectives for SADCC: (a) The reduction of economic dependence, particularly, but not only, on the Republic of South Africa; (b) The forging of links to create a genuine and equitable regional integration; (c) The mobilization of resources to promote the implementation of national interests and subregional policies; and, (d) Concerted action to secure international co-operation within the framework of SADCC's strategy for economic liberation.

To achieve these objectives, the institutional structure of SADCC provides for a small central secretariat and sectoral committees but leaves the primary responsibility of action on implementation of projects and development programmes to devolve on its individual national governments, particularly in critical areas as shown below:

Country	Sector
Angola	Energy
Botswana (headquarters of SADCC)	Crop research and animal diseases
Malawi	Conservation of forests, water and wildlife
Lesotho	Soil conservation and land utilization
Mozambique	SATCC – Transport and communications
Swaziland	Manpower development
Tanzania	Industrial development
Zambia	SADCC fund, mining and economic bulletin
Zimbabwe	Agriculture and food security

As regards its effects on the balance of payments, destabilization has led to a reduction in the volume of exports and a corresponding increase in the volume of imports during the period 1980 to 1985. The *1986 SADCC Macro-economic Survey* offers the following selected estimated losses: (a) transport and energy – $US 970 million; (b) exports and tourism – $US 230 million; (c) smuggling – $US 190 million; and, (d) boycotts and embargoes – $US 200 million.

So far, an attempt has been made to provide an analytical and historical background to the root causes of the political and economic crises of the Southern African subregion. There is an imperative need to look at other real chances of economic recovery through stabilization and structural adjustment measures.

Since the adoption of APPER and UN-PAAERD, African Governments in the Southern African region have continued individually and collectively to use effective mechanisms to implement strategies and development programmes.

At subregional level, SADCC, PTA and MULPOC have put in motion the machinery to upgrade the implementation of LPA, and UN-PAAERD. During the tenth meeting of the Lusaka-based MULPOC held in Lusaka on 12 and 13 March 1987, it was decided that the Lusaka MULPOC be entrusted with the responsibility to monitor and evaluate the status of LPA/APPER/UN-PAAERD at a subregional level. Further-more, a call was made on member states to establish an appropriate national mechanism to assist the MULPOC in its role of monitoring and evaluating LPA/APPER/UN-PAAERD.

At the national level, some Governments in the subregion have taken issue with IMF in their bid to effect structural adjustment measures without a complete breakdown of their economies. To this end, some of the negotiations with IMF have centred on the need for the structural adjustment process to be growth-oriented and to be implemented over reasonable periods with increased and sustained levels of financial support.

In responding to IMF credit terms, countries in the subregion have pointed to the difficulties that cross-conditionality has often caused them. It is the consensus of opinion of the subregional countries that structural adjustment financing would be more effective in the absence of cross-conditionality. In general, in their efforts to achieve the sustainability of some of the reform measures and restructuring pro-grammes, the Southern African subregion has pressed for a more humane approach by IMF/World Bank. Any programme of structural adjustment devoid of considerations of the human dimension would lead to serious political consequences which would, in turn, delay or even reverse the adjustment efforts.

In specific terms, countries like Zambia have recently taken recognizable bold and somewhat risky economic policy reforms. In her efforts to liberalize the economy, and as part of the conditionality of IMF stand-bys and World Bank SECALs, the Government of Zambia took certain measures which included: (a) reduction in the size of the public service and a general freeze on wage increases; (b) a gradual switch from subsidies of a consumer-type to a production one, particularly in agriculture; (c) decontrol of prices; and, (d) auctioning of the foreign currency against the Zambian Kwacha (ZK). In addition, there has been a deliberate bias towards the diversification of the economy – hitherto based on copper as a single major raw material earning the foreign exchange for the country.

Initially, there was strong opposition to such a fundamental shift in economic policy. Various economic groups, such as urban consumers, public sector employees and those with access to foreign exchange had benefitted (at least in relative terms) from the previous system of controls and economic policies and were unwilling to lose their advantages. The Zambia Congress of Trade Unions had maintained a claim that there was a steady fall in real and relative wage levels over the preceding ten years and, while eager for change in economic policies, was reluctant to accept any measures that would further reduce real wages and employment.

The political leadership therefore undertook an extensive effort to build a national consensus for change. During 1983, week-long meetings of UNIP, the ruling Party, were held in each provincial capital to listen to complaints and to hear suggestions for improving the economy's performance.

The overall liberalization of the financial and foreign exchange regimes in Zambia has led to rapid realignment of prices and incentives. The exchange rate depreciated from ZK 2.2 per US dollar pre-auction to ZK8.07 in mid-July 1986 and then to nearly ZK 20 in April 1987. The effects of the depreciating Zambian Kwacha continued to be passed through quickly and fully to domestic prices.

However, there have since been encouraging signs alongside the adverse effects of the reform programmes. For instance, as a combined result of policy changes and good weather, agricultural output had grown by 7.7 per cent per annum during 1983 to 1985. The manufacturing sector also witnessed a rise of 9 per cent of value-added in constant prices – no doubt as a result of a major shift in managerial attitudes. Capacity utilization has also risen from less than 40 per cent to over 50 per cent in the private sector and in parastatals, some of which have shed redundant labour by reinforcing natural attrition. Non-traditional exports have more than doubled.

In spite of these developments, some economists are of the view that the reforms have produced the following negative effects: (a) the auction results in allocation of significant resources to non-essential goods, particularly luxury items; (b) some large bidders are more successful in obtaining auction resources and are driving the auction rate up by bidding irresponsibly; (c) the auction fuels inflation; and, (d) the auction-determined rate is too volatile. The Government, on its part, has continued to keep a close watch on the matter.

This Chapter would be incomplete if it did not touch on the debt repayment crisis which has become a nightmare for many a Third World country. For it appears that no amount of adjustment will get the Third World out of the debt trap. Most of the adjustment strategies and rescheduling plans seem to drive the developing countries into greater indebtedness. Zambia and many other countries in the South African subregion have had to grapple with this problem over and above the menace of destabilization from the *apartheid* regime of South Africa. It is sometimes uncertain whether IMF has anything to do with the so-called adjustment regime or any genuine interest whatever in the economic well-being of the country so affected. More often than not, it sometimes appears as if IMF is solely concerned with the creation of conditions which would ensure the maximum possible repayment of interest on foreign debt, irrespective of the permanent damage this may cause to the country so involved.

Third World countries that have negotiated for rescheduling of debts know too well about the role of the London inter-bank offered rate for money (LIBOR), which no debtor country can question. In this set-up, the debtors have to submit to floating interest rates which can be unilaterally changed by the creditors. They are also subject to variable exchange rates. For example, it is said that between 1985 and 1986 the total debt of the developing countries increased by $US 40 billion because of the revaluation of non-dollar currencies. In the final analysis, repayment of interest takes precedence over all national needs and domestic consumption. Indeed, the current available figures point to the fact that, at worst, adjustment strategies and rescheduling will only drive the developing countries into deeper indebtedness, as has been demonstrated in the test case of Brazil recently. As one prominent economist put it succinctly: '... it is an impossible game: the more you pay, the more you owe. The predators are gobbling up country after country.'

CONCLUSION

As has been clearly indicated in this Chapter, South Africa's total strategy of economic, political and military destabilization of ASNSA has added a more complex dimension to APPER. In order to underline the plight of African countries in their attempt to achieve self-sustaining reform programmes, we have used Zambia as a case study. We have also deduced that the critical and far-reaching consequences on the economies resulting from South Africa's aggression can only be resolved or dealt with effectively through unity and collective self-reliance programmes by the states of the subregion themselves with the assistance of the international community.

On going through this Chapter, one is immediately made to believe that the situation in the subregion, in economic and military terms, favours South Africa. The real status of the equation between the front-line states and South Africa is that although South Africa is strong economically and militarily, it is weak ideologically since more than 80 per cent of its population reject *apartheid*. Because they are strong ideologically, the front-line states are a definite threat to South Africa in that the powerful pan-Africanist ideology of the front-line states is shared by ANC, PAC, SWAPO and other liberation movements determined to destroy *apartheid*. In fact, this powerful pan-Africanist ideology, which symbolizes Black South African aspirations, can be considered as profoundly destabilizing the *apartheid* regime. This weakness is South Africa's Achilles' heel and will certainly contribute to its downfall.

There is also the reverse side of political destabilization to consider. The economic dependence on South Africa by ASNSA also means that South Africa's destabilization tactics are bound to have adverse effects on its own economic performance. South Africa needs a thriving economy to oil its war machinery.

Recently, it has been reported that the severe deterioration in political confidence following the state of emergency in 1985 together with the continued exodus of companies – especially US owned – have both rendered the South African economy more vulnerable and growing weaker in every aspect – particularly in its domestic economic activity, i.e., consumer demand, industrial production, construction and agricultural output which continue to register further declines.

Furthermore, it has been observed by political and economic analysts alike that the South African Government has since 1986 dashed local and foreign investors' hopes that an effective programme of political reforms was underway to boost the flagging economy. To crown it all, it will be recalled that while the Commonwealth Eminent Persons Group was in South Africa during May 1985, the *apartheid* regime decided to attack Botswana, Zambia and Zimbabwe making it abundantly clear to the international community that dialogue with South Africa for peaceful change or a negotiated settlement was futile and that mandatory and comprehensive sanctions were the only alternative towards the dismantling of *apartheid*.

It will be recalled that in 1985, in the face of mounting resistance, with the economy sliding deeper into crisis, the *apartheid* regime of South Africa imposed a state of emergency. Furthermore, the cost of defending *apartheid* both internally and externally has taken up to 30 per cent of GDP, with the official defence expenditure constituting 15 per cent of the budget in 1986.

South Africa's foreign debt is now estimated to have passed a record high of 32 billion Rand. Many observers have made the point that South Africa's economic crisis is not a recession which will ease in a relatively short time and over which the *apartheid* regime will have some degree of control. But rather, it is a fundamental structural crisis which will only be resolved by the restructuring of the social order based upon the will of the majority.

It is evident that the escalation of resistance to *apartheid* by the oppressed black majority, together with the international campaign for sanctions and the complete isolation of the *apartheid* regime are now the most effective factors causing havoc to the South African economy leading to its inevitable downfall.

NOTES

Arnheim, M.T.W., *South Africa After Vorster*, Cape Town, 1979.

Commonwealth, *The Front-line States, The Burden of the Liberation Struggle*, London, 1977.

Commonwealth, Mission of EPG, *South Africa*, Penguin, London, 1986.

EDI/World Bank, *Senior Policy Seminar on Structural Adjustment and the Substantiality of Reform in Sub-Saharan Africa*, Lusaka, 16–20 February 1987.

Evans, W., *The Front-line States, South Africa and Southern African Security*, Harare, 1984.

First, Ruth, *The South African Connection*, Victoria, Australia, 1973.

Geldenhuys, D., *The Diplomacy of Isolation*, Johannesburg, 1984.

Independent Commission on International Issues – *North–South: A Programme for Survival*, Report, London, 1980.

Johnson, Phyllis and Martin David (Editors), *Destructive Engagement*, Zimbabwe Publishing House, Harare, 1986.

McNamara, Robert S., 'African Development: Challenges and Opportunities', Yaounde, Cameroon, 1986.

Namibia, *Perspectives for National Reconstruction and Development*, UNIN, London, 1986.

Nobitshungu, Sam C., *South Africa in Africa*, Manchester, 1975.

Pomeroy, W.J., *Apartheid Axis – United States and South Africa*, New York, 1971.

Ramphal, Shridath S., *The Trampling of the Grass*, Addis Ababa, Ethiopia, 1985.

SADCC, *Macro-economic Survey*, Gaborone, 1986.

The World Bank, *Annual Report 1986*.

The World Bank, *Financing Adjustment with Growth in Sub-Saharan Africa, 1986–1990*, Washington, D.C., 1986.

TABLE 14.1

TOTAL OVERSEAS TRADE THROUGH REGIONAL PORTS IN 1984

(million tons)

Country Port	Angola	Botswana	Malawi	Mozambique	Swaziland	Tanzania	Zambia	Zimbabwe	Total SADCC Countries 1/	South Africa	Total
Maputo (incl. Matola)					0.53			0.53	1.97	0.8	2.77
Beira			0.04	0.35				0.73	1.12		1.12
Nacala			0.19	0.20				–	0.39		0.39
Dar-es-Salaam 2/			0.02			1.15	0.95	–	2.03		2.03
Lobito	0.40		–	–					0.40		0.40
Luanda	0.80		–	–					0.80		0.80
Total SADCC ports	1.2		0.25	1.46	0.53	1.15	0.86	1.20	6.71	0.8	7.51
SA ports	–	0.32 3/	0.58	–	0.23	–	0.58	1.33	3.04	85.0	88.8
Total	1.2	0.32 3/	0.83	1.46	1.76	1.15	1.44	2.59	9.75	85.8	96.3

Source: SADCC

Notes: 1. Lesotho overseas trade remained under 5,000 tons.
2. Excluding bulk oil
3. Estimates

TABLE 14.2

DIRECTION OF TRADE FOR THE NINE SADCC COUNTRIES

(percentage)

	Exports to				Imports to			
	S A D C C		South Africa		S A D C C		South Africa	
	1981	1983	1981	1983	1981	1983	1981	1983
Angola	0.0	0.1(1982)	-		1.2	0.9(1982)	-	
Botswana b/	9.1	8.2	16.6	8.3	6.3	7.4	87.5 a/	81.4 a/
Lesotho b/	0.4	0.1(1982)	46.7	41.3(1982)	0.4	0.1(1982)	97.1	97.1(1982)
Malawi c/	9.9	9.7(1982)	4.7	5.7(1982)	8.1	9.6(1982)	32.2	34.0(1982)
Mozambique	9.6	3.9	2.8	3.5	2.5	5.0	12.5	9.6
Swaziland	2.3	2.6(1982)	34.1	36.9(1982)	0.6	0.8(1982)	83.3	82.9(1982)
Tanzania	0.9	1.0		-	0.5	2.6	-	-
Zambia	4.0	3.5)1982)	0.6	0.3(1982)	5.8	6.3(1982)	15.1	14.5(1982)
Zimbabwe c/	10.8	11.0	21.6	18.5	7.8	8.2	27.5	24.5

Source: Calculated from SADCC Intra-Regional Trade Study Figures. (Interim Report, Phase 1, July 1985.)

Notes:

a. Percentages include goods imported from other countries transshipped through South Africa
b. Belongs to SACU (Southern African Customs Union) together with South Africa
c. Have Preferential Trade Agreement with South Africa

351

TABLE 14.3

TRENDS IN THE PRODUCTION OF MAJOR AGRICULTURAL COMMODITY GROUPS IN SADCC COUNTRIES, 1978–1982

	Angola	Botswana	Lesotho	Malawi	Mozambique	Swaziland	Tanzania	Zambia	Zimbabwe
Food crop production									
Cereals	-8.3	-12.0	-17.9	1.2	-4.8	-3.9	-0.9	-7.0	10.5
Root crops	3.1	0.9	3.7	4.6	2.5	1.3	3.5	1.4	1.7
Pulses	-5.5		4.9	1.3	-5.3	0.5	-1.3	13.3	4.1
Oil seed crops	-1.0	3.9		1.4	0.1	1.0	0.3	-4.6	6.5
Meat	2.5	6.6	3.4	2.2	2.9	2.9	2.0	3.9	-6.2
Milk	0.7	2.8	3.0	3.0	2.6	1.3	1.7	3.4	-1.3
Livestock production									
Cattle	3.0	0.6	-3.0	4.2	1.2	1.1	1.9	4.0	-3.1
Sheep	2.3	9.7	8.5	2.0	2.2	3.0	2.0	5.3	-10.8
Goats	0.5	5.7	9.0	-3.8	1.5	6.4	2.0	2.5	-9.2
Pigs	4.6	-7.5	-7.5	-5.3	1.9	4.3	5.1	3.1	0.1
Fisheries production									
Freshwater and	-2.4	11.0	-14.2	-6.8	50.2		5.7	0.8	29.1
Marine	-13.3				21.9		-4.9		
Shell Fish							6.6		
Forestry production									
Fuelwood and charcoal	2.2		1.2	3.3	4.1	2.5	3.2	2.7	0.7
Industrial roundwood	1.2	2.6		6.4	1.7	-2.6	8.8		6.7
Sawnwood				9.4	-7.9	7.9	-2.2	2.0	9.5
Paper					6.7				7.1

Source: Country tables, basic data on the agricultural sector, Rome, 1984.

CHAPTER FIFTEEN

Gender, Skill and Power: Africa in Search of Transformation

ALI A. MAZRUI
ANDREW D. WHITE

INTRODUCTION

As Africa approaches the third *millennium* of the Christian era, three major transformations are needed and, to some extent, have begun to unfold. Firstly, there is the domestic revolution in relations between the sexes; secondly, there is the need for a revolution in technology and skill all over the continent; and, thirdly, there is the need for transforming Africa's power relations within the global system.

These three revolutions of *gender, skill* and *power* are intimately intertwined. The history of Africa since 1935 is, to a large extent, a preparation for these three revolutions.

A fundamental change in relations between the genders has been occurring partly because of Africa's interaction with other cultures in this period. Islam and Western colonialism came with alternative paradigms of relationships between the sexes. Both the family and African society at large are caught up in these tensions of culture change. It is this question of gender in African society since 1935 that we address first.

GENDER ROLES IN TRANSITION

Africa has since 1935 witnessed significant changes in the role and status of its women. In many traditional cultures, there has been a belief that God made woman the custodian of *fire, water* and *earth*. God himself took charge of the fourth element of the universe – the omnipresent *air*. Custody of fire entailed responsibility for making energy available. And the greatest source of energy in rural Africa is firewood. The African woman became primarily responsible for finding and carrying huge bundles of firewood. Custody of water involved water as a symbol of both survival and cleanliness. The African woman became responsible for ensuring that this critical substance was available for the family. She has trekked long distances to fetch water. The custody of earth has been part of a doctrine of *dual fertility*. Woman ensures the *survival* of this generation by maintaining a central role in cultivation – and preserving the fertility of the *soil*. Woman ensures the *arrival* of the next generation by her role as mother – the fertility of the *womb*. Dual fertility becomes an aspect of the triple custodial role of African womanhood.[1]

What has happened to this doctrine of triple custody in the period since 1935? Different elements of the colonial experience affected the role of the African woman in different ways.

Among the factors which increased the woman's role on the land was wage labour for the men. Faced with an African population reluctant to work for low wages for somebody else, colonial rulers had already experimented with both forced labour and taxation as a way of inducing Africans to join the colonial work force. According to Margaret Jean Hay, wage labour took some time before it began to affect women's role on the land. Her own work was among Luo women in Kenya:

> By 1930, a large number of men had left Kowe at least once for outside employment ... More than half of this group stayed away for periods of fifteen years or more ... This growing export of labour from the province might be thought to have increased the burden of agricultural work for women ... . As early as 1910, administrators lamented the fact that Nyanza was becoming the labour pool of the entire colony ... . Yet, the short-term migrants of the 1920's were usually unmarried youths, who played a relatively minor role in the local economy beyond occasional herding and the conquest of cattle in war. Furthermore, the short-term labour migrants could and often did arrange to be away during the slack periods of the agricultural cycle ... Thus, labour migration in the period before 1930 actually removed little labour from the local economy and did not significantly alter the sexual division of labour.[2]

But Margaret Hay goes on to demonstrate how the Great Depression and the Second World War changed the situation as migrant labour and conscription of males took a bigger proportion of men away from the land. This was compounded by the growth of mining industries like the gold mining at Kowe from 1934 onwards:

> The long-term absence of men had an impact on the sexual

division of labour, with women and children assuming a greater share of agricultural work than ever before ... The thirties represent a transition with regard to the sexual division of labour, and it was clearly the women who bore the burden of the transition in rural areas.[3]

Women in this period, from the 1930s onwards, became more deeply involved as 'custodians of earth'. In Southern Africa, the migrations to the mines became even more dramatic. By the 1950s, a remarkable bifurcation was taking place in some Southern African societies – a division between a male proletariat (industrial working class) and a female peasantry. South Africa's regulations against families joining their husbands on the mines exacerbated this tendency towards *gender-apartheid*, the segregation of the sexes. Many women in the front-line states had to fulfil their triple custodial role of fire, water and earth in greater isolation than ever.

The wars of liberation in Southern Africa from the 1960s took their own toll on family stability and traditional sexual division of labour. Some of the fighters did have their wives with them. Indeed, liberation armies like ZANLA and ZIPRA in Zimbabwe and FRELIMO in Mozambique included a few female fighters. But, on the whole, the impact of the wars was disruptive of family life and of the traditional sexual division of labour.

After independence, there were counter-revolutionary wars among some of the front-line states. The most artificial of the post-colonial wars was that of Mozambique, initiated by the so-called Mozambique National Resistance (MNR or RENAMO). The movement was originally created by reactionary white Rhodesians to punish Samora Machel for his support for Robert Mugabe's forces in Zimbabwe. After Zimbabwe's independence, RENAMO became a surrogate army for reactionary whites in the Republic of South Africa – committing a variety of acts of sabotage against the fragile post-colonial economy of Mozambique.

Again, this development has had implications for relations between the genders. In addition to the usual disruptive consequences of war for the family, RENAMO, by the mid-1980s, had inflicted enough damage on the infrastructure in Mozambique that many migrant workers never got home to their families in between their contracts with the South African mines. The miners often remained on the border between South Africa and Mozambique, waiting for their next opportunity to the mines without ever having found the transportation to get to their families in distant villages of Mozambique.

It is not completely clear how this situation has affected the doctrine of 'dual fertility' in relation to the role of the African woman. One possibility is that the extra long absences of the husbands have reduced fertility rates in some communities in Mozambique. The other scenario is that the pattern of migrant labour in Southern Africa generally has initiated a tendency towards *de facto* polyandry. The woman who is left behind acquires over time a *de facto* extra husband. The two husbands take their turn over time with the woman. The migrant labourer from the mines has conjugal priority between mining contracts if he does manage to get to the village. He also has prior claim to the new babies unless agreed otherwise.[4]

If the more widespread pattern is that of declining fertility as a result of extra-long absences of husbands, the principle of 'dual fertility' has reduced the social functions of the fertility of the womb and increased the woman's involvement in matters pertaining to the fertility of the soil. On the other hand, if the more significant tendency in mining communities in Southern Africa is towards *de facto* polyandry, a whole new nexus of social relationships may be in the making in Southern Africa.[5]

Other changes in Africa during this period which affected relationships between men and women included the impact of new technologies on gender roles. Cultivation with the hoe still left the African woman centrally involved in agriculture. But cultivation with the tractor was often a prescription for male dominance.

> When you see a farmer
> On bended knee
> Tilling land
> For the family
> The chances are
> It is a *she*!
>
> *   *   *
>
> When you see tractor
> Passing by
> And the driver
> Waves you 'Hi'
> The chances are
> It is a *he*!

Mechanization of agriculture in Africa has tended to marginalize women. Their role as 'custodians of earth' is threatened by male prerogatives in new and more advanced technologies. It is true that greater male involvement in agriculture could help reduce the heavy burdens of work undertaken by women on the land. On the other hand, there is no reason why this relief in workload for women should not come through better technology. Tractors were not invented to be driven solely by men.

Another threat to the central role of the African woman in the economy in this period has come from the nature of Western education. It is true that the Westernized African woman is usually more mobile and with more freedom for her own interests than is her more traditional sister. But a transition from custodian of fire, water, and earth to keeper of the typewriter is definitely a form of marginalization for African womanhood. Typing is less fundamental for survival than cultivation. Filing is less basic to the human condition than water and energy. The Westernized African woman in the second half of the twentieth century has tended to be more free but less important for African economies than the traditional woman in rural areas.

The third threat to the role of African woman in this period came with the internationalization of African economies. When economic activity in Africa was more localized, women had a decisive role in local markets and as traders. But the colonial and post-colonial tendencies towards enlargement of economic scale have increasingly pushed the woman to the side in international decision-making. It is true that Nigerian women especially have refused to be completely marginalized even in international trade. But, on the whole, the Africans who deal with international markets and sit on the Boards of transnational corporations are overwhelmingly men. And, at meetings of OPEC – where Muslims predominate – there are additional inhibitions about having even Nigeria represented by a female delegate.

But what is the future avenue which is likely to change the balance between men and women in public life in Africa? The reasons why women are politically subordinate are not to be sought in economic differentiation. Women in Africa are economically very active; women in Saudi Arabia are economically neutralized. And yet, in both types of society, women are politically subordinate. And so economic differences are not the real explanation of political subjection of womanhood.

What is indeed universal is not the economic role of women but their military role. All over Africa (and indeed all over the world) women are militarily marginalized. What will one day change the political balance between men and women is when the military machine becomes bisexual. The Somali army has started recruiting women. The Algerian air force has started recruiting women pilots. Both Muslim societies in

Africa are beginning to give a military role to women. But the future needs more than tokenism in gender roles. In this continent of coups, we may have to wait for the day when the announcement of a coup in West Africa declares as follows: 'Brigadier-General Janet Adebiyi has captured power in a military takeover in Lagos.'

But technology is not only linked to the relationship between men and women in Africa; it is also linked to the wider configuration of power in the world. The period since 1935 has witnessed the emergence of a world divided between an increasingly prosperous northern hemisphere and a persistently disadvantaged southern hemisphere. The concept of 'the Third World' was, of course, born in this period of history – as the North was split between east and west in *ideological systems* and the world between north and south in both *skill* and *income*. In the global context, Africa, in this period of history, has had to look at itself partly in terms of this North–South divide. The continent's global allies have increasingly become the rest of the Third World.

TOWARDS DUAL SOLIDARITY

Two forms of solidarity are critical for Africa and the Third World if the global system is to change in favour of the disadvantaged.

Organic Solidarity concerns South–South linkages designed to increase mutual dependence between and among African or Third World countries themselves. *Strategic Solidarity* concerns co-operation among Third World countries in the struggle to extract concessions from the industrialized North. Organic solidarity concerns the aspiration to promote greater integration between Third World economies. Strategic solidarity aspires to decrease the South's dependent integration into *Northern* economies. While the focus of organic solidarity is primarily a South–South economic marriage, the focus of strategic solidarity is either a North–South divorce, a new marriage settlement or a new social contract between North and South. The terms of the North–South bond have to be re-negotiated.

We start also from the additional basic observation that economic flows are in any case far deeper between North and South than between South and South. On the whole, Southerners do far greater trade with the North than with each other, and have more extensive relations of production with industrialized states than with fellow developing countries. But those economic relations between North and South are distorted by a tradition of dependency involving unequal partnership. The structural links give undue advantage and leverage to the North – and leave the South vulnerable and exploitable.

What then is the way out? How can these two forms of solidarity help to ameliorate the Third World's predicament of dependency and its persistent economic vulnerability?

One of the more neglected areas of co-operation is humanpower and humanpower training. A start has been made in manpower exchange between some Third World countries and in the field of manpower training across Third World boundaries. But the importance of this area has been grossly underestimated.

It is not often realized that the most obstinate line of demarcation between North and South is not income (criteria of wealth) but technology (criteria of skill). The entire international system of stratification has come to be based *not* on 'who owns what' but on 'who *knows* what'. Libya and Saudi Arabia may have a higher per capita income than some of the members of the EEC, but Libya and Saudi Arabia are well below Western Europe in skills of production and economic organization. Indeed, members of OPEC do not even have adequate skills to control or drill their own oil.

Nowhere is this demonstrated more clearly than in Southern Africa and the Middle East. Less than five million whites in South Africa have been able to hold to ransom a black population in the region ten times their own. They have held neighbouring Blacks to ransom both economically and militarily. The main explanation is not simply because South Africa is rich, but because that wealth has been extracted through African labour and *European* expertise. South Africa's neighbours have African labour too. Some of them are also rich in minerals. What the Blacks have lacked indigenously is the superior technology of production and the accompanying culture of efficient organization.

The Middle East is a clearer and more staggering illustration of the power of skill over income. At least since the 1970s, much of the Arab world has become significantly richer than Israel in sheer income. Indeed, the Israeli economy would have suffered complete collapse but for the infusion of billions of dollars from the US and from World Jewry. And yet, in spite of being out-numbered and out-wealthed, the Israelis have retained the upper hand militarily against the Arabs. The supremacy of skill over income and numbers has been dramatically illustrated in one Middle East war after another.

In both South Africa and Israel, the cultural variable is critical. Had Israel consisted entirely of Middle Eastern Jews, the Arabs would have won every war. Indeed, it would not have been necessary to have more than the 1948 war. After all, Middle Eastern Jews are not very different from their Arab neighbours in culture and skill. In a war against fellow Middle Easterners, the numerical preponderance of the Arabs would have triumphed against Jews long before the numerical advantage was reinforced by Arab petro-wealth.

What has made the Israelis militarily pre-eminent is not the Jewishness of 80 per cent of the total population, but the Europeanness of less than half of that Jewish sector. It is the European and Western Jews who have provided the technological foundations of Israel's regional hegemony.

If then the ultimate basis of international stratification is indeed skill rather than income, what is Africa to do in order to ameliorate the consequences of its technological underdevelopment? The more obvious answer is for Africa to obtain the know-how from the Northern hemisphere as rapidly as possible. But there are difficulties. Countries of the Northern hemisphere are often all too eager to transfer certain forms of technology, especially through TNCs, but the South's need for certain technological transfers only helps to deepen relationships of dependency between the two hemispheres.

On the other hand, there are other areas of technology which the North is not at all keen to transfer. Pre-eminent among the taboos is the transfer of certain branches of nuclear physics and technology. The computer is part of the phenomenon of dependency through technology transfer; the nuclear plant or reactor is a symbol of dependency through technological monopoly by the North. TNCs are often instruments of Northern penetration of the South through technological transfer; nuclear power, on the other hand, is a symbol of Northern hegemony through technological monopoly.

The dual strategy for Africa and the Third World is both to learn from the North and to share expertise among each other. Those aspects of technology which are being freely transferred by the North should be 'decolonized' and stripped of their dependency implications as fast as possible. Those aspects of technology which are deliberately monopolized by the North should be subjected to Southern industrial espionage in a bid to break the monopoly. Pakistani scientists have been on the right track in their reported efforts to subject Northern nuclear monopoly to Southern industrial spying. If Pakistan becomes Islam's first nuclear power (as, indeed, it has recently become the first Islamic country to have a woman prime minister), and decides to share the nuclear secrets with a few select fellow Muslims like Egyptians or Libyans, that trend would be in the direction of enhanced technological co-operation among Third World countries.

That is one reason why the brain-drain from the South is not an unmitigated disaster. What would be a catastrophe is a complete stoppage of the brain-drain. It is vital that the South should counter-penetrate the citadels of technological and economic power. The counter-penetration can take the form of African engineers, teachers and professors, medical doctors and consultants, businessmen and scientists working in the North. The North needs to be more sensitized to Southern needs not only by the speeches of Southern statesmen and ambassadors, but also by the influence and leverage of Southerners resident in the North.

In any case, there is no law of gravity which says expertise can only flow from the North to the South. There is no gravitational logic which says that European teachers teaching African children is natural but that African teachers teaching European children is not. The structure of scientific stratification in the world should rapidly cease to be a rigid caste system and allow for social mobility in both directions. Of course, too big a brain-drain from the South northwards could deeply hurt the South – but the trouble with the present level of the brain drain is not that it is too great, but that it is grossly under-utilized by the South itself. Professor Edward S. Ayensu, a Ghanian Research Director at the Smithsonian Institution in Washington, D.C., has argued that there is a large potential pool of Third World experts, resident in the Northern hemisphere, who would be only too glad to serve for a year or two in developing countries if only their services were solicited. What is more, the Northern institutions where they work would, according to Professor Ayensu, be sympathetically inclined towards facilitating such exchanges from time to time if so requested by Third World authorities.[6]

If that were to happen, it would be a case of tapping the brain-drain on the basis of a triangular formula. The flow of expertise would be firstly from South to North, then North to South, and then South to South – often involving the same Southern experts or their equivalents sharing their know-how across hemispheres.

This sharing of Southern experts by both North and South would be a more realistic formula than the tax on the brain-drain which Professor Jagdish Bhagwati of the Massachusetts Institute of Technology has often recommended as a method of compensation by the North towards the South for manpower transfer. Unfortunately, while the North may indeed be willing to share with the South some of its newly acquired Southern experts, the South itself has shown more enthusiasm for borrowing 'pure' Northern experts than for borrowing Southern experts residing in the North. The psychological dependency of the South is less likely to be impressed by an Indian or Nigerian expert coming from the US than by an American expert with far less understanding of the Third World. The American is regarded as 'the real thing' in expertise – while the Indian statistician or Nigerian engineer is deemed to be a mere Southern 'carbon copy'.

Fortunately, all is not bleak. There is some movement of expertise between Third World countries. Dr. Boutros Boutros-Ghali, Egypt's Minister of State for Foreign Affairs, gave the assurance in an interview in Cairo in 1983 that Egypt had 'two million experts' working in other countries, mainly in Africa and the Middle East. South Asia also exports a considerable body of expertise to other parts of the Third World.

Some of the traffic in expertise across Third World frontiers is caused by political instability and economic problems at home. Qualified Ugandans and Ethiopians are scattered in almost all the four corners of the Third World, as well as in the North. So are qualified Ghanaians, Southern Africans, Nigerians, and others.

Then, there is the inter-Third World traffic of experts caused by the magnetism of petro-wealth. The Gulf states have a particularly impressive variety of *human power* from different lands. Two Ghanaian scholars visited the University of Petroleum and Minerals in Dhahran in the Kingdom of Saudi Arabia in the summer of 1984. They were impressed by the Ghanaian presence in the research complex of the University. They were also surprised to learn about '24 highly qualified Ghanaian medical officers working in and around this University town of Dhahran'.[7]

To summarize, there is a *push factor* in some of the less fortunate Third World countries which forces out many indigenous experts in search of alternative opportunities in other countries. But there is also a *pull factor* in the wealthier Third World societies which magnetically attracts workers and specialists from other lands. Together, the two forces are helping to lay down some of the foundations of organic solidarity within the Third World in the field of know-how.

What is lacking is an adequate linkage between organic and strategic solidarity in this field of evolving Third World expertise. A systematic programme which would enable Africa to borrow some of the Southern experts now residing in the North could become an important stage in the evolution of a merger between organic and strategic solidarity.

Behind it all is the realization that the ultimate foundations of international stratification are not income differences, military gadgets, or demographic variations. Ultimate power resides neither in the barrel of the gun nor in the barrel of oil – but in the technology which can produce and utilize both efficiently. A New International Economic Order would be void without a New International Technological Order. Africa needs strategies of solidarity to realize both.

FOUR FORMS OF POWER

But although *the power of skill* is at the moment overwhelmingly in the hands of the North, there are other areas of power which the South possesses but which it has under-utilized. OPEC is an illustration of *producer power*. From 1973 to 1983 OPEC grossly under-utilized its leverage. Instead of using that golden decade to put pressure on the North for fundamental adjustments in the patterns and rules of the world economy, OPEC concentrated almost exclusively on the prices game, a game of short-term maximization of returns.

There is a crying need for other 'producer cartels', no matter how weak in the short run. Cobalt has more promise as a mineral of leverage than copper, and would involve fewer countries. Experimentation in a cobalt cartel could pay off if Zaire asserted herself a little more decisively as an independent power. After all, Zaire has the credentials of being the Saudi Arabia of cobalt when the market improves in the years ahead.

The Third World has also under-utilized its *consumer power*, regionally specific and patchy as it is. The Middle East and African countries like Nigeria are especially important as consumers of Western civil and military hardware, technology and household products. Occasionally, Nigeria or individual Middle East countries flex their muscles and threaten to cancel trade contracts or to refuse to renew them. But such muscles are flexed usually for relatively minor issues – like protesting against the television film *Death of a Princess* or when an Arab or African delegation is snubbed by a Western power. The consumer power of Africa and the Middle East could be used as leverage for more fundamental changes in the exchange patterns between North and South.

The fourth form of power currently under-utilized by the South is *debtor power*. President Julius Nyerere of Tanzania, upon being elected Chairman of OAU in November 1984, identified development, debt and drought as the three leading concerns of the current African condition. Of course, African debts are modest as compared with those of Latin America, but Nyerere identified debt as a source of power and not merely as a source of weakness. At the first press conference after his election, Nyerere lamented that the Third World was not utilizing the threat of defaulting more efficiently to induce Western banks to make more fundamental concessions to the indebted.[8]

It is indeed true that if one owes his/her local bank a few thousand dollars, one is vulnerable – but if the debt is in millions of dollars the bank is vulnerable. Tanzania still owes so little that the country is still very vulnerable. But Nyerere virtually declared that if he owed as much as some of the leading African debtor countries owed, he would simply refuse to pay. (Africa's leading debtor nations include Nigeria, Egypt and Zaire. The debt of Africa, South of the Sahara, was by 1988 over 200 billion US dollars.)

In reality, Tanzania would still be vulnerable unless there was substantial strategic solidarity among both African and Latin American countries. The utilization of debtor power requires considerable consensus among the indebted. The Western banks have evolved a kind of organic solidarity of their own as well as mechanisms of almost continual consultation. The creditors of the North are united – but the debtors of the South are in disarray. Africa and Latin America need to explore the possibility of creating a strategic solidarity of the dispossessed and the indebted – to help induce the Shylocks of the North to make concessions on such issues as rates of interest, schedule of payment, methods of payment, and the conditions for a moratorium or even total debt relief where needed.

Fundamental as all these areas of strategic solidarity are, they are no substitute for organic solidarity in terms of greater trade, investment, and other interactions among Third World countries themselves. Here, the LDCs are caught up in one of several contradictions. In their relations with the North, the LDCs need to diversify their economies. But in their relations with each other, the LDCs need to specialize in order to increase mutual complementarity. Uganda could revive its cotton industry and sell the fibre to Kenya to process into a textile industry. This specialization would help the two countries develop in the direction of complementary specialization. But the imperatives of Uganda's relations with the world economy as a whole dictate diversification of Uganda's industry rather than specialization. This is an acute dilemma which Third World countries need to resolve as a matter of urgency. They need to find a suitable balance between diversification for North–South relations and specialization in South–South trade.

Related to this is the imperative of finding alternative methods of payment in South–South trade. The principle of using Northern currencies for South–South trade has been very stressful. The bogey of 'foreign exchange' has bedevilled Southern economies. Tanzania, Zambia, and Zimbabwe have been exploring possibilities of reviving *barter* as a basis of at least some aspect of their economic relations. Nigeria, in the 1980s, has experimented with 'counter-trade' – exchanging her oil for manufactured goods. The new detente between Kenya and Tanzania also envisages areas of barter trade between the two countries in the years ahead. And if Uganda's cotton did feed Kenya's textile industry more systematically in the future, it would not be unrealistic for Kenya to pay back Uganda in shirts and processed military uniforms, rather than in hard foreign exchange.

Another area of organic solidarity among Third World countries concerns the issue of sharing *energy*. There have been years when Kenya has needed to get a third of its electricity from the dam at Jinja in Uganda. Uganda is still a major supplier of power to Kenya. The Akosombo Dam on the Volta River in Ghana was also designed to be a major *regional* supplier of electricity in West Africa. Unfortunately, the level of water has been so low that far from supplying power to neighbours, Ghana has periodically had to ration power domestically. Ghana has sometimes needed electrical co-operation from the Cote d'Ivoire. Southern African dams like Kariba have had more successful regional roles. They all symbolize a kind of pan-Africanism of energy, organic solidarity through interlocking structures of hydro-electric power.

An integrated European steel complex once served as midwife to the birth of EEC. Indeed, the integrated steel industry was envisioned as an insurance against any future fratricidal war in Europe. If European steel production was interlocked, industrial interdependence was at hand – and separate military aggression in the future would therefore be less likely. In the same spirit, interlocking electrical systems between Third World countries should deepen mutual dependence – and create incentives for co-operation in other areas.

The struggle for a more integrated Africa has encountered many setbacks – from the collapse of the East African Community of Kenya, Uganda and Tanzania to the substantial drying up of the Akosombo Dam. An experiment worthy of Africa's attention and study is South East Asia. The struggle for a more integrated South East Asia is more of a success story – as the Association of South East Asian Nations (ASEAN) has emerged as a major economic and diplomatic force in the affairs of the region. The struggle for a more integrated Arab world is a mixed story – ranging from the positive promise of the Gulf Co-operation Council to the negative internecine squabbles of Arab politics. Libya and Egypt are often close to conflict.

In Latin America, regional integration is also a mixed record. Central America in the 1980s is tense under the clouds of war. On the other hand, Chile and Argentina – through the mediation of the Vatican – have defused the sensitive issue of the Bege channel. Economic co-operation has had its ups and downs throughout the region, but the ideal of greater integration is still a live flame. Africa should watch this distant political laboratory with fascination.

The Northern hemisphere, as a whole, is divided between two economic blocs which coincide with the ideological divide. The split is of course between the socialist world of COMECON/CMEA and the capitalist world of the North Atlantic Treaty Organization (NATO). Africa as a Southern region, on the other hand, is still in multiple fragments. It is now in search of the elusive secret of putting the fragments together. It is in search of the secret genius of cohesion. Strategies of solidarity are but means to an end. The goal is distant and difficult – but Africa's reach should exceed its grasp or what's a heaven for?

But should Africa's 'reach' extend to participation in the politics of nuclear power? Where does Africa fit into these nuclear calculations? How have cultural and racial inequalities affected Africa in the nuclear age? It is to this theme that we must now turn.

AFRICA VERSUS THE NUCLEAR AGE

It is symbolic of the basic African condition that the first form of African participation in the nuclear age concerned a raw material. Uranium is of course as indigenous to Africa as 'the flame trees of Thika' or the baobab tree of Senegal. Africa in the 1930s and 1940s helped to provide the uranium which launched the western world into the nuclear orbit.

To change the metaphor, Africa was in attendance at the birth of the nuclear age. It was in part Africa's uranium from Zaire which helped to set in motion the first nuclear reactor in North America. And for better or for worse, Africa's uranium may have gone into those dreadful atomic bombs which were dropped on Hiroshima and Nagasaki in August 1945. But, of course, Africa had no say in the matter. An African resource had simply been pirated by others – and once again played a major role in a significant shift in Western industrialism.

Not that uranium was all that scarce even in the 1940s. What was significant was that, outside the Soviet Bloc and North America, uranium seemed to be substantially available only in Black Africa. As Caryl P. Haskins put it way back in 1946:

> [Uranium] stands next to copper in abundance, is more abundant than zinc, and is about four times as plentiful as lead ... However, the outstanding deposits are narrowly distributed, being

confined to the United States, Canada, the Belgian Congo, Czechoslovakia and possibly Russia. The fact that the richest deposits of uranium ore occurs in a fairly limited number of places makes international control feasible; but it also foreshadows violent competitive struggles for ownership of the richest deposits (the struggle for oil greatly intensified).[9]

Of course, since 1946 other reserves of uranium ore have been discovered in the world, including in different parts of Africa. African uranium has continued to fill many a reactor in the Western world, and to help create many a nuclear bomb.

The second service (after uranium supply) which Africa rendered to the nuclear age was also symbolic. Africa provided the desert for nuclear tests in the early 1960s. In this case, Africa's nuclear involvement had slightly shifted from a purely indigenous resource (uranium) to a partially geographical context (the Sahara). The transition was from providing indigenous nuclear material to furnishing a laboratory in the desert surrounded by Islamic countries for a Western bomb. At least two of the legacies of Africa's triple heritage (indigenous, Islamic, and Western legacies) were inadvertently involved – from the mines of Zaire to the sands of Algeria.

The third African point of entry into the nuclear age has been through the Republic of South Africa. For better or worse, South Africa has probably become a nuclear power or is close to it. This provides the third leg of Africa's triple heritage – indigenous resources (Africa's uranium), a semi-Islamic testing laboratory (the dunes of the Sahara), and an actual Western productive capability (white South Africa's expertise).

A circle of influence developed. The progress of the French nuclear programme and its tests in the Sahara probably helped the Israeli nuclear programme. This was a period when France was quite close to Israel in terms of economic and technological collaboration. The French helped the Israelis build a nuclear reactor at Dimona and seemed at times to be closer to the Israelis in sharing nuclear secrets than even the Americans were. The evidence is abundant and clear – the French nuclear programme in the late 1950s and 1960s served as a midwife to the Israeli nuclear programme. And French tests in the Sahara were part and parcel of France's nuclear infrastructure in that period.

By a curious twist of destiny, the Israeli nuclear programme, in turn, came to serve as a midwife to the nuclear efforts of the Republic of South Africa in the 1970s and 1980s. Relations between the two countries cooled a little after the Sharpeville massacre of 1960, and when Israel briefly considered the possibility of extending aid to African liberation movements in Southern Africa. But, by 1970, there were clear improvements in economic relationships. And after Black Africa's almost complete diplomatic break with Israel in 1973, co-operation between Israel and South Africa entered new areas, including the nuclear field. When a nuclear explosion occurred in the South Atlantic in September 1979, the question which arose was whether it was primarily a South African nuclear experiment, undertaken with Israeli technical aid, or primarily an Israeli explosive experiment carried out with South Africa's logistical support. A cover-up policy was pursued by both countries, helped in part by their Western allies, especially the Carter Administration in the US. The cyclical nuclear equation was about to be completed. The Sahara had aided France's nuclear programme, France had aided Israel's nuclear design, and Israel had in turn aided South Africa's nuclear ambitions. Kwame Nkrumah's fear of a linkage between nuclear tests in the Sahara and racism in South Africa had found astonishing vindication nearly two decades later. It was in April 1960 that Nkrumah addressed an international meeting in Accra in the following words:

> Fellow Africans and friends: there are two threatening swords of Damocles hanging over the continent, and we must remove them. These are nuclear tests in the Sahara by the French Government and the *apartheid* policy of the Government of the Union of South Africa. It would be a great mistake to imagine that the achievement of political independence by certain areas in Africa will automatically mean the end of the struggle. It is merely the beginning of the struggle.[10]

It has turned out that Nkrumah's thesis of 'two swords of Damocles', one nuclear and one racist, was in fact prophetic. The Republic of South Africa is using nuclear power as a potentially stabilizing factor in defence of *apartheid*. The old nuclear fall-out in the Sahara in the 1960s involved a linkage between racism and nuclear weapons which is only just beginning to reveal itself.

But the cultural and technological inequalities between white and black in Southern Africa affect other areas of security – conventional areas as well as nuclear domains. The Republic of South Africa has used its technological superiority to bully its Black neighbours into submission and into 'non-aggression' pacts. The sovereignty of Mozambique, Angola, Botswana, Lesotho, and even independent Zimbabwe, has been violated from time to time, sometimes with utter impunity. European technological leadership in the last three centuries of world history has been inherited by people of European extraction operating in Africa – and has been used as a decisive military resource against Black Africans. South Africa's neighbours have begun to appreciate what it must feel like to be *Israel's* neighbour – for both South Africa and Israel have seldom hesitated to use blatant military muscle at the expense of the sovereignty of their neighbours.

Again, cultural and technological inequalities have played a part in these politics of intervention. As we have indicated earlier, Israelis have enjoyed military pre-eminence for so long not because they are Jews but because a large part of their population is Western and European. We have argued that, had the population of Israel consisted overwhelmingly of Middle Eastern Jews, the Arabs would have won every single war they have fought with their Jewish neighbour. Numbers would have counted. Middle Eastern Jews in Israel are often more hawkish and eager to fight the Arabs, but the military capability for assuring Israeli victory has come more from their European compatriots. Again, culture has played a decisive role in deciding victory and defeat in military equations.

The danger both in the Middle East and Southern Africa lies in pushing the weak too far. We have already seen how desperate conditions in the two subregions can easily become fertile ground for different forms of terrorism. For the time being, that terrorism in the two geographical areas has not yet gone nuclear. But if the cultural imbalances between the Israelis and Arabs, and between whites and blacks, continue to deepen the sense of desperation among the disadvantaged, we cannot rule out the possibility of their acquiring those nuclear devices one day from radical friends elsewhere. Powerlessness also corrupts – and absolute powerlessness can corrupt absolutely.

But once again, there is one kind of powerlessness whose implications are particularly distinctive – the powerlessness of women on issues of war and peace. Related to this issue is the whole question of the psychology of *nuclear macho*. It is to these sexual questions that we must now return.

THE GENDER OF NUCLEAR WAR

In societies which are vastly different from each other, war has so far been pre-eminently a masculine game. 'Our sons are our warriors' – this has been almost universal. Daughters have had different roles as a rule. Even countries like Israel, which involve women substantially in issues of war and peace, have tended to be protective of women in the allocation of combat duties.

If it is indeed true that there is a pronounced *macho* factor in the psychology of going to war, we cannot ignore the *macho* factor when we are discussing *nuclear* war. Perhaps that is indeed what is distinctive about war in the nuclear age – it has become too important to be left to men. The whole human species is at stake – men, women, and children. And while the human race has managed to survive for perhaps three million years in spite of the violent proclivities of the cave man, nuclear power requires the most fundamental of all human revolutions – a truly androgynized system of social and political power.

It is true that the most famous women rulers in the twentieth century have tended to be 'iron ladies' with a taste for nuclear credentials – Golda Meir, Indira Gandhi as well as Margaret Thatcher. These are the Dahomey Amazons of the Nuclear Age. But, for as long as most societies remain primarily male dominated, the women who succeed in the power game will tend to be approximations of what men regard as tough and heroic. Africa and the rest of the community could only discover the true impact of women on decisions concerning war and peace when the power system as a whole has acquired true sexual balance, commensurate androgyny.

Are we to assume that women in Africa and elsewhere are generally less violent than men? The answer is 'Yes' – though the reasons may be more cultural than biological. Our information is inadequate about the causes, but there is no doubt about the correlation between violence and masculinity. The jails of crimes of violence are a solemn testimony; the wars across history; the concentration camps and their Eichmanns. Of course, the world has also produced brutal women. But, while men and women have had an equal share in determining births, men have had an overwhelmingly larger share in determining deaths. Men and women are co-creators of the human race, but men have often been solo destroyers of large chunks of that race. The female of the species is the senior partner in the progress of baby-making; the male of the species has been the senior partner in the business of corpse-making. In the twentieth century alone, there has been no female equivalent of Hitler, or Stalin, or Pol Pot, or Idi Amin, or the more brutal architects of *apartheid*.

In reality, we cannot be sure that an androgynized power system either in Africa or on the world stage will in fact succeed in moderating the violent inclinations of states. But perhaps nothing short of a gender revolution can stand a chance of containing the nuclear threat to the species. If that does not work either, the future will be grim indeed for the human race as a whole as it faces its own escalating technological capacity for planetary self-destruction.

TOWARDS THE FUTURE

There is one happy prospect that Black Africans can contemplate which the Arabs are denied. Black Africans can contemplate the prospect of inheriting the white bomb of the Republic of South Africa. We are convinced that, before the end of this century, the Blacks of South Africa will probably succeed in overthrowing the regime of white supremacy. In the wake of the racial war which has to precede the Black victory, half the white population would probably have had to leave the Republic. But it seems almost certain that half the white population of South Africa would in the end also still remain behind. Through that other half, South Africa's nuclear capability would be transmitted from white control to Black control.

It is therefore a fair question to ask whether the prospect of a nuclearized South Africa today is a blessing or a curse for the rest of Africa. Is it possible that white South Africa's nuclear bomb is a short-term nuisance for Black Africa but a long-term advantage? Are South Africa's Blacks going to be the legitimate heirs of South Africa's nuclear capability before the end of the century?

There is little doubt that white South Africa's bomb is irrelevant for the survival of *apartheid*. The main threat to South Africa's racist regime is *internal* to South Africa – and the regime is unlikely to use nuclear devices in the streets of Soweto. Such a use would, in any case, precipitate a white exodus – at least as serious a crisis for *apartheid* as the rebellion of Blacks.

But while nuclear power is of marginal significance in the fortunes of present-day South Africa, it may be more significant in the *post-apartheid* era of the Republic. As the new rulers inherit the white nuclear bomb, they will be transformed from the status of being the most humiliated Blacks of the twentieth century to the status of becoming the most powerful Blacks of the twenty-first century. Black-ruled South Africa will of course remain not only one of the richest countries in the world in terms of mineral resources, but also one of the most industrialized in the Southern hemisphere. The nuclear capability will remain part of a wider industrial complex.

But can such 'horizontal nuclear proliferation' be a cure to vertical proliferation? Again, the underlying hope lies in creating the necessary cultural shock for a serious commitment to *universal* nuclear disarmament. In any case, Black inheritance of South Africa's bomb will not be horizontal nuclear proliferation in the usual sense. No new *country* will have been added to the membership of the nuclear club – only a new *race*. For the first time, the nuclear club will have a Black member. At the most, the horizontal proliferation will have been across the racial divide rather than state boundaries. And since Northern nuclear powers are more afraid of South African Blacks handling the bomb than of South African whites doing so, the new Black member of the nuclear club may well precipitate an agonizing reappraisal as to whether the club should exist at all. The racial prejudices and distrusts of the white members of the nuclear club may well serve the positive function of disbanding the club – and dismantling the nuclear arsenals in the cellars which had constituted credentials for membership.

But nuclear disarmament is not enough. There is need to reduce the risk of war. After all, once the 'genie' of nuclear know-how is already out of the bottle, it can be re-utilized if war breaks out – and a new nuclear arms race be inaugurated. The ultimate evil is man's proclivity towards war – and not merely the weapons with which he has fought it.

But what kind of fundamental revolution could stabilize the gains in nuclear disarmament and reduce the risk of war? In order to answer that question we need to ask that other question: what has been the most persistent characteristic of war in all societies, across all time, traversing all cultures?

No, the most persistent attribute of war has not been the consistency of motives – for men have fought for reasons which have ranged from greed to glory, from gold to God, from liberty to land, from sex to soccer. The motives have varied but war has continued. The most current attribute of war has not been its technology either – for we know that the technological range has been from the spear to the intercontinental missile. Nor has war been a peculiarity of certain climates – for men have fought under the blazing sun as well as in snow drifts.

No, the most persistent attribute of war has not been its motivation, technology, organization, goals, or geographical context. As we have indicated, it has in fact been its *masculinity*. But with the coming of the nuclear age, war has become too serious to be left to men. The power system of the world does indeed need to be androgynized. The most poignant of all paradoxes amounts to the following imperative: *If man is to survive, woman has to bear arms.*

Africa originally declared woman as custodian of fire, water, and earth. The nuclear age is redefining the scope of that triple custody globally. Africa once entrusted to woman both the *survival* of this generation and the *arrival* of the next generation through the doctrine of dual fertility. The nuclear age is expanding that responsibility into a planetary agenda for collective self-preservation. Africa's three future revolutions of gender, skill, and power will find their supreme fulfilment when African women take the lead in universal nuclear disarmament and effective arms control. War has for so long worn a masculine mask. Peace may one day unveil a feminine face – perhaps black in complexion.

NOTES

1. Ali A. Mazrui is indebted to the late Okot p'Bitek, the Ugandan anthropologist and poet, for stimulation and information about myths of womanhood in northern Uganda. He and Okot also discussed similarities and differences between African concepts of matter and the ideas of Empedocles, the Greek philosopher of the 5th Century B.C. Consult also Okot p'Bitek, *African Religions in Western Scholarship* (Nairobi: East African Literature Bureau, 1971).
2. Margaret Jean Hay, 'Luo Women and economic change during the colonial period', chapter on *Women in Africa: Studies in Social and Economic Change*, edited by Nancy J. Hafkin and Edna G. Bay (Stanford, California: Stanford University Press, 1976), pp.98–99.
3. *Ibid.*, p.105.
4. There is no doubt that such arrangements occur in Mozambique. What is not clear is how widespread *de facto* polyandry is becoming in South Africa.
5. Mazrui is indebted to the field research and interviews in Southern Africa which accompanied the BBC/WETA television project 'The Africans: A Triple Heritage' (1985–1986).
6. Edward S. Ayensu, lecture on 'Natural and Applied Sciences and National Development', delivered at the Silver Jubilee celebration of the Ghana Academy of Arts and Sciences (Accra), November 22, 1984.
7. The two Ghanian visitors were Professor Alexander Kwapong, Vice-Rector of the United Nations University in Tokyo, and Professor Edward Ayensu of the Smithsonian Institution in the United States. See Ayensu's lecture (mimeo), Ghana Academy of Arts and Sciences (Accra), *Ibid.*
8. The Voice of America's African Service broadcast a recording of both Nyerere's speech and Nyerere's Press Conference. One such broadcast by VOA Africa Service was on Saturday November 24, 1984.
9. Caryl P. Haskins, 'Atomic Energy and American Foreign Policy', *Foreign Affairs*, Vol. 24, No. 4, July 1946, pp.595–596.
10. Kwame Nkrumah, *I Speak of Freedom: A Statement of African Ideology* (London: Heinemann Educational, 1961), p.213.

CHAPTER SIXTEEN

African Development Management Reform: Political and Socio-Cultural Constraints Versus the Neo-Classical Imperative

DAVID F. LUKE

INTRODUCTION

'On our side', African governments told the international community at the special session of the UN General Assembly on Africa's economic crisis, 'we reaffirm our commitment to mobilize all our resources for development purposes and to undertake, individually and collectively, all measures and policy reforms necessary for the recovery of our economies and the revitalization of genuine development to the benefit of all our peoples'.[1] *The African Submission* goes on to outline future intentions and strategies: 'It is our collective and individual determination to make all the sacrifices required for bringing about economic rehabilitation, recovery and development. Accordingly, we will ... take measures to strengthen incentive schemes, review public investment policies, improve economic management, including greater discipline and efficiency in the use of resources, encourage domestic resource mobilization and ensure the broad participation of all our peoples in the veritable fight against poverty, famine and hunger, disease and ignorance.'[2]

This statement captures the new mood of realism on the priorities, policies, institutional and managerial requirements for short- and longer-term development that is now sweeping across Africa.[3] Most African states were, by mid-1986, implementing reform and adjustment programmes in co-operation – in nearly all cases – with World Bank and/or IMF, the UN system and other international development agencies. In the formulation and pursuit of these programmes in the post-crisis era of the late 1980s, African leaders and ruling elites exhibit a new realism on the development prospects of the countries over which they preside. Hence, the *African Submission* emphasizes a commitment to abandon inappropriate policies, identifies the constraints arising out of the 'resource gap' of new money and articulates the need for concerted action in dealing with debt and debt service burdens, declining concessional flows and the persistent downward spiral of the terms of trade of most African countries notwithstanding occasional up-swings. Quite evidently, a rare opportunity for dealing with the region's development problems has been engendered by the current posture of most African regimes.[4]

But this new mood has obviously not been nurtured in a vacuum. It has grown within the present configuration of the African post-colonial state and the framework of a political culture that undergird and continue to provide the bases of personal rule. It has also appeared in a conjuncture – that is increasingly becoming apparent – of fundamental changes in the structure of the world economy that have further marginalized the African region. A corresponding historical shift in ideologies of economic strategy and management is also apparently underway with the consequence of the decline of Keynesianism or interventionism against the growing influence of neoclassicism (and *glasnost* and other liberalizing tendencies in centrally planned economies). It is perhaps still too early to characterize these changes although it is clear that a decline in the role of the state in economic or, for developing countries, development management is not an outcome; but more rather a redefinition of its role. Central to the emerging orthodoxy is the belief that there are strict limits on what governments can do effectively; and governments that ignore such limits, particularly in regard to interventionist mechanisms that constrain rather than enhance the allocative functions of markets, are often rewarded with inefficiencies and intractable difficulties for their efforts.

It is partly with this in mind that the three main sections of this Chapter respectively examine the political and socio-cultural constraints on development management and practice arising out of the present configuration of African post-colonial states; the challenge presented by recent changes in the structure of the world economy and the imperatives of neoclassical economic strategies; and some key aspects of the practical responses by African governments in the management of their economic affairs.

THE CONFIGURATION OF AFRICAN POST-COLONIAL STATES

A recent spate of studies of the post-colonial state and its political and socio-cultural configuration in contemporary Africa has focused on the dubious nature of state–society relations.[5] The problem arises out of what is perceived as a disjointed relationship between the post-colonial state and the society over which it presides. These studies are founded on the premises of the social science of the modern state. In these terms, the state is historically a centralizing force which 'draws in' various aspects of social and economic activities within its scope. Through this process, the state stimulates the development of (and is, itself, further developed by) other ties and interconnections which cut across the economic, social and territorial realms over which it claims sovereignty. Hence the modern state has emerged from its transformation over time with the important features of nation-state (having penetrated but not necessarily dissolved the plurality of cultures and sub-cultures within its 'space') in a world of industrial capitalism (as the dominant mode of economic enterprise). It is in terms of these features that the state is 'modern'; according to Weber it '... has only in modern times reached its full development ... it is best to define it in terms appropriate to the modern type of state, but, at the same time, in terms which abstract from the values of the present day, since these are particularly subject to change.'[6]

As regards the first feature, the modern state has an organic relationship with its (by this point 'civil') society within which social interaction and capital accumulation occurs, fuelled by a range of ideologies and the mechanisms of price, profit and investment in labour and commodity markets. Since these processes do not occur in isolation from similar processes in other states, the second feature, a complex web of international relations between states, is a simultaneous development. If the modern state is also understood to be a community organized for the purpose of government within a prescribed jurisdiction, it develops specialized institutions (collectively referred to as the public sector) for mediating and regulating its economy and society, the competing claims of different groups of individuals as well as its external relations. These institutions or agencies operate through impersonal rules to uphold a consciousness of some concept of 'public purpose'. It is from this consciousness and concept that the state derives its legitimacy.

And in relation to the immediate concerns of this Chapter, to the extent that economic growth – the main if also flawed yardstick of progress – has become a principal objective of governments, economic and development management is a pre-eminent activity of the modern state.[7] Indeed, it is by no means superfluous to argue that a claim to 'statehood' in today's world is also a claim to have this capacity.

The complication which recent studies of African post-colonial states have identified is this: these states are in almost all cases a legacy of colonial rule and not a result of step-by-step state/society transformation. As such they exist in an 'overdeveloped' as distinct from organic relationship with their societies. This incongruity in state formation, as one formulation has it, inhibits the emergence of popular consent; undermines the creation and maintenance of political order, territorial integrity, administrative and institutional capacity; obstructs the generation and allocation of public resources for public purposes; and impedes a regularized exchange of, or succession to, power.

The most common mode of governance that has emerged from this configuration is some variant of personal rule. It arises out a context in which the state has not fully 'drawn in' the plurality of cultural and/or class bases of its society. Accordingly, competing claims from these bases are channelled through kin, clan and ethnic networks rather than mediated by secular political processes.[8] As a mode of governance, personal rule constrains the effectiveness of governmental processes of development management – policy development, planning, organizational design, programming, budgeting, scheduling, processing, staffing, training, personnel and financial management. From the political culture of shared beliefs in the appropriateness of clientelist networks and preferment is derived ambivalent attitudes toward the propriety of bureaucratic processes and institutions.

But this is not to deny that personal rule can be associated with a considerable degree of variance – from country to country – in state/society relations, bureaucratic effectiveness and economic performance. Not to recognize this is to fall into the deterministic trap of lumping all African countries into the same strait-jacket. Ideology and even leadership style of personal rulers accounts for this variance.[9] Thus, a number of African countries combine the features of the overdeveloped state and personal rule with relative economic success and progress; for example, Cameroon, Cote d'Ivoire, Kenya, Malawi, and Morocco; or, among non-African countries, Brazil, India, South Korea, Mexico and Thailand. This suggests that personal rulers and other state actors do have some choice (exercised with varying degrees of political ingenuity and resourcefulness) in the management of state/society relations and the bureaucractic process of economic development.

It is now possible to pull together the implications of the foregoing discussion. Any state that aspires to achieve and maintain a significant rate of economic growth must establish institutional mechanisms through which information is processed to a point of decision, and so that decisions, once made, are implemented and co-ordinated for effect and consistency. Normally falling under the executive arm of government, these institutions are essentially of two kinds: 'substantive' agencies and departments for setting priorities, policy and decision-making, allocation of resources and the implementation and evaluation of programmes and measures, for example, offices of Presidents and Prime Ministers, the cabinet, ministers as well as decentralized units; and 'non-substantive' or 'internal' agencies and departments for applying govenment-wide standards and regulations on financial and personnel matters and working methods, for example, treasuries, budget bureaus, finance ministries and establishments, public service and manpower secretariats and commissions. In any state, moreover, the effectiveness of these institutions and the administrative and managerial processes within them depends at one level on a variety of factors including organizational 'climate and politics' and other informal aspects of bureaucratic life; and, at another level, perhaps also more importantly, on the broader political environment. In the case of African post-colonial states where personal rule and political clientelism is a key feature of the political environment, there is the further difficulty, as noted above, of a political culture of levity toward bureaucratic organization and processes – unless of course special effort is made to 'insulate' them. The recognition of this caveat is an important ingredient of the new mood of realism now sweeping across the region. Accordingly, the *African Submission* refers to the need to improve economic management and for greater discipline and efficiency in the use of resources. Practical action which African governments can take in this regard, and which indeed many are taking, is discussed below. As will be shown presently, this recognition is timely. Recent changes in the structure of the international economy have further marginalized the African region, and revisionist ideologies on the proper role of government in economic or development management have emerged.

ECONOMIC CHANGE AND NEOCLASSICAL REVISIONISM

Future historians writing about this decade will conclude that the 1980s was a watershed in the re-orientation of development strategies in Africa in response to persistent economic difficulties. It has been documented that two-thirds of sub-Saharan African states have under-taken significant reforms in economic policy and management since 1982. While the check-list in Table 16.1 provides the details of the reforms in a number of African countries, Table 16.2 identifies those countries.

The pun on the word 'submission' will also not escape the notice of historians chronicling Africa's economic fortunes during the 1980s. There are good grounds for arguing that African regimes are in effect 'submitting' to the changes in the structure of the world economy that have occurred since the early 1960s and the corresponding revisionism in ideologies of economic strategy and management that had begun to emerge before the recession of 1974–1976 received impetus and became even more sharply defined after the 1980–1982 recession.

TABLE 16.1
TRENDS IN POLICY AND INSTITUTIONAL REFORM AMONG
AFRICAN COUNTRIES

Type of policy action or reform measures taken	No. of countries involved
Countries that have decontrolled producer prices	10
Countries that have frozen hiring or reduced public sector employment	20
Countries that have eliminated public agricultural marketing agencies or permitted private sector competition	13
Countries that have given import of agricultural inputs to the private sector	7
Countries that have privatized some State enterprises	14
Countries that have substantially increased producer prices	21
Countries that have reduced or eliminated agricultural input subsidies	14
Countries that have reduced or eliminated food subsidies	8
Countries that have realigned exchange rates to more closely reflect the real cost of foreign exchange	16
Of the above, countries that have adopted floating market rates	7

Source: West Africa, 30 March 1987, p.625.

In the 20 years since 1960, there have been evident changes in the locus of world manufacturing output and in the relative shares of gross world product of various countries and geographical groups of

TABLE 16.2

AFRICAN COUNTRIES* WITH MAJOR STRUCTURAL REFORM
PROGRAMMES PLANNED OR UNDERWAY AS OF MARCH 1987

Burundi	Mali
Central African Republic	Mauritania
Chad	Niger
Equatorial Guinea	Rwanda
The Gambia	Senegal
Ghana	Sierra Leone
Guinea	Somalia
Guinea-Bissau	Tanzania
Kenya	Togo
Madagascar	Zaire
Malawi	Zambia

* IDA-eligible sub-Saharan African countries.
Source: Overseas Development Council (of the US), 'Should the IMF withdraw from Africa?'
Policy Focus, No.1, 1987, p.6.

countries. As a result, the industrial market economies of Western Europe and North America have lost some ground to a number of 'new-comers' – Japan, most prominent among them, but including two dozen or so 'middle-income' countries and/or NICs. The changes in the relative shares of gross world product were accompanied by a significant change in the composition of the exports of the new-comers – a trend showing an increasing share of manufactures as distinct from resource-based commodities. During the same period, the share of world product of the 'low-income' countries (most of which can be found in Africa) declined, but only marginally; on the other hand, their share of manufacturing output increased and, again, only marginally.[10]

The success of the new-comers – especially Japan and the Asian NICs – was associated with a common set of policies and practices, including a reliance on export markets to generate growth rather than the expansion of domestic markets; the use of foreign capital and borrowings to finance local investment; the provision of a host of market incentives to stimulate agricultural and industrial production; a shift to floating exchange rates; and the exposure of export industries to market forces and international competitiveness.[11]

By contrast, the *dirigiste* import-substitution and/or redistribution strategies which a number of 'poor performers' – low-income and state socialist countries as well as some Latin American NICs – pursued during the same period resulted in high cost and low quality industrial output, neglect of agriculture (and in some cases growing food deficits), worsening income distribution, intractable inflation combined with unemployment and/or underemployment, and thriving underground economies. These effects were especially pronounced in African countries.

In terms of ideologies of economic strategy and management, the success of the newcomers signalled the emergence of apparently viable alternatives to the theories, policies and practices associated with post-war state intervention. As Harris suggests, 'by the seventies, there was no such confidence in the capacity of governments to control their domestic affairs; the market, the invisible hand of a benevolent deity, was everywhere to be seen as the only means of allocating resources efficiently; economic growth and high employment were seen as the gift of the world market, not of domestic management'.[12] The subsequent rise in influence of neoclassicism received impetus from the desperate search of many governments for a formula of adjustment to economic change and the post-recession climate of the late 1970s. But it has to be understood that neoclassical revisionism did not imply a decline in the role of the state in economic or development management. On the contrary, the visible hand of government was very much in evidence orchestrating the policies that had brought about the success of the new-comers and directing adjustment strategies in developing and developed market and centrally-planned economies alike. Some analysts of European and North American adjustments even identified corporatist tendencies in the neo-activism of the state amid premature paranoia over the alleged de-industrialization of these countries.[13] Harris is quite perceptive in asserting:

> Ideologies and their substructure of economic theory are no better than the prejudices of the age and the classes from which they derive, but it is rare for such a complete transformation to take place in such a short time. It is a mark of how conscious most participants are that the change received little systematic attention − it seems that pragmatically one thing led to another ... .[14]

The *mea culpa* of the *African Submission* and its espousal of neo-classical policy and institutional reforms has to be seen as the 'African submission' to new international economic realities (and, as noted above, a parallel to liberalizing trends in centrally planned economies).

The redefinition of the role of the state, the provision of appropriate incentives for increased agricultural and industrial productivity, cutting the fat off the public sector, the re-alignment of exchange rates and, more generally, the application of appropriate strategies reflecting the dynamism of linkages between domestic productive forces and international trade (see Table 16.1) are measures that will – the proverbial all things being equal must be inserted here – provide increased economic activity and growth in the medium term.

But some caveats must be indicated in relation to the foregoing optimism. Firstly, the resource gap identified by the *African Submission* implies that new money for rehabilitation programmes is inadequate.[15] Private commercial lending to Africa has virtually ceased and interest charges on debts have been increasing. According to one estimate, net resource flows to Africa declined sharply from $US10 billion in 1980 to $US4.9 billion in 1985 in current prices. A partial recovery in 1987 to $US7.3 billion is expected in net flows largely as a result of official aid to finance adjustment programmes. About 40 per cent of current debt service payments – estimated at an annual amount of $US 11 billion in 1986–1987 – consists of payments to IMF and World Bank and interest due to other financial creditors which are not eligible for rescheduling.[16] This is now virtually the only debt that is being paid. Secondly, a number of other difficulties stand in the way of recovery in Africa. These include sharp fluctuations in the exchange rate of major international currencies, instability of oil prices (although African oil-importers are currently enjoying relief from high prices), tariff and non-tariff trade barriers (including protectionism in agricultural commodities in North America and through the Common Agricultural Policy in Europe which hurt some existing and potential African exports) and depressed international commodity and mineral markets (with the partial exception of precious minerals).

It is clear that economic reform and development management have become very complex as a result of the limited room for manoeuvre that African ruling elites and policy-makers have. Against such a background, future growth will have to come out of innovations in development management as much as out of increased productivity and export success, hence the need to examine some aspects of the institutional reforms now underway.

DEVELOPMENT MANAGEMENT REFORM

As noted above, primary responsibility for development management normally falls under the executive arm of government. The public sector is a generic term that encompasses the range of institutions and processes that are involved. Its precise organization and the variety of functions undertaken by it varies among countries. Given however its pre-eminent role as an instrument of fashioning and putting public or development policy into effect, public sectors everywhere typically encompass two 'domains' of organization and management.

The first domain, as already mentioned, is the substantive arrangements for the setting of priorities, policy and decision-making, allocating resources and the implementation and evaluation of programmes and measures. The network of institutions and organizations under this category includes:

(a) *Central agencies* that prepare and process information for decision-making by the cabinet, prime minister or president; *ministries, departments and agencies* at other levels of government, including local authorities, which generate and process information for decision-making and policy development at these and higher levels and/or implement policies that have been adopted; and,

(b) *Parastatal agencies* which ostensibly operate at 'arm's-length' from other organizations of the executive branch of government to facilitate a commercial mode of operations, for example public enterprises, or some degree of operating autonomy such as regulatory commissions, advisory councils, etc.

The second domain comprises the 'internal' arrangements for applying government-wide standards and regulations on financial and personnel administration and working methods (it is usual for public agencies outside the public service – local authorities and parastatal organizations, for example – to be given autonomy in these matters but their operations may fall within the purview of public service financial administration). This network of institutions include:

(a) *Institutions of financial management* such as treasuries, budget bureaus and finance ministries; and,

(b) *Institutions of personnel management* such as establishment secretariats, public service and manpower commissions, training facilities and ministries of public services.

The domain of internal arrangements provides the administrative infrastructure for the domain of substantive arrangements but, together, they facilitate the role of government in development management. This role itself essentially encompasses three main activities: *macro-economic management; micro-economic regulating* and *production*. As a manager and regulator, a government respectively sets the macro- and micro-economic framework within which economic agents – in the private and public sectors and hybrids of the two – can operate. As a producer, the public sector directly provides certain goods and services most usually through public enterprises. It should be kept in mind that these activities are effected through the range of public sector institutions, departments and agencies that constitute the domains of substantive operations and internal administrative arrangements. It is not possible within the bounds of this Chapter to provide a full survey of the reforms being undertaken in these domains and activities.[17] But an account is given below of the reform of central agencies and new approaches to macro-economic management.

The Reform of Central Agencies

These provide political executives with staff services and include central bank, budget, monetary, statistical, policy and planning agencies, aid and technical assistance co-ordination bureaus and other staff units. Matters which require action by political leaders are processed and analyzed at these agencies to facilitate decision-making, resource allocation and policy co-ordination. Although these are common functions performed by central agencies everywhere, national circumstances such as administrative traditions, the leadership style of chief executives, and the exigencies of national power politics, among other factors, have resulted in some central agencies being either dominant or passive intermediaries in decision-making at the highest level of government.

Most African states have some version of the central agencies that have been identified. This cluster of economic and financial agencies constitute the nerve centre of national development management. But the ability of these agencies in many African states to function effectively in dealing with external and internal challenges has not inspired much confidence in the past. This is because key central agencies in some countries have simply lacked analytical capacity and have slavishly worked within the parameters of multi-year development plans in spite of the rapidly changing circumstances and environments. Where this has not been the problem, the tendency for personal rulers to fill them with patronage appointments or to take arbitrary decisions irrespective of the impact and consequences for development objectives has undermined the institutionalization of analytical capacity in central agencies.

As part of the new mood, this is now changing. The World Bank's fourth report on sub-Saharan Africa records several instances of institutional reform and new procedures for dealing with external debt and co-ordinating multilateral and bilateral assistance.[18] In Zambia, for example, a Special Economic Unit chaired by the Minister of Finance and composed of senior officials of the National Planning Commission, the sectoral ministries, the central bank, major parastatal agencies, the Cabinet Office, and State House (the Office of the President) was created in 1983 to prepare, co-ordinate and implement the government's policies and efforts to stabilize and restructure the economy following the difficulties caused by the collapse of international copper prices, the country's leading export. According to a 1984 assessment, in the short time since the unit was created, it proved invaluable in instituting policy reforms and it clearly satisfied the long-felt need for a high-level body capable of policy analysis and generating information for quick decision-making.[19]

A number of African countries have, of course, consistently displayed institutional capacity at this level. Botswana, frequently cited as a laudable example of the 'insulation' of bureaucratic institutions and processes and, consequently, of effective development management in Africa south of the Sahara is a case in point. Policy analysis and co-ordination is carried out under the auspices of the Ministry of Finance and Development Planning (which has also been headed by the Vice-President since independence). As the nerve centre of policy development in the government, the ministry acts as a channel of information to the Economic Committee of the cabinet which is the government's decision-making body on development matters.[20]

North of the Sahara, the *Conseil Supérieur de la Promotion Nationale et du Plan* in Morocco brings together staff of various central agencies and ministries not only to facilitate policy development but, in co-operation with the Royal Cabinet (the King's advisers and executive office), the Office of the Prime Minister and the secretariat of the council of ministers, to process information for decision-making by the King and his ministers.[21]

These examples are part of a trend of improving co-ordination and analytical capacity to facilitate more flexible and innovative responses by African governments. The reorientation of central agencies is complemented by new approaches to macro-economic management.

Changing Approaches to Macro-economic Management
The macro-economic framework is composed of a series of interrelated policies that affect all aspects of economic behaviour. The main instruments are fiscal, monetary, exchange rate, credit, wage, price and trade policies which, in combination and along with exogenous factors, help to determine the rate of domestic inflation, the rate and pattern of capital accumulation, resource mobilization and utilization, the amount of foreign exchange earnings, foreign borrowing, the balance-of-payments position and, ultimately, the pace of economic activity and growth.

A central element of neoclassical economic management are policy measures that allow prices in an economy (especially of foreign exchange, credit, labour, infrastructure services including energy and power) to reflect relative scarcity. A strong correlation is presumed to exist between 'getting prices right' and growth.[22] If 'getting prices right' (and conversely, avoiding price 'distortions') in an economy is ultimately a matter of qualitative judgement, the analytical capacity of central agencies to monitor the impact of macro-economic measures and international trends on prices and markets and facilitate necessary adjustments is crucial.[23]

Before the onset of the new mood of realism, this approach to development management was de-emphasized by African regimes which emphasized instead a 'plan of action' of some sort. Many African governments are now in their fifth or sixth planning cycles since independence; for example, Kenya's current (1984–1988) plan is its fifth. But, over the years, experience has revealed the inherent limitations of a comprehensive plan in rapidly changing environments and markets. Available analytical techniques are just not able to cope with the complexities of economic change to produce plans that are up-to-date, relevant and comprehensive.[24]

The limitations of planning as the mechanism of establishing the macro-economic framework became particularly evident during the recession of 1974–1976. It was around this time that analysts identified a 'crisis in planning'[25] with implications of too much emphasis on the plan and not enough on its implementation; over-emphasis on the medium-term; excessive rigidity; and differences in perspective and inadequate communication between politicians, planners and administrators.[26] To be sure, there are pragmatic means of coping with the difficulties. To the extent that a government cannot effect public policy without spending money, and to the extent that the national budget not only encompasses expectations of macro-economic performance but is also the main instrument of public expenditure, the integration of budgeting and the objectives, programmes or projects incorporated in the development plan has long been recognized as crucially important.[27] In addition, the adoption of some variant of performance budgeting by many African countries has led to tighter co-ordination of the linkages between planning and budgeting. Such reforms while compatible with neoclassical strategies do not, however, go far enough in redressing the fundamental problems of macro-economic management in changing environments: how should fiscal, monetary, exchange rate, credit, wages and incomes, price and tariff policies be adjusted in response to change – and this is the perennial conundrum – within the bounds of political feasibility and public policy objectives such as the reduction of inequalities and regional disparities in a country?

Since there are no definitive answers (analytical techniques notoriously fail to provide optimal solutions), political judgements have to be made. But, in de-emphasizing planning and utilizing a problem solving/ policy analysis approach, African governments are beginning to follow the example of the developed market countries and NICs. It has been stressed that this approach requires analytical capability and capacity in central agencies to make the information that is generated intelligible, and a commitment at the highest level of political executives to facilitate necessary adjustments. Institutional arrangements in Zambia, Botswana and Morocco, which have been identified, are a reflection of this requirement.

The problem-solving/policy analysis approach does not imply that planning is redundant. Governments must perforce rely on medium- and long-term forecasting to clarify the priorities of public expenditure and investment, and to give guidance to the private sector. Variables such as GDP, savings, investment, public revenues and expenditures, export, import, capital inflows and outflows, and so on, need to be projected to provide an informed basis for decision-making. And, as regards the main economic sectors, forecasts in such areas as power, energy and transport are vital. Hence, the problem-solving/policy analysis approach does have a need for the programming of public investment and forecasting; it does not, however, leave the policy instruments and options of governments 'frozen' in an environment and markets characterized by change. Moreover, as the evidence from the NICs suggest, this approach also facilitates innovation, a consideration that is especially relevant to the context of limited room of manoeuvre and constraints in African development management.

CONCLUSION

As suggested above, it is by no means superfluous to assert that a claim to statehood in today's world is also a claim to have the bureaucratic capacity to manage effectively and efficiently economic or development objectives. The priority being given by African governments to development management reform is as much an ingredient of the new mood of realism as it is a response to the imperatives of neoclassical economic strategies on the proper role of government that have become a world-wide orthodoxy. The reforms and World Bank/IMF adjustment programmes have a number of interesting implications.

The African post-colonial state is seen as overdeveloped because it has not fully drawn in various economic and social activities within the territory over which it claims sovereignty. It is against this background that personal rule – and an underlying political culture of ambivalence toward a consciousness and concept of public purpose and the propriety of bureaucratic institutions and processes – has emerged as the most common mode of governance. The insertion of neoclassical strategies (the inherent logic of which is to draw in economic activities outside the scope of the state) into this context will enhance the process of state formation and the rationality of bureaucratic institutions; but not necessarily political accountability or popular consent. It was to the economic logic of neoclassicism, its demonstrated effect in the NICs and its impact on international trends that the *African Submission* 'submitted'.

NOTES

1. OAU/UN–ECA, *Africa's Submission to the Special Session of the United Nations General Assembly on Africa's Economic and Social Crisis*, Addis Ababa, 1986, p.2.
2. *Ibid.*, pp.2–3.
3. For a further note on this mood, cf. David F. Luke, 'Development strategies: a new realism' in Group of 78, *Canada and Africa: Common Cause*, Ottawa, 1986.
4. The timing of the World Bank in designating 1986–1987 'a year of opportunity' was excellent. Cf. World Bank, *Financing Adjustment with Growth in sub-Saharan Africa 1986–1990*, Washington DC, 1986.
5. Cf., for example, Robert Jackson and Carl Rosberg, *Personal Rule in Black Africa: Prince, Autocrat, Prophet, Tyrant*, Los Angeles, 1982; Goran Hyden, *No Shortcuts to Progress: African Development Management in Perspective*, Los Angeles, 1983; Richard Sandbrook, *The Politics of Africa's Economic Stagnation*, Cambridge (UK), 1985; and Patrick Chabal ed., *Political Domination in Africa: Reflections on the Limits of Power*, Cambridge (UK), 1986.
6. Cf., Max Weber, *Economy and Society* (vol. 1), Los Angeles, 1978, p.56.
7. Cf., Anthony Giddens, *A Contemporary Critique of Historical Materialism* (vol. 2), Los Angeles, 1985, for a useful discussion of the Social Science of the modern state.
8. For a case-study, cf., David F. Luke, *Labour and Parastatal Politics in Sierra Leone: A Study of African Working-Class Ambivalence*, Washington DC, 1984.
9. This is recognized by the authors cited in note No. 5 above; but the theme is perhaps best developed in Crawford Young, *Ideology and Development in Africa*, New Haven, 1982.
10. The best analysis of these changes is probably Nigel Harris, *The End of the Third World: Newly Industrializing Countries and the Decline of an Ideology*, Harmondsworth (UK), 1986. But see also Chad Leechor *et al*, *Structural Changes in World Industry: A Quantitative Analysis of Recent Developments*, Washington DC (World Bank Technical Paper, Industry and Finance Series) 1983.
11. Cf., For example, Bela Balassa, *Policy Reform in Developing Countries*, Oxford (UK), 1977; Bruce Cummings, 'The origins and development of Northeast Asian political economy', *International Organization* 38 (winter), 1978, pp.1–14; Chalmers Johnson, *MITI and the Japanese Miracle*, Stanford (US), 1982; Miyohei Shinohara *et al*, *The Japanese and Korean Experiences in Managing Development*, Washington DC (World Bank Staff Working Papers No. 574, Management and

Development Series) 1983; and Yung Whee Rhee *et al*, *Managing Entry into World Markets*, Baltimore, 1984.

12. Harris, *The End of the Third World, Op.cit.*, p.155.
13. Cf., for example, G. Lehmbruch and P.C. Schmitter eds., *Patterns of Corporatist Policy-Making*, Los Angeles, 1982; John Goldthorpe ed., *Order and Conflict in Contemporary Capitalism: Studies in the Political Economy of Western European Nations*, Oxford (UK), 1984; P.J. Katzenstein, *Small States in World Markets: Industrial Policy in Europe*, Ithaca (US), 1985; and John Whalley ed., *Domestic Policies and the International Economic Environment*, Toronto, 1985. For liberalizing trends in centrally planned economies, cf., for example, Peter Knight, *Economic Reform in Socialist Countries: The Experiences of China, Hungary, Romania and Yugoslavia*, Washington DC (World Bank Staff Working papers No. 579, Management and Development Series) 1983.
14. Harris, *The End of the Third World, op.cit.*, pp.28–29.
15. *The African Submission*, pp.23–24.
16. Overseas Development Council (of the US), 'Should the IMF withdraw from Africa?', *Policy Focus* No. 1 1987, p.6.
17. For a more detailed survey, cf. David F. Luke, *African Development Management Reform*, forthcoming.
18. Cf. World Bank, *Financing Adjustment with Growth*.
19. Cf. World Bank, *Zambia: Country Economic Memorandum: Issues and Options for Economic Diversification* (a restricted access report), Washington DC, 1984, pp.23–34.
20. Cf. Nimrod Raphaeli *et al*, *Public Sector Management in Botswana: Lessons in Pragmatism*, Washington DC (World Bank Staff Working Papers No. 709), 1984, pp.18–20.
21. Cf. World Bank, *Morocco: Economic and Social Development Report*, Washington DC, 1981.
22. Cf. Ramgopal Agarwala, *Price Distortions and Growth in Developing Countries*, Washington DC (World Bank Staff Working Papers No. 575, Management and Development Series) 1983; and World Bank, *World Development Report 1983*, New York, 1983, pp.57–63.
23. On this issue cf. Bela Balassa, *Policy Reform in Developing Countries*.
24. For a review of the planning experience of developing countries, cf. Ramgopal Argawala, *Planning in Developing Countries: Lessons of Experience*, Washington DC (World Bank Staff Working Papers No. 576, Management and Development Series), 1983.
25. Cf. Michael Faber and Dudley Seers eds., *The Crisis in Planning* (two vols.), London, 1972.
26. For a good review of these problems, cf. Diana Conyers and Peter Hills, *An Introduction to Development Planning in the Third World*, Chichester (UK), 1984.
27. Cf., for example, Albert Waterston, *Development Planning: Lessons of Experience*, Baltimore, 1965; Naomi Caiden and Aaron Wildavsky, *Planning and Budgeting in Poor Countries*, New York, 1974; and United Nations, *Development Administration: Current Approaches and Trends in Public Administration for National Development*, New York, 1975.

CHAPTER SEVENTEEN

The Scientific and Technological Environment for African Economic Recovery and Development

THOMAS R. ODHIAMBO

INTRODUCTION

The state of the economy and well-being of Africa is a matter of grave concern. The Lagos Plan of Action for the Economic Development of Africa, 1980–2000, which was rolled out in April 1980 with so much enthusiasm and promise, has remained a documentary monument for consensus building among a diverse regional grouping of Heads of State and Government, but has produced little tangible impetus for economic growth and sustainable development. The great drought and famine of 1982–1985, which pervaded much of sub-Saharan Africa, galvanized Africa and the world as to this cyclical catastrophe, and led the African leadership to agonize as to what to do to stem the tide of disaster facing the continent and thus make Africa part of the rest of the prospering world. As someone said not so long ago, 'so long as the daily bread is a daily victory there will be enough incentive left to survive'.

It is in this light that one has to view the African economic summit meeting held in Addis Ababa in July 1985, during which the Heads of State and Government of OAU expressed their grave concern for 'the continuing deterioration of our economies which have been severely affected by the deep world economic recession and penalized by an unjust and inequitable international economic system'. They observed that the deterioration of economic performance had been aggravated by severe drought and persistent food deficits; and that they had come to realize that domestic policy shortcomings had played a major role in this development crisis. The Declaration of this economic summit meeting, which has become known as APPER, made at least two far-reaching decisions. First, it reaffirmed that the development of Africa is the primary responsibility of the governments and peoples of Africa – a revealing commitment in the face of the profound dependency of today's African economies on former metropolitan and other dominant economies. Second, the summit committed itself, during the five-year period 1986–1990, to a priority programme which would pave the way to self-sustained economic growth and social development. The three critical measures in this priority programme consist of: measures for an accelerated implementation of LPA; 'special action for the improvement of the food situation and the rehabilitation of agricultural development in Africa'; and measures for resolving Africa's increasing debt burden. The two seminal decisions are an important start in re-directing Africa's strategies for initiating a programme of action which could lead to sustainable development.

The greatest disappointment one derives from an examination of APPER is its un-targeted and anaemic science and technology policy. Sure, the document starts the section on 'Science and Technology' with a firm statement of fact: 'Experience indicates that no country has attained any breakthrough in its economic development without the development of minimum science and technology base'. But then it goes on to suggest measures for implementing a science and technology strategy which fall far short of the measures that could bring about a development transformation of the continent. The core of the medium-term and long-range measures that were proposed by the summit consist of establishing 'national mechanisms and institutions ... to promote the translation of Research and Development results into commercial operations'. While a few areas of critical importance to national development have existing technology which is implementable, and while a few other areas need only adaptive research and development effort to package them into usable new technology, in the vast majority of critical issues related to the tropical environment – such as agricultural and other biological resources, tropical health, and tropical climate – we have a dearth of basic knowledge which could lead to the design of new technology to exploit them on a sustainable basis.

Let us take the example of tropical agriculture. Modern agriculture is the climax of an evolutionary process over the last century or so of Research and Development (R & D) effort under temperate climate and ecology. This has resulted in a highly productive agricultural production system – knowledge-intensive, highly mechanized, and requiring high inputs. This approach has been extended to tropical and sub-tropical areas, of fertile land and uniform conditions and where stable conditions for growing rice and wheat exist, leading to the phenomenon of the Green Revolution. But serious questions have recently been raised whether it can lead to sustainable production systems: indeed, questions are being raised in the temperate regions whether the practice of 'industrialized agriculture' is not leading to the death of soil, the death of forests and, indeed, the death of inland waters. In any event, this approach – which presumes a monocrop production system under irrigation or other stable water regimes – cannot work in tropical African conditions where mixed cropping is the prevalent practice, and where the agronomic conditions are so varied.

As I had occasion to state five years ago, at an International Conference on Chemistry and World Food Supplies held in Manila, a great deal of R & D is needed to lay down a knowledge base required to design the basic technologies needed to accomplish sustainable food production under the more difficult tropical regimes in the humid zones and the semi-arid marginal areas:[1]

> The biological factors of the environment are a constant challenge to crop production, particularly so in the humid tropics. As production intensifies, the problems in this area become more acute. Thus, there are serious disease and insect problems in the humid tropics. Yet, our present technology cannot reduce these constraints sufficiently and on a long-range basis. Indeed, our present perception is that we do not posses an adequate knowledge base to utilize effectively the seemingly abundant resources and opportunities in the tropics on a sustainable basis ... Our knowledge base appears even thinner when we consider marginal lands, where ecological constraints become evidently paramount, and where close to one billion people live out a poor and unfulfilled existence. Major advances in scientific discoveries and crop production have been carried out in the fertile, better endowed lands; this encompasses the areas first swept by the Green Revolution. On the other hand, the new challenge must be to make the marginal lands bloom. Since marginal lands are far more extensive than the fertile ones, even a modest upward swing in crop yields would make a significant dent in the food deficit situation ... The challenge here is a much more difficult task than faced us prior to the Green Revolution.

Science has a vital role to play in priming the pump that would feed the knowledge watershed from which problem-solving technology could be developed and fine-tuned to tackle the specific problems of tropical agriculture (or, for that matter, other technology-oriented African tropical problems). African leaders can no longer afford to deny the vital role of science and technology in national development – just as it has become manifestly evident that science and technology has become a prime mover in the accelerated development of the newly industrialized countries of South Korea, Taiwan, India and Brazil. As Morris Cohen once said, science is a flickering light in our darkness, it is but the only one we have and woe to him who would put it out.

SCIENCE AS PART OF THE AFRICAN SOCIAL MILIEU

A dangerous myth that has developed among twentieth-century Africans is that science is divorced from their culture. But if culture is understood to mean 'how people structure their experience conceptually so that it can be transmitted as knowledge from person to person and from generation to generation',[2] then natural science has always been an integral part of the African traditional culture – except for its disruption as a result of the colonial imposition of a different perception.

Thus, we are at home when Ritter (1955) describes the education of the pre-adolescent Zulu youth during the time of the King Shaka Zulu in South Africa:[3]

> During the adolescent growing up period, the thorough study of nature was quietly proceeding, and a large amount of nature knowledge being gradually accumulated. The small girls, by minding babies, were learning human anatomy, and the care of children; and domestic art and science, equal to their needs, alongside their mothers in the home and on the field. Out on the veld the boys were busy studying the nature of plant and tree, the habits of insects, the peculiarities of rocks, and could soon interpret the meaning of the winds and clouds and mists; and could give the name of the grasses and the medicinal uses of many trees and herbs; could describe the qualities of the different kinds of wood, the shapes of the different types of leaf, and explain the bodily structure of insect, bird and beast within their little world. Thus, through the ages this admirable system of forming character and imparting knowledge continued, until at length was evolved a Zulu race noble of heart, dignified of bearing, with refined manner, and learned in natural science-qualities, alas! rapidly corrupted or destroyed by the advance of European civilization.

What is important to remind ourselves here is that scientific enquiry leads to two types of results; one is knowledge, the other is products (in other words, technology). Whereas the Egyptians and Greeks emphasized pure knowledge derived from scientific research or enquiry (astronomy, cosmology, etc), their successors (the Romans and, much later, the latter-day Europeans) have emphasized technological products (transport vehicles, power-generating equipment, monuments, etc.).

We are therefore witnessing an unfortunate perception which seems to equate science wholly with technology. Because Africans have left few monuments during their long succession of civilizations from the pharaonic times to those of ancient Zimbabwe, it has often been assumed that they had no science, and their cultures have even been labelled as pre-scientific:[2]

> The western cultures are focused on the visually conspicuous, the moving images, the monumental material manifestations. We have arrived at a stage where we conceive the present as the apex of human achievement. We conceive the world as a world of skyscrapers, staggering bridge spans, giant dams, moonflights and supertankers ... Little by little, we have come to believe that civilization is synonymous with stone monuments or other material manifestations.

Twentieth-century Africans should begin once more to investigate nature, to listen to what nature promises, and then we shall know how to work with it so as to achieve sustainability in our development goals. A Russian proverb says it very well: 'don't hurry to reply, hurry to listen'.

MOBILIZATION OF SCIENCE FOR AFRICA'S DEVELOPMENT

A country's greatest resource is its people – educated people, trained people, innovative people, entrepreneurs in all walks of life. A key factor in economic growth is innovation; and the over-arching element in innovation is research (technological, social, marketing). But one needs to be cautious how one uses the technological resources emerging as a result of research. They must be moulded according to the social needs of the society to which they are targetted, if such technology would have a lasting beneficial effect on human well-being, otherwise 'technology and the technocratic outlook are somewhat like hammers and the "law of the hammer": give a child a hammer and it will discover that everything needs pounding ... We need the hammer but not the impulse to over-use it'.[4]

We have, by far, the fewest R & D scientists and engineers compared to any other region of the world. While Africa (excluding Arab States) in 1978 had 53 scientists and engineers per one million inhabitants, Asia (excluding Japan) had 99, Arab States had 202, Latin America (including the Caribbean) had 209, and Europe had 1,632. The comparable figures for the US, Japan, and the Soviet Union were 2,685; 3,548; and 5,024 respectively.[5] Because of the minuscule size of the African scientific community in relation to the enormous agenda for science-driven development in their continent of birth, the African people and their leaders should cultivate their few R & D scientists and engineers, challenge them with worthwhile tasks, establish and nurture an intellectual environment that encourages creativity, provide incentives that they cannot refuse, and honour them. This must be a conscious, definitive political decision. The newly industrializing nations made such a profound decision two or three decades ago; and all the powerful industrialized nations in the North made them long ago – and remind themselves of this commitment time and again. As a leading American industrial mogul recently stated:[6]

> Honor thy inventors and innovators – sweep their path free of even small obstructions instead of throwing up roadblocks that diminish their contributions. Without the creativity of our scientists and technologists we will grow weak in every way ... we will be a helpless giant.

The resources made available to African R & D scientists and engineers are presently meagre, in relation to the monumental development agenda they have to grapple with. Firstly, while Africa (as well as Asia, exclusive of Japan) spends less than $US1.00 on R & D per head of inhabitants, Latin America spends approximately $US5, and the US spends a massive $US200 per head.[5] As a result, Africa makes precious little inroads into the market for the production of goods and services which are technology-intensive. For instance, and in terms of crude indicators, the developing regions account for only 2.8 to 3.2 per cent of world exports of technology-intensive goods; similarly, only 4.6 to 5.5 per cent of imports of machinery and transport equipment arises from South–South trade, whereas 90 per cent come from industrialized countries.[7] Secondly, the African scientists and technologists need a vibrant and responsive communication system – through the formal and peer-reviewed scientific journal; through the informal channels of the scientific conference corridors, letter writing, and the evening discourse; and through regular visits to other laboratories of excellence. However well endowed and equipped a research centre is, it will never produce important work in isolation. The nature of science is that it only grows when unfettered and where scientists can communicate their ideas easily and let them grow in their minds as they plan their next experiments. The national boundaries between African states must therefore be made more porous to visiting scientists; and African scientists must be enabled to travel and communicate with their peers in Africa and other lands:

> An outsider watching a scientist at work will be amazed to discover that the scientist spends most of his time apparently engaged in idle chatter, drinking cups of coffee. But this is the hub of his work. The gathering of information and the exchange of ideas are the essential preconditions for research.[5]

Thirdly, the African scientist and technologist needs time. He needs it as a resource; and he desperately needs the political leadership to understand that the time perspective required for most worthwhile R & D effort to be turned into usable technologies is from 10 to 15 years, even in the agricultural field:[8]

> Research takes time. This is sometimes overlooked by those who are not actively involved in the process or merely dealing with the disbursement of donor funds. Furthermore, research for rural development is multi-dimensional, constituting only one component which is highly biological in nature. Dependent on the type of research, the time framework may last from several decades in basic and strategic research. This may also apply in the development of new technology, for instance new crop cultivars that do not lodge if fertilized. Above all, such applied research is a continuous process which also characterizes the more short-termed adaptive research that is supposed to adjust the new technology to a specific environment. With the addition of time for adoption of new technology, the total process covers a significant period. This has an important implication, namely, the need for a research policy that recognizes the complexity of the problem area and the societal consequences of a certain approach.

What are the prospects for Africa if all these resources are made available to the continent's scientists and technologists?

PROSPECTS FOR SUSTAINABLE DEVELOPMENT

We believe that Africa must design its development policy on the basis of those policies and practices that will lead to sustainable development within a contextual framework that provides for material comfort, moral-ethical well-being, and psychic peace. We cannot predict the future in absolute terms; but we can certainly avoid drifting into a sense of unfulfilled promise that has been painted for the contemporary Western technocratic civilization in such sombre terms by Gabor (1963):[9]

> Science has never quite given man what he desired, not even applied science. Man dreamt of wings; science gave him an easy chair which flies through the air. Man wanted to see things invisible and far; he got television and can look inside a studio. He wanted the transmutation of the base metals into gold, to acquire fabulous riches; he can now be happy if he himself is not transmuted into radioactive gases.

But others, probably more of them than the technocracy doubters, do not agree. They see science and technology opening doors, giving us the probability space for considering other more positive development scenarios; and they affirm definitely that there is no way back to pre-science or non-science days. As Read (1979) states:[6]

> Science and technology have brought us this far. Science and technology must take us the rest of the way or we will all fall back into some nether place of lost dreams and unused opportunity, where the prime pastime will be deciding who was responsible for the Fall.

Consequently, the important question is not what science and technology can do, but how this can be done – and in what way social invention can enlarge the prospects for sustainable well-being in Africa.

NOTES

1. Odhiambo, T.R. 'Biological constraints on food production and on the level and efficient use of chemical inputs', in G. Bixler and L.W. Shemitt eds., *Chemistry and World Food Supplies: The New Frontiers*, Manila: International Rice Research Institute and International Union of Pure and Applied Chemistry, 1983, pp.65–88.
2. Fuglesang, A. *About Understanding – Ideas and Observations on Cross-cultural Communication*. Uppsala: Dag Hammarskjold Foundation (1982).
3. Ritter, E.A. *Shaka Zulu*, London: Longmans (1955).
4. Jackson, M.W. 'Science and Depoliticization', in J. Richardson ed., *Integrated Technology Transfer*, Mt. Airy (Maryland): Lomond Books, 1979, pp.141–149.
5. Clarke, R. *Science and Technology in World Development*, Oxford: Oxford University Press and UNESCO (1987).
6. Read, S.K. 'Food and nutrition', in H.I. Fusfed and C.S. Haklisch eds., *Technology Policy: Perspectives for the 1980s*, New York: New York Academy of Sciences

(1979), pp.71–79.

7. United Nations Industrial Organization, *Industry 2000 – New Perspectives*. New York: United Nations (1979).

8. Bengtsson, B.M.I. *Rural Development Research and Agricultural Innovations*, Report 115. Uppsala: Swedish University of Agricultural Sciences (1983).

9. Gabor, D. *Inventing the Future*. London: Secker & Warburg (1963).

CHAPTER EIGHTEEN

The Scientific and Technological Perspective for African Economic Recovery and Development, With Particular Emphasis on Environmental Aspects

MANSOUR KHALID

INTRODUCTION

In the past, lack of imaginative insights into the complexities of development as an interrelationship between people, resources and environment, coupled with undeterred rummaging around discredited economic models, brought the continent to the verge of disaster. Even failure did not instil in some of our policy makers and economists an element of humility, and dismal results are glaringly before us. Those economic policies that did not take account of Africa's social bio-chemistry, the needs of its most marginalized people, and the charac-teristics and limitations of its eco-system were not only limited in their vision, they were also wrong-headed in their approach. From among those interrelated issues, this Chapter deals with the scientific and technological perspectives emphasizing, in particular, the environ-mental aspects.

Awareness among African policy-makers of the importance to development of science and technology application and environmental protection has increasingly sharpened since the 1970s. The place reserved by LPA for the application of science and technology to development is unparalleled in any other regional development plan. Not only is the chapter on science and technology application the largest and most elaborate chapter of that Plan, references to science and technology application abound in all the sectoral chapters.

On the other hand, consciousness of environmental degradation, particularly following the shuddering agonies caused by the drought of the 1970s, made environment a recurring theme in nearly all African development plans. It took us such agonies to realize, at least intellectually, the fallacy of the stultifying misconception about the marginality of environment in the development process.

But while there was a professed realization of the importance to development of both science and technology and environmental protection, the realization was seldom translated into action. Both issues were abundantly intellectualized but scarcely, if ever, internalized. Chapters on science and technology continue to appear in the preambular parts and normative sections of development plans, only to disappear in the operative sections of those plans. Programmes rarely provide for tools of implementation or elaborate policies for the choice, management, and control of scientific and technological application to development.

A similar situation obtains with regard to the environment. Environmental protection agencies were created in many countries, but rarely armed with the tools of action or empowered to influence decisions on fundamental issues pertaining to the environment. They were, in effect, fashionable adjuncts, out of touch with the institutions that really run the economy and often are also the ones responsible for environmental damage.

Economic policy-makers failed to appreciate fully the interlocking nature of science and technology environment and development in their wider social, cultural and human dimensions. To traditional economists, these links were marginal because they failed the cost and benefit test, in the limited pecuniary sense. Thus, science and technology application to development was only seen as one of several alternatives, weighed in terms of labour and capital intensity available to produce a given product in a more efficient and 'economic' way. It was never recognized as an all-embracing process that affects people's cultural traits and attitudes as well as public institutions and the natural environment.

Equally, environmental issues were viewed as 'externalities', since they have no monetary expression and were not subject to market transactions. This assumption is half-fraudulent if not outright false: economists never account for environmental degradation in figuring the costs of production, nor do they account for the way in which this degradation imperils the potential for future development.

It was precisely because of this yawning gap in perception (not only in Africa) that the UN General Assembly sought to create in the autumn of 1983 a Special Commission, later known as the World Commission on Environment and Development (WCED), to recommend long-term environmental strategies that would take into account the inter-relationships between people, resources, environment and development. This long-term strategy, focused on the year 2000, was to be translated into greater co-operation among developing countries and between countries at different stages of economic and social development leading to the achievement of mutually supportive objectives.

The Commission, in its wisdom, adopted a wider and more liberal interpretation of this mandate for, according to its report, 'the environment does not exist as a sphere separate from human action, ambitions and needs, and attempts to define it in isolation from human concerns have given the very word "environmental" a connotation of naivity in some political circles.'[1]

This is the context within which this Chapter aims at approaching the subject of science and technology in Africa. Inescapably, references are made, here and there, to external and internal economic factors that have a direct or indirect impact on the environment. Those factors shall certainly be dealt with more elaborately in other chapters. However, reference to them, in this Chapter, is necessary if the issue is to be seen within its wider perspective.

SCIENCE AND TECHNOLOGY INTERRELATIONSHIP WITH SUSTAINABLE DEVELOPMENT

Sustainable Development: The Environmental Perspectives

Environmental protection is a function of sustainable development. Sustainability means the capacity to continuously grow, and there are no limits to growth except those imposed by the dialectic laws of nature. In other words, growth cannot be achieved without first identifying the conditions required by the eco-system to endure without giving way.

The idea of sustainability was for some time associated with the growth paradigm, and therefore with a purely economic idea of a continuous investment process that permits the economy to permanently expand. But such a model of growth loses sight of the supply of global resources compared to the growing demand on them by population pressures, higher living standards and the unmet aspirations of newcomers. Emphasis on the acceleration and diversification of material consumption has inevitably put nature under stress; in Africa, the tolerance of the natural system has reached a critical threshold. Sustainable development is only possible if ecological boundaries are not transgressed.

401

WCED has defined sustainable development as a development that meets the needs of the present without compromising the ability of future generations to meet their own needs. This definition contains within it two key concepts:

(a) The concept of 'needs', in particular the essential needs of the poor, to which overriding priority should be given; and,
(b) The concept of limitations to be imposed on patterns of growth, lifestyles, and social organization that curtail the environment's ability to meet present and future needs.

The WCED report noted that the satisfaction of human needs and aspirations is the major objective of development:

> The essential needs of vast numbers of people in developing countries – for food, clothing, shelter, jobs – are not being met, and beyond their basic needs people have legitimate aspirations for an improved quality of life. A world in which poverty and inequity are endemic will always be prone to ecological and other crises... Growth by itself is not enough. High levels of productive activity and widespread poverty can co-exist, and can endanger the environment. Hence sustainable development requires that societies meet human needs both by increasing productive potential and by ensuring equitable opportunities for all.[2]

When the World Conference on the Human Environment met in Stockholm in 1972, it largely reflected the environmental concerns of the industrialized countries. Greater emphasis was then placed on the need to promulgate laws and to design instruments to deal with environmental problems peculiar to countries that are at a particular stage of development. The real environmental problems of developing countries were only considered to the extent that they were also having an impact on developed countries or because their magnitude was such that concern about them was worldwide in character.

For example, the developed countries were focusing mostly on interdependent environmental phenomena, like air and water pollution, and the movement of hazardous wastes. Though such issues impact on developing countries too, the most urgent environmental problems preoccupying them were rapid deforestation, soil erosion, desertification and the destruction of biological diversity.

The most critical African problems were hardly discussed at Stockholm. The most serious and daunting of those problems is desertification. Albeit a global phenomenon, it was most destructive to Africa, with the Sudano-Sahelian zone suffering the most. Countries in this zone are entirely located in arid and semi-arid regions and shall continue to suffer; indeed they are threatened with extinction, following the pattern of ancient civilizations whose economic base was destroyed, if action is not taken. Within the last 50 years, 65 million hectares of once productive lands became desert, and the process is continuing.

Solutions to this problem were not wanting. As early as 1977, the United Nations Environment Programme Plan of Action to Combat Desertification provided both the description and the prescription for both the global problem and the African one. The Plan is based on a set of 28 interrelated recommendations, including (as far as Africa is concerned) the creation of a green belt both north of the Sahara and south of it, from the Atlantic to the Red Sea, and the exploitation of major aquifers in North East Africa. The implementation of that Plan is yet to materialize. For lack of the needed funds, the Plan stands as a testimony to the cynical neglect by the international community in the face of a crisis of such mighty dimensions, a crisis of survival.

The African famine was, in large part, due to this environmental degradation. Famine is not just an African phenomenon nor should it be an inevitability. Great famines of the past occurred in Asia and many African countries were then cited as examples of countries that were able to feed themselves. Today, the situation has changed dramatically. China, India, and Thailand, which once suffered from famine, have become cereal exporters. The experience of these countries, where population was also growing at impressive rates, explodes the stubborn myth that famines are the inevitable result of a crude relationship between rapid population growth and a limited 'natural' carrying capacity of the land.

Survival issues of this magnitude cannot be faced by one country alone, or even by a group of countries: they require an international solution. The inadequacies of present responses convinced WCED that a return to multilateralism is now urgent: 'The challenge of reconstruction after the Second World War was the real motivating power behind the establishment of our post-war economic system. The challenge of finding sustainable development patterns ought to provide the impetus – indeed the imperative – for a renewed search for multilateral solutions and a restructured economic system of co-operation.'[3]

The African famine is a result of an interplay of internal and external factors. The external factors, for which Africa is blameless, are rooted in past colonial legacies, current patterns of international trade and the way African economies are inverted in the international market. More than 60 per cent of African countries' export earnings comes from cash crops and minerals whose prices have been progressively declining while those of manufactured goods soared. Failure to reach international commodity agreements, indeed to negotiate them, has left the African countries in the cruel grip of the international commodity market. And whatever some ideologues may say about the magic of the market-place and the virtues of free trade, global commerce in those commodities is virtually monopolized by three to six corporations, according to UNCTAD: 85–90 per cent in coffee, 85 per cent in cocoa, 90 per cent in forest products, 85–90 per cent in cotton, 60 per cent in sugar, 80 per cent in tea, 70 per cent in bananas, 90 per cent in pineapples, 80–85 per cent in copper, 50–60 per cent in phosphate, and 80–85 per cent in bauxite. This is hardly free trade.

As a result of internationally-imposed unfavourable economic terms, Africa lost more than 20 per cent of the purchasing power of its exports between 1973 and 1983. The ensuing decline in the GNP forced African countries to turn to the international money market, only to be saddled with heavy debt burdens. Debts grew at an annual rate of 22 per cent during the 1970s reaching, by the middle of 1986, about $US70 billion – and this only in sub-Saharan Africa. Though the African debt is dwarfed beside the Latin American one, its impact is more ruinous in terms of human suffering and economic pressure. Annual debt repayments represent between 40 to 100 per cent of foreign exchange earnings in the 1980s. Sudan, for example, would have had to pay 100 per cent of its export earnings in 1985 were it not for debt rescheduling.

Paradoxically, while the impact of the African debt on people and the economy is so devastating, more considerate attention is being paid by the international money market to the Latin American countries, not out of kindness, but because the impact of their debts on the Western banking system is greater. This lack of concern is reflected in the progressive decrease of private capital flow to Africa from the international money market. So, while there was a net inflow of about $US2 billion in 1980 from private creditors; by 1985, Africa became a net loser of $US700 million because of debt repayments, dwindling capital investments and decline in export earnings.

However, there is a mounting awareness of the plight of Africa. For example, the OECD Ministerial Conference meeting in Paris in May 1987 considered ways and means of alleviating the African debt burden, 80 per cent of which originates in Western countries. According to the plan emerging from that Conference, the remaining government loans are to be converted into grants and repayment of officially guaranteed export credits are to be rescheduled for repayment within 20 years with an 11-year period of grace. But, on the thorny issue of interests accumulating on these debts, the OECD countries were divided, with the United Kingdom, Italy, France and Canada pleading for excusing Africa from paying these interests, while the US and Germany disagreed to avoid setting a precedent for other regions.

Another recent action which reflects this awareness is the decision by Citicorp to boost its loan loss reserve by $US3 billion (from 2 to 5 billion US dollars) in view of the inability of Third World debtors to meet repayment schedules, sometimes even after restructuring. This landmark decision will have a profound impact on the US and probably the whole Western banking community. For years, private banks have maintained that restructuring of Third World debts should not impose losses on them and that debtors should be approached on a case by case basis. The decision by Citicorp, whose Third World debts amount to $US15 billion, is in effect reducing the value of its debts by one quarter and making it difficult for other banks to pretend that the world banking community is not responsible for finding ways and means of resolving the problem of Third World debt. On the other hand, the decision shall also impact on the issue of interests since its real meaning is that the true value of Citicorp debts is below their book value of 3 billion US dollars. Debtors, certainly, will not miss the opportunity to claim that interest repayment be scaled down accordingly.

While one appreciates all those efforts, Africa's economic crisis remains a deep one. UN-PAAERD and the Declaration of African Ministers Responsible for Trade and Development Preparatory to UNCTAD VII have all the ingredients of the action needed by the international community to help Africa overcome its pressing economic problems. To these, WCED has added its voice: 'The vast misery brought on by the drought in Africa is now generally acknowledged, and the world community has responded with substantial emergency programmes. But emergency food aid is only a short-term reaction and, at best, a partial answer. The roots of the problem lie in national and international policies that have so far prevented African economies from realizing their full potential for economic expansion and thus for erasing poverty and the environmental pressures that it generates.'[4]

The internal problems, on the other hand, are no less important, if only because Africans have themselves to blame for them. And if some of us feel that Africa has weathered the worst because of emergency aid or debt rescheduling, they may be grossly mistaken. We still need to gaze inwards into regional disparities and distribution of power and influence within the society. Those regional and class disparities increase social tension which is the antithesis of sustainability. There is an inverse relationship between what African plans say about equity and social justice, and what policy-makers do to achieve them. Those plans will count for nothing if they are not coupled with the political will to change course.

Science and Technology Response to and Role in Sustainable Development

Socio-economic development depends on the transformation and exploitation of the natural system by society. One of the most powerful social instruments for the utilization of nature and fostering development is science and technology. Nowadays, the major global issues are at the interface of social and natural systems and are characterized by a strong scientific and technological dimension. But science and technology cannot be developed in a vacuum, they are not a realm of their own. They are the link between humans and nature. And, to make them more responsive to sustainable development, they have to have a new orientation, particularly in the developing world. For our capacity for technological innovation should be greatly enhanced so that it can respond more effectively to the challenge of sustainable development. Also, the orientation of technology development must be changed to pay greater attention to environmental factors.

In this perspective, one of the most striking features of underdevelopment is technological backwardness. A large population in the developing countries still depend on technologies that are incapable of generating levels of income to meet even the most elementary basic needs. These technologies often are also inadequate to transform, without destroying, the natural environment. Moreover, their productive capacity is so low that significant steps cannot be made towards increasing output and improving utilization of the natural environment until they are replaced.

Scientific and technological knowledge and application are necessary if we are to avoid the continuous disruption of the natural system. Although even resource-rich and lightly populated countries may suffer serious environmental disturbance, a shortage of natural resources need not in itself lead to environmental pressure. This can be avoided if technological capabilities appropriate to the environmental conditions of the particular region are introduced.

Science and technology are global phenomena, but their integration in the production process differs between the developed and developing worlds. In the former, such an integration takes place through close linkages with the productive sector, which orient and provide resources for research and development and, finally, 'consume' the resulting innovation. The research and development integration with the productive activity frequently reduces the time-lag between the research phase and the commercial production of innovations, hence accelerating the diffusion phase.

Technology became a commercial good in itself and, as a result, an object of specialization, used by developed countries to retain their influence over raw material sources of production and, in general, over the economic activities of the developing world. This influence has been strengthened by the concentration and monopolization of applied research and technological development, leading to the perpetuation of the dependency of the developing world.

In developing countries, on the contrary, the links between the scientific and technological sectors are very weak, while those between research and development activities and the productive system are almost non-existent. Developing countries imitate, if anything, the organization, structure, purposes and methods of the research and development activities of the developed world, while their scientists and technicians consider themselves as members of the world community of scientists, with loyalties and responsibilities to that community rather than to the home base. Inevitably, the developing countries are precluded from establishing a scientific and technological base linked to their productive activity and conscious of the constraints and potentialities of its natural environment. Scientific institutions consequently become isolated from their socio-economic, cultural and natural environment, and unresponsive to the urgent needs and problems of the population. In the process of penetration by 'modern' technology, the indigenous technological structure is typically abandoned, if not threatened with outright extinction.

Developing countries have thus become consumers of an imported technology which they have done nothing to generate. The assumption is that the absorption of foreign technology can raise the socio-economic system towards higher levels of development. This indiscriminate and uncritical acquisition of alien technology has led to increasing dependency, for the mere assimilation of technology implies the acceptance of a linear concept of development and suggests that the stages that have characterized the development of industrialized countries would have to be replicated in developing countries.

From the environmental perspective, there are additional implications. Modern industrialized societies have developed technologies in accordance with their own peculiar characteristics, their natural and human resources endowment, their historical development, and the interrelationships between their resources, capital and environment.

Critical economic analysis shows that these technologies are not well-adapted to the circumstances of developing countries, but rather to conditions of labour scarcities, capital abundance, and large markets which permit the exploitation of scale economies leading to a reduction of cost per unit of production.

Problems of Uncritical Transfer of Technology: Examples from Agriculture

With particular reference to Africa, one may single out one specific activity in this field; namely, agriculture. Northern agricultural technologies are developed for temperate regions, while Africa is mainly tropical.

This aspect deserves a more detailed examination, if only because LPA has underlined the importance of agriculture to African development and the need to increase productivity in food through the application of science and technology. LPA called on member states to 'direct their efforts for spelling out a strategy for development, which should guide their thinking, planning and action on bringing about socio-economic changes necessary for improving the quality of life of the majority of the people. This objective requires them to invest in science and technology resources for raising African standard of living and for relieving misery in the rural areas ...'. LPA goes on to say that more attention should '... be paid to the role of science and technology in integrated rural development'. This would require, among other things, 'the generation of financial resources and political will and courage on the part of the policy- and decision-makers of the continent to induce profound change with far-reaching effects on the use of science and technology as the basis of socio-economic development as a matter of the utmost importance and urgency at this fateful juncture in history'. No plan could be more explicit on this issue.

Tropical climates affect over 75 per cent of the African continent, the only regions beyond the tropics are the Mediterranean countries in the north, and South Africa, Lesotho and Swaziland in the extreme south. The basic difference between temperate and the tropical regions is that, in the former, temperature mainly determines the potential and constraints of the natural system, while in the tropics the fundamental factor is rainfall variations. Thus in temperate areas temperature determines the emergence of four well-defined seasons, while in the tropical regions, the frequently erratic rainfall determines two types of seasons: the wet and the dry. However, it would be a gross over-simplication to think that all tropical areas have the same features, since one encounters different types of tropical climate, depending on rainfall patterns and their interrelationship with the ecological conditions of each area, for example, soil, altitude, etc.

Roughly, one may identify several climatic zones in tropical Africa: the wet equatorial zone distinguished by constant heat, rainfall, and humidity; the dry tropical zone close to the tropics of Cancer and Capricorn, with a hot arid climate and scarce and erratic rainfall affecting rainfed agriculture. A third zone occupies a middle ground between these two, characterized by an alternating climate, the wet season when the the sun is overhead and the dry season when the sun is lower. The Congo basin, the north coast of the Gulf of Guinea in West Africa, and the coastal areas of East Africa (Kenya and Tanzania) are examples of the first zone; Mauritania, Mali, the Niger, Chad, and northern Sudan are examples of the second; while inland Kenya and Tanzania, and southern Sudan are examples of the third.

Within this rough picture there are other variations; for example, the sub-tropical highlands (over 5,000 feet) that exist in Ethiopia and Central and Western Kenya. In these areas, the altitude introduces changes in the climate with temperatures generally dropping at higher levels, resulting in a reduction of evaporation and humidity. All these climatic aspects interrelate with ecological characteristics, in particular soils that provide specific environmental potentialities and impose certain constraints.

The characteristics of soils in African tropical areas are also different from those in temperate regions, not only because the nutrients in the latter are accumulated in a thick layer of humus, while in the tropical areas there is a rapid circulation of nutrients through vegetation, but also their physical, chemical and structural characteristics are different. Tropical soils frequently have a high content of alumina. The rapid circulation of nutrients and the rapid decomposition of organic matter due to an all-year high temperature results in poor nutrient content and little organic material. Besides, the leaching of nutrients leaves in many places a reddish clay rich in oxides of iron and hydroxide of aluminium which makes the soil unsuitable for agriculture.

On the other hand, the structural characteristics of temperate soils permit them to accumulate water and, since the temperature is moderate, there is little evaporation; the soil continues to have a reserve of moisture for the growing season. In the tropical areas not only does rain fall during short periods, but also high temperatures produce elevated rates of evaporation. So, torrential rains reduce soil capacity for water retention and high temperatures directly result in considerable water wastage.

A large part of the African tropical lands are unreclaimed acid soils or are only used for extensive traditional agriculture and animal grazing with minimum inputs and thus low fertility. Traditionally, those areas are used for cultivation of crops that are soil acidity-tolerant and can adapt to low phosphorus content, like cassava which constitutes one of the most important African food crops.

Another important difference is solar radiation which has an important role in photosynthesis. In the temperate regions of the North, solar radiation is less in winter and more in summer when days are longer. In tropical areas, and particularly near the equator, the length of the day is more or less the same all the year round. So, solar radiation in temperate regions is higher in summer when it is most needed for the ripening season thus having an important effect on productivity. Yields per crop, for this reason, tend to be higher in temperate areas, albeit the yield per day is frequently higher in the tropics than in temperate regions.

Differences between tropical and temperate regions are not only limited to climatology and soil structures, they also extend to biological diversity. Biological diversity is significantly greater in tropical areas. A recent estimation of the US National Research Council indicates that the number of species of organisms in the tropics is twice the number of those existing in temperate areas. However, only 17 per cent of tropical organisms have been studied or identified for taxonomic purposes. The diversity offers, from the point of view of development, great potential, but it also poses some problems.

The problems arise from the fact that this enormous diversity is rampant with noxious species like weeds and pathogenes. Swaminathan reported that rice in tropical areas is facing between 500 and 600 diseases while in temperate areas it encounters not more than 54; in the case of corn the relation is 125 to only 85; in beans, between 250 and 280 to only 52 in temperate areas; and for 278 diseases that tomatoes face in tropical areas they face only 32 in temperate climates.[5] This factor alone represents a limitation on agricultural expansion and poses a challenge to our scientists.

All those reflections have implications for science and technology policies in Africa. One important implication is that the natural systems of the continent, particularly in the tropics, are yet to be discovered; a large part of the available knowledge about these systems has been developed in order to satisfy the demands of the world market rather than local needs. The potential for research in this area is enormous and untapped. A second implication is that agricultural technologies and practices developed in temperate areas cannot be directly duplicated or indiscriminately copied. In other words, uncritical transfer of technology in agriculture is likely to fail or, at least, not reproduce the same good results in productivity.

This is probably why indiscriminate technology transfers have failed to make a substantial impact in the developing countries' agricultural systems. The catalogue of such failures in African agriculture is appalling. As early as the 1940s, the British peanut scheme in Tanganyika (now the United Republic of Tanzania) was one of the most spectacular failures. Here 1.2 million hectares of land were allocated to a giant peanut scheme. The area did not get the needed amount of water. After 10 years, the area was eroded, turning in the dry season into a cement-hard desert. The cost of that project was $US35 million. In this case, planners never considered the recurrent low rainfall and the low water-holding capacity of the soil.

A more recent example from Tanzania is the Hanag wheat project, which cost the Canadian and Tanzanian governments more than $US80 million but provided jobs for only 250 Tanzanians and resulted in accelerated erosion because of heavy mechanization. And it displaced Barbaig pastoralists to poor areas that became rapidly overgrazed, thus deepening the environmental degradation.

An example from West Africa is the Sefo scheme in southern Senegal, which ignored the environmental impact of large-scale mechanical clearing which resulted in high rates of soil erosion, crop loss, and the eventual failure of the project.

Another scheme that failed is the Mopti rice project developed in the delta of the Niger in the Mopti region of Mali during the 1970s. The great variations of rainfall were not considered, so by October 1984 rice was only harvested in 10 per cent of the area because of the strong unimpeded flow of the river.

Also, in the Ejura farms maize project in Ghana, the best Northern technology was applied: improved varieties, mechanization, fertilizers, pest control, post harvest storage, etc. Yet the yields remained well below those expected while costs were higher than planned. An interrelated web of neglected environmental factors explained the failure: heavy mechanized clearing left large areas of soil too much exposed, leading to accelerated erosion. Faced by all those difficulties from the start, the project was condemned to failure.

The Gezira scheme in the Sudan is yet another example of a development that went awry because it ignored environmental considerations. The Gezira is an intensive agricultural scheme which started with good results, creating high hopes only to be dashed afterwards. The scheme heavily depended, for long, on chemical fertilizers and pesticides which resulted in increasing soil debility, chemical contamination and hazards to humans and animals. The government of the Sudan, like any other government, was faced with the paradox of choosing between short-term gain, i.e. increasing production, and the long-term loss reflected in environmental collapse. But not only is that collapse no longer an eventuality, even the short-term gain has become a fallacy. With all those inputs tied to international market trends and foreign currency availability, cultivation schedules were seldom met and the project suffered accordingly.

Serious attempts are being made, with the help of World Bank financing, to rehabilitate the Gezira scheme from scratch but, sadly, the same over-dependence on imported inputs persists; the only saving grace in this rehabilitation effort is the limited action initiated by the FAO to introduce into the scheme elements of biological control and organic fertilization.

SCIENCE AND TECHNOLOGY AND SUSTAINABLE DEVELOPMENT: THE LONG-TERM PERSPECTIVE

Sustainable development, science and technology, and the environment have an important element in common: the long-term perspective. Sustainability cannot be achieved by short-term policies oblivious to the future. It requires an analysis that will anticipate the immediate impact of present policies as well as their long-term implications. Environmental phenomena often mature slowly. The effects of today's actions over the natural environment may only surface in the medium- or the long-term. This poses a challenge to economists who think in terms of short-term gains. Similarly, the recovery of deteriorated ecological systems is a task that requires long periods of time, constant monitoring and permanent and flexible planning and management.

Science and technology is also an activity in which the long-term horizon predominates. The large time-frame is needed for an invention to become accepted and for technological innovation to be diffused. It is also required for technological systems to go through their life cycles; significant effects on nature and society may result from technologically-induced modifications requiring long-term maturation.

The implications of all those considerations are manifold; they derive not only from the inherent nature of the questions at issue but also from the objectives of recovery and sustainable development. Recovery implies actions to solve immediate and urgent needs of Africa, particularly halting the deterioration of the natural environment. This requires short-term actions that would generate immediate

412

positive results. Development, *per contra*, implies a look over a larger horizon and requires different policies. But in both cases scientific and technological policies must be adopted.

The task is complex and the Catch-22 of this situation is how to solve today's urgent problems without jeopardizing long-term development. But neither should the solution of today's urgent needs of the large part of the African people be jeopardized by favouring long-term development, nor need they be in conflict.

From a scientific and technological perspective, Africa must rely for solving its present problems on the available array of technologies and existing institutions and mechanisms. There is no time for the development of innovations, nor for instant modifications of the present institutional setting. Innovations in, and diffusion of, new technologies is costly and time consuming, and with uncertain results. Institutional changes also take time to materialize, especially when change is hindered by those who are concerned more with turf than with societal progress.

The question, therefore, is how to choose from the available set of technologies, the ones that can contribute most to the solution of today's problems without creating rigidities that would impede the adoption of emerging new technologies. This applies particularly to the use of emerging technologies.

In this connection, African scientists are faced with the responsibility of assessing the potentialities of those emerging technologies not only to ascertain their applicability to the African condition but also to ensure participation in the process of their development. Scientists must find answers to questions such as what institutional arrangements are necessary for handling those emerging technologies? What type of human resources are required? And, what are the economic implications of their incorporation in the development process?

In recent years, the idea that mankind is at the turning point of a new technological revolution similar to the industrial revolution has gained more and more adepts. The basic characteristic of this revolution is that it is information- and science-intensive. This characteristic implies a drastic modification in the present prevalent technological pattern.

The informatics revolution is no longer science fiction, it is a present-day reality with a direct impact on the lives of our citizens in its two forms: computer and telecommunication technologies. However, its development and application is largely concentrated in the industrialized world and grows at the rate of 20 per cent annually.

In a recent seminar organized by the North–South Roundtable of the Society for International Development at Scheveningen in the

Netherlands (September 1985) attended by the best available experts both from the North and the South, the seminarists concluded that the primary and urgent need is 'to ensure that developing countries have full access to knowledge of the rapid changes taking place in the information technologies and their applications so that they may develop the capacity to evaluate the implications of these changes.'[6] One area where action is immediately needed and where the impact will be greatest is the development of human resources. The informatics revolution requires a quantum change in each country's education and training systems; and paradoxically, it also helps to facilitate those changes.

Emerging technologies, it is assumed, will have great impact on the development of the Third World, in particular those related to informatics, micro-electronics and biotechnologies. It is often contended, in support of this assumption, that many of the newly emerging technologies are 'natural-resource-augmenting', meaning that they help expand supply of natural resources that can be exploited for economic purposes, particularly those needed for the satisfaction of urgent basic needs. It is also contended that many of the new technologies do not require huge capital investment, and in fact that they can develop in decentralized systems, thus facilitating the process of rural development.

One additional advantage of the new technologies is that they are not necessarily energy-intensive and, in particular, not oil-intensive. They are material-saving and, because their reduced wastes permit a more integral use of raw materials, they have their positive environmental impact.

Equally, emerging technologies, it is maintained, can be applied for the revitalization and upgrading of vernacular or traditional technology and therefore can be assimilated by the population without major cultural conflicts. This suggests that a policy oriented to the merging of new and traditional technology would help avoid the negative aspects of the technological dualism that has so far characterized transfer of technology from the industrialized to developing countries.

The idea of technological blending, or merging of new and traditional technologies, implies a completely different approach to technology policy and planning. The objective should no longer be 'bridging the gap' between technologically advanced areas and those presumed to be backward. It also would not require a long process of socio-economic adjustment and change.

In effect, the concept of merging implies the possibility of a technological 'jump' in which it would be possible to benefit from the advantages of new technologies without having first to undergo fundamental investment in technological infrastructure, as was necessary with the exclusively imported technologies.

The prevailing concept of importation condemns the developing countries to perpetual backwardness. If we persist in that classical approach '... Our future shall always be the past of others' according to a renowned African historian.

Africa, and the developing world in general, are indeed in the horns of a dilemma. For, to quote another distinguished African scientist, Edward Ayensu, 'the economics of the 20th century industrial development have placed the Third World in a double bind. It is suggested that a double bind is always such that it cannot be resolved on its own terms. The way out is to escape from its terms. For the Third World, information technology provides that escape.'[7]

THE INSTITUTIONAL FRAMEWORK FOR SCIENTIFIC AND TECHNOLOGICAL POLICY IN AFRICA

To master the application of technology to the identified priority areas for recovery and sustainable development, African countries will have to reorganize their human and material resources, reorient their policies and modify their institutions. The ingredients of this reorganization and reorientation are to be found in the African Economic Development Master Plan, the LPA.

More specifically, scientific development and technological application depend upon a functional interrelationship among three social sub-systems. The first is the government which synthesizes the goals of the society and has the responsibility to establish priorities and to allocate resources to achieve those goals. The second is the scientific and technological infrastructure made up of research institutions, the scientific community, the educational system and institutions created for extension purposes and for the diffusion of science and technology among the populace. Financial mechanisms and allocation of resources for research and development and the diffusion of science and technology are part of this process. The third is the productive sector which is in fact the most important user of the products of science and technology.

While the government has the responsibility to catalyze the development of science and technology and promote and facilitate their application in accordance with the objectives of development, the scientific and technological infrastructure should provide society with the capacity to create, adopt, adapt and transmit knowledge. The productive sector, both public and private, has also an important role to play in the scientific and technological development directly through their participation in, or support of, research and development activities undertaken by governmental institutions, universities and research centres. Interaction among those three sub-systems is a pre-requisite if science and technology is to become a dynamic factor in development.

Several elements can be identified in this science and technology infrastructure:

(a) The educational system responsible for the production of the human resources needed in terms of quantity and quality;
(b) The quality of research and researchers, and the adequacy of research centres located in the universities, government departments and the productive sector;
(c) The co-ordination and planning of science and technology, and the administrative and financial tools needed for the implementation and management of science and technology activities; and,
(d) The extension system that would carry the results of science and technology to those who need it most, the rural people and the marginalized sectors of society like women.

The situation in Africa in relation to all these elements gives something to ponder. To begin with, the educational system is hardly oriented to the production of a science and technology linked to the environment or developmental purposes. One important task, therefore, is to integrate education into the overall planning of science and technology.

However, this task should be balanced with the most urgent one of reducing illiteracy and educational marginality. And, in promoting literacy, particularly in the rural areas, efforts should be focused on issues like efficient land use, water management, and protection of forests. Special attention in this regard should be given to women whose access to education is still woefully inadequate. Although the issue of women's access to education has been, for the last two decades, a subject of intense research and programmes by UNESCO, the problem still persists. In effect, the problem of women's education can only be solved through a restructuring of the relationship between men and women in a male-dominated society. This is why some African social scientists, for example in the Sudan, are calling for the creation of a social science for women since the prevailing studies look at the problem of women in isolation from issues like religion, sex and economic exploitation.

Also, education barely takes stock of environmental considerations. Basic scientific knowledge is often non-existent in the lower grades of education. At higher levels, education is class-room bound with very little exposure to the field.

To this end the educational system must be restructured, diversified and decentralized. Basic sciences, particularly biology, should be extended to even primary levels. The young should know their environment and its fauna and flora. They should know, from an early age, how to husband and protect it. In higher institutions, students must have the right orientation towards community needs and local people, particularly in rural areas. Both students and scientists can learn from traditional farmers who are more conversant with the local environment. Curricula also should be indigenized for, despite all claims of cultural authenticity, our school curricula, in the large part, are still modelled on Western systems and fail to reflect local realities.

The most important weakness, however, appears to be in the planning, administration and financial mechanisms entrusted with the design and management of science and technology. The adoption of a national policy for science and technology requires an awareness of the pervasive nature of science, which includes non-economic variables like education. The interrelationship between education and science and technology development is not recognizable in economic plans; education always falls by the wayside when it comes to the allocation of resources. It also requires the creation of organs specifically empowered to carry out and control such policy. The work of those organs must be co-ordinated with other institutions responsible for development policy. They must be permanently able and ready to advise policy-makers and planners on matters relating to science and technology. Many African countries have national bodies responsible for research in science and technology, but many of them are not integrated in the overall planning process.

The scientific community itself, largely a product of the type of education just outlined, is a victim of the inherent limitations of that system. It is a sad commentary on our system of education that, in a continent suffering from famine, graduates of agricultural colleges remain unemployed and governments and private institutions feel that they can do without them. Because of their often irrelevant training and lack of exposure to the traditional community, there is no common language between those graduates and the traditional communities nor are they able to develop, *in situ*, technologies appropriate to those communities.

But let us not blame the victims; this situation is a reflection of the obtuseness of the policies of those same governments. It is no wonder, therefore, that many of Africa's scientists feel more comfortable in foreign institutes, on whose models of education they were trained, than they do in their own homeland.

But the lack of dialogue is not only between the scientific community and the local population; there is also an absence of dialogue between the scientific community and policy-makers. Scientists trained in the Western liberal tradition are generally reluctant to be involved in the political process. There is also a widespread opinion among them that science and technology should be free from any intervention and not be subordinated to any political or economic priorities. Scientists, particularly some of the ivory-tower-dwellers of academia, often seek to assume a dominant role, not only in the management and quality control of science and technology application (which is fair), but also in the planning and setting of priorities for such application, which is the domain reserved for policy-makers who are, supposedly, mandated by, and accountable to, the general public.

In the productive sector, one of the most striking characteristics has been the emphasis on the process of linear transfer of technology, and we have alluded to examples of this in agriculture. The industrialization process based on import substitution is no better. In a great measure, it is associated with strong economic protectionism from foreign competition which contributes to the creation of a local entrepreneurship that is not concerned with improving productive capacity and efficiency through local research and development. The situation is aggravated where governmental policies grant almost unconditional terms for importing technology in the form of patents, equipment, semi-finished products, technical personnel and consultants.

All these factors undermine confidence in the internal capacity to supply technology, hence weakening even more the already extremely fragile links between science and technology and the productive systems. This process is not helped by the attitude of foreign industries, particularly TNCs, which have their own sources of know-how and technology to draw upon. Developing indigenous capacities is simply not one of their priorities.

However, one of the greatest inadequacies in our science and technology infrastructure is the shortage in intermediate skills, the indispensable link between the scientists and the end-users in the field. Not only is Africa's grand design for a science and technology revolution threatened, even our immediate goals for self-sufficiency in food production cannot be achieved without paying attention to this miserably neglected field. No agricultural development can be achieved without those who maintain pumps and agricultural machinery, guide farmers in the use of agricultural inputs and diffuse knowledge to the local community on the use of seeds, animal breeding, cropping, etc. Here again, heed should be given to women whose contribution to food production reaches up to 73 per cent in some African countries. Women should have access to training in intermediate skills and be more involved in extension work.

SCIENCE, TECHNOLOGY, AND ENVIRONMENTAL ELEMENTS IN LPA AND UN-PAAERD

Having sketched all those stark realities, what are the perspectives of African recovery and long-term sustainable development, particularly within the framework of LPA and UN-PAAERD?

The LPA, based on the Monrovia Declaration, is a long-term plan for all Africa up to the year 2000, which is already staring us in the face. Its fundamental objective is to establish self-sustained development based on collective self-reliance. UN-PAAERD is a short-term programme to overcome the most serious effects of the economic crisis in Africa aggravated by environmental deterioration, inadaptable structures and negative international economic trends reflected in deteriorating terms of trade and increasing external debt.

So, while the Monrovia strategy and LPA are based on Africa's own effort, without neglecting the extremely important influence of interdependence with the world economy, UN-PAAERD is basically an international effort calling for immediate action by all member states of the UN and full participation of all the organizations within its system.

The different purposes of both programmes call for different policy instruments. UN-PAAERD should only be considered as a complementary effort to the implementation of LPA which, alone, defines the basic strategy for the long-term sustainable development of Africa. The economic, social and environmental crisis Africa is experiencing in fact jeopardizes the possibilities to implement LPA.

Cognizant of those fundamental differences, it is also important to keep in mind that the promotion of science and technology is *explicit* and represents an essential ingredient of LPA. While references to science and technology are rather marginal in UN-PAAERD, they are *implicit* in the recommended actions (e.g. development of capacity for the utilization of resources of energy and the like) or very specific in character (creation of a network of agronomical research stations).

So whereas LPA sets out to revolutionize traditional concepts of science and technology policy application to Africa, UN-PAAERD remains bound to the traditional approach, both in terms of *implicit* science and technology policy as well as the relevance it attributes to the transfer of technology, and the role it assigns to international assistance. LPA also proposes a strategy to produce structural and drastic modifications of scientific and technological patterns in Africa oriented to the reduction of technological dependency (for this is what self-reliance is all about). These aspects are, understandably, missing in UN-PAAERD, given its limited horizon.

In the long term, science and technology development is not only a necessary condition for raising productivity, creating new employment opportunities and increasing incomes, it is an inevitable process. What is yet to be adequately recognized is that technological change should be guided by well-formulated and consistent policies closely linked with development policy, and be well adapted to environmental conditions. The latter aspect is of paramount importance for several reasons: Africa will remain predominantly rural for at least the next 20 years, and its most critical problems today are associated with food production and the rational use of the natural system.

LPA amply recognizes this. It emphasizes agricultural priorities and the need for integrated rural development in order to achieve food security, increase agricultural productivity, arrest rural to urban drift and improve living conditions, particularly in the rural areas. UN-PAAERD also states this view.

However, while both Plans are conscious of the environmental aspects of development, UN-PAAERD, due to its specific short-term and emergency character, only focuses on those environmental issues that are at the basis of the immediate African crisis. Some of those issues, such as desertification, deforestation, restoring arable land and developing a capacity for the utilization of renewable sources of energy, especially biomass, require a long-term approach. At the same time, they need immediate action to stop the serious process of environmental deterioration that is undermining the natural base of development.

The fundamental difference between LPA and UN-PAAERD, therefore, derives from their objectives and characteristics. Whereas LPA pleads in favour of an explicit indigenous scientific and technological policy adequately integrated in national economic development plans, UN-PAAERD is rooted in the traditional approach based on the *implicit* scientific and technological policy. In this approach, science and technology elements are not spelled out and they are dependent on indirect economic policies. And for this reason, there is an imminent risk that UN-PAAERD may reinforce traditional and technological

420

patterns, thus conflicting with the purposes of LPA. This risk is to be avoided, and it is in this context that the scientific and technological aspect of African recovery and development plans should be examined.

For a long time, traditional agricultural policies have been largely based on the idea that increasing agricultural productivity is possible by accelerating diffusion of 'modern' technologies developed in the North. With this understanding, a top-down approach was adopted based on the unrealized expectations of the trickle down effect theory.

Technologies originating in the temperate regions of the North were oriented to achieving economies of scale. But when transferred to African rural areas they tended to by-pass the main producers: the small-scale farmers. Given the importance of small-scale producers in African agriculture and the fact that the vast majority of the African population is rural, while most cultivation is done by women, policies should be geared to stimulating those technologies that can best be used by small producers in order to increase productivity in small agricultural units.

Furthermore, adopted Northern technologies have ignored the characteristics of local climate, ecology and resource endowments, an aspect largely commented on earlier in this chapter. The main instruments of those technological policies have been orthodox short-term economic measures invoking price-fixing, subsidies, tax concessions, overvalued exchange rates, etc. In effect, those policies encouraged the transfer of inappropriate technologies and favoured large producers against small ones, high technology over appropriate intermediate-stage technology, and urban consumers over rural producers.

The shortcomings of those policies were accentuated by the absence of complementary policies to maximize the effect of technology development and application, such as physical infrastructure, research institutes, and appropriate diffusion and extension programmes. It is no surprise, therefore, that the impact of those policies in the agricultural sector has been very meagre, sometimes negative. Productivity remained in general very low and, where it increased, it was not matched by increases in employment and income. Moreover, the indiscriminate use of poorly assessed technologies has damaged the environment, in some cases irreversibly, hence increasing insecurity and deterioration of the natural base for development.

Despite these experiences, the same policies are recommended in UN-PAAERD. These include measures like intensive mechanization and increased use of chemical inputs, without guarding against the ill-effects of those measures. Consequently, the risk exists that the same inappropriate technological measures will be used.

UN-PAAERD also emphasized the need to establish assistance programmes to small farmers 'especially women', placing at their disposal the necessary inputs for increased yields, without indication as to how this should be done, particularly in light of the inadequacies of the educational and extension systems, and the experience of ECA itself in this regard. ECA, long before the adoption of LPA, has done an admirable job in research and data collection but many of its recommendations are yet to be carried out by African governments.

In short, there is a gap between some of the policy statements and the existing mechanisms for their implementation, while there are contradictions between the long-term goals and the short-term policies. There is, therefore, an urgent need for action in two directions. Firstly, efforts should be made to co-ordinate the short-term with the long-term policies. Secondly, available technologies offered by the world market should be evaluated to identify the ones that are best suited to the solution of Africa's immediate problems without hampering the long-term goal of sustainable development.

SCIENCE AND TECHNOLOGY AND AFRICAN DEVELOPMENT

Both LPA as well as UN-PAAERD recognize that the priority area for technology development in Africa is agriculture, for that is where developmental and environmental pressures are most obvious. Earlier, we questioned whether agricultural technologies developed in the industrialized countries of the North were invariably applicable in Africa. Two important implications ensue: first, the need for development of an indigenous agricultural technology and, second, the realization of the potential of South–South co-operation in this regard. Historically, agricultural productivity has only advanced when there was substantial indigenous agricultural research and extension.

Developing indigenous technology cannot be done in isolation from technological development elsewhere. The problem here is not catching up with the advanced countries; rather it is marrying ethno-science with modern science. Science and technology policies in Africa should strive to strike a balance between indigenous technological development and imported technology. Our aim should be the achievement of a technological pluralism in which foreign technology (including frontier technologies) can be utilized side by side with traditional technologies.

African scientists and policy-makers should get over the myth of catching up with the advanced countries in science and technology. As Amiya Baghi notes, countries which respond with a fixed lag to changes taking place abroad can never really 'catch up' with new frontier technologies.[8] With the exception of Japan, most countries, including Western Europe, have often fallen further behind, at some stage, because they failed to perceive correctly the direction of technical change.

Africa should also strive to take part in the development and application of new frontier technologies. Increasing efforts in those technologies are now undertaken by some developed countries in order to redefine international competition and achieve comparative advantages. But these efforts are no longer limited to developed countries; several Third World countries have undertaken aggressive policies to participate in the development of those technologies, e.g. Brazil, particularly with a view to increasing productivity and reducing costs in export-oriented activities in order to retain old, or capture new, markets. This is true even in traditional sectors like textiles and leather which are, of late, reactivated in industrialized countries.

African countries cannot remain indifferent to all this revolution and remain passive importers of technologies. They have to be active participants in its development in order to benefit from 'learning by doing' and reducing, in the process, their technological dependency. The merging of new technology with conventional and traditional technologies is an approach that could permit both a quantitative and qualitative jump by-passing, in some cases, intermediate steps.

This approach is also necessary for integrating Africa's immediate problems: 'urgent recovery' and the long-term goal of self-reliant sustainable development. The short-term goal shall thus be combined with the long-term strategy. Merging of frontier technologies with traditional ones is not only desirable, it is also possible, particularly in the fields of agriculture and food production.

This can be illustrated with a few examples. UN-PAAERD recommends increasing use of fertilizers and chemical pesticides to improve productivity and raise production in agriculture. Obviously, there are immediate results that would be achieved by these methods. However, those methods are energy intensive, and additional reliance on imported energy sources would create a new dependency.

Intensification of agriculture and maximization of crop yields cannot be overemphasized in the light of the increasing demand for food, animal fodder, and edible oils. Modern farming in Western affluent economies achieves high crop yields by sound agronomical practices, including the judicious use of fertilizers, herbicides, insecticides, fungicides, and plant growth factors. So, the enhancement of crop productivity evidently requires the increasing use of those inputs. During 1974–1976, Africa received 948,000 tons of fertilizer (NPK) and, according to FAO scenarios for the year 2000, the requirement will be of the order of 4,083,000 tons to 5,611,100 tons. This increasing use of imported chemicals, in the light of the current African condition, imposes a heavy burden on the scarce foreign currencies available to African countries.

One of the frontier technologies that recommends itself in this regard is biotechnology. The impressively rapid development in biotechnology over the past few years has made available a whole battery of totally new techniques for the plant breeder and agronomist to manipulate. The application of those innovative techniques, given their rapid results as compared to conventional farming methods, holds particular promise for the food-starved population of Africa.

Biotechnology would immensely contribute to the improvement of soil productivity through genetic engineering either by incorporating nitrogen fixing genes, or by the inoculation of nitrogen fixing agents. In many crops, yield is largely governed by the availability of nitrogen. Conventional farming resorts to supplementing the soil with vast amounts of nitrogen, phosphate, and potassium fertilizers. But the draw-backs of those practices are by now common knowledge, e.g. pollution and biologically disruptive effects on the environment, not to mention prohibitive costs.

Not all plants, however, require extraneous macro-minerals to satisfy their metabolic needs, some having naturally evolved the capacity of symbiotic association with specific micro-organisms, highly efficient in their capacity for fixing atmospheric nitrogen. The most biologically significant of these mutually beneficial symbiotic associations is that between legumes and the nitrogen-fixing bacterium, rhizobium, which inhabits nodules along their root system. It has been calculated that less than a kilogram of high quality inoculant, when properly applied, can replace more than 100 kilograms of fertilizer nitrogen per hectare and therefore can save large amounts of foreign currency.

Besides rhizobium, the most important nitrogen-fixing agents are the free-living blue algae; the blue-green algae (BGA) anabaena, and the symbiosis of BGA with the water fern azolla. Blue-green algae can contribute up to 77 kg/n/ha per cropping season when it is fixing nitrogen under non-symbiotic conditions; in symbiosis with azolla, the biological nitrogen fixation can be up to 425 kg/n/ha/100 days. That was successfully experimented in rice cultivation.

In addition, BGAs can operate in a wide variety of conditions with temperatures ranging from 0°C to 60°C, including desert regions where they use early mornings and nocturnal moisture. And not only does the use of BGA in rice fields contribute to reduce dependency on chemical fertilizers, increase paddy yields and improve soil conditions by gradually increasing its organic matter content, it also reduces environmental contamination that usually results from the leaching of nitrogen into ground water.

There is no revelation in many of those practices to African scientists. For example, the inoculation of BGA in rice fields in Egypt has increased biological fixation by 24–48 kg/n/ha and increased yields by 14 to 30 per cent. In other words, consumption of nitrogen fertilizers is reduced by about 30 per cent with the added advantage of increasing crop yields.

Micro-organisms, like BGAs, yeasts and fungi equally constitute a hitherto hardly tapped source of protein that has an enormous potential role in satisfying the long-term needs for food and animal feed. The BGA spirulina was considered a nuisance to the salt extracting industry from the alkaline waters of Lake Texcoco in Mexico until research elsewhere demonstrated its potential value as a source of protein. Interestingly, this discovery came from Africa, from the alkaline ponds of Kanem near Lake Chad. For generations this organism has been harvested as seaweed, sun-dried, and eaten as green biscuit which the Chadians call *dihe*. Consequently, a large plant, producing over 400 tons per year, was set up in Mexico to commercially exploit the organism. The absence of cellulosic outer cell walls, which in spirulina is composed of easily digestible microproteins, the exceptionally high content of proteins, vitamins and minerals, and its non-toxicity, make this algae an ideal food supplement to be mixed with cassava, maize, rice or sorghum.

So what Africans have traditionally known for generations can be improved upon by our scientists using the manipulation techniques of biogenetics. For example, identifying and suppressing the expression of the genes coding for the blue pigment, and producing a white protein which has a composition similar to milk, spirulina can thus be used as a milk substitute.

Algae can also be used as a source of bio-energy. According to Lars Kristoferson[9] of the Beijer Institute in Sweden, 'land-based cultivation of sea algae illustrates possible long-term trends in advanced bio-energy production of particular interest for arid and semi-arid countries. The basic idea is to use coastal wasteland and deserts for growing suitable algae in either shallow ponds or in the sea water spray systems consisting of nutrients, sea water, sunshine and coastal waste-land'. Also, according to the same author, experiments with this type of algae-farming methods have produced yields of up to 150 tons dry matter per hectare per year on a semi-sustainable basis, comparable to extremely high-yield agriculture.

Another innovation in African agriculture is the use of tissue-culture technologies. Tubers constitute an important food crop in many African countries and they are propagated vegetatively or asexually. Frequently, parts of the plant used for propagation are disease-ridden, leading to the contamination of other plants. Tissue culture allows the production of whole plants from single cells. The technique is used to facilitate the propagation of plant cells and plants, and permits the production of uniform disease-free plant material.

Until recently, improvement in plant stock was achieved by the well-established but slow techniques of conventional selection and classical genetic breeding of varieties for high yield and maximum natural resistance to pests and diseases. The drawbacks inherent in these old methods of selective breeding, namely the large dependence on cross fertilization and the restriction of the available genetic pool of sexually compatible and hence closely related plant systems, have been largely circumvented by several ingenious modern techniques.

It is thus now possible to bring about the fusion of two naked somatic cells (protoplasms) of different varieties of crops and to produce, without the intervention of any sex factor whatsoever, viable intact, sexually fertile, whole hybrid plants. The stable propagation of such desirable newly produced hybrids is facilitated by the modern technique of micro-propagation and in-vitro culture of plants, whereby tiny fragments of surface sterilized plant leaf or stem are induced, by the provision of optimal nutrients and growth factors in suitable media, to produce numerous, identical, intact, whole plants. Such cloning techniques not only accelerate and facilitate plant propagation, but also maintain and safeguard the genetic stability of the desirable traits in such new hybrids. Micro-propagation is already being successfully applied to many plants including potatoes, tomatoes and forage legumes.

Tissue culture techniques have already been applied to two important tropical products: cassava and oil-palm tree. Cassava root is a basic food for more than 500 million people around the world and is cultivated mainly in small holdings throughout the tropics. In Africa, cassava is cultivated almost everywhere and it is part of a process of rotation of cultures, in particular with maize and peanuts. It is grown in subsistence agriculture by small farmers and is harvested when other products are out of season or when, due to climatic conditions, their production is insufficient. Africa ranks as the second world producer with 56.6 million tons in 1985, used mainly for human consumption in the domestic market.

Equally, in-vitro propagation has obtained disease-free planting material of cassava at the International Institute of Tropical Agriculture (IITA) in Ibadan (Nigeria) and healthy clones of cassava were deposited by IITA at the Kenya Agricultural Research Institute (KARI) and distributed to other African countries. This is a living example of the application of frontier technologies to African agriculture by African scientists.

Another major African indigenous food crop where research can be developed using modern techniques is sorghum. Sorghum is grown mostly in the semi-arid tropics in the belt stretching from Senegal to Chad in the west, to the Sudan and Ethiopia in the north east, and down to South Africa. Sorghum is the major cereal crop in Burkina Faso, Nigeria and the Sudan and second to millet and maize in Cameroon, Ghana, Mali, Senegal, Chad, the United Republic of Tanzania, Mozambique, and Zambia. According to FAO data, 32 per cent of the world area under sorghum is in Africa, yet Africa produces only 14 per cent of the total world sorghum production. Bad as this is, still worse is that while productivity in sorghum is growing at a high level in the rest of the world, productivity in Africa is not keeping up with the population growth and thus is directly contributing to the critical shortage of food. Between 1971 and 1981 world sorghum yield per hectare increased by 22.7 per cent, while in Africa it only increased by 4.7 per cent.

The International Centre for Research in Semi-Arid Tropics (ICRISAT) has obtained important results in new varieties of high-yield sorghum but, so far, the diffusion process of those new varieties has failed to make an impact on African agriculture. The problem with sorghum is its great diversity associated with different environmental conditions. No single variety is suitable for all African regions and conditions such as resistance to disease, soil quality and drought stress.

Despite these constraints, important results were achieved by ICRISAT with new varieties adapted to specific conditions as can be illustrated in the following examples:

(a) In Burkina Faso, where the average national yield for sorghum is 600 kg per ha, ICRISAT released in 1983 a new variety called Framida which has an average yield of 1811 kg/ha;

(b) In Ethiopia, ICRISAT released a variety called ESIP II with an average yield of 6307 kg/ha, while the national average is of 1498 kg/ha;

(c) In the Sudan, the national yield average is 520 kg/ha but the new variety released in 1983, known as Hageen Durra, has a productivity of 5190 kg/ha; and,

(d) In Zambia, where the national average yield is about 630 kg/ha, ICRISAT released in 1980 the variety ISCV III with a productivity of 7753 kg/ha.[10]

Other examples for Kenya, Senegal, and the United Republic of Tanzania can be found in the ICRISAT reports. They demonstrate that there is a great potential to increase agricultural production in Africa. But this is not achievable without decentralization making research more sensitive to local farming conditions.

But such steps will not convince farmers to use new varieties if they are not assured of good prices. Regrettably, in many African countries, farmers abandon agriculture because it simply does not pay; the existing price support system for food mainly favours town dwellers, the vociferous minority which makes and breaks governments. They demand cheap food as if it were their birth-right. Governments will have to turn the terms of trade in favour of farmers. And, in this respect, one cannot help recalling the relief worker in the Sahel who asked: 'Starve the city dwellers and they riot; starve the peasants and they die. If you were a politician, which would you choose?' But are we as callous as all that?

Be that as it may, indigenous research is vital for African agriculture not only because of its economic returns, but also because of the nefarious effects on the environment that may result from the indiscriminate use of imported varieties. The switch to foreign-bred productive strains is often suggested as one alternative for increasing agricultural productivity in Africa. Those suggestions often emanate from seed companies who promote the products of their private gene banks or from economic planners who are more concerned with the international market than with the requirements of the local population or the characteristics of the local eco-systems.

Apart from the need for an increasing amount of costly chemical fertilizers for new varieties, the most serious danger is the neglect and the extinction of traditional crop varieties well adapted to the local eco-system and highly resistant to local pests. New varieties may have no such resistance, and the more genetically homogeneous the crop fields are, the higher is their vulnerability to pests, diseases or weather changes. The rice homogenization in South East Asia was recurrently subject to devastations for these reasons.

Indiscriminate biological diversification may introduce a new and extremely serious uncertainty into African agriculture. Such uncertainty does not exist in the developed countries that have the technological and economic capacity that permits them to establish warning systems and an adequate mechanism to anticipate and respond to situations produced by that system. And in the eventuality of a crisis, they have the capacity to cope, either because of the availability of strategic food stocks and commodities, or because their economic capacity allows them to resort to the international market.

Africa's situation is dramatically different. Even where a warning system exists and works, it is rarely complemented with adequate institutional mechanisms and does not have the technical and economic capacity to cope with the emergency when it arises. The 1984 famine is a case in point. The famine was not a secret; FAO had been warning about it long before the October 1984 BBC television broadcast which is now popularly credited for starting off the international relief mobilization.

Early warning systems alone are never enough. They should be adequately complemented by technical and economic mechanisms to deal with emergencies. And, in the absence of buffer stocks, there should be an economic capacity to buy on international markets, which tend to react with increasing prices in the case of increased demand. In view of the lack of all that, African countries had no recourse but to appeal to international solidarity. Alas, food aid perpetuates the cycle of misery by eventually flooding the market and reducing the incentive to improve domestic food production. All this goes to prove the wisdom of the call for self-reliance reflected in LPA.

Throughout this Chapter references have been made to new technologies directly applicable to agriculture. Still, we cannot neglect the importance of new technologies that go beyond agricultural development. For example, remote sensing can be used for weather forecasting, evaluation of natural resources and pest control. Equally, the application of informatics and microelectronics, as alluded to earlier, would enhance the efficient use of other technologies, as well as serving agriculture and livestock monitoring. WHO has done some pioneering work in the use of informatics and telematics in health, particularly in the developing countries, and there is something to be learned by other institutions from WHO's experience.

Science and technology is one field where integration is not only desirable; it is an imperative. The majority of African countries are either too small or too poor to afford the full range of scientific research facilities. This problem can only be solved through the establishment of a cluster of regional institutes, made up of national institutions on the basis of their depth and expertise, to deal with the global scientific and technological needs of the continent. Only in this way can we bridge gaps in national capabilities and provide a backup in basic research.

It is worth mentioning here a new initiative which is of particular relevance for science and technology development: the creation of an Institute for Natural Resources for Africa by OAU, ECA, and the United Nations University (UNU). Among the basic functions of the Institute is research in agriculture and mining with three sub-areas in the former and one in the latter. Subjects related to water resources, animal resources and energy are considered for later action.

The Institute will be financed through an endowment fund which is expected to reach the amount of $US50 million. So far, Cote d'Ivoire and Zambia have already pledged $US5 and $US2 million, respectively, and offered physical facilities. France and Italy 2 million francs and $US15 million, respectively, while ADB is considering a $US5 million interest-free loan for four years and UNDP has informally expressed its willingness to provide $US5.6 million to support the programme during the first three years.

However, for the Institute to succeed, it will have to be complemented with national institutions dealing with those areas of activity that are vital for African development. Relevant departments of OAU and ECA should take the lead in launching policies aimed at co-ordinating the efforts of such institutions.

One hopes that, in addition to the co-ordination of research in Africa, the Institute will also lead the way for a meaningful South–South co-operation in fields where the technology of the North is irrelevant to Africa's needs. South–South co-operation is another theme to which we often pay lip service; the vertical penetration (North–South dialogue) cannot be achieved without horizontal integration (South–South co-operation). In the specific field of science and technology, several countries of the South have made strides in research, including those in biotechnology and informatics, either independently or jointly with other countries of the region. Examples of such endeavours are the co-operation between India and China in areas related to energy generation from biomass and natural nitrogen fixation, between Cuba and Mexico for the production of single-cell protein (SCP) from sugar cane molasses and bagasse, and between Brazil and Argentina on biotechnology application to pharmaceuticals. Earlier, we referred to the co-operation between IITA in Ibadan, Nigeria, and KARI in Kenya.

LPA is futuristic in its outlook and long-term in its vision. The rudimentary planning processes of nation-states are not the appropriate tools for the realization of such a grand design. And it is precisely because of this that the first African Economic Summit in 1980 which midwifed LPA, recommended 'the establishment of an African Institute for Future Studies within a period of two years, whose feasibility study was launched by OAU and ECA with the assistance of UNDP'. The Summit could not have been more explicit.

According to the study, prepared by Professor Mahdi El Mandjra, 'advanced public policy analysis is not intended to replace or compete with the existing planning institutions. On the contrary, it is meant to stimulate and extend the national planning exercise in time and space. The two are complementary and mutually-enriching. The imported planning "know-how" is of very limited use unless one takes care first of all of the "know-why".'[11]

One of the most important tasks of this Institute shall be the elaboration of an 'African World Model', both as an exercise of cultural decolonization and a study of Africa's future, were we to cease importing irrelevant development models. The feasibility study underscored that the 'African World Model' will not be envisaged as an entirely normative exercise but as a conceptual framework for examining key development strategies such as 'endogenous development', 'collective self-reliance', 'cultural identity' – all broad themes of LPA – in order to translate them into alternative scenarios over the next 20 years and in specific sectors such as: food self-sufficiency, primary health care, rural development, science and technology, etc. The importance of the creation of this Institute need not, therefore, be emphasized; self-reliance has also an intellectual dimension.

In the end, if there is one event that should have made us all – policy-makers, development planners, and scientists – ransack our conscience it should have been African famine. What more do we need to be morally embarrassed? The issue is not famine, but the way business as usual prevails in some parts of the continent. The causes for the crisis in Africa that brought us perilously close to Apocalypse cannot be all placed on our door, but there are also those causes that are home-grown. If only for the sake of credibility, we have to apply all our energies to solve them. If we are to be taken seriously, we have to take ourselves seriously.

LPA has defined the goals, set the tone, and mapped out the strategy. But while there are leaders who are ready to live up to its goals, in many parts of the continent, the Plan still lies gathering dust in foreign offices. How many African countries have aligned their national plans with LPA? How many African development institutes have initiated studies on African economic integration in order to prepare future planners of Africa? How many of the public opinion moulders in the media are aware of the existence of the Plan, not to mention their potential role in imparting its message to their audience? How many African research institutes are engaged in a sustained and co-ordinated effort, to find indigenous solutions to problems that are peculiarly African? Those are pertinent questions we need to ask ourselves with transparent frankness. Paying lip service to lofty causes would not carry us far. Africa's situation is woesome but woe, in part, is us.

In the end, if Africa's present agonies are not to turn into future horrors, we will have to live up to our commitments. And for that we need the political will and the enlargement of imagination; there is no witch doctor cure for our ailment. As the Reverend Burges Carr, an inspired son of Africa, has recently said: 'The drought has dried up our lands, let it not dry up our dreams.'

NOTES

1. World Commission on Environment and Development, *Our Common Future* (Oxford University Press, 1987), p.xi.
2. *Ibid.*, pp.43–44.
3. *Ibid.*, p.x.
4. *Ibid.*, p.72.
5. M.S. Swaminathan, *Biotechnology and Agricultural Betterment in the Developing Countries* (New Delhi, 1985).
6. Society for International Development (SID), *The Informatics Revolution and the Developing Countries*, North–South Roundtable, 1986.
7. E. Ayensu, 'Science, Technology, Environment and Sustainable Development', Discussion Paper to the WCED (Geneva, 1985).
8. A.K. Bagchi, *The Impact of Micro-electronics Based Technologies: The Case of India*, ILO/WEP Working Papers Series, WEP.2–22/WP.169 (Geneva).
9. Lars Kristoferson, *Report to World Resources Institute*, World Resources Institute Study 5, April 1986.
10. ICRISAT, *Reports 1980–1985*.
11. Mahdi El Mandjra, *Report on the Desirability and Feasibility of Establishing an African Institute for Advanced Policy Analysis and Future Studies*, UNDP, 1982.

CONCLUDING REMARKS

From the analysis contained in Chapters 12–18, and the relevant discussions at the Abuja Conference, a number of conclusions emerge. First and foremost among these, perhaps, is that Africans must look inside themselves and their history to rediscover the mainsprings of positive traditional values and knowledge to transform and sustain their society. The appreciation of history is important since the current crisis is but an intensification of a long and multi-form process of structural maladjustment. Second, clear objectives and priorities must be set in all the interconnected fields of endeavour: political, social, cultural, scientific, technological and economic. Third, the political dimension should be carefully examined in order to understand the constraints and to work out strategies to overcome them. Peace, security and stability are essential pre-conditions for the economic development of the continent as is the mass mobilisation of people in economic and political activities and institutions. Thus, internally within each state, there should be democratization of the development process, the elimination of political subordination, either on grounds of sex, ethnicity or race (as in *apartheid* South Africa), popular participation, social justice and accountability in the use of power. There must be an organic relation between the state and the society, and a conducive social climate must be created for structural change and economic development.

Fourth, development management must be reformed. However, there must be vigilance in this area given the historical position of Africa in the world economy. The pursuit of economic growth policies without due regard to the satisfaction of predominant social needs and the limitations of the continent's ecosystem could lead to even greater crises. In so far as ex-colonial interests are intertwined with Africa's development, the pursuit of growth may only mean the intensification of the dependency syndrome. Appropriate skills and expertise must be developed and/or harnessed among Africans to manage their own development. Fifth, science and technology and environmental protection should play a critical role in the search for transformation and sustainable development. Indigenous science and technology, which hitherto have been neglected, must be promoted and blended with their 'modern' or foreign counterparts. No longer should Africa allow the uncritical transfer of unadaptable foreign technology in a rush to solve its problems. Adequate time and resources must be devoted

433

to scientific research especially in the critical areas of food and agriculture, communication and informatics. Human resources must be developed, utilized and sustained in all the necessary fields. In this regard, a reform of the present dysfunctional educational system is essential to incorporate scientific, technological and environmental knowledge as well as social and cultural values from the early stages. In order to have the desired impact, effective extension systems must be developed using, as necessary, local African languages to bring the results of science and technology to the potential and expected users, especially women and the rural people.

Finally, there is a compelling need for organic and strategic solidarity and co-operation among African countries, and between Africa and the other countries of the South which should be relatively easy to achieve since LPA has made collective self-reliance a cornerstone of Africa's global development strategy. What is needed is vigorous and relentless implementation.

PART FOUR

Structural Change and Long-Term Development In Africa

INTRODUCTORY NOTE

There are three groups of Chapters in this Part. The first, comprising Chapters 19–21, analyses the salient structural features of the African economies and how they have evolved in the post-independence period. The second, i.e., Chapters 22 and 23, examines the nature and efficacy of the structural adjustment process in the African countries. Finally, the third group, made up of Chapters 24 and 25, reflects on the nature of the long-term growth and development that Africa will have to follow in order to move out of the quagmire of development crisis. The basic inter-connectedness of the three groups of chapters lies in their implicit and explicit focus on issues of adjustment processes, ranging from short- to medium- and long-term, and on structural change and transformation in Africa.

Benachenhou, in Chapter 19, surveys the diversity and similarities of problems and experiences in the historical growth and structural transformation of the African economies. Notwithstanding the heterogeneity of African countries in terms of size, human and natural resource endowment, and the initial stages of economic take-off, there are, according to Benachenhou, other important factors that have accounted for a noticeable diversity in performance, especially growth performance. These include the dynamism of the oil sector, the adverse external developments in mineral commodity markets, agrarian policy reforms, local productive capacities and the differing levels of political stability. At the same time, however, he identifies some crucial common structural factors that underlie the social and economic development of all African countries and have resulted decisively in in-built limits to growth, prominent among which are Africa's international economic relations, long-term agricultural stagnation, chronic and perverse under-industrialization, inadequate mobilization of natural resources, and scientific and technological underdevelopment. Benachenhou's analysis is complemented at a more macro-level in Chapter 20 by Phillips which demonstrates that the lop-sided structure of African economies has remained unchanged since independence; a fact which, not unexpectedly, has accounted for the widespread and persistent deterioration of the African economy.

In Chapter 21, Onitiri raises a number of issues that are undoubtedly important to the betterment of Africa's immediate and medium-term prospects. He outlines the different initiatives that have so far been undertaken and identifies some new ones that are still needed. Since IMF and World Bank stabilization and structural adjustment programmes have been an important component of the African reform initiatives, an in-depth analysis of the nature, pit-falls, contradictions and desirable re-orientation of these programmes is undertaken in Chapter 22 by Nana-Sinkam. His reflections are logically followed and enriched by the IDEP *Report on the International Conference on Growth and Structural Adjustment in Africa* in Chapter 23.

It is essentially with Africa's long-term development that the remaining two Chapters are preoccupied. In Chapter 24, Montasser identifies Africa's long-term development problem with the irreversible slow-down of trade as the traditional 'engine of growth', and proceeds on this basic premise to argue for a new engine of growth, based on agriculture, whose implications for structural change he also analyses. Amin follows suit in his insightful contribution in Chapter 25 by compellingly arguing in favour of a new national and popular auto-centred strategy of development.

CHAPTER NINETEEN

Structural Trends in African Economies

ABDELATIF BENACHENHOU

INTRODUCTION

No one can deny that by 1987 almost all the African countries had been unable to lay down the conditions for long-term stable growth of their economies. Trade movements in the 1970s and the expansion of some basic commodity markets made it possible to believe that some countries had at least achieved long-term growth. However, the current crisis has revealed structural loopholes in the economies of the continent and makes it imperative to analyse thoroughly the short-comings of the policies pursued and the new requirements for Africa's economic policy.

The intention here is not to blot out differences or underestimate the results achieved by some countries. Nonetheless, it can be said that the current crisis has in a way brought African countries closer together because of the common problems, the identical external financial difficulties and the fall in investment and the rate of development almost everywhere on the continent.

The first part of this Chapter will examine the diversity in the transformation of African economies over the last 25 years and the results achieved. The second part will examine the common economic problems facing the African continent.

DIVERSITY IN THE TRANSFORMATIONS OF AFRICAN ECONOMIES AND THEIR RESULTS

The heterogeneity of African economies is well known, and there is no need to emphasize it here. African countries differ in size, in the natural, agricultural and non-agricultural resources they are endowed with, in the level of development of their human resources and also, of course, in the level of their per capita income. This diversity, as we all

439

know, does not exclude some kind of link with the generally low per capita income, the prevalence of massive illiteracy and the vulnerability of the ecosystems. At this juncture, it is important to examine the diversity in the economic evolutions on the continent over the last 25 years before concluding that the impact of the crisis compels us to belabour this diversity and before trying to examine the common shortcomings.

The analysis of available statistics, particularly those of World Bank and ECA, makes it possible to distinguish two major groups of countries whose experiences differ greatly from one another. In the first group are countries whose economies have on the average achieved significant annual growth rates above 4 per cent and have, as a result, improved significantly their per capita income. Some of these countries maintain, even at present, these performances, though at a lower rate. This category comprises the following countries: Algeria, Botswana, Cameroon, the Congo, Cote d'Ivoire, Gabon, Kenya, Lesotho, the Libyan Arab Jamahiriya, Malawi, Nigeria, Swaziland, Tunisia and Zimbabwe (Table 19.1). In the second group are countries whose growth rates are low or nil due to various reasons, resulting in a fall of their per capita income. This group comprises: Burkina Faso, Central African Republic, Chad, Ghana, Madagascar, Mauritania, Niger, Senegal, Somalia, the Sudan, United Republic of Tanzania, Uganda, Zaire and Zambia (Table 19.2).

TABLE 19.1
RAPID GROWTH ECONOMIES

Country	1965–1973	1973–1984	1980–1984
Algeria	7.0	6.4	4.9
Botswana	14.8	10.7	9.7
Cameroon	4.2	7.1	5.8
Congo	6.8	8.1	14.5
Cote d'Ivoire	7.1	7.5	0.7
Egypt	3.8	8.5	7.5
Gabon	3.8	2.0	1.5
Kenya	7.9	4.4	3.0
Libya	7.7	3.0	−6.0
Malawi	5.7	3.3	2.3
Nigeria	9.7	0.7	−3.8
Swaziland	7.7	4.4	2.3
Tunisia	6.9	5.5	−
Zimbabwe	9.4	11.7	−

Source: World Bank, World Development Reports, various years.

TABLE 19.2

VERY SLOW GROWTH ECONOMIES

Country	1965–1973	1973–1984	1980–1984
Burkina Faso	2.4	2.9	−0.7
Ghana	3.4	−0.9	−0.5
Madagascar	3.5	−	−1.9
Mauritania	2.6	2.3	2.1
Niger	−0.8	5.2	3.4
Uganda	3.6	−1.3	5.4
Central African Republic	2.7	0.7	4.3
Senegal	1.5	2.6	3.1
Somalia	1.0	3.8	3.2
Sudan	0.2	5.5	0.4
Tanzania	5.0	2.6	0.6
Chad	0.5	−2.6	−6.9
Zaire	3.9	−1.0	1.3
Zambia	2.4	0.4	−8.8

Source: Same as for Table 19.1

The third group comprises the rest of the African countries with poor economic performance and with their per capita income stagnating or growing only slightly.

As far as the first group is concerned, two major factors accounted for the rapid growth of the economies:

(a) First, there was the dynamism of the oil sector and the rapid upsurge in the oil trade which has, until recently, generated, expanded and sustained the growth of African oil-producing countries. The seven African countries which greatly benefitted from the rise in oil price in 1973 and again in 1979/80 were Algeria, Cameroon, the Congo, Gabon, the Libyan Arab Jamahiriya, Nigeria and Tunisia; and,

(b) The second was the expansion of the agricultural commodity markets either at regional or international level. This accounted, to a large extent, for the agricultural growth of some countries like Cameroon, Cote d'Ivoire, Kenya, Malawi, Swaziland and Zimbabwe. The driving force behind the growth of this group of countries was oil and/or agriculture.

It should be pointed out, right away, that the growth of these countries was due mainly to one sector: the oil sector, for some countries, and the agricultural sector, for others. A downward trend in the growth rate of either of these sectors will undoubtedly adversely affect the overall growth rate.

Some countries in this group, however, experienced more diversified growth rates either on account of an initial diversification of the sources of growth, e.g. Egypt and Tunisia, or because of elaborate diversification of the sources of growth, e.g. Algeria and Kenya. We shall come back to this later because the diversification that was introduced did not spare even those countries of the crisis.

The factors which adversely affected the economic growth of the countries in the second group are also well known. Recent developments in the foreign trade sector undermined the growth of the mining countries such as Morocco, Mauritania, Zaire and Zambia. In other countries, it was the agrarian policies, particularly the producer price policies and the management of the exchange rates which led to the stagnation of agricultural growth, the only potential source of development. This was obviously the case in Madagascar, Senegal, the Sudan, the United Republic of Tanzania, etc. In some countries, the international or domestic constraints were exacerbated by the low level of the local productive potential as was the case in the Sahel countries such as Ethiopia, Mali, Niger, Somalia, Uganda and Chad. These countries were affected to a large extent by drought and ineffective food aid policies. The poor economic performance of the countries in this category was worsened by political instability and wars in which some of them, like Ethiopia, Mozambique, the Sudan and Uganda, found themselves caught up.

GROWTH LIMITS AND IMPACT OF THE CRISIS

For various reasons, neither the oil-producing countries nor the rich agricultural countries were able to or managed to pre-empt the adverse effects on their growth and lay down the conditions for a more diversified and stable economic development. They were therefore dependent on their export sectors.

In the case of the oil-producing countries, the most obvious adverse effects were the stagnation, if not the fall, in agriculture and the inadequacy or lack of appropriate technological policies which go with industrialization. The relative agricultural stagnation is a well-known fact in African oil-producing countries (Table 19.3). The availability of external payment resources and the resultant trade overvaluation accounted for the massive importation of food commodities and systematically discouraged the local production of these commodities. Agriculture has suffered from the oil-boom and will take a long time to recover. Even in countries like Cameroon and Egypt, with ancestral farming traditions, the direct or indirect effects of the oil-boom limited the growth rates of agricultural production and geared Egypt toward food aid and Cameroon towards growing food imports. It is obvious that it is not always the lack of agricultural development policies which is responsible for this state of affairs but rather the ill conception of such policies, inconsistency in their implementation and the paucity of the resources mobilized.

TABLE 19.3
AVERAGE PER CAPITA FOOD PRODUCTION INDEX
(1974–1976 = 100)

Country	1982–1984
Algeria	79
Congo	96
Egypt	91
Gabon	**
Libya	84
Nigeria	96
Tunisia	94

Source: Same as for Table 19.1
Note:
** According to World Bank, Gabon's annual agricultural growth rate between 1970 and 1982 was 0.8%.

The second adverse effect on the growth of the oil-producing countries, always linked with the availability of external resources, was the launching of relatively expensive industrial development which, from the technological viewpoint, was overly dependent on the outside world. All the African oil-producing countries have experienced significant industrialization, the programme of which obviously differs from one country to another. The industrial sectors were developed and their activities diversified. The share of the manufacturing industry in the GDP of these countries increased significantly (Table 19.4). No one industrialization resembles another, and the sectoral logic was different. Some countries favoured essentially substitution of locally manufactured goods for imported consumer goods (Congo, the Libyan Arab Jamahiriya, Nigeria and Tunisia) while others favoured the development of industries that manufacture intermediate goods and even industries for the manufacture of capital goods (Egypt and Algeria particularly). This industrialization was expensive and revealed particularly the shortcomings of the technological policy.

443

TABLE 19.4

SHARE OF THE MANUFACTURING SECTOR IN THE GROSS DOMESTIC
PRODUCT, 1984

Algeria	13	Morocco	17
Cameroon	11	Nigeria	4
Congo	6	Senegal	18
Cote d'Ivoire	17	Tunisia	14
Egypt	27**	Zambia	21
Kenya	12	Zimbabwe	27

Source: Same as for Table 19.1.
Note:
** For 1982

The contrast between technological changes and technological development became manifest. The constant importation of equipment, knowledge and skills in periods of euphoria led to significant technological transformations in the domestic economies. However, these transformations were not accompanied by local mastery of the technological development, that is to say the ability of each country to control gradually the nature and rate of its technological imports and replace them partially and gradually with local technological innovations initiated by its industries and research centres. This question of local technological creativity in Africa will be dealt with later as this appears to be the fundamental weakness in African development.

The growth of the rich agricultural countries also reveals two limitations. On the one hand, farmers have not benefitted equally from this agricultural growth, as in Malawi and Swaziland.[1] It was a foreign minority who monopolized the benefits accruing from agricultural growth. In other countries, like Cote d'Ivoire and Kenya, the agricultural growth only benefitted to a lesser degree a group of farmers and a significant portion of agriculture remained outside the growth spiral. Some writers even proved that in countries like Cote d'Ivoire or Swaziland, agricultural growth did not prevent the real income of farmers[2] from falling considerably. The growth was differentiated from the social point of view but this differentiation is not without its effect on the conditions for expansion of domestic markets and the potential development of industries and modern services. Herein lies the second limitation of the pattern.

Apart from Kenya which, for reasons linked among other things to the nature of its agricultural growth, was able to attain a certain level of diversification of its industry, countries with rapid agricultural growth experienced marginal industrialization characterized by local processing of agricultural goods for export and designed to meet the demands of an urban market which, of course, is growing but is still too limited on account of the income distribution system that denies a significant portion of the population access to industrial goods.

Similarly, the technological policies which followed the agricultural and industrial policies were not in the main basically different from those pursued by the oil-producing countries. Looking at the growth limits of the oil and non-oil producing countries, it is not surprising to note that they were affected as seriously as the less dynamic countries in the past. As a matter of fact, the crisis has undermined the foundations of their sectoral growth (oil for some, various agricultural products for others) and has revealed the difficulties facing these countries in repaying their debts. These countries are in fact the most indebted in Africa because the euphoria caused by their sectoral growth prompted them to resort to massive borrowings, convinced as they were that repayment would not pose any major problems since borrowing was only an advance from guaranteed future income. For the majority of these countries, the growth rates either slumped or fell considerably, particularly among the oil-producing countries.

It should however be noted that resistance to the crisis was made much easier due to the high level of economic diversification. Thus, Algeria, Cameroon and Kenya seem to resist the crisis better than Cote d'Ivoire, Gabon, the Libyan Arab Jamahiriya or Nigeria, where domestic markets served as positive substitutes for a diversified production apparatus. Unfortunately, this was not the case in Egypt or Tunisia which based their growth on export sectors that faced crisis at the same time.

In other words, in Africa like elsewhere, there is no mystery in economic analysis: where the overall growth is heavily dependent on one sector and where that sector relies too much on the world market, any variation in the world trade movement will automatically affect the domestic economic activity. Thus, in a way, the crisis has brought African countries closer together. Even though some writers pointed out the correlation between good economic performance and liberal international trade policy, and advocated that Africa should adopt an open door policy, this hypothesis will work only if international trade is stable and if the dynamism of the export sector permeates the other sectors and benefits all segments of the society. The situation in Africa is in sharp contrast to this hypothesis.

COMMON PROBLEMS FACING AFRICAN ECONOMIES

The economic stagnation of some countries and the vulnerability of the growth achieved by others compel us to speak of common problems facing African economies, despite the differences between countries in size, natural endowments and level of development. This diversity should be taken into consideration when examining future prospects and solutions. In the meantime, we shall try to identify the unifying factor of Africa's economic problems and the resultant vulnerability of the continent from the political and diplomatic point of view.

All African countries experience, each in its own way, five major problems which we shall analyse one after the other.

Crisis of Africa's International Economic Relations

The crisis of Africa's international economic relations, though an old one, appears more serious today, with the massive deterioration of the terms of trade and the shortage of outlets. There are at least three aspects of this crisis.

First and foremost, it is undeniably a crisis arising out of the international specialization Africa finds itself in. Gradually, the continent loses ground on its traditional export markets and does not have the means or the will to conquer alternative markets.

Statistics show that the share of African agricultural or mining export products has fallen over the last twenty-five years compared to that of other developing countries, and also to world exports (see Tables 19.5 and 19.6). Similarly, Africa's share of OPEC production and export fell at a time when there was a drop in OPEC's share of the world export. The relative fall in Africa's share of raw materials on the world market was attributed to a number of causes. To some, it was the remote consequence of the bad policies of African governments. These policies impeded export growth either because of export tax on agricultural products or unrealistic exchange rates. To others, however, it is the inevitable consequence of the greater dynamism of other world producers faced with a demand which, in any case, is in relative stagnation. These explanations notwithstanding, the result is the same. Given the magnitude of the problem, it is unlikely that African countries can regain easily their share of raw materials on the world markets, much less increase it in the near future. It should also be noted that countries that have performed well in terms of raw material exports did so, thanks to external factors (OPEC action) or to an appreciable growth in domestic output despite the fall in unit price.

TABLE 19.5

AFRICA'S SHARE IN THE WORLD PRODUCTION OF MAJOR MINERALS

Products	Year	
	1975	1985
Crude oil	10.3*	8.5
Uranium	12	22
Bauxite	12	18
Aluminium	1	1
Copper	20	16
Steel	6	4
Iron ore	6	3
Nickel	2	4
Lead	4	5
Zinc	3	3
Phosphate	23	21

Source: Same as for Table 19.1
Note: * For 1973

TABLE 19.6

EXPORTS OF SUB-SAHARAN AFRICA EXPRESSED AS A PERCENTAGE
OF TOTAL EXPORTS OF THE DEVELOPING COUNTRIES

Exported commodities	1961–1963	1980–1982	1961–1963	1980–1982
Beverages				
Cocoa	81.2	72.8	79.9	69.3
Coffee	26.0	27.4	25.6	25.9
Tea	10.0	10.7	8.7	9.3
Cereals				
Maize	7.9	2.2	2.5	0.4
Oil and seed oil				
Groundnut oil	61.2	35.9	53.8	27.8
Palm kernel oil	91.7	23.2	55.2	
Palm oil	57.0	3.1	55.0	3.0
Others				
Bananas	11.3	3.2	10.9	3.0
Cotton	18.4	20.8	10.8	9.2
Rubber	7.6	4.5	6.8	4.4
Sisal	65.4	60.9	60.7	60.4
Tobacco	22.2	20.3	12.1	11.8

Source: Same as for Table 19.1

Indeed, there is a clear correlation between the growth of volumes exported and the fall in unit prices as evidenced by the massive deterioration of the terms of trade for certain products. Faced with this crisis of Africa's traditional specializations, are there any alternatives on the export markets?

There are those who argue that Africa could substitute some of its raw material exports with industrial exports, as the continent gradually replaces the Asian countries in the manufacture of industrial goods known as goods of the first generation, the production of which depends mainly on the availability of cheap labour. This, however, is far from reality. Current analysis of the evolution of the world market as far as industrial goods are concerned shows that, in the developed countries, there is a trend towards restrictions on demand, protectionist policies and the substitution of locally manufactured goods for imported ones, as well as the diversification of the sources of supply (the socialist countries and other heavily-indebted developing countries in Latin America and Asia). Under these circumstances, and with the exception of Algeria, Kenya and Zimbabwe, one cannot really see how Africa could make a breakthrough on the world market for manufactured goods. As we shall see later, the current level of its industrialization in Africa and the conditions and motivations of direct international investment are not very encouraging, not to mention the low level skills of African labour. It cannot be overemphasized that the development of industrial export goods is elusive and unstable when the export sector has to import the bulk of its equipment and rely on expatriates for the running of the industry. Under the present circumstances, Africa can only specialize in the production of raw materials and the development of its labour force.

The second aspect of the crisis of Africa's international economic relations is linked to its present level of indebtedness. One has to look at both sides of the coin when passing judgement on Africa's debt. On the one hand, it could be said that Africa contracted debt mainly from national or international public institutions and that debt-servicing is therefore relatively limited for many countries as the indebtedness to public institutions would make easier negotiations for debt rescheduling, grace periods and write-offs. However, there is a political price to pay for this. On the other hand, it should be recalled that Africa is among the most indebted regions in the world in relation to its per capita income. For instance, in sub-Saharan Africa, indebtedness per inhabitant represents 41 per cent of per capita product whereas in Latin America it is 49 per cent and only 30 per cent in the Asian countries. It should also be noted that Africa's capacity to service its debt is much more limited on account of the unfavourable situation of its production potential compared to that of Latin America and Asia. In Africa, more than anywhere else, the indebtedness has a negative effect on development because the borrowed monies were not judiciously used or, where they were, the resulting output if they were meant for exports came up against the hard reality of international prices or shortage of outlets. This prompted some people to say, and rightly so, that to be able to pay back its debt, Africa needs development policies and not adjustment policies. As a matter of fact, it is becoming clear that adjustment policies pursued in an inordinate and injudicious manner will further weaken Africa's ability to pay back its debt. The debt crisis is a serious one and the solutions to be envisaged, particularly with regard to ineffective monetary and trade policies, must be examined thoroughly.

The third aspect of the crisis of Africa's international economic relations lies in the widening gap between the average level of technology in the world economy and that prevailing in Africa. In saying this, we are not advocating international technological mimicry; far from it. We are simply highlighting the scientific and technological disparities in the contemporary world. Africa constitutes the weakest link and, as such, is seriously handicapped in its search for a place in international economic relations.

Under these circumstances, the suggestion that Africa can change the conditions of its world trade, particularly its exports, simply by modifying the exchange rates of its currencies, should be taken with much caution. Competitiveness does not come about through currency manipulations. It depends on the effectiveness of the productive structures.

The recent experience of some countries like Cote d'Ivoire or Morocco has shown that devaluation has no impact on the volumes of goods exported because of the quantitative evolution of the markets. Economists know very well that it is competitiveness which determines the long-term exchange rate of an economy and not the opposite. Constant devaluation simply leads to the transfer of international trade benefits abroad and continuous domestic pressure on the living standards of the farmers and on salary earners. It also makes the exporter rich at the expense of the other segments of the society.

Analogical reasoning is always misleading and it cannot be concluded that because currency overvaluation has a negative effect on exports, devaluation will have a positive effect on the same exports. In any case, there is no general rule. African countries must be studied separately taking into account the products, markets, productive structures, etc.

Long-term Agricultural Stagnation

A lot has been said about agricultural crisis in Africa and its causes classified into two major groups. Some are of the opinion that the crisis stems mainly from the management of the price and the exchange rate system. This thesis holds, and it can be assumed that in many countries where agricultural potential is high, what is lacking is the motivation of the producers faced with unjust price policies and inadequate protection vis-a-vis the international market.[3] Analysing this thesis further, some people have concluded that the international price system relating to agricultural products, through its effects on domestic prices, is responsible for Africa's agricultural stagnation because these prices are not at all remunerative and do not make it possible to step up agricultural production. To substantiate this thesis, one can cite the positive experience of countries like Cote d'Ivoire, Kenya and Zimbabwe which had the wisdom to pay to the farmers prices more or less commensurate with effort, and the negative experience of countries like Madagascar, the Sudan and the United Republic of Tanzania which maintained an inadequate price system that completely discouraged the farmers.

There is, however, another thesis which seems more fundamental in explaining the agricultural crisis. According to this thesis, agricultural crisis in Africa is structural and stems from long-term deterioration of production conditions and soil fertility.[4] Its proponents argue that, in the majority of countries, average agricultural output has stagnated or even fallen, and that, more often than not, the agricultural growth achieved (2 per cent on the average in the continent) was due much more to the extension of the areas under cultivation than increase in output per hectare. This is substantiated by the fact that where there has been agricultural growth, only part of this growth can be attributed to agriculture which has mobilized development resources to its advantage. This is certainly the case in the countries of the Magreb as well as in Cote d'Ivoire, Kenya, Malawi and Swaziland.

Behind the agricultural prosperity of some of these countries lurks the technological stagnation of the so-called traditional agriculture. The proponents of this thesis argue in favour of a structural agricultural policy based on public investment in research, training, infrastructure and equipment. The price policy will be an indispensable link but not the sole premise on which agricultural policy should be based. This harmonious relationship between the various components of the agrarian policy seems to constitute the key to agricultural success in Zimbabwe and partially in Kenya. This structural stagnation of agriculture in Africa probably constitutes the first obstacle to any development policy on the continent.

In fact, it is difficult to imagine how domestic markets can expand under these conditions. It is equally difficult to imagine how Africa can sustain a solid industrial development, even partially geared towards export, if the cities continue to depend heavily on imports for their food requirements. Agricultural development is a *sine qua non* for Africa's development and it is gratifying to note that UN-PAAERD lays great emphasis on this aspect of development. However, as we shall see later, agricultural development is not limited to investment in agriculture; far from it. Proof of this is the agricultural performance on the Asian continent due not so much to agricultural investment *per se* but rather to the convergence of different policies towards the same objective, namely growth.

Africa's Chronic Under-industrialization

It was pointed out earlier that the growth experienced by some African countries during the last 25 years has led to industrialization, either in the oil-producing countries or in countries with apparent agricultural prosperity. A closer look, however, shows that Africa's industrialization is marginal.

An analysis of the distribution of manufacturing activities on the continent reveals that 4 countries (Algeria, Egypt, Morocco and Nigeria) account for 67 per cent of the overall industrial production and that seven countries (the first four plus Cote d'Ivoire, Tunisia and Zimbabwe) account for 80 per cent of this production. Similarly, an analysis of the global imports of capital goods shows that five countries; namely, Algeria, Egypt, Liberia, the Libyan Arab Jamahiriya and Nigeria, accounted for 75 per cent of imports in 1984. This distribution of industrial activities shows that the industrial landscape is limited in Africa, and that current industrialization is confined mainly to processing of raw materials for export and the substitution of imported manufactured consumer goods by domestically produced consumer goods for a relatively limited domestic market. Besides, this skeleton industry is affected by stabilization policies which slowed down investment and deprived the existing production apparatus.

With the partial exception of Algeria and Zimbabwe, production links between agricultural and industrial development, on the one hand, and between the various segments of the industry, on the other, are inadequate if not completely lacking. African industrialization is not deep-rooted: its markets are too small, its technology overly dependent on the outside world and its financing uncertain.

Agricultural industry in the wide sense of the term is still under-developed in Africa, and FAO has come up with the conclusion that African agriculture is the most dependent on the outside world for its equipment and its operation, even in the rich agricultural countries. It can also be said that though limited, as already pointed out, African industrialization continues to import large quantities of equipment and raw materials from outside. This under-industrialization has several causes which are becoming more serious.

The first cause seems to be the smallness of the domestic markets, due not so much to the size of the states but to agricultural stagnation resulting in low rural income. It cannot be stressed too often that the success of European or South Korean industrialization lies in the dynamism of the domestic market which, in turn, has sustained the growth of the foreign market.

As a matter of fact, financial difficulties also contributed to Africa's under-industrialization. However, these difficulties, as will be discussed later, stemmed not from Africa's natural poverty but rather from its inability to mobilize its natural resources to finance its development. It has been shown that it is the contrary in the oil-producing countries where, thanks to the review of the oil prices, these countries were able to secure the necessary financial resources for their industrial development. Thus, in Algeria and Nigeria, the share of the manufacturing industry in GDP has continued to grow during the last 15 years.

Inadequate Mobilization of Natural Resource Income

The mining industry in Africa has functioned more or less like an enclave despite the large quantity of mineral resources on the continent. In the early 1970s, the situation was better, as evidenced by the increase in the price of mining products which made it possible for countries with mineral resources to control, partially, the revenue accruing from such resources. However, for many products and, for that matter, for many countries like Botswana, Mauritania, Zaire and Zambia, the situation has changed. The mining industry of many of the countries is in crisis after playing a leading role in the economy. Revenue accruing from mining is vital for Africa's development. Mobilization of income promotes development financing, especially where this income is used to restructure the national economy and develop agriculture. However, control of the mining industry has not made it possible to internalize the financial and technological benefits accruing from the development of this industry. A very large portion of this income was transferred abroad in the form of profits, fees or salaries.

One wonders whether, under the present circumstances, the world market situation is not going to change since the use of ore by the industrial world no longer follows the same pattern as in the past. The African continent seems to have missed the historic opportunity of transforming its natural resources into agricultural and scientific development. Faced with the stagnation of the world market, there is need for concerted action to redeploy Africa's natural resources with a view to ensuring the continent's development.

Scientific and Technological Underdevelopment

Africa's scientific and technological underdevelopment can be examined from several angles. First, Africa occupies a marginal place in the world distribution of scientific and technological know-how which is determined by the number of researchers and the resources earmarked for research and development.

Africa accounts for only 7 per cent of world scientists and engineers engaged in research and development activities, and spends only 4 per cent of the world's resources to this end. The share of Africa's GNP spent on research and development is 0.45 per cent as against 2.2 per cent for North America and 1.9 per cent for Europe. This refers of course to global products which are not of any comparative nature.

Africa has 53 scientists and engineers for every 1,000,000 inhabitants as against 5,000 in the Soviet Union, 3,548 in Japan and 2,685 in the US. These figures should not be a matter of much concern. What should be of concern is the mediocrity of the objectives, results and research development in Africa. Concerning agricultural research, World Bank rightly noted that the problem is, first and foremost, the judicious utilization of existing resources. At national levels, research results are not adequately disseminated in many priority sectors. Local researchers are often under-employed. The objectives lack clarity, the programmes are inconsistent, research management is ineffective and the status of the researchers is poor. In most of the African countries, the researchers have no contact with the farmers and instructors. As a result, they do not care much about practical application of research results.[5] Industrial research, with a few exceptions, is almost non-existent in many countries.

Africa's scientific and technological under-development is due mostly to its general economic under-development. It is obvious that the scientific and technological research objectives of the continent have become less important and less relevant due to the poor level, nature and control of agricultural and research development. For instance, agricultural research into cash crops has continued to receive more resources than research into food crops. Also, the major problems of African ecosystems are not adequately studied and tackled. Besides, industrial research is very inadequate and often completely non-existent because of the very poor level of industrialization. Several observers have noted that, of all the developing regions, Africa is next to the Middle East as the region which buys its technology in the most integral manner and seeks technical assistance most (Table 19.7).

TABLE 19.7

DISTRIBUTION OF WORLD EXPORT OF INDUSTRIAL GOODS AND TECHNICAL SERVICES ACCORDING TO REGIONS OF DESTINATION EXPRESSED IN PERCENTAGES

	1980		1982		1983		1984	
Major regions of destination	E.I. *	S.T. **	E.I. *	S.T. **	E.I. *	S.T. **	E.I. *	S.T. **
Europe and North America	17	15	17	13	19	13	22.1	14.8
Middle East	39	36	42	34	35	35	33	32.3
Asia	14	16	19	19	16	21	22.7	23.2
Africa	15	23	14	24	23	21	15.5	22.6
Central and South America	15	10	8	10	7	10	6.7	8.0

Notes:
* E.I.: Industrial goods
** S.T.: Technical services

Although the recent crisis has dramatically changed the educational situation in Africa, it is a fact that concern for political legitimacy and the often-maintained belief that education alone can generate development have prompted many countries to make considerable efforts in the field of education, a notable result of which is the growing number of school-leavers in a relatively stagnant and declining economic context. Before trying to pass general judgement, it is justifiable at present to assess the relevance of educational strategies in Africa in relation to the nature and seriousness of the continent's economic problems. For example, it will not be out of place to question the priorities laid down for developing the various forms, levels and systems of education, knowing the reality and the complex nature of African development problems.

The rapid school population growth in the rural areas is not commensurate with the development conditions of these areas as evidenced by the large number of people leaving the rural areas for the cities. The development of higher education in a way contributed to the perpetuation of unproductive employment, not so much because of its size but because of the industrial, scientific and technological underdevelopment of the economies. The schools are overpopulated, compared to the economic systems which are deteriorating. Extrapolation of the current development trends of the educational systems and the foreseeable evolution of the economic systems point to a serious dysfunctioning with possible social implications.

In the meantime, suffice it to highlight the growing wastage of human resources due to a rapid development of the educational system which is not commensurate, in most countries, with the economic, technological and organizational capabilities of the countries.

The solution to this problem does not lie in partial, static educational adjustment policies because adjustments are phenomena that will always occur. What is needed as far as the African continent is concerned is the formulation of global strategies in which education is both an initiator and a factor of development. As a subsystem, education is inevitably influenced by other systems which, in turn, it influences.

As a matter of fact, the five characteristics of the African economies just enumerated point to the fact that Africa is at present in dire need of development. Of course this assertion neither negates the diversity of the African economies, nor the fact that some countries have pursued policies which have borne some fruits. However, it can be seen at different levels that the conditions for long-term stable development have yet to be laid down.

CONCLUSION

There are reasons for looking at the future with optimism. The first is that, in spite of the difficulties, some countries have been able to achieve some growth and a certain level of diversification. These countries comprise, among others, Algeria, Cameroon, Kenya and Zimbabwe. These achievements must be preserved, and steps should be taken to ensure that the growth and diversification policies are not affected by stabilization and deflation measures linked with debt-servicing but, rather, are strengthened through improvements in resource mobilization, allocation and utilization processes.

The second is that the international community has come to the realization that debt repayment cannot take precedence over development. The recent discussions at the Paris Club proved that debt rescheduling is necessary. This awareness is necessary, all the more so since each and everyone now knows that Africa's future trade prospects are not bright. This calls to mind Keynes' wisdom when, in the wake of the First World War, he wondered about vanquished Germany's ability to repay its debt and pleaded that rather than taking from its resources already devastated by the war, Germany should be provided with development aid.

Africa's situation is almost similar to that of post-First World War Germany. What Africa needs is development and not adjustment. A more substantial growth will in future increase African countries' ability to repay their debt. However, this is possible only when more coherent and stable development policies are implemented. It is also possible only if Africa does away with endless ideological debates which fill the contemporary world and which lead to economic policies that are of no relevance to the African countries.

The third lies in the increasingly strong political awareness within the African scientific community that the continent will be united and will be strong in future. Some people thought that the recent growth of the rich countries and the current crisis would break up the solidarity called for in LPA. In reality, the recent change in the world economic situation has brought into focus the structural basis of the economic solidarity of the continent. What remains now is action.

NOTES

1. World Bank, *Economic Memorandum on Swaziland.* Washington, D.C.; Kyad, J. and Christiansen, R. 1982, 'Structural Change in Malawi since independence', in *World Development,* May 1982.
2. Chai, D, and Radwan, S (eds), 1983, *Agrarian policies and Rural Development in Africa,* ILO, Geneva; and, Lee, E., 1983, 'Export-led Rural Development: The Ivory Coast' in Chai and Radwan (eds).
3. On Ghana, see Bequele, A., 1983, 'Stagnation and Inequality in Ghana', in Chai and Radwan (eds); and, Tababatai, H., 1986, Economic Decline. Access to Food and Structural Adjustment in Ghana, World Employment Programme Research Working paper, ILO, Geneva. On Uganda, see Jamal, V., 1985, Structural Adjustment and Food Security in Uganda, World Employment Programme Research Working Paper, ILO, Geneva. On Sudan, see O'Brien, J., 1986, 'Sowing the Seeds of Famine: The Political Economy of Food Deficits in Sudan', in Lawrence (ed).
4. Cf *Africa in crisis: The causes, the cures of environmental bankruptcy,* Timberlake, L., Earthscan, London, 1985.
5. Cf *Concerted programme of action for the stable development of Africa South of the Sahara.* World Bank, October 1984.

CHAPTER TWENTY

Structural Change and Transformation of African Economies

ADEDOTUN O. PHILLIPS

THE DETERIORATION

In spite of the fact that structural change and development has been the objective of economic policies of African Government since the first United Nations Development Decade, there is as yet no singular example of significant changes either in the structure of the economy or in the quality of life in African countries. Indeed, the deterioration in social and economic conditions has become so alarming that, in a majority of African countries, survival, not development, has become the preoccupation of governments and the international community.

Whilst the world economy in general has experienced declining growth since the early 1980s, Africa's decline has been the most serious. According to the World Bank Development Report, 1986, the average annual percentage growth rate of Africa's GDP declined from about 4 per cent in 1965 to about 0.3 per cent in 1983. Within Africa, sub-Saharan Africa's GDP has experienced negative annual growth rates since the early 1980s. Matters have been worsened by the fact that this decline has been happening at a time when Africa's population growth rate has been rising. Thus, whilst world population growth rate has tended to decline from a little over 2 per cent in 1965 to under 2 per cent in 1985, Africa's population growth rate has increased from about 2.8 per cent to about 3.0 per cent during the same period. Behind all this development is the fact that, for over two decades, the structure of African economies has hardly changed in such a way as to reflect or engender modernization and development. In fact, several aspects of the structure worsened during this period.

Comparative statistics on changes in the structure of production during the period 1965 to 1984 for Asia, Africa and the industrial market economies are presented in Table 20.1. The Table shows that while the relative shares of agriculture and industry have progressed towards equality in Asia, progress towards industrialization in Africa has been very slow. In fact, the share of industry in Africa increased by only one percentage point during the period.

TABLE 20.1

SECTORAL STRUCTURE OF PRODUCTION BY REGION AND MARKET
ORIENTATION
(as percentage of GDP)

	1965		1984	
	Agriculture	Industry	Agriculture	Industry
Asia	42	28	36	36
Africa	47	15	38	16
Industrial market economies	5	40	3	37
World (excluding non-market industrial economies)	10	38	10	38

Source: World Bank, *World Development Report, 1986*

Furthermore, Table 20.2 reveals that the contribution of the manufacturing sector to GDP is less than 14 per cent in 1983 in any subregion of Africa. Subregional and intra-subregional disparities are also of interest. For example, East and North Africa show relatively higher percentage shares for industrial production than Central and West Africa. Furthermore, imbalances obtain within subregions. Thus, in West Africa, Nigeria alone is responsible for about 74 per cent of agricultural output, 92 per cent of the mining output and 67 per cent of manufactured goods.

TABLE 20.2

STRUCTURE OF PRODUCTION IN AFRICA, 1983
(as percentage of GDP)

Subregion	Agriculture	Mining	Manufacturing
Central	32.4	22.1	9.8
East	34.5	3.2	13.6
North	6.0	25.6	10.6
West	30.7	15.8	7.5

Source: Same as Table 20.1.

Table 20.3 shows that the major sectors of African economies experienced decline in growth rates between 1965 and 1984. Thus, at the end of the period, the growth rate of agriculture (1.1 per cent) was only half the rate at the beginning of the period, and service growth rate declined from about 4.3 per cent to 1.4 per cent. The growth rate of industry suffered the heaviest decline, falling from about 7 per cent to a negative growth rate of −1.2 per cent at the end of the period. In general, African economies experienced the worst sectoral growth rates among developing countries.

TABLE 20.3

SECTORAL GROWTH RATES IN AFRICA IN PERCENTAGES, 1965–1984

Sector	1965–1973	1980–1984
Agriculture	2.2	1.1
Industry	7.1	−1.2
Service	4.3	1.4

Source: Same as Table 20.1

The structure of demand in Africa (consumption, investment, savings, exports) tended to shift against the requirements of growth, development and transformation during the two decades from 1965. For example, in low-income African economies (constituting the bulk of African countries), consumption as a percentage of GDP rose from about 89 per cent in 1965 to about 96 per cent in 1984. Correspondingly, savings fell from about 11 per cent in 1965 to about 4 per cent in 1984. Investment, which rose from about 14 per cent in 1965 to about 19 per cent in 1980, has since declined to about 12 per cent in 1984.

In African economies, to date, growth emanates from the external sector. Exports provided the bulk of foreign exchange and government income, whilst imports bought with export earnings provide the critical inputs for industrial and agricultural activities. Therefore, developments in the external trade sector are critical to a proper understanding of the plight of African economies. Thus, as shown in Table 20.4, exports are dominated by primary commodities and there has been little change in this pattern between 1965 and 1983. During this period, primary commodities accounted for over 90 per cent of the exports of many African economies. Similarly, imports are dominated by manufactured goods, averaging about 70 per cent for most African countries between 1965 and 1983.

Table 20.5 shows that the growth rate of African exports has been

TABLE 20.4

COMMODITY STRUCTURE OF THE FOREIGN TRADE OF SELECTED
AFRICAN COUNTRIES

Country	Primary commodities as % of total value of exports		Primary commodities as % of total value of imports		Manufactured goods as % of total value of imports	
	1965	1983	1965	1983	1965	1983
Cameroon	94	95	20	16	79	84
Cote d'Ivoire	95	89	27	42	74	59
Ethiopia	100	99	18	38	81	62
Ghana	98	**	19	**	81	62
Kenya	89	87	**	49	**	51
Liberia	97	99	28	45	72	54
Malawi	99	**	23	**	78	**
Niger	95	**	24	**	76	**
Nigeria	97	**	18	27	82	73
Senegal	97	**	46	**	53	**
Sierra Leone	39	57	29	64	70	36
Sudan	99	**	32	**	68	**
Tanzania	86	**	**	**	**	**
Zaire	92	**	32	**	70	**
Zambia	100	**	**	**	**	**

Source: Same as Table 20.1.
Note: ** means 'not available'

TABLE 20.5

AVERAGE ANNUAL PERCENTAGE GROWTH RATE OF AFRICAN
EXPORT VOLUME

	Primary goods	Manufactures
1965–1973	4.5	5.4
1973–1980	1.2	2.0
1983	–0.4	2.8

Source: Same as Table 20.1.

declining since 1965. The annual growth rate of primary products, the
dominant portion of African exports, has declined from over 4 per cent
in the 1965–1973 period to a negative level of –0.4 per cent by 1983.
Manufactured export growth rate declined by about one half, from 5.4
per cent to 2.8 per cent, during the same period.

The geographical pattern of Africa's external trade shows an unchanging lopsidedness. Table 20.6 shows that industrial market economies remain by and large the destination of most African exports, although there has been a tendency between 1965 and 1984 for the importance of industrial market economies to decline from an average of about 80 to 70 per cent. Correspondingly, although exports to developing countries trail far behind those to the industrial market economies, their importance has tended to grow for several African countries. However, Africa still hardly trades with Africa. Thus, since the 1970s, Africa's annual share of African trade has been less than 5 per cent of her exports and imports.

TABLE 20.6
DIRECTION OF EXPORTS OF SELECTED AFRICAN COUNTRIES
(as percentage of total)

Country	Industrial market economies		Developing economies	
	1965	1984	1965	1984
Cameroon	93	78	7	22
Cote d'Ivoire	84	70	13	27
Ethiopia	78	79	14	15
Ghana	74	57	9	17
Kenya	69	51	28	47
Liberia	98	77	2	23
Malawi	69	68	30	31
Niger	61	56	39	26
Nigeria	91	73	6	27
Senegal	92	53	7	47
Sierra Leone	92	71	8	29
Sudan	56	40	27	35
Tanzania	66	61	32	35
Zaire	93	92	7	8
Zambia	87	68	11	30

Source: Same as Table 20.1.

The adverse impact of the growth and structure of African trade is compounded by unhealthy developments in Africa's terms of trade over the years. With import prices rising constantly and export prices falling over the long term, the terms of trade have never really moved significantly in favour of Africa since the 1960s. In fact, the average annual percentage change in African terms of trade has been negative since the early 1970s. In 1986, export prices fell to their lowest level in 50 years, resulting in a sharp drop in African export earnings from about $US 60 billion in 1985 to about $US 44 billion in 1986. Much of Africa's debt and development problems are explained by the long-term decline in export prices.

Apart from production and trade structures, several other aspects of Africa's socio-economic structure have continued to give cause for concern. Table 20.7 shows that a relatively high proportion of African population is in urban areas and the drift to urban areas has increased in the two decades since 1960. During this period, the percentage of people in urban areas in most African countries was not less than 30 per cent and, in some cases, was well over 50 per cent. The rapid drift of the rural population to the cities has put tremendous strain on social infrastructures such as housing, power and water supply, and it has had dire consequences for agricultural production since it is the most able-bodied who migrate from the rural to the urban centres.

TABLE 20.7

THE STRUCTURE OF URBAN POPULATION IN SELECTED AFRICAN
COUNTRIES (in percentages)

Country	In largest city		In cities of over 500,000	
	1960	1980	1960	1980
Cameroon	26	21	**	21
Cote d'Ivoire	27	34	**	34
Ethiopia	30	37	**	37
Ghana	25	35	**	48
Kenya	40	57	**	57
Liberia	**	**	**	**
Malawi	**	19	**	**
Niger	**	31	**	**
Nigeria	13	17	22	58
Senegal	53	65	**	65
Sierra Leone	37	47	**	**
Sudan	30	31	**	31
Tanzania	3	50	**	50
Zaire	14	28	14	38

Source: Same as Table 20.1.
Note: ** means 'not available'

Table 20.8 shows another interesting aspect of the structure of African economies. Agriculture has remained the predominant source of employment. The situation has changed only marginally during the two decades since 1960 with over 70 per cent of total employment still in agriculture in most African countries. Services are in most cases more important sources of employment than industry which remains the least important source, accounting for less than 10 per cent of total employment in most African countries.

TABLE 20.8

THE STRUCTURE OF EMPLOYMENT IN SELECTED AFRICAN COUNTRIES

(in percentages)

Country	Agriculture		Industry		Services	
	1960	1980	1960	1980	1960	1980
Cameroon	**	70	**	**	8	22
Cote d'Ivoire	89	65	2	8	9	27
Ethiopia	88	80	5	8	7	12
Ghana	64	56	14	18	22	26
Kenya	86	81	5	7	9	12
Liberia	80	74	10	9	10	16
Malawi	92	83	3	7	5	9
Niger	95	91	1	2	4	7
Nigeria	71	68	10	12	19	20
Senegal	84	81	5	6	11	13
Sierra Leone	78	70	12	14	10	16
Sudan	86	71	6	7	8	22
Tanzania	89	86	4	5	7	10
Zaire	83	72	9	13	8	16
Zambia	79	73	7	10	14	17

Source: Same as Table 20.1.
Note: ** means 'not available'

In other respects, trends in the development process in Africa have been ominous. The much-publicized deteriorating food situation, the marginal and sometimes negative growth in per capita real income, and the decline in real official development assistance are just a few examples of such ominous developments. But few of these surpass the foreign debt-service problems of African countries. These debt problems are themselves largely due to the structural problems which have been described in the foregoing. Africa's foreign debt problem is not so much with its absolute size (which is the smallest among the various continents) as with its servicing. The overall debt-service ratio has risen from about 18 per cent to about 35 per cent of export earnings between 1980 and 1985. But for reschedulings, the ratio would have been much higher. The situation has been worsened by the fact that net financial flows to Africa have been declining. It was about $US 2 billion in 1985, which was only about one-third the level in 1980.

STRUCTURAL CHANGE: THE MAJOR ISSUES

The prospects for economic recovery, structural change and African development must be considered against the background of a number of major issues. First, what is the degree of consistency between the IMF Structural Adjustment Programme to which a majority of African countries have had to submit, on the one hand, and the LPA and APPER on the other hand? Second, there is the crucial role which foreign resource flows are expected to play in the economic restructuring and development process of African countries, and the implications this has for the speed and extent of the adjustment and development. Thirdly, there is need for a reconsideration of the proposals for alleviating Africa's foreign debt burden. Fourthly, there is the role which regional and subregional groupings are expected to play in bringing about structural change and transformation in African economies. We will briefly discuss each of these issues.

The majority of African countries are currently implementing some Structural Adjustment Programme which is often supported by the International Monetary Fund. A typical SAP stipulates, *inter alia*, that government should disengage from active participation in the economy; the majority of quasi-government establishments should be privatized; government expenditure should be drastically reduced; subsidies should be eliminated; public sector employment should be reduced, wages and salaries should be frozen; and the local currency should be devalued. Thus, a typical SAP package tends to be inherently deflationary, if not stagflationary. In fact, so draconian are some of the policy measures under a SAP that they very often give rise not just to deflation or stagflation, but also to social unrest. It is often argued by the designers and protagonists of SAP that the negative effects will operate only in the short term and are necessary for, and will be followed by, long-term development and growth. As yet, there is little empirical evidence to support this expectation.

The policy instruments for SAP and APPER tend to conflict in some major areas. A good example is in their postures towards government involvement in the economy. While the former demands government disengagement, the latter requires the heavy presence of government. The former therefore implicitly questions whether a large role for government is strongly correlated with or contributes to a high level of development. In this regard, the data on government expenditures and overall deficit or surplus shown in Table 20.9 do not appear to support the contention of a relatively heavier presence of government in

464

African economies compared with the more developed economies. In fact, the latter tend to have a heavier presence of government than the former. Besides, the statistics in Table 20.9 also show an increasing trend not only for developing countries of Africa but also for the industrialized countries. The question therefore arises as to whether government should maintain a greater or lesser presence in a developing economy than in a developed one. So far, there do not appear to be significant theoretical or empirical reasons for the role of government to be less in a developing than in a developed economy.

TABLE 20.9

CENTRAL GOVERNMENT EXPENDITURES AS PERCENTAGE OF GDP
IN SELECTED AFRICAN AND INDUSTRIALIZED COUNTRIES

Country	Central government expenditures		Overall deficit surplus	
	1972	1983	1972	1983
Cameroon	**	21.8	**	1.3
Ethiopia	13.7	**	−1.4	**
Ghana	19.5	7.8	−5.8	−2.6
Kenya	21.0	26.6	−3.9	−5.1
Liberia	**	34.9	**	−10.6
Malawi	22.1	32.0	−6.2	−7.7
Nigeria	10.2	**	−0.9	**
Senegal	17.4	26.8	−0.8	−6.0
Sierra Leone	**	21.2	**	−13.8
Sudan	19.2	16.9	−0.8	−4.6
Tanzania	19.7	**	−5.0	**
Zaire	38.6	27.5	−7.5	−3.0
Zambia	34.0	41.5	−0.9	−2.8
United Kingdom	32.7	41.4	−2.7	−5.0
Italy	31.8	52.8	−9.4	−13.4
France	32.5	44.8	0.7	−3.6
Japan	12.7	18.6	**	**
West Germany	24.2	31.1	0.7	2.0
Sweden	28.0	46.9	−1.2	−10.1
United States	19.4	25.3	−1.6	−6.1

Source: Same as Table 20.1.
Note: ** means 'not available'

Data presented in Tables 20.10 and 20.11 show the crucial role which foreign capital was expected to play in the implementation of development plans of many African countries during 1981–1985 and in APPER, during 1986–1990. The resource gap, in quite a number of cases, is so wide that little or no implementation can take place without foreign capital, particularly in the case of IDA-eligible countries which constitute the bulk of sub-Saharan countries. Also, even where the resource gap is relatively small, its impact on the execution of development programmes is critical in view of its role in providing funds for the importation of capital and intermediate goods which must complement domestic resources in virtually every development project.

TABLE 20.10

EXTERNAL RESOURCES REQUIREMENTS OF THE DEVELOPMENT
PLANS OF SELECTED AFRICAN COUNTRIES, 1981–1985

Country	External financing as percentage of total cost of development plan
Algeria	5.0
Benin	82.0
Botswana	13.4
Burundi	82.9
Cape Verde	86.9
Cote d'Ivoire	48.0
Ethiopia	52.9
Gambia	8.9
Gabon	8.0
Guinea	42.1
Kenya	5.0
Mali	97.4
Mauritania	51.5
Morocco	44.5
Niger	57.0
Nigeria	8.5
Senegal	75.0
Somalia	77.9
Sudan	41.0
Tanzania	85.0
Uganda	27.1
Zaire	65.0
Zimbabwe	37.4

Source: UNCTAD Secretariat and development plans of the respective countries.

Africa's Submission to the Special Session of the UN envisaged that out of the $US 128 billion which Africa requires over 1986–1990, $US 46 billion (or an annual average of $US 9 billion) would come from external sources. The World Bank estimates that Africa requires about $US 2.5 billion annually in the form of concessional flows alone during the first three years of 1986–1990. Two years after the adoption of APPER and one year after UN-PAAERD was adopted, the performance of external sources has been much below expectation, as net flows have hardly exceeded $US 2 billion annually.

TABLE 20.11
ESTIMATES OF RESOURCE GAP FOR APPER (1986–1990) FOR
SELECTED AFRICAN COUNTRIES

Country	Cost of programme ($US million)	Resource gap ($US million)	Gap as percentage of cost
Cameroon	361.9	310.0	8.6
Cote d'Ivoire	1,381.5	1,049.0	76.0
Ethiopia	4,880.6	1,982.7	40.6
Ghana	4,724.0	549.0	11.6
Kenya	1,197.0	241.0	20.1
Liberia	374.0	360.0	60.1
Malawi	849.0	510.8	16.11
Niger	1,204.6	691.3	57.4
Nigeria	12,437.0	2,000.0	16.1
Senegal	777.3	260.0	33.4
Sierra Leone	219.1	177.1	80.1
Sudan	2,913.0	750.0	25.7
Tanzania	5,832.0	771.0	12.2
Zaire	5,220.9	759.0	14.5
Zambia	557.3	451.4	81.0

Source: OAU and ECA: *Africa's Submission to the Special Session of the UN General Assembly on Africa's Economic and Social Crisis* (1986).

Yet, the nature of SAPs being implemented by the majority of African countries are such that strong external inflows are required to cushion them until the stagflationary impact of these packages and the ensuing human suffering hopefully change round to growth, development and increase in living standards in the medium and long terms. Without strong external financial support, the various packages are doomed to failure and would result (as they have indeed already done in some countries) in social unrest and political upheaval.

The chances that such strong external financial support would be forthcoming, and soon enough, are so far slim. There are several related reasons for this. First, there is relative lack of knowledge in most potential donor countries of SAP packages being implemented by African countries. Second, even where awareness is substantial, it is neutralized by pervading scepticism. Third, most of the potential donor countries are themselves undergoing internal budgetary rationalizations. Fourth, many of them are increasingly adopting protectionist policies. Fifth, it does not appear that the potential donor countries appreciate that they too have contributed to Africa's problems. Sixth, such is the enormity of Africa's economic problems compared with those of other regions that a certain feeling of hopelessness may have begun to inspire the current responses of donor countries. After all, Africa has been receiving the highest per capita aid, particularly since the 1970s, and nearly half of IDA's concessional flows go to Africa annually. Yet, Africa has remained the poorest region of the world; the only region where per capita incomes are lower today than they were in the early 1960s, and where infant mortality has been rising when it has been falling elsewhere in the rest of the world. Seventh, such are the stringent strings and conditions attached to even the weak flow of the external finance that disbursements invariably fall far short of commitments not only in quantity but also in time. Eighth, bilateral flows, which have been dominant in the past, have yielded dominance to multilateral flows, particularly from international bodies such as the World Bank and its affiliates. However, the current greater importance of multilateral flows does not, in fact, imply larger overall flow. Thus, the World Bank's Special Facility for sub-Saharan Africa has committed only about $US 1.7 billion since 1984. Also, some of the largest bilateral donors are reducing their assistance to Africa, instead of increasing it. For example, US assistance to Africa has fallen from about $US 1 billion in 1986 to about $US 650 million in 1987 (food assistance included). It will not be surprising if other large bilateral donors follow the example of the US.

For at least the eight reasons given above, SAPs in most African countries may well be doomed to result only in stagflation and human suffering without the *quid pro quo* of growth, self-reliant development and rising living standards in the medium and long terms. For the same reasons, the short-term cushion for SAPs mentioned earlier, or what UNICEF has referred to as 'adjustment with a human face', will remain a mirage impossible to realize. Without growth and development, African countries would not have acquired adequate capacity to service their foreign debts without jeopardizing their socio-economic survival.

Debt rescheduling provides a temporary respite but does not really provide an answer; it merely postpones the high debt burden of an already impoverished region. If the scenario painted under the eight reasons given above persists, repeated rescheduling would result, *inter alia*, in scarce trained personnel being distracted and diverted from development duties owing to their involvement in the rescheduling exercise; uncertainty would grow and discourage foreign financial inflow; hedging by foreigners would increase and this might lead to rising cost of importing goods and services. The overall negative impact will be on development.

Unless radical measures are taken, the foreign debt burden will continue to impose a major constraint on resource availability for African development. A casual observation based on Table 20.12 shows that for many African countries, a great proportion (if not the total) of the resource gap during APPER period would disappear if the debt obligations during that period were removed. Clearly, any attempt to resolve Africa's foreign debt problem which does not have the effect of total or substantial cancellation of debt obligations cannot be said to be attacking the problem realistically.

Of course, debt cancellation (write-off or forgiveness) can be opposed on grounds that it may cut off the flow of new money to Africa; that it is preferable to devise methods to ensure wiser use of funds by African countries; and that debt cancellation runs counter to the economic processes of market economies. However, the fact remains that new foreign money which comes in the form of loans, rather than gifts or grants, only increases the debt profile. Additionally, in view of the growing protectionist tendencies in the advanced countries in particular and the world in general, the prospects are dim that 'wiser' policies by African countries would indeed result in substantial increases in foreign exchange earnings to sufficiently ease the burden of the enhanced debt profile. The fact is that the current and foreseeable circumstances of Africa are such that her urgent requirements consist of expanding export trade, rising commodity prices and foreign grants or gifts, not loans. It is for this reason that the Baker Plan, which emphasizes new money in the form of loans (and prescribes continued IMF supervision), tends to lack appeal.

In addition to the foregoing, there are developments in the secondary debt markets which indicate that debt write-off or cancellation is not altogether unacceptable or impracticable. Thus, foreign banks are increasingly selling off their debt claims at substantial discounts in return for token immediate payment. Some are doing so because existing regulations limit the period for reflecting bad loans in their books, whilst some are doing so to cut losses or to reflect genuine revisions in the value of money. For non-bank official lenders, the decision is essentially that of the foreign governments concerned, and there is a sense in which decision at this level can be easier and faster. Indeed, some governments (e.g., in Scandinavia) have acted in this direction. Besides, it is noteworthy that for most African countries, with the major exceptions of Cote d'Ivoire, Nigeria and Zimbabwe, the foreign debt is largely official. Whatever be the case, it has been shown that debt cancellation is not such a detestable impossibility.

After trying unsuccessfully for three decades to rely mainly on the advanced countries for economic salvation, it is time for African countries to begin to look much more seriously elsewhere, particularly at themselves collectively. Regional and subregional co-operation and South–South co-operation ought now to be urgently elevated from the level of rhetoric to the level of imperative action.

In this regard, the first concrete joint imperative action should be in the area of accelerating a joint resolution of Africa's foreign debt problems. African countries should borrow a leaf from the evolution and role of the Paris and London Clubs. Thus, when African countries were contracting the loans which have now become a major block on their way to economic growth and development, they dealt separately with the individual foreign banks or government organizations from where the loans were contracted. The London and Paris Clubs had virtually no role to play then, nor were contracts made with them. Now that African countries have great difficulties with meeting their debt-service obligations and have to negotiate rescheduling, they are individually confronted with a collective front in the form of the Paris and London Clubs. To achieve symmetry and equity, African countries too must co-operate and act in concert on their foreign debt problems by forming an African Club to negotiate with the London and Paris Clubs; and the common strategy and negotiating position of this African Club should be to achieve substantial, if not total, cancellation of Africa's current foreign debt obligations. As members of this African Club, African countries must accept the dire prospect that their debt problem may turn out to be that epochal turning-point in the life of nations which finally make them do those things which they have been reluctant to do for long, but which are necessary for their eventual survival, self-respect and self-reliant development.

African co-operation on foreign debt problems may be easier (because of the singular focus) than co-operation on general economic development. It should, however, serve to revive and invigorate general economic co-operation which is now at its lowest ebb because member states of African economic co-operation schemes have often failed to live up to their respective responsibilities. The various economic co-operation organizations are invariably starved of funds and quite a number of resolutions adopted even at the level of the Heads of State and Government remain unimplemented. Also, proposals for reorganization designed to make the multiplicity of intergovernmental organizations effective have been shelved because of the lack of political will. The result is that the impact which the integration of markets, production process and overall co-operation in a number of other areas would have made on African development has

TABLE 20.12
COMPARATIVE STATISTICS OF ESTIMATES OF FOREIGN DEBT
OBLIGATIONS AND RESOURCE GAP OF SELECTED AFRICAN
COUNTRIES, 1986–1990

Country	Total foreign debt obligation ($US million)	Resource gap ($US million)	Total debt repayment as percentage of resource gap
Cameroon	1,261.3	310.0	406.9
Cote d'Ivoire	4,704.1	1,049.9	448.1
Ethiopia	644.9	1,982.7	32.5
Ghana	486.4	549.0	88.6
Kenya	1,755.8	241.0	728.5
Liberia	537.1	360.0	149.2
Malawi	320.0	510.8	62.6
Niger	452.9	691.3	65.5
Nigeria	1,370.8	2,000.0	685.2
Senegal	1,074.6	260.0	413.3
Sierra Leone	155.7	177.1	87.9
Sudan	3,305.4	750.0	440.7
Tanzania	1,205.4	713.0	169.1
Zaire	2,968.4	759.0	391.1
Zambia	1,763.5	451.4	435.0

not been felt. A collective approach such as in the form of the proposed African Club should serve as the catalyst for reversing current negative trends in African economic co-operation schemes.

The structural change and transformation of African economies can be predicated only on such co-operation and such collective self-reliance. The current stagflationary policies being pursued under SAPs in most African countries cannot provide the basis for structural change and transformation without massive, free and quick-disbursing external financial support, right from the start. Thus far, that kind of support has not been forthcoming and is unlikely ever to materialize, or can come only at 'costs' which Africa would find unacceptable.

CHAPTER TWENTY-ONE

Measures and Mechanisms for a New Momentum for African Economic Recovery and Development

H. M. A. ONITIRI

INTRODUCTION

We live in a world of immeasurable opportunities. So rapid and so spectacular are the shifting frontiers of science and technology that new vistas and new possibilities for the betterment and, regrettably, also for the destruction of human lives, are opening up at a rate that would have been unthinkable only a few decades ago. But it is also a world of tremendous challenges, in which economic survival – indeed political survival – depends, in the final analysis, on the capacity to respond to changing economic and political circumstances, and to take full advantage of new developments in science and technology.

The capacity to respond needs to be qualified. Indeed, it may be more appropriate to speak of the capacity to respond to changing circumstances without paying the ultimate price of total deprivation, starvation and death. Such eventuality is no longer the bad dream of pessimists. In the seven years that have elapsed since LPA and FAL were adopted, millions of Africans, more than half of them children, have paid just that ultimate price because of the incapacity of African countries to respond to external and internal economic changes that have driven many of them almost beyond the periphery of the international economic system.

This is in sharp contrast to what LPA and FAL set out to do, and the direct opposite of all the hopes and expectations embodied in the NIEO. What has gone wrong? What can be done? During the past three years, those questions have reverberated around the globe and have been the subject of innumerable conferences and masses of documents.

Without doubt, the rounds of conferences and dialogues will go on, and still more reports and studies will emerge from the rolling mills of the international system. The mechanism of international economic diplomacy tends to proceed by its own momentum regardless of its productivity and tangible benefits. However, in the final analysis, what will be important for the future – what will constitute a new element that will make a major difference to the present situation – is an honest and concerted effort to implement the decisions, resolutions and undertakings that have clearly emerged from these years of crisis. Many people expect that APPER and UN-PAAERD will subsequently slow down the implementation of LPA and FAL.

This Chapter has a limited purpose. Firstly, it recalls those critical problems that have weakened the capacity of African countries to respond to changing economic circumstances, and which were identified in *Africa's Submission* to the UN General Assembly as 'a vicious interaction between excruciating poverty and abysmally low levels of productivity in an environment characterized by serious deficiencies in basic economic and social infrastructure, most especially the physical capital, research capabilities, technological know-how and human resource development that are indispensable to an integrated and dynamic economy.' Several other problems, such as the instability of export earnings, and the heavy dependence of domestic production and consumption on imported materials, are the direct results of the lack of structural transformation which are further compounded by wrong policy priorities, poor management, and failure to make a real success of the programmes for subregional economic cooperation and integration.

THE CRITICAL ISSUES

What then are those critical issues that are going to determine whether the continent will turn a new corner at the turn of the century and whether the economic and political structures that will shape the lives of the more than 600 million Africans who will enter that century will be robust and secure enough to guarantee the continuity of political independence and the capacity of African countries to provide for the expanded basic needs of their citizens without a shameful and destructive dependence on foreign powers?

One does not have to look very far to identify those critical issues. Reports and studies about them abound in great profusion. More recently, the African submission to the UN Special Session on Africa constitutes new points of departure with prospects directed more to the implementation of specific action programmes than to the production of still more resolutions and declarations.

While the roots of the present crisis are to be found in both external and internal causes, the real initiative for lasting economic and social changes, without any doubt, lies within Africa itself. That is clearly evident from Africa's Submission to the Special Session of the United Nations General Assembly. 'In this battle for survival and development', notes the *Submission*, 'African Governments have recognized the necessity to fully mobilize and utilize all their domestic resources. The co-operation and assistance solicited from the international community is therefore intended to complement the tremendous efforts which African countries have decided to make in the years ahead to put their economies on course.' This full mobilization is to be reflected both in new directions in national economic and social policies and in new efforts to increase the effectiveness of the programmes of regional and subregional economic co-operation. What needs to be monitored carefully is how this declaration is being put into effect and how the supplemental assistance required from the international community is living up to expectations.

Failure of real economic integration is a most serious matter. In a continent which emerged from colonial dependence in such a fragmented state, nothing will guarantee the full mobilization of the continent's immense potential more than a concerted effort to create large economic communities out of the present separate and largely unviable economic entities.

Indeed, African countries were not unaware of these fundamental problems and the adverse economic portents that were looming ominously on the horizon as they gathered to adopt LPA and FAL in March, 1980. What can be said is that the fragile character of African economic structures, the magnitude of the tasks that need to be accomplished to transform the structures and the extremely low capacity of African countries to cope with external shocks, were not fully appreciated. In particular, at the time that LPA and FAL were adopted, four emerging trends that were to weaken the capacities of African countries to implement the measures embodied in these historic documents were clearly noticeable.

First, the prices of the major commodities on which Africa relied for the bulk of its export earnings had turned decidedly downward, while the prices of imported consumer goods, and a wide range of intermediate and capital goods and services on which many domestic activities depended, had risen substantially.

Second, domestic production and consumption had become even more dependent on imported goods and services. Many countries were importing increasing proportions of their food requirements, the struggling domestic industries had become heavily dependent on imported raw materials and intermediate products, and domestic consumption patterns were becoming increasingly import dependent.

Third, in many countries, productivity trends were falling at the same time as pressures were mounting for rapid increases in real incomes and improved economic and social services, a situation which gave rise to further pressures on domestic prices and the balance of payments.

Fourth, the level of foreign debt and debt-servicing obligations in several countries had reached unacceptable levels. Indeed, many countries were already devoting substantial portions of their foreign exchange earnings to the servicing of debts at a time that the need was rising for more imports to devote to capital formation and the maintenance of existing productive capacities.

In spite of these developments, and the wide gap that was clearly evident between commitment and performance at the subregional level, LPA and FAL attached much importance to the progressive extension of economic integration so that it would lead to the formation of an African Common Market and Economic Community by the turn of the century.

It was not surprising therefore that the ink had hardly dried on the adopted documents when the worsening international economic recession, further deterioration of world commodity prices, and the prevalence of droughts in many parts of the continent brought many African economies to the verge of collapse, and led to widespread preoccupation with the problem of crisis-management to the virtual neglect of carefully considered planning for long-term economic and social development.

As it turned out, even those countries that were riding on the crest of the oil-boom at the time that LPA and FAL were adopted did not escape the consequences of these adverse trends. Indeed, the experience of such countries confirms the view that while the limitation of financial resources is undoubtedly a major obstacle to African development, the availability of financial resources, by itself and without the necessary changes in development priorities and in the approaches to economic and social planning, will not bring about the fundamental restructuring of African economies that will guarantee stable development in a world of rapid technological change.

This experience has no doubt led to widespread disappointment and frustrations, but it has not altered the central purpose of LPA and FAL which remain today the major pillars of Africa's development objectives and aspirations. What has changed significantly is the assessment of the amount of effort and the degree of sacrifice that would have to be made at all levels to realize the objectives embodied in those documents. This is evident in the Declaration on the Economic Situation in Africa by the African Heads of State and Government at the Economic Summit of OAU in July 1985. The Declaration which serves as a preamble to APPER notes that: 'while reiterating our full commitment to the principles and objectives of LPA and FAL which are more valid today than ever before, we have focused our discussions at the present Summit on a priority programme that we will concentrate on during the next five years so as to pave the way for national and collective self-reliant and self-sustained growth and development in our continent.'

These five years are probably going to be some of the most critical in Africa's economic history. For what is at stake is whether the continent will enter the twenty-first century with its present fragile structures, which will assure that the tragic and traumatic experience of the drought and famine of 1984–1985, and the misery, degradation and deaths associated with that experience, will become a recurring phenomenon or whether the continent is going to march towards the twenty-first century with a new resolve to build the political and economic structures that will assure better living conditions and expanding opportunities for the vast majority of the African population, and restore the continent's prestige and dignity, in a world that has learnt to expect lots of words but little action from the continent, and that is rapidly losing faith in the capacity of African countries to turn their tremendous potential of natural and human resources, and the advantages and opportunities that those resources confer upon them, into concrete results and achievements.

The hard fact that African countries have to face is that the race is on for the twenty-first century, and all indications are that the clear winners are going to be those who can move with the tide of the tremendous developments in science and technology that is at present sweeping the world, and that has so far bypassed the African countries. Not only are those who rely almost entirely on the possession of abundant raw materials going to find themselves more and more in a disadvantageous position, it is even doubtful whether they will be able to maintain their political independence in the brave new world of the twenty-first century in which the technology of intelligence and warfare, added to the even far greater inequalities of economic strength and power that are likely to open up among countries, is going to make it easier for the stronger countries to undermine political institutions in the weaker states and consequently to impose their will and preferences upon them. Current fears and accusations of neo-colonialism are going to look like child's play in circumstances where science and technology makes it possible for the powerful countries to execute acts of political undermining and sabotage on the weaker ones largely by remote control.

The conclusions and views that are now to be found in many official documents to the effect that most Africans are worse off today than before independence are admittedly the results of impartial economic and statistical analysis, but they are already being used in a most subtle manner to support the argument that many African countries would probably have been better off under colonial servitude than under self-rule. Indeed, as we know very well, the South African whites have always been quick to seize upon the failings of African governments to buttress their argument that only perpetual white rule can save South Africa from collapse.

THE INITIATIVES AND THEIR LIMITATIONS

One should not underestimate what Africa has achieved so far. For example, some of the subregional institutions have weathered serious crises successfully in recent years, and new initiatives for co-ordination and rationalization of their activities are clearly noticeable. It is also important to draw attention to the few but important examples where such institutions have been used successfully to promote concerted action where individual actions would have been much less effective.

One such example was the establishment of a common front for the negotiation of the first Lome Convention with the EEC in 1974. Before the conclusion of that Convention, the EEC had separate agreements with different African countries: the Francophone countries formed one group, while the countries of the EAC formed another group; Nigeria had concluded a separate agreement with the Community, while other African countries were in the queue seeking separate agreements. While the common African front was no doubt facilitated by the entry of Britain into the EEC, the difficulties that African countries had to overcome should not be underestimated, especially as there was a deep division among them on the principle of 'reverse preference.'

A second example came much later in the establishment of the Drought Relief Fund and its successful launching into an operational mechanism to provide emergency assistance to needy African countries.

These are worthwhile achievements but, on the whole, the record of co-operation has been far less than impressive, and African countries have been quite open in drawing attention to their failings in this respect.

Thanks to a sober awareness of the realities of the present situation, the new Declaration of the African Heads of State and Government has not been a dead letter. APPER provides a platform for new initiatives to accelerate the implementation of LPA and FAL, while UN-PAAERD provides African countries with a new opportunity to draw the attention of the international community to the external constraints to African development and to mobilize necessary support and assistance in its struggle to address the critical problems that need to be tackled.

There are at least five areas in which the new initiatives are clearly noticeable:

(a) Increased emphasis on agriculture and food security;
(b) Efforts to promote greater productive efficiency, among other things, through increased privatization and better incentives;
(c) Greater flexibility of exchange rates;
(d) New programmes to reduce import dependence through more vigorous exploration of local sources of raw materials and a deliberate shift of consumption patterns in favour of locally produced products; and,
(e) New efforts to increase the effectiveness of economic co-operation and integration.

The first four measures usually form part of the structural adjustment programmes which many African countries have adopted partly in response to APPER, and partly as a result of agreements with World Bank and IMF. In a few cases, some of these measures are already paying off in increased agricultural production, increased volume of agricultural exports, reduced level of imports, especially of food, and a modest increase in the inflow of foreign funds, especially those repatriated by domestic nationals in response to more favourable official exchange rates. In the vast majority of cases, however, the measures have encountered serious problems. In almost every case, including those countries where some progress has been recorded, problems of unemployment, distorted priorities and worsening pockets of poverty have become sufficiently serious to warrant a re-examination of the instruments and mechanisms being used in pursuit of structural adjustment programmes.

The experience gained so far in the implementation of such measures has given rise to widespread comments and criticisms. First, it has been suggested that many of the instruments have been used so bluntly that they have left the weakest groups in the society, for example children, unprotected, apart from creating other social problems, such as unemployment and serious shortages of essential drugs and other materials required to maintain the efficiency of the vital services. Secondly, in many cases, the increase in export earnings that is expected to result from an increased volume of exports has not been realized because of falling world prices. Thirdly, the adjustment measures have not substantially increased the resources available for the rehabilitation of domestic industries, some of which, in some extreme cases, are still working at less than ten per cent of capacity. Fourthly, the regulations and safeguards surrounding the operation of the flexible exchange rates systems have not been sufficiently strong to prevent the diversion of the limited foreign exchange resources available into less vital imports, or into disguised capital outflows. Finally, the small size of many African economies and the limited flexibility of existing structures have narrowed the scope for policy options in the pursuit of structural adjustment measures. This is why current efforts to enhance the effectiveness of economic integration schemes have a major bearing on the ultimate success of adjustment measures.

NEED FOR FURTHER MEASURES

The experience with the new initiatives clearly demonstrates the need for further measures particularly in two areas: (i) in the modalities for the implementation of structural adjustment measures; and, (ii) in the implementation of new measures to increase the effectiveness of economic co-operation and integration schemes and their contribution to economic development and structural change on the continent. The pursuit of 'adjustment with growth' and the mobilization of increased foreign resources to support it – the twin pillars of World Bank policies on structural adjustment – are necessary but not sufficient conditions for the success of adjustment measures. Furthermore, the insistence on a quick return to a single-tier foreign exchange system and on an almost complete reliance on free markets and price movements alone for regulating the patterns of imports, tend to create new distortions that may not be conducive to the most desirable allocation of scarce foreign exchange resources. For these reasons, more effective safeguards and increased monitoring of the use of the foreign exchange derived from the operations of the new flexible systems may be necessary to ensure that these scarce resources are devoted to real improvements in productive structures. Secondly, in order to ensure that the foreign exchange requirements of vital economic and social services are not squeezed out by less urgent claims because of the operation of the free market mechanism, it may be necessary to take special measures to safeguard such vital services as health and education, or those connected with the maintenance of the economic infrastructure on which the productive efficiency of the economy depends. If, as it has been argued, the difficulty of coping with corruption and leakages would not allow a truly multi-tier exchange rate system to work effectively, then budgetary measures would have to be used to achieve these goals. For example, a substantial part of the nominal increase in budgetary resources resulting from the operation of flexible exchange rates could be used to increase budgetary allocations for the socially necessary goals that might otherwise be disadvantaged by the operation of free markets in foreign exchange.

The need for a new and more comprehensive approach to economic integration in the context of the structural changes that are needed to address the fundamental problems of African economic development is now clearly recognized. Indeed, it would have been expected that the need for closer economic co-operation would be more keenly felt at a time that many of the African countries are facing severe economic difficulties. But, ironically, it is precisely at such a time that the spirit of co-operation tends to falter. Massive unemployment, critical shortages of foreign exchange and of vital material supplies, deteriorating infrastructure, low capacity utilization in domestic industries, and galloping inflation, all tend to increase the number of domestic vested interests who might be adversely affected by trade liberalization and other measures of regional co-operation, thus creating an inward-looking atmosphere that tend to make integration measures more politically difficult to accomplish.

Aside from this, there is also the impact of external pressures, arising from the policies of major trading partners or donor governments, which tend to have different impacts on different countries and which are particularly difficult to resist at a time when the countries involved are facing serious economic problems.

In spite of these difficulties, real progress with the programme of regional and subregional co-operation and integration would have to be made in the next five years if the hopes and aspirations built upon APPER are to be fulfilled. Among other things, this would require more concerted efforts by the member states forming the subregional groupings to co-ordinate their national economic policies. It is in these critical areas that these institutions have to make significant advances if they are to make any worthwhile contribution to the implementation of APPER and UN-PAAERD.

It must not be forgotten, however, that the strength of a subregional economic grouping depends primarily on the strength of the individual economies which it represents. Indeed the success of the new thrust in the direction of greater economic co-operation and integration would depend for the most part on how far member states forming such groupings succeed in addressing their individual development problems, and in part on how far they are prepared to work within the framework of the norms and agreements that they have established collectively at the regional and subregional levels. In this connection, the new shift in the orientation of UNDP support for the subregional groupings during the Fourth Programming Cycle is likely to have a significant impact if properly implemented. It is in this area in particular that a new momentum needs to be generated at the continental level.

THE MECHANISM FOR A NEW MOMENTUM

In the follow-up and evaluation mechanism established for the successful implementation of UN-PAAERD, the actions envisaged at the regional level have been entrusted to 'existing mechanisms', and the twenty-second session of the Assembly of Heads of State and Government has established a framework for the fulfilment of these responsibilities. In adopting UN-PAAERD and in reaffirming its determination to implement it, the Assembly has entrusted the implementation of the Programme at the continental level to the Permanent Steering Committee of OAU, and has requested the Committee, among other things, to:

(a) Work out practical and operational modalities for the follow-up and evaluation of the implementation of UN-PAAERD in close consultation with the UN System and other multilateral funding agencies as well as other organizations; and,

(b) Liaise with the existing national, subregional and regional follow-up and evaluation mechanisms.

If, in the implementation of UN-PAAERD, Africa is to maintain the initiative that it seized in presenting Africa's case to the Special Session of the UN General Assembly, the mandate thus given to the Permanent

Steering Committee would need to be executed with great seriousness and urgency especially in respect of three essential tasks:

(a) Monitoring and evaluation of implementation at national and subregional levels, and taking whatever measures are deemed necessary, including consultations and negotiations, to encourage more effective performance at those levels;

(b) Monitoring and evaluation of performance by donor countries and agencies, in terms of the commitments they have made in UN-PAAERD; and,

(c) Mobilizing the support of UN agencies and other organizations for the implementation of APPER and UN-PAAERD.

If the Permanent Steering Committee is to perform these tasks successfully, it would have to become far more operational than it seems to be at the moment. Three ideas can be proposed for this purpose.

First, the Committee would need to establish task forces to provide it with the analytical information that will assist it to keep in touch with developments at national and subregional levels, and that will prepare options for policy to facilitate the decision of the Committee. Such a task force approach was in fact used by the Committee successfully to prepare the *African submission* to the Special Session of the UN General Assembly on Africa's economic crisis. In the present case, the Committee may find it useful to establish three task forces to deal, respectively, with the three major tasks to be performed, as outlined above. The terms of reference of each task force would be clearly defined and the assistance of UN agencies and other organizations dealing with the subject-matter under consideration will be enlisted.

Second, the Permanent Steering Committee and the Assembly of Heads of State and Government of OAU can make a significant contribution through intensive consultations and negotiations on sub-regional issues. The Permanent Steering Committee may consider establishing sub-committees of itself to liaise or negotiate with member states or subregional groupings on critical problems that may be presenting serious obstacles to the implementation of UN-PAAERD. In actual fact, the establishment of this kind of arrangement would seem to be overdue. Past experience would seem to suggest that many of the critical issues slowing down the implementation of resolutions and declarations passed by African conferences, especially those dealing with regional and subregional co-operation, cannot be resolved except within operational committees.

In Africa's efforts at the regional and subregional levels are to be focused on the crucial issues that will affect the implementation of UN-PAAERD, more time would need to be devoted to detailed negotiations, involving trade-offs and mutual concessions by member states. In particular, subregional groupings, such as ECOWAS and PTA, would need from time to time the kind of high-level interventions that can be provided by sub-committees of the Permanent Steering Committee to help resolve some of the critical problems that have slowed the pace of implementation of their programmes.

It could even be envisaged that, on some particularly difficult issues where the Permanent Steering Committee considers that the negotiations are better pursued at a higher level, it would make recommendations to the Assembly of Heads of State and Government to compose negotiating teams at that level to assist in resolving those issues.

Among the issues that need to be resolved in the co-ordination of economic and social policies, five are absolutely vital if real progress is to be achieved. These are:

(i) Harmonization of procurement policies, including the standardization of models and design, for a wide range of transportation equipment and other expensive machinery and equipment on which African governments spend sizeable proportions of their foreign exchange earnings. Not only would this reduce the unit costs of imports of these materials, it would also facilitate repair and maintenance and pave the way for the eventual manufacture of parts and components within the member countries of the subregional groupings.

(ii) Harmonization of industrial policies, including agreement on the location of a selected group of industries. Though this had always been one of the most difficult objectives to implement, it is an area where progress would have to be made if the common agreement is to make much sense in circumstances where the domestic markets of the individual countries are too small to support viable industrial establishments, and where the level of domestic productivity is not sufficiently high to allow the individual countries to make an in-road into the export markets.

(iii) Harmonization of external tariffs, which would enable the costs of imported industrial inputs and consequently the prices of final outputs in the individual countries to be harmonized.

(iv) Free movement of persons which would contribute to overall increase in productivity even though it may arouse great sensitivities in the recipient countries; and,

(v) Co-ordination of economic and social policies, which would allow divergences in individual plans and programmes to be reconciled before they are implemented.

The various subregional groupings have provisions in their Treaties and Protocols, including specific timetables, that could enable them to achieve these objectives, but in most cases very little has actually been achieved and it would take a new burst of energy to accomplish a substantial part of these goals by the turn of the century when an African Economic Community is expected to take shape.

CHAPTER TWENTY-TWO

General Framework for an Analysis of Economic Adjustment Programmes in Africa with Reference to the Rural Sector

S.C. NANA-SINKAM

INTRODUCTION

IMF stabilization and World Bank SAPs centre on two broad objectives: to correct balance-of-payments deficit of a country, exclusively; and, to achieve external payments reduction with minimized output losses, reduced inflation, improved macro-economic performance and increased economic growth rate.

The main criticism of the IMF stabilization programme is that it concentrates exclusively on the first objective, and even though it could be argued that, in the medium term, there is no contradiction between short-term external payments reduction and economic growth, there is no doubt that concentrating on current account deficit alone is too narrow a target especially if capital inflows are sustainable.

According to World Bank, structural adjustment intends to 'support a programme of specific policy changes and institutional reforms designed to achieve a more efficient use of resources and thereby contribute to a more sustainable balance of payments in the medium and long term, and to the maintenance of growth in the face of severe constraints, and to lay the basis for regaining future growth momentum'.

It should be noted that, for World Bank SAPs, increasing the efficiency of resource allocation appears as a key intermediate goal, but the crucial final objective remains the improvement of the current account deficit while minimizing its growth costs. The objective may perhaps be appropriate, but the question is whether it is specific enough to guide the *design of a SAP which takes into account its impacts on the rural sector of the economy.*

Despite their designation, SAPs recommended for African countries are not based on a structural analysis of the economies but on a limited view of domestic economic structures. As such, the consequences on the distribution of income are not properly analysed.

The neoclassical paradigm of economics, which assumes that economic agents respond better to price incentives and signals in general, is the basis of the philosophy of structural and stabilization programmes. This principle has been largely questioned. Factor price differentials could even stem from imperfect knowledge, racism, factors mobility, sex discrimination, etc.

There is no doubt that IMF and World Bank conditionalities are generally politically sensitive; entailing, as they do, currency rate modification, removal of price subsidies, reduction of imports and investment, cuts in budgetary spending and other demand restraining actions. It has been argued that IMF and World Bank conditionalities have destructive effects whereas the institutions themselves maintain that the conditionalities constitute the medicine which the countries must swallow if they are to restore their economic balance at all. IMF and World Bank's reasoning is theoretically correct and may also be correct in practice. However, the changes it presupposes are so thorough that they cannot be carried out within the 1–3 or even 5 years time frame which characterizes most lendings of the institutions. It is clear that the basic *tool kit* (short- or even medium-term loans conditioned on the implementation of basic changes in the borrower's economic policy and the prompt achievement of prescribed targets) is just not suitable for today's African reality especially with floating exchange rates. The set of IMF and World Bank conditionalities constitute a form of 'technology' which, when imported and applied indiscriminately without modification to suit the African environment, could have long-run negative or disastrous impact on African countries.[1]

In fact, the choice between the appropriateness of 'shock treatments' and 'gradualist' approaches to adjustment in African countries is based on the rapid desire to achieve the external sector objective and not on the welfare losses of rapid dislocation and/or the political impacts and the consequences on the rural sector of the economy. Although privatization and minimization of state participation could improve economic efficiency and reduce some distortions preventing economic growth, they remain forms of organization of economic activity and are, in the final analysis, based on value judgements. In the typical African economy, the financing of the agricultural sector, mainly small-holders, comes from the informal financial (or credit) sector while the industrial sector is financed via the official and controlled markets. This dual characteristic is not taken into account in the sectoral distribution of the burden from financial measures.

In African countries, an optimal production structure in the agricultural sector is more inflexible for the simple reason that the possibility of foreign market foreclosure (sudden price change, embargo for political reasons, increasing protectionism, etc ...) is usually very high. The consequence of this is that African countries, in risk-aversion to foreign income fluctuations, should favour putting more emphasis on agricultural food production and not on exportable goods which stem from static non-stochastic comparative advantage assessment.

Even the argument that international capital flows for adjustment could be increased through international co-operation to allow longer adjustment periods should not be exaggerated. In the face of persistent deficits, external financing does have a role to play in easing the transition period, but this role is limited, since the international credit environment must be considered as exogenously given. The most important thing is to find out which programme really is beneficial to the rural poor and does not, in general, sacrifice the rural sector through the recommended measures.

Although literature abounds with analysis of the theoretical impacts of particular stabilization and structural adjustment policies on projected objectives, very little research has been devoted to: analysing how a wide set of policies interact (or will interact) with each other, both over time and in the long run, especially in the most important economic sector in the African countries, i.e. the rural sector; the formulation of a formal framework which could be used both to evaluate adjustment programmes and to construct a set of optimal consistent policies which take into account the preoccupations of the rural sector; and taking into account the elasticities of response of the objectives to policy actions and/or the international effects of the policies themselves.

All adjustment programmes concentrate on the following elements: the restoration of external balance-of-payments, the elimination of distortions and promotion of macro-economic efficiency; the reduction of high inflation rates; the protection or resumption of output growth; and the minimization of the cost of adjustment to the poorest. However, little attention in the literature has been focused upon the assigning of relative weights to the potentially conflicting objectives, or on ways of adjusting such weights to specific country circumstances.

Efficiency in macro-terms and under static conditions could mean maximizing the present value of output from a given level of inputs or cost minimization if the objective is to achieve a particular social goal. In this context, the factor determining efficiency is the price of inputs and output reflecting relative scarcities. Under dynamic circumstances, domestic interest rates must reflect the cost of foreign borrowing and the labour costs of a unit of output must be internationally competitive.[2]

Efficiency in macro-terms could mean that factor proportions are such that isocost curves are tangent to the production isoquants under given factor prices (price efficiency) or that producers are operating on their production possibilities curve and not inside. It has been observed that, in African countries, peasants will adjust efficiently their product mix and factor proportions to whatever prices they face. This does not imply optimality in terms of income generation but the question remains whether the economy is better off under distorted or undistorted price conditions. Consequently, while some 'distortions' are definitely uneconomic and should be the object of reform, blanket removal of distortions as often suggested in stabilization and structural adjustment programmes only on efficiency grounds should be analysed more seriously by the authorities.

To evaluate the impact of different adjustment policies, the accepted framework must incorporate the elasticities of response of policy variables to policy actions and must also account for interaction effects between policies in a consistent, simultaneous manner, and response lags should be taken into account so as to permit the elaboration of a dynamically consistent set of policies.

There is no doubt that in the majority of African countries, policies followed by the authorities have contributed significantly to the impressive contribution of agriculture to economic growth, considering especially the small and decreasing level of investment in the agricultural sector. The economic development process of many African countries must therefore be agriculture based.

Consequently, it becomes very important to know what are the implications of policies embodied in stabilization and/or structural adjustment programmes for the agricultural sector or the rural sector in general (i.e., removal of price supports, trade liberalization, subsidies, reduction in Government investment and spendings, price stabilization, money supply contractions, different types of distortions, devaluation, etc ...). Conversely, how will real incomes of various economic interests, overall production mix, foreign deficits, government and economic growth, labour migration to the cities and/or modern sectors in response to better income opportunities, be influenced? What are the possible structural elements of the rural sector that might influence and/or be influenced by the programme's measures? Can these elements be changed easily in the short or long run? The importance of the rural sector in the African economies makes the answers to these questions imperative.

STABILIZATION AND STRUCTURAL ADJUSTMENT: THE INSIDE STORY

In the literature, the terms stabilization and structural adjustment are often used recurrently without any clear distinction between them. Sometimes, it is argued that stabilization is a short-run (one to three years) set of policies; that it uses demand management to cause contractions and reduce imports; and that it is the main policy tool of IMF. On the other hand, structural adjustment, used in the structural adjustment loans of World Bank and the External Fund Facility of the IMF, covers a longer period, more than 3 years, and acts on the supply side to increase production and exports. 'Structural adjustment' and 'stabilization' should be thought of as abstract concepts defining opposite poles on a range of different policy approaches, rather than specific policy packages *per se*. It is clear that all such delineations do not fully capture the distinction between stabilization and structural adjustment programmes. There are many elements of complementarity between the stabilization and structural adjustment programmes. For example, IMF standby and External Fund Facility contain measures to be found in any SAP.

The most important features of a stabilization programme *per se* are that it attempts to correct the balance of payments deficit *exclusively* and takes the determining parameters of an economy's response to policy instruments as given, and therefore attempts to manipulate these policy instruments *exclusively* to achieve its *stabilization* objectives within a relatively short-term horizon. Consequently, a typical stabilization programme will concentrate on the contraction of monetary growth and demand, and/or on exchange rate modification to encourage the supply of exports and import substitutes by increasing their relative prices and enhancing their profitability. Needless to say that, in the short term and in the absence of additional and appropriate policy actions, the expenditure switching effects of the devaluation *will* be quite limited. Hence, there is little doubt that achievement of balance-of-payments equilibrium relies upon severe contraction of economic activity through cuts in investment, exploiting to the highest extent possible the strong parameters like imports and output for exports, while ignoring the impact of these measures on the *rural sector* of the economy (food production, transportation facilities between the productive and consumption areas).

The objective of SAP (World Bank or IMF) is to simultaneously achieve payments deficit reduction, the resumption of output growth, and the achievement of structural changes required to prevent future payments and stabilization problems. The approach is to undertake other actions simultaneously to increase the responsiveness of the stabilization objectives to the primary policy instruments. Structural adjustment *may* include: (a) sectoral/micro reforms to *increase the responsiveness of exports and imports* to devaluation; and, (b) budgetary/financial sectoral reforms to *decrease the responsiveness of current account deficits to the growth of output for exports.*

SAPs assume that: (a) there are structural rigidities in the economy causing harsh economic difficulties; (b) domestic distortions prevent efficient allocation of resources and hence the maximization of income; and, (c) the existence of distortions represent bottlenecks limiting growth prospects. In the preparation of SAPs, there seems to be a total lack of an explicit framework of analysis and the different elements mentioned above are not articulated. In addition, even the concept of distortion is not unanimously accepted. Why then should health regulations, administrative structures, etc., be considered as distortions? Why should prices in agriculture which are out of tune with international prices be considered causes of distortions while international prices very often reflect subsidy policies of concerned governments?

Distortions in the agricultural sector in African countries are often due to bureaucratic elements. Thus, merely removing what could be called price distortions may not induce meaningful product response. While in some countries distortions are product market-related, in others factor market distortions are more predominant. In other countries, the existence of both types of distortions makes it difficult to know which of them should be tackled first.

It can be said that the short-run objectives of the stabilization programmes take the parameters of an economy's response to stimuli as given and fixed, while the medium-term objectives of SAPs act on a longer time frame to be able to transform the parameters of response themselves.

Whatever the differences between the two modes of adjustment, the common objective remains to achieve the equilibrium of the external sector, via expenditure absorption-reduction and/or expenditure switching mechanism. *The consequences of the implied measures on the rural sector are not taken as constraints but as residuals.*

490

Absorption-Reduction Mode

The absorption-reduction adjustment mode consists of a decrease in domestic credit creation (reduction of money supply) in order to reduce the current account deficit and contain inflation. This monetary approach stems from the belief that excesses in the demand or supply of monetary balances are adjusted through inflows or outflows in international reserves. In other words, considering nominal income as fixed in the short run, declines in domestic credit creation are assumed to lead to excess demand for money; this can be satisfied only through international reserve inflows, i.e., a surplus in current account and, in the longer run, reduced money supply is believed to restrain inflation. This monetarist rationale, based on Keynesian or absorption-oriented explanation, does not fit in many African countries where current account deficits result from misallocation of resources rather than from a spillover of absorption over supply and into imports. Consequently, domestic credit restraint will not lead to a reduction of trade deficit via the reduction of absorption *per se* but via the reduction of output and activity levels. This approach seems therefore to be an inappropriate medicine to the structural difficulties facing the LDCs, and *the existence of large informal markets for funds, make monetary control very difficult or even impossible in some cases*. Hence, it is doubtful that the monetary targets can be easily attained.

Credit restraint will also lead to an increase in interest rates, working capital, production costs, reduction in output and increases in prices (inflationary effects). Credit restraint programmes may hurt small informal sector firms and certainly the rural sector. In addition, measures to cut consumption subsidies and raise government charges may be detrimental to the poor regardless of their sources of income.

In the formulation of this approach, it is always easier to *reduce investments* than increase government tax revenues or change private consumption/savings decisions. The impact on the sectoral economy and on the rural sector, in particular, is never assessed. The structural adjustment objectives, to reduce the above mentioned rigidities, i.e., sectoral rigidities, ineffective taxation systems, underdeveloped capital markets and financial regulations, remain the achievement of current account balance. The impact of those measures on the rural sector is not a major concern and therefore is not assessed. There is no doubt that all those actions will lead to an important change in the structural distribution of income in the rural sector, a movement toward greater inequality, generally detrimental to the rural poor, and will shift part of that population towards the cities, sacrifice the food production sector and consequently increase the countries' reliance on food imports with its detrimental consequences on the current account position.

Expenditure Switching Mode

Whenever the expenditure switching mode is utilized in a stabilization programme, the most important tool is the 'modification of exchange rate and specifically devaluation in general'. By raising the internal currency price of tradeables *vis-à-vis* home goods, this action shifts production towards the former and demand towards the latter (although to a lesser degree). Since it is assumed that the devaluing country is a price-taker in the world markets, changes in exports and imports will result solely from internal agent decisions.

Contrary to absorption-reduction policies, devaluation is considered expansionary, as it increases production and curtails demand leakages through imports. Technically, one always has to choose between 'maxi-devaluation' and a series of 'mini-devaluation' (sliding or crawling peg) or a combination of both. Any modification of an exchange rate bases its success on a variety of factors. On how much devaluation contributes to inflation, there is no consensus as yet, but it depends upon the share of tradeables in the country's GDP, the degree of substitutability between tradeables and non-tradeables, and on the degree to which workers and firms can pass cost increases on to consumers in the economy. The supply response of exporters is an important factor in the effectiveness of devaluation. Since LDCs are generally price-takers, and because of external stockpile of many of the LDCs primary export products, the response could be very slow and their primary exports may be expected to show a very low short-run elasticity while manufactured exports from middle-income LDCs show quick response.

It is doubtful that changes in import demand and import-substituting supply resulting from devaluation will be very important to trade deficit reduction. In fact, LDCs have a great variety of import quantity restrictions. For example, years of tariff protection have already suppressed the importation of most consumer goods and other essentials. In addition, the effect of currency devaluation is to lower the profit margins of import licences more than to raise the price of imports to consumers. The question here is how do we compensate the government revenue losses due to a lower taxable income for licences, and/or lower taxable imports. The major imports remaining are essential intermediate goods and capital goods with inelastic demand, and these cannot easily be produced locally in the short run.

However, despite the above criticism, there is some efficacy in the medium term in spurring net exports. The degree to which the contractionary effect of a devaluation offsets its expansionary impetus reflects sectoral rigidities inhibiting full supply and demand response to the exchange rate modification. Two important parameters in essence determine this response: the elasticity of export supply with respect to the price changes of tradeable goods and the elasticity of import demand. One of the objectives of the structural adjustment policy is to enlarge these elasticities as well as to more directly shift resources into the tradeable goods sector.

In support of the expenditure-switching mode, SAPs utilize 'trade liberalization'. The adoption of this element is based on the fact that high tariff and non-tariff protective barriers have dominated the economic management of LDCs. This policy has had the effect of raising costs, lowering productivity and introducing other distortions including incentive biases against exports. However, trade liberalization, which is intended to bring about greater micro-efficiency and aggregate output in the medium term, may and often does cause loss of activity. The persistence of government income-losses and the lack of compensation from elsewhere would bring about the reinstallation of tariffs and other barriers (in part to protect the failing parastatal enterprises, 'white elephants' which have to be subsidized). Finally, high tariffs on some imported capital and intermediate goods, and inputs such as fertilizers (since the final objective of liberalization is the unification of tariffs), *would have detrimental impacts on the cost structures of enterprises and especially in the rural sector's productive scheme.*

The liberalization of price controls is often another important element of structural adjustment. It could also have short-run destabilizing consequences. In fact, many developing countries in Africa have a large number of parastatals or public enterprises with monopoly, and the sudden liberalization of prices will force them into bankruptcy unless the government subsidizes them. Even where there are oligopolistic elements, it will take a long time for prices to adjust downward to clear the goods and labour markets. A certain gradualism may therefore be necessary, especially in the rural sector where the potential impact of those measures should be clearly understood.

QUESTIONING THE BASIC FOUNDATION OF THE STABILIZATION AND STRUCTURAL ADJUSTMENT PROGRAMMES OF IMF AND WORLD BANK

It is true that in a fully integrated economy, all policies and objectives will interact with each other (either positively or negatively) but, considering the economic structure of African countries, one can always single out from IMF and IBRD adjustment programmes a set of potential conflicts. Some of these are: (a) the lack of well-elaborated medium-term perspectives; (b) objectives which conflict with policy instruments because of lack of sufficient elaboration and careful exploration of trade-offs; (c) the programmes have multiple objectives and instruments, but the multi-directional links and interactions are only informally and loosely established; and, (d) partial analysis dominates the programmes but the process hardly allows the tracing of the general equilibrium interactions in the economy despite the recommended policies. The lack of cost analysis of the conflicting objectives and the severity of some measures impair the credibility of the package of adjustment policies and very often lead to the breakdown of the programme.

Altogether, there are about six groups of policy measures which appear frequently in stabilization and structural adjustment programmes (see Annex 22.1). The absence of an integrated general framework for the interactions of possible conflicts and trade-offs has been one of the major reasons for the failure of the implementation of some of these programmes and why the models behind those programmes were not made to do what they are being blamed for not doing. So far, it has been assumed that moving prices towards equilibrium, and restructuring institutions to conform to undefined but accepted operating efficiency norms could help in addressing those conflicts and trade-offs.

Stabilization, Financial Liberalization versus Growth/Investment

In general, structural adjustment follows a standby programme, the objective of which is correcting imbalance between aggregate demand and supply created by international mismanagement and/or external shocks. This is done via the adjustment of demand and supply. However, supply adjustment usually takes time, hence the main burden of stabilization programmes falls on the demand side via the reduction of money supply growth rate. *It is assumed that contraction of demand and reduction in capacity utilization and output would be compensated by an autonomous increase in agricultural output due to favourable weather conditions!* Certainly, credit for working and fixed capital would decrease, discouraging new investment, hence curtailing severely any supply adjustment. It could be argued that the contractionary period would be short, but its length and the economic and social costs (especially in the rural sector) could be of utmost economic and political importance.

One of the main characteristics of African countries is that the share of agriculture in the total public expenditure is always quite low compared to the share of agriculture in GDP. Except under extreme cases of stochastic changes in harvest, agricultural food production does not contribute to short-term crisis of the types which prompt IMF and, subsequently, World Bank adjustment programmes. However, lack of incentives, exogenous problems, reduction of appropriate levels of investment of resources in the agricultural sector and problems of internally generated technology can weaken agricultural growth rate and bring pressure on the balance of payments in the long run.

Subsidies versus Public Sector Surplus

It has been pointed out by international studies that export-led rather than an import-substituting industrialization policy is more relevant to the performance of the industrial sectors and overall national economies. This demonstration has pushed some LDCs to introduce important export-subsidy policies (e.g. Kenya 20 per cent and Zambia 9 per cent). The optimization of economic growth can be achieved in the short run only if subsidies to encourage diversification are made available to all sectors of the economy, including agriculture.

Because of the need to boost exports and bring about a rapid adjustment of the exchange rate and/or balance of payments, it is often suggested in some adjustment programmes that exports receive direct subsidies (sometimes interest rate subsidies are granted to export sectors). Granting or even reducing subsidies goes in conflict with increasing public sector surplus (reduction of public firms' subsidies will increase the cost of those firms).

A position on a supply function curve which is upward sloping for major food products is not automatically an indication of a structural problem or of a need for structural adjustment. International prices, in addition to exchange rate departure from an equilibrium value and other factors such as obstacles to free trade which often dictate the need for adjustment measures embodied in stabilization programmes, do not represent the correct criteria at all. In fact, international prices could be and often are just the reflection of subsidy policies prevailing in the major exporting countries, the EEC and US being cases in point.[3] African countries should reduce the use of this traditional method of determining internal pricing policy. It is even unfortunate that African countries still believe that the application of international pricing mechanism can bring about an efficient long-term allocation of resources at the international level, especially in the agriculture sector. While it is true that a small country cannot influence its terms of trade, it still would be wrong to accept distorted international prices as the opportunity cost of a product especially in the agricultural sector.

Privatization versus Liberalization of Interest Rates and/or Increase in Tax Revenues

Because of the macro-objectives of stabilization and structural adjustment programmes, and the existence of many 'white elephants' in African countries, there is an increasing tendency to make privatization one of the major objectives of IMF and World Bank programmes. Unfortunately, this objective goes simultaneously with liberalization of interest rates and an increase in tax revenues. *The assumption is that a sufficient array of investment opportunities with high rates of return will always exist, which is not true.* Consequently, in the short run, there will be a reduction in the investment rate and expansion of output. Here again, the conflict between objectives is evident.

It has been argued that raising nominal interest rates instead of reducing the money supply growth would represent a better way to foster growth rate in the short run.[4] In African countries, in general, the rate of inflation tends to be on the high side which makes interest rates on agricultural credit negative in real terms. Adjustment programmes usually require those rates to be made positive or less negative. There is little doubt that in those countries, maintaining real positive interest rates during high inflation periods will reduce producers' real net incomes and/or cause producers to adopt input-saving technologies. This will certainly reduce the growth rate of the sector's gross output.

Trade Liberalization versus Reduction in Balance of payments and Budget Deficit

Trade liberalization, for example through tariffs reductions and unsupported by appropriate supplementary policies, will reduce government revenue and increase imports which, in turn, will increase budget deficits and balance of payments deficit.

Trade liberalization alone, without adequate measures to reduce the costs of imported inputs such as markups, intermediaries' benefits etc., would not bring about the expected results. Price controls, which are often politically motivated, usually benefit mainly intermediaries but not the rural peasants. Food security assistance and additional food imports could be used to reduce the impacts of large fluctuations in the prices of mass consumption food products. Those products have important political significance which justifies the control of imports and prices. Any change in that set-up, which should be the appropriate move, must make provisions for reasonable substitute policy measures. By the same token, replacing import quotas with tariffs and/or unifying tariffs, without protecting export products, would not yield the expected results. Tariffs may protect some producers while being detrimental to others; comparative advantage may not be just a question of yes or no for those producers.

If there was free trade by all trading countries, the 'time' international opportunity cost of a product would reflect its international price. Unfortunately, international prices are themselves distorted because of agricultural price policies of the various trading countries concerned. The problem with most African countries is that the price policies they have set up do not relate optimally to what is assumed to be the objective.

IMF and IBRD Programmes versus Employment and Income Distribution

In general, these programmes include exchange rate modification, reduction in output and investment, and elimination or reduction of subsidies. Exchange rate depreciation will shift resources from non-tradeables to tradeables, or from labour-intensive to capital-intensive technologies. Hence, export-promotion tends to reduce employment although in some cases a compensation may come from exportables being more labour-intensive than importables. There is no doubt that decreases in output and investment will have a detrimental impact on employment. Finally, the removal of subsidies and/or liberalization of prices will create adverse effects on income distribution, especially in the rural sector and among the low-income consumers. In this domain, the cost-benefit of alternative adjustment paths should be brought out more explicitly. Furthermore, IMF and World Bank, through their SAPs, are suggesting the need to bring down personnel costs to a reasonable and manageable level compatible with revenues, either through early retirement and reduction of salary and/or freeze of recruitment in the public sector. Considering the present economic structure of African countries with the dominance of public sector, this prescription, though valid, will not bring any lasting solution to the problems crippling the African economy, especially in the agricultural sector. There is no doubt that if things were working properly, there would be a shortage of staff in this sector.

The political-economic equilibrium trap caused by migration from rural to urban areas is well known. In fact, this common situation increases the urban unemployment leading to political pressures to maintain or increase subsidies for urban basic mass consumption of food products which, in turn, encourage more migration. This 'trap' will jeopardize any stabilization programme having the reduction of urban subsidies as one of the major objectives. In general, the policy measure consists of an artificially low cost of living in urban areas through holding down farm prices below the international level; an implicit kind of taxation! Elements such as the above have not been taken into account in analyzing the supply functions, the equilibrium prices and the resulting adjustment measures needed especially in the agricultural sector.

All these measures are dictated by the sole objective to move towards more market-oriented economies by removing economic activity from the 'inefficient' administration of government. One cannot change mentalities and the prevailing environment overnight. In many cases, interventionism (export subsidies and/or multiple exchange rates) might be considered as a second-best solution. No single country has developed its agricultural sector without subsidy. The question is mainly: what is the optimum level of subsidy? The problems with subsidy are: its high administrative costs, the development of vested interest groups which will oppose its removal, and the fact that if it acts directly on value-added, it will violate GATT articles and invite hostile reciprocation. Even credit subsidies to exporters tend to shift investment towards relatively capital-intensive techniques.

CONCLUSION

At this crucial moment when African countries are reconsidering the philosophy underlying a viable and sustainable economic and social development, a detailed analysis of the impacts of IMF and World Bank recommendations on the rural sector of African economies will represent an important contribution to the implementation of APPER and UN-PAAERD. Since the middle of the 1970s, African countries have been using the two institutions' stabilization and structural adjustment programmes; some countries have in fact gone to IMF and World Bank more than once. It is clear that with or without IMF and World Bank, African countries have to adjust. With the information that is already largely available and case studies that could be undertaken of three or four countries, it should be possible to provide countries with manageable options to choose from, in the interest of a sound and sustainable economic and social development process with beneficial impact on the *rural sector*.

Because of the present structure of the African economies, all adjustment measures used by IMF and World Bank have serious impacts on *the rural sector of the economy*. This sector is the most important in many countries and the changing income structure in that sector brought about by the implementation of adjustment measures should be clearly analysed and understood. If not, all stabilization and structural adjustment programmes are bound to fail and even the apparent temporary success will be just an illusion! It is clear however that even if IMF and World Bank wanted to undertake such a study on the impacts of their stabilization and/or structural adjustment programmes on the rural sectors of African economies, these institutions do not have the tools and/or the qualification to do it.

It is well-known that designing a multiple-objectives policy framework is not an easy task. Let us assume that there exist policy objectives which are positively correlated in response to any given instrument, so that the attainment of any objective necessarily implied progress toward achieving the remainder. In such a case, there will be little difficulty, since certain objectives are negatively correlated and the effect of each instrument on all objectives is not always positive. Hence, there is need for using multiple instruments, some being assigned to help eliminate the negative effects of the others. Any coherent programme should consider explicitly the multi-directional links and effects. Below are some of the pertinent areas.

What should be the degree of response of the objective variables to a given change in an instrument or package of instruments? What should be the short- and long-term elasticity values of: (i) imports and exports, with respect to the exchange rate; (ii) inflation, with respect to money stock and exchange rate, and, (iii) saving and investment, with respect to interest rate? Only the inflationary problem is considered in stabilization and structural adjustment programmes, because inflation has been seen mainly as a monetary phenomenon.

Policy instruments could have indirect effects on other objectives. In fact there may be serious conflicts between the adjustment of exchange rate and inflation in the sense that cost-push effects, i.e., of public firms' output prices, could be the main contributor to the general price level. Very often, the output prices of the public enterprises are liberalized but no measure is taken to improve the efficiency of those

499

enterprises. Consequently, they pass on their inefficiencies through the prices of the basic intermediate and capital goods they produce. Cost-push factors should therefore receive due consideration.

We have seen that liberalization of interest rates will increase cost of borrowing for both working capital and fixed capital and will negatively affect investment in the private sector. What type of policy instruments should be used to eliminate those negative side effects? For the case of liberalization of interest rates, one could try to reduce the intermediation costs of the banking sector (reduction of transaction tax on credit for example) but the oligopolistic conditions or lack of competition in that sector could prevent the cost-reduction from being passed on to borrowers. Thus, the banking structure of the country has to be taken into account.

It would be important to know whether the policy measures should be introduced simultaneously or sequentially. What has been the time lag of the response of the key macro variables and targets to policy variables? Can they be time-phased? The answers to these questions would have important bearings on the speed of adjustment.

If IMF programmes are based on general equilibrium analysis, there is a serious lack of partial equilibrium analysis. Both IMF and World Bank programmes are formulated around various economic, institutional and social objectives which are linked to a multitude of policy instruments. Since contemporaneous and inter-temporal interdependence is a key feature, there is need for an efficient integration of partial and general equilibrium analyses so that all interactions and consistency are present. In addition, all this should be placed in a well elaborated medium-term perspective in order to guide the policy actions and institutional improvements towards the desired medium-term goals. Such procedure could constitute the basis for alternative growth paths in terms of chosen macro-performance indicators and time-phased consistent policy instruments. Specific issue-oriented analysis of direct, partial-equilibrium relationships linking policy instruments to performance indicators should be combined with the use of a policy-oriented economy-wide modelling framework to study the interactions of instruments and indicators in general equilibrium context. Unfortunately, most of the models developed in IMF and World Bank are research-oriented, developed for specific tasks, while what is needed here is an operational tool, supported by research and located in a user oriented environment. Such a framework has to be a flexible policy modelling system with many choices (number of sectors, objectives, policy instruments, equation specification, adjustment mechanism, etc.). This framework should be oriented towards policy analysis rather than projections, help work out contemporaneously and inter-temporally consistent macro-policy packages, and help analyse major issues rather than enumerate objectives and instruments. This framework would serve as an element of dialogue on the diagnosis of problems, the types of instruments and the speed of adjustment, and make explicit the implicit assumption embodied in policy analysis while at the same time providing insights into the behaviour of the economy.

The above analysis points to the necessity of following certain steps in setting up an adjustment programme:

(i)   Sound analysis of the structural characteristics of the economy prior to adjustment programmes. The difference here is between 'structural characteristics' and 'economic characteristics'. Emphasis should be put on the agricultural sector, the prevailing system of protection and incentives, the behaviour of the export sector, resource mobilization, the public sector (including central government, budget), statal and para-statal enterprises, etc.

(ii)   The structural analysis should bring out the need to set specific objectives in specific areas to eliminate distortions and promote economic efficiency while minimizing the cost of adjustment on the rural poor. To reach these objectives, some intermediate objectives could be set. Once these intermediate and final objectives have been set, macro and micro instruments to fulfil the objectives have to be discussed and adopted, taking into account their capabilities to temper the unavoidable conflicts among policy objectives, the trade-offs, and the link between policy instruments and performance indicators.

(iii) Mobilization of resources and speed of adjustment: optimal level of financing of adjustment, keeping in mind that too much foreign financing can be harmful. Its role is to ease the transition process. The international credit environment must be taken as given. Maximum efforts should come from within. Cost and benefit analysis of both external and internal financing should be made independently.

(iv) Determining whether to opt for 'shock treatments' or a 'gradualist approach': shock treatments may be politically more appropriate while a gradualist approach would better fit the search for economic benefits. There are pros and cons for both approaches to the time dimension of adjustment. In African countries, the elements of the necessity to give time to rigid structural parameters to adjust, the avoidance of welfare losses imposed by

501

strong and rapid dislocation, extreme contractionary restraints, excessive output price fluctuations and sudden increase in unemployment, all make the gradualist approach more convenient. Unfortunately it helps build up political resistance. Sometimes a once-and-for-all application of some policy measures could reduce the risk of political failure. In conclusion, a combination of the two approaches could prove more amenable, and, anyway, the problem must be handled on a country by country basis. Nevertheless, within the framework of APPER and UN-PAAERD, African Heads of State and Government have shown their political will. Consequently, with the basic assumption that there is strong political commitment to adjustment, gradualism would be most appropriate for African countries.

ANNEX 22.1

MAJOR POLICIES AND RELATED MACRO-INSTRUMENTS/OBJECTIVES USED BY IMF AND WORLD BANK IN SAPs, AND INDUCED MICRO INSTRUMENTS IN THE RURAL SECTOR

A. *Monetary Policy*
(Institutions using it most: IMF)

Related macro instruments/ objectives	Induced micro instruments in the rural sector
– Money supply objectives – Interest rates structures – Credit ceilings (short- and long-term) – Inflation targets – Real positive interest rates – Capital reform markets to attract financial savings – revaluation of assets	– Targets for distribution of credit to rural sector contradictary – Interest rates for the agricultural sector become expensive in real terms (high) when the target is to reduce the level of inflation. Hence reduction in real incomes and in the sector's growth rate of outputs

B. *Fiscal Policy*
(Institutions using it most: IMF)

Related macro instruments/ objectives	Induced micro instruments in the rural sector
– Reduction of expenditures – Modification of tax and tariffs structures – Changes in subsidy structures – Fiscal substitutes for exchange rate modification	– Increase allocation of funding to agriculture and social services at the expense of infrastructure and especially government buildings – Reduction in current expenditure and public investment – Increased taxes and other charges – Introduction and/or changes of tariffs in the rural sector – Modification of subsidy structure – Reduction of salary levels and/

502

Related macro instruments/ objectives	Induced micro instruments in the rural sector (cont'd)
	or of staff of rural-related ministries and institutions – Restructuring of agricultural institutions with a view to changing expenditure levels – Measures to improve public agricultural enterprises performance in order to reduce government budgetary burden

C. *Price Policy*
(Institutions using it most: IMF and IBRD)

Related macro instruments/ objectives	Induced micro instruments in the rural sector
– Modification of exchange rate – Changes in wage policy – Modification of interest rate structure – Fiscal substitutes for exchange rate changes – Theory of the second-best due to many non-economic objectives and other justifiable elements causing price distortions – Reduce domestic demand by curbing monetary expansion through the limitations of credit to the public sector from the central authorities	– Tariffs on imported goods – Change in rural wage structure and rural interest rates – Various sets of administered output and input prices. Price incentives for farmers but since higher staple food prices will have detrimental impact on the poorest strata there is need for transitional measures such as targeted subsidies – Agricultural supply function for all major food products is upward sloping (Tunisia, Egypt ...), which makes it very difficult to set a realistic protective tariff level in the absence of import quota; necessity of a general equilibrium model to compute the optimal internal product and factor prices in the face of all possible justifications – Reduce public investment. Introduce tax reform and price liberalization. – Limit employment in the public sector. Reduce the number of public enterprises – Rely on market forces – Let the prices adjust to the trend value of world prices with intervention limited to settling guaranteed floor prices or levying an export tax depending on the year of low or high prices

D. *Policy on Trade*
(Institutions using it most: IMF and IBRD)

Related macro instruments/ objectives	Induced micro instruments in the rural sector
– Trade liberalization – Export subsidies for export promotion – Rationalization of foreign exchange, tariff and quotas – New tariff structure – Flexible exchange rate and periodical review in co-ordination with IMF. Action on marginal deposit requirements and on central bank rediscount rate. Changes in institutions' structure to promote exports	– Increase public investment in the agriculture field – Removal of some subsidies in the rural sector, subsidizing exports production to the detriment of food production – Foreign exchange objectives – No doubt that trade liberalization is, in the short run, inconsistent with the balance of payments improvement because of its impact on import bill (agricultural exports *will not* expand rapidly during the adjustment process with or without exchange rate modification) – Tariff protection or export subsidies? Unless there are appropriate policy substitutes, it will be potentially risky to dismantle domestic and import controls for mass consumption of food products as in countries such as Morocco, Tunisia, Egypt, Madagascar, Senegal – Improve mechanism for determining agricultural producer prices

E. *Reform of Institutions*
(Institutions using it most: IBRD)

Related macro instruments/ objectives	Induced micro instruments in the rural sector
– Managerial rules in monetary sector, statal and parastatal enterprises; change in the structure of investment in the parastatals – Training programmes at different levels – Improvement of managerial capabilities at selected levels and in selected sectors – Abstract factor	– Improving management in the rural sector – Training in the agricultural sector – Elimination of intermediaries by introducing reforms in the agriculture structures (such as marketing boards ...) – Introducing research in the rural sector – Abstract factor of adjustment process

F. *Sectoral Studies and Further Research*
(Institutions using it most: IBRD)

Related macro instruments/ objectives	Induced micro instruments in the rural sector
– Although the majority of structural adjustment programmes contain sectoral policy instruments, there is no general and integrated framework for a meaningful analysis of their interactions – Use of economic analysis in project evaluation – Introduce new and more adapted investment criteria – Balance of payments gap – Amount of foreign resources from other sources; debt servicing; capacities; absorptive capacity; quotas of member countries and institutions' quota policy regarding use of its resources – Often depend on the capacity of the national authorities to negotiate – Prudent debt management, and better debt statistics – Allow no commercial arrears – Try to reschedule – Limit commercial credit	– Measures suggested in the rural sector are not integrated in a general framework. They are also in conflict with other policy instruments – The final objective remains the equilibrium of the external sector and foreign savings – Improve medium-term planning and research capabilities – Measures to reach optimal distribution – Serious conflicts between level of needs and of amount imposed by quota system – More emphasis on apparently quick-yielding sector or projects, the final objective remaining the rapid equilibrium of the external sector. The cost-benefit criterion is at the global and not at the sectoral level

NOTES

1. The present observation is based on general analysis of IMF's stabilization and Extended Fund Facility programmes and World Bank Structural adjustment programme as implemented in some African countries (Burkina Faso, Central African Republic, Cote d'Ivoire, Egypt, Equatorial Guinea, Ethiopia, Gabon, Ghana, Kenya, Liberia, Madagascar, Mauritania, Mauritius, Morocco, Rwanda, Senegal, Sierra Leone, the Sudan, Togo, the United Republic of Tanzania, Zaire and Zambia).
2. See World Banks, Development Report, 1983 (pp.42–43).
3. No country has developed its agricultural sector without a certain degree of subsidy! Subsidy policies have intensified in major industrial countries in recent years and are setting up an economic 'war' between EEC and US and even among the EEC countries themselves, especially in the agricultural sector.
4. Mckinnon R.I., *Money and Capital in Economic Development*, Brookings Institution, 1973.

CHAPTER TWENTY-THREE

Report on the International Conference on Growth and Structural Adjustment in Africa

IDEP SECRETARIAT

The International Conference on Growth and Structural Adjustment in Africa took place in Dakar, Senegal, on 4 May 1987. It reviewed Africa's present economic situation and future prospects, with a focus on the prospects and policy requirements of agriculture-led economic recovery in Africa, and examined also the financing requirements and policies for growth and structural adjustment in Africa. The following is a summary of the proceedings of the Conference.

THE OPENING STATEMENTS

In the various statements addressed to the opening session, it was noted that since the early 1980s the majority of African countries had undertaken adjustment programmes involving mainly the control of aggregate demand. However, these efforts, supported in most cases by bilateral and multilateral financial institutions, had not been very fruitful owing to the unfavourable international environment which included factors such as the slow-down of world economic activity, the instability in the international commodity and financial markets, the prolonged and drastic fall in export earnings from primary commodities as well as increasing debt burden.

The African countries were naturally all too aware that they are an integral part of the world. But the sad reality is that, although some efforts have already been made to recognize and provide solutions to the negative effects of the international environment on the African continent, a lot remains to be done or achieved. In this regard, the need to effectively support the efforts of the developing countries through exceptional financing was emphasized, as was the urgent need to review the African experience of SAPs so as to come to very clear conclusions on at least three critical questions, namely: (a) What are the real benefits – if any – of the various adjustment programmes attempted by the different African countries? (b) What are the avoidable and inevitable transitional and other social, political and economic costs, and how can their effects be minimized? (c) Who reaps the benefits and who bears the burden of the stabilization and structural adjustment programmes in Africa?

It was emphasized that while there was no controversy regarding the necessity for structural adjustment, there seemed to be no unanimity of views with respect to the content, time paths and emphasis of the needed structural adjustment in the African economies. The orthodox IMF-inspired adjustment programmes have generally focused on short-term policies aimed at demand management, with elements such as currency devaluation, ceilings on budgetary deficits, wage freeze, reduction or elimination of subsidies, streamlining of public enterprises, tax reforms, liberalization of the market forces, price incentives for agriculture, credit control, interest rate adjustment etc., predominating. However, the experience of African countries that have undertaken structural adjustment programmes between 1980 and 1985 shows that the performance on the basis of most social and economic indicators is mixed, with partial success stories and absolute failures. The indications so far are that structural adjustment programmes, as traditionally conceived and implemented, may not have the inherent capability of rectifying any of the structural weaknesses in the African economies since such disequilibria are often more intensive and extensive, and more often than not, have tended to be both internal (endogenous) and external (exogenous) structural weaknesses.

Doubt was expressed as to whether the usual IMF-type prescriptions could effectively deal with balance of payments adjustments in Africa. Even if these policies were to bring about some supply response, the actual balance of payments improvement would depend critically on prevailing international commodity prices. On the question of exchange rate adjustments and the effects of devaluation, the African experience did not seem to have conformed to the classical model. In most African countries, both exports and imports, particularly imports, are price inelastic, and under such conditions, one devaluation tends to necessitate another resulting in a chain reaction of inflationary pressures.

In the light of the above, the need for alternative policy guidelines for an appropriate structural adjustment approach for Africa was stressed. It was also considered necessary to ensure that policies were implemented in the context of recovery and growth rather than retrenchment. Achieving such growth would, in the context of the African economy, entail accelerated rates of capital formation in carefully selected sectors, diversification of production, domestic and intra-African trade; as well as achieving greater regional co-operation, all of which are issues that have already been articulated in a coherent manner by both APPER and UN-PAAERD.

SUBSTANTIVE SESSIONS AND ISSUES

Africa's present economic situation and future prospects

The three main background papers on this theme were: (i) 'Growth and Structural Adjustment in Africa: A Global Perspective', (ii) 'Economic Outlook for Africa', and (iii) 'Adjustment and Growth in sub-Saharan Africa'.

The first paper noted that the African economy, after having achieved a high rate of sustained growth over a decade, from early 1960s to the 1970s, came to a standstill at the turn of the 1980s, and the performance of a number of the African economies since then has been very poor. This phenomenon constitutes a source of major concern for many policy makers both at the national and international levels.

The paper broadly noted that the major 'engine of growth' in Africa during the decade of high growth has traditionally been the exports of primary commodities to the main trading partners (i.e., the developed market economies). It was the pace of primary commodity exports that set the level and pulse of economic activities. However, since the early 1970s, the momentum created by this traditional engine of growth has followed a steady downward trend with a profound effect on growth in the African economies. If the present trend in international markets (particularly, the fall in demand and prices for primary commodity exports) continues, then new development strategies to cope with this basic organic factor would have to be devised.

According to the paper, the vast agricultural resource base of many African countries points to the potential role of agriculture in growth. The recent drought and famine that afflicted some African countries have highlighted the importance and urgent need for accelerated agricultural growth. As part of the policy requirements for accelerated agricultural growth and its interrelationship with overall growth, greater emphasis must be placed on sectoral balance and regional co-operation including intra-regional trade. There must also be increased investment in agriculture. Other policies include pricing, credit, marketing and the building up of both soft and physical infrastructure. Reforms in the land tenure system are also important. However, a critical analysis of the framework underlying the design of structural adjustment policies shows that the viability and efficacy of these policies to deal with the African situation and its structural characteristics are below expectations. Therefore, while structural adjustment is a necessity, its constituent policies must be reoriented to take into consideration both internal structural features as well as the constraints imposed by external factors, policies and trends.

The second paper reviewed the recent economic developments in Africa and their underlying factors as well as the implications for the short- and medium-term outlook for Africa in general and sub-Saharan Africa in particular. It concluded, in general, that the African countries experienced serious economic and financial imbalances, particularly in the late 1970s and the 1980s. These imbalances were partly the result of adverse exogenous developments such as declining terms of trade, slow growth in industrial countries, high international interest rates, and the rise in protectionism. The impact of the external shocks was compounded by inadequate domestic policies especially with regard to fiscal, monetary, exchange rate and pricing policies, as well as economic restrictions. The difficult situation was complicated by structural weaknesses and the damaging impact of recurrent droughts, particularly in the Sahelian region, and resulted in high rates of inflation, large external current account deficits, mounting debt and debt service obligations, and a sharp drop in economic growth.

As a result of these difficulties an increasing number of African countries embarked on implementing adjustment policies aimed at reducing domestic and external imbalances, increasing incentives for production and promoting growth and exports under IMF-supported adjustment programmes. Subsequent to the implementation of these adjustment policies some progress had been achieved in terms of GDP growth, inflation, current account balances and the debt situation for sub-Saharan Africa during 1984–1985. But the year 1986 was a difficult one for Africa with a worsening of the terms of trade and the external resource flow situation, leading to deterioration in the economic and financial conditions in most of the African countries.

The overall outlook for Africa in the short and medium term depended not only on the external environment (e.g. the evolution of the terms of trade, and weather conditions), but also on the pace and quality of adjustment programmes undertaken. Regarding the international environment, the prospects were not perceived as encouraging, as growth in industrial countries was projected to pick up only slightly, and demand for the export commodities was not expected to pick up significantly. The prices of primary commodities were likely indeed to remain weak in the immediate future and to improve only moderately in the medium term, while the debt service burden in Africa was projected to remain high.

To tackle these challenges, the paper sees co-ordinated efforts of the African countries themselves, the donors and creditors and multilateral institutions, particularly IMF and World Bank as crucial. African countries should persevere in implementing wide-ranging adjustment programmes, including well-designed investment plans that would aim at mobilizing additional domestic resources, improving efficiency in the allocation of resources, and reducing socio-economic distortions, but these efforts needed to be supported by adequate concessional financing from donors and creditors as well as reduced protectionism.

The third paper gave an overview of the evidence of slow growth in sub-Saharan African countries in the past decade which included exogenous factors such as drought and terms of trade as well as the domestic policy environment. In order to address such problems, many African countries had undertaken policy adjustments with some common themes. It was noteworthy that these new policy directions had been taken courageously, offering new possibilities and, at the same time, continually creating new dilemmas.

One major theme of the adjustment process in Africa has been the re-orientation of the role of government in the economy towards vital areas such as infrastructure, education, health, population, agricultural research and ecology. On infrastructure, the past imbalance between construction and maintenance has led to a massive deterioration of the existing infrastructure. For a number of countries, there is now a new policy focus on rehabilitation and maintenance. In education, the past emphasis on higher cost options needs to shift to improved efficiency and quality. For example, provisions have to be made for adequate learning materials at the primary school level and lower cost options need to be developed, particularly at secondary and higher levels.

Other critical areas for government involvement are health and population. The inadequacy of basic health services was aggravated by policies which concentrated on health care facilities in urban and high-cost hospitals. There was, therefore, need to shift priorities towards the delivery of minimum health care, such as immunization and other elements of child care, and the expansion of access to community-based primary health, particularly in the rural areas. On population issues, the cost of extending access to family planning information through local government, community and private initiatives is not great. The public sector must, therefore, assume this role, particularly in the rural areas where the government is the major provider of modern health care. While most governments have recognized the threat of deforestation, the scope for design and implementation of government programmes to date has been far from adequate. Providing tree seedlings for rural families to plant and maintain may be sufficient in some contexts, but, in other more hostile environments, reforestation must be combined with other policies including those on livestock, land re-settlement and irrigation.

The major challenge in the re-orientation of the role of government is that the vital government activities identified need to be performed in the context of an overall reduction in the extent of government involvement in the economy. One critical dilemma is how to facilitate the transition of public sector manpower to the productive sectors. There is also some apprehension as to whether the private sector can respond adequately in those areas where the government was previously active. The concentration by government on vital functions and the reduction in the overall scope of government is, in itself, insufficient to encourage growth and development. The government must create an incentive framework involving, *inter alia*, the aligning of key prices with economic realities. Such realignment must include the exchange rate, interest rates and agricultural producer prices. In addition, the institutional framework must be improved for effective delivery of services, including marketing and transport. Over and above these, the government must remove controls and concentrate on broad economic strategic planning.

The main conclusions on the theme of Africa's present situation and future prospects were that:

(a) There is no controversy about the necessity for structural adjustment in the African economies. However, Africa's partners, i.e. the donor countries and the international financial community in general, still had to demonstrate their willingness to assist Africa.

(b) There is a general consensus about the nature and main causes of the African economic crisis. The economies are characterized by serious economic imbalances: low and negative per capita income growth, high rates of inflation, large current account deficits, and a heavy debt burden. These imbalances were, to a large extent, the result of adverse exogenous developments: declining terms of trade, slow growth in industrial countries as well as farm support policies, the rise in protectionism in these countries, and high

511

international interest rates. The impact of these external shocks was compounded by inefficient domestic policies: fiscal, monetary, exchange rate and pricing policies, and intensified controls and restrictions. These were complicated by structural weaknesses and rigidities: marketing and distribution bottlenecks, social constraints, fragile political systems, civil wars and natural hazards such as the recent drought and desertification.

(c) Doubts exist concerning the validity of the usual IMF-inspired SAP as the panacea for sustaining growth of the African economies. Some aspects of the Programmes seem to have adverse effects. For example, exchange rate adjustments and devaluation may not be able to deal effectively with balance of payments maladjustments because both imports and exports are in general, price inelastic. The import bill may remain high under a liberalized trade regime. And while export supply may respond to higher producer price incentives, in some cases, actual balance of payments improvements depend critically on prevailing international commodity prices. As commodity prices collapse or commodity substitutes are discovered, the balance of payments may deteriorate even further. The African experience does not appear to have conformed to the orthodox model of exchange rate adjustments and devaluation.

(d) Primary commodity exports acted as the engine of growth for African economies in the 1960s and early 1970s. The prospects for the short- and medium-term outlook for this engine of growth are rather bleak. This is because growth in industrial countries is projected to pick up only slightly, with demand for primary export commodities and prices remaining weak.

(e) While primary commodity exports cannot continue to be the engine of growth, the role of agriculture as a potential source of growth is envisaged. The African economy, particularly the sub-Saharan region, is still predominantly rural and agricultural. An agriculture-led growth strategy would entail the following: (i) A comprehensive programme for the attainment of food self-sufficiency in the basic staples of the continent; (ii) Production of raw materials to feed the growing industrial complex made up of food processing, textiles and other agro-based industries; (iii) African countries maintaining at least their share of primary commodity exports in world trade; and, (iv) Developing intra-African and interregional trade and co-operation to expand the market for agricultural products.

(f) The desirable policy package of an appropriate adjustment programme has been coherently stated in APPER in terms of specific growth policies oriented towards Africa's priority sectors. Structural adjustment policies can best be implemented in the context of recovery and growth rather than retrenchment. This, in turn, would necessitate accelerated rates of capital formation in the priority sectors as identified in APPER; diversification of production and domestic and intra-African trade; and achievement of greater regional co-operation.

(g) The constraint on growth emanating from the debt problem and debt service can be removed only by *long-term* debt rescheduling on a concessional basis rather than the current short-term relief programmes.

(h) Appropriate action is required at the next GATT Round towards a global arrangement on tropical commodities similar to the ACP-EEC stabex programme. Such action should aim at stabilizing income from primary tropical commodity exports in the face of deteriorating terms of trade.

(i) The role of the government needs re-examination to enable it to support a flexible, growth-oriented and developing economy. The government has vital functions to perform especially in the areas of infrastructure, education, health, population, agricultural research and ecology, all of which are critical to development and there is no substitute for government involvement and leadership. It would seem desirable that the government divests itself from those areas in which the private sector has comparative advantage so that the vital government activities can be performed in the context of an overall reduction in the size of government within the economy.

Agriculture-led Economic Recovery in Africa: Prospects and Policy Requirements

The two main papers on this theme were: (i) 'Stimulating Agricultural Growth in sub-Saharan Africa'; and, (ii) 'Structural Adjustment Policies and Agricultural Growth in Africa'.

The first paper stated the general premise that the rehabilitation of the agricultural sector through policy reforms can provide the necessary conditions for short-term growth, although sustained growth in agriculture depends on medium- to long-term measures. It analysed the policies of World Bank with respect to the agricultural sector noting that, after 1980, World Bank had gradually shifted away from agricultural project investments towards lending in support of long-term policy reform and institution building objectives. The main vehicles for policy-based lending continued to be the agricultural adjustment loan and the general structural adjustment loan which usually included a major agricultural component. Most agricultural adjustment loans of World Bank in Africa involved import credits conditioned on institutional reforms. The loans also involved reforms of trade regimes, tariffs and interest rates, price incentives, as well as divestiture of parastatals.

The paper argued that while the policy reforms associated with agricultural adjustment loans are essential for creating the necessary climate for growth, they are inadequate to ensure sustained agricultural development since agricultural development was essentially predicated on such key variables as: appropriate technological advance; institutional development; and efficient market structure. The role of technology should be identified as the main 'engine of growth' in agriculture, especially within the context of land and labour intensive agriculture, where yield-augmenting technologies have a progressively greater relevance. In the African context, the strategy for augmenting crop yields had to address three principal problems: weak research capacity; absence of timely and predictable availability of water for crop production; and inadequacy of draft power on the farms.

The strategic role of the land tenure system in sub-Saharan African agriculture needed to be examined. Security in the cultivation of land, if not ownership, was also a major determinant of farmer response to development incentives and willingness to invest in land improvements. Communal ownership and private property rights are basic elements of the right to land, including the right to use land and to inherit, sell or rent land.

A review of marketing systems for inputs and outputs in the agricultural sector was also necessary. In the areas of education, research, rural infrastructure and health, the role of the public sector is particularly crucial, since these are public goods. But in the realm of marketing of agricultural goods, private firms and farmers' cooperatives have the advantage as they respond directly to price and market signals.

The second paper argues that the deteriorating performance of sub-Saharan African agriculture has often been attributed to inappropriate pricing and marketing policies. As a consequence, restructuring the incentive framework through pricing and institutional reforms, including marketing, had been the priority in most adjustment programmes. However, the strong emphasis on macro-economic management, particularly public finance, and the control of public expenditure in adjustment programmes had adversely affected agriculture. For example, the emphasis on reduction and elimination of subsidies had negatively affected fertilizer, pesticide and other critical inputs that are required for improved performance in sub-Saharan African agriculture. Also, most price reforms under adjustment programmes are usually justified, first by the supply response they elicit and, secondly, by the apparent benefit of a shift towards tradeables, in particular exportables. Yet, in practice, this was not always true, as illustrated by two cases where price reforms had contradictory results. In Ghana, for example, when producer prices for cocoa had declined precipitously, major price increases were required to stem the declining output as well as to raise government revenues. True to the theory, when producer prices were raised after 1983, output levels rose by over 35 per cent. However in the Sudan, the effect of the 1978 devaluation was to depress output of all exportables; production remained largely conditioned by factors such as climate, input availability, transportation bottlenecks, power supply problems and, most importantly, labour shortages at the peak seasons.

A review of aggregate supply responses to price changes reveals generally low price elasticities. An empirical investigation covering nine sub-Saharan African countries over the period 1972–1981 revealed statistically significant elasticities of not more than 0.2 for two out of the nine countries. Other short-term price elasticities were between 0.2 and 0.4 while long-term elasticities ranged between 0.6 and 1.8. With price elasticities of this order, it must be evident that any policy that remained almost entirely dependent on price shifts for achieving growth would not be successful. The mechanistic application of price policy in the reform process also has other dangers if other considerations such as foreign exchange earnings, government revenues and income distribution questions are taken into account. This is likely to be particularly true if price reforms are only partial and global prices and demand are not taken into account. It must be noted that the terms of trade for sub-Saharan Africa, although fluctuating between 1968–1986, have largely worsened, while current projections suggest that prices of primary commodities are likely to remain depressed. In short, simply expanding output of traditional primary commodity exports is unlikely to be a long-run solution, either in terms of foreign exchange earning or as a specific agricultural sector strategy.

In effect, the overall impact of price related interventions on agricultural production will be restricted if certain conditions are not met. First, it must be realized that supply responses are held back not only by climatic constraints but also by institutional and infrastructural factors. In a number of countries, civil war is an important factor, while productivity levels in general are relatively low because of the lack of productivity-enhancing technologies.

The overall conclusions of the Conference on the theme of agriculture-led recovery were as follows:

(a) There is need to avoid generalizations of problems and solutions for African agriculture due to disparities among countries as regards institutional frameworks; infrastructure; inputs, including water, pesticides and fertilizers; state of the arts and knowledge; agricultural credit availability at the appropriate interest rates levels; and factor constraints such as skilled labour for the management of modern farms, external credit availability to meet the needs of perennial crops;

(b) The deficit ceiling requirements of the conventional adjustment programmes do not take into account capital and input (fertilizer, pesticide) requirements. There must be scope for financing agricultural input and capital requirements in any appropriate SAP;

(c) Productivity in agriculture as well as agricultural growth and development incentives, including inputs, information and institutions. To these must be added the need for appropriate technology, including adaptive and applied research to specific agro-ecological zones, water resources management strategy and substitution of draft and animal power for human labour;

(d) The creation or strengthening of agricultural research institutions must be a priority. Most agricultural research is presently funded by foreign donors, and it should be underscored that while the Asian 'green revolution' was based on a break-through in production technology of high-yielding-variety of a single crop, namely rice, in Africa, it is necessary to achieve a scientific break-through in at least five different staple food crops if the heterogeneous food-eating habits in the different subregions are to be satisfied;

(e) There is a food crisis in Africa, with the growth rate of food production lagging behind population growth. The acquired eating habits have also compounded the problem and continue to generate the need to divert resources into food imports, thus preventing their use for capital and intermediate goods imports. There is, therefore, a need to change Africa's food-eating habits and to achieve food security and food self-sufficiency;

(f) The land tenure system and water rights issues pose problems that inhibit agricultural growth. The example of the Gezira system in the Sudan where land and water rights are communally shared could be usefully emulated by other African countries;

(g) There is need for a comprehensive water management policy including drainage and small-scale irrigation as opposed to the conventional emphasis on large-scale irrigation schemes. Most of Africa's agriculture is rain-fed, and yet there is evidence that the major constraint behind the slow agricultural growth is lack of timely availability of water. Thus, the main solution would be the internalization of technologies that reduce the inordinate dependence on capricious weather conditions; and,

(h) The cost of irrigation agriculture is a major constraint on agricultural growth. There is concern regarding cost estimation procedures of the major engineering consulting firms which tend to discourage many African governments from irrigation schemes. Senegal has had the experience of employing military engineering in land reclamation and irrigation works along the Senegal river basin. This had reduced costs significantly to about CFA 300,000 million per ha. instead of the estimated cost of about CFA 3 million per ha. from foreign engineering firms. The use of military engineering or cost-reducing alternatives might constitute a viable way for expanding irrigation in Africa.

Financing prospects and Policies for Growth and Structural Adjustment in Africa

On the theme of financing prospects and policies, two presentations were made on (i) 'Funding of Structural Adjustment Programmes in Africa'; and, (ii) 'Financing Needs of sub-Saharan Africa'. The first presentation noted that, in general, all IMF-supported programmes emphasize an integrated approach, involving major economic variables. In this context, the analytical framework adopted by IMF was not strictly monetarist as in the 1960s. The present programmes emphasize financial aggregates such as domestic credit, public sector borrowing and external debt, as well as key elements of the price system, including the exchange and interest rates, and, in some cases, prices of commodities that bear significantly upon a country's public finance and foreign trade situation.

IMF looks at the totality of objectives and their consistency over the short, medium and long term, and it is in this way that IMF monitors the pace of adjustment and growth prospects. In addition, the implications on social, political and distribution effects are taken into account.

The overall performance of a country during the period of a stand-by or extended facility, in support of the country's adjustment programme, is monitored with the help of performance criteria. While the general thrust of these criteria is similar for all member countries – Latin America, Asia, Africa – the specific targets recommended are usually country-specific. The choice of the criteria is dictated by several considerations, including the economic and institutional structure of the country, the availability of data, and the desirability of focusing on broad macro-economic variables. IMF manages a number of facilities including: stand-by agreements, extended fund facility, enlarged access policy, compensatory financing facility, buffer stock financing facility and the structural adjustment facility established in March 1986 to provide balance of payments assistance to low-income developing countries on concessional terms of an interest rate of 1/2 or 1 per cent, and a five-year grace period with semi-annual repayments over the subsequent five years. An eligible member seeking to use the structural adjustment facility must develop a medium-term policy framework that embodies the major objectives and policies of a three-year adjustment programme.

In the second presentation, it was pointed out that World Bank has, on its part, concessional IDA resources and the Special Facility for Africa for the low-income countries of sub-Saharan Africa. Over the immediate and medium term, however, these resources are inadequate especially in view of the fact that, on a net basis, there was a decline in net capital flows to these countries during 1986 because of the decrease in net official non-concessional (including IMF) and private loans. In addition, projections indicate that more concessional aid flows are required in the years 1988–1990 for the economies to grow under the anticipated deterioration in the external conditions.

Based on present trends in resource availability, additional annual concessional flows are required from both multilateral and bilateral sources. Replenishment of IDA would be one source. IMF's recently introduced Structural Adjustment Facility, available on concessional terms largely to African countries, is another source. But more would still be required from bilateral donors. However, the external financing issue is not only one of new flows but also of resolving the external debt problem; and debt relief needs to be harmonized. Any increases in aid and export earnings will have to be used to support growth and development and not just to reduce the debt burden. Another critical factor is the terms associated with external financing. Given the difficult fiscal situation facing most countries, concessionality is of paramount importance if current resource needs and debt servicing are to be redressed.

A complicating factor in the resolution of the debt problem is the growing multilateral share of debt service, including the large IMF obligations, which cannot be addressed through rescheduling. Given the desire of the international community to see IMF remain a short-term lender, the implications of servicing IMF debts have to be taken into account in the financing plans of official creditors. This raises the issue of the importance of increased non-project assistance within the financing package. Non-project finance is critical not only for debt service but also for general inputs to support rehabilitation and re-orientation of the productive sectors, and both bilateral and multi-lateral aid must be refocused in this direction. This does not, however, preclude the financing of long-term development projects such as those in education, health and ecology. Particularly for the middle income countries, commercial banks must be fully brought in as partners to restore growth.

The Conference made the following conclusions with regard to the financing prospects:

1. There was a widespread perception that IMF conditionalities involve preconceived performance criteria of mechanistic targets that are applied indiscriminately to all countries. The consensus was that there is need to avoid such mechanistic targets except where they are supported by sound empirical investigation.

2. There was unanimous agreement that among the major constraints to self-sustained growth in Africa was the burden of debt and the net transfer of capital. Widespread concern was expressed about the financing modality, particularly the efficacy and short-term frame-work. It was emphasized that there should be a movement away from short-term to long-term credit, including longer grace periods.

3. Long-term concessional financing is crucial if growth and structural adjustments are to be attained simultaneously. The Bank's IDA resources and its Special Facility for Africa as well as IMF Structural Adjustment Facility are highly commendable concessional sources. However, additional annual concessional flows are still required from other multilateral and bilateral sources.

4. There was also an urgent need to raise the level of domestic resource mobilization. Interest rate policies were needed to stimulate the mobilization of financial savings. Expansion in branch banking, development of rural and mobile banks as well as simplified deposit, withdrawal and borrowing procedures are some of the institutional reforms that can enhance the mobilization of resources.

5. For the middle income countries (Nigeria, Cote d'Ivoire, Kenya, etc.) which have no access to concessional financing, commercial banks must be brought in to provide the necessary funding. Other

resources are the export/import credit banks and agencies that specialize in the financing of international trade.

6. On the issue of privatization and divestiture of public enterprises, it was suggested that in designing investment codes, account must be taken of the various tax incentives and their implications for lost tax revenues. An assessment must also be made of the benefits flowing from foreign investments compared with the profits repatriated. Privatization should not necessarily imply foreign take-over of state enterprises by multinationals; local take-over could also be contemplated in a programme where there are incentives for the growth of indigenous enterprises.

OVERALL CONCLUSIONS OF THE CONFERENCE

The main conclusions of the Conference, as highlighted during the final panel discussion, were as follows:

1. It is the responsibility of African governments to design their own SAPs. In a majority of cases, the African countries do not have prepared programmes thus giving an opportunity to IMF to hand out a recipe with its own conditions.

2. The task of preparing a growth-oriented structural adjustment programme is a national responsibility. The government leadership should provide the political direction on the goals and objectives of the programme. Technicians should then be mobilized to translate these into a national plan or programme. IDEP and ECA should popularize this idea and develop the technical capacity to offer consultancy services to African governments in this regard. There should be collaboration among key pan-African institutions (IDEP, ECA, ADB and others) in developing growth-oriented programmes that can satisfy the needs and aspirations of the African governments and peoples, and assist them in the negotiations with donors and the financial community.

3. It is necessary for African countries experiencing internal and external imbalances to undertake structural adjustments to correct these imbalances. The weight of exogenous factors in generating and sustaining the stagnant or negative growth rates resulting from these imbalances is very heavy. The main factor has been the secular deterioration in the prices paid for primary commodity exports, as a result of low growth in the demand for primary products, the rise in protectionism and farm subsidies in OECD countries as well as the increasing use of substitutes in manufactures based on primary

commodities. There must, therefore, be policy reforms in the African economies to counter the dependence on primary commodity exports as the engine of growth. These reforms include internalizing development by developing agro-based processing industries and seeking more effective intra-African and inter-regional trade and co-operation.

4. Internal constraints have compounded the problems underlying the deteriorating growth performance of African countries. For many years, many African economies have been subjected to political and social changes as well as inappropriate fiscal, monetary, exchange rate, pricing and other adverse economic policies. Further, it has not often been emphasized that growth requires increasing domestic saving and investment. Where external resources are not available, there is need to reduce consumption in favour of capital investment expenditures.

5. In agriculture, there must be greater intensification of land and labour use, together with emphasis on yield-augmenting technologies. There is also need for a comprehensive water management policy that can assure perennial water supply in adequate quantities. The social structure and land tenure systems also require reforms to ensure security to the farmers.

6. There is a 'we/they' syndrome prevailing in relations between African governments, on the one side, and donor governments and agencies and the financial community in general, on the other. However, it should be recognized that African governments are part shareholders of World Bank and IMF, and that the two institutions have the mandate to promote world development of which the development and growth of the least developed sub-Saharan region is an integral part. The institutions must thus understand that increased concessional financing from World Bank, IMF, and other multilateral and bilateral sources, as well as commercial bank sources, is urgently required. The possibility of recycling the balance-of-payments surpluses of Japan and Germany for the financing, on concessional terms, of Africa's debt and development must also be given serious consideration.

CHAPTER TWENTY-FOUR

Growth and Structural Change in Africa: A Global Perspective

ESSAM MONTASSER

INTRODUCTION

The major engine of growth for African countries has traditionally been exports of primary commodities to main trading partners, i.e., the Developed Market Economies (DMEs). It is the pace of primary commodity exports which set the level and pulse of economic activities. However, since the early 1970s, the momentum created by this traditional engine of growth has followed a steady downward trend. As would be expected, such a development has had a profound effect on growth in the African economies.

This is at the heart of the observed current economic stagnation in the majority of African countries. Other factors and policies which influence economic growth in Africa have been superimposed on this background. The interrelationships between these factors and policies and the gradual demise of the main source of growth are assessed below. Alternative growth strategies and policies to cope with the situation are also explored.

The Chapter is divided into three parts. The first deals with long-term growth and examines the nature of the international transmission mechanisms, including that of primary commodity exports as an engine of growth. Part two discusses the structural adjustment policies being pursued at present by most African countries. It assesses the analytical framework underlying the design of these policies, its viability and efficacy to deal with the African situation and its underlying structural characteristics. The third part focuses on agricultural growth. The vast agricultural potential in many African countries points to a possible agriculture-led growth strategy and the recent drought and famine that afflicted some African countries have highlighted further the importance and urgent need for accelerated agricultural growth.

LONG-TERM GROWTH

The International Transmission Mechanism

Historically, international trade has served as a global engine of growth after the industrial revolution in Europe in the nineteenth century. The pattern of growth was based on the needs of the early industrializing countries. They needed raw materials for their growing industries and food to satisfy the resulting rise in income and demand for food. On the other hand, outlets for the surplus industrial output had to be sought.

The outcome was a rapid growth in international trade between the industrializing European countries and the areas of new settlement, on the one hand, and the rest of the world, on the other. The pattern of trade was based on importing primary commodities from the latter in exchange for industrial goods. This pattern of exchange was accompanied by a parallel and reinforcing pattern of capital movements between the two country groupings. The capital required to develop and produce the requisite primary commodities was provided by the users.

The value of exports of the primary commodities-producing countries always exceeded the value of their imports, thus allowing for the servicing of capital imports. Imports of industrial goods were limited to luxury consumer goods used by a small percentage of the population, indigenous and foreign. The above description characterized the situation in many African countries up to the early sixties.

Such a historical pattern of growth of production and trade, and the resulting dichotomization of centres into primary producing and industrial, developed and underdeveloped, centre and periphery, constituted the foundation of a number of development theories and models.

Development theories on stages of growth pointed to an initial stage of growth in which primary commodity exports serve as the 'engine of growth'. Other related theories emanated from the consequences of this pattern of production and trade, and its impact on price relations between manufactured and primary commodities, i.e. the terms of trade. Many argued that there are long-term trends towards deterioration in the terms of trade against primary commodities and hence unequal distribution of the gains from trade between the industrialized countries and the primary commodity-exporting ones.

Estimates of the relation between growth in industrial production in the DMEs and demand for primary commodities from the LDCs was shown to have exhibited a stable parametric value over the last hundred years or so. The relative rates of growth were such that when the former grew, the latter grew at a slightly lower rate. The precise growth elasticity of primary commodity exports in relation to that of industrial output was estimated to be 0.87. W.A. Lewis, in his famous Nobel Prize acceptance speech, puts the relationship between more developed countries (MDCs) and LDCs growth as follows:

> The principal link through which the former control the growth rate of the latter is trade. As MDCs grow faster, the rate of growth of their imports accelerates and LDCs export more. We can measure this link. The growth rate of world trade in primary products over the period 1873 to 1913 was 0.87 times the growth rate of industrial production in the developed countries; and just about the same relationship, about 0.87, also ruled in the two decades to 1973. World trade in primary products is a wider concept than exports from developing countries, but the two are sufficiently closely related for it to serve as a proxy. We need no elaborate statistical proof that trade depends on prosperity in the industrialized countries. More interesting is the evidence that the relationship was quantitatively the same over a hundred years, so that the two-thirds increase in the rate of growth of exports of primary products from LDCs was no more or less than could be predicted from the increased rate of growth of MDC production.[1]

A lower rate of growth of primary commodity exports, however, does not necessarily mean a lower rate of growth of total output in the exporting countries. Rapid growth in international trade and primary commodity exports exerts a multiplier effect on growth of output and income of the producing countries. Statistical evidence indicates that the final outcome on both the exporters and importers of primary commodities is a similar rate of growth of the two country groups.

However, since the recession of 1974, the role of primary commodity exports as an engine of growth started to decline. Growth in output, industrial production and trade of the DMEs was halved after 1974 from 8 per cent to 4 per cent and, in more recent years, it has been halved again to 2 per cent or less. This decline, as would be expected, reinforced an earlier trend towards declining real prices of primary commodities and deteriorating terms of trade.

The decline in the quantum and prices of primary commodity exports underlies the observed decline in growth, particularly in the predominantly primary commodity-producing countries. The prevailing medium-term outlook points to a continuation of this trend. This is also supported by the present policy orientations in the DMEs avoiding high rates of growth generated by reflationary policies for fear of renewed inflation, and for environmental considerations which also tend to slow growth.

In recent years, particularly since the early seventies, the international transmission mechanism between developed and developing countries has acquired new dimensions. The rapid growth and globalization of international financial and capital markets, their greater integration and deregulation generated a surge in capital movements. This was brought about partially by efforts to recycle petro-dollars which served to provide the requisite finance for the deteriorating external balances of LDCs. The resulting rise in borrowing and accumulating debt of the LDCs as well as capital flights increased substantially their integration into the international financial markets, and, thus, made them more vulnerable to fluctuations in international financial policies and market conditions.

The inflationary trends in the world economy which characterized the 1970s, the unprecedented rise in interest rates, fluctuations in international currency rates – all these have had a profound effect on the macro-balances and economic growth of the indebted countries. These international developments and policy trends gradually started to exert a negative effect on financial resources inflows and growth in the LDCs. Initially, as noted earlier, they provided the necessary finance to cope with declining export proceeds, rising import prices, etc. However, soon after, net resource inflows started to taper off. While real growth in financial inflows decelerated until it came to a complete halt in recent years, outflows have increased steadily. This has led to a negative net inflow in many countries.

The decline in financial inflows has been fuelled by the slow growth as well as decline in oil prices (with negative effect on aid and workers' remittances from the oil-exporting countries), among other things. At the same time, steadily mounting debts and debt servicing burden, capital flights, etc., accelerated the rate of growth of outflows.

The decline of primary commodity exports as an engine of growth was therefore reinforced by new types of externally generated policy waves and negative transmission mechanisms. This is the fundamental background and genesis of the presently observed decline in growth, particularly in Africa.

Growth in real GDP in Africa averaged over 5 per cent per annum during the period 1960–1975, after which it started to decline. For 1975–1980, the rate was 3.7 per cent and, for 1980–1984, 1.2 per cent. For sub-Saharan Africa, the average growth rate since 1973 was less than 2 per cent, and for the more recent years, it went down to zero or below. The pattern of growth of the sixties and early seventies was characterized by rapid industrial growth, mainly mineral products, whereas agricultural growth was positive but modest. On the other hand, capital formation grew at a rate faster than output, and the rate of growth of exports exceeded that of imports. This more or less was the general picture, which does not preclude, needless to say, certain country variations around this general trend.

As for the structures of production and trade, primary production for sub-Saharan Africa constituted around half the total output, and with the exception of a few countries, manufacturing accounted for less than 10 per cent. On the utilization of output, gross domestic investment averaged 15 per cent or less. At the same time, the share of exports in GDP declined substantially in the non-oil-exporting African countries to less than 20 per cent. Over three-quarters of exports are taken by the DMEs, Africa's main trading partners.

As for the level and pattern of change of OECD trade with Africa, there has been no major change since the beginning of the seventies. Africa accounted for 4 per cent of the total (global) trade of OECD. The continent's position was the same in 1983, with the minor qualification that the share of Africa's exports to OECD countries in the total imports of the latter increased to 5 per cent. This is due mainly to the inclusion of oil exports.

The more important aspect of the Africa–OECD trade pattern is the decline in the share of Africa's exports of primary commodities to OECD (as percentage of total OECD imports of primary commodities), from 7 per cent in 1971 to 5 per cent in 1983. The import of this indicator is that, not only is Africa being affected by the global downward trend of primary commodity exports (both quantum and prices), the continent is also losing ground to other regions of the world in this domain. Another explanation could be supply limitations due to the extended drought and its aftermath in Africa.

It must also be mentioned that the share of Africa's manufactured exports to OECD in the latter's total imports of manufactures remained at the level of 1 per cent during the period 1971–1983. The share of OECD manufactured exports to Africa (as per cent of total) also remained at the level of 4 per cent throughout the same period.

The marginal rates of growth of production of many major primary commodities have been negative. For the rest, the rates of growth have been, on the whole, 2 per cent or less. Since the turn of the eighties, the number of commodities whose production growth stagnated or became negative has increased.

With regard to export performance, the number of commodities showing a negative marginal rate of growth is significantly more than that in production. This trend is further accentuated in the period after 1984. Needless to say, oil should be treated as a special case.

This accords well with the changes in international demand mentioned earlier. It also accords with the recent trend in Africa of a slight shift in agricultural production towards domestic use rather than export cash crop. Such a trend has been perhaps precipitated by both international and internal market conditions. International demand is declining, and national populations are rising, while aggregate production is decelerating.

The persistent decline in international prices of primary commodities was perhaps to be expected due to a number of factors. First is the sharply declining growth of manufacturing output in the DMEs which is the major determinant and source of demand for primary commodity exports. To this must be added the technological developments which are raw materials saving, and change in the structure of output of the DMEs favouring services relative to commodity production (the share of services in GDP of this group of countries increased from 56 per cent in 1965 to 62 per cent in 1984 and the trend is continuing). Last, but not least, the phenomenal technological revolution in agricultural production in the West leading to a sharp rise in agricultural productivity and production must be taken into account.

It should also be noted here that the DMEs' share in primary exports (other than oil) is over 60 per cent, particularly so in agricultural and food products. Accordingly, their pricing policies for these products determine the level of international market prices. The policies followed towards agricultural pricing have a considerable effect on international market prices of these primary commodities and on LDCs' exports and market shares.

To sum up, the evidence shows that for the majority of the African countries, primary production is predominant with a share in total output of more than 50 per cent, while manufacturing activities are still at an early stage of development. As for the structure of exports, primary commodities constitute more than 90 per cent of the total. In other words, Africa, on the whole, is still dependent on growth of primary commodity production and exports for income growth.

The bulk of Africa's trade is with the DMEs which absorb three-quarters of Africa's total commodity exports. With respect to primary commodity exports, the DMEs account for over 80 per cent. The manufactured exports of the LDCs account at present for a small share in total commodity exports. In 1982, its share was only 6 per cent. Of

Africa's total manufacturing exports, the DMEs absorbed 75 per cent in 1970. This share declined in 1982 to 69 per cent. In the meantime, the share of manufacturing exports to LDCs increased from 17 per cent in 1970 to 26 per cent in 1982.

From the above, it can be safely concluded that Africa's past output growth performance was closely tied to growth in the DMEs. The main link in this regard has been trade in general, and primary commodity exports in particular.

During the 1960s, both Africa and the DMEs grew at virtually the same rate of 5–6 per cent per annum. The same relation was also sustained during the 1970s and early eighties, with growth declining to 3+ per cent and then to 1+ per cent. As for trade, when industrial production and trade in the DMEs were increasing at rates of 7 and 8 per cent respectively, African exports, particularly primary commodities (with the exclusion of oil), expanded at a slightly lower rate.

However, while historical/statistical evidence supports the above hypotheses of the trade transmission mechanism and its magnitude, the relation has been complicated in recent years by a number of factors. Some of these factors were exogenous; others were endogenous.

As we have seen earlier, there has been a steady decline in primary commodity production and exports as the engine of growth in Africa over a long period. It has now reached a standstill, with both quantum and prices either stagnating or declining in absolute terms. The loss of growth due to this factor was further accentuated by the extended drought that afflicted a number of African countries. This affected not only agricultural trade, but also subsistence production, consumption and levels of economic activities in general. It also decimated a substantial portion of agricultural assets.

Amongst the other factors that had a strong bearing on Africa's economic situation and growth were, needless to say, the aforementioned unfavourable developments in the DMEs: rising inflationary trends, protectionism, rise in interest rates, exchange-rate fluctuations, decelerating direct investment and financial flows in general. Related to these are also the internal policies followed by the African countries in the face of the unfavourable external factors.

The African internal policy responses to changes in the external environment could be summed up as follows. The rise in oil prices after 1973 and the subsequent rise in the rate of inflation in the DMEs turned the external terms of trade sharply against the non-oil-exporting African countries. This had a negative income effect on them. Such a situation could not be dealt with through allowing internal market prices of imported goods to rise and other adjustment mechanisms in order to curtail imports and consumption and, thus, bring about a new macro balance. This was felt difficult from all points of view: economic, political and social, given the low level of average income and consumption. It would lead to a serious cut in consumption and the standard of living of the great bulk of the population. Accordingly, governments chose to absorb the shock themselves through large-scale subsidization. Budgetary expenditures on subsidies increased from negligible amounts to constitute a major portion of public expenditure reaching, in certain cases, billions of dollars. In some countries, the net indirect taxes, after allowing for subsidies, became negative.

Such a policy approach was made possible by a massive inflow of financial resources. These flows took different forms, ranging from ODA from the OECD countries to private bank loans and suppliers' credits. In addition to that, labour movements from oil-importing countries to the oil-exporting ones brought to the former substantial resource inflows in the form of workers' remittances. Also, the oil-exporting countries were generous in providing aid to the non-oil-exporting countries.

The situation for the African oil-exporting countries was different. The rise in their oil prices and income permitted a sharp rise in consumption and investment, as well as imports. It also allowed large-scale subsidization as a means of distributing oil income. In the early years following the oil price rise, these countries' external trade balances showed a surplus and hence large foreign exchange reserves were accumulated. But soon after, with rapid domestic expansion and rising imports, the external balances became negative again. Reserves were gradually depleted and external debts accumulated.

A stock assessment of the cumulative effect of these policies was that it left most African countries, including the oil-exporting ones, with large macro-imbalances, distortions and numerous inconsistencies between such variables as productivity levels and wages, prices and incomes, saving and investment, output and employment, export and import growth, a huge external debt and income distribution.

To sum up, the African countries first lost their main source and engine of growth, namely primary commodity exports. This was compounded by the onset of the oil price rise and international inflation which turned the terms of trade sharply against them, particularly the non-oil-exporting countries. To this was added the devastating effect of the drought. All these factors led to increasing resort to external borrowing. The latter trend was facilitated by recent changes in international financial markets and policies. Financial resources were abundant and easily available, partly as a result of accumulated petro-dollars and the need to recycle them, but also as a result of other sources such as capital flights from LDCs, etc. The emergence of Euro-markets, and the globalization and deregulation of international financial markets and institutions were pivotal in this regard. The building up of the external debt added a new factor and made Africa more vulnerable to a new set of externally generated influences; namely, rising interest rates and the cost of debt servicing.

The recent fluctuations in international currency exchange rates also added to the arsenal of international variables affecting the growth performance of African countries. While the changes in the exchange rates of European currencies *vis-à-vis* the US dollar have benefitted some African countries and harmed others, their appreciation together *vis-à-vis* domestic currencies has had a negative effect on internal investment. Domestic policies of overvaluation of national currencies in Africa, coupled with high real interest rates in inter-national markets, stimulated capital flights abroad. However, it must be pointed out that such flights were also precipitated by internal instability, inadequate and unstable macro policies, low returns and unfavourable environment for investment and, last but not least, political risks.

In the light of the above, a question related to the sources of growth in Africa imposes itself. If primary commodity exports are no longer serving as an engine of growth, what transmission mechanism could or should be substituted for it?

The answer to this question is that investment is the most appropriate motor that can propel the African economy into growth. The African economy being at an early stage of development requires large invest-ments to build up its productive bases and infrastructure. The decline of primary commodity exports as an engine of growth signals the end of complete dependence on the bounty of nature to export its produce and generate income and growth. Even agricultural growth, if it is to be achieved, requires large investments in both production and infra-structure. At the same time, the manufacturing sector is still small and has a modest export capacity. A strong industrial production base has barely started. In addition to this, growth of services is a function of the growth of commodity production and the resulting growth in income. Diversification of production and trade may, therefore, become a necessity for growth.

The growth of capital formation in Africa in the post-independence period has been extremely low. As is shown in Table 24.1, the real rate of growth of net capital formation during the period 1971–1984 for continental Africa was negative. If we add the impact of factors such as drought, desertification, deforestation and soil erosion, among other things, we find also that the resource base of the continent has been eroded. Wars and other types of social strife have contributed to the decline of both capital and other assets, including natural resources.

TABLE 24.1

FIXED CAPITAL FORMATION IN AFRICA (AT CONSTANT 1970 MARKET PRICES), 1970–1984[a]

Year	$US billion
1971	144.9
1972	142.8
1973	140.9
1974	139.4
1975	137.8
1976	136.0
1977	135.0
1978	133.9
1979	133.1
1980	133.4
1981	133.3
1982	132.9
1983	132.6
1984	131.9

Note:

a The capital stock series were derived from available gross fixed investment series for Africa (excluding South Africa) for the period 1970–1984 at constant 1970 prices. The base-year figure for investment was converted from a flow to capital stocks using a capital/output ratio of 4. Then sectoral depreciation rates were estimated which resulted in the applied weighted average of 5 per cent per annum. Both the capital/output and depreciation assumptions constitute rather low estimates. Scenarios with higher estimates brought out a sharper decline in capital stocks. Independent estimates were also made for a number of sub-country groups.

It is therefore safe to conclude that primary exports as an engine of growth is at present fully inoperational. At the same time, present investment levels hardly allow for replacement of depreciation of the present capital stock. If investment is to serve as a growth propeller, it must grow at a much faster rate. Given the external balance position, much greater mobilization of domestic savings and trade growth will be required.

GROWTH AND STRUCTURAL ADJUSTMENT STRATEGIES AND POLICIES

The Analytical Framework

As mentioned above, developments in international trade and payments and fluctuations in the external terms of trade since the early seventies brought about major changes in the external balances of many countries and regions. This, in turn, necessitated a surge in capital movements and basic changes in its structure and pattern. The international financial system adjusted to this situation with new institutions, instruments and policies. In this regard, one can cite the recycling of petro-dollars, the emergence of Euro-dollar markets, globalization and integration of banking, financial and capital markets, and greater movement towards deregulation and free movement of financial flows, tax havens, etc.

These developments bore important consequences for international economic management and structural adjustment policies. For the LDCs, they brought about a huge external debt, unsustainable internal and external macro economic imbalances, as well as price and cost distortions, changes in income distribution etc. They also gave a forward push to integrating the LDCs into the international financial system via the huge accumulated external debt.

The decline in the LDCs' growth and their inability to service their external debts posed a major threat to the stability of the international financial system. This issue became particularly important and pressing when oil prices began to rise. The declining growth of the LDCs, the rising external debt, their declining ability to service the debts, and the threat that such a situation posed to the international banking and financial systems, necessitated urgent action. Structural adjustment programmes accordingly were propagated.

The initial deflationary effect of these programmes was felt to be counter-productive since it lessened the indebted countries' ability to service their debts and caused increased social and political resentment on the part of these countries. James Baker, United States Treasury Secretary in Reagan Administration, took the lead to announce publicly the need to reconcile structural adjustment policies with growth, and urged banks to provide the necessary financial support. To realize this goal, co-operation is required between national and international policy-makers. Adequate international financing is also

532

required to fund and facilitate structural adjustment and reconcile it with growth.

But to make efficient use of the resources available, national or international, and achieve the goal of combining growth with structural adjustment on a sustainable basis would require proper diagnosis, prescriptions, time-tables, phasing, etc. Also, because of the inter-action between internal and external factors, structural adjustment policies must take both factors into consideration explicitly. This requires an appropriate analytical framework.

Accordingly, to take the first step in discussing broader issues related to growth and structural adjustment, some light must be shed on an implicit or explicit underlying analytical framework and how it applies to Africa.

Within the overall programme of structural adjustment and growth, there is a kind of implicit division of labour between IMF and World Bank. Because of a great deal of overlapping and interdependence between ends and means, on the one hand, and within the means themselves, on the other, this division of labour is only a matter of emphasis. In essence, the two programmes are complementary and constitute an integrated package. In spite of the above, the two institutions do not have a uniform analytical framework to design and assess their respective policy prescriptions. In practice, co-ordination takes place mainly at the operational policy levels.

IMF, by virtue of its mandate, is concerned with financing short-term balance of payments disequilibria of member countries and policy reforms aimed at reducing them to sustainable levels. This naturally influences the choice of its analytical approach. This is basically a monetarist (asset) approach to the balance of payments which analyses changes in the external balance in terms of stock adjustment in the money market.

According to this approach, the balance of payments is divided into three related accounts: (a) the current account which includes the balance of trade as well as those of factor and non-factor services; (b) an autonomous capital account, which records autonomous transactions in assets between residents and non-residents; and (c) the balance of official finance, which is a residual account balancing the other two. When there is a deficit in the external balance (total of the first two accounts) it must be accommodated by an equal and opposite flow in the balance of official flows. This can be through external borrowing, running down reserves, etc.

A deficit in the external balance can be financed internally, either through changes in cash balances held by non-monetary authorities (change in velocity of money) or through borrowing from monetary authorities. Lending by the monetary authorities would increase money supply. Therefore, an external deficit, unless sterilized by the monetary authorities, would always involve increase in money supply and domestic credit. The impact of such an increase is to nullify potential corrective mechanisms, particularly a rise in interest rates that may have been aimed at curtailing aggregate demand and expenditures.

Related to the theory underlying national output and absorption, the above relation could be expressed as follows:

$$BOF = (Y - E) + (Ar + Ap)$$

In other words, a surplus or deficit in the balance of payments as measured by a positive or negative balance of official finance (BOF) is the outcome of the balance on current account reflecting the balance between total output (Y) and total expenditure (E) plus the balance of autonomous capital receipts (Ar) and payments (Ap).

Correcting the external imbalance and bringing it down to a sustainable level necessitates 'financial programming'. This consists of certain targets in the form of 'monetary ceiling', raising of interest rates and currency devaluation. These measures are often supplemented by targets for budget deficits to be achieved either through reducing expenditures or increasing revenue. The whole package is often referred to as a 'demand management' strategy or policy.

But for these demand management policy prescriptions to bring about the desired effect, a flexible and efficient market price mechanism will be needed. Market prices (both commodity and factor) must reflect and communicate changes in interest rates, relative import and export prices, etc. It must bring about the desired reduction in total expenditure through allowing the rise in import prices to be reflected in both consumer prices and producers' costs. It must also affect the reallocation and switching of resources in line with changes in costs and profit margins. This is mainly the domain of World Bank's 'Structural Adjustment Policies'.

But over and above the reform of the market price mechanism through greater rationalization, elimination of subsidies, raising of agricultural producer prices etc., World Bank is also concerned with sectoral investment. A greater balance between output and expenditure need not necessarily be brought about only through reduction in expenditure. It could also be realized through growth in output. This latter could be achieved through more efficient use of resources (higher productivity, elimination of bottlenecks and increased levels of investment). This constitutes the growth component of structural adjustment policies prescribed by World Bank.

But while there is a theoretical approach underlying IMF's demand management policy diagnosis and prescriptions, World Bank has no overall analytical framework. Its main analytical tool is a two-gap prototype model which was devised in the early eighties and since then has been in use. Its main function has been to test the outcome of alternative policy scenarios and estimate the external capital requirements of borrowing countries.

There remains also the question of whether and how the analytical tools, findings, parameter estimates, projections, etc., of World Bank and IMF are related. One conclusion could be, however, derived from the fact that there is no overall analytical framework which relates short-term policies, whether 'demand management' or 'structural', to medium-term objectives of growth and structural change. For example, while World Bank may estimate or even recommend a certain level of external resource requirement there is no guarantee, whatsoever, that they would be realized. This frustrates the process of structural adjustment which is designed on the basis of agreed-upon levels of financing.

Other analytical shortcomings of the present orientation of structural adjustment policies need also to be pointed out. Policies normally reflect not only the contemporary predominant political realities and thinking, but also the impact of past economic growth patterns and experiences on economic thinking. More precisely, the depression of the 1930s and the Second World War produced a number of development theories and policy prescriptions which aimed at guiding policy-makers in formulating development strategies and policies. These include the theories on: 'Balanced growth', 'Structural inflation', 'Big push', 'Vent for surplus', 'Unbalanced growth', 'Import substitution', etc. Being products of the depression years and the Second World War, they were characterized by 'export pessimism' and thus advocated economic approaches consistent with stagnant export proceeds and were therefore inward-oriented. They also pointed out certain structural features and rigidities characterizing the LDCs that are not amenable to neoclassical marginalist analysis.

'Export pessimism' which underlined the above-mentioned theories proved to be unfounded. Furthermore, other factors and policy approaches towards planning, industrialization, demand management, market prices, etc., brought certain negative results and created macro-imbalances and inflexible economic structures which choked growth in the countries that followed inward-oriented economic strategies. This was in sharp contrast to the rapid growth achieved by those who followed export-led strategies. These developments therefore undermined the inward-oriented development strategies and their underlying economic thinking.

At present, economic thinking tends to revert once again to 'export pessimism'. Slow growth in the DMEs' output, declining demand and prices of primary commodity exports of LDCs, surplus agricultural output in the international market and the trend towards protectionism in general in the DMEs, and market trends are all feeding the 'pessimism'. Consequently, they seem to revive interest in earlier alternative strategies. Needless to say, this revival of alternative strategies to export-led growth does not have to be biased against exports as has been the case in the past.

Structural adjustment policies as conceived at present seem to pay no attention to the above changes in international economic trends and their influence on economic thinking and policies. They suffer from a time lag. They still advocate unequivocally an export-led strategy and orientation. But how can this be achieved if international markets are not growing, international demand for primary commodities is declining, and world markets are clogged with agricultural food products and surpluses? This concern is over and above the fierce competition among industrialized countries for manufacturing markets and exports and the accelerating trend towards protection of domestic markets. This question is particularly pertinent for Africa. While generalizations here are difficult due to the great diversity of African countries with regard to size, levels of development and income, resource base etc., however, for the majority of African countries, there is still the dependence on primary production and exports for growth. For such countries export 'pessimism' is warranted. As primary exports have ceased to serve as an engine of growth, there is need to develop new sources of growth.

From the point of view of the larger and more industrialized African countries (for example, Egypt, Nigeria and Zimbabwe) industrial growth for both domestic markets and exports must be accelerated. For them, export-led growth constitutes the main source. Also, their growth could serve to generate regional growth via trade and other regional transmission mechanisms. In other words, they could serve as regional growth poles.

However, it must be emphasized that whether it is export 'pessimism' or 'optimism', accelerating export growth is inevitable. At the early stages of development, economic growth of countries with narrow production bases is import-intensive. Accordingly, economic growth requires quite often an even higher rate of growth of imports. If the external balance is to remain within the limits imposed by external financing, both export promotion and import substitution must grow. Under conditions of 'export pessimism', regional and subregional export markets must be expanded to make up for the slow growth of exports to international markets.

Structural Adjustment and Structural Change: A Medium-term Perspective

At present, the African economies on the whole are growing at average rates below population growth (1–1.5 per cent per annum). Their rates of investment are also low, at around 15 per cent of GNP. Real investment must grow faster than output if growth is to accelerate. Thus, for many African countries, the share of investment in GDP needs to be nearly doubled. Assuming a marginal productivity of investment of 20 per cent, a rise in the share of gross fixed investment in GDP from 15 to 25 per cent for example would add two percentage points to the rate of GDP growth (i.e., from 1.5 to 3.5 per cent).

In the light of the initial narrow mono-crop type of production structures, economic growth is likely to be accompanied by rapid growth in imports. Past experience in many African countries showed a real rate of growth of imports close to that of output. Rapid urbanization and the need for rapid growth of internal demand as one of the sources of overall growth will put additional pressures on import growth.

This is in sharp contrast to the growth prospects of exports in the medium term. The difficult external and internal conditions and environment for export growth warrants some expectation of a widening external gap in the current account.

The situation is further accentuated by the need to service the external debt. In recent years, financial outflows and inflows have more or less balanced out with no net external resource inflows. If we add to the above the autonomous capital account balance, including capital flights, the external imbalance is increased significantly.

Market structures and institutions in many African countries are embryonic and still growing. However, an additional facet characterizing many of them needs to be added, viz., their monopolistic organization. Many factors contribute to this situation, prominent among which are the small size of the market, industrial incentives and protection, exclusive franchise or licence, subsidized credit and inputs, etc. This has important implications for SAPs ranging from distorted market prices and profit margins, barriers to trade and competition, overvalued exchange rates, among others. Thus, regulating market structures and guaranteeing freer competition and movement of labour and other resources would greatly enhance the efficacy of both micro and structural policies. It would also contribute to a more equitable income distribution.

The predominant indigenous formal business enterprise structure in most African countries is either wholly public or joint public/private. The economic situation in the post-independence period and the role of governments as the spearhead of the modern sector, and its responsibility for satisfying rising national aspirations for development, entailed heavy dependence on public enterprises as a vehicle of development. It also brought about a particular orientation towards the role of these enterprises and their management system.

Public enterprises were encumbered with numerous objectives. Aside from their role in production, they had also to perform additional functions related to labour absorption, income distribution, national economic control, etc. In short, they have been required to play a catalytic role in production as well as act as welfare instruments.

While public enterprises have fulfilled their initially assigned roles, this was often at the expense of their profitability. Policies involving high costs, low prices, inflexible and cumbersome management, all led to erosion of profit margins and many have been forced to operate at a loss. In spite of government finance of their capital, many were not able to maintain their recurrent costs and had to depend on the government budget and government-guaranteed bank loans to continue operations. Gradually, this began to constitute a major financial and unsustainable burden. A major step towards structural adjustment is to re-invigorate this main economic growth vehicle so that it can operate economically.

Rehabilitation of public enterprises requires many changes. Some relate directly to their management systems, employment, price and trade policies, to mention only a few. But it also relates indirectly to the market price system, laws and regulations, and the overall economic environment and incentive systems within which they operate.

These structural policies are pivotal in making the public and private enterprises operate efficiently. When this goal is achieved, it would go a long way towards encouraging productive private investment at home instead of the present trend towards capital flight and investment in international financial markets.

The other important growth vehicle is banks. Their main function is to mobilize savings and financial resources in general for investment.

But banks, particularly the national banks, have suffered from the same constraints which affected public enterprises in general. They have been used in many cases as public fiscal agents and welfare instruments. The outcome is that they are at present encumbered by portfolios of unrecuperable assets. Banks are therefore hindered from playing their traditional role as efficient intermediaries between savers and investors.

To re-invigorate the banks is a more difficult task. While it will be necessary to change their management systems and regulatory frameworks and policies in general, this will not be sufficient. Their payments and lending services need to be revamped and restructured.

When the multinational banks started facing the situation regarding their loans to LDCs, immediate action was taken by their governments to bail them out. They were allowed, through a combination of tax deductions, retained profits and other policies, to write off risky debts. Similar actions could be taken by African governments to gradually rehabilitate their own banks. Thus, in addition to market reforms, public enterprise and bank reforms will have to feature in structural adjustment policies because they are major agents and vehicles of growth. There is also the issue of foreign aid, which is an equally important factor in African development as it is the main source of financing investment. Yet, at present, the productivity of foreign aid is quite low. More than 50 per cent of aid is allocated to types of expenditure other than investment, thus adding to external debts without generating the necessary growth for debt servicing. Other problems relate to the long time-lags in aid disbursement procedures, costly project studies, long gestation periods of some projects and inefficient external and internal institutional frameworks. All these require streamlining and restructuring if this factor is to achieve the requisite level of productivity and generate enough resources for debt amortization.

As regards the size of external aid, the net total resource inflows to Africa at present are either negligible or negative in certain cases. Even a moderate rate of income growth of 3–4 per cent per annum for Africa will require much greater net resource inflows. To achieve such a goal, major international actions and initiatives would be required. Surplus countries like Japan and West Germany have a major role to play in this regard. Earlier, when the US was in a similar position, it generated international growth, co-operation and development via investing part of its external surplus in initiatives such as the 'Marshall Plan'. It was also the investments of the US multinational companies in Western

Europe which laid the foundations and provided the resources for policy reforms that set the stage for European co-operation and integration.

The present external surpluses are invested in financial assets, mainly in the US, because it is a safe haven with low risks, high returns and a relatively favourable economic environment. Such conditions and incentives need to be created in Africa so that some of these surpluses can be channelled towards financing development in Africa. This would not only contribute to growth and balance in the world economy, it would also greatly alleviate the present external financial shortage which is a constraint on African development.

The fact that the African economy at present has no growth engine makes structural adjustment policies difficult and possibly disruptive. To reconcile structural adjustment with growth, it needs to be geared more towards growth. It would also have to take into consideration the structural features confronting the African economies, both internally and externally.

The outlook for external growth, international demand for primary commodities and financial resource inflows is not very bright. This requires orienting structural adjustment policies towards diversification of sources of growth. Maximum efforts are to be exerted towards expanding international exports of both primary commodities and manufacturing.

Another source of growth would be via internal demand. This requires a pattern of investment allocation, demand management and structural policies to achieve consistent growth propensities of output, imports and exports. There is a substantial potential for growth via import substitution particularly in food products and processed agricultural products.

Another important source of growth would be via intra-regional and subregional trade. At present such trade is minimal. Mechanisms and policies for accelerating intra-African trade need to be created. Prominent among such measures would be subregional clearing arrangements and joint ventures. At a later stage, co-ordination of macro-economic policies would be essential.

In the past, regional co-operation was thought of mainly as a means of overcoming the small size of domestic markets for manufacturing. At present, the emphasis on agricultural growth, coupled with shrinking potential for exports, imposes the need for greater internal use at the national and regional levels for agricultural products. The African countries vary quite widely in their agricultural growth potential, and this constitutes a useful basis for intra-African trade and growth.

Achieving regional co-operation requires also co-operation in production. Complete reliance on intra-African trade liberalization would not be sufficient. The exportable surplus has to be created first. Also co-operation in production via the establishment of intra-African joint ventures and transnational enterprises would avoid past problems in the way of co-operation, such as allocation of gains to participating countries. For many African countries, especially the smaller ones, regional co-operation is no more a choice but an essential condition for growth.

AGRICULTURAL GROWTH, POTENTIAL, PATTERN AND POLICIES

Growth in Agricultural Resources, Output and Trade

Agricultural output in Africa has virtually stagnated over the last 15 years or so. In many countries there was an absolute decline in output. The unprecedented drought that afflicted many countries and regions in the continent contributed to this decline. However, it is not the only reason; other factors and policies too contributed to such an outcome.

Africa's (excluding South Africa) agricultural output increased during the period 1970–1983 from $US17.7 to $US19.3 billion at constant 1970 prices, i.e. a rate of growth of 1 per cent per annum. For sub-Sahara Africa, the rate of growth over the same period was close to zero. Output increased from $US13.5 to $US13.7 billion.

The declining growth in agricultural output was underlined by a decline in resources. The arable land area for the whole of Africa declined from 166.0 to 152.1 million ha. during the period 1961–1983. This is partly due to a sustained and steady trend towards desertification. Also, intensive cultivation in certain areas without care for soil fertility led to soil erosion, decline in fertility and the shifting of such land from crop production to pasture land. Levels of rain and water availability also played a role in this regard. The decline in the arable land area is even more pronounced in certain subregions, such as the Sudano-Sahelian where it decreased from 44.3 million to 29.3 million ha. over the same period.

The decline in water inputs needs no documentation. Drought and declining precipitation over large areas of Africa affected all sources of water, both surface water and underground water.

With regard to capital, no reliable time series exists on investment in agriculture over the period covered by the analysis. However, indirect evidence about declining levels of capital formation in general and certain occasional policy trends towards giving higher priority to the modern sector and urban capital formation would make us conclude that investment in agriculture was not at a level adequate to contribute to real growth in output. Other types of agricultural assets, like livestock, soils, forests, etc., declined in absolute terms.

Economic policies towards agriculture, in terms of price, credit, trade, exchange rates, etc., are felt to have been biased against agriculture and have acted as a disincentive.

One must also mention certain structural factors at work. One such factor would be the land tenure system. Such a system, while performing an important and positive social function, and quite compatible with a subsistence agricultural system, is not consistent with growth in investment and a commercially-oriented agriculture. Another important factor is the present production subsistence system in which rain-fed shifting cultivation predominates. Such a system is also not compatible with efforts to raise productivity and preserve soil fertility. At the same time, growth in productivity is a prerequisite for investing in agriculture. One can also add the over-concentration on the cultivated area while large areas of arable land are left unutilized. This is an outcome of the lack of requisite infrastructure and the historical pattern of spatial growth in Africa.

All these factors are interrelated and make change difficult. They require well tailored policies, acting on a number of areas simultaneously. And the time horizon for achieving set-out goals cannot but be a long-term one.

In contrast with the stagnating or declining agricultural production in Africa, population growth rates steadily accelerated. Between 1960 and 1985, African population (again excluding South Africa) increased from 278 to 553 million inhabitants, i.e. doubled.

The continent's rate of population growth continues to be on the rise. It increased from 2.2 per cent at the turn of the fifties to 3 per cent at the turn of the eighties. At present, it exceeds 3 per cent and thus ranks as the highest growth rate in the world. Africa is still at the beginning of its demographic transition with a young population, high and rising fertility rates and declining mortality rates. As the latter two are highly correlated, the dynamics of population growth point to a sustained high rate of population growth, at least until the end of the century.

The divergence in the rates of growth of population, on the one hand, and agricultural production and resources, on the other, led to a rising population–resource (food) imbalance. Agricultural production per capita declined from $US49.6 to $US38.2 during the period 1970–1985, a decline of about one-third. On the other hand, cereal production per capita declined from 0.14 to 0.10 metric tons during the same period.

Rising population and income per capita meant a rise in food demand, while domestic production steadily declined. Naturally, this outcome required dependence on trade to fill the domestic demand–supply gap. This meant a widening agricultural and food trade gap. Food imports increased from $US1.3 to $US11.0 billion during the period 1970–1983, while exports increased from $US2.7 to $US5.6 billion. The external trade food balance changed from a $US1.4 billion surplus to a $US5.4 billion deficit.

The deteriorating external food balance came on top of rising costs of energy imports and sharply deteriorating terms of trade for the non-oil-exporting African countries. It thus contributed significantly to the continent's balance of payments deficits and rising external debt.

Resuming economic growth and achieving greater external balance requires agricultural growth, among other things. The majority of the African population is rural, and depends on income in agriculture. Also, expanding internal markets for industrial goods is essential if any substantial growth in manufacturing is to take place, but this depends largely on growth in rural income. Industrial growth for home markets would also create a base for industrial exports. Meanwhile, services would also grow in real terms when there is real growth in commodity production and real income.

The interrelation between energy supply and agricultural growth is also well recognized. The main source of energy in Africa is fuel wood (a forest product) which constitutes 90 per cent of energy consumption in rural areas. Furthermore, a by-product of controlling the surface water potential of African rivers is the generation of hydro-power. It is estimated that Africa's exploitable potential hydro-power capacity amounts to one-third of the world total (35.4 per cent), that is 1630 billion kwh. Less than 5 per cent of this potential is at present utilized. Harnessing Africa's rivers and surface water potential would contribute to both agriculture and energy production.

Agricultural Growth Potentials

Africa is depicted, on the whole, as being a water-deficient continent, especially relative to other continents. This has been underlined by recent droughts in the continent. However, available evidence contradicts such impressions, particularly if the continent's water resources are assessed in relation to population growth and development requirements. While certain areas or regions inside Africa are water-deficient, continent-wide resources are abundant but under-utilized and undeveloped. For a better utilization of this crucial resource, co-operation among African countries is needed. The notion that Africa is a relatively water deficient continent is based on the following general indicators. First, water per unit of land (agriculture and non-agriculture) is the lowest in the world; second, while Africa's rainfall levels are high, the continent's coefficient of evaporation is the highest in the world. Third, and as a result, the coefficient of runoff (i.e. excess of rainfall over evaporation divided by rainfall) is the lowest in the world.

As Africa is still relatively less densely populated in comparison with other continents, the runoff/population rate in Africa is amongst the highest in the world. Water per capita amounts, on average, to 8318 m^3 per person in Africa, a level which is significantly higher than that in both Asia and Europe, but lower than in America (North and South). A closer look at the continent's water resources and at its geographical allocation and relation to both land and people presents a clearer and more concrete picture.

Total potential water resources are estimated to be 3,069 km^3 : 2,285 km^3 from surface water, and the rest (784 km^3) from fresh ground water. However, its geographical distribution is quite uneven. Twenty-one countries account for 90 per cent of the continent's total water resources, while the remaining thirty-one account for the rest. Even within the water-rich group the Cameroon, Central African Republic, Congo, Nigeria, Zaire and Angola (6 countries) account for over 50 per cent while Zaire's share alone is 25 per cent. Most of the water-surplus countries fall in the equatorial and humid tropical zones of West and Central Africa.

This uneven water distribution is not, however, parallel to the continent's subregional and national agricultural and food producing capacities. Firstly, it is more evenly allocated by the continent's net-work of rivers which transports water from water surplus areas in countries (often upstream) to water-deficient ones (downstream). Account must also be taken of arable land and population distribution. A number of countries which may not be counted among the water-rich have a high land potential. Others which may have medium land and water resources have small population. Note here that the water-rich areas are inhabited by over 60 per cent of the total population in the continent.

FAO has attempted to simulate the population support capacity for the various African countries and subregions, given their agricultural resource base and potential. It assumed three alternative policy scenarios for the utilization of this capacity, viz. low, intermediate and high intermediate inputs use. The low level of inputs corresponds more

TABLE 24.2

RELATIVE IMPORTANCE OF IRRIGATION IN SELECTED AFRICAN COUNTRIES

Country	Irrigated area as % of the country's area under temporary and permanent crops
Egypt	98.6
Gambia	11.9
Madagascar	32.0
Mali	7.8
Mauritania	12.0
Mauritius	13.1
Morocco	9.5
Somalia	7.2
Sudan	14.1
Swaziland	21.7

Source: *FAO, Consultation on Irrigation in Africa – Needs and Justification of Irrigation Development*, Lomé, Togo, 21–25 April 1986

or less to the present levels and practices. The intermediate one requires higher levels of application of fertilizers, animal power and equipment. Finally, the high level of inputs corresponds to modern farming using methods and systems adapted to the African environment.

The three alternative policy scenarios were translated into average yields per unit of land; then outputs were converted into K cal. Based on the assumption of 2325–2400 K cal/person/day, the population carrying capacity of various countries and regions was estimated. The general conclusion is that there are no resource constraints on present agricultural growth in Africa at the aggregate level. However, it must be pointed out that there are African countries, particularly in North Africa, to which the above conclusion is not applicable. Furthermore, agricultural development and growth is sought after not for sheer sustenance of numbers, but as a means of overall development and raising standards of living and consumption levels.

An important element in the growth of agriculture in Africa is the role of irrigated agriculture. The presently irrigated land area in Africa is very limited in comparison to the potential. It is estimated to amount to only 5.2 per cent of the total area under temporary and permanent crops. Also, the geographical distribution is very uneven. Four countries, Egypt, the Sudan, Madagascar and Nigeria account for 70 per cent of the total irrigated area. Egypt alone accounts for 31 per cent, while 72 per cent of the total irrigated area is located in the Mediterranean and arid North Africa where irrigated agriculture assumes a significant percentage of the total cultivated area (14.7 per cent).

However, in spite of the smallness of irrigated agriculture relative to total land area, its weight in production is substantially larger. The share of irrigated agricultural production to total production in 1980 amounted to 20 per cent. This stems naturally from its higher productivity, although about one-third of the total irrigated area is traditional, with minimum water control and low-level use of inputs.

One can therefore safely conclude that the agricultural growth potential of Africa is enormous, but that this potential is unevenly distributed. Furthermore, its realization requires much greater emphasis on regional co-operation and co-ordination, and a host of appropriate policies, ranging from investment and other inputs to pricing, credit, marketing and building up of both soft infrastructure (agrarian reform) and physical infrastructure.

Economic Policies for Agricultural Growth

As already pointed out, agricultural growth requires substantial acceleration of the rate of investment in that sector. However, to achieve that goal, investment must be able to realize a reasonable rate of return, regardless of who is investing. But, to make investment in agriculture profitable, productivity must significantly be above the present average subsistence level. This requires more intensive use of intermediate inputs (fertilizers, pesticides, etc.), capital and labour. Prices of agricultural produce must cover these higher costs and leave a reasonable return to the producer. A steady rise in agricultural production would also bring about a rise in tax revenues, and help to finance the build-up of infrastructure required to put the agricultural sector on a sustained growth path.

However, an essential question must be asked as to the pattern of utilization of the potential increase in agricultural output since such growth must be paralleled by equal growth in effective demand. Since international demand for Africa's agricultural products is not expected to grow at the desired rates – the agricultural surpluses of the DMEs and their price policies make any increase in agricultural exports from Africa to the international markets a very difficult task – it could safely be concluded that the bulk of any increase in agricultural output must be utilized domestically or exported to regional markets. But domestic utilization, which is the main immediate source, requires growth in effective demand, which in turn, requires accelerated income growth in general and urban income in particular.

Growth in agricultural costs and prices would have the initial effect of reducing urban effective demand for agricultural products rather than the contrary. Thus, a more balanced growth between agricultural and industrial output is needed. This is further reinforced by the fact that an increase in agricultural output and income will generate a rising demand for non-agricultural goods and services, which must be provided for basically through domestic production. At a time of slow export growth, imports must be greatly constrained. An additional outlet for the increase in agricultural output could be through intra-African trade. Each subregion could specialize in the production of and trade in commodities in which it has comparative advantage.

The moral then is that sustained agricultural growth requires growth in urban production and income. In other words, it requires also industrial growth. The two must go hand in hand. As for the relative rates of growth of the two sectors, it must be left to forces of demand and supply. The job of economic management is to facilitate the process, create the proper environment and build up the necessary mechanisms. Amongst the latter are the strengthening of market institutions and mechanisms, and rationalizing the prices system.

Other structural policy requirements are needed in the areas of land tenure and water rights systems if investment is to take place. Given the important social and welfare functions of the present communal land tenure system, changes would come only gradually, and dual systems could be envisaged in the short and medium term. An example of such an arrangement is the Gezira project in the Sudan. Equally successful alternative solutions exist in other parts of Africa, all of which need to be studied to see to what extent the lessons derived from them could be emulated or modified. Another set of requirements relates to soft infrastructure, i.e. credit and marketing systems, supply of immediate inputs, insurance, etc. Lastly, physical infrastructure, in particular transportation and storage, would be needed if agricultural growth is to be realized on a sustained basis.

But, even with this selected short-list of requirements for agricultural growth, the tasks involved, though implementable, are difficult. A number of interrelated building blocks have to be maintained. First, agricultural growth must go hand-in-hand with industrial growth and urban-based economic activities. The relations between the rural and urban populations are multi-faceted and complex. The two populations are in fact an integrated whole. Wives and parents may remain on the land while husbands and children work in urban centres. Major portions of earnings of the latter are transferred to their kinship in rural areas. Shifts between the two areas are frequent. Past experiences in the West and in Japan show that industrial growth preceded agricultural growth, helped its finance and provided it with incentive goods. Second, macro-economic and structural adjustment policies and management systems must aim at balancing the growth propensities of agriculture and industrial production, domestic use, exports and imports. Third, given the uneven distribution of agricultural resources in Africa, intra-African co-operation is essential. Some sort of complementarity needs to be established; this would create the base for expansion in intra-regional trade which would contribute to overall growth. In certain cases, such complementarity is inevitable, for example, among river and lake basin countries, or between groups of small countries in a subregion. Fourth, macro-economic management and policies must strive to enhance international competitiveness if Africa is not to lose its share in international markets, as has already begun. A minimum growth of exports to the DMEs is essential if economic growth is to be resumed. It is also necessary to have access to the requisite financial resources which cannot be generated domestically. In this regard, control of inflation, exchange rates, income policy, etc., are very instrumental. Fifth, in the light of the complexity of Africa's agriculture and its varying and sometimes conflicting requirements, an institution is needed to co-ordinate and monitor policies, mobilize the necessary financial resources for it as well as achieve the necessary regional co-operation. Establishing regional Agricultural Development Banks for Africa would serve this purpose very well and would accelerate the process of agricultural growth in Africa. Africa is greatly starved of financial intermediaries of this kind in comparison with other regions in the world.

CONCLUSION

The African economies are, on the whole, not growing. The main problem is the decline of their 'engine of growth', namely, primary commodity exports, both in quantum and price terms. If the present trend in international markets, demand and prices for primary commodity exports and light manufactures produced in Africa continues, then new development strategies to cope with this basic organic factor will have to be devised.

Economic growth in developing countries with open economies like those of Africa require at least an equal rate of growth of imports. If exports cannot be expanded, due to international demand constraints, then the external gap will widen and growth will be arrested. That corresponds to the present trend in Africa towards declining external financial inflows (in real terms) and rising outflows.

548

Imposing the presently conceived structural adjustment policies on economies whose hearts are hardly beating would accentuate the contractionary forces in the economies rather than reverse them. This would be so at least in the short run. Medium-term prospects would thus have to focus on alleviating undesirable structural changes in the basic organic relations and generating sources of growth.

Possible alternative strategies to the primary commodity export-led strategy would have to aim at diversifying sources of growth. Increased inward orientation of growth, as an intermediate strategy, would be necessary to avoid export and market price biases.

Structural adjustment policies need to be designed with the above ends in mind. It must also be pointed out that, in a sense, structural adjustments are themselves by-products of growth. This is another reason for the difficulty emanating from implementing structural adjustment policy remedies in stagnant economies. Lastly, international financial inflows constitute an important factor in achieving growth, and their absence would require radical internal policy reforms and painful social and political adjustments.

New approaches to structural adjustment in the LDCs, particularly in Africa, are needed. Innovative thinking and action could transform the present challenges and problems into successes and achievements. A quotation from one of the pioneers of Development Economics, A.O. Hirschman,[2] is highly illustrative in this regard:

> Orthodox policy prescriptions for the disrupted postwar economies of Western Europe – stop the inflation and get the exchange rate right – were often politically naive, socially explosive, and economically counter-productive from any longer-run point of view. The innovators who, to their lasting credit, proposed the creative remedies embodied in the Marshall Plan and, in justification, propounded novel doctrines, such as the 'structural dollar shortage', soon became unduly doctrinaire in turn.

The suggestions made above are by no means intended to be doctrinaire. Their only aim is to provide solutions compatible with the present economic problems the African countries are encountering in the face of declining international demand for their exports and the difficult international financial situation.

NOTES

1. W.A. Lewis, 'The Slowing down of the Engines of Growth', *The American Economic Review*, Sept. 1980, pp. 555–564.
2. See G.M. Meier and D. Seers (eds.) *Pioneers in development*, World Bank/Oxford University Press, 1984, p.89.

CHAPTER TWENTY-FIVE

The Interlinkage Between Agricultural Revolution and Industrialization: Alternative Strategies for African Development

SAMIR AMIN

This Chapter starts with the recognition that globally the development strategies implemented in Africa since independence have neither aimed at achieving the priority task of an agricultural revolution, nor really aimed at any significant industrialization; basically, they extended the colonial pattern of integration in the world capitalist system. The catastrophic results are now obvious. Moreover, the Western inspired policies of so-called 'readjustment' to the new conditions created by the global crisis (through IMF and World Bank recipes) would only worsen the case. Hence, another development, fundamentally based on a popular alliance, is the only acceptable alternative. The priority target of achieving an agricultural revolution requires, for sure, industrialization. But the pattern of industrialization would have to be quite different from the conventional one. This Chapter tries to show in which respects this pattern of needed industrialization presupposes some form of 'delinking' from the system governing the global economic expansion of capitalism. The national and popular content of development, in its turn, can hardly be imagined if no significant change is considered in the direction of a democratization of the society, allowing for an autonomous expression of the various social forces and creating the basis for a real civil society. Simultaneously, the weakness of African states, to which reference is made in the Chapter, calls for co-operation and unity without which any national and popular attempt would remain extremely limited and vulnerable.

THE FAILURE OF THE 'MODERNIZATION' STRATEGIES

Twenty years ago, when most of the African countries were attaining independence, the view prevailing at that time, even among Africans, attributed underdevelopment on the continent to an historical backwardness which was to be overcome simply by redoubling efforts aimed at progress in a previously defined and known direction. What the national liberation movement, such as it was, was blaming the colonizers for was precisely the fact that they were not up to the task.

The African 'left' and 'right' were convinced that independence was a sure guarantee of and a sufficient precondition for the acceleration of the modernization process. The liberal thesis considered that maintaining a large opening or access to foreign capital was the means to accelerating growth. The government's role was precisely to create more favourable conditions likely to generate new opportunities for capital investments by accelerating education and training, so feared by the colonizers, as well as the modernization of both infrastructure and administration. The socialist thesis of the time, suspicious of foreign capital, was that the government was itself to compensate for the lack of capital, specifically with a view to effectively speeding up the modernization process. In other words, the socialist thesis was not rejecting either the 'modernization' perspective or integration into the international division of labour.

Both theses shared the same basic views concerning the neutrality of technology, i.e., both were arguing that the direction of modernization could be and was known: a mere glance at both Western and Eastern advanced societies would illustrate the similarity of a number of objectives in terms of consumption, organization of production, administration and education. The 'socialists' were probably more sensitive to issues like national independence, which is why they were on their guard against the recourse to foreign capital. They were also probably more sensitive to issues related to income distribution and the priority of collective services. But the 'liberals' retorted that capitalism would also solve these problems and, moreover, would gradually lead to democratization of social and political life. Both theses were finally based on the same West-centred and technicoeconomistic view, the common denominator of a popular version of marxism and the best of bourgeois social science.

Only 15 years ago protests were still rare and unwelcome, considered as peasant utopias and culturalist nationalisms. It is true that, because of a lack of sufficient support, the protesters were often guilty of such weaknesses.

The outcome of the real history of the last two decades has been such that the two theses have been systematically called into question today. It is this two-fold historical 'frustration' that gives the thesis of unequal development the strength it is gaining.

The thesis of unequal development began by the affirmation that underdevelopment, far from being a 'backwardness', was the result of integration into the world capitalist system as an exploited and dominated periphery, fulfilling specific functions in the process of accumulation at the centre of the system. This integration, contrary to superficial points of view, did not date from the colonial scramble for Africa at the end of the nineteenth century, but from the very beginning of mercantilism in the eighteenth century, a period when Africa was 'specialized', through the 'slave trade', in the supply of labour power which, exploited in America, was to speed up the process of capital accumulation in Atlantic Europe. This 'specialization', apart from its horrors, was leading to a regression of local production systems as well as State organizations and, moreover, was to mark the ideology of the societies involved in this shameful trade with features which will remain for a long time.

The thesis of unequal development proceeded with its analysis by trying to understand the mechanisms by which capital, dominant on the world scale, was subordinating pre-capitalist modes of production while distorting them. Whereas the ethnological mainstream was carrying on its research on the singularities of African societies, trying to isolate them conceptually, the thesis of unequal development was laying stress on the integration of apparently 'traditional' rural societies in the process of capital accumulation. It was in this manner that, in the first half of the 1960s, the essential characteristics of the modes of formal domination of capital over the African rural world were defined. It was shown how, in the 'trade economy', the technical and commercial systems of control were depriving peasant producers of their own control over the means of production, of which they were still the formal owners, in order to extract a surplus of labour transformed through commodity trade into profit for the capital of the dominating monopolies. It was shown how the driving back of peasants into the intentionally small reserves in South Africa and Zimbabwe was intended to supply cheap labour to industries, mines and plantations.

These analyses lead to a consideration of a fundamentally different alternative of a development based on popular alliance between workers and peasants. The way was thus opened for a positive rethinking of all the issues of development: orientations of industrialization, the question of State and Nation, etc. Within this perspective, industry is meant to support the technical and social revolution in the rural area. This inversion of priorities also, by the force of circumstances, involved fundamental revisions at the level of reflection on consumption models, the articulation of big and small industries, modern techniques and artisanal and traditional techniques, etc. A positive content could be given to a strategy of delinking, i.e. of refusal of the imperatives of the international division of labour, heretofore considered as inevitable necessities.

The seed was sown. But it could not germinate unless it fell on fertile soil. For ideas become realities only if they are supported by effective social forces. However, the ground is becoming increasingly solid. The old movement of national liberation, whose objective was political independence, has exhausted its potentials. The 50-State Africa, to whose creation it contributed, finds itself in a number of dilemmas: a dilemma of economic development whose contrasted effects are ever more explosive with urbanization and mass unemployment, agricultural stagnation, soil deterioration, famines and massive imports of food products and growing external dependency; a dilemma of national construction; a political dilemma of imitative democracies giving way to tyrannies, single parties of national construction giving place to military and bureaucratic cliques; an ideological dilemma of capitalist liberalism and bureaucratic socialism which do not answer any needs of the popular masses; a cultural dilemma involving imitative education with all its dysfunctionality; and the imposition of the foreign languages of colonization as a vehicle of alienation, as ineffective as it is unbearable.

The reason is that the old movement of national liberation was in fact a bourgeois movement even though it was able to mobilize peasant masses, and even though its petty bourgeois component had given the illusion of a possible socialist prospect. The newly emerging movement will be that of peasants and workers, by the force of circumstances. It will probably inevitably assume populist forms in a first stage while the seed sown has not yet germinated.

The present crisis of the imperialist system obviously enhances all these contradictions. The solutions offered by the system imposing its 'adjustment' policies are no answer to the real questions. There is no alternative to a strategy of national and popular reconstruction, which is self-centred and delinked from the world capitalist system.

554

THE TOP PRIORITY: AGRICULTURAL REVOLUTION, BUT HOW? – CRITIQUE OF THE CONVENTIONAL 'WISDOM' OF WORLD BANK

The failure of 'development' has been more dramatic for Africa as a whole than in any other region. In fact, Africa has not yet started its agricultural revolution without which no further stage of development can be considered. The production and productivity per rural family have been almost stagnant for long and might have even started declining in many places. Therefore, the outvillage migration is not the result of a relative overpopulation created by some agricultural progress, even if socially unequal, but, on the contrary, it is a desperate runaway of the whole population to escape from famine. This type of migration generates a monstrous type of urbanization with no hope of industrial employment, since it does not provide any means of financing new activities. Simultaneously, African countries, with very few exceptions, have not started entering the industrial age from any point of view: neither a minimal network of inter-related industries exists anywhere, nor a minimal financial and technological capacity is provided to pursue any consistent industrial policy. Elsewhere, in many areas of Latin America and South, South-East and East Asia, such minimal tasks have already been accomplished, even if in chaotic, regionally and socially unequal ways and, hence, inadequate from a national and popular viewpoint.

This failure has, for sure, deep roots, both precolonial and colonial. But in no way can it be considered that the post-colonial decades have started reversing the negative processes and even involutions.

The task of achieving the agricultural revolution is therefore the priority target for the decades to come. This is a very complex task and, obviously, multi-dimensional. It has technological dimensions such as: what types of equipment and other inputs (control of water, use of chemicals, etc.) can bring simultaneously significant increases in production per capita and per acre? These technological choices imply the design of adequate supportive economic policies: the choice of price and income systems ensuring the rationality of the choices they induce, the choice of the supportive industrialization priorities, the pattern of financing etc. These policies, in turn, bear complex social and political consequences: on how the various types of social control in rural areas (land property and use, rent and wage system, co-operatives of producers of a variety of types, from lower to higher forms, etc.) command the direction of change (or make it impossible ...), or how the types of social control in place are the historical result of social power balances and imbalances (particularly the result of the relation of the state to the rural communities and their components), and through which political moves they could be changed, how the various types of social control on trade systems and industry (state, basic collectivities, private national capital, transnationals, etc.) combine with the need for agricultural changes, etc.

On none of these aspects, and less on how they interrelate, are the lessons from the historical experiences – be it that of the developed West, East, Latin America or Asia regions – transferrable as such to Africa today. There are many reasons for this limited possible use of the lessons of history: differences in land availability, differences in pre-modern patterns of social organization and levels of productivities, differences in available industrial technologies, etc. Similarly, the lessons from other experiences of industrialization, whether in the perspective of the world division of labour or conceived in a way 'delinked' from it, whether based on private capital initiative or on state intervention, are of a limited significance in the dramatic case of Africa.

Yet, precisely perhaps because the task is totally new and the challenges too complex, recipes are suggested hurriedly by agencies notably from the UN family, World Bank and major bilateral agencies. Many of these recipes do not meet the test of experience, hence the cascade of shortlived 'fashions'. Those who, in the name of 'immediate efficiency', do not recognize our deep ignorance of what can be done, easily substitute for the need of deeper studies their 'theological' beliefs, whether in the market efficiency (as if some minor changes in prices would create *ipso facto* adequate incentives), or in the state efficiency (without questioning enough the historical, political and cultural dimensions of the state).

Considered from the global perspective of today's world system, the failure of African development bears further dramatic consequences. The weakness of the continent, both at economic and financial levels (extreme food, technological and financial dependency) and – perhaps consequently – at political and military levels, encourage cynical attitudes, allowing the world powers to give priority to their geo-strategic views without being compelled to pay due consideration to local forces and interests. This weakness, combined with the global strategies of the world powers, creates hence an additional unfavourable set of conditions for internal changes.

A glaring example of how 'theology' is substituted for the scientific analysis of the roots of the African failure to achieve its agricultural revolution is provided by the famous World Bank Report on

'Accelerated Development in sub-Saharan Africa'. One expected, in that respect, World Bank to come up with a critique of local social and economic systems and the world system of the division of labour, responsible for this African failure. One even thought that World Bank would make some sort of self-criticism, since for the past twenty years it has supported most of the basic principles underlying the development system that is now being called into question. Not at all – World Bank attributes the failure entirely to the African governments, who are accused of having held agriculture in contempt and given far too much priority to industry!

Therefore, the strategy proposed by World Bank is perfectly summed up as follows: 'The internal structural problems and external constraints impeding African economic growth have been exacerbated by domestic policy inadequacies ... trade and exchange-rate policies (which) have over-protected industry, held back agriculture ... the public sector has become over-extended ...' upon which World Bank goes on to suggest a strategy of adjustment to the demands of the world system, based on exports (agricultural and mining commodities), supported mainly by devaluation measures and by resorting to a larger measure of liberalism, accompanied by offering greater scope to private initiative. A carrot, that of doubling external aid in real terms during the eighties, is dangled to bring countries to accept these principles of 'healthy' management.

Low agricultural productivity in Africa is a platitude. What the World Bank report does not say is that this low productivity, which goes hand-in-hand with the land-extensive type of agriculture, was – and still is – economic from the point of view of the world system of the division of labour. It allowed the West to acquire raw materials without having to invest in its colonies. It has been clearly shown that this mechanism is responsible for having impoverished the land and thus brought about poorer yields. The transition to intensive agriculture, a necessity today, implies an increase in the world prices of raw materials, if they are to be exported: land, like oil or water, is no longer an 'unlimited' resource, but one that is becoming scarce.

Yet, World Bank has only managed to discover three ills from which Africa suffers: overvalued exchange rates, too high a level of taxation of farmers, and excessive growth in administrative expenditure.

It is clear that if prices in foreign currencies are maintained, devaluation would allow the exporter to obtain more in the local currency. That is a pleonasm. However, one cannot conclude either that devaluation would bring about equilibrium in the balance of payments without control, or that prices in foreign currencies would remain stable if the

African countries devalued their own currencies. Experience has repeatedly shown that in many Third World countries the whole range of local prices tends to adjust to the import prices and that, therefore, the effects of devaluation both on comparative price structures and on the balance of payments are cancelled out. The absence of a self-reliant and autonomous economic structure explains this generalized contagion, which reflects the way in which the local systems are dependent on the world price system.

It is true that peasants in Africa are subjected to a considerable degree of 'hidden taxation' – the difference between the export price, the real cost of internal marketing deducted, and the price paid to the producer. But where else would the state raise these resources if this margin were abolished and if the country were to give priority in its development to the production of such export commodities as suggested by World Bank? Why not reduce consumer taxes (e.g. on coffee) in the developed countries for the benefit of the African peasant? Clearly, such hidden taxation reflects the local states' 'anti-peasant' bias, but this bias is a consequence of the nature of the states' relations with the world system. The anti-peasant feature is not that of the local state alone but that of the global system of exploitation within which this state functions.

By failing to carry the analysis of the system any further, the World Bank condemns itself on the subject of public expenditure as on others, distributing advice that is hardly efficient and suggesting ways and means of tinkering with the economy in order to reduce this expenditure (by very little). Such savings are invariably made at the expense of the poor, in contradiction to the fine speeches about 'basic needs'. Moreover, does not IMF, a close partner of World Bank, always impose devaluation, austerity and a reduction in the standard of living of the poorest sections of the population? 'Real prices' (world prices being the supreme reference) and the abolition of subsidies for the most basic consumer goods always operate against the interest of peoples.

On the other hand, is industry in Africa really 'overprotected'? Will not reducing such 'overprotectionism' of an industry which is still the most fragile in the world surely reduce even further its already negligible rate of growth?

Wages in Africa are said to be 'too high' and those of Bangladesh are held up as a model. Does World Bank see the future in terms of the bangladeshization of the Third World? And how does one reconcile this statement with that on satisfying 'basic needs'? Besides, there is no discussion on industrialization strategies, and import substitution is considered as, by far, the superior option (no attention is paid to the fact that this strategy reproduces and reinforces inequalities in income distribution) although it is said to have been 'badly applied' in Africa because it too often required state intervention (without which, despite World Bank's pious hopes concerning 'entrepreneurs', the rate of industrialization would have been even lower). World Bank also recommends processing mineral resources for export, although it is a known fact that such processing swallows up considerable capital without leading to interaction between the exploitation of the resources and national development. It also recommends light export industries. Have the disasters of the textile industries in Morocco and Tunisia been forgotten which, after having followed such 'recommendations', saw the doors of Western markets firmly closed to their products? As for the industrialization required to ensure agricultural development, this is one aspect which World Bank is, apparently, quite unaware of.

THE ALTERNATIVE STRATEGY: AUTO-CENTRED AND DELINKED NATIONAL AND POPULAR DEVELOPMENT: THE NEED FOR INDUSTRIALIZATION TO SUPPORT AGRICULTURAL REVOLUTION

Instead of the false and metaphysical opposition between agriculture and industry, one should look into how they are interlinked in the 'modernization' theory and practices, and popular strategy. For the agricultural revolution requires industry to make it possible, although not the type of industries developed (poorly) until now in Africa.

To try to schematise the opposing auto-centred model/ extraverted model, a four sector analysis had been proposed: (a) Production of the means of production; (b) Production of goods for mass consu.nption; (c) Luxury production/consumption; and, (d) Exports. The 'auto-centred' model is defined as that which is mainly governed by the interlinkage of sectors (a) and (b), and the 'extraverted' model as that which is mainly determined by the interlinkage of sectors (c) and (d). This analysis leads to a major conclusion: in the auto-centred model labour remuneration (wages and peasants' incomes) must necessarily increase according to the rhythm of the progress of productivity. On the other hand, in the extraverted model, the labour remuneration can be delinked from the productivity growth. Thus, the following conditions would seem to apply: (a) the development of a country from the contemporary Third World cannot be achieved through the adjustment of its economy to the requirements of the international division of labour but, on the contrary, through the delinking of this economy as opposed to the international division of labour; (b) this delinking is a necessary (but not sufficient) condition for an auto-centred development which remains impossible if it is not intended for the people (that is, if the benefits of the productivity rise do not go straight to the greater majority); and, (c) on the other hand, a growth that mainly benefits a minority is only possible on the basis of an 'extraverted' development (not always and everywhere possible), and indeed does call for such a development, which is more effective for this objective than an 'auto-centred' model. In the contemporary Third World, therefore, the achievement of auto-centred development will require nationalist regimes and democratic and popular participation.

It is now possible to see that the policies implemented in Africa during the sixties and seventies have been mainly 'extraverted'. Bearing in mind the contrasts and differences, one could at least recall that in this vast continent, which has known different political regimes and numerous changes, there have been four sets of experience: (a) The 'stagnation' cases, associated with a lack of natural resources and/ or a stagnant world demand for these resources; (b) The 'stagnation' cases, in spite of the existence of such resources, either potential (but well-known), or even exploited (and at times on a large scale); (c) The cases of 'relatively marked growth', at times even high, associated with the exploitation of these resources, either by the multinationals or by the national state; and, (d) The cases of 'marked growth', in spite of the fact that the exploited resources (then often agricultural rather than mining resources) are 'moderate', due in general to an extensive opening to the exterior; this 'marked growth' being associated with an uneven distribution of its benefits.

In that frame of the conventional economic analysis, one identifies some driving activities of the effective growth when it has existed: (a) oil and mines first; (b) export agriculture (relatively rich – coffee, cocoa – or poor – groundnut); (c) light consumption industries managed in an acceptable way, established by multinationals or the state, modern in their techniques, and responding to the internal market (import substitution); (d) a lively building sector (linked to the accelerated urbanization and to 'prosperity'); (e) administrative expenditure conceived in very classical terms, miming the West in its form and to one degree or another, the so-called 'social' (education first), growing at a sustained rhythm; and, (f) tertiary activities (trade, finance ...), nearly always also more vivid in their growth than the other sectors. When the global growth has been slight, zero or negative, it has often been attributed to an insufficient dynamism of (a) and (b) and/or to a doubtful character of (c) above. If, in addition, (e) and (f) have been pushed, then the interlinked double crisis of public finances and balance of payments ineluctably worsen the situation. The lack of dynamism of (a), (b) and (c) is attributed either to the evident short-comings of the country or to its lofty 'nationalism' which refuses foreign capital, a 'rare' factor. It is, or can be, aggravated by the unconcern of the 'elite', its 'corruption', etc.

A steadily backward agriculture, almost always stagnant (except in the products of the export sector), is incapable of releasing a marketed food surplus up to the standard of the urban effective demand. In the most extreme cases, it becomes increasingly difficult for the rural world to feed itself. These disasters or shortages are easily attributed to the climate (drought) or to the careless administrative bureaucracy of the rural world. We rarely get into the analysis of the draining policies on the rural world which these conventional global strategies of growth imply necessarily.

In these experiences, industry has been hardly ever the driving force of the growth, but widely the product of a response of adjustment to the latter, whose chain effects are limited: (a) upstream, through the basic industrial shortage and the weak inter-industrial integration; and, (b) downstream, through the uneven character of the incomes it distributes. If industry restricts itself to a definite number of production units in a position of quasi-monopoly on a small market, and the units provide consumption goods for middle classes, the industry, even if efficiently managed (that is, without need for subsidies and with prices competitive with those of imports) is only derived, and is not a driving force.

The alternative option of a national and popular 'auto-centred strategy' rests first on the principle of distribution of income as evenly as possible, especially between rural and urban sectors, between the modern sectors with higher productivity and the backward ones. The surplus of production over the remuneration of labour thus equalized constitutes an excess which, if it is national and retained for accumulation, permits guaranteeing a marked growth and a parallel and even progression of the popular consumption. The structure of demand, constituted in this way, would show priority in basic needs and orient the productive system towards the satisfaction of the latter.

Without entering into an illusory description of concrete details of measures to be taken to implement a development pattern of this type, one can assume that:

(a) It not only implies declaration of the 'agricultural priority', but also its effective implementation. This priority requires that other

561

activities with higher productivity should not be an opportunity for the distribution of incomes which exceed those distributed in agriculture. The reason for this being that the demand is structured in such a way that the satisfaction of the needs expressed by the privileged would necessarily absorb an essential part of the means available for accumulation at the expense of agriculture;

(b) It implies that industrialization be first conceived to maintain the progress of productivity in agriculture: production of adequate inputs (fertilizers, equipment etc), infrastructural works (irrigation, transport), preserving and processing of the produce, etc. It then ensures that this industry satisfies the non-food consumption needs of the rural and urban population, on a basis as egalitarian as possible. It is understood that we cannot give up this national industry in substituting it through imports because imports have to be paid for through exports, and the comparative advantages are those which result from the price and income system of the world order, which in turn, is in conflict with the political coherence outlined above. Import must, therefore, at each step, be reduced to the strict minimum;

(c) It implies therefore national and popular forms of social organization of production: the control of peasants over agricultural projects, real co-operatives (which should not be a way of draining the rural areas, depriving the peasants of their hold on production), institutions of collective bargaining of agricultural prices, the national control of industries, a national wage policy, the redistribution of the means of financing on a country scale etc. It is difficult to imagine how, for instance, the multinationals would find a place in this organisational pattern, except to provide, in time and under strict national control, some limited models as to production or organization;

(d) It implies that technological relations be not reduced to mere 'transfers'. It is in fact a question of creating an inventive capacity, not for reasons of cultural nationalism, but simply because the available techniques, especially the more advanced ones, are not neutral with regard to the range of products, the structure of demand to be satisfied (Western patterns), the price and income structures which control the profitability of these techniques, etc; and,

(e) It implies limited external relations which are radically different from those derived from the various industrialization strategies of import substitution, or export industrialization. The import substitution is based on an already actual demand, in a structure of

562

income distribution characterized by very strong inequality; and on this basis respects the principles of the profitability (with at most some arguments of 'moderate protection of infantile industries' during a brief transition). Therefore, it cannot but displace imports towards the intermediate goods (the industrial apparatus remaining non-integrated), and sophisticated capital goods (as the demand to be satisfied, in competition with the imports reproduces the Western capital exacting consumption model). It thus remains 'extraverted'. On the other hand, national and popular 'auto-centred' industry is not built in response to a pre-existing demand; but is created on the basis of the satisfaction of peoples' needs (incomes policy) and intermediate and derived capital needs. The import, which subsists, aims at filling the gaps, in the range of these derived needs, reducing progressively their relative importance (but not necessarily their absolute bulk). It binds, therefore, the external relations to the logic of internal accumulation. As for export industry, it is, by its very definition, extraverted. More especially because, forced to compete with the industry of advanced countries on their own homeland, it must import advanced technology extensively. This explains why the NICs, which are the most advanced in that direction, are also the most indebted: the export industry does not alleviate the situation of the foreign balance (contrary to the argument put forward to that effect, by World Bank in particular); it aggravates it.

It implies the building up of a national structure of interdependence of price and financing means which is in conflict with the very principles of the criterion of micro-economic profitability. In fact, the auto-centred industry, if it must comply with the peoples' needs, must accept the juxtaposition of the very uneven productive units – modern industries, semi-mechanized manufactures, and handicrafts manufactures. The unit of labour remuneration and that of prices thus entail unequal surplus. It must be redistributed so as to avoid the polarization of progress in the modern units; and, on the contrary, to finance the progressive modernization of the backward sectors with the surplus of the modern sectors. This is hardly possible on a vast scale without large public property: the private national enterprise and, a fortiori, the multinational subcompany cannot accept, at this level, to detach itself from profitability. As we know, they act in a directly opposite sense: in destroying the non-competitive cottage industry, they have contributed in increasing unemployment and at the same time depriving the population of useful products.

CONCLUDING REMARKS

The Chapters in this Part constitute a bridge that spans the analytical preoccupation with short-term stabilization issues and the arena of fundamental structural change and long-term social and economic transformation. In undertaking such a crossing, the inevitable necessity of an immediate transition from continual economic degeneracy to recovery has been appropriately emphasized. That Africa must undertake some form of structural adjustment is not in doubt, what is questionable is the efficacy of the traditional SAPs recommended to the African countries by IMF and World Bank. The overriding conclusion of the Chapters is that African countries must eschew ineffective economic orthodoxy and search for new initiatives predicated on emerging new economic realities both from within the domestic structures of the African economies and from without. Only then will Africa come to experience the social and economic recovery that is so urgently needed for sheer survival and as the launching-pad for long-term development.

While economic systems go through some form of cyclical fluctuations over time, the African continental economic experience so far seems to be unidirectional, with a cumulative tide and trend towards deterioration and decline. The inevitable questions, therefore, are: What went wrong with the African development machinery? What must be done now to rectify the errors and traumas of the past?

With regard to the first question, the Chapters offer a number of insights. First, it is clear that the root cause of Africa's development crisis lies in the failure to transform the national economies for over two decades. Second, the slow-down in Africa's traditional engine of growth, namely, trade with the developed countries, brought the African economy almost to a halt. Third, and as argued by Samir Amin in particular, the seeds of economic disaster were first sown when the African economy was integrated into the international division of labour, thus entrenching the economies into a framework of unequal development. But, above all, the Chapters pragmatically acknowledge that Africa itself also made errors, especially with regard to agricultural development or the lack of it.

It is clear by now that the challenge of recovery must necessarily hinge on economic reconstruction for long-term development, and sustained commitment to a new focus of social organization, economic management and political stability. What is required in Africa, more than ever, is a development process that centres on developing the capacity to understand, predict, respond flexibly to and manage *change*: whether the changes are external or internal. In operational terms, it consists in mobilizing and transforming resources (natural, human, financial, institutional) in a consistent and efficient manner to fulfil socially-satisfying ends, and in breaking the embedded structural rigidities. It entails knowledge and skill of all kinds, social organization, leadership, technology (inventive, creative, adaptive, and applied). The new economic structure for Africa must hinge on a new structural articulation of interrelationships between and among agriculture, industry and subregional and regional co-operation such that agriculture will no longer be the engine of growth only because of the agricultural export commodities. But, rather, it will be the driving force of African development and the rhythm of economic growth since it will be based on national, popular and auto-centred functionalism, and in such a way that it will engender higher and more evenly distributed income which will result in higher accumulation and a progression of popular consumption. This movement will, in turn, support an industrialization process that is consciously geared towards enhancing productivity in agriculture and the satisfaction of non-food consumption needs. But, given the limits to national potentialities, the twin pillars of agriculture and industrialization will need a third pillar, i.e., that of subregional co-operation, to sustain the new process of economic dynamism within which countries will move towards greater specialization and, at the same time, reinforce trade among themselves. It is only when such an integrated development structure is set in motion – which must be soon – that the viability of the African economy would have been established.

PART FIVE

African Economic Co-operation and Integration

INTRODUCTORY NOTE

Following the attainment of political independence, and especially in the 1970s, there have been various attempts at promoting economic co-operation and integration in Africa. The attempts were prompted both by structural weaknesses inherent in the multiplicity and fragility of the newly-emergent national economies and by the stark realization of the pressing needs for subregional and regional approaches to, and solidarity on, development issues in an increasingly difficult, if not hostile, international economic environment. Economic co-operation and integration indeed constitutes one of the essential pillars of LPA and FAL, both of which provided for the eventual establishment of an African Common Market, leading to an African Economic Community by the year 2000. It is against this background and the prominence and reinforcement given to the spirit of African economic co-operation and integration both by the drought-related emergency and the social and economic crisis that has engulfed the region since 1980 that the eight Chapters in this Part have sought to address the issue of economic co-operation and integration as a crucial aspect of the challenge of African economic recovery and development. The focus is on two main issues; namely, the impact of the colonial heritage on the existing economic and integration schemes, and the various approaches to economic co-operation and integration and their relevance or appropriateness to Africa's political, cultural, social and economic conditions.

The main emphasis of virtually all African integration schemes has been on a traditional market integration approach rather than the production-focused strategy. But, as the contributions by Louis Sangare, Makhtar Diouf, Arthur Hazlewood, Walter Kamba and Peter Robson in Chapters 26–30 amply demonstrate, this is like 'putting the cart before the horse'. Their analyses point both to the prematureness and inadequacy of the market integration approach in the particular context of underdeveloped Africa, and the dangers that such a strategy has in reinforcing and strengthening the horizontal extensions of some of the existing vertical linkages of the continent with the advanced industrialized countries of the North.

The almost unanimous verdict and, may be, not altogether unexpected conclusion reached in the various Chpaters is that the success of African economic groupings has so far been rather limited, with little or no impact on the economic growth of the co-operating countries; not even the limited objective of intra-African trade expansion has been achieved. Thus, the suggestion from contributor after contributor is that the market integration approach needs to be reinforced by the production approach to economic integration in order to enhance the derivable economic benefits. And there is no shortage of ideas as to the required modalities, ranging from the down-to-earth to the purely visionary, although the consensus would seem to be on payments reforms, the development of suitable infrastructure for regional economic co-operation and economic restructuring through the promotion of joint ventures in the priority areas of agriculture, agro and basic industries, transport and communications and energy.

Additionally, the fact that current African efforts at economic integration have more often than not resulted in costly bureaucratization and proliferation of inter-governmental organizations has prompted suggestions about new co-operation structures and modifications to existing ones. Hence, Makhtar Diouf argues in favour of only one broad inter-governmental apex organization at each subregional level, while Arthur Hazlewood, in Chapter 27, stresses the importance of indigenous NGOs and individual and corporate economic actors in the private sector as essential ingredients of effective economic co-operation arrangements in the African context.

CHAPTER TWENTY-SIX

The Essential Role of Regional and Subregional Institutions in African Economic Co-operation and Integration

MAKHTAR DIOUF

Many IGOs have been established in Africa in recent years to promote co-operation and integration with a view to enhancing economic development. As we speak of the economic crisis in Africa and of recovery programmes, it is certain that these IGOs are the first to be concerned.

To appreciate their role and utility in Africa's economic life, past and present, we shall situate them in the historic context of their creation and evolution; in other words we shall see what internal and external factors were responsible for their creation and development. To do this, we shall distinguish three major periods: the two past decades 1960–1970 and 1970–1980, and the present decade, beginning 1980. We shall next attempt a brief review of African integration and conclude by making a number of recommendations.

THE 1960–1970 PERIOD: MODEST BEGINNINGS

It is at the very beginning of this period that the two major regional IGOs, OAU and ADB, were established.

OAU, a basically political and pluralist organization, has only very distant links with Nkrumah's Pan-Africanist project of a United States of Africa (1964) and with Cheikh Anta Diop's project of the Federal States of Black Africa (1960). Both men envisioned the future Africa as being like the US of America or the Soviet Union, that is, with a single, federal-type government. Both men very early drew attention to the impossibility of achieving true economic development (that is, on the cultural, political and economic levels), within the framework of the micro-states born out of the balkanization of Africa.

OAU turned out to be a largely political grouping, and, in fact, has never really been seen as a foremost instrument of economic development. It is hardly an exaggeration to say that the economic dimension appeared only with the LPA. The role of co-ordination and harmonization of the economic policies of states, set forth in OAU Charter (Article 2 paragraphs 1 and 2), never found the least application.

On the other hand, the establishment of OAU helped to put an end to many abortive attempts to create political groupings based on ideology (Ghana–Guinea–Mali union, Casablanca Group, etc). All this was in accordance with a non-declared principle of specialization, whereby OAU took charge of political co-operation and economic co-operation was left to subregional organizations existing or yet to be created.

ADB was quite a different proposition because its design was originally based on the system of the UN (Economic and Social Council) where the problems of economic development were as worrying then as they are today.

Paradoxically, while they were setting up structures of regional co-operation, the new African states were unable to establish new institutions at subregional levels. The IGOs of economic integration that saw the light were merely continuations of the experiences born during the colonial period:

(i)   In Southern Africa, the South African Customs Union, comprising Botswana–Lesotho–Swaziland sought to continue after independence an experience which dates back to 1910;

(ii) In East Africa, the Kampala Treaty (1967) gave a legal basis and new dynamism to the EAC created by Great Britain in 1917;

(iii) In Central Africa, the treaty establishing UDEAC, with a new member, Cameroon, replaced in 1964 the Paris Treaty (1959) which established the Equatorial Customs Union (UDE) a few months after the dissolution of the Federation of French Equatorial Africa; and

(iv) In the French-speaking part of West Africa, the scenario was the same: following the dissolution of the Federation of French West Africa (March 1959) the Customs Union of West Africa was established (June 1959); it was replaced in 1966 by the Customs Union of West African states, with essentially the same provisions.

The narrowly-focussed co-operation IGOs that were established during this period were only continuing the experiences born of the colonial period: the Inter-State Committee for Hydraulic Studies (1960), the International Organization against African Migatory Locusts (1962), the Joint Organization for the Fight against Acridian and Fowl Plague (1965).

This first decade of independence in Africa was not one of regional economic integration: on the entire continent, only three economic communities can be counted whose origins go back to the colonial period and which function with very small general secretariats. This lack of enthusiasm for regional integration is due to a number of reasons:

(i) The tasks of construction and consolidation of the nation-state were regarded as priorities; consequently, there could be no question of allocating substantial financial and human resources to regional organizations at the expense of national needs. And these nationalistic feelings went hand-in-hand with the distrust of Nkrumah's Pan-Africanist ideas;

(ii) Some countries had no colonial experience of regional integration; and,

(iii) In the existing economic communities, the process of regional integration was blocked: in the EAC, because the independence of the states had exposed the contradictions (unequal industrial development) which for a long time existed between Kenya and its partners; and in UDEAC and UDEAO, the states embarked very timidly upon the process of horizontal integration, clearly preferring vertical integration with Europe within the framework of the Convention of EEC.

THE PERIOD OF THE 1970s EUPHORIA FOR ECONOMIC INTEGRATION

The period of the 1970s was unquestionably one of the euphoria for economic integration. A number of events are responsible for this:

(a) In 1970, the 3rd summit of non-aligned states held in Lusaka recommended regional integration as a priority development strategy.

(b) In 1973, the onset of the recession, with the first wave of oil price hikes and the beginning of drought in the Sahelian countries, triggered a sense of solidarity among many African governments.

(c) In 1974, the UN General Assembly's declaration of a new international economic order called attention to the need for a South–South dialogue.

573

(d) In 1975 the signing of the first Lome Convention, following Britain's entry into the Common Market, brought the French-speaking states and the English-speaking states together for the first time, but within a system of vertical co-operation. The merit of that was to facilitate their coming together to form subregional groups.

In Central Africa, UDEAC treaty was revised in 1974 to revitalize the organization and extend its activities to new areas of co-operation like agriculture and transport. The Economic Community of the Great Lakes was established (1976) to put back on the rails an old instrument of integration set up in 1925 by Belgium between her colonies of Congo and Rwanda-Burundi and which independence had put an end to.

In West Africa, three economic communities were established within the space of three years: CEAO (1973), the MRU (1974), and ECOWAS (1975). Most of the co-operative organizations with limited objectives were established during this period: Liptako Gourma Authority (1971), OMVS (1972), Permanent Inter-State Committee for drought Control in the Sahel (CILSS) (1973), WARDA (1970), OMVG (1976) etc. This proliferation of IGOs meant that ECA had to decentralize its activities, particularly as regards the direction of economic co-operation: in 1977, the UNDATS, created at the beginning of the 1970s, became the MULPOCs which cover each of the five subregions.

However, this period also saw the break-up of the EAC (1977); but this event must be seen as pointing to the impossibility of achieving an exclusive market integration in the context of under-development.

On the whole, and unlike in the preceding decade, the African states (especially those of West Africa) went in more open-handedly for regional IGOs of integration and co-operation.

THE 1980s: THE SETTING OF THE LPA

The beginning of the 1980s was marked by the advent of LPA which put forward economic integration as a prime factor of inward-oriented development. The LPA unquestionably helped to bring ECA more to the fore of African public opinion and to give OAU an economic dimension and an image that is a little less 'political'. The objective of an African Common Market advocated by LPA required first the establishment of economic communities in each of the five subregions of the continent. The IGOs of economic integration established during this period are more or less meant to fulfil this condition:

(a) ECCAS (1983) which comprises, among others, the members of UDEAC and those of CEPGL;

(b) PTA (1983) exceeds by far the geographical limits of the former EAC whose over-extended size led to a break-up in 1985, with the creation of the Indian Ocean Commission;

(c) The Indian Ocean Commission (1985) was set up to take account of the island character of the countries of the subregion; and,

(d) Alongside PTA, there is also the experience of SADCC (1980) born out of the concerns caused by the negative impact of the proximity of the Republic of South Africa.

SADCC and the Indian Ocean Commission are two IGOs whose establishment was not envisaged under LPA, but which was dictated by reality. On the whole, the period of the 1980s has been marked by a certain lull in the establishment of IGOs, compared to the preceding one. This period also marks a turning point, being one of serious reflection on issues of African integration.

The beginning of the 1980 decade marks also the end of the First Lome Convention; the disappointments arising from this type of co-operation, which five years earlier was presented as a model for the needs of economic development, are certainly of a nature to strengthen the community spirit of the African political leaders. But the economic crisis and the debt burden are also there to vitiate any attempts at new financial commitments in the way of integration structures. The only alternative is to streamline those that already exist. ECA therefore undertakes appraisal missions at the request of subregional political authorities: UDEAC (1981), West Africa (1982), CEPGL (1984). Unfortunately, we cannot avoid observing that these studies have not been followed by any decisive actions to streamline and improve the efficiency of the IGOs concerned.

RESULTS OF REGIONAL ECONOMIC INTEGRATION IN AFRICA

Was the progress that was made in establishing new structures of integration and co-operation accompanied by progress in the process of integration itself? What has been the impact on the economic development of the countries concerned? It is the problem posed by LPA which makes such questions necessary. In fact, the objective of an African Common Market for the year 2000, and the contribution of regional integration to inward-oriented development, are possible only if the existing structures of integration are efficient. Unfortunately, such has not been the case and this is due to a number of reasons. The process of economic integration had a bad start: the

African economic communities all adopted at once the market integration model. In a developed environment like EEC, restrictive trade practices (customs duties, quotas ...) are practically the only factors likely to curb the development of trade considered as a priority objective. But in a context of underdevelopment, trade must not be treated as a priority objective as the major problems are elsewhere; i.e., in lack of complementarity of industrial products, deficiency of the means of transport and communications, absence of adequate means of payment for trade exchanges, obsession with unequal development in less developed member countries, fear of budgetary losses where carriage charges constitute the bulk of the resources of states, etc.

On account of these persisting constraints, all African attempts at integration have so far ended in failure. This is the sad fact. We must face the fact that no progress has been made toward market integration. While it took the EEC about a decade to attain the status of a customs union, the economic communities in Africa have not yet gone beyond the elementary stage of customs preferential area in the best of cases (flat tax system in UDEAC, regional co-operation tax system in CEAO), and that has happened over a very long period. Up till now, there is neither a customs union nor even a free trade-zone in Africa. Geography and history (even in its colonial phase) have helped to weave links of integration that are much more visible between certain African countries: such as is the case between Cote d'Ivoire and Burkina Faso, Senegal and Mali, and Senegal and Mauritania.

Inter-community trade has been negligible, at least if we look at its development in constant and not current prices as the African economic communities statistics usually do in order to swell them up artificially. It is, moreover, significant that the African Trade Ministers meeting in Brazaville in October 1985 recommended that the share of intra-African trade be increased to 10 per cent over the next ten years; a target that is at once modest and ambitious. Besides, one may ask whether the official intra-community trade exceeds the unrecorded border trade which costs the states nothing. It is to be recalled that in the EEC, intra-community trade represents at least two thirds of the total trade of the member-countries.

The overall impact on economic development and even on short-term economic growth has been imperceptible. No serious statistics can report improved economic performance in the member-countries of the economic communities, by taking into account all the objective comparative data.

Because they adopted an inappropriate integration strategy, the African economic communities are left with heavy bureaucracies which only function for themselves, with no feedback on the sub-regional economic environment. The only relations with the economies of member-countries exist at the level of state contributions: high financial contributions, and also human contributions which, unfortunately, can be negative, as often happens where a state sends into an IGO, on the basis of exclusively political criteria, nationals who are far from having the requisite technical qualifications. What places the organization at a serious disadvantage is the fact that, when the staff do have the requisite qualifications, they are unable to give the best of themselves in an organization that is inefficient, and it is the countries of origin which are the losers.

On the whole, African economic integration becomes an operation of cost without benefit; the accounting cost being the financial contributions of states while the opportunity cost is the economic and social investments which could have been financed with these resources at the national level. Management of economic integration in Africa therefore constitutes a permanent challenge to the most elementary principles of economic calculation. Instead of being a factor for development, African integration tends to become a hindrance, owing to the financial burden that it imposes on the budgets of states without any significant results. In terms of financial analysis, these contributions must be regarded, not as ordinary recurrent expenditures, but as capital expenditures from which one should expect to earn minimum economic returns.

CONCLUSIONS AND RECOMMENDATIONS

This appraisal of African experiments at integration is neither severe nor pessimistic. It reflects a reality which it does not pay to conceal, especially in a forum where the subject of discussion is Africa's economic recovery. For regional integration to be effective as a factor for development, the recovery must also cover the strategy of integration, as follows:

(a) Adopt a plan of integration by projects in priority areas: agriculture, industry (agro-industry and heavy industry), energy, transport and communications, currency and finance. In fact, the obstacles which hinder market integration in Africa are nothing but indices of under-development. Logically, regional integration as a development strategy must make them its targets. And these clearly identified subregional projects would have a better chance of attracting donors. ADB would thus find itself called upon under the preamble and Article 2 of its Charter to stress the financing of multinational projects of economic integration;

(b) Make effective the reduction of the number of IGOs so that each subregion has a single economic community in which the sectoral co-operation IGOs will emerge as mere divisions. This will make for rationalization and co-ordination of activities and also substantial savings in the costs of general secretariats. Only obstacles of a subjective nature stand in the way of the realization of this idea;

(c) Undertake periodic audit of operations in the general secretariats of the IGOs so as to direct their resources towards concrete tasks connected with identified development projects;

(d) Lastly, involve OAU more actively in the process of regional economic integration by making it play the role of co-ordination and harmonization assigned to it by its own Charter (Article 2, paragraphs 1 and 2).

NOTES

1. ECA (1981) *Appraisal Mission of UDEAC and Prospects for Expanding Economic Co-operation in Central Africa.*
2. ECA (1983) *Proposals for Strengthening Economic Integration in West Africa.*
3. ECA/OAU (1980) *Lagos Plan of Action.*
4. Cheikh Anta Diop (1960), *Les fondements économiques et culturels d'un Etat fédéral,* Afrique Noire (Présence Africaine, Paris).
5. Makhtar Diouf (1985), *Intégration économique – Perspectives africaines* (Nouvelles Editions Africaines – Paris/Dakar).
6. Kwame Nkrumah (1964), *Africa Must Unite* (Payot, Paris).

CHAPTER TWENTY-SEVEN

Economic Integration: Lessons for African Recovery and Development

ARTHUR D. HAZLEWOOD

INTRODUCTION

The continued attachment to economic integration as an instrument of progress is to be found not only in the pronouncements of African nations and institutions, but also in those of international bodies including EEC and World Bank, as well as, of course, the UN. Even in the very process of dissolving the EAC, the former partner states agreed 'to explore and identify further areas for future cooperation and to work out concrete arrangements for such cooperation'.

A major reason for this continued hope in integration as a developmental mechanism is the difficulty, for so many countries of Africa, in seeing much in the way of an alternative. So many countries are economically so small – with such small and such poor populations – that production for the domestic market alone must be extremely restricted. Domestic production for such small markets will be at extremely high cost if economies of scale are of any importance. Without access to the larger market area that could be created by measures of economic integration, it is impossible to see how the economies of these small countries could be developed and diversified. Without access to a larger market for new productive activities, these countries will remain tied to the world economy as producers of primary commodities and importers of manufactures. Within its limits, the above argument is valid and important, but as it will be explained later, it reflects too restricted a view of the potentialities of economic integration of, and cooperation between, the countries of Africa.

This Chapter begins by referring to the variety of possible kinds of integration and cooperation in terms of African examples. It examines the operation of these schemes in an attempt to learn the reasons for their less than satisfactory performance, or their downright failure. Important issues in the improved design and operation, and in the aims and spheres of operation, of integration schemes are then suggested. It is asked what outsiders might do to help and what Africa must do to help itself.

FORMS OF 'INTEGRATION' IN AFRICA

Economic integration schemes are not new to Africa. They were a feature of the colonial regimes, before the era of independence and economic development. However, it was with independence that the developmental possibilities of integration came to the fore.

If the term 'integration' is allowed to refer to any arrangements of cooperation between the countries of Africa, or between particular institutions within those countries, then examples of integration abound. It is important that the term 'integration' should be used in this very wide sense, because it may be that the scope for progress in integration, and for its contributing to the solution of Africa's problems, is not greatest through the comprehensive arrangements to which a narrow definition of the term would have to be confined.

Most attention has been devoted to the various 'communities' on a subregional basis that exist or have existed. But many of the inter-state arrangements in Africa deal with particular products or services. Some are concerned with particular export products. Others deal with transport and communications, and with services such as re-insurance and tourism. Some are open to an all-Africa membership; others are on a subregional basis. Not every country participates in every institution that it could join.

The Inter-African Coffee Organization, the Cocoa Producers Alliance, the African Groundnut Council, the African Timber Organization are among organizations concerned with particular products. There are the Pan-African Telecommunications Union and the African Postal Union, the Union of African Railways, the Organization for the Development of African Tourism and the African Reinsurance Corporation. Central bankers meet under the auspices of the Association of African Central Banks. Although the fact does not diminish their importance, these associations of national institutions with a common functional interest would not count as integration arrangements except under the broadest definition of the term.

More obvious instruments of economic integration are monetary unions and clearing systems: West African Monetary Union; West African Clearing House; Central African Monetary System; Central

580

African Clearing House. Then, there are the development banks, which may be operated as instruments of economic integration, but to a greater or lesser degree according to the nature of their investments: Development Bank of the Central African States; East African Development Bank; ADB. The various organizations concerned with particular rivers must also be mentioned. They include OMVS, OMVG and the River Niger Basin Authority.

The most complete and comprehensive examples of integration between states, at least in their design and intention, are the various communities and economic unions. The EAC, until its collapse, was perhaps the most developed of these arrangements. UDEAC is a long established and surviving organization. More recently established are CEAO, ECOWAS, and PTA. Of a different nature from the economic unions and communities but holding the possibility for an important development of integration of the members is SADCC.

ECOWAS is large (in the number of countries it embraces) and potentially of great importance, but it has not achieved much. CEAO is small, and has done something, even if not very much.

There are 16 members of ECOWAS, which came into formal existence at the end of 1975, including the six countries which are the members of CEAO and the three which are in the Mano River Union. The population of the sixteen amounts to nearly 150 million, of whom 85 million are Nigerian. Its origin is to be found in Nigerian initiatives, with such motives as to reduce the dependence of the subregion on the developed countries, to provide post-oil options for Nigerian development, and to reduce the influence of France on the francophone countries of West Africa.

The establishment of a customs union is a central feature of the ECOWAS treaty; a 15-year time-table was prescribed, comprising a two-year stand-still for tariff changes, an 8-year period for reduction and eventual elimination of intra-community import duties, and then five years during which a common external tariff was to be established. Quantitative restrictions were to be eliminated over ten years. The treaty also provides for a Fund for Cooperation, Compensation and Development, and for harmonisation of agricultural and monetary policies and of industrial development plans and incentives. But how all this is to be achieved is not set out in the treaty. The approach is said to be 'flexible and pragmatic' and was necessarily so if agreement on the treaty was to be reached. The result was a Treaty that in effect left all implementation measures still to be worked out and agreed.

CEAO represents the third attempt of the states of the former French West Africa at an integration grouping. It came into effect in 1973, and is an ambitious arrangement going in principle far beyond a passive or negative integration scheme for the liberalisation of trade. It was partly inspired by France and undoubtedly represents, in part, an attempt to establish a counter-weight to Nigeria and to her attempts, which resulted in ECOWAS, to establish a grouping embracing both anglophone and franco-phone countries. It comprises 6 countries with a total population of 34 million, of which 14 million are in Cote d'Ivoire and Senegal, which between them account for 70 per cent of the group's GNP. Manufacturing within the group is dominated by TNCs, and Cote d'Ivoire accounts for more than 60 per cent of group exports of manufactures.

EAC was established in 1967 by a treaty which put on a new basis the integration arrangements that had been inherited from the colonial past, and added new elements, particularly those designed to restrict the disequalising effect between the countries of the common market. Despite these 'equalising' instruments, the Community soon ran into difficulties, and within ten years it had broken up.

EAC was unusual in that it was not only a preferential trade group, but was also responsible for the operation of major transport and communications services – railways, ports, airways – and had a range of research and other functions. A development bank for the Community had been established, and there were elaborate arrangements for consultation and cooperation on planning and other matters. As a result, the dissolution of the Community was a long and complex process, requiring agreement on the allocation of very large assets and liabilities, accompanied at times by far from cordial political relationships between the former members.

SADCC, with a membership of nine states – Angola, Botswana, Lesotho, Malawi, Mozambique, Swaziland, Tanzania, Zambia and Zimbabwe – came into being at a summit meeting in Lusaka in April 1980, the month of Zimbabwe's independence. Its integration aims were adopted in the context of the dependence of most of the members, in one way or another, and in particular in terms of transport, on South Africa. The pressure for cooperation came from the felt need to diminish that dependence.

SADCC is not confined to a particular aspect of economic development. Its approach is very different from that of EAC, or ECOWAS. A major focus of its efforts is the coordination and pledging of aid funds through an annual meeting of members with donor countries and international organisations.

One way in which SADCC is distinctive from other integration arrangements in sub-Saharan Africa is in the manner in which responsibility for particular functions has been allocated to particular members. To quote simply a few of the major matters with which SADCC deals, transport is allocated to Mozambique, food security is the responsibility of Zimbabwe, and industrial development to United Republic of Tanzania. A small secretariat, under an executive secretary, has been established in Botswana, but the individual member states are responsible for pursuing the activity in the sphere (or spheres) they have been allocated. The Summit of Heads of State is the supreme body of SADCC, and under them a ministerial Council is responsible for policy and for the coordination of activities.

In November 1980, SADCC held its first pledging meeting, attended by representatives of some thirty governments and bilateral aid organisations and nearly 20 multilateral donor agencies and international organisations. Very substantial funds were pledged, though it was not all 'new money', some of the funds pledged being already components of various donor programmes. Nevertheless, the pledging of the funds in the framework of SADCC programme was a significant support for the integration movement. More than half the total pledged was from the ADB.

The funds pledged in 1980 were to a very large extent for transport, though they were far from meeting the estimated need. They amounted to no more than a third of the estimated total need of funds for transport and communications projects, and eighty per cent of that total was for rehabilitation and upgrading, not for new developments. A Southern African Transport and Communications Commission (SATCC) was established to manage the transport programme.

The pledging meetings are an annual function, the most recent being held in February 1987. The importance of further transport development to reduce dependence on South Africa remains evident. At the 1987 meeting it was estimated that sixty per cent of the traffic of members' external trade was either directly with South Africa or in transit through South African ports.

PTA began in 1981 as an initiative of the ECA and came into formal existence with the signing of a treaty in 1981. Nine countries – about half the total potential membership – signed at that time, though subsequently other countries acceded and the present membership stands at 15. Most members of SADCC are also members of PTA.

PTA's basic objective is the establishment of preferential trade relations between the members. In this regard, it is planned that all barriers to trade should be removed by 1996. A PTA Clearing House, operating in the Reserve Bank of Zimbabwe, was set up in 1984, and a Development Bank was established in 1986. PTA is therefore a scheme, relying on its bureaucracy to implement the provisions of a formal agreement.

The most ambitious scheme for the development of intra-African trade, as well as for other elements of economic integration, is LPA. LPA looks forward to 'the eventual establishment of an African Common Market leading to an African Economic Community'. Industrialisation is a central feature of LPA, with a 'fundamental role' for 'intra-African industrial cooperation' in the establishment of 'major industrial complexes' and 'multi-national industries in Africa'.

Intra-African trade expansion 'is meant to constitute the mainstay for the present strategy', and LPA's document provides a long list of the measures proposed. Existing preferential areas are taken into account; non-tariff barriers are allowed for; the need for improved transport is recognised; and so on. These measures are all sensible enough, though there may well be incompatibilities within such a comprehensive list of desirabilities. And the proposals are all at a level of generality without reference to specific policies or political obstacles, and with a totally unrealistic time-table. There is also the surprising omission from the list of aims and mechanisms of any reference to the less-developed members of preferential areas and to mechanisms for dealing with their problems. True, 'the least developed African countries' have a Chapter to themselves, but this does not deal with their position in a preferential area with more-developed countries, although this has always been the Achilles heel of integration schemes. There is, indeed, a reference to 'ensuring that no undue advantage is taken of the liberalisation process', but if that is meant to refer to the process of 'cumulative causation' which benefits the more-developed, it is an unusually coy way of doing so, and it is not linked to any proposals for corrective mechanisms. Nor does there seem to be even a hint of the problem, let alone a solution, in the Chapter dealing with industry, which is the sector in which the problem is most likely to be generated.

But even if the proposals were entirely comprehensive and totally compatible, there would remain the question of realism. LPA sees the way towards an Africa-wide common market and economic community as being paved by the establishment of preferential trading areas on a narrower geographical basis. But it does not examine the problems faced by the associations that already exist or have existed, nor suggest how their activities can be made to succeed. Governments have committed themselves to LPA, it is true, but they have committed themselves to other arrangements for economic integration in the past, without properly pursuing their commitments.

ACHIEVEMENTS AND PROBLEMS OF INTEGRATION IN AFRICA

Disappointment with the achievements of integration in Africa is as widespread as the continued belief in its virtues and importance. It would be no exaggeration to say that Africa's experience with integration schemes over the last twenty years has been the experience of failure, and that the achievements of integration have been slight or non-existent.

The outstanding failure, most observers would agree, particularly because it was a collapse from such a high order of integration, has been that of EAC. There had been even closer integration before political independence had been achieved, and there was a history of disagreement between the three countries. The Treaty of 1967 was an attempt to halt the process of dissolution by providing an administrative structure appropriate to the era of independence and mechanisms for achieving an acceptable distribution of the benefits and costs of integration. It reflected not a coming together, but an attempt to keep together, though with altered and looser links than had existed.

The mechanisms of the Treaty failed to halt the process of dissolution. There was no single reason why the Treaty failed. A number of interacting influences and issues, including some that could not have been foreseen by its framers, caused the member states to lose interest in keeping the Community alive. The mechanisms for dealing with the unequal effects of the common market proved inadequate; issues of transport co-ordination were disruptive; the operations of state trading corporations were believed to be discriminatory; there were different attitudes towards development through TNCs; the fact that the Heads of State could be called upon to make decisions on contentious matters discouraged compromise at a lower administrative or political level. In addition, there was the disruptive effect of the Amin regime in Uganda.

In the end, the partner states came to see no firm footing of mutual advantage in the existence of the Community. Cooperation came to be seen, not as a positive-sum, but as a zero-sum or even negative-sum game, so that the members would be no worse off, and perhaps better off going it alone.

SADCC has succeeded in raising substantial aid funds for its programmes. It has concentrated on the major issues in the region's development. Yet, the transport situation in the region is becoming more and more difficult, and cooperation in food security has not been able to prevent the desperate scarcity that is developing in 1987. It must be said, however, that this situation cannot be attributed to inadequacies in SADCC or SATCC; it is created by political and military circumstances that cooperation in transport administration and operation alone, or in food security plans, cannot be expected to overcome.

There is no reason to think that SADCC would have made more progress if it had planned to establish a preferential trade area. In fact, there are undoubtedly advantages in this neglect of what is so central to most integration schemes. There would certainly be complications if SADCC began to deal with such matters. Three of its members, Botswana, Lesotho and Swaziland (the BLS states), are joined with South Africa in the Southern African Customs Union (SACU). This customs union is the contemporary form of a long-established trade and customs relationship between the component territories, dating from 1910. It involves free trade between the members with a common external tariff and, since its revision in 1969, a measure of fiscal compensation for the BLS states. The existence of SACU would involve difficulties for any move towards tariff and trade integration among the countries of SADCC. It is to be noted that BLS have not signed the PTA agreement.

Although the omission of tariff and trade issues from the activities of SADCC has enabled it to proceed with less difficulty than would have been likely if it had attempted to deal with these matters, their absence must also be seen as a glaring gap in its integration plans. The gap may not provide a barrier to progress until perhaps a somewhat distant future, but once progress has been made with the more immediate problems of food security and transport, and such matters as co-ordinated industrial development become relevant, then the need for preferential trade will become apparent. It would not be impossible to provide it by negotiation on a commodity by commodity basis, rather than by broader-based preferences. Though of course, by then, the progress and extension of PTA may have gone a long way towards dealing with the matter.

PTA has progressed in its membership, and includes all but a few of the potential member countries. In other respects progress has been slow. The clearing house exists but has been used for only a small part of the transactions arising from trade within the Area. The development bank has not attracted a full membership, though it is too early to expect great activity. There have been reductions in customs charges to establish preferences within the Area, but non-tariff barriers in the form of licensing, exchange controls and bureaucratic administration remain. Enthusiasm for the scheme among the governments does not seem to be great, if that may be deduced from the small attendance of

Heads of State at 'summit' meetings. Only four attended the meeting in Lusaka at the end of 1985, and decisions on important matters had to be deferred. It is true, as was remarked earlier, that in contrast with SADCC, PTA can make progress through the actions of civil servants, without ministerial action, and may as a result be less disturbed by political problems. Nevertheless, a firm commitment to the implementation and extension of integration by governments is ultimately essential for success, and one may wonder if at present it exists among the members of PTA.

There is one issue – technical, but raising political and ideological issues – to which it is worth drawing particular attention. That is the rule of origin which products have to satisfy if they are to qualify for preferential treatment. A similar issue exists in ECOWAS. To obtain preferential treatment as local products, goods must be produced by firms that are managed and owned by nationals of the country in which they are located, a firm being counted as locally owned if not less than 51 per cent of its equity is in the hands of nationals. A great deal of manufacturing in PTA countries, in Zimbabwe for instance, is undertaken by TNCs, whose products do not satisfy this rule of origin. It has been agreed that Zimbabwe should have a two-year adjustment period to allow companies to become localised. The extent to which localisation will deter investment in industry and the growth in intra-African trade in manufactures, is a matter for consideration.

ECOWAS has established an institutional structure, agreed on various protocols and conducted studies. Uniform trade and customs documents have been devised. But there seems little sign of actual implementation. The tariff stand-still period began with a delay, and though formally the second intra-trade tariff reduction period has begun, nothing has been done. There needs to be a schedule for trade liberalisation, a compensation scheme for revenue losses resulting from trade liberalisation, and measures of fiscal harmonisation. The adoption of all these measures is made difficult or ineffective by the continued absence of a common structure for indirect taxes and common rules of origin, and the existence of quantitative controls and foreign exchange restrictions. Nor has any action been taken on industrial and fiscal harmonisation, the measures and policies for 'positive integration'. Given the absence of these, it is perhaps just as well that nothing has really happened in the way of 'passive' or 'negative' integration, the liberalisation of intra-ECOWAS trade.

CEAO treaty provided for the establishment of a common external tariff within 12 years, free trade in local unmanufactured products, and a preferential tariff for intra-group trade in manufactures, fixed product by product and enterprise by enterprise. Fiscal compensation is payable for loss of revenue (to the extent of two-thirds of the loss) from importing goods under the preference. There are clauses relating to a common industrial programme, fiscal incentives and policies towards TNCs etc.

Since the treaty, a common customs and statistical nomenclature has been adopted, together with a harmonised and simplified structure of customs duties, which is a necessary first step towards a common external tariff. Quantitative restrictions, however, have not been dealt with. Nor has there been any progress with positive integration measures, such as industrial planning on a regional basis to avoid uneconomic replication of industries, and even in the field of customs it is unlikely that the timetable for establishing a common external tariff will be met.

Progress has been made with the granting of preferential tariffs, and the pattern of preferential rates has been in favour of the less-developed members' products. The preferential rates, on average, range from 40 to 60 per cent of the external duty rates, but there are some much larger preferences, and some much smaller (where there is a competing industry in the importing country, for instance). The great majority of the enterprises affected, mostly foreign-owned, are located in Cote d'Ivoire and Senegal. They have favourable balances in intra-group trade in manufactures (the two together account for over 90 per cent of intra-group exports of manufactures) and the other countries have deficits. There is little specialisation between countries in manufacturing production, and little intra-industry trade between countries.

In the relationship between CEAO and ECOWAS we have the problem of Africa-wide integration in miniature. The two groupings have different tariff nomenclatures and their fiscal compensation arrangements are not immediately compatible. The Treaty of Lagos requires the extension of most favoured nation (MFN) treatment to member states, which would have the effect of breaking down the preferences that have been established within CEAO (and in the Mano River Union, for that matter), even though the members of CEAO might wish to maintain and intensify the closer cooperation they might achieve within their smaller grouping.

There are important differences between ECOWAS and CEAO rules of origin used to determine what counts as a domestic product for preferential tariff treatment. The conditions relating to the content of domestically-produced raw materials and local value added are not greatly different. The problem arises over the requirement for the provision of capital by citizens. ECOWAS requires a high and, over time, increasing proportion of the capital of the producing enterprise to be in the hands of citizens, if the product is to qualify as domestically-produced. Very little of the manufacturing capacity in Cote d'Ivoire and Senegal would qualify, whereas Nigerian enterprises would be able to take substantial advantage of preferential access. Furthermore, with a very limited supply of locally-generated investment funds, a strict citizenship provision (despite the desirability, in principle, of extending domestic ownership of the manufacturing economy) would undesirably restrict investment in and the growth of the manufacturing sector in most member countries.

Of course, if the rules of origin have obviously disequalising effects among ECOWAS members, it can be assumed that some members will implement the trade liberalisation provisions only reluctantly and slowly. The adverse consequences of liberalisation in advance of other measures will therefore not be experienced – but this provides comfort only in a topsy-turvy way, because it is a way of escaping the costs which also destroys the benefits. In this respect, it is much the same in CEAO. The preservation under CEAO rules of a member's right to protect itself from its partners simply means – until measures to equalise competitive strengths are effective – that losses are avoided by preventing anything much from happening.

It is not to be supposed that the elements of incompatibility between ECOWAS and those of its members which are associated in CEAO cannot be resolved. However, if such difficulties can exist in reconciling the arrangements and interests of a sub-group with those of a larger group to which all the members of the sub-group have committed themselves, what pitfalls might there not be in the way of an Africa-wide association? It is not an easy road that the countries of Africa have before them.

Corresponding issues of compatibility arise in connection with attempts to foster cooperation and integration on an even wider stage. An important element in the UN programme for Economic Cooperation among Developing Countries (ECDC) is the negotiation of the Global System of Trade Preferences (GSTP). The outcome of these negotiations is seen as a significant increase in the volume of South–South trade. But is GSTP compatible with existing arrangements which provide, or plan to provide, preferences between groups of countries which will participate in the GSTP negotiations? It is not politically possible, or at least not very easy, or not very comfortable, for international officials, to pursue a scheme which is incompatible, or which even weakens existing arrangements between groups of member states. However, it is not easy to see how preferences under GSTP can do anything but (in this respect) weaken the preferential arrangements of regional groupings. If country A gives a tariff concession to an outside country, B, it could reestablish its preference with country C, a member of its tariff group, by a further cut in its tariff against C. But its concession to B would then be fraudulent. Country B gave something in return to A on the assumption that A's tariff concession would give B access to A's market. But the cut that is then made in A's tariff against C will deny that access to B. This is the crux of the argument, and even this crudely expressed version shows the weakness of the view that GSTP and regional groupings are compatible. To say they are is like saying that it is possible to discriminate in favour of everyone. It is a contradiction in terms. Not everyone can be preferred – a preference to all is a preference to none.

The argument for compatibility is on stronger ground when it refers to the existence of non-tariff fields of cooperation in regional groupings, industrial coordination, etc. It is important that GSTP is supposed to deal with non-tariff barriers as well as with tariffs. However, the difficulty of dealing with the non-tariff barriers must be recognised. They are various and complex, and although it might be relatively easy to abolish them completely, a partial removal or reduction, corresponding to a tariff concession, would be extremely difficult because of the difficulty of measuring the effect so as to determine 'mutuality'.

Given the fact that GSTP negotiations may be expected to take a very long time indeed, it would appear that the countries of Africa, despite the difficulties, should rather look to the fostering of preferential trade between themselves, and to making their various schemes of integration and cooperation work.

NEED FOR A NEW APPROACH TO INTEGRATION IN AFRICA

During the last few years there has been a good deal of comment, stimulated doubtless by the continued belief in the virtues of integration. There was also some disappointment at its failures in practice, which calls for a new approach to integration.

Some observers of the experience of integration schemes in Africa have drawn the conclusion that the whole 'production approach' is inappropriate. This conclusion cannot be accepted. It would not be helpful to abandon the idea that development, and the contribution integration could make towards it, requires an increase in production (as well, doubtless, as changes in its distribution), though production, it must be remembered, is not only of goods, let alone only of manufactures.

In fact, the proposal to abandon a 'production approach' appears to move entirely in the wrong direction. If it needs to be put in such terms, it would be more valid to say that there should be a move *towards* a *production* approach, *away* from a purely *trade* approach. Integration theory was developed as an aspect of international trade theory. Production was of course an implicit component of the argument: trade theory demonstrated how the availability of trade as against self-sufficiency could result in a more productive allocation of resources, so that world production was increased and all trading partners could be better off. The theory also demonstrated how the situation would be worse if there were protection rather than free trade. Integration theory demonstrated the circumstances in which partial free trade – free trade between some trading partners with barriers maintained against the rest – brought an improvement over general protection, and the circumstances in which it did not. This was the purpose of the analysis of the 'trade creating' and 'trade diverting' effects of a customs union. So it cannot be said that production was ignored – the production effects were the basis of it all – but nevertheless, the focus was on trade and tariffs. The production effects were taken to be the consequence of the tariff changes, the response, not the driving force.

The dominant characteristic of the comprehensive integration schemes, as with most theorising about integration, has been their focus on trade between the members. And within that emphasis on trade, an emphasis on trade in manufactures. It is easy to see why schemes have these characteristics. Trade is, after all, the medium through which economic relationships are established with other states: those relationships are most obviously established, operated or expressed through trade. There may, of course, be a relationship of lending and borrowing, but that relationship is still, fundamentally, given effect by trade: the transfer of resources that the lending/borrowing relationship is designed to achieve must take place through trade.

The emphasis on trade also followed naturally from the predominance of external trade in the monetary economies of the countries of Africa, with such trade overwhelmingly in primary products on the export side and in manufactures on the import side. The need to break the mould of external trade, to escape from this colonial pattern of exports and imports, was seen as an essential ingredient of development. Intra-African trade was seen as one way to achieve this change. Such a view of the development process also explains why intra-African trade in manufactures has been, at least implicitly, so central a feature of what integration arrangements have been designed to achieve. The existing structure of production within each country of Africa provided primary products for export to the developed countries. The development of a new pattern of trade required the development of a new pattern of production. Intra-African trade could not be based on the existing structure of production – there was nothing to be gained from, and no scope for a switch of primary product exports from extra- to intra-African destinations. Intra-African trade has to be based on, and to provide the market for, new production – the production of manufactures. Changes in the structure of production and in the pattern of trade were inter-related and reinforcing features of economic development. Development required a change in the pattern of production, and a change in the pattern of external trade; intra-African trade would provide a market for the new industries, and the new industries would provide the products for intra-African trade. The establishment of customs unions and common markets among groups of African countries was seen as the mechanism to bring about this reorientation of trade and production.

It must not be thought, however, that, either in the analysis of the problem in academic writings or in the design of integration schemes, the establishment of tariff preferences for intra-African trade was taken to be enough. It would be quite wrong to think that only in recent comments, stimulated by the failures of experience, have the inadequacies of this approach to the design of integration schemes in Africa been noted. Far from it. Twenty years ago, for example, in a study of Integration and Disintegration in Africa, it was remarked that:

> ... integration is not simply a matter of lowering tariffs. The existence of tariffs is not the sole, or even the primary impediment to trade between the countries of Africa. The main reason for the low level of trade is to be found in the economic structure of the countries (and in) ... the fact that the 'infrastructure' for intra-African trade is generally lacking.

And that was by no means the first statement of such a proposition. There was plenty of emphasis on the need for the development of appropriate infrastructure to enable trade to be conducted. The inappropriateness of many transport facilities for intra-African trade, designed as they were for extra-African trade, was fully recognised. The need for the planning of industrial development within the integrated area to minimise the danger of an industrial structure in which

592

the same industry was established in several of the member states, each producing at an extremely sub-optimal scale, was also recognised. Joint industrial planning was one of the mechanisms suggested for dealing with what was seen as a major problem of integration schemes: the unequal distribution of the benefits and costs of the scheme among the members. Much thought and ingenuity were devoted to such issues. And, in the world of practice, the Treaty for EAC, to take a leading example, was concerned to support the trade regime not, indeed, with joint planning, but certainly with the coordination of national development plans and other measures.

It has been suggested that the importance of trade in an integration scheme would be diminished by investment in small-scale 'appropriate technology' and, further, that technical change may be in the direction of reducing the importance of economies of scale. It is true, of course, that the 'market size' argument for integration schemes in Africa would be diminished in importance by a pattern of development in which economies of scale were small. And the benefits of intra-African trade would be correspondingly diminished. Whatever the sphere of activity, the benefits of integration must derive either from specialisation or from economies of scale; efficient national self-sufficiency would render integration otiose. However, it is somewhat fanciful to suppose that in many manufacturing processes economies of scale are likely to become unimportant. The argument from market size will therefore remain an important basis for economic integration so far as the development of manufacturing industry is concerned. Nevertheless, it is salutary to be reminded that the development of manufacturing and trade in manufactures do not provide the only basis for economic integration.

In arguing for a shift of emphasis from trade to production it is essential that production is understood in a wide sense. It is not an emphasis on manufacturing production – or at any rate on manufacturing production alone – that is required. Of extreme – one is inclined to say of supreme – importance in the present situation is agricultural production, particularly of food. Then there is a whole range of services, of which transport is the most immediately and directly relevant to integration.

The integrated development of transport and communications is of enormous importance. It cannot be said that it has been neglected. ECA has been extremely active in devising plans for the development of transport with an intra-African focus. Transport and communications inevitably had an important role in EAC, because of the inheritance of joint rail, air, postal and telecommunications services.

Transport, as was stated above, is a major question for SADCC, and the greater part of the funds allocated within SADCC programmes is for transport. Nevertheless, it may be concluded from the condition of African transport systems, and particularly for intra-African routes, that far more needs to be done. The situation in southern Africa remains desperate, and African transport routes remain directed outside Africa.

Until transport is more fully developed and more effectively operated and maintained, it can reasonably be argued that customs controls and such like are much the less important barriers to economic integration. Of course, integration is a complex matter, all parts of which are closely interconnected. Just as the removal of tariffs will not amount to an effective move towards economic integration if there are insuperable transport barriers between the economies, so will the opening and improvement of transport between the countries be an ineffective move towards integration if there remain customs and other government-made barriers. In an ideal world a removal of the different barriers would go hand in hand. In practice, it seems likely that a shift of focus towards the improvement of transport and communications would result in greater progress than further emphasis on customs arrangements.

Let it not be supposed, however, that a proposal for an emphasis on transport is a proposal for an easy option. Far from it. Recent experience – failures in maintenance, lack of spares, discarded machinery, and so forth – suggests that transport improvement (whether with an international, national or intra-African focus) presents a challenge with which African governments are not yet adequately coping.

It should also not be supposed that to increase the relevance of transport routes for intra-African trade means simply to push ahead with grand designs for trans-African highways, and the like. Small-scale developments to reduce the isolation of rural communities and to ease the carriage of crops to markets also have a part to play in what should become a more prominent component of integration schemes: agriculture.

Trade in agricultural produce, and particularly in food-stuffs, may be expected to, and certainly should in the future, play a larger role in intra-African arrangements. Agriculture has been neglected in integration schemes for several reasons. The market for agricultural primary products was abroad, neither within the national economy nor in other countries of Africa. Most food was consumed by the producers, not marketed. In any case, the food that was marketed was not traded to a significant extent outside the national boundaries, and was therefore not relevant to regional arrangements. Food marketing within the national economy was subject to so many controls that the designers of integration schemes did not see their way open to bring such trade within their arrangements, even if they had thought it important to do so. In EAC, for example, agriculture was effectively excluded from the common market because of the incompatibility of free inter-state trade with the national marketing arrangements and control of internal trade for some products of major importance.

The food crises in Africa in recent years have increasingly revealed the inadequacy and inappropriateness of this view of African agriculture and in particular of the production and distribution of food. Recent experience has forced attention on the need to increase food production so as to achieve self-sufficiency on average over a number of seasons. For each country to aim to produce enough food for its own needs in every season would be neither attainable nor desirable. An important role in the maintenance of self-sufficiency must be played by storage of food between good and bad seasons, and within years, between months of plenty and months of dearth. The costs of self-sufficiency on average, through storage, could be much reduced if such a food security policy were based on cooperation between a number of countries rather than attempted by each country in isolation. Account could then be taken of different seasonal patterns in different countries and of a differing incidence of crop failure through drought or other causes. Cooperation and intra-African trade in foodstuffs could also provide the benefits of a degree of specialisation in different crops, countries being normally in surplus in some crops and in deficit in others. For these reasons, agriculture, and particularly the production, storage and distribution of foodstuffs for consumption within Africa, must play a much more important part in the design and operation of integration schemes than has been the case in the past. Another matter, less attended to than it should be, is 'technical assistance' between the cooperating countries. Technical assistance, or technical cooperation as it is now commonly called, is too often, even automatically, thought of as something received by the Third World from the 'developed' members of the world community. One would not wish to minimise the importance and value of technical cooperation or technical assistance of this kind, though there are many tales of inappropriate advice based on the circumstances of the developed country. The continuation and extension of technical cooperation with the developed countries is clearly of great importance, and it could be an important support for the integration schemes of the African countries if directed that way, and not solely to national objectives.

But technical assistance should be available not only from the developed countries. It could be provided between the countries of Africa, and between members of an integration scheme. It is, of course, easy to see the political difficulties if, within an integration scheme, a predominance of technical assistance personnel came from one or a few of the members. The fear of domination that might be engendered by such a situation – a fear which can be considered as part of the wider problem of the generation and magnification of inequalities among the partners – could make technical assistance from the developed countries preferred to that from partners in the integration scheme. It might be taken as a measure of the success and progress of integration that some countries were able to overcome such fears and the others to make it evident that there was no basis for them. In any case, there is another alternative to 'north–south' technical cooperation in the form of a more general 'south–south' flow of technical assistance. There is a successful example of such an arrangement in the Common-wealth Secretariat's Commonwealth Fund for Technical Cooperation (CFTC), which organises an intra-Commonwealth flow of technical assistance, much of it 'south–south'. It is a model that could be utilized more widely and in other contexts.

The 'handling' – if it may be put that way – of TNCs is a sphere of activity in which south–south technical assistance could be of particular value. In developing countries there is something of an inferiority complex with respect to TNCs. The almost ritual reference to TNCs in relation to almost any topic appears to indicate a belief that the countries of the south are bound to be dominated by them, unless they destroy them – by nationalisation. The impression given, in other words, is that it is believed, even if subconsciously, that the multi-nationals are all-powerful, and the countries of the South are inevitably weak. This attitude seriously underestimates the bargaining power of the host governments, especially if they act in concert. Multinationals must be expected to aim to get as much out of their activities as they can. It is up to the governments of the host countries to regulate and control them, to lay down the rules under which they may operate, so that the host countries benefit substantially from the companies' activities.

This is where south–south technical cooperation may come in. Smaller countries, in particular, cannot easily field the technical, legal and economic expertise which is essential if successful negotiations are to take place with a multinational over the conditions under which it may operate. But other countries of the South have such expertise, and it should be made available to the countries which need it.

Moves towards economic integration among African states could affect the operations of TNCs in different ways. On the one hand, the larger market that would be likely to be one outcome of integration would be more attractive for investment by transnationals than the more restricted markets of a number of small countries. The increased attractiveness of the larger market to TNCs, with an increase in the dangers associated with their predominance, could be used as an argument against market integration. Purely local, small-scale production would, it is true, be likely to suffer less from the competition of TNCs in small, purely local markets. But to argue the advantages of remaining small, inefficient and poor because of the dangers that might be associated with larger-scale, more efficient production, is to give way to that inferiority feeling to which reference was made above. It must be remembered that integration, as well as increasing the attractiveness of the integrating states to TNCs, also increases states' ability to deal with them. The increased bargaining and negotiating strength of a grouping of states would weaken the power of the TNCs and could achieve a significant shift in the distribution of the benefits of TNCs' activities between the companies and the host countries.

In the context of integration arrangements the benefits of the TNCs' operations could be considerable. Much trade in manufactures is in intermediate products, and is intra-industry trade. Trade between branches of TNCs could therefore be an important feature of intra-group trade in manufactures and in manufacturing production.

The larger market accessible to a producer within an integration grouping may be expected to make investment more attractive and production more successful. With all the 'infant industry'-type problems that manufacturing faces in African countries, it is important to reduce as far as possible the additional deterrent of a small market. Preferential access to the market of the whole area is one way towards this end. But price is not the only element in the non-competitiveness of local, African products. Demand for a product is also a function of its quality in a technical sense (does it do its job as well as, or break down sooner than, a corresponding product?), and what might be called consumer – or more broadly, buyer – attachment, i.e. 'tastes'. But 'tastes' are not given from outside the economic system, and are only partly a reflection of technical quality (that is certainly so for consumer demand, but also, even if to a lesser extent, for buyers of intermediate products and even capital goods). The substantial premium which Raleigh bicycles at one time commanded in West Africa was no doubt due in part to their technical superiority, but it has been said that an important element was the symbol of the rampant lion under which they were sold. The establishment of a brand name can have a powerful influence on demand.

The trouble is that at the moment, the foreigner 'has all the best tunes'. There is no reason why this situation cannot be changed. Africa must improve its own 'music'. It should become smart to buy local. Moves towards market integration should therefore be accompanied by powerful attempts to establish buyers' loyalty to African products. Perhaps discriminatory controls on advertising and other forms of sales promotion would be one way to help to establish demand for African products. In these days, when restrictions on trade are so widely deplored, can there be objection if imports fall because consumers prefer local goods? After all, the consumer is King. It would be essential that in developing such a demand, the various members of the integration area should cooperate and not compete.

Consideration of the demand for local products makes it necessary to revert to the position of the TNCs. What should be treated as an 'African product'? The rules of origin of ECOWAS would be likely to limit drastically the products of TNCs that would count as local. It may be wondered if that would be beneficial, given the possibility of improving the distribution of benefits between the companies and the host countries.

TOWARDS A NEW APPROACH OF ECONOMIC INTEGRATION

The role of the international community

Economic integration schemes in Africa have received much support from outside Africa. The UN system has played a major part in propagating the idea of integration. World Bank has provided finance for integration projects, such as the development of intra-African transport routes. Individual developed countries have provided technical assistance and finance for integration schemes. The pledges made under SADCC are examples. Yet the policies and activities of developed countries can work against the progress of integration.

Loans and grants made to individual countries within the context of their national plans could be for projects which are inconsistent with an integration scheme. There could, for instance, be a wasteful duplication of production facilities, with several members of a group of countries establishing a productive capacity sufficient to serve the whole group. Such duplicate productive capacity could, in fact, have been established with each country assuming that it would serve the whole group. Aid tied to the products of the donor would hinder the process of integration if the tying diverted demand to the donor from other countries in the group. Such a possibility is particularly strong with commodity aid and barter deals. Aid for transport improvements between the recipient country and the outside world, not matched by corresponding improvements in its links with its partners in an integration scheme, also works against the progress of integration.

Both donor country aid agencies and international institutions are better adapted to deal with individual countries than with groupings of countries. Aid is negotiated in terms of country programmes and provided on application from the government of a particular country. This arrangement does not make it easy to give the preferential treatment for regional projects that is necessary if integration is to be vigorously pursued, and if the support of aid donors is to be evident. To favour regional over national projects in their applications, recipient countries would need to be more strongly committed to integration than has generally been the case. And to deal with a group of countries would involve more complicated negotiations and require a reorganization of the approach and methods of donors and recipients alike.

The allocation of a larger proportion of aid through international and regional institutions would possibly be a way to give greater support to the integration process. But it would not automatically do what is needed. Changes in the way these institutions themselves work, so that they focus more directly on the integration process than they might otherwise do would be required. That such a change might be needed is suggested by the fact that the projects in which the East African Development Bank invested, at any rate during the life of EAC, did little towards the Bank's aim of making the economies of the partner states more complementary.

The work of World Bank, the major international investment institution, during the time of EAC, also indicates the scope for changes beneficial to the progress of integration. Although World Bank provided large funds for transport and communications, which were Community functions, the importance of supporting the economic integration of the partner states was not its main focus. This lack of focus on the integration process is suggested by the fact that Community Affairs were handled, as a kind of side attachment, by the staff concerned primarily with one of the member countries of the Community.

A different approach would have been required to make World

Bank a major support of the integration process. The Community would have had to have the place of a major country in the Bank's organisation, in fact it would have had to be treated as a kind of 'super-country', with which the Bank dealt not only with respect to projects for Community institutions like the railways, but also for projects in the individual partner states. The concern with these projects would have been necessary to assist in the establishment of a pattern of lending to the East African countries that would contribute to their integration and discourage competitiveness in activities where economies of scale are large. It may be remarked that the willingness of the East African countries to accept this kind of coordination of borrowing would have been an indication of their own commitment to the integration process.

For World Bank to have operated in this way, the Bank's staff would have had firmly to believe in the importance of regionalism and integration as means to development, and to have been committed to their success. Given such a commitment within World Bank, the Bank itself could have contributed to the establishment of a corresponding ethos within the member countries of the Community. Through its Economic Development Institute, and perhaps in other ways, World Bank could have fostered among politicians and civil servants an understanding of how their countries could benefit from a properly operating Community. Strong public support for integration, which was by no means widespread in East Africa at the time, could be a potent factor in its success, and World Bank could have helped to form it.

These opportunities for a major role for World Bank in the promotion of integration, though no longer of relevance to EAC, suggest what could be done to promote the success of the various groupings that now exist.

If countries and institutions outside Africa are to play their part in support of integration in Africa, they must be convinced of the virtues of integration. Its failures cannot but shake their conviction. It must be sustained by continued presentations of the case for integration and by the example of the countries of Africa in their determination to push ahead.

The paramount role of African countries

Whether or not integration succeeds will be decided by the countries of Africa themselves. Outsiders can do no more than to assist, to provide some lubricant for the mechanism of integration; the motive force must come from within Africa. That motive force will be lacking however unless there is a widespread conviction among the peoples of Africa – it is not enough for a few politicians and senior civil servants to be convinced – that cooperation among the countries of Africa is an important component in the drive to a better future.

It must be emphasized that the case for integration, for a particular country participating in an integration scheme, rests on the benefits that country itself will obtain from integration. The case for integration is not a case for helping others; it is a case for helping oneself. However, it must be appreciated that integration will not benefit one country, or at any rate not for long, unless it also benefits the others: the case for integration arises from self-interest, but the pursuit of self-interest requires the interest of others to be simultaneously served. Integration will not succeed unless every partner benefits, because any one who thinks he will not benefit will not participate, and there will then be no integration. The benefit is for everyone or no-one.

Because no-one will benefit unless all benefit from integration, arrangements to ensure an acceptable distribution of the benefits are of fundamental importance. It must be admitted, however, that no schemes exist, ready made, that guarantee such an outcome. All kinds of devices have been tried to favour the weaker partners and to redistribute the gains so that all perceive that they gain: fiscal compensation, partial protection, preferential allocation of public investments, and so on, but without conspicuous success. It seems unlikely that there is any package that can be put together in advance to ensure that all partners remain satisfied. There will need to be frequent renegotiation of the terms of a partnership. The statesmanship of the cooperating states will be revealed by their flexibility and tolerance in such negotiations. It is to be expected, and certainly to be hoped, that their willingness to compromise will be stimulated by their knowledge that they are faced with the choice of surrendering some of their potential gains from integration – or all of them.

The acceptable distribution of the benefits is the grand issue of integration schemes. There are many other issues, which often themselves bear on that grand issue, decisions which may determine the success of a scheme. This Chapter can deal with only one or two. For example, the nations of Africa will have to decide whether the way to progress lies through 'community'-type institutions, covering a great range of functions, or in more narrowly-focused organisations. The scope of a community-type integration scheme need not, of course, include all activities that might be relevant. The members could, for instance, agree to exclude some that would be likely to prove particularly contentious in operation. But even such a restricted community is identifiably different from an institution at the other

601

extreme, restricted to a single sphere of activity. There is no doubt that the more comprehensive schemes have the potential of yielding the greater benefit. There is equally no doubt that they are the more difficult to operate, and require the greater commitment of the members. To put it in specific terms, a scheme like SADCC may survive and succeed simply because it aims to do less. The countries of Africa must decide the strength of their commitment to integration.

To emphasise the potential advantages of comprehensive schemes – if they work – is not to argue against more limited arrangements. The establishment of a number of limited schemes, each concerned with its own particular function or functions, could deal not only with the issue of which functions should be integrated, but also with that of the number of countries which should participate. Such groupings could be of variable size according to their purpose, and thus deal with the issue of whether an integration group would be best with many members or with few.

In the design of schemes concerned with different, and possibly overlapping, aspects of integration there is the danger of establishing incompatibilities, a danger which increases with an increase in the number and variety of organizations. The number of intergovernmental organizations is very large – in West Africa, alone, there are more than thirty – and the number could probably with advantage be reduced. But a decision on that would need detailed investigation, and no proposals can be offered here. What can be said, however, and must be said forcefully, is that the organizations must not be allowed to operate so as to frustrate the operations of others. Where there are substantial overlaps in the areas of interest and responsibility of different organizations, effective operation demands that each knows what the other is doing, and what it plans to do. In other words, there must be cooperation among the cooperators.

Probably the most important requirement for progress in economic integration in Africa is the political will to make it succeed. Past inadequacies and failures can be attributed to a great extent to the absence of such a will. This view of the matter has been attacked as attributing an unwillingness to pursue integration plans to irrationality when, given the failures of the past, such behaviour is entirely rational. One can see the point. Nevertheless, political will is a useful expression which emphasizes the need for a vigorous, long-term commitment to integration, if its benefits are to be achieved. Of course, political will is a shorthand expression requiring definition and elaboration in each particular circumstance. In general, it may be taken to refer to a firm belief that integration is in the *national* interest, particularly in the longer term, and a determination or willingness to bear the short-term costs so as to obtain the benefits. Governments will be unwilling to accept the costs of integration if the scheme is likely to break up before its longer-term benefits can be realised. An evident determination of the partners in the enterprise to pursue the integration process and to make it succeed is the most certain way to ensure that it does succeed.

A political will to succeed, a determination on the part of governments, is not enough. Indeed, a degree of insulation of the process of integration from politics could be advantageous. It would be better if every move in the game were not liable to become a political issue between the partner-countries. There is an important role, therefore, for non-governmental institutions, and for the 'private sector'. After all, in countries where production is not predominantly in the hands of government, it is the private sector that must respond to the integration process and implement the changes in production that are the aim. Non-governmental institutions should be recruited to play a part in developing support for integration. The formation of a federation of Chambers of Commerce in PTA countries is a small move in the right direction. The need to develop a consumer preference for 'local' brands, that is, products of the cooperating countries, to which reference was made earlier, provides an obvious role for the private sector.

But, however important the role of the private sector, the process of integration must begin with and be sustained by governments and politicians. Regional economic relations must be given a central role in the activities of governments, which must adopt an administrative structure that gives to those responsible for pursuing integration the weight and power they must have if they are to succeed. And they, once given that power, must ensure that decisions are carried out – which is far from the case today – and that inefficient administration in the relevant spheres – in customs and related transactions, for instance – does not constrain the effectiveness of integration measures. Ministries of regional or intra-African affairs must be the responsibility of senior ministers, and must be a major part of their work. Regionalism, integration and cooperation, whatever it is called, will not succeed if it is seen as a matter of secondary importance; secondary, say, to the important concerns of relationships with the US, with Britain, with France, with the EEC. In short, there must be more power to the integrators.

This Chapter has taken the view that there are rewards to be won from economic integration, and that it would be unacceptable defeatism to conclude from the failures of the past that the problems cannot be overcome. It is this potential for the integrating nations as a whole and individually to benefit that leads to the conclusion that integration has a part to play in meeting 'the challenge of economic recovery and accelerated development' in Africa.

It would, however, be unfortunate if it came to be thought that integration had a major part in the short term to contribute to economic recovery and development. That is not the case. Integration cannot provide 'a quick fix'.

Some measures or forms of integration will, it may be accepted, yield beneficial results more speedily than others. Some forms of cooperation in the distribution of food, for example, are not only of great urgency, but could bring early results. Other forms of integration, particularly the establishment of economic communities, however great the potential benefits in the longer term, cannot be expected to make much of a contribution to African recovery in the short term. Their role will be to remove constraints on the future development of the cooperating states. Other policies must put Africa on the road to recovery; integration can then become a major force driving her along the road of development. The fact that the major gains are expected only in the longer term is no argument against the urgency of action now. Unless progress is made with integration in the short term, the long term will never come.

CHAPTER TWENTY-EIGHT

The Dilemma of Increased Economic Co-operation Among African Countries

WALTER J. KAMBA

STRUCTURAL WEAKNESS OF AFRICAN ECONOMIES

At the beginning of African independence in the 1960s it was correct to ascribe all the ills of the continent to the plunder of the colonial system. This is still true and vivid for those African states that only became independent a decade and half ago, and resoundingly true for South Africa and Namibia still struggling under settler colonialism. However, for Africa, a fundamental and apparently lasting phenomenon of these ills was already encapsulated in the colonial system's development of the colonies primarily as part of the economic reproduction process of the 'mother countries', i.e., the metropolitan economy. The flow of commodities and services was directed to the then 'mother countries'. Both the character and structure of this flow, the nature of the reproduction process, have not been changed. As Africa has remained a source of raw materials and market for a limited range of consumer products, interlinkages among the African countries have remained small. Through the transport system, imposition of huge taxes and custom duties on goods imported from Africa and re-exported, the African region, like other developing regions of the world, has developed a vertical division of labour with the countries of the North to which it has been bound for a long period.

In the wake of the dramatic impact of the 1983/1984 drought and the subsequent international-induced crisis, Africa has recognized that these crises are a manifestation of the fragile nature of its socio-economic structure. It is also recognized that, unless the fundamental factors underlying Africa's economic and social crisis are attacked at the root through durable and long-term structural transformation, Africa will remain the sick child of the international community. This means that Africa must look inward to mobilizing its own human, physical and financial resources. In reality, how does the international community come to the rescue or assistance of African governments in undertaking its long-term structural transformation? It is quite true that African countries cannot accomplish this complex task without the active support of the international community, but by far the larger balance of the task of transformation is in Africa's court.

The basic economic structures of African countries inherited after independence have not fundamentally changed. Most of the continent is still heavily dependent on the export of a narrow range of primary commodities. At the heart of the dilemma of Africa is the low productivity of the African economy, heavy dependence of domestic production on imports, failure to diversify into new exports, the absence of domestic linkages and, above all, a de-industrializing procurement policy by Africa's public sector, including its armed forces. Within the national framework of most African domestic markets, it is impossible to set up an economic-size enterprise in basic industries: iron and steel, cement, paper, agricultural machinery and implements, varieties of chemical industries, intermediate and capital goods. Because of this constraint of economies of scale which is initially felt in satisfying the market at the national level, there is subsequently the low level of exchange of goods and services among the African countries. What then remains is the minimal horizontal production structure in a limited range of consumer goods and non-existence of vertical integration in basic industries, intermediate and capital goods within the African region.

AFRICA'S EXPERIENCE IN REGIONAL COOPERATION

In the 1979 fifth session of the Manila conference the Secretary-General of UNCTAD underlined:

> There are two dimensions to the concept of economic cooperation amongst developing countries. The first relates to the need for extending and expanding trade and other linkages amongst these countries; the second to the need for them to cooperate with one another in bringing about changes and improvements in their relationships with the rest of the world. Each of these aspects is gaining in importance against the backdrop of the evolving international economic situation.

From the documents of the UNCTAD General Conferences in Nairobi (1976) and Manila (1979), the focus of UNCTAD had been on:

(a) measures to establish a global system of trade preferences among developing countries; (b) cooperation among state trading companies; and, (c) creating multinational marketing enterprises for developing countries. Africa has played a key role in these positions of cooperation by the developing world. By itself, Africa has taken the stage even further by defining her strategic tasks, tactical approaches and technical guidelines for cooperation.

A number of factors, notably, historical ties, flows of market information, transport links and the role of TNCs in international trade, have tended to favour the vertical trade links between Africa and the developed countries and thus act as barriers to the growth of trade among the African countries. How is it that over the last two decades expanded linkages among African countries have not overcome the vertical integration intermediated by the TNCs? Why is it that as the efficiency of commodity and capital relationships and communications improve amongst our countries, this significantly improves the conditions for the transnational activities? Africa's regional cooperation experience seems to point to the direction of strengthening horizontal extensions of the existing vertical linkages spearheaded by TNCs. The concept of 'collective self-reliance' was and is basically contradictory. Transnationals, settled in our member states, may enhance their influence of events through regional integration, especially the common market and monetary zones, etc.

Africa cannot employ a laissez faire attitude in its approach to regional cooperation. Besides, if Africa decides to choose from existing models of regional integration that have appeared in the literature and/or those that have been practised elsewhere, these models will not succeed in Africa. Such an attitude implies that the principal problem facing our continent is the economic problem. This approach subordinates political and social problems to economic questions. Hence, regional cooperation strategies seem to conveniently by-pass the existing problem of lack of complementarity between our individual economies and the lack of building measures on decisive, progressive socio-economic changes in the political and economic programmes. The success of any NIEO and regional economic cooperation programmes will depend on the existence of dynamic national new orders.

How seriously do our multi-sectoral regional programmes take into account, as their first step, the implementation and monitoring of the national plans' fulfilment of their regional targets? The unemployed and hungry people in our countries cannot be left out of our cooperation programmes. What is still lacking is the inward-looking posture by our individual countries for those mechanisms inherent in our economic relations that could become essential motive forces for the transformation of the African economy. In the end, Africa cannot continue postponing vertically integrated production programmes which will be responsible for changes in trade and exchanges in the next decade except at its peril.

Africa has since the 1960s stressed the importance of relations within the framework of regional or subregional economic cooperation. The nature and structure of established forms of cooperation are mostly in the spheres of trade and infrastructure. Closer mutual economic ties in the sphere of production itself are still occupying a subordinate position. It is obvious that continued neglect of the latter leads to retention of the *status quo*. At present, only about 5 per cent of the foreign merchandise trade of the African countries is intra-African.

PREREQUISITES FOR ACCELERATING ECONOMIC INTEGRATION

The concept of economic development based on 'collective self-reliance' is now well articulated in African documents and needs no further elaboration. However, bonds of inherited international division of labour still persist in Africa's real economic and social programmes. More often than not, dependence on the capitalist world economy continues to play an important role in the functioning of the national economy. For example, the goods produced for the market in many of our countries are nowhere near the form and volumes required to satisfy the market. The subsistence economy still satisfies a considerable part of the total consumption of the population. National economic and social development requires the acquisition of goods from external markets. This applies to almost all capital goods, intermediate goods, transport, machinery and equipment, electrical goods, spare parts and an increasing amount of consumer goods, including foodstuffs. The items required by the construction sector, for the expansion of social services and cultural establishments, as well as the hardware needed by the armed forces are imported.

Underdevelopment in our economies is still largely explained by the wide divergence between resource-use in the economic sectors, and satisfaction of domestic market demand and needs. Indeed, this divergence in resource-use has already spelt untold disaster in Africa's ability to produce food. Africa has in the past put practically all her agricultural research and extension funds and efforts on trying to raise productivity of export crops and less effort into food production. The correction of this misallocation of resources must not miss the point of the balanced allocation of resources across all the economic sectors that will make Africa technologically independent and able to sustain the reproduction of her material, human and cultural resources.

The inherited mono-production still dominates, without becoming part of the internal reproduction process. Most often, over 90 per cent of African ores and industrial raw materials from agriculture are exported. It would also seem that whilst the economic bonds binding Africa to the international economy have negative effects, Africa is caught in the mechanisms of the international economic system, and the overall result is essentially to hinder its efforts to overcome under-development and bring about greater economic independence. Collectively and at individual levels, African states are aiming at economic cooperation in order to reduce their unilateral foreign-trade dependence on the industrialized countries.

CHAPTER TWENTY-NINE

Economic Co-operation in Africa: Role and Relevance of Regional and Subregional Institutions

J.M. MWANZA

INTRODUCTION

The seventeenth century metaphysical poet John Donne said: 'No man is an Island, entire of itself'. This is indeed true for developing countries, particularly those of Africa which is the most balkanized continent, in the sense that the achievement of rapid development is virtually impossible through any strategy characterized predominantly by autarchism. Most African countries are small in terms of population or geographical size, or both. As such, although the attainment of self-reliance has been a major goal of development in practically all these countries, the countries do not have adequately developed physical and human resources to achieve self-reliance on a national basis. They have, therefore, little choice but to become open and outward-looking in their quest for resources for national development. The promotion of exports and inflows of foreign aid and investment are two of the essential constituents of such efforts.

However, over two decades of experience have revealed that this type of openness, resulting in incomplete integration into the world economy, has not brought the expected benefits to African economies and has often served to aggravate the problems facing them. Indeed, it has been suggested that the prevailing International Economic Order and the Global Recession have negatively affected the performance of African economies especially since 1978. It is also believed that the prospects for primary produce and simple manufactured exports, and for aid and external borrowing are worse in the 1980s than in the 1970s.

Given the rather limited prospects, significant development through a purely inward-looking national approach, on the one hand, and an increasingly gloomy environment for aid and trade, on the other, the greatest promise of development for African countries seems to lie in mutual co-operation among themselves, beginning at subregional and regional levels and extending to the continental level as envisaged in the LPA. Regional co-operation has the merit of being at once outward-looking and inward-looking; outward-looking from a national point of view and inward-looking from a collective point of view. As such, it affords wider access to resources for individual countries that can consequently become self-reliant on a collective basis.

It has often been said that one of the main reasons why 30 years of aspirations of economic co-operation in Africa have achieved so little in practice is the fear on the part of many African states of losing their national sovereignty and control over their internal economies. Ironically, it is the failure to adequately foster regional co-operation that has led to several African countries today losing control over their own economic affairs which are being increasingly dominated by international economic institutions.

This Chapter first outlines briefly the nature of the present international environment and its impact on the economies of African countries. It then provides an assessment of the potential for regional co-operation in the context of two regional institutions in the Eastern and Southern African region, namely, the SADCC and PTA, and identifies measures required to ensure the viability of these institutions.

EXTERNAL ECONOMIC ENVIRONMENT

Africa has undoubtedly been suffering due to a number of adverse external factors over which she has virtually no control. The global recession that began in the late 1970s and spilled over into the 1980s produced a number of repercussions whose collective and cumulative impact in Africa was on the terms of trade, the current account position (see Table 29.1) and the external debt.

International prices for most exports from Africa have shown a declining trend (see Table 29.2). The only exception is oil whose price rose sharply in 1973 and again in 1979–1980. And since most African countries are oil importers, this contributed significantly to their current account deficits. An increase in their oil import bill from $US1.4 billion in 1978 to $US3.1 billion in 1980 led to a rise in their current account deficits from $US4.7 billion in 1978 to $US6.5 billion in 1980.

In the *African Submission*, OAU and ECA have estimated that, in real terms, commodity prices in 1982 were at their lowest level since

TABLE 29.1

PER CAPITA GNP GROWTH RATES, CHANGES IN TERMS OF TRADE AND
CURRENT ACCOUNT BALANCE FOR AFRICA, 1981–1985

	1981	1982	1983	1984	1985
Per capita GNP growth rate	−1.3	−2.4	−2.7	−2.8	−0.4
Annual percentage change in terms of trade	−11.8	−0.9	4.8	5.0	−5.6
Current account balance (in billions of dollars)	−6.3	−5.5	−4.4	−4.6	−5.1

Source: World Bank: *'Towards sustained development in sub-Saharan Africa: A Joint Programme of Action'*, 1984, Washington, D.C.

TABLE 29.2

ANNUAL AVERAGE PERCENTAGE GROWTH RATE IN PRICES FOR SELECTED
COMMODITIES, 1970–1982

Commodity	Price change
Petroleum	20.1
Copper	−7.2
Iron ore	−4.6
Coffee	1.8
Cocoa	3.0
Sugar	−2.7
Tea	−2.8
Groundnuts (meal)	−4.1
Groundnut oil	−4.0
Beef	−4.1
Maize	−4.2
Cotton	−1.9
Tobacco	−1.2

Source: World Bank: *'Towards sustained development in sub-Saharan Africa: A Joint Programme of Action'*, 1984, Washington, D.C.

1940, and that, between 1980 and 1983, the cumulative foreign exchange losses from the sharp fall in commodity prices reached some $US13.5 billion, equal to about 2 per cent of total output in this period. Further, in 1985, Africa's foreign exchange earnings fell despite a 2 per cent increase in the volume of her exports. This was due to an 11 per cent fall in the price of non-oil primary commodities.

Industrialized countries have been subjecting exports from developing countries to higher degrees of protectionism. No doubt, after the Tokyo Round of GATT in 1978, the average tariff level of industrial countries has been reduced to between 4 and 8 per cent. But this reduction in tariffs has been more than offset by the growth of non-tariff barriers (NTBs).

It is pertinent to point out here the asymmetry between the policies prescribed for African countries by international financial and development institutions, which are *de facto* institutions of the Western countries, and the policies pursued by the latter countries themselves. While most African countries have been urged to pursue export-oriented policies, the protectionist policies of the Western countries themselves thwart Africa's efforts to make her exports penetrate the latter's markets. For example in Zambia, not only is copper price today the lowest in decades but, more significantly, in April 1986, Zambia became one of the copper suppliers removed from the Generalized System of Preferences (GSP) which waives tariffs on the import of listed goods into the US. This was because of an increase in Zambian copper sales to the US to $US87.9 million, well above the $US68.00 million ceiling at which the GSP status is automatically suspended. Actually, because of the pressure from the US copper industry, protectionist measures are taken against Third World producers.

The same situation prevails with respect to exchange rates. African countries are advised to effect massive depreciations of their currencies to make their exports attractive. But the depreciation in several cases may have to be carried to almost meaningless levels in order to make the export products competitive in the industrialized countries' markets owing to the latter's protectionist policies. And such depreciations, while facilitating exports, are bound to have severe consequences in terms of domestic inflation and debt burdens. For example, it has been estimated that the threshold rate at which Zambia's garment exports would become competitive in European markets is ZK16 to a US dollar, but the same exports become competitive in countries within the region at around ZK8 to a US dollar. Apart from protectionism, cost differences in terms of international and internal transport, storage and retailing also account for such a situation. It is likely that a similar situation prevails in respect of exports of other African countries. This, in itself, presents a case for developing regional trade instead of placing too much optimism on extra-regional and extra-continental markets.

The increase in international interest rates has served to worsen the debt position of several African countries. In this regard, it is estimated that during 1979–1983, without the additional interest payments, public debt outstanding would have been lower by 16 per cent for Cote d'Ivoire, by 11 per cent for Zambia and by 11 per cent for Malawi. There has also been a drastic reduction of financial flows to Africa during the 1980s. The net transfer of funds to Africa which was $US8.6 billion a year during 1977–1978 became negative during 1984–1985 ($US–5.4 billion per annum on the average).

In addition to the above-mentioned macro-economic factors, the import of technology and technical know-how from the West and the concomitant import of inputs and equipment whose prices have been rising (vis-a-vis falling prices of Africa's exports) have also engendered problems of foreign exchange scarcity, distorted domestic patterns of production with minimal internal linkages, and persistently enhanced external dependency. For Africa to break through this dependency syndrome, there is need to take full advantage of existing opportunities within subregions and the region as a whole.

SADCC AND PTA

In 1980, SADCC was established, and among the main aims are the creation of genuine regional integration and the reduction of economic dependence especially on the Republic of South Africa.

The PTA came into being as a result of a Treaty signed in Lusaka in December 1981 and comprises 20 potential member states of which 15 are actual members at present. Although the main objective of PTA is to promote regional trade and create a regional common market, it also provides for inter-state co-operation and specialization of basic and strategic industries, production of food crops and livestock, science and technology, human resources and the creation of inter-country transport and communication networks.

So far, most African countries have traded little with each other. For most SADCC and PTA countries the major trade has been with countries of which they were erstwhile colonies, and for the Southern African states in particular, South Africa has also been a major trading partner. Within SADCC region, the United Republic of Tanzania is the only country that has not had any trade links with South Africa. Even after the formation of PTA, trade within PTA region is estimated not to have exceeded $US1.00 billion in 1986 – a rather insignificant figure for trade among 15 countries.

Limitations of institutional, management and technological capacities of individual countries have inhibited adequate realization of the region's productive capacity. For instance, SADCC region has hydro-power potential of about seven times of what is developed today and 15 times the current production. Through co-operation and concerted action, the region may be in a better position to rehabilitate and expand its productive capacity.

In its 1986 report on mining facilities, the Commonwealth Secretariat highlights a number of potential areas of cooperation in SADCC region including: (a) expanding production capacities on items already produced by the region so that new technologies are generally not required, and imports of equipment are reduced; (b) manufacturing within the region of items that have high volume import-substitution potential and would, in general, require the acquisition of no new technology; (c) taking full advantage of the adequate raw materials of the region for the expansion plans envisaged; (d) devising significant programmes for expansion of the manufacturing, reconditioning and repairing of mining machinery within the region; and, (e) taking advantage of the existing opportunities within the region for the rationalization of existing facilities to the mutual benefit of member countries.

Economic co-operation along the above lines should be particularly useful in reducing technological dependence and the saving of precious foreign exchange that is today being spent on importing equipment from the traditional foreign sources.

Inter-country specialization in the production of intermediate goods can also serve to ensure a wide market for each country's goods. PTA has initiated inter-country specialization in the production of iron and steel products so that each national plant can virtually count on the entire PTA market. Also, since PTA region is well-endowed with raw materials, such as phosphates for the manufacture of fertilizers, plans are under way for inter-country specialization in fertilizer production.

Food security is another area where regional co-operation can prove beneficial. For instance, due to military aggression by South Africa leading to disruption of agricultural production, Angola and Mozambique have been facing serious food shortages. Lesotho and Zambia have also been facing food shortfalls. In contrast, Malawi and Zimbabwe have large maize surpluses. These surpluses could possibly be traded with the food-deficit countries in return for oil or other agricultural products.

WHAT NEEDS TO BE DONE TO MAKE REGIONAL INSTITUTIONS MORE EFFECTIVE

In the first place, even the existence of two institutions like SADCC and PTA with many members in common and with overlapping objectives and functions can make room for conflict and duplication of efforts. As we have seen, PTA goes beyond being merely a preferential trade arrangement and aims at developing production, technology, transport and communications. Likewise, recent thinking within SADCC is that it is necessary to focus not only on production but also on trade.

It is, therefore, essential that overlapping of functions between SADCC and PTA be kept to a minimum. To some extent, this is at present taken care of by differences in approaches between the two institutions in the area of trade. While PTA aims to promote trade through a blanket reduction or removal of tariffs, SADCC advocates bilateral trade in terms of specific products, e.g. Angola's oil and the United Republic of Tanzania's coffee or Zimbabwe's steel and Malawi's tea.

All the same, countries which are members of both SADCC and PTA can face embarrassing situations. For example, the clause relating to 'rules of origin' in the PTA treaty requires discrimination against goods manufactured substantially outside PTA region. How would a country which is a member of both PTA and SADCC deal with the products from a SADCC member who is not a member of PTA?

It is also essential to ensure that economic benefits of integration are equitably shared among countries. Within SADCC this objective has been pursued by the administrative arrangement of dividing the SADCC programme of action into 12 sectors with each sector being co-ordinated by a member state. Thus, industry is co-ordinated by the United Republic of Tanzania, mining by Zambia, transport by Mozambique, etc.

But this sectoral distribution of functions among member states at present seems to be suffering from lack of effective co-ordination due to financial and manpower constraints in the individual countries. It is the responsibility of the particular country entrusted with the task of co-ordinating a given sector to maintain the sector's secretariat in terms of salaries and facilities. Since most of the countries are undergoing a general economic crisis, their financial allocations towards the upkeep of an efficient secretariat may not always be adequate.

If SADCC's programmes are to be conducted efficiently, the sector co-ordinating units will have to be strengthened so that they could respond to the 'push' received from member states while, at the same time, they give the necessary 'pull'. There is therefore need for strengthening manpower planning in the region. Presently, most of the original SADCC sectoral discussion papers are written by paid expatriate consultants and not by the secretariat.

As mentioned earlier, trade in PTA region has not significantly increased. Part of the reason for this is the same as why African countries are unable to promote their exports in the developed countries, namely, non-tariff barriers. But while the non-tariff barriers in the developed countries assume the form of explicit quantitative import restrictions, 'voluntary' export restraints, and so on, they exist in African countries by way of deliberately protracted and bureaucratic controls. For instance, businessmen in country X may wish to import from country Y. But the government in country X may considerably retard this process by delays in the issue of the necessary import licences. Such barriers need to be removed.

Regional organizations, at least during the initial phase, would not have enough funds to finance all their projects and would, therefore, need additional resources from external sources. However, bilateral and multilateral donors may influence both the scope and the location of a given project, on the basis of the feasibility study they often request before agreeing to fund such a project. This, in turn, can provide an opportunity to the donor agencies to thwart the very objectives of regional integration and co-operation. For example, donors may try to fund projects only in those countries which are in line with their own political ideology, and, by corollary, avoid funding projected in countries where they do not want to assist. This can be achieved in subtle ways. As illustrated by Mupawaenda (1985), 'one envisages a situation where a donor pushes for a feasibility study before agreeing to fund a project in a particular country. The resultant research report may be presented in a way which justifies a preconceived idea that the proposed projects should not be located in that country where there is a base of some kind.'

African countries need therefore to guard against such policies of 'divide and rule'. Considerable political will would be required for an individual country to refuse funds from a donor country or organization when the latter's motives are not in line with its own objectives. This is not to imply that all extra-regional donor agencies and countries are not above board in their intentions. Indeed, the success of regional co-operation in Africa requires financial and political support from the international community.

INTERNATIONAL SUPPORT FOR REGIONAL CO-OPERATION

There is need to develop a better international environment by providing better prices for Africa's exports and removing non-tariff protectionist barriers. Africa also requires a substantial alleviation of its debt burdens. Current SADCC regional debt is estimated to be about $US16.5 billion, constituting over 60 per cent of GDP and 250 per cent of exports. Hence, one way in which international agencies can provide financial assistance is through a more sympathetic consideration of requests by African states for debt rescheduling or even cancellation.

The most significant political-cum-economic factor operating in the Eastern and Southern African region is the presence of *apartheid* South Africa. Due to South Africa's support for armed rebel groups in Angola and Mozambique, and intermittent military incursions into the frontline states, the region has been considered as unstable by foreign investors and the credibility of regional projects is also undermined.

It is true that most of the countries in the southern African region are highly dependent on the Republic of South Africa and, in turn, South Africa has been using this factor as a pressurizing instrument. South Africa has recently announced a commercial boycott of Zambia and Zimbabwe and the threat of deportation hangs over the thousands of SADCC nationals currently working in the Republic of South Africa. But it must also be recognized that if economic sanctions are applied by SADCC states on the Republic of South Africa, the latter will also not be insignificantly affected. Even though the African market accounts for only a small percentage of South Africa's total export market, several South African sectors would definitely suffer if this market suddenly disappeared. The ideal situation would be the imposition of mandatory sanctions by the Western countries on South Africa, with concomitant financial support especially to the vulnerable economies in the region.

REFERENCES

Commonwealth Secretariat (1986): *Mining equipment manufacturing, repairing and reconditioning facilities in SADCC region: Preliminary study*, Matthew Hall, Ortech Ltd.

Economic Intelligence Unit (1986): *Country Report*: Zambia, No.3.

Roster, U. (1986): *Regional co-operation to improve food security in Southern and Eastern African countries*, research report number 53, International Food Policy Research Institute.

Krumm, K.I. (1983): 'The external debt of sub-Saharan Africa: Origins, magnitudes and implications for action', *World Bank Staff Working Papers*, No.741.

Mupewaenda, A.C. (1985): 'Some consideration of regional co-operation with reference to SADCC', paper presented to SADRA II workshop, Lusaka.

Mwase, N. (1985): 'The Eastern and Southern African Preferential Trade Area (PTA): Towards a subregional economic union', paper presented at SADRA II workshop, Lusaka.

Ndegwa, P., Mureithi, L.P. and Green, R.H. (1983): *Report of Symposium on Development Options for Africa in the 1980s and beyond*, SID, Nairobi.

Nogues, J., Olechowski, A. and Winters, L.A. (1986): 'The extent of non-tariff barriers to industrial countries' imports', The World Bank Economic Review, vol.1, pp.181–199.

Saasa, O. (1985): 'Southern Africa Development Co-ordination Conference: A Critical Analysis of Problems and Prospects', paper presented at SADRA II workshop, Lusaka.

SADCC Energy Quarterly (1987): Vol.5, No.13.

UNICEF (1987): The State of the World's Children, 1987, Oxford University Press, U.K.

CHAPTER THIRTY

Variable Geometry or Comprehensive Automaticity? Strategies and Experience of Regional Co-operation in Sub-Saharan Africa

PETER ROBSON

INTRODUCTION

Virtually without exception, all recent internal or external action programmes or guidelines for sub-Saharan Africa assign a major development role to economic integration and regional co-operation. The case for such economic co-operation is compelling and it can surely only be reinforced by recent definitions of priorities. In isolation, most small poor sub-Saharan states have extremely constrained development options. Their balanced development – and certainly any strategy that assigns any significant role to import-substitution – demands larger markets. For most countries, this points to some form of regional co-operation. This has long been recognized, and regional economic integration and co-operation have constituted an element of sub-Saharan African development strategies for more than two decades. Yet, the contribution of integration to development has not so far been great, and in some cases may even have been negative.

This brief contribution has three parts: (i) an outline of salient aspects of recent experience with regional co-operation in sub-Saharan Africa; (ii) a consideration of what that experience realistically suggests – assuming that present approaches and structures are maintained – with respect to the potential contribution of regional co-operation to overcoming the present crisis in much of sub-Saharan Africa, and in particular, to attaining the industrial policy objectives set out in recent action programmes for accelerated development; and,

(iii) a discussion of some indicated priorities for the improvement of performance.

STRUCTURES OF ECONOMIC INTEGRATION AND CO-OPERATION IN AFRICA

The following focuses on West, Central and Equatorial Africa, where a sufficient range of experience exists to bring out most of the salient issues. SADCC does, however, represent a different and potentially fruitful approach which should not be ignored.

Organizations for economic co-operation in West Africa are of four main types: (i) economic communities such as MRU and ECOWAS; (ii) natural resource development organs such as the River Basin and Lake Commissions; (iii) common service organizations providing technical or research services to their members; and, (iv) financial institutions such as the central banks of the West African Monetary Union and the West African Development Bank. There is much overlap in the membership, functions and objectives of these bodies. A far-from-inclusive count (ECA, 1984) enumerates more than 30 such organizations in West Africa alone. In addition to the three economic communities, CEAO, MRU and ECOWAS, a fourth, Senegambia, is in the process of formation. The formation of another, a Benin Union to consist of Nigeria, Ghana, Togo and Benin, has been suggested (ECA, 1984) in the context of a rationalization of economic co-operation arrangements.

Equatorial and Central Africa possess three economic communities: UDEAC, set up in 1964 (which shares a common currency and central bank); the *Communauté économique des pays des Grands Lacs* (CEPGL), set up in 1976; and ECCAS, which was formed in October 1983. ECCAS groups together 10 member states, i.e. the members of UDEAC and CEPGL plus Equatorial Guinea and Sao Tome and Principe. It is the counterpart of ECOWAS for Central Africa.

In West Africa, CEAO and ECOWAS, though having the same basic objectives, have adopted very different strategies. It is useful to compare them and to evaluate their respective merits. In Central Africa, similar types of problems arise; UDEAC itself has many similar features of CEAO and, on the other hand, ECCAS is clearly likely to confront some of the problems encountered by ECOWAS.

621

ECONOMIC COMMUNITY OF WEST AFRICA (CEAO)

CEAO is the most solidly established of the West African communities. It was established in 1973, under the Treaty of Abidjan, and comprises Cote d'Ivoire, the Niger, Burkina Faso, Mali, Mauritania, Senegal and, since its admittance at the summit meeting in October 1984, Benin.

The CEAO Treaty requires the establishment of a customs union, but although a so-called common external tariff has been adopted, this so far represents only a small component of the aggregate duties that are imposed on imports. At its present stage, CEAO is best described as a preferential trade area in which trade is, in principle, free for *produits du cru* and is partially liberalized (by the granting of tariff preferences and the elimination of non-tariff barriers) in respect of manufactured products of local origin. This arrangement is capable of avoiding the distortions that would otherwise be produced by free trade with widely divergent national tariffs.

The integration of product markets through trade liberalization is buttressed by a scheme which provides compensation for losses from trade diversion arising from trade liberalization. Compensation is not provided for any losses that might arise from trade creation, but, in CEAO, this is immaterial since each country can effectively protect its high-cost industries by limiting the tariff preference it accords to its partner state under the special regime (termed the *Taxe de coopération regional* – TCR) that can be applied to manufactured products of Community origin in place of the import duties that would otherwise be levied. The rates, applied by mutual agreement, fall mainly within a band of 40 to 60 per cent of the tariffs applied to countries outside the Community, but some are as low as 10 per cent and a few are as high as 90 per cent. They are fixed for each industrial establishment, and normally discriminate in favour of the Community's less developed members which, with one exception, are land-locked.

Intra-Community trade is a relatively low proportion of total trade (12 per cent in 1983) and only a proportion of this trade is in manufactured products. Of the latter, however, a growing proportion is covered by TCR arrangements. Thus, in 1981, the share of TCR imports in total manufactured imports from the Community was 42 per cent for Burkina Faso; 42 per cent for Mali; 70 per cent for the Niger; 78 per cent for Senegal; and 55 per cent for Cote d'Ivoire (no comparisons are available for Mauritania since 1976). In 1981, Cote d'Ivoire's share of the preferential exports had risen to 70 per cent of the total, while the share of Senegal had fallen to 23 per cent. In this trade, Senegal and Cote d'Ivoire enjoy substantial surpluses with their partners, and this is the case also in total Community trade in manufactures (which is relevant for the contribution key to the compensation fund); all the other countries have deficits.

A valuable feature of this arrangement is that each country effectively retains its policy flexibility and autonomy with respect to the establishment of new industries. Consequently, even before the industrial harmonization envisaged by the Treaty is attained, a participating country's interest is unlikely to be damaged by the operation of the Community. This is an outstanding example of 'variable geometry' in economic integration. It is a workable basis for limited economic cooperation, and it minimizes distributional difficulties and harmonization problems. But a corollary is that the opportunities it affords for generating economic gains are likely to be modest by comparison with those that would *in principle* be available from more ambitious schemes.

ECONOMIC COMMUNITY OF WEST AFRICAN STATES (ECOWAS)

ECOWAS is without doubt the most ambitious grouping in sub-Saharan Africa. This 16-country grouping, which was inaugurated in 1975, includes the member states of MRU and CEAO, together with Nigeria, Ghana, the Gambia, Benin, Togo, Guinea-Bissau and Cape Verde. Together, these states constitute a geographical zone larger than Western Europe. ECOWAS includes some of the richest and most populous countries in Africa, several of which possess immense mineral resources. It also includes a majority of the poorest countries in Africa.

ECOWAS is governed by the Treaty of Lagos which includes a number of time-tabled commitments with respect to (i) a tariff standstill; (ii) trade liberalization; (iii) fiscal harmonization; and, (iv) the introduction of a common external tariff. Since 1981 the Community has been endeavouring to implement the second of these commitments. The time-tabled commitments are coupled with untime-tabled obligations to adopt wider policy measures of 'positive' economic integration, including industrial co-operation.

The ECOWAS Treaty is very elaborate (modelled on the Treaty of Rome), but it left most substantive issues to be resolved subsequently. As an integration strategy this approach has many precedents, though nowhere else has it been pursued so rigorously. Such an approach, perhaps inspired by functionalism, evidently does not induce difficulties to disappear; it merely puts off the need to resolve them. It is unfortunate that, having devised a Treaty whose general provisions are coherent and ultimately mutually reinforcing, the Community should nevertheless have been led by its provisions to give priority initially to market integration and free competition – when market signals, because of widespread and severe distortions, are likely to be so misleading – and to neglect the positive policy measures on which the success of the integration process must ultimately hinge.

ECOWAS cannot yet be said to have a development strategy, except in the limited sense that competition and the free working of market forces are to be facilitated. It has no common external tariff and, unlike the case of the Treaty of Rome, there is no indication in the Lagos Treaty as to how one is to be reached. The Treaty moreover requires trade liberalization to take place in advance of tariff harmonization, unlike the procedure followed in most other groupings where either liberalization has been made conditional on prior tariff harmonization (so providing a stimulus to the formation of a common external tariff and avoiding possible misallocations of resources that might otherwise be produced), or other devices were adopted to avoid distortions (as in CEAO and UDEAC).

In themselves, the implementation of time-tabled measures of trade liberalization would almost inevitably operate adversely to the interests of the least developed members. They would suffer both from trade diversion and from trade creation: their imports of many products from the rest of the world would be replaced by higher cost products of the import-substitution industries of their more advanced ECOWAS partners and, in addition, their own import-substitution industries would tend to be vulnerable to competition from their partners.

The Treaty does contain provisions designed to ameliorate these problems which, if left unchecked, would certainly result (as they have elsewhere in Africa) in a maldistribution of the costs and benefits of integration, and ultimate collapse. The principal provision, which is to come into force synchronously with trade liberalization, provides for fiscal compensation for revenue losses incurred in the process of trade liberalization. A specific scheme was agreed by a decision in 1980 (A/DEC 19/5/80), which should approximately compensate the least developed member states for the 'impact' national income losses (reflected in tariff revenue losses) which they would incur as a result of trade diversion. The provisions do not, however, compensate for any income losses that may arise from a curtailment of production in any import-substitution industries that the least developed members may possess – that is, from trade creation.

ECOWAS has also agreed that in implementing its trade liberalization provisions, the less advanced countries may pursue a slower timetable than the more advanced members, although they will still have to complete the process by the same terminal date.

The Treaty contains other provisions that are designed to ensure that the interests of the Community's less developed members are protected. Thus, although the Treaty emphasizes measures designed to avoid the distortion of competitive forces and to promote uniform market conditions so as to give full scope to specialization, it also stresses the need to promote a fair and equitable distribution of benefits. In relation to that objective, ECOWAS Fund for Co-operation Compensation and Development has a key role. It is through this Fund that in the first place compensation for revenue losses is to be provided. In addition, the Fund is to promote development projects in the less developed members of the Community.

There are other provisions in the Treaty from which the Community's least developed members might also expect to benefit, such as the industrial development provisions which might limit the polarization of development that has characterized integration-induced development in other less developed groups. However, although the customs union obligations are firm and time-tabled, and the procedures are largely worked out, the broader policies of industrial development, and the special emphasis on projects in backward members, remain in the realm of aspiration. If the experience of other African groupings is any guide, it will not prove easy to implement them.

In respect of policies towards foreign direct investment, ECOWAS, nudged by Nigeria, evidently seeks to develop a more positive and radical approach than those of CEAO and MRU. Indeed, bargaining with multinationals appears to have been very much in the minds of those who devised the provisions of ECOWAS Treaty. Ultimately, any useful policy in this field will have to rest on a prior harmonization of investment incentives and of industrial development programmes, since it is basically the lack of harmonization of these key policy areas which accounts for many of the effects or abuses of which ECOWAS countries (in common with other developing countries) complain and which may tip the balance of benefits unduly in the favour of the foreign investor. So far, however, the principal step taken within ECOWAS has been to add a local participation provision to its rules of origin. In itself that is likely to exacerbate the problems of its less developed members, and without a prior harmonization of investment incentives, it cannot be expected significantly to ameliorate the problems posed by foreign direct investment (of which ownership is only one aspect). For the time being, indeed, the provision simply has the effect of rendering any trade liberalization commitments nugatory, since those countries (e.g. Nigeria and Ghana) which can meet the participation requirement are unable to export competitively in West Africa, whereas those which account for the bulk of intra-ECOWAS exports (e.g. Cote d'Ivoire and Senegal) cannot meet the ownership requirement.

THE PERFORMANCE OF EXISTING ECONOMIC CO-OPERATION ARRANGEMENTS

It is difficult to assess the costs and benefits of existing arrangements for integration in sub-Saharan Africa. Many of the relevant factors cannot be quantified and even for those that can be, there is the difficulty that the costs usually make themselves evident promptly, whereas benefits accrue chiefly in the long term. Nevertheless, it is important to attempt a broad evaluation of existing programmes and strategies in order to determine what weight can realistically be placed on their future contribution and, more importantly, to try to discern what policy reforms or changes in emphasis seem to be indicated if they are to play the role expected of them.

For that purpose there is need to have clear in mind how integration can make a contribution to development. At the purely economic level the key object of integration is to expand the opportunities for investment that will profit the African peoples, and that will contribute to the mobilization of their underemployed resources. To this end, rationalization of the emergent structure of production is indispensable. That has to be undertaken in such a way as to take care of the interests of all participants, in particular of the less developed members. To do this, a variety of instruments, agreements and compromises will be required.

The West African economic communities that have been established, and are in the process of being established, are from these points of view, very comprehensive. But they have failed to address problems in the right order; they have often given priority to policy areas which are of little immediate relevance; and they are apt to overburden particular instruments by requiring them to perform too many functions. These points may be illustrated by the experience of CEAO and the programme of ECOWAS. To some extent, similar problems are present in UDEAC, and can be anticipated for ECCAS.

CEAO has made substantial progress towards implementing its treaty provisions in customs affairs. It has adopted a common customs and statistical nomenclature. Agreement has also been reached on a simplified and harmonized structure of customs and internal indirect taxes. The specific measures for trade liberalization and trade expansion involving the duty-free circulation of most *produits du cru* and preferential treatment for manufactured products originating in the area have been implemented and have facilitated a growing and now substantial amount of intra-group trade. An absence of exchange problems because of the common currency (except for Mauritania) is also a favourable factor for economic integration in the subregion. Much progress has also been made with the elimination of non-tariff barriers and specifically, of quantitative restrictions, though some of the latter remain in defiance of the treaty (particularly in textiles). In other fields of co-operation, such as agriculture and transport, progress so far has been less obvious, though steps have been taken to develop regional training and research institutes, and several useful Community projects, e.g. in the field of fisheries.

But any significant rationalization of industrial production is absent. There is little inter-country specialization on particular products or product ranges and thus little intra-industry trade. In numerous sectors of industry, plants are replicated, and production takes place on a smaller scale than the size and structure of the regional market would permit. The advantages of integration are thereby dissipated insofar as they derive from specialization and the exploitation of scale economies. Uneconomic replication has occurred in textiles (despite the interlocking links of a number of the multinationals involved), pharmaceuticals, plastics, food industries, electrical products (i.e. batteries) etc.

In UDEAC, a strikingly similar situation is found. In UDEAC the *taxe Unique* operates in a very similar way to the TCR. A number of TNCs that operate in CEAO – Bata, Riegel, Schaefer – are also active in UDEAC, and, as in CEAO, they account for a very high proportion of sales in a number of industries.

The plant replication found in these two groups is not to any significant extent an inheritance from a pre-integration era. It has largely grown up and continues to develop in the face of arrangements for integration. It has been buttressed by a failure to harmonize national investment incentives, and it reflects, in particular, the absence of any regional industrial development programme or any concerted regional approach towards foreign investment and multinational enterprises.

It is clear that both domestic and international forces have interacted to produce market segmentation and plant replication in CEAO. No matter how the responsibility for the outcome is assigned between these forces, the effect is undeniable. It is to rob integration of much of its hoped-for benefits, and to hinder the attainment of important subsidiary objectives of development policy such as the creation of inter-industry linkages.

The experience of CEAO and UDEAC, in these and other respects, makes it difficult to believe that they have had a major development impact so far. And, more important, there are few signs that the factors which impede an improvement of that impact are currently accorded much attention by policy makers and politicians of the participating countries. A World Bank initiative a few years ago which would have tried to identify the possibilities for regional industrial co-operation in CEAO seems to have been quietly discouraged. Nevertheless, despite its limitation, CEAO's approach (and to some extent this also applies to UDEAC) has two important merits which are capable of being built upon: (i) it is capable, as noted, of avoiding the distortions that would otherwise be produced by trade liberalization undertaken against the background of initially very diverse tariffs; and, (ii) it provides a workable basis for co-operation in the stage prior to industrial harmonization. Of course, it could justifiably be argued that even with policy reforms, the markets of both CEAO and UDEAC are too small to produce really significant benefits anyway – a point which leads to a consideration of the role of the broader groupings such as ECOWAS and ECCAS.

Since its establishment, the principal achievement of ECOWAS has been to create an institutional framework for a customs union. An ECOWAS tariff nomenclature has been adopted and common customs documentation has been developed. A range of important protocols needed to give effect to treaty provisions in respect of trade and customs have also been adopted, thus giving operational content to some of the more general provisions of the Treaty. In its ECOWAS Fund, the Community possesses an institution of potentially great importance for promoting positive integration, development and balance. Nevertheless, the Community's present strategy displays crucial weaknesses that will have to be overcome if progress is to be made and benefits are to be realized. These weaknesses substantially contribute to one of the most widely criticized aspects of ECOWAS; namely, that the decisions it adopts at the level of Heads of State or Ministers almost invariably fail to be implemented by action at national level.

The weaknesses of ECOWAS stem from many factors, but there are two which are closely connected with the integration strategy that is being followed, namely: (i) the priority accorded to trade liberalization and the automaticity of the process; and, (ii) the lack of simultaneity in the obligations and benefits implied by the Community's programme.

Although the classical trade liberalization approach to integration among developing countries has long been discredited, ECOWAS treaty nevertheless gave priority to trade liberalization on an obligatory, automatic 'across-the-board' basis, and its explicit economic strategy emphasizes the liberation of competitive forces. But the framework within which competition would operate is, as yet, fortuitous because there is no agreed general structure of protection (to be provided ultimately through the adoption of a common external tariff and harmonized investment incentives). The ECOWAS programme of automatic trade liberalization would come into effect – if it does – against the background of national protective structures that are diverse, and generally very high, but which in any case have not been constructed with the needs and opportunities of a regional market in mind. It is very difficult to predict the effects of liberalization in such a framework, but there are no *a priori* grounds for supposing that its resource allocation and developmental effects would be favourable. Although any adverse distributive effects resulting from trade liberalization in this rather unsatisfactory context should be largely offset by the Community's compensation scheme, that in itself cannot justify the pattern of trade which might result. That pattern remains essentially unappraised (and indeed unappraisable to the extent that it will depend on ownership just as much as comparative advantage). The compensation scheme also can do nothing to mitigate the economic distortions that may be encouraged in both importing and exporting countries if such trade liberalization were to be implemented.

The second weakness is one that primarily concerns the less industrially advanced members of ECOWAS, although to some extent it affects all. Despite the treaty's emphasis on protecting the interests of the less advanced members, it cannot be said to offer the prospect of doing so adequately. The time-tabled obligations of the treaty concerning the customs union constitute measures from which the industrially less advanced members are unlikely to benefit; rather, they can confidently expect to suffer through the trade creation and trade diversion that results. The measures from which they might hope to benefit – in particular differential action through the Fund to promote their industrialization, and perhaps fiscal and industrial harmonization – are not time-tabled and no specific proposals have yet been considered to give them operational content. Experience elsewhere in Africa will hardly incline less developed members to underrate the difficulties of devising and implementing such measures. All things considered, it is not surprising that at least the (numerically dominant) less developed members of the Community should have been tempted to hang back from implementing formal commitments to liberalize trade until they are assured that their interests will otherwise be safeguarded.

In any case, little can be expected of the trade liberalization programme in itself, even if it were to be implemented. It may be an exaggeration to claim (ECA, 1984) that 'most countries of the region have nothing to trade with anyway'. Sierra Leone, Liberia, Cote d'Ivoire and Senegal do have surplus industrial capacity in relevant products, although their products in some cases, even at full capacity, seem likely to be uncompetitive even if free of tariffs. But it is surely true, as the ECA report emphasized, that the development of productive capacity is one of the most pressing problems of integration.

Apart from these considerations, the impact of trade liberalization commitments, even if fully implemented, would be limited for two further reasons. First, those countries of the region which enjoy revealed comparative advantage would often be excluded from the regional market by the local ownership requirement of the rules of origin; second, if that hurdle is overcome, there remain the problems of currency restrictions and the lack of convertibility of the currencies of several members of ECOWAS such as Nigeria, Ghana and Sierra Leone. The maladministration of these restrictions almost inevitably discriminates against intra-group trade. Rather late in the day, ECOWAS has turned its attention to the inconvertibility constraint. Its initially espoused solution, limited convertibility for intra-regional trade, seems (perhaps surprisingly) to have been received approvingly by the European Commission, but at least it might be better than the promotion of counter-trade.

One further problem must be noted at this point. This concerns the relations between ECOWAS and CEAO and MRU (and the prospective relations between UDEAC, CEPGL and ECCAS). The failure of collaboration amongst the West African institutions is notorious. At the level of the economic communities, co-operation between ECOWAS and CEAO is virtually non-existent. Until now each grouping has tackled similar problems often at the same time but independently and without consultation. This has resulted in different solutions even to the same technical problems, which present later problems of harmonization. Thus, to cite only early initiatives, there are three customs nomenclatures, three different rules of origin, two different and incompatible compensation systems, and two different and yet to be reconciled systems of trade liberalization. To deal with these and related problems ECA has recommended a substantial remodelling of the organizational structure of the subregional institutions for economic integration (ECA, 1984). At the economic community level, the creation of a new one – the Benin Union (to include Nigeria, Ghana, Togo and Benin) – was tentatively proposed. This suggestion was in the context of a more general proposal that would have assigned *all* members of ECOWAS also to one or other of the more compact groupings that would be closer to the interests of members. Thus the Gambia and Cape Verde would join CEAO, and Guinea-Bissau would join the MRU. This approach was seen as opening the way to a greater concentration of effort on promoting integration and development through the smaller and more intimate communities, rather than through ECOWAS itself. The subsequent demand by Benin for admission to CEAO, and its acceptance by that Community, underlines the attraction of smaller communities, although in a manner which constitutes a further challenge to the position of ECOWAS.

FUTURE FOR CO-OPERATION AND INTEGRATION IN SUB-SAHARAN AFRICA

In the light of recent experience, it is difficult to avoid the conclusion that the economic community approach to integration is likely to be unconstructive if there is no redirection of effort and institutional reform in existing schemes and an avoidance of over-ambitious strategies in others now in their formative stages. Five aspects suggest themselves:

(i) Emphasis needs to be given to the development of a suitable infrastructure for regional economic co-operation. This has been a constant theme of analysis and policy declarations for 25 years, but it bears repetition since it remains so basic. Infrastructure links among African countries after more than a quarter of a century of post-independence initiatives still frustrate trade and wider forms of co-operation in posts, telecommunications and transport. Posts and telecommunications are often much worse than at independence. At the financial level, intra-West African clearing arrangements can involve almost unbelievable delays of up to four to six months before final payments. The costs involved in delay and lack of prompt information constitute a major obstacle to intra-regional trade;

(ii) The development of more effective instruments and arrangements for industrial co-operation is a second vital requirement. Indeed, an ability to develop effective instruments for industrial co-operation, and to use them, is likely to be the single most crucial determinant of the future contribution of integration to sub-Saharan economic development. It is necessary to be realistic about what can be achieved, and which paths can be followed. In East Africa, a group of just three countries found it impossible to implement a very limited industrial plan. In the Association of South-East Asian Nations (ASEAN), countries currently find it difficult to agree on the establishment of a handful of large-scale industries to serve the regional market (admittedly the foreign capital/multinational enterprise problem manifests itself – notably in Singapore – in a much more extreme form than it does in most of Africa). To make progress in West and Central Africa, and hopefully in other parts of Africa too, it may be necessary to encourage much more limited and flexible arrangements for industrial co-operation than have hitherto been envisaged (perhaps between smaller groups of as few as two or three countries): perhaps overlapping groupings, and possibly resting on joint financial participation in capital, profits, tax revenues and even manning. To facilitate such initiatives may entail some modification of established treaties of co-operation, and perhaps the creation of smaller sub-groups such as the proposed Benin Union. Initiatives of this kind would have to be handled cautiously if the process is not to be ultimately counter-productive. Community or sub-Community (for the smaller groupings) which would look towards some long-term rationalization of production on a regional basis would certainly be needed, and it would be indispensable that fiscal incentives should be provided to encourage the following of such guidelines;

(iii) Community guidelines for industrial development initiatives should clearly be based on a realistic appraisal of the strengths of the subregion (or smaller areas within it), of the comparative strengths of individual countries within it, and on some very broad agreement on the level and structure of protection towards which it would be reasonable for the region to work. The data on the basis of which such guidelines could be formulated have not been collected or evaluated in West, Equatorial or Central Africa. (World Bank's research programme of the early 1970s on this subject for West Africa was not carried out for a sufficient number of countries, and has not been followed up; the UNDP-financed ECOWAS exercise of 1979/1980 was diffuse, lacked firm direction and specification, and conspicuously failed to produce any useful guidelines). We can all agree, no doubt, that the really crucial factors in the progress and performance of integration are the political will to integrate and a willingness to compromise. Nevertheless, there can equally be no doubt that the lack of relevant studies in Africa can be – and almost certainly *is* currently – an important constraint to constructive decision-taking. It is surely futile to expect constructive advance if structures and priorities are not apt, and if the implications of policies cannot be perceived by member countries. Decisions to integrate that are not well-grounded will either be counter-productive or will fail to be implemented;

(iv) A fourth requirement is for payments reforms. For most countries outside the two monetary unions these are indispensable if trade co-operation is to be feasible, although perhaps with new forms of industrial co-operation *some* existing payments problems could be circumvented. The problem in the short term is to administer payments restrictions in a way that does not discourage intra-regional trade; in the longer term, it is to reduce the need for the restrictions themselves. As to the latter, there is mounting evidence that those African countries which have undertaken policy adjustments to restore equilibrium in their balance of payments during the past decade have not suffered in terms of growth rates of real GDP or consumption. If this is really so, and comes to be more widely perceived, then some of the apparently immovable obstacles to progress on this front may be lessened. Limited convertibility – the current nostrum – would appear only to introduce further distortions into a system in which price systems are so riddled with distortions already that they cannot, without major policy reforms, provide a dependable guide to intra-regional specialization and rationalization. A solution involving a major extension of existing monetary unions is unlikely, but small extensions have taken place in Equatorial Africa, and others that cannot altogether be excluded may help modestly;

(v) Finally, to take another dimension altogether, the structures within member states for reacting to and for developing integration initiatives need to be strengthened. The problems outlined in the ECA report mentioned earlier are well recognized and some countries are reported to be experimenting with new structures in an attempt to deal with them. It cannot be overemphasized – as the ECA Report rightly stresses – that development projects are, and will long remain, largely the responsibility of individual member states. These states must therefore be involved initially, continuously and intimately in any workable integration programme. Attempts to integrate from above are unlikely to make a significant impact.

In the light of the performance of African regional integration initiatives during the past two decades, can one be optimistic about the likelihood of progress on any or all of these fronts? There are several factors in the current situation that might suggest a more optimistic prognosis than past experience appears to warrant. First, the protracted economic crisis is forcing domestic adjustments which hitherto could be put off. Paradoxically, the lack of will to give real priority to intra-regional adjustments and compromises and to the development of practical integration strategies could, for this reason, conceivably prove to be less of an obstacle during the next decade than it has been during the past decade. Second, there currently appears to be a renewed awareness on the part of major donors and aid agencies of the value of regional integration and of the need to provide external support for regional policies, projects, and institutional reform. There are perhaps therefore grounds for guarded optimism that internal and external forces in combination can produce the realignment and rephasing of priorities that will be necessary if co-operation and integration in Africa are to play the role they could in helping to overcome Africa's acute developmental problems.

CHAPTER THIRTY-ONE

The Challenge of Economic Integration in Africa

LOUIS SANGARE

INTRODUCTION

The economic structure of African countries is essentially characterized by its lack of integration. These countries have no physical cohesion and are under-equipped. They have no proper heavy transport network or electrical installations. The links between agriculture and industry, and between industry and transport are minimal.

African economies lack the intermediate goods required for establishing a solid infrastructure, or for modernizing the key sectors. The construction of dams to provide water and hydro-electric power, the building of roads and railways, the supply of water to the towns, the erection of power lines, all require the initial development of basic industries (steel, aluminium, petrochemical and chemical industries) to provide metal shuttering and sheeting-piles, cement, rails, piping, pylons and cables. The absence of a sound industrial base has other serious consequences. There is no modernization in agriculture due to lack of modern agricultural inputs: fertilizer, pesticides and agricultural machinery.

The industrial sector in Africa consists largely of a series of light import-substitution industries, isolated from one another, but all linked to basic industries abroad for their supply of intermediate products. Thus, such an industrialization process can hardly generate the industrial base required for building a self-sustained economy.

The lack of basic industries is a major constraint to the development of African countries. More specifically, African economies are caught in a vicious circle of stagnation. Since the intermediate products required are imported, African economies depend heavily on export of primary commodities (agricultural produce and mining resources) to finance such imports. In any case, the continuing deterioration of the terms of trade makes this development strategy illusory.

There are two main reasons for the lack of basic industries in Africa, namely, the small size of national markets, and the low productive capacity of individual African economies.

The efficiency of basic industries producing on a large scale is largely dependent on the size of the market available. Most African countries are the results of dismantled colonial entities. Thus, the resulting small states are unable to process their strategic resources.

On the other hand, the small and poor African countries have low performance capabilities for the following main reasons: weak political and administrative structures, lack of financial and technical resources, inability to mobilize significant amounts of funds for carrying out major projects, and the absence of a skilled workforce. In Africa, economic integration on a subregional basis thus seems to be the quickest way for these small states to achieve accelerated economic development. This would increase their ability to carry out large economic projects and have access to a subregional market large enough to support large-scale industries producing intermediate and capital goods, which would in turn lead to the achievement of food self-sufficiency as well as the modernization of the key sectors of the economy.

The first part of this Chapter reviews the process of the creation of small African communities by the former colonial powers in order to preserve their basic interests. The second part deals with the global approach to integration advocated by LPA and FAL. In the third part the subregional integration strategies are examined in each subregion. The fourth part examines measures required to address the political problems related to the implementation of economic integration programmes in Africa. Finally, in the fifth part, is a perspective analysis of a future continental economic community.

THE MARKET INTEGRATION APPROACH

The colonial powers soon realized that the African states would not be slow in reacting to the policy of dividing the continent into small states. They were, therefore, quick to suggest systems of economic integration which were unsuitable for African countries in the sense that they prevented the formation of large federal groups but helped to preserve their colonial interests. In this respect, the former French colonial power proposed, on 9 June 1959, the creation of the Customs Union of West Africa (UDAO) after dissolving the *Fédération de l'Afrique occidentale française* (ACF) on 3 March 1959 on the eve of independence of the West African countries under French control.

In 1966, UDAO was renamed as UDEAO with the intention of

making it an instrument for trade co-operation. However, UDEAO has not succeeded in its function as a free-trade zone, because each member State continued to tax imports from the other partners. And, in 1973, CEAO replaced UDEAO, with the aim of embarking on a real economic co-operation. The same colonial power set up, in 1959, in central Africa the Equatorial Customs Union (UDE) after dismantling the *Fédération de l'Afrique équatoriale française*. UDE became, in 1964, UDEAC. Similarly, CEPGL is, in actual fact, only the continuation of an economic union created between Rwanda, Burundi and Zaire by Belgium in 1925.

The subregional communities mentioned above were based on strategies for market integration as in Western Europe. However, the economies of these underdeveloped subregions of Africa have nothing in common with Western Europe which, when the common market was being established, had a well-integrated industrial structure and a diversified heavy-transport system. The industrial production capacity of the European states simply needed a wider market in order to increase and diversify production. The European countries correctly identified the factors limiting their production systems and conceived a model of economic integration based on market integration.

For the African economic communities referred to above, the priority given to market integration was premature. These economic communities have developed schemes for the removal of customs barriers while their member states either at national or at subregional levels do not have production, transport and communications systems capable of intensifying trade. The situation of transport in the subregions of Africa is an obstacle to the development of trade. It is characterized by enclaved zones which are only linked with the ports for the export of primary commodities to, and the import of manufactured goods from Europe. Moreover, all essential air freight is carried by non-African airlines.

Only few lateral links have been created between the member countries of the African subregions, by road, rail or sea. The railway, in particular, which is an important factor in economic development as the main transport system for mining and industry, has remained neglected in Africa, with no link between French and English-speaking countries. The telecommunications system is also in a disastrous state.

Furthermore, the current economic structures of the member states of the African economic communities, oriented towards imports, are not conducive to increasing intra-community trade. Leaving aside the difficulties of transport and telecommunications, the low agricultural productivity and the little progress made in animal husbandry in the field of improving breeds and the treatment and preservation of meat and fish are obstacles to the development of trade. Subsistence agriculture has been totally neglected. Agricultural investment in fertilizer, pesticides, machinery and storage facilities has been mainly to the benefit of agricultural export commodities.

The industrial development strategies adopted by the member countries are also hardly suited to improving trade. Countries in the same subregion have established almost the same range of industries, most of them of an import-substitution nature.

Intra-African trade is only about 4 per cent of all African trade as there is not much to trade among countries. Even if all the measures advocated by the economic communities for the promotion of trade were applied, this ratio would hardly reach 10 per cent, which would still be insufficient to form a viable basis for integration through trade. Consequently, the subregional economic communities must give less emphasis to trade liberalization. They must restructure their national and subregional production systems, by creating a subregional transport and telecommunications infrastructure, by developing new production capacities in industry, and by increasing agricultural productivity.

Another aspect of the existing economic communities is that the most developed partners find themselves in a position to export certain industrial goods in the community market duty-free, whereas these same goods, when they come from an outside country, incur customs duty. This market integration scheme, which gives no priority to the basic industries, reinforces the position of the foreign private sector in the African countries and increases economic domination from abroad. It also has the disadvantage of accentuating the disparity in the levels of development of the member countries.

In conclusion, the abolition of customs duties, quotas and other restrictions without a corresponding removal of the physical obstacles to the distribution of goods, and without subregional production being distributed harmoniously within the economic community, will, in the short term, result in the breaking up of that community. In fact, the states which have a more developed production system will benefit from the situation at the expense of the poorer counries. The removal of customs duties and the establishment of a common external tariff, without a subregional production system being set up, may also facilitate the capture of these markets by MNCs.

THE GLOBAL APPROACH TO ECONOMIC INTEGRATION AS CALLED FOR IN LPA AND FAL

LPA proposes measures intended to transform the structure of the African economies with a view to setting up an economic system basically oriented towards satisfying the needs of the economies and populations, and to stimulate a process of economic development which would be endogenous and self-sustaining. The global approach to economic integration, as adovcated by LPA, tackles the real obstacles to the economic development of the African subregions, especially with respect to physical infrastructure, agriculture, industry and trade.

Development of Physical Infrastructure

The opening of lines of communication between the member states is a prerequisite to the exploitation of the basic strategic materials, especially those located in the hinterland. In view of the necessity to develop a heavy transport system for the needs of the industrial base, priority would have to be given to the improvement of navigable waterways (rivers and lakes) and to increasing coastal shipping. Also, railway lines must be developed and rail-networks connected.

The development of telecommunications systems is also an essential factor for reinforcing the cohesion of the subregional economic areas. This includes the maintenance of national networks and the inter-connection of the earth stations networks of the subregion. The African satellite project, intended to ensure reliable communications across the whole of Africa, must quickly become a reality.

Energy resources are also essential components in the integration of the subregional economic entities. In this regard, it is necessary to ensure the full exploitation of the hydro-electric energy potential of the subregion and devise a comprehensive programme of interconnections of power lines within each subregion, in order to meet primarily the needs of the basic and capital goods industries.

Agricultural Development

Subregional economic integration requires a vigorous agricultural development programme. The economic integration strategy will only be effective if it is based on a subregional agricultural development policy leading to self-sufficiency in food and the improvement of agricultural and livestock productivity. Emphasis should be placed on subregional co-operation in terms of agronomic research for stimulating agricultural productivity. This co-operation will be based on the specialization of national agronomic research centres in improved seed and plants for the main food crops, notably maize, sorghum, plantain, manioc, etc. Livestock development requires co-operation, including such aspects as specialization of countries and intercountry co-operation in the field of animal selection for improved production capacity of existing breeds and increased tolerance to different diseases; the fight against animal diseases; the production of vaccines and the manufacture of quality food concentrates based on primary local produce; and training.

Industrial Development

Industry is the main integrating factor of subregional economic co-operation. First, the industrial sector must contribute to the increase in agricultural productivity, through the setting up of industries producing fertilizers, pesticides and agricultural machinery.

Secondly, the industrial sector must contribute to the modernization of the priority economic sectors. Indeed, the establishment of a solid industrial base with key industries of iron and steel, aluminium, chemical and petrochemical products is necessary for triggering a rapid, self-sustaining process of economic development. This industrialization process is also essential to support energy development (production of cables, manufacture of pylons and transformers), the major infrastructural projects, the construction of transport facilities and basic capital goods.

Trade and Finance

The present framework of community trade must be reinforced by the creation of a clearing house and even by pursuing the convertibility of the currencies of the subregion, with the aim of creating conditions which would stimulate to a certain extent the intra-community trade. However, the freedom of trade between the member states must be planned progressively. The granting of preferential treatment to highly competitive consumer goods, common foodstuffs and certain durable goods may slow down the process of industrialization in the LDCs in the subregion and aggravate the trade imbalance in the subregional economic communities. Such a situation would be incompatible with the *raison d'être* of the community.

AN OVERVIEW OF POSSIBLE SUBREGIONAL ECONOMIC INTEGRATION STRATEGIES

In light of the global approach to subregional economic integration recommended in LPA and FAL, it is important to determine at the level of each subregion the main potentials on which integration programmes should be based. These potentials should constitute the basis for the strategy to accelerate the integration process.

The West African Subregion

The West African subregion has a number of advantages:

- A potentially wide market of 130 million inhabitants (equivalent to the population of Japan, or to that of France and the Federal Republic of Germany combined) which could sustain large-scale investment projects, notably in heavy industry;
- Two large and distinct ecological zones, which give rise to different types of agriculture: ground-nuts, cotton, millet and sorghum, in the savannah countries (Sahel); coffee, cocoa, cabbage palm, plantain and manioc, in the forested countries (Sudano-guinean zone). Rice is grown and consumed throughout the subregion;
- A relatively flat topography, which facilitates the construction of roads and railway lines. However, the interconnection of the railway networks is made difficult by differences in the gauges of the anglo-phone and franco-phone countries; and,
- A large sea-board, which is favourable to the development of coastal trading and sea fishing, taking into account that West African coasts have the highest fish density in the world.

West Africa has only three land-locked countries: Burkina Faso, Mali and Niger, each linked to at least two coastal countries.

Another advantage is the great variety of mining resources: oil (Nigeria), phosphates (Senegal, Togo), iron (Liberia, Mali and Mauritania), bauxite (Guinea-Conakry), Uranium (Niger), etc., which is extremely favourable to the development of a true industrial basin. The subregion does, however, suffer from a relative handicap in terms of energy: there is no huge hydro-electric potential such as the river Zaire in Central Africa or the river Zambezi in Southern Africa, and the exploitation of the four great rivers (Niger, Senegal, Mano and Gambia) has only just started.

These advantages have not been fully used to the benefit of subregional economic integration for the following reasons:

- The total lack of economic co-operation between member countries in production, especially in basic industries, while the distribution of industrial complexes of iron and steel, bauxite, oil and gas on the basis of comparative advantages could provide the basis for trade at the subregional level, and for rapid economic development;
- The lack of adequate transport links between the countries of the subregion, notably East–West;
- The fact that there are different non-convertible national currencies; this monetary problem does not exist in CEAO where six countries use the same currency. Within ECOWAS, this situation might reasonably be improved by better functioning of the Clearing House set up in 1976, and a net improvement in the telecommunications network; and,
- The existence of a large number of IGOs (around thirty) which are often competing. These fall into two large categories: (i) Multipurpose IGOs mainly economic communities (CEAO, MRU and ECOWAS); (ii) Limited objective IGOs for the exploitation of river basins (OMVS, OMVG and the Niger Basin Authority), for agriculture (WARDA) for campaigning against predators (Joint Anti-Locust and Anti-aviarian Organization), for monetary co-operation (West African Monetary Union; West African Clearing House), for development financing (West African Development Bank), etc.

In West Africa, the economic integration strategy should be directed first of all to reinforce the physical integration of the economic area of the subregion by constructing roads across from east to west, with priority given to the N'Djamena–Dakar and Lagos–Nouakchott roads along the coasts, so as to promote economic relations between such countries as Niger, Mali and Mauritania. The isolation of land-locked countries prevents them from producing intermediate goods for export to the coastal countries. Hence, the interconnection of the railway networks of the subregion is of primary importance for integration. In this regard, the following interconnections are necessary: Bamako–Sikasso–Bobo; Dioulasso–Abidjan; Ouaga–Anie–Parakou–Niamey; Ouaga–Tamba–Ansongo–Ouaga–Tamba–Ansongo; Lagos–Cotonou –Lome–Accra–Abidjan; and Bamako–Kouroussa–Kankan–Conakry.

The second integration factor should concern the management of the river-basins of the subregion: Niger, Senegal, Gambia, Mano, Volta, etc. especially in view of the desertification process in the subregion. In addition to providing energy, management of river basins could enable the controlling of water flow for navigation throughout the year, the irrigation of significant areas of cultivable land, and the supply of water to people and cattle. However, the production of hydro-electric power should be given priority within the overall exploitation of river basins, as it constitutes the economic factor which will justify the development of irrigated areas. West Africa must systematically concentrate on the provision of hydro-electric installations at sites of importance to the community and on the interconnection of national electricity grids in order to satisfy the requirements of the countries with poor energy resources and to exploit the mining resources which would not otherwise be exploited, notably iron and bauxite.

The present hydro-electric installations are in the basins of the River Senegal (Manantali), the River Gambia (Kekreti, in Senegal, Kouya in Upper Gambia, etc.) the River Mano (Cavally), the River Konkoure (Souapiti and Amaria), the Volta (Bui and Akossombo). It would be desirable to connect Akossombo with the hydro-electric installations of Nigeria (Kainji) and develop the hydro-electric potential in the loop of the Niger (Kandadji, Tossaye, Labezanga and the West site). A plan for the interconnection of these lines should be drawn up and the following links should be made: Liberia–Sierra Leone with the Mano River installation; Ghana–Cote d'Ivoire, which would optimize the most important installations in the two countries; the power stations at Ayame and Kossou, 50 MW and 174 MW respectively, Taabo, 210 MW, Buyo, 165 MW, and Soubre, 288 MW in Cote d'Ivoire. Akossombo, 512 MW, then 768 MW in Ghana; Ghana–Burkina–Cote d'Ivoire; Togo–Benin–Nigeria, which, with the Ghana–Togo–Benin link, on the one hand, and with Cote d'Ivoire, on the other, would connect Nigeria with Cote d'Ivoire; Liberia–Cote d'Ivoire with the Cabally installation; and Mali–Burkina with Cote d'Ivoire.

Thirdly, the above two factors will, undoubtedly, enable an industrialization process which should aim at: increasing agricultural productivity by the exploitation of river basins; the manufacture of agricultural inputs, and production of appropriate means of transport; speeding up the development of the subregion by expanding the transport network, the installation of facilities on urban sites, and extending power link-ups; and developing a capital goods sector with priority given to the manufacture of agricultural goods and machinery, transport equipment and industrial machinery for processing agricultural products, machinery and electrical equipment.

This economic integration strategy in West Africa requires that ECOWAS be recognized as the only economic integration entity in the subregion and that the respective roles of other intergovernmental organizations in West Africa be redefined. The primary role of ECOWAS will be to formulate a multi-sectoral master plan for the integration of the economic sphere of the subregion and to prepare sectoral master plans for the main sectors: transport and communication, energy, agriculture and industry. A subregional monetary and finance policy must also be defined.

The multi-sectoral co-operation organizations and the organizations dealing with the development of one single sector should revise their action plans so that they fit in with the overall ECOWAS programme. ECOWAS should be solely concerned with the strategy for the integration of the national markets of the subregion: planning the abolition of customs duties between the states and the establishment of a common external tariff.

The Central African Subregion

A major characteristic of the subregion is that CEPGL countries (Burundi, Rwanda and Zaire) are cut off from the rest of the Economic Community. In addition, Zaire, a huge country, has several regions suffering from economic isolation because of the inadequacy of the transport system. Also, the Central African Republic and Chad incur high transport costs due to their land-locked position.

On the other hand, the subregion has a great hydro-electric potential. The current surplus capacity of the Inga II hydro-electric power station is more than 1,600 MW and could be used for the building of a sound industrial base in the Community.

The first objective of the economic integration strategy for the Central African subregion must be the exploitation of the Zaire/Congo river basin. The energy potential of the river is estimated at about 84,000 MW, the bulk of which is concentrated in the Matadi–Kinshasa stretch of the river.

One site alone, Inga, currently in construction, represents more than 30,000 MW of potential power. Moreover, the river basin is rich in minerals and mining resources: oil and gas, iron deposits, bauxite, manganese, phosphate, potassium, salt, coal, etc. The abundance of cheap hydro-electricity and the presence of mining resources (iron ore, bauxite) should make it possible to build an industrial base in the basin of the Zaire/Congo and its main tributaries for iron and steel complexes and aluminium foundries. Electricity from Inga may also be used for the production of phosphoric acid, and superphosphates, and thereby turn the basin into a centre of dynamic industrial and agro-industrial development which would transform the economies of the member countries of the ECCAS. An inventory should be drawn up of the installed power capacity of the member countries, as well as the hydro-electric projects which have already undergone feasibility studies, and an assessment made of the viability of a programme for interlinking the power lines in the subregion.

The second priority is the opening of transport links between the member states, in particular between their capitals. At the same time, it is imperative that the isolated regions (Great Lakes, Chad, Central African Republic, the islands of Sao Tome and Principe) be opened up without delay by the development of air transport, especially air freight. Moreover, the development of a heavy transport system in the subregion requires the improvement of the main navigable waterways (rivers or lakes) and the development of coastal shipping. Finally, over a longer period of time, it is necessary to develop the railways and link the rail networks.

Thirdly, in the agricultural sector, emphasis should be put on subregional co-operation in research so as to stimulate agricultural productivity. There is need for an inventory of the national agronomic research centres (on seed selection, plant disease) which could serve as the basis for co-operation. In livestock management, research into trypanotolerant breeds of cattle and the use of vaccines would seem to be suitable areas for the development of co-operation.

Finally, in the industrial sector, the basic aim must be the increase of agricultural productivity by modernizing the agricultural sector. A number of priority industries should be encouraged including the production of fertilizers and pesticides and the manufacture of agricultural machinery. At the same time, it would be necessary to establish an industrial base by the development of certain basic industries: iron and steel, and aluminium given the availability of raw materials and cheap hydro-electric power. This industrialization must, in particular, support the development of the energy sector (production of cables, manufacture of pylons and transformers), the large infrastructural projects and the construction of transport facilities and essential capital goods.

The East and Southern Africa Subregion

The subregion of East and southern Africa is characterised by its great hydro-electric potential and immense mining resources. However, in the majority of countries, the average standard of living of the population is relatively poor and the growth rate of the national product is very low. The main reasons are the lack of economic links among the countries and the economic sabotage by South Africa.

The hydro-electric potential of PTA is estimated at some 106,000 MW. The capacity of existing installations in the subregion is however around 6,392 MW, or only 6 per cent of the available potential. Most of

645

these hydro-electric resources are concentrated in the Zambezi basin, whose technically exploitable potential is estimated at 16,023 MW. Almost 30 per cent of these resources are concentrated in two countries of Southern Africa (Angola and Mozambique) which do not belong to PTA but are members of SADCC. Angola has the greatest hydro-electric potential, with 23,000 MW, followed by Mozambique (15,000 MW), Zambia (12,000 MW), Tanzania (9,500 MW), and Zimbabwe (3,800 MW). In East Africa, Madagascar has the greatest hydro-electric potential, with 20,000 MW, followed by Ethiopia (12,000 MW), Kenya (6,000 MW) and Uganda (1,200 MW).

Angola, Mozambique and Tanzania possess iron ore, natural gas and cheap power, and could produce iron and steel by the direct reduction process, while Zambia and Tanzania could produce steel by using coal as the reducing agent. Moreover, the subregion is endowed with some high grade bauxite deposits, iron, copper, cobalt, coal, gypsum, limestone and other minerals.

The subregion has also abundant raw materials for the manufacture of three types of fertilizers based on phosphates, potassium and ammonia. Likewise, natural gas is found in Tanzania, Mozambique, Ethiopia, Angola and Rwanda; phosphate deposits in Tanzania, Uganda, Burundi, Zimbabwe and Zambia; and potassium deposits in Ethiopia. In addition, Ethiopia, Mozambique and Zambia currently produce a large amount of electric power, which could be used for fertilizer production.

The agricultural potentials are also quite impressive. Although the subregion suffers from periodic drought, at least two countries, i.e., Zimbabwe and Malawi, have a production surplus of maize, the basic foodstuff in the subregion. Botswana, Zimbabwe and Kenya are large producers of beef cattle and export meat to EEC. Agricultural research is very advanced in Zimbabwe and Kenya and the other countries could gain substantial advantages from the progress made in agricultural technology in these countries.

Although it was long believed in the subregion of PTA that the abolition of customs barriers between the states would immediately stimulate intra-community trade and the process of subregional economic integration, certain member states of the PTA rightly opposed the speed with which the abolition of customs barriers was progressing. Their fear was that the removal of customs barriers could result in a polarisation of development in favour of the more developed member states. This fear was well-founded, as free trade does not have integration effects, but rather aggravates the disparities in development within a community composed of unequal partners. What is of greatest importance is the promotion of production and productivity within the subregion by the effective exploitation of the immense natural resources available, through joint efforts by the member states.

However, for the subregion to exploit profitably its immense natural resources, there is need to examine the physical integration of the community, through the construction of a subregional transport and communications network, increased hydro-electric power and the development of the interconnection of power lines. There is need for several road links as the subregion has eight land-locked countries. Also, the great hydro-electric potential should lead to a bold subregional policy of hydro-electric development. The increase in energy production must be accompanied by a programme to link the subregion's rich energy resources with the principal centres of energy consumption (industrial areas, large agricultural and agro-industrial units and member states poor in energy resources).

In the field of industry, the power currently produced at Cabora-Basa, at the Kariba dam and on the Kafue river provides the opportunity to increase the steel production of PTA, to promote aluminium production and set up the subregional industrial units necessary to stimulate rapid economic development. Steel production will stimulate the development of rail transport by the production of rails and the manufacture of rolling stock; it will also enable the production of pipes for the construction of pipe lines for the oil industry. The production of sheet steel will also enable the setting up of industries for the manufacture of transport equipment, agricultural machinery, pumps, equipment for water-supply, tanks, industrial machinery for sugar refineries, cement factories, the textile industries, mining, etc.

Finally, the economic integration strategy will only be effective if it is based on a subregional agricultural development policy of food self-sufficiency and the improvement of agricultural and livestock productivity. Co-operation in agronomic research will provide improved seed and plants for the main food-crops, notably maize, sorghum, banana, plantain, manioc, etc. The improvement of livestock management will require three specific measures: the specialization of countries and inter-state co-operation in the area of animal selection for the improvement of productivity in existing breeds and to increase the tolerance of the animals to various diseases; the specialization of countries and inter-state co-operation in the campaign against animal diseases; and the production of food concentrates based on locally produced raw materials.

POLITICAL PROBLEMS RELATED TO THE EFFECTIVE
IMPLEMENTATION OF SUBREGIONAL INTEGRATION
PROGRAMMES

The implementation of the economic integration programmes broadly outlined above requires that the political leaders of the member states depart from their present nationalist standpoint and develop a community spirit. Of course, presently, member states automatically give priority to national projects which directly concern their own economy and people, and community measures are examined by each member state from the point of view of its exclusive interests.

The rule of majority is also a major constraint in the functioning of community institutions such as the Conference of Heads of State and Government, the Council of Ministers, the Intergovernmental Commission of Experts and the Technical Committees. As community decisions are often aimed at lessening the dependence of the subregion on foreign countries, some community members come under pressure to oppose such decisions. Thus, decisions are limited to measures which do not harm anybody and which promote foreign interests; such as abolition of customs duties when there is in fact no subregional production capacity. And if there is no general consensus of opinion on community matters, the decision process is blocked. This basically explains why the African economic communities are not in a position to undertake politically the fundamental measures which will bring about profound changes in their economic structures.

The Need for a Community Parliament

It appears from the above that there is a serious vacuum in the system of political decision-making for the implementation of economic integration projects. There is need for a mechanism which would guaranteee that measures taken by the community authorities are in the interests of the community and those of the states. Therefore, the establishment, within these communities, of a community parliament endowed with legislative powers in certain areas and consultative powers in others, would help to establish the community spirit. The parliament should be made up of three types of representation: from the Council of Ministers, from the legislative assemblies of the member countries, and from the general population. Experts in economic integration should also participate in the parliamentary decisions, but without voting rights.

These assemblies should be able to discuss three types of issues: (i) the technical problems involved in economic integration – subregional transport and telecommunications projects; multinational hydro-electric development projects; agricultural projects of community importance and industrial economic integration projects; (ii) problems concerning the abolition of customs duties between the member countries and all questions of tariffs, except that the parliament will have no legislative powers in this area; and, (iii) political questions concerning the future of the community and the movement towards African federations or confederations.

Attempts to obtain the explicit agreement of each member country to all the problems of integration, technical or political, must be avoided. A distinction must be made between problems which can only be solved amicably by consensus and those which can be resolved without the explicit agreement of each and every member country. For example, it is not necessary to obtain a consensus of all the member countries before starting a basic industrial project or deciding on the construction of a dam. Nor does the co-operation of the member countries concerning seed selection or the improvement of cattle breeds require unanimity among the member states. There is also need to strengthen the executive power of the communities by having in place decision-makers who have a vision of the future of the community. The chief executives must have an understanding of the problems of economic integration, and the conviction and determination to carry through the implementation of the integration projects.

The Need for a Policy of Realism: the Establishment of Co-production Enterprises

It would be difficult to stimulate the process of economic integration based only on the resources (financial, skilled work-force, etc.) of the African micro-states. Already, several economic integration groupings are stagnating because the majority of their members cannot provide the financial contributions necessary for the normal functioning of their secretariats, far less to finance the studies required for the setting up of certain large-scale projects. Also, given the largely open nature of African economies, the goods and services produced by the economic communities must be competitive both in terms of costs and quality in comparison with those of the industrialized countries.

All this explains the absolute necessity and urgency of creating co-production enterprises, in the form of African MNCs, linking state, institutions and private African individuals with partners from the North and South, notably the industrialized countries of Latin America and Asia, for the development of the priority economic sectors of the

African countries. Indeed, the use of capital from the North for the construction of dams, to ensure the navigability of rivers and lakes, coastal shipping, hydro-electric installations, etc., would enable African enterprises not only to exploit systematically the African natural resources, but also to facilitate the integration of state markets and increase the revenue of the African states. Under these conditions, it would be completely logical that the countries which helped the subregional economic communities to create an infrastructure suitable for the exploitation of their natural resources should also be the ones involved in the transformation of their raw materials. The strategy of economic domination by the former colonial powers, based on the export of intermediate and capital goods and the importation of raw materials from the colonies, would thus be fundamentally reversed.

With respect to North–South co-operation, a number of economic reasons should lead the subregional economic communities to establish co-operation agreements with other developing countries with a view to creating African co-production enterprises. In this regard, several oil-producing countries have accumulated large financial resources which exceed their absorptive capacity for investment. It may be in their interests to invest in the priority sectors of the African countries to ensure a constant flow of profits. Also, some industrialized countries of the Third World are endowed with real abilities in the field of export techniques to thwart the protectionist measures taken by several developed countries. Others have succeeded to a great extent in mastering certain areas of technology which the developed countries are reluctant to pass on because they wish to monopolize the production and commercialization of certain products. With the setting up of African co-production links with these southern partners, the African countries will be able to have access to a wider range of products necessary for the acceleration of their economic development.

Finally, some non-African countries of the South do not possess certain key industrial products. The Gulf states do not produce enough wood for their needs. The consumption of aluminium in most Asian countries exceeds local production. It would be advantageous for these countries to form agreements with the African countries for participation in the capitalization of African co-production enterprises, in order to satisfy their economies' needs for these key products. This kind of participation will enable the scale of production of the African multinationals to increase, and for their productivity to improve and the competitiveness of their products on the international market to be enhanced.

THE MOVEMENT TOWARDS THE CONTINENTAL ECONOMIC COMMUNITY

The effective establishment of the continental economic community between now and the year 2000 will depend on two important preconditions. First, the creation of the continental community must be perceived as an evolving phenomenon rather than as a *de facto* situation. This means that, as of now, there must be some strategic orientation of regional programmes on which the foundation of the community could henceforth be built. The implementation of these regional programmes should help to reinforce the process of subregional integration. Second, with the understanding that the real foundations of the continental community are the subregional economic communities, the consolidation of these subregional entities will provide the conditions for a solid continental structure. The creation of a continental economic community before the year 2000 requires that the subregional communities should be transformed into political federations, if not confederations, in order to give the necessary cohesion to the continental community.

The Main Themes of the Continental Community

The basic principles of economic integration as applied at the subregional level remain valid at the regional level: consolidation of regional economic cohesion, and the establishment of a regional production capacity. The regional programmes will come under two main headings:

(i) Consolidation of the cohesion of the regional economic area

The first project of intra-regional co-operation that is likely to strengthen regional economic cohesion would be the creation of a common African market for hydro-electricity. The potential for hydro-electric production on the African continent is close to 2,690 thousand million KWh and the technically exploitable potential would be 1,630 thousand million KWh per year, which is more than one third of the technically exploitable hydro-electric resources of the world (5,000 thousand million KWh per year).

The African hydro-electric potential is, however, not evenly distributed. The subregion of Central Africa alone has a potential of at least 744 thousand million KWh per year, i.e. approximately 46 per cent of the total potential of the continent, while North Africa has only 5 per cent, West Africa around 10 per cent, East Africa 22 per cent, and

Southern Africa around 17 per cent. Obviously, the hydro-electric potential of Central Africa is a major advantage for the rapid economic development of the continent.

The continental strategy for the development of hydro-electric power should be to bring Inga, the most powerful site in the world, up to its installed capacity of 40 million KW, and have it produce 300 thousand million KWh. The next step would be the inter-connection of Inga-Cameroon (installation at the Ogooue sites, 30 thousand million KWh) and Nigeria (Kainji – 800 MW, Sapele – 720 MW, Chiroro – 600 MW, and Jebba – 545 MW). This inter-connection is fundamental for Nigeria and the whole of West Africa because of this subregion's relatively meagre hydro-electric power potential. The second line of inter-connection from Inga, across the Shaba should reach the valley of the Zambezi, where there is a technically exploitable energy potential of 16,023 MW.

Next, the continuation of the inter-connection programme within PTA is a priority because of the hydro-electric potential of different countries of this subregion: Angola – 28,000 MW, Mozambique – 15,000 MW, Zambia – 12,000 MW, Tanzania – 9,500 MW, Zimbabwe – 3,800 MW, Kenya – 6,000 MW, and Ethiopia – 12,000 MW.

The second area of intra-regional co-operation is the expansion and implementation of the UN decade for Transport and Communications in Africa. This programme was conceived at the regional level and its implementation is effected at national and subregional levels. The regional planning of the transport and communications sectors must guarantee regional economic cohesion.

The problem of coastal shipping should be the subject of a regional project. The creation of a coastal shipping company serving the African coasts would be a strategic tool for the development of the continent, notably in terms of the transport of heavy goods: iron ore, bauxite, coal, pig iron, steel, copper, aluminium and its semi-products, food-stuffs such as maize, rice, millet, etc. The African satellite project is the second intra-regional co-operation project. Putting African satellites into orbit to facilitate communication between all the countries of the continent would, progressively, create an African awareness. It would break down the barriers between the subregions and contribute substantially to exchanges of all kinds: linguistic, commercial, cultural, etc.

(ii) The establishment of a regional production capacity

One area of intra-regional co-operation could be the identification and promotion of a number of development projects of continental importance in the development of essential sectors. For example, in the industrial field, it is conceivable to plan a restricted number of continental industrial enterprises involved in the production of rails, the construction of locomotives, the manufacture of trucks, rural transport equipment, etc. Similarly, research into advanced technology should be carried out on a regional scale: space research, medical research, etc.

The Development of Subregional Economic Communities towards the Constitution of a Continental Economic Community

The implementation of the projects proposed in the fields of transport and telecommunications, and hydro-electric installations in the sub-regions, as well as in the productivity sectors – industry and agriculture – will lead to initiating the economic integration process. Greater cohesion of the community area and the installation of electric facilities in the community will lead to the harmonious and balanced develop-ment of the member states. The distribution of development zones throughout the community and the creation of community production centres in each member country will intensify intra-community trade by increasing the efficiency of the structure of production in these countries. Movement of individuals within the community would consequently become an accepted fact by all the countries. A new community mentality will be born in the diverse African populations. This strategy of economic integration which enables countries that are not viable individually to attain rapid development will lead irresistibly to a political union. This political union will occur when the policy of economic integration has its initial success. First of all, the economic communities must prove that they are the real answer to the continuing crisis on the continent. Then, each country will understand the futility of national sovereignty and be ready to join with the other states for a better future.

The achievement of political unity should be carried out in stages. Initially, confederal states should be formed. African constitutionalists should devise the type of confederal state which corresponds best to the demands of African subregional development: consolidation of the physical integration of the subregional economic area and the setting up of a subregional production capacity. This confederal state will give less importance to international political questions which have little impact on the rapid development of the subregion. On the contrary, economic matters of common interest, concerning the consolidation of the internal integration of the state through the development of transport and communication and the installation of facilities within the confederal territory will receive priority. Certain large industrial projects will be declared community projects and their implementation brought under the control of the confederal institutions. Meanwhile, a strong confederal army will be established for the defence of confederal territory. At this stage, all the community integration groups within the confederal state will have to become technical organizations for the implementation of economic integration projects conforming to the master plans and the economic policies conceived by the confederal state. The confederal Assembly will be strengthened in the sense that it will be composed, on the one hand, of elected representatives of the confederate states, and, on the other hand, of representatives elected directly by the electorate of the states.

A confederal executive body from this Assembly will be set up to replace the general secretariat of the community. The confederate states could have different political orientations. The most important thing about their *raison d'être* is the control of priority natural resources within the subregions and their exploitation for the rapid development of the countries of the subregion and the well-being of the population of the confederal states.

The confederal state will concern itself with all important projects that are not within the sphere of the African micro-states. These areas of confederal state intervention concern initially the main infrastructures of community importance, and without which the growth of the small African states could not be accelerated. These include the construction of main confederal transport links, the exploitation of sites with the greatest hydro-electric potential, and industrial processing of strategic natural resources. The form of exploitation of these natural resources must allow for effective state control. A confederal monetary and banking system will also be set up.

The transformation of the confederal state into a federal state will be justified when there exists within the subregion a solid subregional infrastructure, a real subregional production capacity and the efficient movement of people and goods. The creation of the federal state will be expressed by a consolidation of legislative and executive powers and the strengthening of the federal institutions and services. It is superfluous at this stage to attempt to give a detailed description of the institutions and spheres of control of this federal State. What is essential is to note that a proper policy of economic integration will necessarily lead to a political union which should be progressively strengthened. Finally, it should be stressed that there can be no continental economic community unless the subregional economic communities form such a political union.

CONCLUDING REMARKS

Economic co-operation and integration remains a desirable and essential tool of collective self-sufficiency and self-reliance in Africa, as well as a critical strategy of continental long-term economic growth and development.

Existing subregional economic groupings and inter-governmental organizations for economic co-operation have often not yielded much economic benefits or produced significant results even in the area of intra-African trade expansion. They have put too much emphasis on market integration instead of production and development of physical infrastructure, and have allowed legitimate goals of strengthening national sovereignty to degenerate into national egoism which, in many cases, has proved detrimental to the development of community spirit. The proliferation of economic groupings and the lack of political commitment to co-operation and integration have brought to the fore the issue of sustainability as most co-operation arrangements have increasingly been confronted with financial difficulties, even at the level of routine day-to-day operations. All these shortcomings point in the direction of reform and rationalization of structures and functions of existing co-operation arrangements, and, above all, the need for a re-examination of strategy, involving the reinforcement of the market integration approach with the production approach that seeks to alter the structures of co-operating economies through greater focus on projects and programmes, and the operation of joint ventures and African multinationals. For, in the long term, structural change would seem to be a prerequisite for effective economic co-operation and integration in Africa. At the political level, there is need for African countries to renew their commitments to economic integration in more practical terms, and to ensure that there is greater co-ordination and less dissipation of integration and co-operation efforts at sub-regional levels. In this regard, non-governmental organizations should be made more concerned and involved with the integration process, and encouraged to incorporate the concept in their respective activities, while the international community need to pay greater attention to the problems of integration in Africa and to intensify their technical and financial support of African multinational projects and programmes.

The Long-Term Prospects of Co-operation Between Africa and the International Community

INTRODUCTORY NOTE

The overall position of Africa in the world economic system would seem to have become increasingly marginalized and much more peripheral since World War II. Africa's contribution to world production and global exchange decreased rather than increased in importance while its dependence on the world economic system has intensified. Viewed against this background, both the unique display in UN-PAAERD of a new understanding of Africa's development problems, and its implications for a new pattern of relationship between Africa and the international community should be welcomed. That the international community entered into a broad political commitment to assist Africa to achieve economic recovery, rehabilitation and reconstruction by taking appropriate collective international action to complement African domestic efforts was in itself a new and remarkable development in international economic solidarity.

Given the implicit 'New Deal' for Africa that is encompassed in UN-PAAERD, what are the long-term prospects for co-operation between Africa and the international community? In Chapter 33, Adedeji views the issues of debt, export earnings and resource flows as three inter-related ones which, unless addressed and tackled together within the framework of a concerted approach that offers a lasting solution to the debt problem, stabilizes export earnings and ensures increased resource flows commensurate with growth and development requirements of African countries, are likely to vitiate the process of recovery and development. The same view is more or less echoed in Chapter 35 by the Commonwealth Secretariat notwithstanding the noticeable differences of emphasis.

That there has as yet been little concrete evidence of the practical and whole-hearted support of the international community for the ongoing process of reforms in the African countries or ever likely to be what many would consider an adequate response, even in the near future, is the grim conclusion of Chapter 34 by Sewell and Gambino.

True enough, there have been certain positive measures and actions on the part of the international community since the adoption of UN-PAAERD, but these would seem to have been rather too little in relation to Africa's needs, and more than counterbalanced and out-weighed by the conjunctive persistence of certain negative forces and influences in the international arena.

The same pessimism about the prospects of international support for Africa's reform and development efforts underlines the analysis by Shaw and Carlsson in Chapter 32. Based on differing assumptions as to the emerging global political economy and the prospects of inter-national co-operation with Africa, Shaw and Carlsson project three alternative scenarios of African development as far as the rest of the century is concerned, ranging from the optimistic to the pessimistic. Their conclusion, it would seem, is that the current structural adjust-ment preoccupations of such international development and financial institutions as World Bank and IMF may turn out, in the end, to be necessary corrections on the path towards such indigenous directions as self-reliance and self-sustainment which have been and are still being advocated by ECA and OAU.

In Chapter 36, Tevoedjre reassesses the whole concept of co-operation between Africa and the rest of the word, viewing with cynicism and scepticism the existing structure and system of co-operation between Africa and the North. To avoid further dishar-monious development, increased absolute dependence and marginali-zation and exploitation of Africa, Tevoedjre calls for a rethinking and a new philosophical approach that will guarantee new and rewarding forms and strategies of co-operation between Africa and the rest of the world, the essential dynamics and elements of which will be solidarity in partnership, reciprocity of interests and associative dynamics anchored on extra-governmental forces, agents and actors in the local communities of the co-operating countries. Consequently, horizontal exchanges and dialogue within the South–South context are to be preferred to conventional pyramidal relations as the first steps of a new phase and framework of genuine co-operation structures.

CHAPTER THIRTY-TWO

Issues in and Prospects for Co-operation Between Africa and the International Community

TIMOTHY M. SHAW
JERKER CARLSSON

INTRODUCTION

... in spite of the unique expressions of international solidarity with Africa in 1986, there is as yet little evidence of concrete international measures in direct response to the commitment entered into in UN-PAAERD ...

One of the significant developments in Africa in 1986, on the positive side, is the transition from a uniformly disastrous situation to one that is distinctly marginally better, at least for some countries ... On the negative side, there was a slump in Africa's export trade in 1986, unprecedented perhaps since the Great Depression, resulting in a catastrophic drop in export values and an escalation in the deficits on the current account.

Adedeji's new year message, 1987[1]

One year after the minor achievement of a near 'consensus' at the UN Special Session on Africa's economic crisis,[2] the diplomatic horizon is becoming darkened with growing clouds of frustration. Notwithstanding the possibility that recipients and donors talked past each other last June in New York, the encouragement of false hopes induced by a range of conditionalities is about to generate disappointment and alienation among African regimes and peoples alike. Extra-continental concern has yielded, with the apparent dissipation of the drought, to both popular and official indifference. So, the proposed 'contract' between the continent's representatives and external agencies is more elusive than ever: conditionality has not yet led to enhanced support for African structural adjustment.[3] If the international community fails to meet its side of the tacit 'compact', then 'reform' is likely to flounder for lack of political and financial support: endangered domestic 'coalitions' require external encouragement.[4] Thus, twelve months after the diplomatic agreement of the Special Session, the position of the African continent in the new international division of labour remains as problematic as ever. Indeed, the continent's marginality and vulnerability is quite apparent and is unlikely to be moderated whether structural adjustment is efficacious or not.

However, whilst reform may not induce dramatic changes in Africa's economies, it may do so for its politics: harassed reformist coalitions need international recognitions as well as resources. In short, the tenuous consensus of mid-1986 is in danger of being disowned by African states as international resources seem to be unavailable in either the magnitude or the immediacy required. As protectionist pressures mount in the North, Africa's own liquidity crisis will intensify with profound implications for the viability of reform coalitions and the vitality of informal associations. If structural adjustment is not supported and sustained well before the end of the 1980's, then Africa may be forced to revert to its self-reliance as outlined in the first economic summit in Lagos at the beginning of the decade.[5]

The conjuncture of the mid-1970's of energy, currency and technology 'shocks' has yet to generate a definitive relationship between Africa and the world political economy. Nevertheless, as Adebayo Adedeji's mixed new year assessment for 1987 has indicated, Africa's place in the emerging international division of labour is hardly privileged or promising. Rather, the global periphery may become ever more marginal in a post-industrial period. Yet, not all African states are similarly situated, with profound implications for regional cohesion. And, as the continental condition evolves, so African studies as well as African policies are in a state of flux, with important implications for future *praxis*.[6]

This Chapter examines the present characteristics of the global and continental economies before projecting alternative scenarios: the optimistic, realist and pessimistic. In so doing, we are all too well aware that orthodox economics is in a state of disarray as current problems have proved to be resistant to monetarist and welfarist prescriptions alike. Nevertheless, the world economy of the 1990s is likely to differ significantly from that of the 1960s when Ghana, now 30 years old, symbolized Africa's reclamation of independence. Yet the incidence of the cycle of expansion and contraction will be uneven, both between and within states: some countries, companies and classes in Africa will be more adversely affected than others with important implications for *praxis* as well as for analysis and policy.

We adopt a dialectical perspective here in two ways. First, we treat diplomacy and security as functions of shifts in the international division of labour; i.e. issues in the UN, IMF/IBRD, Non-Aligned Movement, Commonwealth, GATT and ECA/OAU are functions of contradictions between and within Africa's political economies in their relations with the rest of the global community.[7] And second, as adversity is the parent of invention, we recognize the resistance and creativity of Africa's peoples; even if official reform and restructuring are neither sufficient nor sustainable, Africans retain resources of initiative and survival. The expansion of the informal sector is impossible to document and calculate with accuracy but at least the continent's statespeople and scholars should come to recognize and embrace rather than deny or repress it.

These two forms of dialectical response are neither mechanistic nor marxist but rather represent attempts to capture current realities and to inform emerging scenarios. We also come to suggest another emerging dialectic or sequence. The so-called consensus between World Bank and ECA, *Accelerated Development in sub-Saharan Africa* (known as Berg Report) and *LPA*[8] and their successors,[9] is, we believe, endangered and misplaced. Rather than seeking some elusive consensus among disparate and divergent positions we come to conclude that the conditions (not conditionalities!) of World Bank and IMF are likely to be met by the end of the 1980s so that Africa will be forced back upon its own meagre resources in the 1990s; i.e., *LPA* has not been displaced, it was just premature.

In short, any analysis of the continent's relations with the global community has to treat: (i) inequalities within and between Africa's varied political economies; and, (ii) dialectics between global economics and politics. The degree to which 'internal' economic pressures impact upon 'international' political discourse is apparent in the ongoing debate in UN/IBRD systems over Africa's debt. Notwithstanding the difficulties of precedent, conditionalities, environment and democracy, the current Secretary-General's 'Wass group' on 'financial flows' and the fifth 'Please Report' for World Bank both focus on debt: how to reduce the drain of financial resources out of the continent so that the redirection and reinvigoration of Africa's economies and polities can proceed. Unless substantial real resources are provided for the continent before the end of the decade, any prospects of effecting and sustaining structural adjustment over the medium term will be lost. The real economic as opposed to ecological crisis has only just begun:

can the world community support Africa's recovery until at least the end of the century? Because of Africa's marginal position in the global political economy, we are sceptical except, perhaps, for a few countries, classes, corporations and coalitions.

INTERNATIONAL ECONOMY IN THE MID-1980s

The global political economy which is emerging for the final decade of the twentieth century is quite different from that which was designed and established after the Second World War. The major features of this post-Bretton Woods situation which have profound implications for Africa's development possibilities in the 1990s compared with, say, the 1960s, include the following:

(i)   growth will be uncertain and sporadic;
(ii)   growth will be unevenly distributed between and within countries;
(iii)   technological change will dramatically impact upon the demand for and price of raw materials from Africa;
(iv)   foreign exchange sales will continue to fluctuate and external debt will accumulate;
(v)   foreign assistance will increase slowly but its terms will become more interventive: human needs and rights, environment and gender, etc.;
(vi)   foreign investment will decline in total and change in content: from direct to portfolio;
(vii)   the Pacific Rim will replace the North Atlantic as the primary centre for innovation, accumulation and exchange; and,
(viii) protectionism as well as strategic tension in the North will undermine North–South exchanges and expectations.

In short, the benign and optimistic era of expansion in the post-independence period has long since gone and may never return; hence the centrality of GATT's current Uruguay Round which may include services as well as manufactures. The decade of the 1990s – post-neocolonialism? – is unlikely to be either as benign or as optimistic. Rather, it will pose a series of challenges for the periphery, which will be compelled to rethink its development assumptions and directions: more or less self-reliance? more or less privatisation? more or less stability? The current discussions and uncertainties within IMF/IBRD, GATT/UNCTAD and South Commission are just the beginning of the new international division of labour.

The post-Bretton Woods order poses profound problems for both analysis and *praxis* everywhere but especially in the Third and Fourth Worlds. Despite the pretensions and intentions of IMF and World Bank, it is not yet clear whether they can recapture the degree of economic order and growth realized, in a very different economic and strategic context, in the 1960s. Thus, the African states have now to plan in an environment of considerable uncertainty and volatility. The unsteady context became most apparent as droughts and conflicts increased the prospect of famine over the last decade. Both before and after the second Sahel drought, the continent had already begun to identify new constraints and possibilities: from *LPA* to *APPER*.

Yet these and other official, ideological declarations constitute only one part of an emerging redirection. For just as the new international division of labour has resulted in changed expectations and relations among and within the advanced industrialized states, so it has caused dramatic shifts in the Third World, notably the rise of informal sectors, including smuggling and black marketeering; i.e. post-colonial has yielded to non-colonial states or even non-states. The official re-evaluation and unofficial redirection have not always been entirely compatible – *de jure* or *de facto* privatization and subnational or regional integration? – but together they mark a turning-point in the African condition: from post-colonial to post-neocolonial periods.

Thus the major imponderable, with some significance for policy options, is the balance in Africa's difficulties between pre-crisis mismanagement and intra-crisis problems: i.e. the degree to which crisis management or structural adjustment, on the one hand, and fundamental change in political economy, on the other, will produce results. Probably, the balance between inherited institutions and crisis issues varies between states. Certainly, the degree to which current antidotes are applied successfully will vary depending on causality. Likewise, the degree to which they will be supported or tolerated by domestic constituencies differs between states.

Several of the features apparent in the new division of labour are interrelated: free and fluctuating exchange rates along with indigenization and nationalization have encouraged portfolio rather than direct foreign investment; unstable and increasing costs of petroleum encouraged alternative sources of fuels to oil and gas; new technologies lead to an expanding global services sector and a decreasing salience of colonial-type commodities. Hence, the problematique of policy redirection: to treat short-term crisis or long-term conjuncture?

In most factors identified as central to the new division of labour, Africa tends to be the least favoured or involved continent: in terms of debt, industry, services, technology, etc., Africa trails Asia and Latin America. But some of Africa – e.g. Algeria, Cote d'Ivoire, Kenya, Zimbabwe – are more engaged in such divisions than others, although the beneficiaries within even these states are few and the costs high. Thus, the post-Bretton Woods order is more inequitable at global, continental and national levels, with profound implications for African viability and stability, as we will see.

As Africa marked the centenary of the Treaty of Berlin and ECA its silver jubilee, EEC was 30 and OECD turned 25. Yet the latter's Secretary-General, Jean-Claude Paye, exhibited regret and apprehension at the demise of Bretton Woods, recognizing that interdependence generates uncertainty unless it is structured. He pointed to the imperative of 'reconciling solidarity and vulnerability'[11] so that no future shock can disrupt the overall situation. But managing such complexity is problematic despite advances in communication and information.

It is already axiomatic that economic trilaterality (i.e. US, EEC and Japan) has been superseded by multipolarity, with the NICs eroding the status and distance of the already industrialized: the conundrum of 'graduation'. Yet, despite the promise of South–South exchange, much of the South still concentrates on the old North rather than the new frontiers of capitalism concentrated around the Pacific Rim: time-warp of the nationalist generation. And nuclear bipolarity has not yet yielded to wholesale proliferation despite tendencies in that direction. Interdependence has yet to transcend established North–South interregional lines by facilitating Africa's relations with Asia's NICs.

Multilateralism is under threat if not suspension everywhere as trade wars and protectionism lead to bilateral stances. Of all the continents, Africa with its 50 states benefits most from multilateral contexts and loses most from bilateral contests. Any attempt to restore multilateralism should be based on Africa's needs – e.g. NICs graduation into OECD if they invest in the continent? – and on Japan's recognition – the world's pre-eminent financial centre is now Tokyo rather than London or New York.

Despite the unanticipated windfall – for most of Africa as well as of the world – of a dramatic decline in energy prices in the mid-1980s, the recovery in the North has been slow: persistent unemployment despite reduced inflation and increased indebtedness despite currency fluctuations. Ronald Reagan's rearmament binge has not financed a global recovery; rather, it has produced a massive US debt in just a couple of years, leading to excessive imports from Japan and the Pacific Rim, initially of goods, now of investment. The long-term response to US vulnerability is not currency realignment but a fundamental shift in patterns of production: US and other Western investment in Japan, Taiwan and South Korea plus Pacific investment in the US and EEC. Despite the protectionist rhetoric, the long-term trend is towards increased inter-OECD investment rather than exchange: trilateralism lives! If the US debt was controlled or Pacific Rim investment diverted in favour of Africa, then a new contract for the continent might be prepared; the draft agreed in New York a year ago is presently in danger of being honoured more in the breach, in part because it lacked an institutional expression.

The marginal gains secured by the OECD in the wake of OPEC have not spilt over to advance the South. Instead, as noted below, South–South relations have become more problematic as their centrepieces – OPEC oil and NICs, industrial exports in exchange for labour and commodity imports – have contracted. When combined with declines in foreign assistance and investment, except on specific, structural or portfolio terms, respectively, the 1980s have been anything but auspicious for the South. As the 1986 *OECD Economic Outlook* indicates, by contrast to more optimistic IBRD positions, even after a decade of marginal or negative growth:

> The main counterpart to the OECD's terms-of-trade gain has been a loss to the *developing countries* equivalent to as much as 3 per cent of their combined GNP. Faced with this development, as well as reduced access to financing from private sources, many developing countries cut back their imports sharply over the past year – at a time when some of them had not fully digested earlier import reduction. The OECD projects that import compression will continue in many of these countries, albeit at a slower pace, over the year to come, even if their terms of trade do not change significantly, because a pick-up of capital flows to most of these countries appears unlikely.[12]

The euphemism of 'import compression' can be translated, of course, as increased infant mortality and malnutrition in the Third World and decreases in life expectancy and basic needs satisfaction. The new rhetoric of 'adjustment with a human face' or 'growth for basic human needs' merely disguises palpable declines in POLI scores, which are likely to be exponential rather than transitional.

Thus, Gerald Helleiner is quite right to be pessimistic, asserting that IBRD's structures may be insufficiently cautious: 'sober as the World Bank's 1986 report is, it nevertheless significantly *understates* the degree of Africa's problems'.[13] He warns, in particular, that:

The most immediate constraints upon improved sub-Saharan African economic performance are undoubtedly foreign exchange and the difficult international economic environment. There is plenty of room for policy improvement in many countries, but even the best performers in Africa are at present struggling with acute foreign exchange constraints. Unfortunately, the international prospects are not bright ... no knowledgeable observers now predict any recovery in real agricultural or metals prices over the remainder of the 1980s.[14]

However, while Helleiner warns that the real crisis now is 'institutional desertification' in which African regimes reveal uncertain capacity 'to right themselves and their economies, to redress the enormous losses already suffered and to resume orderly progress',[15] he fails to recognize the range of innovative informal adaptations at subnational levels: regional, peasant, female and technological adaptations; and the dialectic of African political economies despite (or because of?) the vacillation of incumbent governments.

The remaining commodity sector can be characterized as a particular form of 'casino capitalism' as the long-term trend is towards a secular decline in relation to manufactures (as well as to debt and services); i.e. a transfer from South to North. Yet a few countries, classes and commodities may enjoy short-term windfalls in, say, oil (Middle East war), coffee (frost in Brazil), or gold (currency instability). But such bonanzas do not compensate for overall long-term trends; they merely camouflage them. Compensating schemes like the Integrated Programme for Commodities of UNCTAD or the Compensatory Financing Facility of the IMF are moribund already, although EEC's Stabex scheme has been helpful if insufficient. And because of extreme dependence on one commodity in a few cases, the foreign exchange and debt implications have been quite devastating:

> Commodity prices in real (purchasing power) terms are now at their lowest levels since the 1930s; overall, they also failed to rise significantly with the sharp upturn in world economic activity during 1985–1986. By mid-1986 the overall average was (in nominal terms) a quarter below that of 1980 ... Between 1980 and 1985, the dollar value of merchandise exports from Zambia fell in every year ... Between 1970 and 1984 the ratio of debt-service repayments to total export receipts deteriorated five to nine-fold in Jamaica, Kenya, Mauritius, Nigeria, Uganda and Zimbabwe.[16]

Although by global standards Africa's debt is modest – still less than

US$300 billion – the development implications of escalating payments are considerable: over 35 per cent of regional GNP and 25 per cent of exports. *APPER* drew attention to some of the causes and consequences:

> We are fully aware of the fact that shortcomings in development policies have contributed to the present debt crisis. However, it is evident that the major causes of our countries' debt-servicing problems are external ... These include, *inter alia*, the deteriorating terms of trade ... unprecedented rise in interest rates, sharp exchange rate fluctuations, deteriorating terms of borrowing and the reduction in the flow on concessional resources, the combined effects of which result in net capital outflow for most of our member States. In this regard, the 26 African LDCs have been the most seriously affected.[17]

Africa's debt may be modest *in toto* but it has grown faster than that of other regions and is more official than private; hence the centrality of the Paris rather than the London Club negotiations and the roles of World Bank and IMF. Africa's regular and repeated negotiations and reschedulings have not (yet?) meant recovery. They have, however, become a national and bureaucratic preoccupation, especially for states in decline. As Tom Callaghy notes, 'An important psychological side effect of these foreign economic relations is that scarce talent is constantly preoccupied by negotiations with external actors about adjustment issues, while attempting to implement previous agreements.'[18]

Despite the centrality and symbolism of the debt, however, Callaghy cautions that no dramatic developments are likely on either side. Rather:

> Modest expectations are in order on both sides. African states cannot expect any major beneficial structural or procedural reforms in the international political economy on the part of their Western creditors. Likewise, the latter cannot expect any significant restructuring of African regimes and economies or substantial improvement in their economic and debt performance. Western actors clearly determine most of the rules of the game, shaping the parameters of action, but African regimes do have some autonomy and room for maneuver.[19]

Although Africa's debt remains small by global standards, it has 'grown faster than that of any other region': up 20 to 25 per cent in the 1970s. Its ability to manage this debt may be equally modest – initially many African states had little idea of how much they owed – and as the state has shrunk, so its ability to repay has also contracted. Belatedly, World Bank seems to be appreciative of the centrality of debt as well as of exchange rates, so its next Africa Report due in early 1988 will focus on it and on regionalism, another overlooked dimension. Likewise, the UN Secretary-General is finally establishing a group of eminent persons on debt – the Wass Committee – which will no doubt also animate the South Commission on its establishment. Africa's debt has not yet been discounted as a major feature of the new debt market,[21] presumably because it is too small and 'official', but South Africa's massive private debt might yet be so traded.

African debt, like that of other regions, is not, of course, uncontroversial in origin. Be that as it may, one possible means for the continent to reverse the capital flow, other than major incentives and ready convertibility, is to lay claim to Africans' overseas investments, which are not inconsiderable. Even if only a proportion of these were available as collateral then the debt crisis would be eased; and reverse flows would help shore-up lagging exchange rates. 'Third World communities' within the North have potential not only as policy pressures and foreign exchange suppliers but also as guarantors of future investments. Without such external interest, and in the absence of a developed national bourgeoisie[22] in most countries, privatisation is likely to remain merely an aspiration: there is insufficient internal saving to permit private purchases except at bargain-basement prices.

Foreign capital flows to Africa, which were never massive contrary to dependency assertions, have declined for a series of reasons. First, 'aid fatigue' in the North (let alone in the East and OPEC, two sets of rather mercurial donors) has led to reduced and conditional aid for purposes of emergencies, allies and structural adjustment only. Second, declarations of indigenization and nationalization made investors apprehensive, especially when alternative opportunities existed. Third, the new international division of labour has reduced demand for African minerals and markets, both of which lost their attractiveness. Fourth, and finally, partly in response to Third World nationalism, MNCs began to unpackage their investment. New patterns of foreign direct investment include sets of contractual arrangements for licensing, management, turnkey, subcontracting, leasing or franchising contracts. Such packages attempt to minimize risks and foreign exchange costs, and often involve MNCs from EEC or NICs. These open up a range of possibilities which may now become more commonplace in a period of privatization. Such new forms of unbundled packages offer the potential of enhanced host country control depending on certain conditions, notably 'the relative bargaining strength of host country elites *vis-à-vis* their international counterparts':

> This, in turn, depends on such factors as the size and dynamism of the local market, the state of local technological, managerial and entrepreneurial capacity, and the dynamics of global inter-firm competition.[23]

Of course, Africa tends to lack these characteristics through which to attract and regulate external interests and investments. The continent's marginality is most apparent, then, in its inability to secure sufficient internal financial support even in a period of visibility.

Even the IMF's Group of 24 recognizes that liquidity is elusive despite strenuous efforts at adjustment, calling for the use of SDRs as incentives:

> ... even when developing countries have pursued strong adjustment policies – as evidenced by the decline in their current account deficits – this has been insufficient to secure them bank credit or access to commercial markets.
>
> The liquidity needs of many developing countries could be met in the present circumstances, however, if there were an allocation of SDRs.[24]

Hopefully, the Wass and Please Reports will echo the imperative of greatly increased resource flows if structural adjustment is to be sustained let alone successful. Without them, most of the continent's countries and states will be forced back once more onto their own devices, as indicated in our concluding scenarios.

AFRICA AND THE SOUTH

As indicated already, one principal structural feature of the Second United Nations Development Decade was the changing organization of world production. Already, by the early 1970s, international production had surpassed international trade as a vehicle for international economic exchange; i.e., the combined production of all MNCs abroad is now greater than the total value of goods and services that enter into trade between countries.

This international process has interacted with two other phenomena. First, the internationalization of production has tended to run parallel with the process of economic differentiation in the South. The minority of rapidly growing countries in the South are those that have been most clearly integrated into this emerging international network of production relations. And, second, the petro-dollar-fuelled expansion of international capital markets during the late 1970s and early 1980s contributed to an increased involvement by international finance capital with multinational-controlled/owned productive enterprises, often in an alliance with the peripheral state.[25] The new tripartite collaboration, between international finance capital, MNCs and the state in the South, articulates international relations of production which are wholly consistent with escalating costs and risks characteristic of present-day raw-material explorations and industrial ventures.

The new-found wealth of the petroleum exporters and the rather sophisticated production structures of the NICs meant profound changes in the established structure of the South. Developing countries outside this group, by contrast, are still largely dependent on agriculture while more than two decades of 'development' have left them poorer than they were before. A classification of countries, along the lines of the present structure of the world economy, would yield the following categories:

A – Large, in terms of geographic size, population and economy, industrialized countries;

B – Small industrialized countries;

C – Newly Industrializing Countries;

D – Developing countries with a traditional peripheral structure, but possessing raw materials of strategic value; for example, petroleum;

E – Developing countries with a traditional peripheral economic structure, usually based on agriculture or non-strategic minerals; and,

F – The least developed countries, whose economies are heavily dependent on resource flows (aid and loans not private capital) from the industrialized world.

Categories A and B comprise what is commonly referred to as the North. Category C – the NICs – consists of countries that have clearly moved out of the South and have ambitions to advance to industrialized status, thus placing themselves in one of the first two categories.

The pattern of global industrialization, particularly in the last decade, has been responsible for a great divergence in economic performance within the South. The Latin American diversifying economies and the export-led South-East Asian economies, together constitute the NICs. According to OECD, there are ten in this group, none of them in Africa: Brazil, Greece, Hong Kong, Mexico, Portugal,

Singapore, South Korea, Spain, Taiwan and Yugoslavia. A definition of the common characteristics of the NICs would refer to: (i) rapid penetration of the world market for manufactures, (ii) rising share of industrial employment, and, (iii) increase in real GDP per capita relative to the more advanced industrial countries.[26]

What structural developments characterize these NICs? Their pattern of development generally involves a heavy reliance on imported capital-intensive techniques and a neglect of food production. The problem of the marginalization of a large number of urban and rural poor from economic life is then said to be the result. Other studies indicate that there is no firm evidence for the view that high growth rates inevitably generate greater inequality, though there is some evidence that income inequality first increases and then decreases with development (the Kuznet's curve).

The last three categories, D–F, constitute the traditional developing countries, where economies are still based on a 'neo-colonial' production pattern; i.e., export of primaries and import-substitution based industries. All African countries are found within this group, although most of them belong to categories E and F.

The related hierarchization of the South[27] has thus created countries with more or less permanent stagnation tendencies, as well as countries with structural characteristics which increasingly resemble the North and with favourable (although not very high) growth rates. The growth performance of countries within the Fourth World, or the categories D–F, has deteriorated in both relative and absolute terms when compared with that of the more advanced countries in category C. Needless to say, most African countries share this experience of stagnation or decline.

In conclusion, then, judging by measures of economic production and trade performance, there has been apparent economic differentiation in the South into, on the one hand, economies experiencing growth and structural change and, on the other hand, stagnant, or even declining economies, with traditional peripheral structural characteristics; and this economic differentiation is associated with the degree and type of integration of such countries into the capitalist world economy. An analysis of Africa's relations – diplomatic and strategic as well as economic – with the international community must take new world structure into account, as the type of category predetermines the character of foreign policy and external relations.[28]

Political developments in the South do not always follow economic realities directly; however, there is usually a time-lag at the political level, namely the formation of appropriate organizations and actions.

The achievement of South solidarity is a case in point. Thus, in contrast to the diverging economic situations experienced by the countries of the South, they managed to forge a greater political unity than ever before during the early 1970s through various institutional venues; e.g. the Group of 77 and the Non-Aligned Movement. The success of South leaders in presenting a united front manifested itself for the first time in the formulation of the demand for a NIEO in 1974, when economic divergence was already apparent.

The theme of collective self-reliance, central to the NIEO, contains the crucial element of economic co-operation. This has two aspects: first, the notion of co-operation for enhancing the developing countries, collective bargaining power *vis-à-vis* the outside world and, second, the notion of intensifying trade and other linkages. However, the imperative of collective self-reliance also reveals the Achilles heel of the NIEO ideology. It is an ideology uneasily balanced upon contradictory principles: greater interdependence between rich and poor worlds and independence from the former by the latter; i.e., better links with the rich world as well as delinking from it.

Following the NIEO debate, a new element came to be included in the Northern strategy: internal reform and redistribution in the South. Redistribution of resources between the countries of the South (at the time, particularly a transfer of wealth from the oil-exporting to the oil-importing developing countries); and domestic redistribution within them. There was a link between international redistribution and internal reform. Without the latter, the former would not have any effect on the economic development of the poorest countries or peoples of the South. The Brandt Report formulated this in terms of concessions for international redistribution being made conditional upon internationally-recognized measures of internal reform.

The need for internal reform has already been recognized by radical Third World spokespersons. However, they have made the central point compatible with dependency logic, that the unequal pattern of income distribution inside the South has been generated by these countries' manner of insertion into the total world economy, and that this in turn presents bottlenecks for further South economic development. The 'basic needs' approach was the logical outcome of this new orientation in the Northern strategy. The conditionality associated with this approach was attacked by the Group of 77 who called it diversionary and unacceptably intrusive.

After 1975, the emerging facts of economic divergence among South countries made it difficult to translate general NIEO demands into specific policies, and to maintain unity at any level other than rhetoric.

On the part of the North, it readily seized upon the opportunities to contribute to an increased hierarchization of the South, with accompanying differences in political goals. The North came to propagate the new perspective of global management for an 'interdependent' world. This perspective was designated to forge and legitimize closer links between international business and global institutions, on the one hand, and repressive regimes of fast-growing developing countries, on the other. Within this perspective, the twin problems of global inequality and poverty were redefined as problems arising not so much from international economic relations as from domestic social injustice and lack of internal reforms. Hence the new emphasis on 'human rights' and 'democratic development'.

Characteristic of the dialectic between economic change and political debate has been the recent formation of two new South organizations. First, in an attempt to contain the impact of divergencies at the level of political economy, the Non-Aligned Movement approved the creation of the 'South Commission' at its 1986 summit in Harare: an important development in the encouragement and articulation of a distinctive Southern perspective on global issues, symbolizing intellectual and political autonomy. And, second, under Nigeria's sponsorship, a group of 'like-minded' or 'like-positioned' NICs have formed a 'Concert of Medium Powers': Newly *Influential* Countries. These 16 intermediate states are concerned to revive multilateralism and encourage international development and peace by serving as a bridge between North and South: a diplomatic and strategic aspect of 'graduation'.

Significant differences in the approaches of national governments of the North and of international financial institutions like IBRD, IMF and OECD need to be noted. The latter appreciate the importance of balanced economic development among all the regions of the world. Consequently, they advocate structural changes in international economic relations, superficially much along the lines demanded by the South in NIEO. By contrast, the former do not employ such a long-term global perspective as they are more concerned with immediate short-term measures. Beneath this surface alignment between the South's contemporary ideology and 'globalist' capitalist ideology there exists an important difference, however. Whereas the South aims towards national economic independence, the globalist concept of a world economic system aims at supra-nationalism; i.e., national versus international capitalisms.

The distinctive thing about this globalist approach has been its increasing mix with international assistance programmes. One concrete manifestation of this has been the basic needs approach. Measures for the international redistribution of wealth have been made conditional upon the implementation of redistributive policies within the South. This aspect of the 'basic needs' approach strikes at the heart of the economic sovereignty of South nations. It marks the first step towards an international social policy designed to complement the global management of an increasingly internationalized system of world production: Keynesianism for the twenty-first century?

The great divide between the Third World countries is between, on the one hand, those countries which have either the resources (oil, or non-fuel, scarce minerals) or the industrializing markets that permit continued participation in contemporary world economic exchanges, and, on the other hand, those countries which have not. During the last ten years a considerable expansion has taken place in the exchange between the NICs and the rest of the South. The initiative has usually come from the NICs themselves as the objective needs of their economic structures have required a rather determined strategy for developing alternative markets to the North.

The economic relations that have developed under the guise of 'South–South' are markedly 'neo-colonial' in character, where Africa performs its traditional role as a supplier of primary goods and as a market for industrial products.[29] In certain cases, e.g. India–East Africa relations, technical assistance programmes have also been involved. In other cases, e.g. Brazil–Nigeria relations, strict trade arrangements predominate. It has been argued that this South–South exchange possesses certain qualitative aspects which differentiate it from traditional North–South patterns. For example, it has been claimed that the terms of trade would be 'fairer' to the South, compared with traditional North–South exchange, and that technologies and goods would be more appropriate to the needs of South markets. Yet little quantitative evidence is available in support of the first argument, and there are indications that the terms of trade are not substantially more beneficial to the weaker partner in this type of South–South exchange. However, it may very well be that we are dealing with more suitable forms of industrial technology (paradoxically enough, usually produced by Northern companies from their new locations in the South).

More importantly, though, these relations cannot be said to contain any better prospects for structural change in the traditional peripheral structure of African economies than would traditional North–South exchange. Rather, we would argue, the main advantage to Africa from dealing with the NICs is that such relations create new outlets for its products; possibilities for developing alternative trade arrangements and access to alternative sources of technological know-how. Thereby, Africa would probably also gain from a better bargaining position *vis-à-vis* the North, a subject for the South Commission.

The dynamic element in a C–D–F relation lies, therefore, to a considerable extent in the role of growth-pull performed by the C-countries, the NICs. Their growth dynamics can, through South–South relations, be transferred to participating African countries, admittedly without significant structural development effects, at least not in the short to medium term: a revisionist form of NIEO.

Recent developments in the world economy have made it clear, however, that the South has increased its importance for the North as well as NICs as a market for exports of manufactures and especially of engineering products, for which traditional outlets in the industrial countries are declining.

The petro-dollar period meant excess capital available to international financial markets, albeit for a limited term. However, the low-income countries have found it increasingly difficult to obtain general-purpose loans from these private capital markets. This is the reason why it is increasingly being urged that official lending should discriminate in favour of the low-income countries, who lack both private investment and private debt; i.e. the imperative of sufficient liquidity for Africa as it presently exports rather than imports international capital.[30]

AFRICA

Although we are primarily concerned here with Africa's external economic relations and their diplomatic repercussions, these cannot be separated from changes within the continent's political economy, especially at regional, national and sub-national levels. Obviously, the imperative of reform and restructuring lies in the failure of previous development policies and contexts. But the incidence and impact of stagnation or contraction are uneven in Africa as elsewhere: some states and peoples have endured more than others. Likewise, the costs and benefits of reform and devaluation are uneven. Therefore, support for adjustment – the identification and manipulation of majority coalitions – is problematic. Moreover, given the contractions in living standards already suffered by most Africans – declines in incomes, services, basic human needs and expectations – scepticism is a natural response to dramatic devaluations and privatizations.[31] Finally, if the current direction is not vindicated in the early 1990s then alienation is likely to be widespread, with profound social, political and strategic implications.

African economies remain, despite considerable post-independence efforts, largely agricultural in concentration and external in orientation, characteristics which World Bank and IMF seek to foster rather than transcend. And the rest of the world economy is increasingly preoccupied with its own persistence and expansion. The coincidence of externally-oriented reforms with international protectionism is hardly auspicious unless Africa can produce new products which can find new market niches, along the lines of successful manufacturers and commodity exporters from the NICs to Cote d'Ivoire. And it remains quite unlikely that all 50 states could adjust successfully simultaneously given commonalities among their products and positions: the 'fallacy of composition' argument.[32] Moreover, the mutual impacts of reforms and protectionism on continental exchange are important, if neglected, elements in any African revival: will reoriented production reduce intra- and inter-African exchange even further?

The juxtaposition of international and continental trends does not, at first sight, appear to be promising: global protectionism induced by low levels of growth and continental recession caused by underdevelopment, underfinancing and drought. The orthodox projection from such an inauspicious conjuncture would surely be limited prospects for African development, because of Northern preoccupations and lack of interest: OECD isolationism based on new technologies and relationships.

However, three alternative scenarios can be identified for Africa based on apparent trends and interests, as indicated in our final section. First, the World Bank's 'optimistic' preference of 'reform' based on new coalitions and resources may be realised, at least in some selected African states: Northern re-engagement. Second, OAU/ECA official and 'realistic' definition of self-reliance may be approached given the Northern retreat: continental, regional and national self-reliance centred around a group of core African states. Third, and finally, an unofficial and somewhat pessimistic conception of development may triumph: the decline if not demise of the state in Africa accompanied by a set of alternative structures – informal economies based on exchange, credit, women and adaptive, especially agricultural, technologies in which rival systems flourish, often across national borders, so exacerbating the shrinking of the post-colonial state.

Clearly, these three alternatives to any NIEO or even Lome IV are unlikely to be effected easily. Rather, some mix of them is likely between and within states. As indicated in the earlier discussion, some countries, classes and companies identify more readily with World Bank or South Commission perspectives. Likewise, some interests encourage reform coalitions; others official self-reliance; and yet others advocate informal survival strategies. These may co-exist for a while, as had occurred in Africa in the 1980s, and official strategies may indeed attempt to incorporate the unofficial; but whether they can be rendered compatible over the medium term is another question. Nevertheless, we would suggest that, given inadequate financial and political resources, no single solution is possible. How, then, to minimise friction or tension between these three alternative propositions?

This section projects possible future directions in Africa's relations with other countries in the South (excluding the so-called NICs) on the basis of the experience gained so far with respect to established political and economic relations. Few new insights or strategies will be provided as the future seems to carry very little potential in this regard. We shall merely extrapolate from recent trends and stress factors that are seen to be key variables for developing these relations to contribute something of substance to the continent's development. Let us immediately clarify that this type of relation on the part of Africa largely concerns relations within the continent itself. Relationships with D–F countries outside Africa have been, and will continue to be, rather insignificant, the rhetoric of Third Worldism notwithstanding.

It should also be stressed that the immediate potential for economic relations among D–F countries is relatively small. The expansion of intensive economic linkages requires a common political effort to achieve economic development before enhanced natural pre-conditions for exchange will exist. This is related to the need for economic diversification and the resulting higher degree of complementarity among the economies due to differences in structural characteristics. This is the primary reason why economic exchange between C countries, on the one hand, and D–F countries, on the other, has expanded during the recent decades.

The history of Africa's South relations in the post-war period shows that the contemporary international division of labour has provided few opportunities for South–South exchange to develop. Africa was integrated into the world economy along classical North–South lines. Very little with respect to joint South political initiatives was undertaken, except for the formation of large ostensibly supra-national bodies, like OAU and ECA, which have had, as it turned out, little impact on strategy and policy formulation on national levels, even after the articulation of collective strategies from 1980 onwards. Economic flows between Africa and other countries in the South were virtually non-existent, and intra-African relations were not much greater, except in the special case of Southern Africa. In more recent times, largely from the 1970s onwards, the character of these relationships did begin to change to a certain extent. Not that Africa started to increase contacts with non-NICs in other continents, but rather that important attempts were made towards improving as well as creating new forms of intra-African contacts on the political as well as economic levels. In particular, the formation of different regional organizations was seen, like ECOWAS and PTA, as containing rather ambitious goals beyond loose political alliances and development arrangements, such as SADCC. Naturally, the emergence of such organisations must be seen as important milestones in the integration of Africa, although their sustainable impact remains in question.

So, notwithstanding these important achievements, it is equally clear that very little in terms of concrete practical gains has yet resulted. Economic flows among African countries are, at best, at a modest level, in spite of a continuing series of attempts to facilitate them through an increasingly diverse set of trade agreements. In political terms, these organisations have served an important role as fora for diplomatic and strategic issues of common interest to the region. However, little in the form of concrete action has resulted, except of course with regard to the questions of South Africa and Namibia.

Concerted action within the framework of subregional groupings started at independence, around 1960, after the break-up of colonial and settler arrangements. The main objective of such groupings was the creation of complementary economic structures, which would bring about the integration of subregions and raise the levels of income and employment in partner countries. The emphasis was originally on the reduction of barriers to intra-group trade which, however, was found to favour the more advanced countries and proved to be ineffective as a major instrument of integration. Increasing use has therefore been made of other instruments, particularly various forms of co-operation in respect to infrastructure, investment and production.

The history of African groupings in the 1960s and 1970s reflects this general evolution. However, a new departure was made in 1980 – based on the legacies and limitations of the previous two decades – LPA – providing a distinctive framework for national and collective self-reliant policies designed to bring about the integration of major African subregions through self-reliance and self-sustainment. World economic changes since 1980 have strengthened the case for self-reliant policies, but have also compounded the problems of giving effect to LPA. The coincidence of global and continental economic and environmental crises has forced African countries to concentrate simply on keeping their economies going through different stop-gap measures. It has rather effectively prevented the formulation and implementation of long-term collective strategic goals along the lines of LPA, although, as we suggest below, the intensity of the crisis may yet necessitate return to and revival of LPA.

The emphasis of LPA is on planned public action. Its fundamental principle is that of self-reliance, national and collective, which is translated into the following policy objectives: (a) Satisfaction of basic needs; (b) Creation of productive employment; (c) Strengthening of technological and management capabilities; (d) Ensuring African control over natural resources; and, (e) Bringing about self-sustained development, which in turn is based on the attainment of self-sufficiency in food. The ultimate goal of LPA is an African Common Market and, later, an African Economic Community by the next century.

In spite of the difficulties and diversions, a lot of preparatory work has been undertaken and progress has been realized in respect of the establishment of major subregional groupings, whose principles and objectives are broadly consistent with LPA, ECOWAS (1975), PTA (1981), CEEAC (1983), and SADCC (1980). Taken together, these groupings account for roughly 40 out of the 44 independent sub-Saharan African states, some of whom belong to more than one organisation.[33]

SADCC possesses certain features that distinguish it from other similar groupings. This is so not only because of its extensive programme, but also because of its institutional set-up in which (i) sectoral activities are decentralised, i.e. programme formulation and co-ordination are assigned to individual member states; (ii) ministerial committees are established for major areas of on-going activities; (iii) proposals for action are put forward by governments and inter-governmental bodies only; and, (iv) the central secretariat is small. These particular features of SADCC arrangements reflect the objectives of ensuring government involvement, initiative and control by higher political authorities. This, along with sustained extra-regional interest and support, is most probably one major cause as to why SADCC has performed remarkably well in terms of tangible results. Few, if any, of the more traditional groupings can display an equivalent record. A contributing factor to this success story is, of course, the rather substantial inflow of resources from donor countries, one that is closely linked to the South African issue, which is a particular feature of SADCC programme: reduced dependence on the apartheid economy.[34]

Industrial development is considered to be the main vehicle of integration, necessarily associated with increased trade among partner countries, and LPA emphasized the establishment of core industries producing intermediate and capital goods. A high priority is attached to the establishment of multinational enterprises, but not MNCs. These require efficient operational planning by governments within the framework of subregional and regional plans. Industrial co-operation was given a further boost through the formulation of the Programme for the Industrial Development Decade for Africa (1980s), a dramatic contrast with World Bank's emphases on agriculture and commodities.

The fact that Africa's different and continuing attempts to develop intra-African relations have met with limited success naturally has historical roots. The colonial and then neo-colonial experience created linkages to spheres of interest not conducive to the furthering of intra-African relations. The African countries have not possessed the technical/administrative resources necessary for promoting and developing regional exchange programmes. Furthermore, the organizational forms chosen for such programmes have often prevented their consolidation and integration into national development strategies (those of SADCC are a possible exception). The accelerating crisis of the late 1970s onwards forced national governments to make national crash-programmes a first priority and thus contributed to the wide gap between the ambitious dreams of regionalism and the imperatives of national development.

The prospects for successful regional economic relations on the continent are not necessarily dim, however. The deepening crisis and the relative ignorance of the North with respect to support measures to stimulate renewed growth of the African economies has ironically emphasized the need for continental self-reliance strategies. However, even if historical experiences have not been too encouraging, there is today a renewed awareness of the need to continue to make intra-continental relations an important priority.

However, the development and sustainment of such relations require that the economies have something to offer each other. The peripheral status of almost all African countries implies that the degree of complementarity is small indeed. There are, nonetheless, countries that have achieved a fairly advanced level of industrial development, e.g. Cote d'Ivoire, Kenya and Zimbabwe. These countries stand to secure immediate benefits from the further opening-up of intra-

African channels for goods and capital. However, within the framework of the capitalist development process still characterising Africa today, the creation of regional markets will only serve to reproduce and aggravate the inequalities of peripheral capitalism. The Myrdal concept of 'cumulative causation' will thus be operational. In consequence, unless counteracting measures are taken, Africa's continued development will imply an increased hierarchization where differences in economic strength and structure will become more pronounced; in other words, a parallel continental process to that which has already occurred in the international economy. The critical issue is whether these stronger economies will act as growth poles and carry the weaker ones with them, or whether the weak ones will be increasingly marginalized: the dialectic of fast and slow growers.

This raises the question of whether regional exchange programmes should contain devices for redistributing resources so that the participating countries develop on a more 'equal' basis. In this sense, the more developed economies would be held back while the less developed countries would develop faster and catch up; in other words, to contain or reverse the same problematique that was the main contributory factor to the collapse of EAC.

Trade among African countries accounts for only 3 to 4 per cent of their total trade. This extremely low level of intra-continental trade is mainly due to lack of complementary South–South economic structures. But it also reflects the persistence of commercial and other South–North ties between former colonies and metropolitan centres. Intra-African preferential treatment of goods would help in overcoming the negative impact of this factor and also in translating co-operation on the capital and production side into increased exchange between African countries. LPA also proposed that African countries should accord each other most-favoured-nation treatment. Questions may, of course, be raised as to the compatibility of 'free' trade with planning on the production side.

By contrast to the continued elusiveness of continental exchange, the countries of Africa need to deepen their relations with the NICs. A projection of the experiences of the last decade shows the potential in the latter regard. This group of countries offers alternatives with respect to trade, technology transfer and, to a certain extent, capital flows in the form of direct and portfolio investments. The foundation for such links is the existence of complementary economies. Such relations do not contain any larger potential for structural change so, in this sense, they do not differ qualitatively from traditional North–South relations. Intra-African exchange has so far been less impressive, partly because of sheer economic facts (primary-producing countries with little industrial capacity have little to gain from this type of exchange) and partly for historical reasons.

From experience, it is possible to specify the pre-conditions that must be at hand if such relations are to develop favourably:

(a) African economies must be able to offer each other something by way of complementary exchange. The possibilities for complementarity that exist today must therefore be mobilized through information, transportation facilities and trade arrangements that take account of the most common barriers to trade (for example non-convertible and unstable currencies);

(b) Regional organizations and their programmes must be better co-ordinated with national economic plans to ensure effective implementation. Today, there is an apparent conflict between national crisis packages and sustainable regional strategies. The LPA is a case in point. It has remained long-term and macroscopic and has not been translated into short-term implementation steps. Thus, the package of policy instruments to be employed in the short run in a way consistent with LPA has not been developed in specific country contexts. In the absence of such policy packages the vacuum is being filled by World Bank/IMF export-oriented, free trade and market-based strategies;

(c) Extended intra-African economic relations will have to consider and contain increased hierarchization between African countries;

(d) The emphasis of LPA on industrialization should remain. However, the importance of agriculture for creating a surplus used for such industrialization purposes must continue to receive priority in the short term; and,

(e) The role of the public sector needs to be revised not primarily for ideological reasons, but from the point of view of efficiency. Africa lacks the effective technical/administrative bureaucracy which can be found in most NICs. Consequently, the private sector must assume primary importance in all productive activities. Meanwhile, responsibility for the formulation of coherent development plans must still rest with the public sector in a new division of power. The scenario described above takes as its point of departure Africa's immediate problems; i.e., the revival of agricultural and industrial production. Thus, the focus must lie on production rather than distribution.

As relations with the North carry little growth potential with regard to resource flows in general, trade must shift towards the South. Any realization of the potential of South–South relations must take into account the development dynamics of capitalism, again for sheer pragmatic reasons; i.e., getting back on the road of continued growth.

This development path will in all likelihood mean increased hierarchy and unequal distribution of the gains from expanded production. Marginalization between and within countries is compatible with this perspective. On the other hand, it can equally well be argued that the marginalization of Africa's population cannot go much further, when levels of production have deteriorated and the means of production have been run down so seriously.

The stand-off between LPA and World Bank's *Agenda* as alternative and essentially antagonistic world views[35] moderated over the first half of the 1980s as drought demanded attention and successor documents on both sides moved towards a middle ground: APPER and *Financing Adjustment with Growth*, respectively. This new consensus or at least truce was most apparent in the run-up to the Special Session in mid-1986 for which OAU/ECA submission identified sets of both endogenous and exogenous factors responsible for the contemporary malaise.[36] Yet although APPER recognizes short-term and indigenous problems it, like LPA before it, still emphasized longer-term, exogenous causes as primary:

> ... the current battle to save lives and to reduce the impact of hunger and famine should not be the only focus of international support and co-operation. Otherwise, the international community will be unwittingly contributing to making the emergency a permanent phenomenon.[37]

Likewise, in explaining why LPA has been difficult to implement, APPER points to inherited external dependence, insufficient resources, elusive regionalism and structural problems. It points in particular to a set of 'extraneous factors':

> the widespread, severe and persistent drought; the acceleration of the desertification process; persistent and destructive cyclones in the Indian Ocean; and the intensification of destabilization attempts from South Africa on neighbouring African countriès, especially the Front-line States.[38]

Yet, it also suggests that 'if most of the measures recommended in LPA had been implemented, the ravaging effects of the current world recession and drought on African economies would have certainly been minimized'.[39] Thus, Africa's leaders criticize both themselves and the international system for the non-implementation of LPA, which is itself symptomatic of depressed and extroverted political economics.

If there is a new uncertainty and modesty in explanations and expectations of the global economy there is considerable apprehension about the probable trends in Africa, a continent in great and seemingly exponential difficulty.[40] This is reflected in a new official openness towards policy failures and reforms as well as in a revisionist mood among scholars as well as statespersons.

African studies as well as African states have begun to reflect this new post-crisis conjuncture. To be sure, established perspectives are restated still[41] and no agreed paradigm has yet emerged to replace the demise of 'modernization' or 'decolonization': no intellectual as opposed to political 'consensus'. Yet there is a new foment and excitement as novel issues are identified and debated, if not resolved: debt, environment, gender, informal sector, privatization, reform. And a range of possible frameworks has been conceived and considered, from dependence and democracy to corporatism and capitalisms.[42]

Africa is, then, at the crossroads. Temperamentally, its leaders are inclined to opt for greater self-reliance, recognizing that further extroverted integration is unlikely to be either possible or profitable. Pragmatically, however, the pressures to accept structural adjustment structures are intense, leading to supposedly short-term compromises in the interest of external support, approval and advice. And the apparent options available to Africa may yet change if protectionism intensifies in the North because of slow growth, especially of employment, and if exponential debt leads to nationalist measures against Japan and the NICs. Unless freer trade is advanced everywhere, Africa may have no choice but to become more self-reliant, nationally and continentally. Ironically, however, it has postponed such an advance towards self-reliance under pressure from external agencies which themselves lack the resources to deliver the massive amounts of concessional assistance needed to perpetuate extroversion: $US1.5 to 2.5 billion shortfall.[43] Structural adjustment thus raised hopes which it cannot begin to satisfy, especially if the majority of eligible states opt for 'reform': the fallacy of composition.

One indicator of the new consensus is the agreed but ambiguous concept of 'reform' itself which seems to have superseded more controversial terms such as 'self-reliance' or 'structural adjustment'. Somewhat akin to 'basic human needs', reform passes the buck back from an unyielding world economy to impoverished peripheral polities. In particular, advocates in World Bank of reform expect local ruling classes to assemble political 'coalitions' to effect change – the usual mix of devaluation, de-subsidization, privatization, etc. – when the terms of such adjustments are usually quite unacceptable to the majority of the population. Thus, a new 'contract' is required between donors and recipients, based on mutual acceptability, in which resources as well as conditions for reform are agreed.[44] Otherwise, reform will lead to repression or instability: the food riots syndrome. World Bank cannot excuse its past policy mistakes any more than African regimes, despite attempts to do so: 'governments in Africa must be seen to have the prime responsibility for designing their adjustment and investment programmes and for co-ordinating aid and other financial flows'.[45]

Although there is a new, albeit fragile, consensus on the imperative of 'reform', there is considerable divergence and disagreement about how to define its content: from purist *laissez-faire* to pragmatic interventionism; i.e. from minimal to substantial if not maximal state 'intervention'. The range of issues stretches from exchange rates, subsidies, regulation and ownership to sectoral balancing. Peter Hopcraft favours the middle ground, at least in the area of grain marketing, between abandonment of marketing boards (as in Nigeria and elsewhere) and their expansion: the case-by-case consideration of liberalization, removal of price controls and subsidies, and termination of international controls on food. He advocates a residual role for government in terms of management, basic human needs and emergencies, while supporting the prevailing revisionist mood:

> Parastatal monopoly and official control over grain marketing does not have a good record in Africa. African grain marketing policies and institutions are now turning, sometimes deliberately, sometimes by default, to more indigenous and open systems. The institutions involved are flexible, self-financing and self-managing. They are also low-cost, responsive to economic opportunities, often quite small, and frequently run by women.[46]

Despite the pressures to proliferate adjustment in Africa, scepticism remains about the appropriateness and efficacy of reform over the medium term especially if defined to include basic human needs because of global resources and national reservations. Notwithstanding assertions of compatibility between World Bank and ECA proposals reflected in the convergence of the former's third report and the latter's *Priority Programme*, the longer-term viability of reform is still in some doubt. As a recent ODI *Briefing Paper* suggests 'the World Bank's overriding emphasis on the importance of the price mechanism raises the risk of neglecting infrastructure and other long-term constraints to growth'.[47] And if the 'liquidity gap'[48] is not bridged by novel and expanded forms of finance (e.g. from the Pacific Rim and the Socialist states) then the promised benefits of postponed consumption may never materialize, leading to 'back-sliding' from agreed packages:

> So far the shock of adjustment has been accompanied by relative political stability. This may suggest no more, however, than the capacity of most governments to ride out a squall. Once these changes are seen to be more or less permanent, governments are likely to face mounting political opposition to these reforms – a reflection that makes the lack of a long-term strategy for African development the more serious.[49]

And yet, as in the modernization era of 'trickle-down' theory, there still seems to be a widespread assumption amongst policy-makers that basic human needs will be met through renewed growth if not through redistribution. Nevertheless, despite accolades from the American State Department about successful adjustment,[50] all the evidence in Africa points to the contrary: declining per capita incomes lead to reduced taxation and national revenue and so poorer roads, hospitals, schools and other services. The slack is being picked up, if at all, by informal institutions, notably by national and transnational NGOs. The profit-oriented MNCs may have largely abandoned the continent, but non-profit transnationals have taken their place. The so-called 'success stories' after such a short period of adjustment need to be treated cautiously: success for whom and for how long?

Although there is widespread international recognition that the series of shocks over the last 15 years constitutes a turning point in the global political economy, there is a peculiar reluctance to recognize correlates such as the vitality of Africa's informal sector and the related vulnerability of the continent's economies. The old assumptions about neocolonial dependence – Africa was important enough to be rescued – were undermined by oil shocks and debt negotiations and Africa's survival became closely linked to that of the informal sector. And, yet, the political and personal 'internalization' of these changes did not really occur despite drought and decline; LPA was grafted on to the established orthodoxies. Rather, it was not until the early 1980s when structural adjustments were demanded that official African perceptions changed, albeit reluctantly. And even today, there is a lingering romanticism, despite all the evidence to the contrary, that the continent can still return to the halcyon days of the 1960s.

If these issues constitute a new 'radical' agenda for African studies,[51] a new 'orthodox' agenda has been defined and proselytized by World

Bank: reform rather than anything more revolutionary. The World Bank's package, along with that of IMF, of devaluation, deregulation, privatization, revival of commodity exports, and debt reschedulings has transformed the policy framework during the 1980s. Aspirations and arrangements which were unthinkable in the 1970s are now regarded as commonplace; growth is considered rather than development, and adjustment rather than consolidation. This reform conundrum has led to an unseemly and unprecedented rush towards floats, auctions, privatizations and renegotiations: the old days of state sectors, parastatals, controls and basic human needs seem to be gone forever. The literature is now replete with comparative analyses of adjustment and anticipations of expansion – from Ghana and Zaire to Somalia and Zambia despite emerging cautionary tales.

However, some critical sceptics remain, albeit in the minority[52] and the radical perspective may yet return to prominence if the new orthodoxy proves to be inappropriate and inadequate for the continent's crisis. In short, the Berg Report and LPA (and their successor documents) may indeed be compatible, at least in sequence. As difficulties arise with structural adjustment, mainly because of an ungiving world economy, so the necessity of self-reliance will become apparent once again; i.e., the supposed consensus bought time for reforms to work but if these fail to be efficacious then LPA and APPER would exist as welcome fall-backs.

If World Bank is concerned about mobilizing domestic coalitions in Africa to support reform in the short term – why should the peoples of Africa welcome restraint programmes when they were hardly invited, except perhaps in Nigeria's great 'IMF debate'?[53] – then it should be even more perplexed about securing such support, or even permissiveness, in the longer term. For, as contraction comes to be seen as normal, so popular reactions and resistance will intensify: from religious extremism to food riots to populist associations. To be sure, some of the continent's difficulties predate restructuring. But the scape-goat will be external – IMF/IBRD – rather than internal – rapacious or inappropriate leaders. Debates about the efficacy and objectivity of IMF conditionalities will continue to rage[54] but unless Africa has more than a few 'success' stories, internal opposition will build up against external deficiencies: a return to dependence as effect if not cause.

Stability or otherwise of leadership and policy is, to be sure, a crucial ingredient but the issue remains whether it is a dependent or independent variable. And its characterization is integrally related to mode of analysis, with substructuralists treating it as result and super-structuralists as cause. Clearly, the set of factors identified by Dharam Ghai are interrelated and reinforcing as the sets of fast and slow growers both indicate. But the balances between politics and economics, and between internal and external factors remain controversial. Callaghy, amongst others, suggests that remarkably little instability has been caused, thus far, by IMF conditionality, particularly where regime legitimacy is high.[55]

The role of the state, however conceived, is central in both instances of fast and slow growth, and between NICs and LDCs. The new orthodoxy on the former suggests that the *dirigiste* state is crucial to rapid and sustained industrialization whereas, on the latter, World Bank now calls for the shrinking of the state. Nigel Harris' rhetorical volume on the NICs – *The End of the Third World*[56] – reflects the former, albeit with comparative elements – the Asian 'gang of four' are quite dissimilar in recent history and political economy. Likewise, Peter Evans' seminal study of Brazil's 'triple alliance' suggests a central role for the state in semi-peripheral industrialization.[57]

Nevertheless, if some of the Third World cannot be cavalierly dismissed from the new international division of labour, 'Third Worldism' is increasingly hollow and vulnerable. In particular, the issue of 'graduation' from Third to First Worlds is complicating current North–South relations, particularly in GATT's current 'Uruguay Round'. Ironically, it was such co-operation which Henry Kissinger sought in the early 1970s as a response to OPEC's invigoration of the South. However, in the mid-1980s, the very success of the NICs is undermining not only the South but also the North: protectionism is contrary to graduation; international and national capitalisms are in competition.

Yet, the silence of World Bank's restructuring – contraction of the state – rather than ECA's reformism is apparent in recent national development documents. Characteristic of the influence of World Bank is Kenya's return to agriculture-based export promotion in which renewed growth will be based on coffee and tea exports. Industry is de-emphasized, along with state control, while the informal sector is recognized as the basis of employment. Basic needs will be met as a function of resumed growth – a fanciful 5.6 per cent per annum until 2000 – and of continued 'Harambee' initiatives while family planning will be encouraged. In short, the bases of Kenya's 1989–1993 Development Plan are to be found in World Bank's new orthodoxy rather than ECA's old idealism.[58] Regional co-operation is not addressed and the redefined mixed economy is to leave basic human needs to the vagaries of the market place: privatized welfare. In short, the Kenyan state, like most high-growth success stories in Africa, is redefining itself in minimalist terms, leaving development to 'trickle down' from anticipated economic revival rather than being central to politics and plans.

Notwithstanding the generally unhelpful character of the global economy and ecology over the last one or two decades, the differential performances of African political economies has led ironically to a rediscovery of politics and policies as variables: ways in which different leaders, sectors, classes and industries have responded. A succinct comparative analysis in this genre is provided by Dharam Ghai, who contrasts groups of fast and slow growers, recognizing distinctions among each according to reliance on minerals and agriculture and to basic needs performances. He concludes that political instability, export performance, terms of trade, resource inflows, foreign aid, natural resource endowment, role of the state and appropriate policy framework are all salient factors, with an emphasis on the first and last. Ghai argues that 'robustness' of economic performance is crucial with, of all the fast growers, Kenya being the most 'robust'.

The major structural constraints on Africa are, however, external and environmental as well as internal. Reginald Green points to the profound ecological challenge facing the continent, including successes like Kenya, as population growth without economic expansion serves to disrupt established land–people equations as well as optimistic World Bank/IMF extrapolations. The famine period of the 1970s and 1980s may, then, become normal rather than occasional as exponential desertification affects weather patterns in both long- and short-terms: 'By the mid-1990s, if present trends continue, the 1983–85 'famine' years will be looked upon as 'good' harvest years compared with the poor harvests that followed.'[59] Green cautions against any expectations of general, fast rehabilitation and redirection, given Africa's social history and the basic, ecological and economic causes of contemporary declines:

> the root (sic!) problem is not any African disrespect for nature but the combination of rising populations, limited land of reasonable quality, and the failure to devise sustainable intensive cropping or pastoral systems. The traditional African ... pastoral systems were ecologically sustainable but only with low population/land ratios.[60]

The fast-growing political economies of the 1980s may become, then, the ecological catastrophes of the 1990s. We turn, in conclusion, to three distinctive medium-term scenarios.

CONCLUSIONS AND SCENARIOS

The continuing African crisis, compounded by tensions in the global economy, means that the rest of the 1980s are likely to be crucial in relation to the continent's development prospects.[61] Domestic reform is not enough; external support is critical. If Africa meets the terms of its conditionalities but international institutions and donors fail to meet theirs, then the implicit contract lapses, with profound implications for Africa's directions and prospects. Conversely, if cross-conditionalities are met on both sides then at least some African political economies may yet revive and grow. A final possibility, not discussed in either diplomatic or academic circles, is that Africa will become, because of the uneven incidence of contraction, stagnation and expansion, a more unequal continent. This trend towards inter- and intra-state inequalities has already been intensified over the last decade – from OPEC and coffee windfalls to drought, devaluation and deflation – but the new concentration on 'reform' has overshadowed notions of declining basic needs and rights, let alone exponential ecological decline. In this concluding section we revive the themes of formal–informal, changing technologies, and international diplomacy–political economy dialectics in abstracting three possible scenarios for the remainder of this century: optimistic, realistic and pessimistic, respectively.

The new orthodoxy of IMF/IBRD 'reform' – debt rescheduling and structural adjustment with *de facto* cross-conditionalities – has now been adopted by the majority of African and industrial states. It promises transformed policies and economies: the package of devaluation, deregulation, privatization, and commodity exportation. Its emphasis is on growth rather than development and it is permissive of authoritarian regimes providing they follow its dictates. The new 'multilateral colonization' is quite unconcerned about non-compliant States – a new pattern of differentiation on the continent? – and has yet had insufficient time for testing: Ghana and Zaire are amongst the early purported 'success' stories. World Bank/IMF assumption, even assertion, is that devaluation[62] and deregulation will serve to revive and restructure African economies so that foreign exchange income from commodity exports[63] will finance debt repayment and industrial rejuvenation. This new orthodoxy is, we believe, *optimistic* mainly because there is little evidence that the global economy is expanding sufficiently fast to absorb Africa's exports of raw materials. And it is so preoccupied with Northern trade wars and NICs graduations that Southern development is low on its agenda. Unless new forms of assistance and investment are forthcoming – debt for equity? SDRs/aid from NICs? democratic and environmental development? – the implicit 'contract' will remain unfulfilled because of Northern perfidy not Southern procrastination. The African agenda has been transformed because of World Bank/IMF and related donor conditionalities, which the continent may attempt to meet while Northern partners fail to match. But if reform does not generate sustained revival then social coalitions supportive of the new regime will evaporate or be alienated with profound implications in near and long terms, as indicated in the final, third scenario. In the latter, authoritarianism is disapproved of whereas in this official projection, some militarization may be necessary to advance adjustment.

Given alternative ECA/OAU proposals for greater self-reliance, somewhat side-lined in the first half of this decade by IBRD Reports and reforms, Africa's exponential marginality in the global economy along with the minority of non-adjusting governments may yet renew their relevance and salience. If adjustment packages are not sustained, because of regime exhaustion or social opposition, on the one hand, or external indifference or protectionism, on the other, then Africa may once again be thrown back onto its own devices. Because of prevailing Northern preoccupations, we consider the rediscovery of self-reliance to be *realistic* rather than idealistic given the dictates of international diplomacy. World Bank has always asserted that its reforms were shorter-term and economistic and so compatible with longer-term and developmental ECA reformations. The transition from reform to restructuring may occur around the end of the decade if IBRD fails to mobilize sufficient international resources to meet its side of the tacit bargain. Moreover, non-adjusting states may have meanwhile enhanced their national self-reliance while adjusting regional powers may be strengthened sufficiently to once again encourage regional self-reliance. And if the World Bank fails to deliver, then continent-wide collective self-reliance may be a necessity rather than desiderata. The only level or form of self-reliance which may not be either recognized or facilitated is that of sub-national, informal enterprise, the centrepiece of our final, *pessimistic* scenario.

If neither World Bank reform nor ECA self-reliance is realized, then a more pluralist or anarchistic scenario is possible if not desirable; neither African nor international bourgeois interests would gain if a variety of informal, populist, proletarian even guerilla formations were released. Yet if devaluation and adjustment fail and self-reliance proves elusive, then social reactions could be multiple: the state could shrink further, informal exchange and credit could expand, black markets might revive, and a variety of bandit or guerilla warlords establish *de facto* 'micro-states'. To be sure, such a pessimistic scenario is not only unlikely, it would be both fragmented and resisted: the external agencies which declined to support reform adequately might yet contain violent opposition, especially if East–West interests were stimulated and injected into essentially development situations of disinterest in militarization under scenario one. The trend towards domestic authoritarianism would be intensified to protect vulnerable bourgeois privileges, and African 'peace-keeping' operations might be stimulated, as a distinctive form of continental self-reliance. Whilst such a scenario is problematic, it does at least represent a logical correlate of underdevelopment. And it might lead African studies back to some of its earlier, presently overlooked, concerns with inequalities as well as with adjustments: class and ethnicity as well as reform and trickle-down.

In conclusion, any estimation and evaluation of Africa's future position in the international community cannot escape from an inheritance of dependence and underdevelopment which has resulted in contemporary marginalization and vulnerabilities to cycles of ecology and economy. Thus, the dialectics of diplomacy/security with political economy and of formal–informal responses will undoubtedly continue, along with the primacy of links with the North, even if South–South relations, particularly those involving NICs, increase in salience marginally. The importance of the latter, along with intra- and inter-African relations, will only increase as North–South connections decrease, either because of Northern protectionism or preoccupations or because of Southern preferences and resources. In retrospect, then, the current structural adjustment preoccupations of World Bank and IMF may appear to be necessary corrections on the path towards self-reliance and development which ECA and other indigenous directions identified. To be sure, 'distortions' in Africa had become widespread and extreme but the external prescription consistently ignores changes in the global division of labour. As Northern preoccupations and preservation predominate, so Africa's self-sustainment will become an imperative. The lingering question remains whether this will be state-determined or a function of privatizations of the heights of the economy and recognition of the resilience of the ubiquitous informal sector.

A final footnote about a novel, responsive trend in Africa comparable to that in other parts of the Third World and related to both official and informal privatization: demands for democratic development. Last spring, a group of eminent Africans again posed the question 'Which way Africa?' Their declaration called for three, interdependent fundamentals: 'democracy, development and unity'.[64] In situating Africa's economic crisis, they implicitly responded to World Bank conditions:

> The development of Africa cannot, under existing conditions, result from closer integration into the world economy ... Rigorous management of financial and monetary resources is indispensable for development and democracy in Africa and presupposed the participation of the people in the decision-making process ... Full repayment of our countries' debts would seriously mortgage our future and deprive Africa of the resources it needs to develop, while the adjustment policies involved might well destabilise the African production and social systems in the long term.[65]

NOTES

1. 'Adedeji's message', *West Africa* 3618, 12 January 1987, 57; reprinted from Adebayo Adedeji, 'Preliminary Assessment of the Performance of the African Economy in 1986 and Prospects for 1987' (Addis Ababa: ECA, January 1987).
2. See 'UN Programme of Action for Africa's Economic Recovery and Development', *Africa Recovery*, February–April 1987, 12–14.
3. See Robert J. Berg and Jennifer Seymour Whitaker (eds.), *Strategies for African Development* (Berkeley: University of California Press, 1986).
4. See World Bank encouragement of 'reform' through supportive 'coalitions'.
5. See Adebayo Adedeji and Timothy M. Shaw (eds.), *Economic crisis in Africa: African perspectives on development problems and potentials* (Boulder: Lynne Reinner, 1985).
6. See Timothy M. Shaw, *Towards a Political Economy for Africa: the dialectics of dependence* (London: Macmillan, 1985).
7. See Timothy M. Shaw, 'The Non-Aligned Movement and the New International Economic Order' in Herb Addo (ed.), *Transforming the World-Economy? Nine critical essays on the NIEO* (London: Hodder and Stoughton, 1984), 138–162 and 'The Non-Aligned Movement and the New International Division of Labour' in Kofi Buenor Hadjor (ed.), *New Perspectives in North–South Dialogue: essays in honour of Olof Palme* (London: Third World Book Review, 1987).
8. See IBRD, *Accelerated Development in Sub-Saharan Africa* (Washington: World Bank, 1981) and OAU, *Lagos Plan of Action for the Economic Development of Africa, 1980–2000* (Geneva: International Institute for Labour Studies, 1981).
9. See IBRD, *Toward Sustained Development in Sub-Saharan Africa* (Washington: World Bank, 1984), *Financing Adjustment with Growth in Sub-Saharan Africa, 1986–1990* (Washington: World Bank, 1986) and OAU, *Africa's Priority Programme for Economic Recovery 1986–1990* (Addis Ababa, 1985).
10. See ODI and Ronald K. Shelp, 'Trade in Services', *Foreign Policy*, 65, Winter 1986–87, 64–84.
11. Jean-Claude Paye, 'OECD: analyst and catalyst', *OECD Observer* 144, January 1987, 6.
12. 'Highlights from the *OECD Economic Outlook*, December 1986', *OECD Observer* 144, January 1987, 36.
13. G.K. Helleiner, 'Economic Crisis in Sub-Saharan Africa: the international dimension', *International Journal* 41(4), Autumn 1986, 794.

14. *Ibid.*, 750.
15. *Ibid.*, 749. See also Gerald K. Helleiner (ed.), *Africa and the IMF* (Washington, 1985).
16. 'Commodities and the Commonwealth', *Commonwealth Currents*, December 1986, 9.
17. *African Priority Programme for Economic Recovery* 5. See also John Loxley, *The IMF and the Poorest Countries* (Ottawa: North–South Institute, 1984).
18. Thomas M. Callaghy, 'Between Scylla and Charybdis: the foreign economic relations of Sub-Saharan African states', *Annals of the American Academy* 489, January 1987, 158.
19. *Ibid.*, 162.
20. *Ibid.*, 151. See also Edward V.K. Jaycox *et al*, 'The Nature of the Debt Problem in Eastern and Southern Africa' in Carol Lancaster and John Williamson (eds.), *African Debt and Financing* (Washington: Institute for International Economic Affairs, 1986). Special Report Number Five, 47–62.
21. See Richard S. Weinert, 'Swapping Third World Debt', *Foreign Policy* 65, Winter 1986–87, 85–97.
22. See Paul M. Lubeck (ed.), *The African Bourgeoisie: capitalist development in Nigeria, Kenya and the Ivory Coast* (Boulder: Lynne Reinner, 1987).
23. Charles Oman, 'Changing international investment strategies in the North–South context', *CTC Reporter* 22, Autumn 1986, 55.
24. Arjun Sengupta and A. Vasudeva, 'Reform of the international monetary system: recent developments', *Third World Affairs 1987* (London: Third World Foundation, 1987) 9. On the controversies raging around the IMF see Jahangir Amuzegar, 'The IMF under fire', *Foreign Policy* 64, Fall 1986, 98–119 and ODC, 'Should the IMF withdraw from Africa?' (Washington: Policy Focus, 1987).
25. For more on this thesis see Ankie Hoogvelt, *The Third World in Global Development* (London: Macmillan, 1982).
26. There is a burgeoning literature on the NICs. For overviews see Jerker Carlsson and Timothy M. Shaw (eds.), *Newly Industrialising Countries and the Political Economy of South–South Relations* (London: Macmillan, 1987).
27. See Bahgat Korany, 'Hierarchy within the South: in search of theory', *Third World Affairs 1986* (London: Third World Foundation, 1986) 85–100.
28. See Timothy M. Shaw, 'Peripheral Social Formations in the New International Division of Labour: African states in the mid-1980s', *Journal of Modern African Studies* 24(3), September 1986, 489–508.
29. See Carlsson and Shaw (eds.), *The Newly Industrialising Countries and the Political Economy of South–South Relations*.
30. See 'Should the IMF withdraw from Africa?'.
31. See Richard Sandbrook, *The Politics of Africa's Economic Stagnation* (Cambridge: Cambridge University Press, 1985) and Olusola Akinrinade and J. Kurt Barling (eds.), *Economic Development in Africa* (London: Frances Pinter, 1987).
32. See Tony Killick, 'Adjustment with Growth in Africa? Unsettled questions of design and finance' (London: ODI, February 1987).
33. For overviews of regionalism in Africa see, *inter alia*, S.K.B. Asante, *The Political Economy of Regionalism in Africa: a decade of ECOWAS* (New York: Praeger, 1986); David Fashole Luke, 'Regionalism in Africa: a short study of the record', *International Journal* 41(4), Autumn 1986, 853–868; Domenico Mazzeo (ed.), *African Regional Organizations* (Cambridge: Cambridge University Press, 1984) and R.I. Onwuka and A. Sesay (eds.), *The Future of Regionalism in Africa* (London: Macmillan, 1985).
34. For the debate over SADCC see, *inter alia*, Douglas G. Anglin, 'Economic Liberation and Regional Co-operation in Southern Africa: SADCC and PTA', *International Organisation* 37(4), Autumn 1983, 681–711 and 'SADCC after Nkomati', *African Affairs* 84(335), April 1985, 163–181, and Thandika Mkanda-

wire, 'SADCC Co-operation: problems and prospects', Yash Tandon, 'SADCC and the PTA: points of convergence and divergence' and Ibbo Mandaza, 'Some Notes and Reflections on SADCC' in Timothy M. Shaw and Yash Tandon (eds.), *Regional Development at the International Level: Volume 2 African and Canadian Perspectives* (Washington: University Press of America, 1985) 93–144.

35. See David Fashole Luke and Timothy M. Shaw (eds.), *Continental Crisis: the Lagos Plan of Action and Africa's Future* (Washington: University Press of America, 1984). Dalhousie African Studies Series 2), Robert S. Browne and Robert J. Cummings (eds.), *The Lagos Plan of Action vs. the Berg Report: contemporary issues in African development* (Washington: Howard University Press, 1984) and John Ravenhill (ed.), *Africa in Economic Crisis* (London: Macmillan, 1987).

36. 'Africa's Submission to the Special Session of the UN on Africa's Economic and Social Crisis' (Addis Ababa: OAU/ECA, March 1986. E/ECA/ECM.1/1 Rev.2) 7–9.

37. *Africa's Priority Programme for Economic Recovery*, 4.

38. *Ibid.*, 13.

39. *Ibid.*, 12.

40. See Timothy M. Shaw (ed.), *Alternative Futures for Africa* (Boulder: Westview, 1982) and, with Olajide Aluko (eds.), *Africa Projected: from recession to renaissance by the year 2000?* (London: Macmillan, 1985).

41. See the disappointingly orthodox crop of standard texts on African politics: Richard Hodder-Williams, *An Introduction to the Politics of Tropical Africa* (London: George Allen and Unwin, 1987), J. Gus Liebenow, *African Politics: crises and challenges* (Indiana: Indiana University Press, 1986), Roger Tangri, *Politics in Sub-Saharan Africa* (London: James Currey, 1985) and William Tordoff, *Government and Politics in Africa* (London: Macmillan, 1984).

42. See *inter alia*, S.N. Sang-Mpam, 'The State–Society Relationship in Peripheral Countries', *The Review of Politics* 47(4), Fall 1986, 596–619, Julius E. Nyang'oro, 'On the concept of "corporatism" and the African state', *Studies in Comparative International Development* 11(4), Winter 1986–87, 31–54, Julius E. Nyang'oro and Timothy M. Shaw (eds.), *Corporatism in Africa: comparative analysis and practice* (Boulder: Westview, 1987) and John Sender and Sheila Smith, *The Development of Capitalism in Africa* (London: Methuen, 1986).

43. *Financing Adjustment with Growth in Sub-Saharan Africa*, 4.

44. See 'Compact for African Development: Report of the Committee on African Development Strategies' in Berg and Whitaker (eds.), *Strategies for African Development*, 557–585.

45. *Financing Adjustment with Growth in Sub-Saharan Africa*, 4–5.

46. Peter Hopcraft, 'Grain marketing policies and institutions in Africa', *Finance and Development* 24(1), March 1987, 40.

47. ODI. *Briefing Paper*.

48. J.D.A. Duddy, 'Third World liquidity needs: a new look', *Third World Affairs* 1987, 22.

49. ODI. *Op.cit.*

50. See Robert M. Press, 'Economic reforms bring hopes and risks to Africa', *Christian Science Monitor* 79(101), 21 April 1987. See also 'Reform statistics study', *West Africa*, 3629, 30 March 1987, 625 and 'Should the IMF Withdraw from Africa', 6.

51. See Nzongola-Ntalaja *et al. Africa's Crisis* (London: Institute for African Alternatives, 1987) and James H. Mittelman and Donald Hill, 'IMF Conditionality, State Autonomy and Human Rights', *International Studies Association*, Washington, April 1987.

52. See, for example, Norman P. Girvan, 'Adjustment via Austerity: is there an alternative?', *IFDA* Dossier 45, January–February 1985, 45–54 and *Development and Peace* 7(1), Spring 1986, 57–63.

53. See Timothy M. Shaw, 'Nigeria Restrained: foreign policy under changing political

and petroleum regimes', *The Annals of the American Academy* 489, January 1987, 40–50.

54. See Amuzegar, 'The IMF under fire' and Henry S. Bienen and Mark Gersovitz, 'Economic stabilisation, conditionality, and political stability', *International Organisation* 39(4), Autumn 1985, 729–754.

55. See Callaghy, 'Between Scylla and Charybdis', 159–160.

56. See Nigel Harris, *The End of the Third World: Newly Industrialising Countries and the decline of an ideology* (Harmondsworth: Penguin, 1986).

57. See Peter Evans, *Dependent Development: the alliance of multinational, State and local capital in Brazil* (Princeton: Princeton University Press, 1979).

58. See Republic of Kenya, *Sessional Paper Number One of 1986 on Economic Management for Renewal Growth* (Nairobi: Government Printer, 1986).

59. Reginald H. Green, 'Food policy, food production, and hunger in sub-Saharan Africa: retrospect and prospect', *International Journal* 41(4), Autumn 1986, 769.

60. *Ibid.* See also Timothy M. Shaw, 'Towards a political economy of the African crisis: diplomacy, debates and dialectics' in Michael H. Glantz (ed.), *Drought and Hunger in Africa* (Cambridge: Cambridge University Press, 1987) 127–147.

61. For a succinct and readable overview of the current range of issues see the UN's *Africa Recovery* 1, February–April 1987.

62. See Ravi Gulhati *et al.*, 'Exchange Rate Policies in Africa: how valid is the scepticism?', *Development and Change*, 17, 1986, 399–423.

63. Dramatic devaluations have indeed served to undermine regional black markets, such as those around non-convertible currency regimes like Ghana, Kenya and Nigeria. However, just as in the Caribbean and South East Asia, the production and exportation of illegal drugs may come to be a major means for enrichment through the 'fix' of 'forex'. See Olusegun Obasanjo, 'Debt and the Third World', *New York Times*, 15 April 1987.

64. See 'Which Way Africa? For Democracy, for Development, for Unity. Declaration on Africa', *IFDA Dossier* 54, July 1986, 35–45.

65. *Ibid.*, 43. For a critical analytic introduction to these issues see Mahmood Mamdani and Wamba-dia-Wamba, 'Social Movements, Social Transformation, Democracy and Development in Africa', *Newsletter of International Labour Studies* 32–33, January–April 1987, 26–29.

CHAPTER THIRTY-THREE

The Challenge to the International Community of Sustaining Africa's Economic Recovery

ADEBAYO ADEDEJI

INTRODUCTION

At the formal opening of the twenty-first session of ECA and twelfth meeting of its Conference of Ministers held in Yaounde (Cameroon), this time last year, I made bold to assert that the African economies were at the crossroads and that the most significant and peculiar attribute of being at the crossroads is that one is forced to make a deliberate and calculated decision as to the turning which one should make, and having made the choice, of the imperative necessity to pursue it to its logical conclusion. That choice, I suggested, must be made by Africa in the form of a package of at least five commitments which African Governments and people must irrevocably undertake.

These are: (i) that African Governments must indeed and in fact give the highest priority, in their rehabilitation and recovery programme, to the rural sector in general and to food and agriculture development in particular; (ii) that African Governments must continue to make genuine efforts to improve the management of their economies, to rationalize their public investment policies and to promote the most efficient utilization of resources; (iii) that African Governments and people must accept to impose greater sacrifices on themselves by adopting appropriate austerity measures, so as to achieve greater mobilization of domestic resources through both private and public savings and through the adoption of necessary fiscal and monetary reform measures; (iv) that our Governments must continue the process of undertaking essential policy reforms, difficult and painful as they are; and, (v) that Africa must demonstrate in every practical way its recognition of the need to bear the burden of its development, even in spite of the very low standard of living of its people – a low standard of living that has fallen even further as a result of the cumulative impact of the poor economic performance of the past 10–15 years and the disastrous consequences of the Great African Drought Disaster of 1983–1985.

Having designated the year 1986 as Africa's year with destiny, the year when Africa must begin to demonstrate to itself and to an increasingly cynical world its resolution and total commitment to this package, and as the year when the people and Governments of Africa, finding themselves at the economic crossroads, must take the path of honour and integrity to will an economic future of recovery and growth for themselves, it was most important to monitor very closely developments in various national economies by undertaking empirical investigations to ascertain the overall picture that would emerge at the end of the year 1986, not only in terms of macro-economic aggregates, not only in terms of the usual socio-economic indicators but also – and most importantly – in terms of qualitative changes in policies and programmes and in the management of the economies. Hence, ECA sent a comprehensive questionnaire to all member States. The preliminary analysis of the questionnaire is the subject of Chapter 2 – an earlier version of which had been submitted to the ECA Conference of Ministers during their 1987 session in April.

AFRICA'S RESPONSE AND PERFORMANCE IN 1986

Through the ECA annual *Survey of Economic and Social Conditions in Africa 1985–1986 and ECA/ADB Annual Economic Report, 1987*, the picture which has emerged on the basis of the main economic indicators is the transition of the economic performance of the continent from the uniformly disastrous situation of the past years to one that is distinctly marginally better. Unlike in the past when there was hardly a redeeming feature in Africa's economic firmament, 1986 saw a large number of African countries achieving positive growth rates and a significant improvement in food production. Africa had record harvests. For the first time in more than a decade and a half, agricultural output grew in 1986 by more than three per cent and, also for the first time in many a year, the problem was how to dispose of exceptional food surpluses internally.

This is not to suggest that the overall food deficit situation of Africa has disappeared. While a few countries are approaching the food self-sufficiency ratio, food deficits still persist on the continent as a whole. Indeed, many African countries – particularly those which still have pockets of drought, a large population of refugees and/or are suffering from civil strife – will need increased food aid in 1987 to meet their structural food deficits. While the standard of living of Africans as a whole did not improve in 1986 as total regional output grew by only 1.3 per cent in 1986 against a population growth rate of nearly 3 per cent, while Africa's major economies – many of which are also oil-producing and oil- and/or mineral-exporting countries – experienced negative growth rates, and while, therefore, it will be premature to conclude that Africa is now out of the economic doldrums, one cannot, nevertheless, escape the conclusion that the Africans and their leaders have accepted the challenge and are rising to it and are, at last, determined to take the path of honour and integrity to will the recovery of their economies.

Indeed, ECA's Preliminary Survey on the Implementation of APPER and UN-PAAERD gives credence to this emerging trend. The questionnaire which was designed in five parts focused on: (i) general issues related to the implementation of APPER and UN-PAAERD; (ii) immediate measures to enable African countries to cope with future emergencies and catastrophes; (iii) short-term measures to assist in Africa's economic recovery and development; (iv) financial resource mobilization; and, (v) modalities and mechanisms for implementing and monitoring both programmes.

The questionnaire also followed closely the structure of both APPER and UN-PAAERD in another respect. It was structured in such a way as to obtain information on the main priority areas which, as we all know full well, are (i) food and agriculture; (ii) other sectors in support of agriculture; (iii) drought and desertification; (iv) human resources development, planning and utilization; (v) policy reforms; and, (vi) refugees and displaced persons.

The responses to the questionnaire – both in terms of the number of countries and in their geo-political spread as well as in the facts and information provided – have been quite encouraging. As of today, 34 out of ECA's total states membership of 50 have completed and returned the questionnaire to us. Twenty-two of the responding countries are LDCs and all the seven economic and ecological sub-regions into which ECA has divided Africa, i.e., the Indian Ocean island countries, East Africa, Southern African states, Central Africa, the Sahel, non-Sahelian West Africa and North Africa – are well represented in the responses. This is why we are confident that the overall picture which emerges from our analysis of the responses is typical of the trend which is discernible throughout Africa today.

And what is this overall picture like? On the canvas are writ large determination, commitment, and sacrifice; the making of painful choices, and unprecedented political courage; and the will to pull

Africa up by its bootstraps. Country after country introduced policy reforms and undertook adjustment programmes which have imposed more sacrifice on their people and which have had dire political consequences. The overall picture therefore is one of African leadership, one after another, their Governments and their people rising to the challenge posed by APPER and UN-PAAERD.

The Survey shows that 97 per cent of the countries that have responded have adopted the same priorities as APPER and UN-PAAERD; it shows that many countries have adopted stabilization programmes (43 per cent), structural adjustment programmes (70 per cent), and overall economic rehabilitation programmes (17 per cent). It is, of course, the case that structural adjustment programmes have been in existence in some countries for a number of years now, and their impact is being increasingly felt. As far as immediate measures are concerned, 50 per cent have created or maintained national emergency preparedness mechanisms; 47 per cent are instituting effective early-warning systems, and 50 per cent have established national food security systems while 87 per cent have adopted price incentives for agricultural products.

On short- and medium-term measures, 80 per cent of the countries indicated that they had raised substantially the level of investment; 13 per cent have plans to do this by 1990. Seventy-three per cent had already established or strengthened agricultural credit institutions while only 47 per cent had already taken measures to provide incentives to encourage rural savings. The responses also reveal interestingly encouraging developments in the field of the introduction of mechanization of agriculture (67 per cent); development, dissemination and encouragement of modern inputs and methods (87 per cent); improving and expanding storage capacity (70 per cent); and strengthening or creation of a network of agronomical research stations (73 per cent).

I could go on quoting from ECA's Survey of what the responses are in other areas which I know are of interest – in the domain of the management of the economy, encouraging the private sector, establishment of a national population policy, of measures to mobilize domestic resources and of efforts to liberalize the investment codes. Substantial information has also been made available through responses to the questionnaire on the modalities and mechanisms which have been put in place at the national level for the implementation and monitoring of APPER and UN-PAAERD. The ECA's Survey has thus made available a wealth of data and information and an overall picture. The current survey is a baseline one and it is ECA's intention to update it regularly and to extend its coverage and its depth as part of its monitoring function. Meanwhile, a close study of the Survey is highly recommended. It is the first document of its kind – providing comprehensive information as to what is taking place at the national level – that will be available since UN-PAAERD was adopted on 1 June 1986 and indeed since APPER itself was adopted in July 1985.

From all the information and data – qualitative and quantitative – available, there can be no doubt about the overall picture which is discernible both from the analysis of the questionnaire and from our Survey of Economic and Social Conditions in Africa. This unmistakable picture is that, at least for once, Africa is matching its rhetorics with deeds and promise with performance. In *Africa's Submission*, both OAU Council of Ministers and ECA Conference of Ministers pledged on behalf of the continent Africa's determination 'to face and overcome the twin challenges of survival and development ... to make all the sacrifices for bringing about economic rehabilitation, recovery and development (and) accordingly ... take measures to strengthen incentive schemes, review public investment policies, improve economic management, including greater discipline and efficiency in the use of resources, encourage domestic resource mobilization and ensure the broad participation of all our peoples in the veritable fight against poverty, famine and hunger, disease and ignorance'.[1]

THE RESPONSE OF THE INTERNATIONAL COMMUNITY

What, in the face of the heroic efforts made by Africa, have been the responses of the international community? What is the nature of the international economic environment in which Africa has had to pursue its economic recovery and development goals during the past twelve months? What has become of UN-PAAERD as far as the implementation of the commitments of the international community is concerned since the adoption of the Programme on 1 June 1986? After examining the performance of Africa in the fulfilment of the commitment its leaders and Governments undertook, we cannot but X-ray the performance of the international community, particularly of Africa's development partners.

First and foremost, the international economic environment was even more hostile last year than it had been for many a decade. As I said in my end-of-year assessment of the performance of the African economy, the slump in Africa's export trade in 1986 was unprecedented perhaps since the Great Depression of the inter-war years, resulting in a catastrophic drop in export value and in an escalation in the deficits on current accounts. In one single year, the value of Africa's merchandise exports declined by about 29 per cent from $US64.0 billion in 1985 to $US45.0 billion in 1986 as a result of the fall in prices of exports because of the collapse in the commodity market; export volume having fallen by a mere 3.0 per cent. The export earnings of the nine African oil producers fell by a record of 36 per cent while those of non-oil producers crashed even further by 39 per cent in 1986.

Also, in 1986, the external debt problem and debt-servicing obligations assumed unmanageable proportions. Africa's disbursed and undisbursed foreign debt – which is estimated to be about $US200 billion by the end of 1986 – amounts to 44 per cent of its total GDP and 190 per cent of its total export earnings. Debt-service ratio now exceeds 30 per cent of GDP on the average and is much higher for many low-income countries. For over 25 per cent of African countries, the debt-service ratio exceeds 50 per cent and, in some cases, more than 100 per cent of export earnings. For example, debt-service obligations of the Sudan in 1986 were estimated at about 300 per cent of the value of its export of goods and services. It is for this reason that actual repayments have in fact been much lower and rescheduling of repayments has been more frequent. Indeed, indications are that unless and until some broad agreement on the debt issue is reached, the prospects of an increasing number of countries defaulting will loom larger and larger. And, worse still, the prospect of a sustained and sustainable African economic recovery will be in constant jeopardy.

With the debt-servicing obligations of African countries now between $US14.6 billion and $US23.0 billion, and with export earnings falling by about $US19.0 billion in 1986, the African economies have been drained of resources to the tune of between $US33.6 billion and $US42.0 billion in one year. In the face of such a huge drain – such 'outflow' – the capital inflows of $US12.0 billion in 1986 seem rather insignificant. Therefore, unless the African commodity problems are addressed and unless the continent's debt-servicing obligations are tackled, resource inflows will have little impact and seldom any meaning. And of course the implementation of APPER and UN-PAAERD will become a nigh impossibility.

ADDRESSING THE COMMODITY PROBLEM

Let me deal with these two cancers in Africa's political economy in some detail. In UN-PAAERD, it was agreed that there is a need for the international community 'to deal with commodity issues taking into account the special interest of the African countries'. Given the precipitous fall in the prices of virtually all of these commodities in 1986, what more opportune moment for action can exist? It is certainly not beyond the capacity of the international community to devise an imaginative package that can address Africa's perennial commodity issues.

The EEC and ACP countries came out with the STABEX as the single most significant innovation of the Lome Convention. STABEX has developed into a significant source of compensatory finance in the face of falling export earnings from products included in the scheme. STABEX is a particularly constructive response by EEC to the perceived need to 'do something' to assist primary producers in associated states. In the words of Claude Cheysson, former EEC Commissioner for Development, the scheme is both a sickness and unemployment insurance: compensation where earnings have declined as a result of local production problems (sickness) and compensation as a result of falling prices or reduced demand on the world market (unemployment).

Of course, the scheme has its many shortcomings and pitfalls. Its product coverage is limited. By not covering processed commodities, it is acting to preserve the existing division of labour between EEC member states and ACP member states. The scheme also suffers from insufficiency of funds – a situation which no doubt accounts for the evolution of the rather arbitrary system of dependency threshold, the principal purpose of which appears to be to reduce the cost of the scheme to the EEC. Finally, the scheme does not cover minerals. Therefore mineral exporting countries are discriminated against. Needless to add that SYSMIN – the special financing facility for mineral products – is a poor substitute for STABEX.

But in spite of their limitations and their deficiencies STABEX and SYSMIN are innovative responses by EEC and ACP countries to deal with the commodities problem. Within the context of UN-PAAERD, cannot the international community come out with a similar innovative scheme which will draw from the experience of STABEX and SYSMIN for Africa?

ADDRESSING THE EXTERNAL DEBT PROBLEM

The African debt problems also deserve similar innovative approaches. Again, in UN-PAAERD, the international community 'recognizes the magnitude of Africa's debt and the severe and restrictive burden which this has placed on many African countries. *It realizes that measures have to be taken to alleviate this burden* (emphasis added) and to enable those countries to concentrate on the full implementation of priorities.'[2]

In view of this recognition, the time is due for the international community to come out with a package of measures that will be addressed uniquely to Africa's debt problem. The thirty-first meeting of IBRD/IMF Development Committee held on 10 April 1987 also gave recognition to the severe problems of indebtedness facing Africa and agreed that for many African countries 'additional measures were needed to improve their capacity to service their debts and at the same time, undertake growth-oriented programmes'.[3] The time has therefore come for remedial actions. Indeed it is already overdue.

In this connection, we must applaud the initiative that has been launched by some members of the Paris Club to work towards realistic rescheduling terms for the 'poorest nations undertaking strong growth-oriented adjustment programme'. While the move to stop keeping African debtor countries on a short leash is to be welcomed, longer rescheduling periods alone will not be adequate. Debt-relief measures addressed to the realistic solution of African problems must be comprehensive enough to accommodate the three proposals which we made in *Africa's Submission* last year. These are: (i) conversion of ODA debts and interest obligations into grants; (ii) consolidation of non-ODA official debts and service payments thereon due over the period 1986–1990 of UN-PAAERD and APPER into long-term loans payable over 30–40 years on concessional terms with a 10-year period of grace; and, (iii) improving the existing framework for commercial debt renegotiation. Capping and reducing interest rates for commercial debts as well as consolidating debt-servicing payments for these debts and their repayment over a long period of time on concessional terms must be part of the comprehensive approach.

In addition to the Paris Club and the London Club members adopting this package, both the Bretton Woods institutions – World Bank and IMF – must also, insofar as the debts owed them by African countries are concerned, adopt and implement similar measures. At present, these institutions are prevented by their rules from even rescheduling repayments of debts and debt-service obligations. Hence, in order to ensure that countries do not default, they give Structural Adjustment Loans or Facility, a substantial part of which is merely recycled back to them for settlement of debt obligations.

CONCLUSION

Unless the twin problems of commodity prices and external debt are addressed, UN-PAAERD will be a sham particularly insofar as the response and commitment of the international community are concerned. While the replenishment of IDA 8 to the tune of $US12.4 billion and the decision to allocate 45 per cent thereof to sub-Saharan Africa is most welcome, this measure is only meaningful within the context of the package that addresses the commodities issues and the debt problems. For, without doubt, the recovery programme will be stillborn unless action is taken by the international community on these twin problems.

In conclusion, the package which I am urging the international community to put together in response to Africa's needs would therefore consist of the following four principal components:

(a) Support and stabilization of earnings for commodities and minerals that are of primary interest to Africa at reasonably remunerative levels – i.e., a system analogous to EEC/ACP STABEX and SYSMIN;

(b) Comprehensive measures to deal with the debt and debt-servicing problems;

(c) Measures to ensure that both World Bank and IMF can reschedule on a long-term basis the repayment of the debt and debt-service obligations owed them by Africa's debt-distress countries; and,

(d) Measures to ensure the flow of net concessional resources at a level adequate to cover Africa's requirements for recovery and development.

Fortunately, there is a growing awareness among some developed countries that such actions are urgently required. It is therefore my earnest hope that such countries will take the lead in organizing concerted response from those donor countries that are like-minded. In this connection, the forthcoming annual meeting of the Group of 7 in Venice in June 1987 will provide an opportunity for the most advanced Western industrialized countries to put together a package that will address the vital issues of recovery and development in Africa.

Last year the entire international community adopted by consensus UN-PAAERD. The sceptical world did not think Africans meant business. Now that they have demonstrated their commitment, will the international community rise to the challenge of sustaining the continent's economic recovery and development? The answer to this question, in operational terms, will have decisive impact not only on the future of Africa but also on the future of our world community.

NOTES

1. *Loc.cit.*, pp.1–3.
2. United Nations General Assembly, *United Nations Programme of Action for African Economic Recovery and Development, 1986–1990* (A/RES/S.13/2), page 16.
3. *Development Committee Press Communique* (mimeo), p.3.

CHAPTER THIRTY-FOUR

Prospects of Implementation of UN-PAAERD by the International Community

JOHN W. SEWELL
ANTHONY W. GAMBINO

INTRODUCTION

Twelve months ago, the international community and African Governments agreed to an historic compact, pledging both sides to UN-PAAERD. African Governments made a series of far-reaching commitments to economic reform and the rationalization of their own economies. In return, bilateral donors and multilateral development organizations accepted a large role in Africa's recovery and in assisting African nations to move beyond recovery to the development of their immense human and material resources.

As part of UN-PAAERD, the international community agreed upon a number of principles, most importantly to:

(a) increase external resource flows to Africa, with an estimated $US9 billion in external resources needed annually between 1986 and 1990 to fulfil the various programmes of rehabilitation and development planned across the continent and contained in APPER;

(b) give priority to programme over project aid, including balance-of-payments support, with assistance allocated according to the priorities of the recipient countries;

(c) provide aid in a regular, predictable, and timely fashion;

(d) increase the grant element in development assistance;

(e) seek greater involvement of qualified African personnel and more substantial training efforts in donor programmes;

(f) intensify co-operation and co-ordination among donors;

(g) support the concessional windows of multilateral development institutions, including a speedy eighth replenishment of IDA at a level in accord with Africa's needs, and continued support for ADB and African Development Fund; and,

(h) ensure that no African nation undertaking an adjustment programme would find itself a net exporter of official capital to any donor country.

The international community recognized the potential need for extraordinary measures to alleviate the debt burden of particular African states, with priority given to sustainable economic growth over full debt-servicing on rigid schedules.

UN-PAAERD also stressed the importance of improvements in the world economic environment, calling on the international community to: (i) adopt policies for sustained, equitable, non-inflationary growth in the world economy, including the elimination of protectionism, particularly non-tariff barriers, encouragement of African exports and economic diversification, and improved access for tropical products within the framework of GATT; and, (ii) take comprehensive action on commodity issues, including commodity agreements and arrangements, compensatory financing, and programmes to increase Africa's capacity to process, market, distribute, and transport its exports.

The magnitude of Africa's development crisis and the broad positive response by African countries stand in contrast to the response by the international community which to date has been far from sufficient. This is particularly true for some of the largest donors such as the US.

The response of bilateral donors and multilateral organizations is particularly disappointing given the far-reaching reforms already made by many African nations. The wisdom of these difficult yet critical policy changes – particularly those affecting agricultural and food policies and the size of the public sector – has been recognized by the international community. But Africans made many of these wrenching adjustments on the basis of an implicit understanding that the international community would do more than simply applaud in response.

These shortcomings, however, should not cause pessimism yet. Nor should they diminish the importance of gains already achieved. The next twelve to twenty-four months will be crucial in determining if this fragile compact is to be sustained and strengthened. Despite the uncertainties and disappointments, Africans and outsiders concerned about Africa's development need to intensify pressure on international institutions and rich-country governments to fulfil their end of last year's accord.

ACHIEVEMENTS TO DATE

Twelve months is not a long time to gauge the progress in implementing an international agreement, particularly when a large number of governments and multilateral agencies are involved. Some accomplishments on the part of the international community, however, can already be noted:

(a) The outcome of the UN Special Session represented agreement between Africans and donors on the diagnosis of Africa's problems and measures needed to resolve them – a considerable achievement given recent *disagreements* over these same issues. It reflects a growing realization – not yet fully present in actions – that restarting sustained growth in Africa is the key challenge facing those concerned about international development.

(b) The major donor countries have been increasing the grant element in their ODA worldwide for more than a decade, and all indications suggest that this trend will continue. ODA make up the bulk of the international community's financial flows to sub-Saharan Africa in 1984 – underlining the importance of this trend.

(c) Grace periods for debt repayment have been lengthened, with Canada, for instance, providing a five-year grace period on debt repayment for the poorest African nations. Some Western donors have already softened the terms of loan repayment; an agreement between Egypt and its major creditors contains a five-year moratorium on repayments with generous rescheduling thereafter. Zaire also has recently received generous terms. These could be the first in a series of more realistic programmes of debt relief for Africa.

(d) Agreement on the eighth replenishment of IDA at $US12.4 billion, with at least $US6.2 billion earmarked for Africa. Although not as high as some had hoped, this figure does provide substantial funds for African recovery and development. Africa received $US3.6 billion under IDA-VII; so it stands to receive nearly 75 per cent more in current terms under IDA-VIII.

(e) World Bank appears ready to inject greater attention for the poorest people in the design of its programme and project loans including Structural Adjustment Loans to African nations. A new acceptance of targeted interventions to protect the poorest and most vulnerable people from the harshest effects of economic adjustment should help provide critical sustenance for Africa's poorest people.

(f) Japan is increasing its aid to Africa. Although still at relatively low levels, Japanese aid has gone from a few million dollars in 1970 to nearly $US300 million today.

(g) More and more nations have adopted measures against South African *apartheid* and to encourage development in the nine member nations of SADCC. Sweden has decided to cut off all commercial relations with South Africa, the US has a stiff sanctions law against South Africa, and a number of other governments, including those of Canada, other Commonwealth nations, and Japan, have taken measures in support of long-standing efforts by Africans to end *apartheid*. The Nordic countries have taken the lead in aiding SADCC member states in their struggle to develop despite South African destabilization efforts.

SHORTCOMINGS IN THE INTERNATIONAL RESPONSE

African countries have estimated that a total of $US128.1 billion will be needed between 1986 and 1990 to implement APPER. With $US82.5 billion estimated as available from internal sources, $US45.6 billion will have to come from external sources, or roughly $US9 billion annually.

Using a different yardstick for measurement – that of restoring import volumes to levels prevalent in 1980–1982 – World Bank estimates that the twenty-nine poorest sub-Saharan countries will require roughly $US13 billion in external resources per year from 1986–1990. This total depends upon assumptions about high African growth rates and increased export volumes which already appear to have been too optimistic. Even with these assumptions, an annual shortfall of $US2.5 billion remained for external actors to fill over and above predicted inflows of external assistance. If IDA and other multilateral concessional agencies covered $US1 billion of this gap, as World Bank suggested, a $US1.5 billion gap would be left for bilateral agencies to close.

This World Bank estimate of Africa's needs is based on a return to a level of imports deemed adequate to prevent further declines in living standards, that is, for recovery, not development. African development would, even with full success in World Bank terms, still be a goal for the 1990s and the century beyond.

Although the various measures of estimating the resource shortfall are not comparable, all observers seem to agree that an enormous shortfall in external resources continues to hinder African recovery and development.

Africa received roughly $US11 billion in net disbursements of ODA in 1985 (the last year for which reasonably complete data are available) from the member nations of DAC, multilateral organizations, member states of OPEC, and Arab-financed agencies. (This $US11 billion is total net ODA for all projects, and therefore not comparable to the $US9 billion in yearly external assistance called for by APPER.) Between 1981 and 1985 net ODA disbursements increased in real terms at a yearly rate of 5 per cent. Multilateral aid grew most strongly – by 7.3 per cent per year. Bilateral assistance from DAC members grew by 5.8 per cent, while aid from OPEC members – after peaking in 1982 – shrank – 18.2 per cent per year.

Sixty-three per cent of total aid in 1985 was bilateral assistance from the OECD countries, with the US and France accounting for 45 per cent of total bilateral aid. Multilateral assistance equalled 31 per cent of the total; IDA is the largest multilateral donor, providing 30 per cent of this. OPEC countries accounted for 6 per cent of total ODA.

Aid from the centrally managed economies is provided at compara-tively low levels – about three per cent of total aid to Africa – and is concentrated in a small number of countries. At an estimated $US300 million annually, their assistance is roughly at the same level as that of Canada.

The 1986 report of the DAC noted that 'the largest single aid source over the past decade has been France, followed by the US, IDA, the European Development Fund, Germany, and Canada. The Nordic countries are major donors, especially in East Africa. Italy and Japan have recently become major new bilateral sources.'

Development assistance to Africa appears to have levelled off in real terms in 1986 and all indications are that any real increase in 1987 will be small. Various estimates of requirements continue to show a substantial resource gap. Flows from the OECD countries are likely to remain at today's levels or increase marginally in real terms over the next 2–4 years. Aid from the centrally planned economies is not only at low levels, but often is ill-suited to Africa's developmental needs.

Africa received only $US1.1 billion through private commercial channels in 1985, dramatically down from levels prevalent in the early 1980s. Total net non-concessional flows (public and private) to Africa fell from $US7 billion in 1982 to $US3.3 billion in 1984, with three countries – the Cote d'Ivoire, Nigeria, and Zaire – accounting for over half of the 1984 total. For 1985, this figure is estimated at $US3.5 billion. This drop in real non-concessional flows is unlikely to turn around until the process of African recovery is over and strong African development can restart.

As in other areas of the developing world, concern is growing over the flight of capital out of Africa to the developed countries. For certain countries, such as Sudan and Zaire, the amount of capital that has fled approaches, or perhaps even exceeds, the country's official debt. It appears probable that no substantial inflows of private, non-African capital will occur until African capital begins to return home in quantity.

Private investment in Africa must become attractive both to draw back the African flight capital that sits in industrial country banks, and, thereafter to attract foreign capital. Part of this process requires more progress towards reaping the benefits of economic co-operation and integration. This was the central idea contained in LPA and is even more important now than when that seminal document was written.

Perhaps the most serious, immediate problem facing most countries in sub-Saharan Africa today is how to deal with the crushing burden of debt repayment. Over 90 per cent of Africa's debt of $US95 billion is owed directly to or guaranteed by official sources – either creditor country government agencies or international institutions. The squeeze on African recovery will be particularly sharp in 1987, with debt-servicing hitting its highest level of the decade – roughly $US11 billion. The unfortunate confluence of low commodity prices, negligible flows of commercial capital, and no substantial increase in ODA makes this debt-servicing level untenable.

A key issue here concerns the role of IMF. IMF emerged in the late 1970s and early 1980s as an important participant in Africa's balance-of-payments picture. But the earlier transfers now are coming due, and in 1986 repayments to IMF grew rapidly, causing overall net flows to Africa to turn negative by about $US400 million. This trend will continue unless this urgent question is addressed very shortly.[1]

The resource gap can be closed in two ways: via more external resources or a smaller external claim on African resources. Aid can be increased, debt relief provided to reduce Africa's repayments to bilateral and multilateral creditors, or some combination of these two adopted to close the gap.

It now appears highly improbable that additional resources on the scale needed will be furnished before 1990. As a result, debt negotiations assume an even greater importance, since they provide the only space where resources for African recovery and development can be fruitfully sought. Fortunately, purposeful action to address this issue now appears more and more likely.

Particularly damaging to African countries – and beyond their control – is a slowdown in Western growth rates. The IMF recently reduced its estimate of growth in the OECD countries from 3.5 to roughly 2 per cent. This will adversely affect both the willingness of many Western countries to increase levels of assistance to Africa, and the prospects for growth in markets for Africa's exports.

The situation of low commodity prices will not change in the near term, and will continue to exacerbate Africa's current account problems. World Bank projections suggest that prices for beverages will decline, prices of cereals, fats and oils, and metals and minerals will remain the same or increase slightly, while the price of petroleum is projected to jump by more than 70 per cent between 1987 and 2000. Market rationalization agreements which could result from GATT negotiations will not come into effect before the early 1990s, too late to help reduce this obstacle to African recovery.

Many Western governments and specialists are wary of the utility of commodity agreements, and there is virtually no support in the industrial countries for commodity agreements. The UNCTAD pro- gramme laboriously negotiated a few years ago is unlikely to be implemented. Compensatory financing schemes that require govern- ment resources directly conflict with the desire for higher levels of concessional assistance.

Over the next few years it is probable that protectionism will grow among Western nations. Trade legislation in the US threatens to disrupt world patterns of exchange. This trend, however lamentable, must be recognized and incorporated into Africa's development plans.

Some progress on donor co-ordination has occurred in Africa, particularly with the organization of more CGs to act as 'a central mechanism for aid co-ordination, providing a confidential forum for the exchange of information, ideas and comments among aid givers and receivers, and permitting a common assessment to be made of relative needs and performance'.[2] Much remains to be done, however, and, as on the larger issues of recovery and development, Africa must take the lead.

A focus on rationalizing aid flows and development projects seems promising as a way to increase regional co-operation in Africa. Without well-functioning regional co-ordination, the smaller nations of Africa will find it nearly impossible to develop and diversify their economies.

As the Chairman of OECD's Development Assistance Committee points out, African governments themselves will have to take on the task of co-ordinating aid flows, just as Asian governments assumed this crucial task in the past. In the interim, however, there are actions that can be taken to improve aid co-ordination. A number of them can be found in the report of the Informal Consultation on the Progress of the

Recovery of Africa held in Bommerswik, Sweden last October and sponsored by the North–South Roundtable.

Tied aid continues at unacceptable levels. In 1984–1985, Austria, Italy, the United Kingdom, France, and the US tied more than 50 per cent of their total ODA.[3] In addition to tying aid, too much assistance still is determined purely on a political, rather than developmental, basis. So it is with many donors – the US sends relatively massive amounts to two countries, Egypt and Israel; France concentrates on its former colonies, not to speak of its continuing overseas territories and departments; Arab donors emphasize *their* frontline states; and the Soviet Union and other like-minded countries send two-thirds of their assistance to sub-Saharan Africa to Ethiopia.

In one sense, aid untying is easy; it can be accomplished through unilateral actions. But each bilateral programme will be reluctant to move on this unless all do the same. This means that international leadership by World Bank and one or two major donors such as the US is imperative. Similarly, donors need to balance their political interests with overall interests in a stable, growing Africa.

THE SITUATION IN THE UNITED STATES

Prospects for favourable action by the US in support of African development are not good in the short term, although the longer-run situation may be somewhat more favourable. Aid levels for Africa are caught up in largely unrelated political debates concerning the need to reduce the federal deficit, the relative priority of domestic social programmes versus military activities, and the balance between foreign aid for short-term political and military programmes, predominantly in the middle income countries, and longer-term programmes for development in the poorer regions.

Foreign aid voted by the US Congress rose from $US9.9 billion in 1980 to $US14.8 billion in 1986. But almost all of the increase has gone into security assistance programmes in the Middle East, Central America, and a few other Asian and Southern European countries. Only a few African countries have benefited from these trends in US aid allocations.

US assistance to Africa declined by more than 25 per cent between 1986 and 1987, while total US aid declined by less than 20 per cent. Aid from the US to Africa will in all probability continue to shrink for the next two years; but it is critically important that this not be taken by Africans as an irreversible trend.

Until the US deals with its budgetary problems, the debates will be over how to divide a shrinking quantity of foreign aid funds. Full funding for the Middle East is a given, and special priority is given to the requests for a small number of countries, including those of Central America and those perceived to be of strategic significance for the US, such as Pakistan and, in Africa, Kenya, Sudan and Zaire. Once aid funds for these countries of primary interest are allocated, a decreasing share is left for the rest of the developing world, including Africa.

One issue of great importance to Africa – full US participation in the eighth replenishment of IDA, now hangs in the balance. The Reagan Administration requested the full amount needed to fulfil the first payment of the US share, but constraints in the overall national budget, a strong anti-foreign aid element within the Congress, a weakened President, and other factors, merge to produce strong forces to reduce the level of IDA below the Administration's request. This issue remains unresolved, and will be fought in the US Congress over the next four months. It is possible that the US contribution to the first year of IDA-VIII could be as low as $US400 million instead of the pledged $US950 million.

In light of the above analysis, it might seem paradoxical to suggest that interest in African recovery and development is far from dead. Stirred by Africa's development crisis and by public concern, a group of legislators from both parties have introduced the African Famine Recovery and Development Act. Drawing on the work of a number of groups, most notably the report of the Committee on African Development Strategies (a private, high-level commission on African development) and studies by environmental groups, the legislation writes into law a long-term commitment to African assistance at a higher level. In addition, the bill provides a much more flexible bilateral aid programme designed to meet the needs and wishes of Africans, and permits debt rescheduling for low income African countries. Perhaps, most importantly, it would help to 'protect' Africa from the current budgetary squeeze by setting the amount of bilateral aid to be sent to African countries.

The Reagan Administration incorporated many of these ideas in its proposal this year to the Congress to create a special Development Fund for Africa. The Administration requested aid levels of $US500 million for Africa in 1988, but due to budgetary exigencies, it is unlikely that this fund will receive more than $US400 million. Moreover, it appears practically impossible that this level of funding will be reversed before 1989, primarily due to concern about the US Government's budget deficit.[4]

Africans should not take this as a sign of reduced US interest in, or commitment to, African development. The battle between a Democratic Congress and a Republican President is centred on a different issue – the shape of the federal budget. In this battle, foreign aid levels have become a weapon, to be used by both sides as each threatens to resist the other on domestic issues such as whether or not to raise taxes. In this environment, the ability and willingness of African governments to keep pressure on US Congress and the executive branch, both by their own efforts and by allying with sympathetic supporters in the US, is very important.

American public support for African development is a more favourable element in this picture. The support by Americans of private and public efforts to deal with the African crisis of 1984–85 was unprecedented both in terms of public concern and private financial contributions to groups working in Africa. Grants by private voluntary agencies to developing countries worldwide reached $US1.5 billion in 1985, with roughly $US1 billion going to sub-Saharan Africa.

Furthermore, Americans favour aid to Africa as a priority for US assistance. A recent survey of US public opinion on development indicated that a majority of Americans continue to support US economic aid to developing countries, with 'a strong preference for those types of US economic aid programmes that most recognizably aim to deliver help directly to poor people'. Africa was identified as the 'highest priority' for US assistance by a plurality of Americans.[5] Evidence from opinion polls in Europe, Canada, and Australia also suggests that the citizens of these nations support development aid, with Africa as their highest regional priority.

Nevertheless, the economic and social advances made by many African nations are not well understood in the US. For too many Americans, Africa remains the continent of famine, poverty, and corruption. Some private American groups work to correct these misperceptions, but, as elsewhere, more efforts are needed.

This situation provides Africans and their governments with an opportunity to make a measurable impact on debates in the US over development policies towards their countries. Friends of Africa note with some regret that African efforts in Washington do not appear to have any important impact on our debates over development assistance. This is certainly not true of other countries and regions that are considerable recipients of American aid! To bolster their effectiveness in the US, African states and organizations should reconsider their activities, and make alliances with like-minded groups. Important potential allies include American environmentalists, church groups, private development organizations, and other NGOs supportive of African development efforts.

THE NEED FOR FURTHER ACTION

Any candid assessment of actions taken by the international community to implement their end of the implicit bargain resulting from last year's Special Session on Africa has to contain more pessimism than optimism. But only one year has passed, and some achievements have been realized and should not be ignored. In other areas, particularly debt relief, helpful action is likely.

Above all, the important, albeit implicit, conclusion of the UN Special Session needs to be reinforced: Africa now faces an unprecedented set of problems that call for urgent co-ordinated international attention and special measures that recognize the inadequacy of 'business as usual'. In the next twelve to twenty-four months, those concerned about Africa's development should mobilize efforts to press for more positive actions.

To further the implementation process, more formalized monitoring of and reporting on activities within and outside Africa should be instituted. Perhaps DAC could evaluate the response by the international community while ECA co-ordinates analysis of African actions.

Concessional assistance remains crucial to Africa's short-term prospects for recovery and longer-term prospects for development. Yet, prospects for increased concessional flows are not good in the near term. The situation is made even more crucial by Africa's debt crisis – many countries are paying more back to rich country creditors than they are receiving in new funds for development. This perverse situation urgently needs to be resolved.

The choices are conceptually simple, even if politically difficult. Donors can provide new financing, or debt relief on past official flows, or some combination of both. Fortunately, recent statements and actions give hope that new measures to address these debt problems may be in the offing. One year ago, UN-PAAERD suggested, somewhat tepidly, that 'the international community is determined to assist African countries in their efforts to deal with their financial constraints'.

Bilateral and multilateral creditors now appear ready to consider debt relief for many African nations. Instead of traditional stretchouts of repayments without important concessions, many governments are beginning to explore official debt relief by converting some loans into grants or by adopting generous grace periods and interest rate reductions. In 1987, legislation was introduced in the US Congress to provide a five-year grace period and interest rate relief on official US bilateral debt owed by the poorest African nations. Recent Paris Club reschedulings have been for multi-year periods.

Action also is taking place at the multilateral level. World Bank has created a new post at the Vice-President level to co-ordinate efforts to help resolve the debt crisis, and has consolidated all personnel working on Africa into one division. These changes should permit World Bank to work more effectively for African economic recovery and development. In addition, in June, Western leaders at the Venice economic summit meeting will discuss ways to make Africa's debt burden manageable. The fact that Africa's debt problems are on the agenda of this high-level meeting which usually focuses on industrial country problems could foreshadow dramatic action by donor countries in the short term to permit African recovery by 1990.

The UN Secretary-General has formed a special panel of 'wise men' to advise him on helping debt-ridden African countries resolve their debt problems. This high-level group should contribute concrete ideas on new solutions, including some form of debt *relief*.

IMF in particular needs to take action, and its member governments need to augment IMF's resources for African adjustment assistance at reduced interest rates, and by adopting more flexible repayment schedules. IMF also should strengthen its co-operation with World Bank and other multilateral development organizations.

Finally, IMF should aim for no worse than a net neutral financial position between itself and the poorest African nations. This was not the case in 1985, when eleven African countries had negative net flows with IMF. Without firm action this situation will continue, and could worsen, particularly as interest charges on outstanding debt owed IMF create additional strains.

Aid donors not yet deeply involved in Africa should be encouraged to participate more fully. The most obvious donor with under-utilized capacity is Japan. A substantial increase in Japanese assistance to Africa beyond present low, albeit growing, levels, could help re-ignite growth. Official and private statements, including those of Prime Minister Nakasone during his recent visit to Washington, indicate that Japan is ready to increase greatly its assistance to developing countries. African governments, international agencies, and other OECD governments should encourage and assist the Japanese to become more deeply involved in supporting African development.

TABLE 34.1
IMF NET FLOWS BY COUNTRY, 1980–85
($US millions at 1983 prices and exchange rates)

		1980	1981	1982	1983	1984	1985
LOW-INCOME		460	1113	658	1089	450	191
of which:	Ghana	−12	−11	4	278	215	122
	Zaire	16	104	120	128	107	66
	Zambia	7	358	−49	80	78	−19
	Madagascar	46	36	57	12	18	−4
	Malawi	29	27	2	26	18	7
	Senegal	45	59	44	28	17	15
	Liberia	20	52	71	55	16	−7
	Niger	–	–	–	33	15	16
	Sudan	132	168	46	162	14	−5
	Togo	20	8	–	23	13	7
	Sierra Leone	0	28	–	23	11	−4
	Somalia	7	30	35	51	−3	26
	Mauritania	16	4	17	−2	−9	−3
	Kenya	65	26	147	96	−12	54
	Uganda	34	129	92	108	−17	−65
	Ethiopia	–	76	23	−19	−21	−31
	Tanzania	18	−12	−10	−20	−25	−5
MIDDLE-INCOME		75	468	492	472	99	−72
of which:	Zimbabwe	40	43	–	164	83	−21
	Cote d'Ivoire	15	377	127	179	14	−38
	Cameroon	−16	−10	−3	13	7	–
	Congo	−6	−8	–	4	3	–
	Nigeria	–	–	339	83	–	–

Source: Organization for Economic Co-operation and Development
Note:
– Denotes Zero or negligible.

Similarly, the centrally-planned economies should be encouraged to do more for Africa. Their aid levels remain low with programmes concentrated in a small number of countries. Historically, these governments have maintained that, since they had no colonial involvement in Africa, they should not be asked to provide large amounts of aid. The same logic could, of course, be used by the US and Japan, and this weak rationalization for insufficient assistance to Africa should no longer be accepted. Eastern Europe and the Soviet Union should play a larger role in supporting African development.

Other important issues have a longer gestation period. For instance, The Uruguay Round of trade negotiations under GATT will address agricultural trade, and this could help African agriculture, not by increasing export possibilities, but by moving towards agricultural price policies which better reflect underlying production realities. Present trends in the developed countries, which amount to the pursuit of a policy of import substitution in agriculture, are beginning to come under more pressure, with the possibility of a transition to a more rational system of world agriculture sometime during the 1990s.

Short periods of high prices for some commodities should not lull nations into diminishing essential efforts to diversify their economies. Other commodities, particularly minerals such as copper, are experiencing long-term secular declines in world demand, with any price improvements highly unlikely.

Producing countries should centre their planning efforts on taking advantage of any temporary surplus by, insofar as reasonable, investing earnings in efforts to diversify away from production of these commodities, recognizing that concentration on production of primary products is not a long-term sustainable strategy.

If the opportunities discussed above are to be seized, Africans and their governments need to keep the pressure on international organizations and donor governments. This means that African governments and organizations must do a much better job than in the past of telling their own story about the hard steps they are taking, the progress they are making, and the potential that lies ahead. They should work with their natural allies in the OECD countries – particularly the US – in legislatures, political parties, NGOs, and businesses involved in Africa. In addition, a permanent 'representative for African development' in Washington to deal both with the US government as well as with IBRD and IMF could bring considerable returns.

CONCLUSION

We return to our initial assessment. The short-term outlook is not overly bright, but this is not a time for pessimism. Over the long term, UN-PAAERD's importance is grounded in consensus over a twin strategy: (i) changes within African countries to transform their economies; and, (ii) support from the international community for recovery and sustained development.

Africa's actions over the next two years will greatly affect the willingness of outsiders to contribute more substantially to Africa's future; the consensus over problems faced and solutions needed should be carefully preserved. In the end, the durability of the compact between the international community and Africa rests on African leadership – leadership both by example and through insistent pressure on the international community to hold to its role in this agreed-upon agenda for Africa's future.

NOTES

1. See 'Should the IMF Withdraw from Africa?', by Maurice J. Williams, ODC Policy focus, No.1, March 1987.
2. DAC, 1986 report.
3. *Ibid.*
4. The Administration's proposals stemmed from a little-noticed 'Presidential Initiative on Ending Hunger in Africa', issued by President Reagan without fanfare in March 1987. It also recommends long-term 'framework agreements' between donors and each African country, and a more flexible stance on debt relief.
5. Christine E. Contee, *What Americans Think: Views on Development and United States – Third World Relations and Interaction*, Overseas Development Council, 1987.

CHAPTER THIRTY-FIVE

Long-Term Prospects for Co-operation Between Africa and the International Community

COMMONWEALTH SECRETARIAT

INTRODUCTION

An assessment of the long-term prospects for co-operation between Africa and the international community must begin by emphasising the fact that the region's economic crisis extends beyond drought and famine. There was ample rain, the best in a decade, across much of the African continent in 1985. Total agricultural production and food production increased during the year, though an estimated 15 million people are still at risk from famine. For the first time since 1980, some GDP growth was achieved in sub-Saharan Africa in 1985. Nonetheless, even in that year, population was still growing faster than output and average incomes declined, albeit more slowly than in earlier years, and the pace of decline is likely to have gone up again in 1986. For Africa, 'recovery' so far has only meant an abatement of the rate of decline.

The outlines of Africa's current economic crisis are well known. Declining output levels, high inflation and widening current account deficits are symptoms of the overall deterioration in Africa's economic activity over the past decade. Average growth of per capita GDP slowed from 3.7 per cent a year in 1965–73 to 0.5 per cent a year in 1973–80; over 1980–86, per capita GDP fell on average by 3.7 per cent. Inflation has remained high at over 15 per cent throughout 1980–86; and the combined current account deficits have increased from an average of $US5 billion during 1973–80 to an average of $US10 billion during 1980–86. The increases in the deficits have, by and large, not been financed by a net inflow of medium and long-term debt, but rather by a build-up of short-term debt, a draw-down on reserves, purchases from IMF, the accumulation of payments arrears and debt rescheduling. More importantly, the size of the deficits understates the magnitude of Africa's problem. The deficits would have been much larger had imports not been massively cut, breaking growth but avoiding even more serious balance of payments problems.

The origin of some, although not all, of Africa's problems lies in the past. The colonial structures that many newly independent countries inherited were often ill-adapted to serve the new development challenges. Transport and communication networks were geared to serve former metropolitan markets and the production emphasis was more often on the export of minerals and agricultural commodities to these markets than on domestic food production. Twenty-five years later, weaknesses in the development of food crops, of agriculture in general, and of domestic manufacturing still remain a basic structural characteristic shared by many African countries. Poverty has compounded the development problems faced by governments.

The ability of African governments to shape their political and economic future has been made even more difficult by a series of shocks. Of these, the most adverse in scope and duration have been the two oil shocks and their aftermaths. The sharp decline in output and accelerated rates of inflation in the industrial countries after each oil shock resulted in reduced demand for Africa's exports and a weakening of commodity prices. As a result of the increased cost of imported oil and the demand of essential imports of food, fertilizers, oil and producer goods, compounded by low world demand for Africa's exports, African economies experienced widening current account deficits. The severity of the external environment can be gauged from the fact that income losses due to the deterioration in Africa's terms of trade were as much as 10 per cent of GDP in 1974–75 and again in 1979–82. Some countries registered losses as high as 25 per cent of GDP during the latter period. By contrast, the income losses of the industrial countries due to adverse terms of trade were approximately 2 per cent of GDP after each oil shock. The third shock for these countries was the deep recession of the early 1980s from which many have never recovered. Stagnant concessional and declining non-concessional flows, reduced export opportunities and sharply decreased imports, all compounded development problems.

Domestic policies also played a part in Africa's economic decline: the lack of support for agricultural development through pricing and other supporting policies; overvalued exchange rates that discriminated against exports and tended to favour the urban population over rural areas; high levels of protection for urban industries; mounting fiscal deficits; and a variety of burdensome government interventions in the production process that slowed Africa's growth. Such policies, by and large, have exacted the inevitable penalties – an erosion of productivity and entrepreneurial energy. And that, inevitably, has exacerbated long-term structural problems and has translated into sluggish economic growth.

The long-term outlook for sub-Saharan Africa is bleak. World Bank has made growth projections for various regions of the developing world. Its 'high case' scenario for the decade 1985–95 assumes that many of the worldwide checks to growth in the past ten years have been overcome, and developing countries have improved their economic policies. In such promising circumstances, developing countries as a whole would enjoy an average growth of 3.9 per cent in per capita incomes per year; but for sub-Saharan Africa, per capita growth would be a precariously low 0.7 per cent a year, and most of this would not be realised until the second half of the decade. The 'low case' scenario assumes that industrial countries continue to grow slowly (at 2.5 per cent), trade barriers increase and capital flows remain depressed. In such circumstances, sub-Saharan Africa is projected to show zero growth in per capita income over the coming decade.

This Chapter examines some of the critical development problems which impede the reversal of economic decline in sub-Saharan Africa and considers the co-operation required between Africa and the international community if the decline is to be halted and consumption and living standards gradually increased. The central message is that the current situation is desperate and is not likely to improve without a major concerted effort by African countries and their development partners. The key challenges include: innovative ways to deal with the debt crisis; improvements in the trade and external environment; adequate support to ensure growth alongside adjustment; and the removal of some long-term constraints to development. The Chapter looks at these challenges for Africa, primarily from the perspective of the 29 low-income countries of sub-Saharan Africa.

DEALING WITH THE DEBT CRISIS

In terms of developing countries' overall indebtedness, which was approaching one trillion US dollars at the end of 1985, the indebtedness of sub-Saharan Africa appears modest at first sight. At the end of 1985, the total stock of sub-Saharan Africa's debt was $US85.6 billion, of which $US65 billion was held by official creditors. But this picture is misleading. It is the data concerning the size of the debt in relation to these countries' GNP and their capacity to service this debt that provide a truer picture of the overwhelming debt problem faced by these countries. The debt ratio doubled in the three year period 1980–83 to over 200 per cent and has stayed at that level since. Total debt as a proportion of GNP was 55 per cent. For the 29 low-income sub-Saharan countries, the figures are even more dramatic. At the end of 1985, debt represented 425.5 per cent of annual exports and 80 per cent of their GNP – virtually twice the level of indebtedness of developing countries as a whole.

It is important to distinguish between the major debtors, mainly those in Latin America, with obligations principally to commercial banks, and the poorer countries, especially those in sub-Saharan Africa, with mainly official or officially-guaranteed debt. This latter group have debt-servicing problems which are, in some cases, more onerous than those of Latin American countries. But since African debt is much smaller in total than that of the major debtors, and since most of it is owed to Western governments rather than to banks, it has so far received less international attention. Default by one or more of the large debtors could pose a threat to the international financial systems; African debt is unlikely to do so.

Another important feature of sub-Saharan African debt has been the large proportion of the debt service owed to the multilateral development institutions and IMF. For example, World Bank estimates that, for a number of countries in the region, 50 per cent or more of their debt service is owed to these institutions. World Bank credits have not been rescheduled in the past in order to preserve the Bank's preferred creditor status. There has been reluctance on the part of all World Bank members to permit rescheduling as this could affect the cost at which World Bank borrows and, in turn, the cost of its lending to developing countries. IMF drawings are neither reschedulable nor cheap – they are provided at about 6 per cent interest currently (variable at six-monthly intervals), and are usually repayable within 5–7 years. In addition, because of the revolving nature of IMF credits, net flows from IMF to low-income Africa have shifted from over $US800 million annually in 1981–83 (when a number of drawings were made) to negative flows in 1986 and beyond. Several sub-Saharan African countries have consequently found themselves in arrears on payments to one or the other institutions or both. Because of arrears to IMF, Liberia and Sudan were declared ineligible for further IMF credits at the end of 1986.

Bank lending has also collapsed. While the amount of bank credit provided to low-income African countries has always been modest, since 1983 even these modest flows have halted. Since 1983, these countries have been making net repayments to the financial markets, as indeed has sub-Saharan Africa as a whole. For example, the region received net transfers of $US2.3 billion from the financial markets in 1982, but by 1985 it was making net payments of $US2.9 billion.

The end-result has been that total debt service payments for sub-Saharan Africa have risen from $US5 billion (including $US0.8 billion to IMF) in 1980 to $US9.6 billion (including $US1.5 billion to IMF) in 1986. In 1987, after taking account of the anticipated rescheduling payments, total debt service payments are expected to be $US10.8 billion (including $US1.8 billion to IMF). Including debt service payments to IMF, the debt service ratio is expected to have risen from 16.7 per cent in 1980 and 35.8 per cent in 1986 to 37.7 per cent in 1987. The debt-servicing outlook beyond 1987 remains particularly bleak for low-income African countries. Multilateral and bilateral concessional assistance loans made in the 1970s are now coming due for repayment, so that these countries will face continuously rising amortisation obligations in 1987–97.

While Western governments have begun to recognize the seriousness of the debt-servicing problem of African countries, the policy response has so far been short-term and piecemeal, consisting largely of successive short-term debt reschedulings by official creditors. The pace of such reschedulings has accelerated in recent years. There have been 57 reschedulings by 23 African countries in the decade to 1986, including 13 alone in 1986; 14 African countries have had a series of debt rescheduling agreements, each one arranged 12–18 months apart. However, with the exception of Cote d'Ivoire, no African country has been able to negotiate a multi-year restructuring agreement (MYRA).

Most official reschedulings of debt have taken place under the auspices of the Paris Club – an *ad hoc* group of Western creditor governments. One of the problems with this forum is that only official debts owed to Western governments are considered. This means debts owed to governments in Eastern Europe and, more importantly, payments owed to the multilateral development institutions and IMF are excluded, as is debt owed to private creditors. As a result, often around half of an African country's debt is ineligible for rescheduling.

Besides the problem of the short duration of the period for which debts are rescheduled (the consolidation period) and the limited amount of debt eligible for rescheduling, the current procedures and mode of operation of the Paris Club have posed a number of problems. For example:

– creditors generally agree to a meeting only after debt-servicing problems have reached a critical stage. There is little willingness to work towards preventive action.

- interest rates on non-concessional rescheduled loans (which are bilaterally negotiated after the Paris Club has completed its work) are usually set at market rates, which in practice can be higher than those on the original loan.
- considerable time often elapses between reaching agreement in the Paris Club and the signing of bilateral agreements. During this period, export credit agencies have often been reluctant to resume cover. Even when rescheduling is completed, there may be prolonged delays before export credit is resumed.
- finally, the Paris Club mechanism was not designed, nor has it been used, to assess African countries' development requirements as well as debt-servicing capacities. There is often little or no co-ordination within creditor governments between officials in the Treasury responsible for debt reschedulings and those in aid Ministries. As a consequence, there is no overall consideration of the minimum external flows from all sources required for debtor countries to be able to meet debt-servicing requirements and to ensure economic growth.

There is an overwhelming need to approach Africa's debt problem in a more comprehensive fashion. The problem cannot simply be seen as one of coping with short-term balance of payments and liquidity constraints but has to be recognised as one closely related to long-term poverty, the solution of which requires the fundamental transformation of these economies.

There have been some important recent developments. It is highly encouraging that a number of developed country governments are increasingly recognising that a much more determined and long-term effort is needed to alleviate the debt burden which is crippling Africa's recovery. The recent proposals announced by Britain's Chancellor of the Exchequer, Nigel Lawson, in April 1987 illustrate the type of longer-term and concerted efforts that are required, although even these may not be far-reaching enough if growth is to be resumed and sustained in sub-Saharan Africa. The Lawson approach consists of: (i) the conversion of aid loans into grants by those donor governments that have not already done so; (ii) the rescheduling of official debt over longer periods of up to 20 years as well as longer grace periods; and, (iii) a reduction in interest rates to a few points below market levels on outstanding debt.

Another encouraging initiative is that of the UN Secretary-General who announced in April 1987 the establishment of a working group 'to propose concrete solutions for Africa's financial problems' by the end of 1987. It is to be hoped that this group will be able to arrive at practical and politically acceptable proposals that provide both the debt relief and financial flows so urgently needed by Africa.

One step, on which there is already a large measure of agreement, is the cancellation of repayment obligations on development assistance loans. Several donors, including Britain, Canada, Germany and the Scandinavian countries, have already converted bilateral aid loans into grants for a number of low-income countries, as proposed in UNCTAD resolution of 1978. It is important for other donors to follow, and for all donors to ensure that this relief is extended to all low-income indebted African countries.

Additional measures are urgently needed to deal with other official bilateral debt and debt owed to multilateral creditors. Agreement on a reduction in interest rates to well below prevailing market rates will be important as will longer rescheduling periods and more generous grace periods. For some countries, the relief may still not be sufficient and more far-reaching proposals may be needed, including the writing-down of a considerable portion of the official debt. This proposal is not as radical as it sounds. Western creditors, in 1966 for example, agreed to reschedule all of Indonesia's outstanding debt for thirty years at no interest; there was even a provision for a further postponement of repayments, if warranted by balance of payments considerations.

Another question that needs to be addressed is that of the multi-year restructuring of debt. So far, creditors have not been willing to consider MYRAs for African countries on the grounds that successive reschedulings, evolving according to the particular needs and circumstances of each debtor, are more flexible than MYRAs. In the case of Cote d'Ivoire, the only African country to negotiate one, Paris Club creditors have not rescheduled interest but have only rescheduled successively smaller amounts of principal. By contrast, under recent successive rescheduling agreements, 95 per cent of principal and interest on loans from governments and on guaranteed export credits has been rescheduled. While the successive rescheduling agreements may be more generous in their terms than MYRAs, they can place a major burden on the resources of already stretched governmental machineries. Each rescheduling creates an enormous amount of work for the rescheduled countries – both in the background work required before the negotiation as well as in the follow-up negotiation of terms and interest rates with each bilateral creditor. There is also much greater uncertainty for the government in planning its debt payments, if it (and creditor governments) knows further rescheduling will be necessary but does not know what the terms will be.

Action is also required on the other major portion of Africa's official debt – the debt owed to World Bank and regional development banks, and payments due to IMF. A number of ideas have been under consideration by governments and it is now urgent to come to common conclusions on what must be done. The exact form of the proposal is not as important as its end-result – an increase in the net flows from these institutions to low-income Africa. It may, for example, be necessary to extricate IMF from its position as a creditor to the poorest countries, and to replace its generally short-term focus with a longer-term perspective. A new policy framework should combine medium-term adjustment and policy reform with adequate net flows. World Bank should play a strengthened role in mobilising resources, ensuring needed debt relief and assisting the poorest debtors in setting out the appropriate adjustment and development framework.

The need to maintain trade finance to these countries is also critical to their ability to keep their economies moving. Despite the exclusion of short-term trade credits by export agencies from reschedulings in an effort to ensure these flows are not interrupted, it has not always been possible for the country undergoing rescheduling to maintain or to regain cover in a timely fashion. It may therefore be necessary for creditor country governments to look not only at the rescheduling requirements of low-income Africa but to support what would amount to non-market operations of their export credit agencies in providing short and longer-term export credits.

Problems relating to the uncertainty of financial flows to these countries underline the need for closer co-ordination between debt relief and aid. Under the current pattern of discussions, where aid levels are often indicated before an agreement is reached on debt relief, larger aid commitments have often been offset by harder terms on debt restructuring. One way to integrate the two areas of policy would be to bring together in one forum the different representatives of developed country governments handling aid and debt in order to ensure adequate aid and debt relief, as was done through the case of India (1968/72), Pakistan (1973), and more recently Mauritania (1985).

OVERCOMING TRADE CONSTRAINTS

Commodity production and exports play an extremely important role in Africa's economic performance; and most of the constraints posed by Africa's trade relate to export commodities, which account for around 80 per cent of the region's total export earnings. In the 1960s and throughout the commodity boom of the early 1970s, Africa's export performance was quite satisfactory, but after the first oil shock, it slipped badly both absolutely and in relation to other developing regions and it has never recovered. While part of the difficulty stems from poor domestic performance, particularly in the agricultural sector, many of the constraints lie beyond the control of either individual countries or the region as a whole. International action and co-operation are essential to reverse the downward trend.

Volume growth of trade (excluding Nigeria) averaged only 0.6 per cent a year in the period 1973–80, and it declined for the next three years. In 1985, it rose by a modest 2 per cent. Slow volume growth has been characteristic of the weakness in Africa's export performance. The region's share of the non-fuel exports of developing countries fell steeply from 18.0 per cent in 1960 and 18.6 per cent in 1970, to 9.2 per cent in 1978 and has not recovered. More seriously, Africa lost market share in those commodities which form its staple exports. Africa's share of world exports of cocoa fell from 80 per cent in 1961–63 to 69 per cent in 1977–79; of groundnut oil, from 54 per cent to 41 per cent; and of palm oil, from 55 per cent to only 4 per cent. This poor volume performance has been exacerbated by the decreased purchasing power of these exports – a trend which has been consistently downward since the 1970s. As a result, the total export earnings of sub-Saharan Africa (excluding Nigeria) have remained at around $US25 billion each year since 1982 – which is no higher than the 1978–80 average and well below the single peak-year figure of $US30 billion in 1980.

Oil is particularly important – about half of the total regional GDP for sub-Saharan countries comes from the oil-exporting countries. The sharp decline in oil prices in 1986 has hit these countries badly, with losses to exporters of around $US7 billion. To some extent, this loss has been compensated for by the reduced oil import expenditures of some $US2 billion for other countries in the region. Overall, the effects on individual countries have varied considerably. For example, the losses have been primarily concentrated in Nigeria, while the benefits of lower prices have been important for others such as Ghana, Kenya, Tanzania, and Zimbabwe. The negative indirect regional effects, including lower oil-related foreign investment, reduced expatriate worker remittances and decreased local demand, must also be taken into account.

The disappointing export receipts have resulted in a sharp decline in import performance – a problem exacerbated by debt-servicing difficulties. The decline in import volumes in the 1980s has been the major cause of the significant under-utilisation of existing capacities in the agricultural and manufacturing sectors and in the deterioration of the economic infrastructure, as well as in social services. The negative impact of sub-Saharan Africa's terms of trade has been such that, in 1985, they were 10 per cent below the 1970 levels for the region as a whole; with over 20 per cent average falls in some countries (including Zambia, Sierra Leone, Ethiopia, Zaire and Liberia). This represents an accumulated loss of approximately $US11 billion in the period 1980–85.

While the causes of this disappointing trade performance are not all exclusive to the sub-Saharan region, some special features can be distinguished. For most countries in the region, the major underlying problem has been their dependency on a limited range of primary products. In addition, poor agricultural performance has led to increased food imports, decreased exports of agricultural goods and a deterioration of the external payments situation. The 1970s and early 1980s saw falls in the export volumes of cocoa, coffee, groundnuts and their oils, oilseed cake and meal, palm kernel oil, palm oil, seasame seed, bananas, cotton, rubber and sisal. In all of these products, the sub-Saharan countries' share of developing country exports fell reflecting an inability to compete in a difficult overall market situation. A similar pattern is evident for non-agricultural commodities; for example, the region's exports of copper, iron ore and zinc decreased from 1970 to 1982, a period in which world trade in these products increased.

Another significant factor that has contributed to the region's poor trade performance is the instability and ongoing decline in commodity prices, mainly due to the decline in overall world demand for commodities. Commodity prices, excluding fuels, were at the end of 1985 twenty-two per cent below 1980 levels and the 1980 level was itself twenty per cent below the average price level of the 1960–80 period. This reflects two main problems. The first is technology and the lesser use of commodities in modern technological processes. The impact of increased recycling (in steel and aluminium); reduced stock holdings and more flexible purchasing patterns by major consumers; the introduction of new technologies, including the substitution of new inputs (e.g. optical fibres replacing copper in telecommunications; plastics and ceramics replacing metals in automobiles) have all increased in recent years. This has resulted in a partial 'delinkage' of economic growth from commodity trade, so that recovery in the industrial countries has not resulted in increased demand and/or prices for many commodities.

Second, it reflects increasing protectionism in the major consumer countries, notably in EEC and the US – often allied to increasing domestic production support measures for the same or substitutable commodities – which has had a significant impact on sub-Saharan exports. Developing country commodity exporters face high tariffs in industrial countries on their major processed commodities, such as cocoa, coffee, tea, beef and fish, manufactured tobacco, leather products, processed aluminium and copper. These tariffs pose a serious barrier to efforts by sub-Saharan African countries to diversify into higher value-added processing of their commodities. Tariffs escalate with each successive stage of processing and entry is made even more impregnable by similar escalations of non-tariff barrier structures.

The price decline is also partially a result of the pressures of over-supply, which have affected most commodity markets. Of Africa's major commodity exports, only coffee has seen some price rises. On the other hand, commodities such as sugar, tea, copper and tin (and potentially cocoa) have large stocks or surplus capacity overhanging these already depressed markets. In some commodities, developing countries, including some in sub-Saharan Africa, have found themselves contributing to the oversupply situation as they have no other significant exports to earn badly needed foreign exchange.

The price situation has been exacerbated by the ineffectiveness, and in some cases collapse, of international commodity agreements. The only agreements which now contain economic (price stabilisation) provisions are cocoa, natural rubber and coffee (the last being currently non-operative). In particular, the debacle of the International Tin Council has demonstrated the difficulty of attempts to support commodity prices. Buffer stocking and other market interventions designed to stabilise or improve commodity prices have been unable to withstand the downward price pressures, which have affected commodities in recent years. The compensatory financing mechanism of IMF has not proved adequate to the task of meeting the export shortfalls of the developing countries in the 1980s and, more recently, has only been available when an IMF stabilisation programme has been in place. The Lome Convention's Stabex scheme for the stabilisation of the export earnings of the Africa–Caribbean–Pacific (ACP) group of countries quickly ran out of funds in the face of its first serious test in the early 1980s (and has, so far, not been effectively revised or improved).

Another cause of the deterioration in commodity prices is the impact of exchange rate variations, adding to dollar price fluctuations and creating uncertainty. The existence of high interest rates has also had a damaging effect on commodity prices largely through changes in stock holdings patterns, including the unloading of existing stocks.

There are a number of measures that can be taken to help reverse these trends. At the national level, it is important that increased policy attention be given to improving the contribution of the commodity sector in GDP, in particular, through the expansion of agricultural output. With nearly four-fifths of Africa's population dependent on agriculture for its livelihood, increased agricultural production is essential for any meaningful improvement in living standards. Whether such production should be export-oriented or utilized for domestic consumption depends, in part, on international markets and, in part, on country circumstances. In either case, increased production would contribute to the easing of foreign exchange constraints, either by the reduction of food imports or by increased returns from exports. There is also a need to reassess national policies in industry; high-cost import substitution has grown up behind quotas or tariffs in individual countries of the region.

However, sub-Saharan trade prospects are largely dependent on the expansion of the world economy and improved international co-operation in the trade field. There is already growing recognition that a return to liberalised world trade, and an improvement of the rules under which such trade is conducted, would be of benefit to all countries, developed or developing. The newly-launched Uruguay Round of multilateral trade negotiations in GATT is an opportunity for 'rolling back' existing protectionist measures as well as for addressing the rules of the trading system. The multilateral trade round must, however, address specific interests of sub-Saharan countries. In particular, it must give adequate attention to more liberalised trade in agriculture, tropical products, and natural resource products, as well as to trade rules governing safeguards, dispute settlement procedures and provisions for differential and more favourable treatment of developing countries. Progress in the trade round should be supplemented by unilateral liberalisation, wherever this is possible.

Similarly, attention must be focused on improving existing special trade agreements between countries of the region and the industrial countries. Individual countries should assess whether the benefits of wider liberalisation in the Uruguay Round would be offset by the consequential erosion of preferences they have under such special agreements as the Lome Convention. A related area of long-term co-operation is the Generalised System of Preferences. The expansion of the product coverage to include key commodities would be of benefit to the region as would improvements in the rules of origin to allow for greater regional 'cumulation' of content for qualifying preferences. The ongoing negotiations for the establishment of the Global System of Trade Preferences among developing countries offer increased prospects for South–South co-operation in this field and for the expansion of Africa's external trade.

There is also a need to revitalise the international debate on commodities, including work in UNCTAD on the Integrated Programme for Commodities (IPC). There should be increased efforts to develop commodity agreements, where these are feasible. Equally, work should be done on other 'flexible' forms of producer/consumer co-operation, such as study groups, to review long-term trends and market conditions and provide forums where the interests of producers and consumers can be discussed and reconciled. An area that requires special attention is the strengthening of compensatory financing mechanisms for countries experiencing temporary export shortfalls. Besides possible improvements in the existing facilities, particularly the IMF facility, the possibilities for setting up new mechanisms, with adequate support of major industrial countries, should be seriously considered. Some proposals have already been advanced in UNCTAD and should be studied further.

However, such mechanisms cannot alleviate problems resulting from the downward trend in the long-term demand for commodities. African countries must ultimately encourage the expansion of non-traditional exports and the industrial sector, including the processing of commodities, in order to reduce the region's dependency on a limited range of exportable commodities. Given the financial and resource constraints of the region, progress can only be achieved in the medium to longer term. Increased international support is critical in assisting the commodity upgrading and export diversification process; equally important will be the negotiation of improved access for these products in industrial country markets.

ENSURING GROWTH ALONGSIDE ADJUSTMENT

The decline in African economic performance and the unfavourable external environment is reflected in the protracted balance of payments difficulties that many countries in the region are facing. Since the late 1970s, many countries have found themselves obliged to negotiate with IMF short-term stabilisation programmes – usually of 12 months duration – often one following the other. IMF's own assessment of its programmes has not been that of unqualified success. For example, of the 1980–81 programmes in sub-Saharan Africa, only about a third attained the targets designed to reduce current account deficits and only a fifth reached the targeted level of economic growth. The longer-term success of these programmes in generating sustainable growth is even less certain.

The truth is that the cost of pursuing too short-term an approach to adjustment in sub-Saharan Africa has been severe. Often the deflationary adjustment measures necessitated by short-term balance of payments arithmetic have resulted in the 'import strangulation' of many African economies. Import volumes of sub-Saharan African countries declined – for example, over the period 1980–86 by an average of 8 per cent per annum. This has not only made the investment required for recovery impossible, but has damaged the limited and painfully accumulated existing capital stock. In many instances, it has resulted in unnecessary output losses because of under-utilisation of partially import-dependent productive capacity. Moreover, the market-related interest rates and the 5- to 7-year repayment terms of IMF loans have meant that IMF debt now represents a substantial proportion of the total debt for many African countries.

But improved IMF programmes alone would not be enough. IMF must work with the resources that are available to it. Moreover, its short-term programmes and repayment periods were never designed to deal with the basic poverty and long-term structural problems facing Africa. While IMF could have been more imaginative in making use of the extended fund facility – a facility with a three-year programme period – even that facility in its conception lacked the flexibility in its objectives and targets that most developing countries needed. In addition, its interest rates were again those of the market. Since its establishment in 1974, nine countries in sub-Saharan Africa did negotiate programmes under it, but its rigid manner of operation and an almost compulsive focus on precise short-term targets meant that five of the nine programmes were cancelled before expiration and others were not renewed.

It has only somewhat belatedly been recognised that sub-Saharan Africa's difficulties were structural in character and that what the region needed was a longer-term approach to adjustment combined, in the case of the poorest countries, with concessional funds. The joint Programme of Action launched at the September 1984 World Bank/ IMF annual meetings sought to correct the causes of Africa's economic decline through the improved formulation and implementation of rehabilitation and development programmes, together with more closely co-ordinated donor assistance to support national priorities and programmes. For the poorer IDA-eligible countries, a special assistance facility was also set up in World Bank, with donor contributions of $US1.5 billion to supplement assistance of $US3 billion from

IDA-7 over the period 1984–87. Resources under IDA-8 will continue to be concentrated on sub-Saharan Africa; the region is expected to receive $US5.6–$US6.2 billion in the 1987–90 period. So far, 22 of the 29 poor (IDA-eligible) countries in sub-Saharan Africa have embarked on major programmes of structural reform or are close to initiating such programmes. In some countries such as Ghana, Senegal, Zaire and Zambia, these efforts have been underway for several years; in others, such as Sierra Leone, Tanzania and Gambia, programmes with World Bank have recently begun.

The need to provide concessional assistance to poor countries suffering from protracted balance of payments difficulties and willing to implement courageous policy reforms was further recognised when a Structural Adjustment Facility (SAF) was set up in IMF in 1986. Eligible countries are to develop jointly with the staff of IMF and World Bank a three-year policy framework outlining their medium-term objectives, main macroeconomic and structural policies, and financing needs. Six sub-Saharan African countries have so far negotiated such programmes; the process has been facilitated by the fact that these countries already had or have simultaneously negotiated a stabilisation arrangement with IMF. While it is too early to assess its performance, one of its shortcomings is that, because of its informal linkage with stabilisation programmes, its programmes may suffer from the same type of short-term bias that has applied to normal IMF programmes. They also tend to be fairly complex to negotiate because of the involvement of World Bank as well as IMF. Moreover, with resources limited to 47 per cent of quota over a three-year period, funds available under the SAF are tiny when compared with the 280 or 345 per cent of quota available under the Fund's normal facilities. The SAF clearly needs more resources if it is to provide adequate concessional balance of payments support to sub-Saharan African countries undertaking adjustment.

Clearly, both IMF and World Bank are deeply involved in sub-Saharan Africa's pursuit of major structural reforms and balance of payments adjustment. Questions have, however, arisen about which institution should play a lead role in Africa, and about whether the lending conditions of one or the other institution have been or should be made preconditions for lending by the other – the issue of cross-conditionality. These issues, while significant, are, however, subsidiary to the two basic questions that need to be addressed when considering structural reform and balance of payments adjustment in sub-Saharan Africa. First, what should be the content of the adjustment programme and second, what level and type of financing is necessary to support these efforts.

Fortunately, there is now broad agreement on the main elements of reform that are needed. The focus should be on the supply side and aimed at increasing efficient export production as well as import substitution. Supply side measures should be supported by responsible monetary and fiscal policy in order to expand savings and investment. There is also widespread agreement on the main elements of previous supply side policy error in Africa. In fact, the common elements in the approaches to Africa's policy requirements by the multilateral institutions and bilateral donors now far outweigh the differences. While the timing and sequencing of the required policies as well as the role of non-price measures to support price incentives pose some differences, it would be misleading to exaggerate these conflicts among policy-makers who otherwise agree on the broad direction of change.

There may nonetheless be sharp disagreements between longer-term development strategies and medium-term structural reform. Issues such as the degree of outward orientation of the economy, the role of government, longer-term industrialisation policies, the degree of tolerable income inequality are as much political as economic issues. Donors who have firm views as to the appropriate longer-term strategies may be tempted to insist on measures in programmes that reflect their views. Rightly or wrongly, the international institutions and some donors are seen by many African countries as pursuing longer-term objectives that are not in accord with their own. Unnecessary confusion between the requirements for medium-term adjustment, on which there can be relatively easy agreement, and the appropriate longer-term development strategy, on which may be sharp differences, can risk aborting an African recovery. In current circumstances, therefore, disagreements over the long-term strategies should, and frequently can, be set aside in the interests of progress on medium-term structural reforms.

Take, for example, the relative roles of the public and the private sectors. There is undoubtedly now widespread agreement, even in African policy-making circles, that governments have frequently and inappropriately overextended the public sector. But it would be counterproductive to push private sector expansion too fast or too far. Inefficiency in public monopolies does not necessarily create a case for private monopolies. The mix of state and private sector activity varies and should vary, with the specifics of individual countries' economic, political and administrative structures. Indeed, many public sector enterprises were set up because the private sector offered inadequate services or no services at all. For external agencies to push national governments too far on this or other such issues could risk the credibility of otherwise sound and agreed programmes.

For the programmes of structural reform to succeed, they must aim for some modest growth in living standards. After years of declining per capita incomes and consumption, adjustment measures must offer some hope of improved living standards. It may, for instance, be appropriate to define the objectives in terms of annual per cent growth rates which provides – say – at least a one per cent per annum growth in per capita consumption. This would clearly have implications for the length of the programme period and for the financial requirements to sustain such growth. But if countries are prepared to undertake such courageous and politically risky programmes, it is essential for the international community to provide the necessary resources to ensure the modest growth in per capita income needed to sustain long-term efforts.

Even with modest targets, there is concern that the necessary quantum of financial assistance may not materialize. The 22 sub-Saharan African countries with World Bank-sponsored SAPs saw only a modest increase of 8 per cent in their aid flows from OECD countries in 1985 over the 1984 levels. While preliminary estimates suggest these flows increased again in 1986, it is nonetheless clear that resources remain inadequate to achieve basic growth objectives.

World Bank has estimated, for example, that to maintain the 1986 per capita consumption levels during 1987–1989 for six countries – Madagascar, Niger, Senegal, Tanzania, Zaire and Zambia – an additional $US700 million per annum would be required over and above the expected net aid flows of $US2,510 million, the anticipated reschedulings of their debt, and an export growth of 50 per cent over the period. This is a tall order by any account. The requirements would need to be all the greater if per capita consumption is to grow by at least one per cent per annum. For low-income Africa as a whole, World Bank estimated that at least $US13.5 billion per annum of concessional flows and debt rescheduling would be needed for Africa to pursue economic adjustment and achieve a modest level of growth (3–4 per cent of GDP) during the 1986–1990 period. This analysis assumes that a resource gap of at least $US1.5 billion per annum would be filled.

To support adjustment programmes, donors must not only increase their aid budgets but concentrate their assistance as far as possible on low-income countries implementing adjustment programmes. Undoubtedly, the highest returns in Africa are typically to be reaped from the provision of untied foreign exchange for increased inputs for the rehabilitation and full utilisation of existing capital stock rather than the creation of new capital. Despite widespread agreement that, in current circumstances, more non-project aid is required, there seems to have been a significant shift away from overall programme aid toward sector aid.

Growth prospects in sub-Saharan Africa have been affected not only by inadequate resource flows but an inhospitable environment. If industrial countries continue to grow at about 2.5 per cent per annum – rates very similar to those achieved during 1980–1986 – or if the 2 per cent per annum growth in export volumes projected for these countries does not materialise, income per capita in Africa could decline. Increased co-ordination of macro-economic policies of major industrialised countries designed to achieve sustained world growth is also critical for African countries.

REMEDYING THE LONG-TERM CONSTRAINTS ON DEVELOPMENT

While Africa's immediate needs are for the rehabilitation and the expansion of its productive sectors, the region faces a number of long-term constraints on development. These include an inadequate transport infrastructure, a low level of human resource development, rapidly rising population, creeping deforestation and desertification, and a poor level of agricultural research. Donor support is essential not only for African countries' medium-term structural reform efforts, but also to address these long-term constraints.

Sub-Saharan Africa has never been equipped with adequate transport infrastructure. This inadequate infrastructure in many countries is rapidly reaching the end of its effective life. Without improved infrastructure, production-oriented strategies cannot succeed. Financing requirements for rehabilitation, reconstruction and expansion are massive. In addition to rural feeder networks, the region's main import and export supply routes need major investment. In the case of SADCC countries particularly, improved supply routes are imperative if these countries are to reduce their dependence on South Africa.

The population of sub-Saharan Africa is growing faster than that of any other continent. Its growth has accelerated from an average of 2.3 per cent a year in 1960 to 3.1 per cent today. The population problem in Africa is not that there are too many people but that the explosive growth in population is putting increasing stress on resources.

Lower rates of population growth may well be the most important requirement for sustained development in Africa. The progress achieved so far in sub-Saharan Africa is limited in relation to the task ahead; governments at present finance a very small share of family planning expenditures. Increased donor support is vital. Currently, only 0.5 per cent of ODA is directed at family planning activities in Africa, much less than 1.5 per cent for all developing countries.

Appropriate population strategies are also critical for human resource development. While health conditions in sub-Saharan Africa have improved in the past two decades, the limited financial resources mean that access to health care is extremely limited in most African countries. Greater emphasis is clearly needed on primary health care in rural areas. Donors could also help finance primary health care projects, perhaps by funnelling a larger share of their resources through NGOs which, in a number of African countries, already serve as a useful vehicle for providing such care.

As with health, the education sector is suffering a reversal in both the quantity and the quality of services it provides. Primary enrolment rates declined in 12 poor countries during the 1980–83 period. Additional resources are clearly needed to maintain the momentum of primary education both to meet enrolment requirements of a growing population and to ensure the adequate supply of books and other requirements.

Degrading of land – soil erosion, declining soil fertility and rapidly increasing desertification – is now posing one of the most serious challenges to large parts of Africa. The area of forest and savannah woodland has declined since the turn of the century and there have been major losses in farm tree stocks. The decline in tree stocks is accelerating under several influences – consumption of fuelwood is rising with population growth, so is land clearance for subsistence agriculture, thereby reducing soil moisture and increasing soil erosion. Seedlings and mature trees have been lost to ill-managed livestock, and commercial logging has gone on without adequate reinvestment in forest reserves.

The World Commission on Environment and Development has argued that it is poverty which is the major source of environmental stress, so that the main remedies are to be found in mechanisms that raise living standards and reduce pressures leading to overcropping and overgrazing, the elimination of forest cover for firewood and the spread of urban squalor. Requirements include increased resource flows to African countries, growth-oriented adjustment, redistributive policies designed to give priority to basic needs and measures to reduce population growth. Within this general policy framework, there is need for African governments to ensure that there is a better integration of natural resource management with country economic planning, and for donors to ensure that new investments contribute to sustainable development. In particular, a high proportion of funds should go to projects where the objectives of growth, poverty alleviation and environmental production are complementary.

In Africa, most farming remains at rudimentary subsistence levels and major advances in agricultural research, such as those that revolutionised wheat and rice cultivation in Asia, have not taken place. There has been no breakthrough for millet, which accounts for 80 per cent of cultivable land in the Sahel and other dry areas; nor for most root crops, which are the basic staple food in Africa. A long-term programme to strengthen agricultural research in sub-Saharan Africa must aim to build up scientific knowledge, to strengthen the country level institutions and to make better use of existing local research capacity. A short-term priority has to be the adaptation of existing technology to local farm conditions. While donors have funded much of the agricultural research in Africa, their policies have not only led to duplication of effort but compounded the problem by frequently changing priorities and making unrealistic demands for immediate results. While World Bank's special programme for African agricultural research is a good beginning, the financial implications for the effective adaptation of new technology go far beyond the resources currently being allocated for this purpose.

AN AFRICA-WIDE EFFORT

Clearly, part of the solution to sub-Saharan Africa's economic crisis has to come from the North, which alone can provide the large-scale development assistance, debt relief and balance of payments financing which is urgently needed. But, with imagination and vision, greater co-operation within Africa, in the context of strengthened South–South co-operation, could form part of a positive response to the crisis. What might be involved is a programme of action in the three broad areas of critical importance to African development – food and agriculture, trade and industry.

At the centre of Africa's current crisis is the problem of hunger and, in some countries, famine. The need for adequate food supplies must remain in the forefront of African policy makers' concerns. To a large extent, the remedies lie with national governments in correcting existing policy distortions. But this is only part of the answer. There is need for new technology in the form of better seeds, cheap and appropriate fertilizers, and improved distribution for agricultural inputs and output. Because of the similarity of crops and ecological conditions, African countries could mutually benefit from subregional co-operation. Joint efforts are appropriate for new research into drought resistant seeds and other vital inputs. Regional training programmes – of extension officers, agronomists and postgraduate specialists in new biotechnologies – are another potential area for co-operation. New advanced technology aids to agriculture – satellite reconnaissance, for example – require regional co-operation.

The objective is not to establish new subregional or regional institutions. Africa already has several regional institutions. What seems to be needed is a systematic review of the impact of current agricultural research in the region and the main issues and problems requiring urgent resolution and concerted action. Such an exercise could also form the basis of practical South–South programmes of technical assistance, for the success stories in other parts of the Third World may have relevance for Africa. For example, India has successfully developed some 15 semi-arid zones; that technology might be adapted to Africa. Co-operation in the field of regional food security is also important – this could include early warning systems for food production shortfalls, especially in areas close to national borders but far from capitals. The establishment of regional buffer stocks is another possibility.

There is also scope fo renewed efforts at the regional level in the trade field. Past efforts have achieved less than their original intentions; in part, this reflects a genuine motivation which exceeded either the resources available or the ability of regional authorities. It also reflects the impact of external pressures which were not perceived at the time of the launching of these efforts. While some of the constraints still remain, they are now more clearly recognised and can be more realistically addressed. Major constraints include the vast differences in the levels of industrial development, in the resource bases and in the overall financial and trade infrastructures of the individual countries of the region. With constraints of such magnitude, only a gradual and selective approach can hope to build a base for long-term sustainable results.

For instance, it is probable that a generalized tariff-cutting approach to trade liberalisation between member countries may not, for the present, be a viable approach for the sub-Saharan region; what may, however, be possible is a more selective approach. There seems to be scope for programmes of sectoral or product-based regional trade liberalization which do not place unequal burdens on individual member countries or cause significant increases in overall costs. Obviously, the scope for such liberalisation, and the scale of benefits are, in part, related to the foreign exchange savings which would accrue. This is, in turn, linked to the need for improved regional clearing and payments schemes. Existing schemes have highlighted the difficulties arising from persistent imbalances in trade flows between economies of differing strengths and from shortages of foreign exchange. Only if these problems are adequately addressed, and where necessary supported by external assistance, can such schemes be expected to function in an effective manner. There is also a need to investigate the potential for greater harmonisation of import procedures and long-term import needs to facilitate trade within the region. This could incorporate such basic issues as the harmonization and simplification of documentation or could eventually involve joint purchasing of imports.

In industry, experiences of regional co-operation in Africa have so far produced very few practical results. One of the basic problems has been that countries have found it hard to agree on the allocation of large-scale industry among member countries and on the level of access to regional markets such industries should have. But, so far, very little attention seems to have been given to promoting an investment process that would involve patterns of specialization between small- and medium-size enterprises in different partner states, associated with the strengthening of indigenous entrepreneurship. Co-operative arrangements and joint ventures between such enterprises could be encouraged to take advantage not only of scale economies within the intra-group market, but also in international markets, including the possibility for joint sub-contracting with outside firms. The vision has to be three-dimensional: national, South–South and international.

Such an approach requires concerted policies with respect to the promotion of joint investment activities, including the development of indigenous entrepreneurship and the provision of pre-investment services and export promotion facilities to small firms. This in no way diminishes the importance of seizing opportunities for joint action in setting up large multinational enterprises, where such opportunities exist. It also does not imply a less active role for governments in the integration of production.

The effective implementation of measures of regional and inter-regional co-operation inevitably poses the problem of financing. In this area, however, ADB could play a larger role. As a continent-wide organisation, whose resources are currently being increased substantially, it is well suited to channel financial resources to selected regional development projects with development potential and to act as a catalyst to encourage other donors and private lenders to do likewise.

CONCLUSION

The challenges for Africa and the international community are formidable. Action is required on virtually all fronts. Some of it is urgent and required to survive the immediate crisis; other action is longer-term but equally essential if the basis for sustained growth into the twenty-first century and beyond is to be laid. African countries have their own internal agendas to pursue in undertaking the necessary transformation and reform of their economies. But it is clear that they will not succeed, or will be far less likely to do so, without the generous and sustained support of the international community.

High on the priority list will be adequate financial and technical support to African countries in the formulation and implementation of growth-oriented adjustment programmes. Not only must such programmes meet balance of payments objectives, structural change criteria and income distribution considerations, but they must ensure that the environmental, social and the long-term economic objectives are steadily pursued so that the next generation faces a more promising world. But aid to economic programmes will not be enough. Debt relief is also an essential part of the co-operation needed from the international community. Under-development, poverty, and the long-term nature of Africa's problems means that Africa, by and large, is unable to service non-concessional debt. New and imaginative solutions to reduce the debt burden and increase the overall flow of resources are required. Greater co-ordination among donors on how to meet overall financial requirements (aid and debt relief) would be an important element of the process.

A more favourable external environment is equally crucial. Higher growth in developed countries through improved co-ordination of policies is needed if these countries are to become more amenable to increasing concessional and private flows to Africa and to reducing protectionism. Access to markets is essential if Africa is to move away from its enormous dependence for exports on a small range of commodities to become a more diversified exporter of processed commodities and other products.

The list of requirements is long. Intra-regional co-operation and international co-operation must work hand in hand if Africa is to reverse its decline and move forward to self-sustaining development.

CHAPTER THIRTY-SIX

Africa: The Search for Alternative Forms of Co-operation

ALBERT TEVOEDJRE

INTRODUCTION

Several meetings have been organized in 1987 at the initiative of governments or international organizations to discuss issues which, despite their apparent diversity, indeed express one and the same concern: a review and change of strategies in co-operation. Such concern could be conceptualized by the following formula: a priority of our time ... alternatives to co-operation ... why and how?

In analysing the critical situation of the African continent, there is need to rethink the whole concept of co-operation between Africa and the rest of the world. The inevitable conclusion is that the way the system of co-operation has operated in recent years has made the Third World in general and Africa in particular aid-recipients and further marginalized by the present crisis.

Until now Africa has accepted the 'charitable aid' of the rich countries. However, this begging position in international co-operation has become particularly uneasy in a crisis situation where egocentrism is the rule of the day and only the crumbs from the master's table or the smallest share of the benefits are the new forms of international co-operation.

The debt-ridden countries of Africa are maintained in their role as suppliers of raw materials and incapable of creating, for themselves, the capital accumulation required for their economic recovery. Hence, the present dramatic situation. Furthermore, the major international actors are mainly concerned about maintaining the *status quo*, in the face of the growing number of 'losers' who will one day become aware of their common plight and organize themselves to overturn a system which oppresses them. The first alarming signs of this 'rebellion', such as the new attitude of the Latin American countries to debt repayment, have begun to appear.

The period of prosperity of the 1960s and early 1970s had encouraged the myth of 'catching-up' in the sense that a massive transfer of ideas, technology and capital from the North to the South would enable the latter to catch up with Western societies, on the understanding that the latter are the only points of reference. For that purpose the North would provide logistical support, propagating its ideologies, providing its food, transferring its technologies, selling its weapons and using its armed forces throughout the world as a watchful and stringent form of co-operation.

But, today, this has not materialized and, contrary to the expectations, the gap has continued to widen both within and among the countries, and has been compounded by the effects of the crisis in the South.

The centre itself, as defined by Samir Amin, no longer has the means of maintaining its own periphery while at the same time protecting itself from that periphery. The major adjustments have had unforeseeable and uncontrollable consequences: over-production, over-capitalization, unemployment and inflation in the North; proletarization, disappearance of traditional economies and underutilization of machinery and modern equipment in the South. This generalized ill-planned development therefore threatens both the South and the North.

And yet no solution is in sight for collectively emerging from the crisis and vicious circle of debt. Everyone expects with naive confidence that the US will show the way to recovery and share with the world their hegemonic success. There is no basis to believe, however, that the recovery of the US will be followed by that of the other continents. The Third World in particular would be very wrong to believe in the benevolent generosity of the creditor countries in helping them overcome their economic crisis.

In this context, it has become imperative to find new forms of co-operation. Even if this democratic and generous idea is not yet well perceived, the antagonistic situations and the conflicting relations generated by the present international system pave the way for alternatives and call for innovative efforts.

BASIC PRINCIPLES OF THE NEW FORM OF CO-OPERATION

Two main issues must be addressed in the search for new forms of co-operation. First, there is need to create in the countries that are victims of the present system, counter-authorities, and forces of resistance, capable of standing up to the powerful, at least to question their unilateral and undisputed role as arbiters of the world order. Since these clusters of resistance derive their power from the indigenous population, they should first and foremost count on the solidarity and dynamism that comes from togetherness.

The second objective is to encourage the development of those communities for whom co-operation has meant more often than not exploitation without anything in return. In this respect, initiatives should come from social actors in the micro-societies where some play a crucial role in social and economic relations. It is at that level that societies can find solutions and solve their problems. As Henri Rouille D'Orfeuil very rightly observed: 'Against the modes of production and technologies that exclude local resources, particularly people, and which amass capital and then suck it out should be set the modes of production and technologies that are able to mobilize all local resources: labour force, know-how, local materials, renewable energy and which because they are remunerated locally contribute to the reconstruction of local economies.'[1]

The purpose of co-operation is therefore to encourage popular dynamism and to provide them with opportunities to develop and become autonomous and effective. It will be balanced and adapted to realities if the different partners realize that under-development in the South and ill-planned development in the North are closely linked; only genuine collaboration of all can steer the world economy away from the present impasse.

THE SHORTCOMINGS OF THE PRESENT CO-OPERATION FRAMEWORK

After the Second World War, co-operation was initially conceived by the centre as a means of consolidating or even expanding its influences, by globalizing economies and political strategies. This was to be achieved through two major tactics: impose foreign concepts and models on the Third World, and develop it by bringing in elements which should play the dual role of mooring it safely into the market economy and thus creating the conditions for its dependence. Economic, technological and military co-operation was thus to make the development of the periphery a carbon copy of the centre through a massive transfer of know-how and goods; development and economic growth were becoming interchangeable without taking into account such indicators as quality of life or the state of the social fabric.

In this way, what has traditionally been called co-operation represented an attempt by the centre to monopolise the mode of development, impose its concept of modernization and integrate all resources, both human and material, into a system which it could dominate. Two very important aspects of such co-operation were carried out through education, as a medium for disseminating Western ideologies and ways of thinking; and the training of workers so as to introduce men to machines and technologies of the industrialized countries thereby opening up markets to capital goods and other products.

It is therefore obvious that the three components of traditional co-operation, i.e. military, economic and technical, are inextricably linked and depend one upon the other. So-called technical co-operation indeed depends greatly on economic assistance which enables the developing countries to acquire the necessary machines and experience to put into practice methods acquired through North–South transfers, while military assistance is supposed to help protect markets and frontiers so as to safeguard each country's place in the international system. In other respects, governmental or private co-operation, through TNCs, thus steers the entire world economy towards the direction acceptable to the centre, by making the latter a reservoir of knowledge and capital goods, the mentor of international management.

But the failure is so glaring that the whole system today shakes from its foundations. Economic growth has either not been achieved or has benefited only a small minority and, in any case, the development of the Third World countries has not followed the expected scenarios. Rather, the calamities of poor peoples, hunger, malnutrition, disease, low life expectancy, social and political marginalization, and unemployment are today endemic in those societies forgotten by the huge world economic machine.

The dependence of the masses on the few privileged ones has increased. The subjugation of the peripheral economies under the control of the centre, the submission of the elites of news media, and educational establishments to foreign norms and concepts has worsened, making those countries pawns of distorted order.

The so-called harmony of an international development based on laws and formulae that can be transposed without any restrictions, easily absorbed by all societies and controllable at both macro- and micro-economic levels is most unacceptable. Today, endogenous development is being advocated instead, with emphasis being placed fundamentally both on the uniqueness of each environment and on the impossibility of transferring willy-nilly one model from one situation to another. There is no doubt that the main error of conventional co-operation was its short-sightedness in respect of the innovative capacities, the accumulated knowledge and the creative genius of those Third World societies, built up by centuries of history and often perfectly adapted to their environment. By under-estimating this heritage and its inner strength, while over-estimating the flexibility and the capabilities of Western countries to integrate systems, goods and capital, the centre introduced into the evolution of these societies, an element of imbalance which encourages them to seek hypothetical solutions in an irrational imitation of other societies, elevated to the level of a myth, instead of making use of their own resources.

The main error of these traditional forms of co-operation is that they do not confront problems in a way that would make people forgo privileges in favour of the satisfaction of basic needs for all.

For this reason, the Third World would not, and could not, harness its most precious resources – its abundant, talented and resourceful manpower. Furthermore, it has forgotten its traditional crafts, its know-how, acquired through a long period of practice, to the benefit of imported know-how; the indirect consequence being that, faced with the failures and difficulties of grafting the two together, those people have somehow lost confidence in themselves and retarded the innovations required for the promotion of their native culture. This culture was, however, not really challenged and its neglect and disgrace were definitely unjustified. It would have been more pertinent to question the relevance of the scraps of the imported culture and the expediency of adopting them. It is therefore necessary to introduce new forms of co-operation to counter the negative tendencies and learn to discern better what is in the best interest of the countries concerned.

THE NEW FORMS OF CO-OPERATION

No genuine co-operation is possible within a servant/master or exploited/exploiter relationship; any situation reinforcing established forms of subjugation should therefore be completely reviewed. Relations cannot be sustained except within a framework of equality between partners having respect for each other, even if their respective strengths are not identical in economic or military terms. It should be noted, however, that co-operation will be easier between countries with similar potentials, having identical characteristics and the same types of problems. For that reason, South–South dialogue is definitely preferable in the first phase to North–South dialogue which inevitably entails an aid dimension. It is therefore essential to encourage horizontal exchanges in lieu of pyramidal relations.

From the aforesaid, co-operation is first and foremost a reciprocal commitment between two peoples, aimed at pooling together their energies and resources to achieve their legitimate aspirations. Consequently, each of the two parties should have full autonomy over his decisions and responsibility over his actions. Each should be able to mobilize without hindrance his people and resources in a manner best suited to his needs. In this regard, E. Oteiza speaks of 'auto-responsibility'.[2]

The process of co-operation as it was defined above is clear. The first step will be to create the conditions for re-focusing the political and economic strategies of each nation. This is a prerequisite, and it presupposes that the Third World countries should be able to increase their creative capabilities and self-sustained production of knowledge to be used for solving their specific development problems.

The time has now come to redefine development. It would be totally self-deceiving to reduce it to the mere concept of economic growth. Development should appear as a complete endogenous phenomenon incorporating technical processes and cultural elements that cannot be transposed. It requires, furthermore, the effort and participation of the entire population and the development of all the available resources. It aims at the development of people through the fight against servitude, social injustice and poverty.

Output that meets the actual demand of the masses is the only one that can satisfy their basic needs. On the one hand, this implies the mobilization of the entire population to make known their social needs and direct the productive machinery accordingly, and, on the other hand, it implies a modification of the social structures to ensure that the whims of a minority will no longer predominate.

In this context, co-operation should be supported by two mechanisms: solidarity in partnership and associative dynamics.

The associative dynamics is based on the fact that the imported administrative model from Western countries is in crisis. This model presupposed that the bureaucracy assumed responsibility for all the services and thus met all the basic needs of the population: education, health, urban services, assistance to industry and agriculture. The myth of the provident state which is deep-rooted in the countries of the North proved inoperative in developing countries where its ineffectiveness is there for all to see. And, indeed, this technocratic model requires a 'rich' administration, whereas the resources of such an administration are meagre in the Third World; its domestic resources (tax receipts) are low owing to the low standard of living of the majority of the people; and its external resource flows (international co-operation, tourism, returning migrants) hardly grow. Besides, international aid today has some misgivings about giving financial support to expensive state machineries destabilized by the ever-growing debt servicing burden.

Under such circumstances, the credibility of the public service is seriously in doubt and many opportunities are therefore left to parallel and especially associative initiatives. In terms of co-operation, these initiatives have been chanelled through the NGOs. Despite the several errors made by NGOs, they should be encouraged in their efforts at conceiving and implementing a new form of co-operation. In the face of the social destitution of pilot projects of traditional co-operation making these sectors simple parentheses in a future that is heavily compromised by the international order, the NGOs endeavour to emphasize popular dynamics and encourage the integration of innovations into a receptive social fabric. In this way they encourage flexibility in projects, continuity of operations and their dissemination through examples in the communities concerned. By rejecting one sole concept of development, the NGOs try to harness local potential through its specificity.

The associative environment thus participates in efforts to seek and experiment with new strategies of co-operation, in which actions are to be guided by various principles which call for some generalization:

- Replace transfers, within the framework of relations based on unconditional dependency, by actions of solidarity and a cross-conditional partnership which commits the two partners into reciprocal contacts;
- Organize the receiving environment so as to create autonomous and creative dynamics, and encourage discernment in the face of external innovations. Only when the inputs are totally appropriate will the venture be successful; these should be in line with methods well adapted to the rationale of local evolution and respond to the real needs of the people;
- Promote the strengthening of a collective identity through a re-interpretation of traditional practices and authority and a readaptation of the history of the community;
- Stimulate alliances among partners of the South, or for instance, between farmers from both the North and the South, since they are all confronted with survival problems, through non-governmental co-operation;
- Reinforce the economic space of the local population, so as to provide them with the means for negotiation;
- Promote the restoration of a collective control over equilibria through the rational management of means of production and space.

In any case, this extra-governmental co-operation, which is embedded in an organized population, pursues the objective of an endogenous development so as to restore and strengthen neglected local strategies and find a balanced and autonomous mode of community assertion. This type of co-operation will prosper in those societies that are free from international enslavement and ready to take responsibility for their choices.

These associative methods seem the more adapted to the African environment since the strength and richness of community traditions are well known. Although those links are disappearing in the main cities, they are still very much alive in the villages, where they continue to weave the web of the community organization. These traditional institutions could possibly be directly involved in development activities, provided they reflect the aspirations of the beneficiaries. Too often these opportunities have been exploited in bad faith or diverted by a group of local rulers who take advantage of their relations with their western counterparts without any benefit for the population.

The objective is to mobilize the direct partners or, in other words, the entire population, so as to turn it into solid and responsible actors, in lasting and coherent development projects. Beyond display projects and monetary and technical feats, co-operative assistance is beneficial only if it strengthens the dynamic evolution of the systems concerned and supports the development of their social mix. This is why D'Orfeuil suggests that NGOs emphasize, 'on the one hand, the mobilization on a long-term basis of the associative partners and their powers of negotiation vis-a-vis governmental institutions, and, on the other hand, the definition of the contents, based on the knowledge of local production systems and their evolution process, the definition of adaptable innovations; and finally the dissemination and extension of the action outside the limits of the initial micro-realization'.[1] These efforts should help reverse the relationship of dependence and assistance which never benefits those most in need but destroys solidarity links. Again, as stated by D'Orfeuil 'the gift project, apart from destroying the productive fabric, provokes a redistribution of social power to the benefit of the local intermediaries of the aid'.[2] This type of permanent subordination should therefore be rejected and replaced by real participation of co-operation in the community efforts.

The challenge of a genuine partnership, attentive to the demands of the societies concerned, founded on negotiation and respect of reciprocal interests shall be taken up. A number of prerequisites must evidently be fulfilled before a positive and loyal dialogue can begin: in particular, the countries of the Third World should be capable of sharing the knowledge required for an accurate evaluation of their potential. Paradoxically, the major TNCs often have much more information on the raw materials and various sources of energy in the developing countries than do these countries themselves, thus placing them in a situation of absolute dependence vis-a-vis policies regarding the exploitation of those resources and, in fact, their entire economic policy. It is therefore necessary to first disseminate widely all the information necessary among the countries concerned to enable them to better control their own wealth. Free access to data banks and clarity of transactions are indispensable if all those involved in a negotiation are to have the same chances of being heard.

These are the basic requirements for establishing contracts of solidarity among the different partners: exchange of information, consultations, technical advice, co-ordination of interventions will be effective and relevant means of supporting the development of African countries, and at the same time allowing them the necessary autonomy.

To co-operate is to free ourselves from crippling realities and to come together and set up networks that free man from overwhelming constraints preventing him from fighting for survival wherever he may be.

Finally, it is to be noted that no co-operation is possible unless it is based on 'ability to liberate man', on the most authentic values of the partners involved, and on the right of peoples to live in peace in an environment enriched and made propitious by themselves to become their legitimate heritage. Co-operation, be it from the East or the West, should be perceived as an act of unambiguous solidarity, as the condition to live together and share together. Failing that, it would reject its own objectives and methods and would renege on its own self.

What is needed is a new philosophical approach. Some time ago, calling for new ethics in co-operation, I wrote in 'Le Monde' of 15 June 1978: 'warped co-operation, divorced from the demands and aspirations of the people, distorted towards privileges (non-essential needs par excellence) would be taking a serious risk; it would revive the right of the people to revolt against oppression'. The disastrous and often irreparable effects of this risk are such that it will never be too early to co-operate in other ways.

Only by acting together can the new instruments of common development be devised so as to achieve physical, moral and social well-being for all, and to establish a redefined international order and intelligent forms of co-operation for the benefit of the people.

NOTES

1. H. Rouille D'Orfeuil, *Coopérer autrement*, L'Harmattan, coll. Bibliothèque du développement, Paris, 1984, p.11.
2. Cf E. Oteiza, 'Le développement par la coopération technique entre les pays du tiers monde' in *Travail et Société*, Vol.3, No.3–4 juil/oct. 1978, p.478.

CONCLUDING REMARKS

The existing system of international co-operation is not in the least beneficial to Africa, and there is need therefore for Africa to re-evaluate and re-define the basis, the objectives and the nature of its future co-operation with the rest of the world. In so doing, however, a distinction must be made not only between the North and the South, but also between national governments, NGOs, multilateral and international organizations as far as the prospects for co-operation are concerned. If, for instance, Africa believes, as indeed she does, in the existing international organizations, then she must participate meaningfully in bringing about the required and necessary changes and reforms that will ensure that those institutions are utilized to the maximum for the benefit of Africa. Given the dramatic and uneven impact of the changes in international economic growth and fortunes on the African economies, there can be little doubt that Africa's future relations with the countries of the North pose serious problems and challenges. As for South–South co-operation, this would seem, on the surface, to open wider avenues for Africa, but opinion is divided as to whether Africa really stands to benefit much from such co-operation for now except in terms of enlarged markets for primary export commodities. In effect, Africa's marginalization in respect of the world economic system may not as such be confined to North–South co-operation; it extends even to South–South co-operation, the future prospects for which, given the extremely narrow range of NICs among African countries, may not be that bright.

As for North–South co-operation, there have been, in recent years, a number of positive developments which tend to augur well for the future relations between Africa and the North. These include some of the decisions and agreements of the Venice and Toronto Summits of the seven most highly industrialized countries, Lome III, and changes in approaches by EEC and OECD countries regarding aid flows to sub-Saharan Africa. Nonetheless, the real choice for Africa reposes neither in complacency nor the exclusive devotion of energies to the pursuit of South–South co-operation or in indefinite bargains with the international community of the North; rather, Africa needs to reassess its own needs and to organize accordingly its development efforts. By refocusing its energies on producing what it consumes in addition to what it can profitably export, by avoiding consumption of what it does not produce, by developing larger markets through subregional economic communities and by seeking to overcome the constraints of transport, communications, customs barriers and disharmonious monetary systems, all of which inhibit and create obstacles to intra-African trade, Africa can improve the capacity for more meaningful and mutually-beneficial co-operation with the rest of the world and genuine bargaining with the international community, North or South.

PART SEVEN

Epilogue

CHAPTER THIRTY-SEVEN

Will Africa Ever Get Out of its Economic Doldrums?

ADEBAYO ADEDEJI

A mid-term review and evaluation of the implementation of UN-PAAERD was undertaken by an *Ad Hoc* Committee of the Whole of the General Assembly of the UN from 15 to 23 September 1988 in accordance with the Assembly's resolution 42/163 of 8 December 1987. Its report and recommendations, which were submitted to the 43rd session of the General Assembly, were the subject of a full-dress debate by that august body in November of the same year. Indeed, the continuous monitoring of the implementation of UN-PAAERD was provided for in the programme itself and in the resolution by which it was adopted by acclamation by the 13th special session of the General Assembly. Such monitoring was envisaged at three distinct levels – national, regional and international. Each African country was required to put in place appropriate monitoring mechanisms at the national level. At the regional level, monitoring was primarily the responsibility of ECA, assisted by a UN Inter-Agency Task Force (IATF) consisting of the specialized agencies and organizations most directly concerned with the four priority sectors of the Programme – i.e., food and agriculture sector; sectors in support of food and agriculture (industry, transport and communications, etc.), environment (protection and the combat against drought and desertification); and human resources development. Thus, apart from ECA, the core membership of IATF consists of FAO, WFP, International Fund for Agricultural Development (IFAD), United Nations Fund for Popula-

763

tion Activities (UNFPA), ILO, UNDP, World Bank, IMF, UNCTAD, ADB and UNIDO. Recently, International Civil Aviation Organization (ICAO) has at its own request been admitted to membership.

For the purpose of monitoring the response of the international community, with particular reference to their specific commitments and obligations, and of ensuring effective co-ordination among them, the UN Secretary-General established a Steering Committee chaired by the Director-General for Development and International Economic Co-operation, with the ECA Executive Secretary as its Deputy Chairman and consisting of UNDP, UNFPA, World Bank, IMF and United Nations Department of International Economic and Social Affairs (DIESA). The IATF serves as the operational arm of the Steering Committee.

The *Ad Hoc* Committee of the Whole of the General Assembly, in conducting a comprehensive mid-term review and appraisal of the implementation of UN-PAAERD, had before it three main documents: Report of the Secretary-General on the mid-term review of the implementation of UN-PAAERD; The Khartoum Declaration: Towards a Human Focused Approach to Socio-Economic Recovery and Development in Africa; and an OAU document entitled: 'Mid-Term Assessment of the Implementation of UN-PAAERD, 1986–1990'.

As was adequately reflected in the Secretary-General's report and was of course generally well known, the mid-term review and appraisal of UN-PAAERD was conducted against a backdrop of a continuing deterioration in the overall economic situation in Africa. This unyielding economic crisis was taking place in spite of the courageous and impressive efforts on the part of the majority of African countries to pursue and strengthen significant policy reforms and adjustment measures designed to improve economic performance and to bring about accelerated recovery and development, as well as in spite of the many important initiatives taken by the international community in support of Africa's efforts.

The massiveness of the response of African countries is poignantly illustrated in Table 37.1, the only Table contained in the body of the report of the Secretary-General. This Table is reproduced here to show the extent, scope and generally universal nature of the response. The measures selected to illustrate the seriousness with which Africa took UN-PAAERD are: (a) policy reforms; (b) putting in place early warning systems; (c) public enterprise reforms; (d) the share of agricultural investment in total public investment (the target being 20 to 25 per cent); and, (e) population policies.

TABLE 37.1
SUMMARY TABLE OF SELECTED REFORM MEASURES TAKEN BY
AFRICAN GOVERNMENTS

	Policy reforms	Early warning systems	Public enterprise reforms	Share of agricultural investment in total public investment (20–25%)	Explicit population policies
Indian Ocean Island countries					
Comoros	x			x	x
Madagascar	x		x	x	x
Mauritius	x		x		x
Seychelles					
East African countries					
Burundi	x		x	x	x
Djibouti					
Ethiopia	x	x	x	x	x
Kenya	x		x		x
Rwanda	x		x		x
Somalia	x	x	x	x	x
Sudan	x		x	x	x
Uganda	x		x	x	x
United Republic of Tanzania	x	x	x	x	
Southern African countries					
Angola					
Botswana	x	x	x		
Lesotho	x	x			x
Malawi	x	x	x		
Mozambique	x				
Swaziland	x				x
Zambia	x	x	x		
Zimbabwe	x	x		x	
Central African countries					
Cameroon	x		x		x
Central African Republic	x		x	x	
Congo	x		x		x
Equatorial Guinea	x				x
Gabon	x				
Sao Tome and Principe	x	x		x	x
Zaire	x		x		x

TABLE 37.1 (continued)

	Policy reforms	Early warning systems	Public enterprise reforms	Share of agricultural investment in total public investment (20–25%)	Explicit population policies
Sahelian countries					
Burkina Faso	x				x
Cape Verde	x	x		x	x
Chad	x				
Gambia	x		x	x	
Guinea Bissau	x	x	x	x	x
Mali	x	x	x	x	x
Mauritania	x		x		
Niger	x	x	x	x	x
Senegal	x	x	x	x	x
Non-Sahelian West African countries					
Benin	x		x		x
Cote d'Ivoire	x		x	x	x
Ghana	x	x	x		x
Guinea	x	x			
Liberia	x		x	x	x
Nigeria	x		x		x
Sierra Leone	x		x	x	x
Togo	x		x	x	x
North African countries					
Algeria	x	x		x	x
Egypt	x				x
Libyan Arab Jamahiriya	x	x		x	x
Morocco	x	x		x	x
Tunisia	x			x	x

Source: ECA 1987 and 1988 surveys on the implementation of APPER, UN-PAAERD, and data collected by the UNDP/World Bank/ECA project on development programmes and aid flows.

Yet, in spite of this massive response, in spite of the restructuring process that has been initiated and despite the policy reforms that have been introduced, the economic performance of African countries during 1986–1988 has generally been disappointing. During the first three out of the five years of UN-PAAERD, GDP growth rate has consistently fallen below population growth rate. Thus, the fall in per capita income which has been the plight of Africa since 1980 has continued. The performance of the agriculture sector continues to depend largely on the weather, and thanks to favourable weather conditions, the growth rate in this sector in 1986 and 1988 surpassed the population growth rate during the same years. On the other hand, mining growth rates have remained consistently negative until 1988 while recovery in the manufacturing sector continues to be elusive. As I stated in my annual end-of-year review and assessment of the performance of the African economy in 1988 and the prospects for 1989, 'the cumulative impact of persistent economic crisis in Africa during this decade (the 1980s) in the face of high population growth rate has been a sustained deceleration in the standards and conditions of living of the average African. Today, his/her per capita income is only about 80 per cent of what it was at the beginning of the decade in 1980.'

TABLE 37.2

GROWTH RATE OF GDP AND GDP PER CAPITA AND OF VALUE ADDED IN AGRICULTURE, MINING AND MANUFACTURING IN AFRICA, 1980–1988

	1980–85	1986	1987	1988
GDP	0.6	1.0	2.5	2.5
GDP per capita	−2.5	−2.0	−0.5	−0.5
Agriculture	1.5	3.8	1.1	3.8
Mining	−2.5	−0.1	−3.3	2.3
Manufacturing	3.4	−3.0	5.3	3.2

Source: ECA

Thus, natural disasters, pervasively low levels of productivity, low capacity for mobilization of domestic resource, inefficient utilization of resources, particularly human resources, and high dependence on imports are some of the factors responsible for the continued poor performance of the African economy. But the most devastating of these factors are the collapse in the commodity market and the inexorable rise in the prices of imported manufactured goods. For instance, in 1986 – the very first year of UN-PAAERD – Africa lost over $US19 billion in foreign exchange earnings due to the dramatic fall in commodity prices. In the same year, prices of imports increased by about 20 per cent.

Thus, in spite of the commitment of the international community to improve the external economic environment, the latter has remained very hostile since 1986. For its part, the international community had agreed that, given the dimensions of international and external problems facing Africa, it was obvious that Africa must be given full support in implementing UN-PAAERD. Specifically, the international community had committed itself (a) to make every effort to provide sufficient resources to support and supplement African development efforts; (b) to improve the quality and modality of external assistance and co-operation; and, (c) to improve the external economic environment (particularly through the expansion of trade and by dealing urgently with the commodity and debt problems).

Unfortunately, as already noted, the external environment has aggravated the recovery process. Although the developed countries as a group have had a period of uninterrupted growth of output over the past six years, Africa has not benefitted at all from this. The trickle-down theory has not worked. It has not worked because of Africa's lack of manufactured exports which have enjoyed high elasticity of demand in the developed countries, and its dependence on commodity exports with their increasingly inelastic demand. The prosperity in the industrialized economies has not had any spread effect in Africa because its trading relationship with the developed world is primarily with Europe where growth has been slower than in North America and Japan. And, as if these were not enough, Africa's exports were constrained by protectionism and subsidies in the developed countries.

But perhaps the most serious impediment in the recovery process has been the failure of the international community to provide resources in adequate flows to support Africa's efforts. Resource flows to Africa in 1986, 1987 and 1988 were grossly inadequate. As is shown in Table 37.3 below, net resource flows to sub-Saharan Africa at 1986 prices and exchange rates were $US2.3 and $US1.9 billion less in 1986 and 1987 than they were in 1982, respectively. When it is remembered that Africa has asked for an additional $US9.1 billion every year in resource flows in implementing UN-PAAERD, this has meant a shortage of $US11.4 billion in 1986 and $US11.0 billion in 1987. Little wonder that the recovery process has hardly begun.

Yet, in UN-PAAERD, the international community, after noting that Africa would need an additional sum of $US46 billion through external resources to augment their domestic resources, committed 'itself to making every effort to provide sufficient resources to support and supplement the African development effort'. The donor countries were specially singled out in the document as having agreed 'on the importance of increasing development assistance to Africa, its improved quality and effectiveness'. In spite of all this, resource flows to Africa at best stagnated. As net-ODA (disbursements) to sub-

TABLE 37.3

NET RESOURCE FLOWS (DISBURSEMENTS) TO AFRICA, 1982–1987
(Billions of current US dollars)

	1982	1983	1984	1985	1986	1987 a
Sub-Saharan Africa						
I. OFFICIAL DEVELOPMENT FINANCE (ODF)	10.8	10.6	12.0	11.9	14.9	18.2
1. Official development assistance (ODA) of which:	9.1	9.0	9.4	10.6	12.9	
Bilateral disbursements	6.6	6.4	6.6	7.3	8.9	
Multilateral disbursements	2.5	2.6	2.8	3.3	4.0	
2. Other ODF of which:	1.7	1.6	2.6	1.3	2.0	
Bilateral disbursements	1.1	0.9	1.8	0.5	1.2	
Multilateral disbursements	0.6	0.7	0.8	0.8	0.8	
II. TOTAL EXPORT CREDITS	1.9	1.5	0.0	0.8	0.4	
1. DAC countries of which: Short-term	1.8 / 0.2	1.4 / 0.5	X / −0.1	0.7 / 0.4	0.3 / 0.6	
2. Other countries	0.1	0.1	X	0.1	0.1	
III. PRIVATE FLOWS	3.7	2.0	0.4	2.2	2.2	2.3
1. Direct investment (OECD)	1.0	0.8	0.6	0.5	0.7	
2. International bank lending	2.0	0.5	−1.0	0.8	0.5	
3. Total bond lending	–	–	–	–	–	
4. Other private	–	–	–	–	–	
5. Grants by non-governmental organizations	0.7	0.7	0.8	0.9	1.0	
Sub-total for sub-Saharan Africa	16.4	14.1	12.4	14.9	17.5	20.5
North Africa	2.2	2.2	2.4	3.0	2.4	2.4
Total Africa	18.1	16.3	14.8	17.9	19.9	22.9
	At 1986 prices and exchange rates					
Net resource flows to sub-Saharan Africa	19.8	17.1	15.4	18.3	17.5	17.9

Source: OECD
Note:
a. Preliminary estimates.

Saharan Africa, in particular from countries such as US, Sweden, the Netherlands, Italy, Denmark and Belgium (to mention only a few), fell between 1986 and 1987, it was not surprising that attention was focused more on how to restore the pre-UN-PAAERD level than on how to realize the additionality in resource flows that UN-PAAERD had made imperative if the process of recovery is to be launched and sustained. As I stated before the US Congressional Sub-Committee on Africa of the Committee on Foreign Affairs:

> the commitments which the international community has entered into are not only extensive but are in fulfilment of their declared desire to assist Africa to launch long-term programmes for self-sustaining socio-economic development and growth ... The challenge which is now before us is its full and vigorous implementation so that when the time comes for the distinguished Secretary-General of the United Nations to present progress reports on the implementation of the Programme to the General Assembly at its forty-second and forty-third sessions in 1987 and 1988, respectively, he can report that both the African Governments and the international community are vigorously and faithfully fulfilling the commitments which they entered into during the Special Session.[1]

Unfortunately, that warning went unheeded by the international community as donor countries, one after another, followed the US lead by reducing, in real terms, their resource flows to Africa even before the ink had dried on the paper on which UN-PAAERD had been written – thus making a mockery of the so-called shared partnership between Africa and the donor community. The rule of the game of the partnership was as explicit as it could be. Africa acts and the donor community responds commensurately through its own donor reforms and increased levels of assistance. It is a mutual pact, with both sides having binding obligations. 'Alas, the international community has not yet fulfilled its part of the bargain', so stated the Khartoum Declaration. 'African economies continue to be threatened on every front by catastrophic debt, collapsed commodity prices, stagnating concessional flows and crippling terms of trade. Because the frontline of recovery is the human dimension, the human dimension is at greatest risk. If structural adjustment with a human face does not succeed, then the failure, in considerable measure, will be laid at the feet of the international community', so concluded the Khartoum Declaration.

Indeed, the debt trap and the SAP conditionality for obtaining resources from the donor countries constitute two major albatrosses around the necks of African countries. Without removing the debt trap and relenting on the insistence that African countries should adopt IMF/World Bank-approved SAPs, recovery and development on a sustainable and sustained basis will continue to elude most, if not all of

FIGURE 37.1
NET RESOURCE FLOWS TO SUB-SAHARAN AFRICA
($ bn, at 1986 prices and exchange rates)

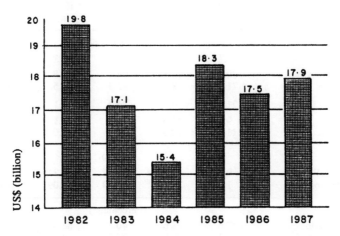

Source: OECD

Africa. Little wonder that three years after the adoption of UN-PAAERD, progress in implementation has been painfully slow. In spite of the fact that the international community had recognized that 'the continued improvement of the external environment and a strong economic adjustment effort may not be sufficient to allow many African states to service their debt while establishing the basis for sustainable growth'. In such circumstances, the international community pledged itself to 'assist African countries in their efforts to deal with their financial constraints'.

We have already established that resource flows to Africa decreased in real terms during the first three years of UN-PAAERD, i.e., in 1986, 1987 and 1988. Since the debt service problem has therefore not been dealt with through financial flows, let us examine what direct debt relief measures have been granted and their impact on resource outflows from Africa as this constitutes the only other way of dealing with debt service problems.

On this score, the Secretary-General in his report on mid-term review of the implementation of UN-PAAERD acknowledged that the international community has taken some initiatives to lighten the debt burden of low-income African countries. However, he added, 'less progress has been achieved with regard to middle-income countries.

771

TABLE 37.4
DEBT AND DEBT-SERVICE OBLIGATION OF AFRICA, 1984–1988

	1984	1985	1986	1987 a	1988
	(Billions of US dollars)				
Total debt	*152.1*	*174.4*	*190.0*	*220.3*	*230.0*
Sub-Saharan Africa	80.6	95.5	98.1	119.8	125.8
North Africa	71.5	78.9	91.9	100.5	104.2
Debt service	21.7	24.3	26.4	26.1	29.3
Sub-Saharan Africa	9.9	12.0	13.7	14.1	16.9
North Africa	11.8	12.3	12.7	12.0	12.4
	(Ratio)				
Total debt/GDP	0.57	0.52	0.62	0.71	0.81
Total debt/exports	1.94	2.05	2.89	3.09	3.14
	(Percentage)				
Debt service ratio	27.6	28.6	40.2	36.8	40.0
Sub-Saharan Africa	26.1	27.3	36.2	34.6	40.0
North Africa	29.1	29.9	49.9	39.2	40.1

Source: ECA estimates.
Note:
a. Preliminary.

Even those measures that have been taken have provided primarily temporary relief. The debt problem has not yet been dealt with in a manner that provides a durable solution.'[2] Table 37.4 provides a graphic picture of the evolution of the debt and debt servicing situation in Africa from 1984 to 1988. During this period, Africa's debt had increased by 51 per cent. Between 1985 and 1988, it increased by 32 per cent. The rate of increase slowed down from 1987 onwards – thanks, *inter alia*, to the lack of credit-worthiness and access to credit markets by many an African country.

No doubt, even more alarming is the fact that the Debt/GDP ratio has moved from 0.57 in 1984 to 0.81 in 1988 while the Debt/Export ratio has reached the overwhelming proportion of 3.14, with the debt service ratio averaging 40 per cent. ECA estimates that in both 1989 and 1990 – the last two years of UN-PAAERD – these figures will be higher and the situation will become severely aggravated as Africa perforce faces the need to increase borrowing in order to service new debt maturities, and to reduce arrears in debt service obligations which may increase even further if the upward trend in interest rates which reappeared in 1988 in the creditor countries is maintained in 1989 and 1990. A six to ten per cent annual increase in Africa's external debt in both 1989 and 1990 is therefore projected by ECA. Thus, at the end of UN-PAAERD, Africa's debt burden is likely to be around $US300 billion – unless, of course, an imaginative and comprehensive solution is arrived at in 1989. The average debt service ratio will, with the anticipated further decline in export earnings, be pushed up to a new high and so will be the total debt service obligations which might exceed $US37 billion in 1990.

In the face of these grim prospects, the measures that have been taken to ameliorate Africa's excruciating debt burden, though welcome, seem extremely insignificant, if not puny. Specifically what are these measures? And what has been their impact – projected or actual? But, before answering these questions, it is essential that we should first and foremost remind ourselves of the magnitude of the debt and debt servicing problems that these measures are designed to solve.

In the OAU/ECA *Africa's Submission*, the debt servicing obligations during the five-year period of the recovery programme were projected as in Tables 37.5 and 37.6 below. Although the difficulties of estimating Africa's debt burden are enormous, they are further compounded by differences in definition. While some calculations are limited only to official credits and publicly-guaranteed commercial debts, others define the external debt obligations to include private non-guaranteed long-term debt and arrears, short-term debt and such items as IMF repurchases. Accordingly, Table 37.5, which defines the debt and debt servicing obligations in a comprehensive manner, shows that the annual average debt servicing obligation of Africa during the 1986–1990 period is $US24.516 billion.

On the other hand, according to Table 37.6, which encompasses only official credits and publicly-guaranteed commercial debts, the average annual debt servicing obligations are estimated at $US14.633 billion.

Whatever definition is preferred, the gravity of the African debt servicing obligations is indisputable. It ranges between about $US15 billion and $US25 billion, annually. It is this excruciating burden that debt relief measures are needed to ameliorate, particularly as ECA projections contained in these two Tables have turned out at least for the years 1986, 1987 and 1988, to be conservative. The debt burden has increased during these years at a rate higher than the growth rates in output and external trade. From $US200 billion in 1986, it rose to $US218 billion and $US230 billion in 1987 and 1988, respectively. Thus, during the first three years of UN-PAAERD, Africa's external

TABLE 37.5

SCHEDULED DEBT-SERVICING INCLUDING PRIVATE NON-GUARANTEED DEBT

(annual average during 1986–1990)

	billions of US dollars	
IDA-eligible countries (25) (reported by World Bank)		
Principal	3.910	
Interest	3.967	
Sub-total		6.877
Other IDA-eligible countries (4) (ECA estimates)		
Principal	0.357	
Interest	0.109	
Sub-total		0.466
Non-IDA-eligible sub-Saharan Africa (8) (reported by World Bank)		
Principal	5.268	
Interest	4.229	
Sub-total		9.497
Other Non-IDA-eligible sub-Saharan Africa (8) (ECA estimates)		
Principal	0.305	
Interest	0.127	
Sub-total		0.432
North Africa (5) (ECA estimates)		
Principal	5.377	
Interest	1.867	
Sub-total		7.244
Total (50 countries)	24.516	

Source: ECA

debt had increased by 15 per cent. It must be emphasized that this phenomenal increase has not been due to Africa's success in new borrowings for new investment. Indeed, many countries have lost their credit-worthiness and access to credit markets. The aggravation of the burden of debt has been due to borrowing to service new maturities as well as attempts to reduce arrears in debt services. It has also been due to recent escalation in the rates of interest and to changes in exchange

TABLE 37.6

PROJECTED DEBT-SERVICE OBLIGATIONS EXCLUDING PRIVATE
NON-GUARANTEED DEBT
(annual average during 1986–1990)

	billions of US dollars	
Official credits		
Principal	24.692	
Interest	12.674	
Sub-total		37.366
Commercial credits		
Principal	28.080	
Interest	7.721	
Sub-total		35.801
Total debt-service		
Principal	52.772	
Interest	20.395	
Grand total		73.167
Annual average of debt servicing payable		14.633

Source: ECA

rate parities. Indeed, the pace at which Africa's debt obligations are mounting is very frightening. Debt is dislocating not only the economic structure of many African countries but also their political and social fabric.

It is in the light of these dire circumstances of the debt problem that we must now examine the various solutions that have been adopted by the creditor countries and their impact. Let us begin with the conversion of ODA loans to grants for the LDCs.

The conversion of ODA loans to grants has been accepted since the adoption in 1978, by UNCTAD Trade and Development Board, of the well-known resolution 165(S-IX). By 1985, $US2 billion loans had been converted into grants. Since UN-PAAERD was adopted, a number of creditor-countries (Finland, Sweden, the United Kingdom of Great Britain and Ireland, Canada, and Federal Republic of Germany) have either already taken similar actions or have announced their intention to do so. But not all creditor countries have converted the entirety of their ODA loans into grants. Indeed, there is an element of arbitrariness in the choice of countries to benefit from such conversions. The choice is more often based on political rather than economic

775

considerations. It is therefore not surprising that conversions to date affect only a sixth of Africa's ODA debt. Even more significant is the fact that the rate of actual conversion since 1986 appears to have slowed to about half the average annual level in earlier years.

Rescheduling of matured debt repayment and due debt service obligations is a second way of obtaining debt reliefs although many people now agree it is postponing the evil day and adding to the debt burden. ODA debt reschedulings take place under the auspices of the Paris Club while commercial debt reschedulings are handled by the London Club.

With regard to Paris Club reschedulings, more debts have been rescheduled since 1986 than was previously the case. According to the report of the UN Secretary-General on mid-term review of UN-PAAERD, 'during 1986–1987, the total amount of African debt consolidated through Paris Club agreements was $US25.6 billion and covered 20 countries, compared to a total of $US8.4 billion in 1980–1985. The Paris Club has also begun to provide more favourable treatment for the poorest, most debt-distressed countries with regard to the amounts covered by agreements and the repayment terms.[3] The lengthening, since 1987, of the grace and maturity periods to 10 and 20 years, respectively, for a growing number of countries marks a major departure from previous practice.

However, these measures have failed to address the fundamental problems of reducing the stock of debt and of increasing concessionality for countries that do not have access to the capital market. Debt reschedulings that fail to incorporate an element of debt reduction in order to reduce the weight of future obligations create more problems in the long-run than they solve. Besides, the present arrangements are not adapted to debtors' capacity to pay nor do they have medium-term perspectives in terms of recovery and development. They are, more often than not, linked to the adoption of IMF/World Bank-sponsored and/or approved SAPs rather than to medium- or long-term fundamental transformation of the African economies. Finally, the reschedulings do not include any reduction in the interest rates on rescheduled official non-concessional debt.

The seven major industrialized countries (US, West Germany, Japan, Great Britain, France, Canada and Italy) at their 1988 Toronto Economic Summit established a virtual umbilical link between re-scheduling official debt and the adoption of IMF/World Bank SAPs. The Toronto Agreement 'would allow official creditors to choose among concessional interest rates on shorter maturities, longer repayment periods at commercial rates, partial write-offs of debt service obligations during the consolidation period or a combination of these options'.[4] The estimated debt relief provided under the Toronto Economic Summit Declaration was only about $US500 million in 1988. Its impact was therefore minimal.

With regard to commercial debt, some relief has been provided by the commercial banks to countries with this type of debt. Since 1986, the amount of such relief has risen substantially. The improvements in London Club reschedulings for Africa include: (a) longer repayment periods; and, (b) decreases in the spreads used to calculate interest charges on adjustable rate loans. But these improvements have had limited impact as they are a far cry from the proposals which were put forward in *Africa's Submission* and repeated in the African Common Position on External Debt adopted by the third extraordinary session of the Assembly of Heads of State and Government of OAU on Africa's external debt crisis. These include: (a) improving the existing framework for commercial debt renegotiation; (b) capping and reducing interest rates for commercial debts; and, (c) consolidating debt-servicing payments for these debts and their repayment over a long period of time on concessional terms. The African proposals for the securitization of commercial debt have yet to be taken up.

But the area where no progress whatsoever has been achieved is with respect to debt owed to multilateral creditors – IMF and World Bank. Debt owed to these institutions has neither been rescheduled nor written off. The result is that they have, particularly IMF, become net recipients of resources from Africa. Since 1986, there has been a sharp turn-around in IMF net lendings as repayment of an increasing amount of drawings made in the 1980s fell due. In that year, net outflow of resources from Africa to IMF amounted to $US0.5 billion. By 1988, it had increased to over $US1.0 billion. Thus, during the first three years of the implementation of UN-PAAERD, net outflows totalled about $US2.0 billion. There is, no doubt, an urgent need to remove the heavy burden faced by the African countries in servicing debt due to the Bretton Woods institutions.

Indeed, from the foregoing analysis, it will have become abundantly clear that all the efforts so far taken have had little significant impact on the alleviation of Africa's debt burden. Had, for example, all bilateral ODA debts been converted into grants, the debt servicing burden of Africa would have been reduced by between $US3.7 and $US7.6 billion every year. The consolidation of non-ODA official debts and service payments thereon into long-term loans repayable over a period of 30–40 years with a ten-year period of grace could bring an additional debt-servicing relief of between $US4 and $US6 billion per annum.

Capping and reducing interest rates for commercial debt as well as consolidating debt-service payments for this category of debt and agreeing to a long-term repayment arrangement on concessional terms will further reduce the debt servicing burden particularly for the middle-income countries. Specific measures will also need to be undertaken to provide relief in servicing the debt of both World Bank and IMF.

While there is general agreement that unless the debt problems of African countries are addressed in a comprehensive and imaginative manner, the political will to do so is still lacking. This is the only reason for the *ad hoc* measures of little significant impact that have so far been taken. The magnitude of African debt and debt-servicing obligations, from the point of view of the creditor countries, is nothing to write home about; but addressing them in an imaginative and comprehensive manner will have quite a disproportionately beneficial effect on the vulnerable and fragile African economies. Measures that do not address the problems of reducing the stock of debt as well as servicing obligations while at the same time restoring the credit-worthiness and access to credit markets will not contribute significantly to the recovery process in Africa. The need to take the debt bull by the horns becomes more desperately urgent every day.

Unfortunately, rather than doing this, there has developed, on the part of some creditor-countries, a tendency to link debt amelioration, however marginal, with the adoption of an IMF/World Bank-approved SAP. Such linkage, to say the least, is most unfortunate. This linkage was made explicit and categorical during the mid-term review of the implementation of UN-PAAERD in September 1988.

While both APPER and UN-PAAERD emphasized the need for policy reforms on a massive scale in Africa, they had in mind reforms designed to address the fundamental causes of the crisis. As is stated in *Africa's Submission*, the African crisis is due 'principally to insufficient structural transformation and economic diversification that are required to move the continent away from inherited colonial economic structures, typified by a vicious interaction between excruciating poverty and abysmally low levels of productivity, in an environment marked by serious deficiencies in basic economic and social infrastructures'.[5]

Accordingly, APPER focused on policy measures in the field of food and agricultural development, particularly measures designed to increase levels of both productivity and production. Eight areas of concentration were specifically identified: (i) increased food production; (ii) arable land development and land improvement; (iii) livestock and animal product development; (iv) mechanization; (v) storage and marketing; (vi) agricultural research and extension; (vii) water resource management and low-cost irrigation schemes; (viii) reafforestation programmes and drought and desertification control; (ix) better agricultural pricing policies; (x) effective credit and adequate input support and delivery systems; (xi) establishing national subregional and regional food security and food processing systems; (xii) diffusion of appropriate agricultural technologies and improving rural transport; and, (xiii) making peasant farmers, especially women food producers, genuine economic actors.

Similar policy reform measures were identified for other sectors that will facilitate the achievement of these thirteen objectives. These are: (i) the development and rehabilitation of agro-based industries; (ii) the development of transport and communications; (iii) improving the distribution channels for domestic and intra-regional trade; (iv) reversing the present consumption pattern in favour of goods produceable in Africa, given its climatic and environmental endowments; and, (v) improving generally the management of the African economy.

With regard to the last objective, the specific measures envisaged were (i) improvement of public management systems, institutions and practices; (ii) improvement of the performance of public enterprises; (iii) greater mobilization of domestic savings; (iv) improvement of financial management and fiscal administration with a view to promoting the efficient use of resources, and cutting – if not totally eliminating – wastage and resource misallocation; and, (v) better management of the foreign debt and external assistance. It was also explicitly stated that the positive role of the private sector would be encouraged through well-defined and consistent policies.

Appropriate recognition was given by African governments to the centrality of the human factor in the recovery and development process. Policy measures envisaged in APPER in the pursuit of the objective of the efficient development, planning and utilization of human resources and the effective participation of the people in the development process include greater emphasis on education at all levels to ensure that skills, knowledge and attitudes that are developed are relevant to developmental needs, control of the brain-drain and the promotion of socio-political stability, and the guaranteeing of human rights, i.e. the creation of an enabling environment for development.

It will be seen from all these objectives that nowhere in the recovery plan did the traditional SAP, whether supported or initiated by IMF and World Bank or developed endogenously, feature in our calculation as to how to bring about economic recovery and transformation in

Africa for the simple reason that the basic objectives of traditional SAPs are the pursuit of fiscal, trade and price balances as ends in themselves and as virtually complete sets of means to production increases. The policy instruments of the traditional SAPs are, as is well known, mainly exchange rate adjustment, resulting in most cases in repeated currency devaluation, increase in interest rates, control of money supply and domestic credit and reductions in government expenditure, particularly expenditure on the social sector – education, health and social welfare – the so-called soft sector.

Apart from diverting attention from focusing on the fundamental basis of the continuing underdevelopment of Africa, traditional SAPs have not only failed to achieve their limited objective of external equilibrium and fiscal balance, but they have also most seriously aggravated the human condition and torn apart the fabric of the African society. They have separated the pursuit of these short-term objectives from the long-term transformational goals. They constitute the very antithesis of achieving these long-term development objectives.

Since the Abuja International Conference and, indeed, as one of the direct consequences of that Conference, there has been an emerging consensus that structural adjustment must have a human face. The pioneering work of UNICEF in this connection must be acknowledged. And the impact of another ECA-sponsored international Conference on the *Human Dimension of Africa's Recovery and Development* and the *Khartoum Declaration* which was the outcome of that conference has been particularly significant in bringing about that consensus, and in forcing an agonizing reappraisal by the sponsors of SAPs. But marginal changes are not enough. What is required are fundamental rather than cosmetic changes. What we need is a complete refocus on domestic development and the total integration of short-term objectives with medium- and long-term development goals. This will compel us to pursue relentlessly the policy measures enunciated in APPER and LPA, some of which have been enumerated in the preceding pages. It will logically and inevitably oblige all concerned – particularly multi-lateral financial, monetary and development institutions to put all the emphasis on Africa's domestic and intra-regional market, rather than on the external market, on domestic factor inputs rather than perpetuate the dependency syndrome, and on the creation of an internal enabling environment and dynamics instead of being overly concerned with external and internal financial and monetary balances. It will also compel all concerned to devote energy and resources on how to engineer a fundamental restructuring of the African economies instead of perpetuating the neo-colonial monocultural export production system at a time when the external demand prospects are dismal. It is in order to help in developing a new consensus along these lines that the recent efforts of ECA in trying to design an African alternative to the traditional SAPs have been dedicated.[6]

In concluding, it will have been clear so far that unless certain conditions are fulfilled and certain factors and forces unleashed, the five-year period of both APPER and UN-PAAERD – 1986–1990 – will have passed without having any significant impact on the African economic crisis, without getting Africa out of its economic doldrums. There is, therefore, an urgent need for renewed and vigorous efforts on the part of all parties concerned – African people and governments, the donor community, the creditor countries, and multilateral financial, monetary and development institutions – to make sure that the expectations raised in June 1986, when the UN General Assembly solemnly adopted UN-PAAERD by consensus, are not frustrated.

The *Ad Hoc* Committee of the Whole of the UN General Assembly which undertook the mid-term review and assessment of the implementation of UN-PAAERD also reached the same conclusion when it concluded that 'the Programme of Action provides an important framework of co-operation between Africa and the international community and all parties wish to reaffirm their commitment to the Programme ... Dealing with the African crisis is a priority concern for the international community and the United Nations. It is therefore a matter of urgency that the promising actions that have been taken by all parties concerned to implement the Programme of Action should be strengthened and accelerated. Sustained and unfaltering efforts made by the African countries must be matched by substantial and urgent efforts by the international community to provide support to them at the required levels and to create an international environment favourable to the process of reform and restructuring.' This conclusion was endorsed by the General Assembly at its 43rd session when it adopted, by consensus, the report of the *Ad Hoc* Committee.

Thus, if the international community becomes more vigorous in its support of UN-PAAERD, if the debt-servicing problems are imaginatively tackled, if the reverse flows of resources are tackled, if the conventional SAP is replaced by an adjustment programme for socio-economic transformation and if, above all, African countries pursue relentlessly the goals and objectives of LPA and FAL and APPER, then the prospects of Africa getting out of its current economic doldrums will become brighter. Although these are powerful and heroic ifs, they are not unrealizable. It all depends on the level of commitment of all the parties concerned.

NOTES

1. Statement at the Hearing of the Sub-Committee on Africa of the Committee on Foreign Affairs, U.S. Congress on long-term development needs in Africa and the U.S. Response, 7 August 1986.
2. Document No.A/43/500 of 10 August 1988, p.40.
3. Document No.A/43/435/19974, Annex 1, paras.29–30.
4. *Ibid.*, p.4, para.14.
5. ECA, *African Alternative to Structural Adjustment Programme (AA-SAP): A Framework for Transformation and Recovery.* Document No.E/ ECA/CM.15/6, March–April 1989.

Abuja Statement on Economic Recovery and Long-Term Development in Africa

An *International Conference on Africa: The Challenge of Economic Recovery and Accelerated Development* was convened in Abuja, the new Federal capital of Nigeria, from 15 to 19 June 1987, for the purpose of making an in-depth review of Africa's recovery process and prospects for long-term development.

Such a review and assessment was both crucial and timely, taking into account the time that had elapsed since the adoption of APPER and UN-PAAERD in 1985 and 1986 respectively. The Conference was also deemed timely in view of the gravity of the economic situation facing Africa, in spite of the efforts in the implementation of the recovery programmes. It has accordingly become necessary to undertake a critical assessment of actions that had so far been taken by Africa and the international community in their implementation, with a view to identifying what progress had been made and the constraints that were impeding Africa's economic recovery and long-term development. This Statement reflects the conclusions and recommendations which have emerged from this review and assessment. It draws attention to the emerging trends, opportunities and constraints and puts forward concrete and practical proposals for generating sustained recovery and growth and bringing about structural transformation of the African economies.

Over 200 African and world experts and scholars, government officials and policy-makers from 36 countries, 24 organizations from the United Nations system and 28 African and non-African inter-governmental and non-governmental organizations participated. To assist the Conference in its task, several issue- and policy-oriented papers and studies were submitted as background documentation. The diversity and very high level of participation provided a unique opportunity for a balanced exchange of ideas and reasoned recommendations. The Conference was therefore appreciative of the initiative and effort by the Executive Secretary of ECA in organizing this important Conference. The Conference was also appreciative of the co-sponsorship by the Federal Republic of Nigeria and the co-operation of the Organization of African Unity and the African Development Bank.

The Conference was particularly honoured that His Excellency Major General Ibrahim Babangida, President of the Federal Republic of Nigeria, Commander-in-Chief of the Armed Forces, and His Excellency Colonel Denis Sassou Nguesso, President of the People's Republic of Congo and Chairman of the OAU, personally addressed the Conference. The Conference was greatly encouraged by the message of the Secretary-General of the United Nations, His Excellency Javier Perez de Cuellar. The Conference welcomed the statement delivered by Madame Monique Landry, Minister of External Relations of Canada, reflecting Canada's interest in, and support for, Africa's recovery and development.

The Conference proceedings were conducted in seven plenary sessions and several group discussions. While detailed proceedings will be published in due course, this Statement brings out the highlights of the issues, conclusions and recommendations for action. The Conference hopes that African Governments and peoples and the international community will take prompt and appropriate actions to implement the recommendations.

OVERALL ASSESSMENT OF THE SITUATION

Progress, problems and prospects in the recovery process

The review of the progress made in the implementation of APPER and UN-PAAERD was at three levels: action taken by African Governments; action taken by African regional and subregional organizations and institutions; and action taken by the international community. The Conference noted that the measures undertaken so far by African Governments included, among others, higher public investment in the agricultural sector, reduction in public expenditure, reduction of subsidies and transfers, greater incentives to farmers and domestic manufacturing, restructuring of public administration, reform of public enterprises, squeezing of public sector wages and reform of the exchange system. These measures have so far yielded some positive results in a number of countries, particularly in improved agricultural production and in the rationalization and better utilization of resources. More than anything else, these measures have demonstrated the limitations and constraints that need to be removed if the process of recovery is to gain any momentum on a sustainable basis.

The collapse of international commodity prices has drastically reduced the actual and potential earnings from an increased volume of commodity exports; the expected inflow in the level of resources to support the recovery process has not been forthcoming to the extent that they can have an adequate impact on the situation; and additional external debt-service burdens have put serious limits on what can be mobilized to promote domestic reconstruction and development as envisaged in APPER and UN-PAAERD. The net effects of these are the aggravation of balance-of-payments problems and the dire need for external resources; thus forcing many countries to implement structural adjustment programmes aimed at correcting current financial imbalances. To date, 28 African countries are implementing such measures.

In many countries, the period of the adjustment programme has been too short to allow for a realistic evaluation and, in any case, there is hardly any country that has been able to mobilize adequate resources to support its adjustment programme. What has become evident, however, is that unless structural adjustment programmes are closely related to the wider objectives of APPER and UN-PAAERD, and unless more substantial resources can be mobilized to support the programmes, there is great danger that the process will have a negative impact on growth, living standards, employment, social development and political stability.

The Conference was gratified to learn that subregional concerted approaches to the promotion of the recovery process had begun to emerge. For example, the Authority of Heads of State and Government of ECOWAS had pledged individual and collective support to initiate a West Africa-wide recovery process through a joint plan of action to be launched on 8 July 1987. Such a programme would concentrate *inter alia* on subregional food security, drought and desertification control and water resources development and management.

Similar efforts have been made in other subregions, particularly in Southern Africa under the auspices of the SADCC, where concerted efforts particularly designed to counteract the destabilizing policies of South Africa have preceded both APPER and UN-PAAERD. These concerted efforts focus especially on strengthening the subregion's alternative transport and communications structure, the development of food security, strengthening of the subregion's capacity, securing social and economic infrastructure, reducing the subregion's dependence on South Africa, and the promotion of co-operation in the fields of trade, industry and energy.

The Conference also noted with satisfaction the substantial increase in the authorized capital of the ADB which would be available to finance projects in response to priorities of APPER and UN-PAAERD. The Conference also welcomed the growing role of ECA and OAU in promoting the objectives and monitoring of the implementation of APPER and UN-PAAERD.

Africa and the international community

While it is generally agreed that much of the effort and resources required for implementing the recovery programmes and bringing about long-term development in the region will have to come from African countries themselves, the Conference recalled that the contribution of the international community had been underscored as being critical during the thirteenth special session of the United Nations General Assembly on the critical economic situation in Africa. African countries had estimated their external financial needs for the recovery programmes at $US45.6 billion for the five-year period and their external debts servicing requirements conservatively estimated at $US14.6 billion annually, thus bringing the average annual external resource requirements under UN-PAAERD to between $US24 billion and $US34 billion on the assumption that commodity prices remained at the 1985 level. While it did not commit itself to these figures, the international community did undertake to make every effort to provide sufficient resources to support and supplement Africa's development effort and agreed that measures had to be taken to alleviate Africa's debt burden.

The Conference noted with satisfaction that a number of positive steps had been taken since last year. These include (a) the replenishment of IDA resources to the tune of $US12.4 billion and the decision to allocate 45 per cent thereof to sub-Saharan Africa; (b) the increase in the level of the grant element in ODA by some developed countries to the hard pressed low-income African countries; (c) the cancellation of ODA debts by some donor countries in favour of some least developed African countries. The Conference also welcomed the recent decision of the thirteenth Summit meeting of the seven most industrialized market economies of the West, held in Venice, Italy, from 8–10 June 1987, that consideration should be given by the Paris Club to the possibility of applying lower interest rates to the existing debts of those African countries that were undertaking adjustment efforts and that agreement should be reached on longer repayment and grace periods to ease the debt burden. It also endorsed the proposal submitted by the Managing Director of IMF to the Summit for a significant increase in the resources of the structural adjustment facility over a period of three years beginning 1 January 1988.

While the Conference would wish to express its appreciation for these efforts, there is some concern that they may not be adequate to meet the external resource needs of Africa for its recovery programme, particularly in the face of the dramatic fall in commodity prices and the escalation of debt burden obligations. The Conference is also of the view that the approach so far to the African external resource needs is rather *ad hoc* and partial in nature and therefore likely to have limited impact. What is required is a comprehensive approach to the debt problem and aid flows that would provide the financial resources required for economic recovery and development in Africa.

Delegates noted the continuing decline of primary commodity prices including oil. They also noted the grim prospects for future commodity prices which would increase the already substantial need for resources in African countries. In view of the sizeable magnitude of the resource needs of those countries, however, they called on the industrial countries to make special efforts to increase the flow of capital and concessional aid, to remove protectionist barriers and structural rigidities in their economies and to create an international environment conducive to growth-oriented structural adjustment and increased trade.

The Conference stressed the importance of South–South co-operation in Africa's economic recovery and long-term development. Such co-operation was particularly essential in bringing about the structural changes required for self-reliance and self-sustained development. The main areas outlined included the building up of appropriate technological capabilities through technical assistance, interregional trade among developing countries and human resource development.

In view of the foregoing analysis, the Conference came to the conclusion that the prospects for recovery depended on the concentration of efforts on such issues as (a) sustainment of domestic policy reforms; (b) continuation of the efforts to improve economic management; (c) ensuring that structural adjustment programmes were consistent with the objectives and priorities of the recovery programmes; (d) the alleviation of the debt burden; (e) the intensification of the search for a solution to the commodities problems; (f) the removal of the constraints on achieving fully adequate levels of official development assistance; and, (g) the amelioration of the impact of acts of political and economic destabilization on the recovery of the countries of southern Africa. Accordingly, the Conference devoted a considerable part of its time to an in-depth study of those issues in group discussions. The recommendations contained in the latter part of this Statement were derived from those detailed discussions.

Long-term development prospects

The second part of the Conference was devoted to reviewing Africa's prospects for long-term development in the light of the experience of the past seven years since the adoption of LPA and FAL in April 1980. The Conference undertook this review in the light of the historical, socio-cultural and political situation of Africa as well as the scientific and technological perspectives. It came to the conclusion that Africa's long-term development must be based on a fundamental structural change which would not happen by itself and which therefore had to be engineered by the Africans themselves as envisaged in LPA. In accordance with APPER, the food and agricultural sector should constitute the base of structural change with the African countries gradually reducing the importance and significance to their national economies of exports of primary commodities while increasing the role of domestic and intra-African production relationships until the latter became more dominant and the former more marginal.

In order to achieve such a structural change, Africa must take measures to overcome its scientific and technological backwardness. However, the Conference believed that structural changes at the political and cultural levels would also have to be engineered. In a situation where rapid changes were taking place in the geopolitical and technological world order, Africa would have to contend with the pace, content and turbulences of global structural shifts. The continent must also gear itself to respond to the long-term demand prospects for its primary commodities and endeavour over time to move out of the present structure of the export-oriented primary commodity system. However, the continent's ultimate future had to remain firmly rooted in its own uniqueness and diversities, in its cultures, in its peoples and in its natural resources. An improvement in the capacity to respond to these changes must therefore be an essential component in Africa's long-term development strategies.

Africa's history and recent experiences confirm that the future prospects of the continent will not hinge simply on issues of economic growth and financial flows. It will require a refocusing of the African ethos and a regathering of all African forces. Africa, as an entity in the world, will have to derive its strength from its internal socio-cultural authenticity, territorial and political cohesion and economic viability based mainly on endogenous forces.

New political perspectives are also imperative for setting into motion the process of African progress. A viable development strategy for Africa should be predicated on a comprehensive programme of social transformation which requires vision, resolve and commitment on the part of the African leadership. The democratisation of the African society and increased accountability of those entrusted with power are vital for the mobilization of greater popular participation. For such necessities to become realities, African political perspectives *vis-à-vis* external political and economic interests will also have to be sharpened to become more decisive and enlightened so that the destiny of Africa is assured to be in the hands of the African people.

Overcoming scientific and technological underdevelopment will be one of the critical preconditions for Africa's economic maturity in the coming twenty-first century. To achieve this task, Africa will have to depend less on technology transfers that only deepen its dependency. It must, instead, make consistent efforts to develop, acquire, adapt and internalize such technologies and scientific knowledge that will enable it to make full and effective use of its resource endowments and in relation to its needs. Two areas that will have to be focused upon include the enhancement of African research and innovation and their institutionalisation in the fabric of society and the development and fuller utilization of African scientific and technical skills.

Given the present political and economic fragmentation of the continent, it will be difficult if not impossible for Africa to realize its vision without collective self-reliance, economic co-operation and integration. Although the process of co-operation in Africa has been going on for some time, it will require strengthening and rationalization. Efforts at African integration can bear fruits only if African countries honour faithfully their commitment to integrate their economies particularly through productive activities. It is only in this way that the objective of an African Economic Community can be achieved.

CONCLUSIONS AND RECOMMENDATIONS

In the light of the foregoing analysis, the following conclusions and recommendations are proposed for the most careful consideration of African countries and the international community.

Measures for accelerating the recovery process

(a) *Sustaining domestic policy reforms and improvement in economic management*: African countries must continue to pursue structural policy reform measures, taking into account the need to minimize the adverse social impact of such measures and to take into account the human dimension of adjustment; ensure that budgetary cuts do not affect the development of social infrastructure, particularly health and education services; and put greater emphasis on the rationalization of government institutions, with a view to ensuring effective and efficient contribution of the public sector to the recovery process. In the light of the recommendation of the Niamey Symposium on Grass Root Development, African Governments must create favourable conditions for decentralization of decision-making, and for delegation of authority and responsibility for increased access to resources so as to broaden the participation of all groups of the population in the recovery process.

(b) *Structural adjustment programmes and the recovery process*: African countries must sustain and accelerate the process of economic recovery by increasing the level of investment in agriculture, developing rural transportation with greater emphasis on low-cost transport equipment and promoting agro-allied industries. They must ensure that structural adjustment programmes are consistent with the requirements for recovery and growth. They are urged to undertake, with the assistance of African regional institutions, concerted efforts to exchange information on their negotiations with international financial organizations and donors on policy reform measures and structural adjustment programmes. They must also take appropriate measures for controlling capital flight and the brain drain from Africa.

(c) The ECA Secretariat should constantly monitor, through in-depth studies, the impact of structural adjustment programmes on medium- and long-term development; and,

(d) At the subregional level, collective approaches to recovery and development within the framework of the existing sub-regional economic communities should continue to be devised and vigorously implemented.

Debt and debt service payments

In view of the severity of the debt-servicing problem in many countries in Africa and its dire implications for recovery and development prospects, new efforts will be needed to deal with this problem, particularly in so far as low-income countries are concerned. These efforts should include:

(a) Lower interest rates on existing debts, which, in rescheduling agreements, could be critical in some cases; longer repayments and grace periods to ease the debt-service burden as agreed upon at the recent Venice Summit should be pursued;

(b) Conversion into grants of bilateral government-to-government debt and interest obligations for low-income countries undertaking structural adjustment programmes where this has not already been accomplished;

(c) Repayment of debt in local currency could be considered; and,

(d) Conversion of debt and debt-servicing obligations into investment portfolios and equity.

Development assistance

In addition, there is an urgent need for increased aid flows that will provide the resources required for recovery and development. In this connection, the Conference welcomes the recent initiative of the UN Secretary-General to establish a High-level Advisory Group on Resource Flows to Africa which will make practical recommendations to ease the debt burden and increase resource flows to the continent. The Conference also welcomes the new initiatives by some major bilateral donors to increase resource flows to Africa. African Governments and institutions and other development programmes should offer to assist these countries in establishing and expanding their activities in Africa.

In addition to all these, the Conference is putting forward the following policy options for serious consideration:

(a) Further increase of bilateral aid and more effective use of these flows for recovery and development;

(b) A significant increase in additional concessional resources through multilateral institutions. In this regard, special support should be given to proposals or agreements to triple the Structural Adjustment Facility and replenish IDA and the African Development

Fund at higher levels and to allocate substantial parts thereof to Africa;

(c) Consider the possibility of issuing new SDRs in relation to development needs;

(d) With the assistance of ECA, ADB and the African Centre for Monetary Studies, consideration should be given to the possibility of setting up an African consultative machinery to enable member states to exchange information and harmonize their positions for the meetings with creditors in the Paris and London Clubs.

Commodities, trade and price stabilization

Within the overall context of Africa's recovery and accelerated growth, the Conference arrived at the following conclusions: (a) Intra-African trade offers substantial opportunities for trade expansion, and increased production; thus one way of reducing the vulnerability of the economies is to intensify efforts towards subregional and regional co-operation in trade including trade in commodities; (b) Existing initiatives in international co-operation in commodities need to be continued and strengthened, especially as regards the operation of the common fund; (c) There is a link between commodity, price level, external debt and the need for international resource flows; and, (d) Over the past ten years there have been marked rigidities in the trade policies of industrialized countries towards Africa, especially with regard to trade in processed or semi-processed commodities, a trend which has proved detrimental to Africa's efforts to shift away from commodity dependence. In the light of these conclusions, the following proposals were addressed to specific target groups, namely, the African Governments, the international community and international institutions.

(a) *African Governments* should:

   (i)   Initiate supply rationalization measures so as to bring production and supply of their commodities in line with long-term demand trends; to this end, Governments should take steps to promote new domestic and export demand for their primary commodities through increased market research, development measures and improved market information systems;

   (ii) Diversify efforts while avoiding repeating costly mistakes or creating new surplus situations; the diversification should include the use of locally available raw materials for production instead of relying on imported ones;

   (iii) Examine the prospects for the increased use of counter-trade as a measure to promote intra-African trade expansion, including trade in primary commodities without having to use scarce external currencies.

(b) The *International Community* should:

   (i) Ensure that the Uruguay Round of negotiations enables the granting of more liberal access to industrial country markets of African exports, including tropical products. The possibility of a more rational system of world agricultural trade in the 1990s should be encouraged;

   (ii) Continue to discuss especially at the forthcoming UNCTAD Conference, the problem of commodity price changes, seeking measures to deal with the problem of reduced income as African countries undertake long-term structural adjustments;

   (iii) Give further consideration to expanding donor participation in Stabex schemes to include other OECD donor countries.

(c) *International organizations and institutions* should bear in mind, where structural adjustment and other programmes undertaken under the auspices of the multilateral financial institutions are targeted to achieve external balance, that the reference prices on which the programmes are based are, themselves, subject to short-term distortions; therefore, less rigidity in the price assumptions is necessary. The Conference urges full discussion of issues related to commodities, trade and the special problem of least developed countries at the forthcoming UNCTAD Conference.

Political and economic destabilization and the consequences for economic recovery and development

The Conference recognized that peace, security and stability are necessary pre-conditions for Africa's economic development. Recovery and economic development efforts in the countries of the southern African region members of SADCC have been, and continue to be, frustrated by the racist regime of South Africa and its continued policies of aggression and political and economic destabilization. To achieve peace, stability and security in this region the Conference recommends the following:

(a) Continuation of the campaign to ensure divestment by all transnational corporations in South Africa;

(b) Full implementation by African countries of the measures identified in APPER in support of the national liberation movements and the SADCC countries;

(c) Support to the efforts of SADCC countries to strengthen co-operation among themselves and reduce their dependence on South Africa, particularly through maximum support to the SADCC Programme of Action and its plans for alternative transport and communications routes, food security and manpower development;

(d) Increased assistance by the international community to the SADCC countries to allow them to implement their recovery programmes and cover the cost of aggression and destabilization policies of South Africa, which was estimated to have cost the region over $US2 billion annually; and,

(e) International and regional development and financial institutions should increase their co-operation with, and assistance to, SADCC countries.

As a result of the continuous aggression by the South African regime and its support of destabilization activities in Mozambique, and the current drought affecting large areas in that country, Mozambique is facing a serious economic emergency. Thousands of people are facing severe famine. The Conference urges more urgent humanitarian relief, especially food aid and shelter as well as assistance in removing the fundamental cause of instability.

Prospects for long-term development

As far as the prospects for accelerated and long-term development are concerned, the general conclusion of the Conference is that Africa needs a new approach to its political economy. This should involve more coherent and more clearly thought out principles to guide its development process and to provide a framework for more efficient resource mobilization. In this context, recovery must also mean economic reconstruction for long-term development which, in turn, calls for new forms of social organization and economic management and the bridging of economic and social disparities.

The Conference therefore decided to forward the following recommendations to African countries:

(a) The internalization of the productive forces and the growth impetus, as well as increased and effective self-reliance and co-operation on a regional basis;

(b) Intensification of popular participation in the economic development process and the promotion of social justice and distributive equity;

(c) Recognition of the fundamental role of women in the development process;

(d) Development and enhancement of African research and the encouragement of the process of technological and scientific innovation and adaptation;

(e) Ensure consistency of the development process and environmental sustainability;

(f) Greater reliance on African technical and scientific skills and entrepreneurship; and,

(g) The political, social, administrative and cultural dimensions that are conducive to long-term development must be created to ensure the success and sustainability of the development process.

Economic co-operation in Africa and between Africa and the international community

In order to reverse the disappointing experience with economic integration and to ensure that the process of integration contributes more effectively to economic development and structural change, African countries should embark on a comprehensive approach to economic integration involving (a) the rationalization of existing co-operation organs in each subregion, and their effective mobilization for co-ordinated planning and development at the subregional level; and, (b) the pursuit of measures for the close co-ordination of economic and social policies at the subregional level as well as for the joint planning and development of community projects in the key economic sectors.

The current effort to harmonize the activities of the multinational institutions established under the aegis of OAU and the ECA should be accelerated with a view to ensuring that their institutions act in support of the comprehensive approach to economic co-operation and integration.

The comprehensive approach to economic co-operation should be accompanied by new efforts to promote closer collaboration with other developing regions, in particular the newly industrialising countries (NICs) which are now in a position to provide African countries with an effective programme of technical co-operation in support of sectoral planning at the subregional level in the key economic sectors.

Realizing that, in the final analysis, the pursuit of self-reliant and self-sustaining development on the continent would demand a new pattern of economic relationship with the developed countries, involving new trade structures and new efforts to promote foreign investment in Africa, African countries should devise appropriate mechanisms for promoting collaboration between the different productive sectors in Africa and those in the developed countries.

Follow-up actions

The Conference would be most grateful to the President of the Federal Republic of Nigeria and the Chairman of OAU for bringing the recommendations of this Abuja Statement to all forthcoming appropriate major international forums. The Conference particularly referred to the forthcoming Twenty-third Assembly of Heads of State and Government of OAU, as well as the Summit of Francophone countries, the Commonwealth Conference and the fourteenth Summit of the seven most industrialized countries, that are scheduled to be held in Canada. The Conference also requests the Secretary-General of the United Nations to bring the document to the attention of the forty-second Session of the General Assembly.

The Executive Secretary of ECA should follow-up on the implementation of the above recommendations taking into account the consideration that would be given to them by the above main international forums. One of the major challenges that faces Africa is how to sustain international public interest in Africa's long-term development through continuous and effective communication that will reach all levels of society. This is a challenge that faces the Governments of Africa as much as it faces the UN in general and its regional arm, the ECA, in particular. It is therefore imperative that it should be addressed in a comprehensive manner. In this connection, ECA can, with necessary financial support, play a catalytic role.

Vote of thanks

In conclusion, the Conference wishes to reiterate its appreciation for the generous hospitality of the Nigerian Government and people in providing the necessary facilities for the meeting. Its deliberations and conclusions were particularly enlightened by the inspiring addresses of the President of the Federal Republic of Nigeria, the President of the People's Republic of Congo and Chairman of OAU, and by the enriching message of the Secretary-General of the UN.